# RICHARD ROLLE: PROSE AND VERSE

EARLY ENGLISH TEXT SOCIETY
No. 293
1988

men maye deye. for þat loue maketh þe as siker of heuyn when
þou deyest as þou now art of helle. ffor þe fyr of loue hath brent
away al þe rust of syn. and I wene fro þou or I or any be
broght in to þis ioy of loue we mow nat lyue longe aftir
as oþer men doth, bot as we lyue in loue: also we shal dey
in ioy and passe to hym þat we haue loued. In þis degre of
loue al drede al sorowe al wo al ydel ioy and al wikked de
lites is putt fro us and we lyue in swetnesse of heuyn.
Thynk euer to lest and to be bettyr and bettir and þat wil gif þe grace
to loue hym as he doth another. Our lord yeueth nat
to men and women fayrhede richesse and delites for to set þair
hertes þon and dispend þam in syn. bot for þay shold knowe
hym and loue hym and þanke hym of al his yiftes. þe more is
þair shame if þai wreth hym þat he hath gyffen to þam
many yiftes in body or in soule. ffor þi if we couait
to fle þe peyn of helle and þe peyn of purgatorie us bihoueth
restreyne us perfitly fro þe lustes and þe lykynges and fro þe ill
delites and þe wicked dedes of þis lif. and þe world is so
rowe be nat in us. bot þat we hold al our hertes fast on
Ihesu crist and stand manly agayns temptacions. Now
I write a songe of loue þat þou shalt haue delite in when þou art
louynge Ihesu crist.

**M**y songe is in seghynge: my lif is in langynge:
til I þe se my kynge. so fayr in þi shynynge: so
fayr in þi fayrhede. Into þi light me lede. and in þi loue
me fede. In loue make me spede. that þou be euer my mede.
When wil þou cum Ihesu my ioy. and keuer me of kare. And gyf
me þe þat I may se hauynge for euer more. Al my couei
tynge war comen. If I myght to þe fare. I wil no þynge
bot only þe þat al my wille war. Ihesu my sauyour Ihesu
my comfortour of fayrnesse þe flour. my help and my sokour
when may I se þi tour. When wil þou me kall. Me lan
geth in to þi hall. To se þe þan all. Thi loue let it nat
fall. My hert peyneth þe pall. þat stiddeth us in stall.
Now wax I pale and wan. ffor loue of my leman. Ihesu
both god and man. Thi loue þou lered me þan. when I to
þe fast ran. ffor þi now loue I can. I sitt and synge of

# RICHARD ROLLE: PROSE AND VERSE

*edited from MS Longleat 29 and related manuscripts*

*BY*

*S. J. OGILVIE-THOMSON*

*Published for*

THE EARLY ENGLISH TEXT SOCIETY

*by the*

OXFORD UNIVERSITY PRESS

1988

*Oxford University Press, Walton Street, Oxford OX2 6DP*
*Oxford New York Toronto*
*Delhi Bombay Calcutta Madras Karachi*
*Petaling Jaya Singapore Hong Kong Tokyo*
*Nairobi Dar es Salaam Cape Town*
*Melbourne Auckland*
*Associated companies in Beirut Berlin Ibadan Nicosia*

*Oxford is a trade mark of Oxford University Press*



*British Library Cataloguing in Publication Data*
*Rolle, Richard*
*Richard Rolle: prose and verse edited from Ms. Longleat 29 and related manuscripts.*
*—(Early English Text Society; 05293).*
*1. Mysticism*
*I. Title II. Ogilvie-Thompson, Sarah*
*III. Series*
*242.2'2 BV5080*
*ISBN 0-19-722295-1*

*Set by Joshua Associates Limited, Oxford*
*Printed in Great Britain by*
*Richard Clay (The Chaucer Press) Ltd,*
*Bungay, Suffolk*

# CONTENTS

## PLATES



Reproduced by permission of the Marquess of Bath, Longleat House, Warminster, Wiltshire.

# PREFACE

I am grateful to the Marquess of Bath for permission to publish from his manuscript, and to his former librarian, Miss Jane Fowles, for her advice on the Thynne papers. My thanks are also due to the librarians and staff of the Bodleian Library, University College, Oxford, the University Library of Cambridge, the libraries of Trinity, Magdalene, and Gonville and Caius Colleges, Cambridge, the Fitzwilliam Museum, Professor Takamiya, the British Library, Lambeth Palace Library, Westminster School, the Cathedral libraries of Hereford and Lincoln, the University libraries of Edinburgh, London and Yale, Trinity College Dublin, Chetham's Library, the Huntington Library, the Pierpont Morgan Library, the Bibliothèque Sainte Geneviève, and Miss Christina Foyle and her husband Mr Batty, all of whom have allowed me access to their manuscripts, or supplied me with microfilm.

I remain indebted to Miss Celia Sisam and the late Professor Eric Dobson, who supervised the greater part of this edition in its thesis form. I should also like to thank Dr Bruce Mitchell, who read part of the book in typescript and made many helpful suggestions. Finally, no editor of Rolle can fail to pay tribute to Hope Emily Allen, whose researches have paved the way for all subsequent work.

# ABBREVIATIONS

| | |
|---|---|
| Abbott | T. K. Abbott, *Catalogue of the Manuscripts in the Library of Trinity College Dublin* (Dublin, 1900). |
| Arntz | Sr. M. L. Arntz, *Richard Rolle and þe Holy Boke Gratia Dei* Elizabethan & Renaissance Studies, 92: 2 (Salzburg, 1981). |
| BL | British Library. |
| Black and Macray | W. H. Black and W. D. Macray, *A Descriptive Analytical and Critical Catalogue of the Manuscripts bequeathed unto the University of Oxford by Elias Ashmole, Esq.* (Oxford, 1845). |
| Borland | C. Borland, *A Descriptive Catalogue of the Western Medieval Manuscripts in Edinburgh University Library* (Edinburgh, 1916). |
| *Census (Supplement)* | S. de Ricci and J. Wilson, *Census of Medieval and Renaissance Manuscripts in the United States and Canada* (New York, 1935 and 1937); *Supplement* by C. U. Faye and W. H. Bond (New York, 1962). |
| Colledge and Walsh | E. Colledge and J. Walsh, *A Book of Showings to the Anchoress Julian of Norwich* (Toronto, 1978). |
| Comper | F. M. M. Comper, *The Life and Lyrics of Richard Rolle* (London, 1928). |
| *Comp. theol. ver.* | *Compendium theologicae veritatis*, attributed originally to Albertus Magnus, but now thought to be the work of Hugo Argentinensis and written *c.* 1265. |
| Coxe 1852 | H. O. Coxe, *Catalogus Codicum Manuscriptorum qui in Collegiis Aulisque Oxoniensibus hodie adservantur* (Oxford, 1852). |
| d'Ardenne | S. R. T. O. d'Ardenne, *Þe Liflade ant te Passiun of Seinte Iuliene* (Liège, 1936, reprinted EETS 248, 1961). |
| Doyle | A. I. Doyle, *A Survey of the Origins and Circulation of Theological Writings in English in the 14th, 15th and Early 16th Centuries with Special Consideration of the Part of the Clergy Therein*, 2 vols (unpublished Ph.D. thesis, Cambridge University, 1953). I should like to thank Dr Doyle for allowing me to |

| | |
|---|---|
| | have a copy made of this most valuable work of reference. |
| EETS | Early English Text Society. |
| *English Writings* | H. E. Allen, *English Writings of Richard Rolle* (Oxford, 1931). |
| Gradon | P. Gradon, *Dan Michel's Ayenbite of Inwyt* EETS 278 (1979), vol. ii. |
| Halliwell | J. O. Halliwell, *An Account of the European Manuscripts in the Chetham Library Manchester* (Manchester, 1842). |
| *Handlist* | Ralph Hanna III, *The Index of Middle English Prose. A Handlist of Manuscripts containing Middle English Prose in the Henry E. Huntington Library* (Cambridge, 1984). |
| HBS | Henry Bradshaw Society. |
| Heseltine | G. C. Heseltine, *Selected Works of Richard Rolle* (London, 1930). |
| HMC | Historical Manuscripts Commission. |
| Hodgson | P. Hodgson, *Deonise Hid Diuinite* EETS 231 (1955). |
| Horstman | C. Horstman, *Yorkshire Writers: Richard Rolle of Hampole and his Followers*, 2 vols (London, 1895). |
| *IMEV (Supplement)* | C. Brown and R. H. Robbins, *Index of Middle English Verse* (New York, 1943); *Supplement* by R. H. Robbins and J. L. Cutler (Lexington, 1965). |
| James 1900–4 | M. R. James, *The Western Manuscripts in the Library of Trinity College Cambridge* (Cambridge, 1900–4). |
| James 1907–8 | M. R. James, *A Descriptive Catalogue of the Manuscripts in the Library of Gonville and Caius College Cambridge* (Cambridge, 1907–8). |
| James 1923 | M. R. James, *Bibliotheca Pepysiana. A Descriptive Catalogue of the Library of Samuel Pepys, Part III, Medieval Manuscripts* (Cambridge, 1923). |
| James 1930–2 | M. R. James, *A Descriptive Catalogue of the Manuscripts in the Library of Lambeth Palace* (Cambridge, 1930–2). |
| Jordan | R. Jordan, *Handbuch der mittelenglischen Grammatik* (Heidelberg, 1925; translated and revised E. J. Crook, 1974). |
| Kane | G. Kane, *Piers Plowman: the A Version* (London, 1960). |

| | |
|---|---|
| Kane and Donaldson | G. Kane and E. Talbot Donaldson, *Piers Plowman: the B Version* (London, 1975). |
| Ker | N. R. Ker, *Medieval Manuscripts in British Libraries* I–III (Oxford, 1969–83). |
| Lewis and McIntosh | R. E. Lewis and A. McIntosh, *A Descriptive Guide to the Manuscripts of the 'Prick of Conscience'* Medium Ævum Monographs New Series XII (Oxford, 1982). |
| Macray 1862 | W. D. Macray, *Catalogi Codicum Manuscriptorum Bibliothecae Bodleianae Partes Quintae Fasciculus Primus viri Munificentissimi Ricardi Rawlinson* (Oxford, 1862). |
| Macray 1878 | W. D. Macray, *Catalogi Codicum Manuscriptorum Bibliothecae Bodleianae Partes Quintae Fasciculus Secundus viri Munificentissimi Ricardi Rawlinson* (Oxford, 1878). |
| Macray 1883 | W. D. Macray, *Catalogi Codicum Manuscriptorum Bodleianae Pars Nona codices a viro clarissimo Kenelm Digby* (Oxford, 1883). |
| ME | Middle English. |
| *MED* | H. Kurath, S. M. Kuhn and J. Reidy, *Middle English Dictionary*, vols. A–R (Ann Arbor, 1956–). |
| *MLR* | *Modern Language Review*. |
| OE | Old English. |
| *OED* | *Oxford English Dictionary.* |
| OF | Old French. |
| OHG | Old High German. |
| ON | Old Norse. |
| OTeut | Old Teutonic. |
| Perry | G. G. Perry, *English Prose Treatises of Richard Rolle of Hampole* EETS OS 20 (1866). |
| *PL* | J. P. Migne, *Patrologia Latina* (Paris, 1844–64). |
| *PMLA* | *Publications of the Modern Language Association of America.* |
| *Promptorium Parvulorum* | A. L. Mayhew, *The Promptorium Parvulorum: the First English–Latin Dictionary* EETS ES 102 (1908). |
| *Quarto Catalogue* | H. O. Coxe, with additions by R. W. Hunt, *Bodleian Library Quarto Catalogues, II, Laudian Manuscripts* (Oxford, 1973). |

| | |
|---|---|
| *RES* | *Review of English Studies.* |
| *RL XIV* | C. Brown, *Religious Lyrics of the XIV Century* (Oxford, 1924, revised G. V. Smithers, Oxford, 1952). |
| *SC* | F. Madan, *A Summary Catalogue of Western Manuscripts in the Bodleian Library at Oxford which have not hitherto been catalogued in the Quarto series* (Oxford, 1895–1937). |
| *Speculum Christiani* | G. Holmstedt, *Speculum Christiani* EETS 182 (1933). |
| ULC | University Library of Cambridge. |
| Warner and Gilson | G. F. Warner and J. P. Gilson, *Catalogue of Western Manuscripts in the Old Royal and King's Collections* (London, 1921). |
| *Worcs. Misc.* | N. S. Baugh, *A Worcestershire Miscellany compiled by John Northwood* (Philadelphia, 1956). |
| *Writings* | H. E. Allen, *Writings ascribed to Richard Rolle and materials for his Biography* Modern Language Association of America 1927; reprinted New York, 1966. |

# INTRODUCTION

As early as 1927 the importance of the Rolle texts in MS Longleat 29 was recognized. H. E. Allen, the pioneer of modern Rolle studies, stated that the manuscript 'must have been derived from manuscripts of authority because it contains rare texts and gives the surname of Rolle's favourite disciple'.[1] However it has never been considered as a base text for an edition because of its non-Northern dialect, and its relative inaccessibility[2] has discouraged previous editors from using it for collation. This edition is intended to complement that of Miss Allen; it cannot represent the language of Rolle dialectally, but it can and does restore a significant number of correct readings.

The manuscript contains the three English epistles *The Form of Living*, *Ego Dormio* and *The Commandment*, two short prose pieces *Desire and Delight* and *Ghostly Gladness*, five lyrics generally accepted as Rolle's work, the poem *Sweet Jesu*, and a fragment of prose which I have identified as part of a meditation on the Passion found in its entirety in MS Cotton Titus C xix. The last two do not form part of the canon established by Miss Allen, but I hope to have justified their inclusion here.[3] All these works are apparently dedicated to Margaret of Kirkby, the colophon reading 'Explicit tractatus Ricardi heremite de Hampolle ad Margaretam reclusam de Kyrkby de amore dei', which might suggest descent from an autograph collection made for her.

In 1958 Lord Bath permitted me to study Longleat 29 at the Bodleian library, and it was there that the late Neil Ker verified that its main hand was also that of MS Bodl. e Museo 232. This manuscript contains the meditation on the Passion sometimes attributed to Rolle, and in the hope that its text would prove as authoritative as that of its sister volume it was decided to include it in this edition. Unfortunately that hope has not been substantiated. It is not a bad text, but it clearly does not evolve from the same source as the Rolle texts in the Longleat manuscript, a fact which can only reinforce the doubts about Rolle's authorship. However a fully edited version of the work does not exist elsewhere, and it has therefore been retained.

[1] *Writings*, p. 34.

[2] The manuscript is in the private library of Lord Bath at Longleat House. He has been most generous in allowing me to consult it and to publish from it.

[3] See further pp. lxxxix–xci, xlix.

## ALPHABETICAL TABLE OF MANUSCRIPT SIGLA

A Ashmole 1524 (*Form* MS 29)

Ad BL Add. 37790 (*Form* MS 31, *Ego Dormio* MS 11)

Ad$^{2}$ BL Add. 37787 (Lyrics MS 7)

Add ULC Add. 3042 (*Meditation* B MS 4)

Ar Arundel 507 (*Form* MS 30, *Ego Dormio* MS 12)

B Bodley 110 (*Form* MS 17)

B$^{2}$ Bodley 938 (*Form* MS 25)

B$^{3}$ Bodley 423 (*Form* MS 39)

Br Bradfer-Lawrence 10 (*Form* MS 43, *Ego Dormio* MS 8, *Commandment* MS 12)

C Caius College 669 (*Form* MS 13)

Ch Chetham 6690 (*Form* MS 27)

D Digby 18 (*Form* MS 15)

Dd ULC Dd v 64 III (*Form* MS 9, *Ego Dormio* MS 7, *Commandment* MS 5, *Ghostly Gladness* MS 2, Lyrics MS 2)

Dd$^{2}$ ULC Dd v 55 (*Commandment* MS 14)

Do Douce 302 (*Form* MS 40)

E Edinburgh University 107 (*Form* MS 37)

F Foyle, Beeleigh Abbey (*Form* MS 21)

Ff ULC Ff v 40 (*Form* MS 11, *Commandment* MS 6)

Ff$^{2}$ ULC Ff v 45 (*Form* MS 32)

G Bibliothèque Ste-Geneviève 3390 (*Form* MS 4, *Ego Dormio* MS 6)

H Huntington HM 127 (*Form* MS 23)

H$^{2}$ Huntington HM 502 (*Form* MS 35)

H$^{3}$ Huntington HM 148 (*Commandment* MS 9)

H$^{4}$ Huntington EL 34 B 7 (Lyrics MS 10)

Ha Harley 1022 (*Form* MS 28)

He Hereford Cathedral P i 9 (*Form* MS 14)

Hh ULC Hh i 12 (*Form* MS 34)

Ii ULC Ii iv 9 (*Form* MS 18)

Ii$^{2}$ ULC Ii vi 40 (*Form* MS 42, *Commandment* MS 11)

Ii$^{3}$ ULC Ii vi 55 (*Form* MS 33)

L Lansdowne 455 (*Form* MS 12)

La Lambeth Palace 853 (*Form* MS 44, Lyrics MS 3)

Ld Laud misc. 210 (*Form* MS 22)

Ld$^{2}$ Laud misc. 524 (*Form* MS 38)

Lt Longleat 29 (*Form* MS 1, *Ego Dormio* MS 1, *Commandment*

MS 1, *Desire and Delight* MS 1, *Ghostly Gladness* MS 1, Lyrics MS 1, Meditation A MS 1)

- Lt² Longleat 32 (*Form* MS 41, *Commandment* MS 10)
- M Pierpont Morgan M 818 (*Form* MS 19)
- Mu Bodl. e mus. 232 (*Meditation* B MS 1)
- P Pepys 2125 (*Form* MS 20, *Ego Dormio* MS 9, *Commandment* MS 8)
- R Rawl. A 389 (*Form* MS 3, *Ego Dormio* MS 2, *Commandment* MS 2)
- R² Rawl. C 285 (*Form* MS 10)
- Ro Royal 17 B xvii (Lyrics MS 8)
- S Simeon, BL Add. 22283 (*Form* MS 5, *Ego Dormio* MS 3, *Commandment* MS 3, Lyrics MS 6)
- T Trinity College Cambridge B 14 38 (*Form* MS 8)
- T² Trinity College Cambridge B 15 17 (*Form* MS 24)
- T³ Trinity College Cambridge O 1 29 (*Form* MS 16, *Commandment* MS 13)
- T⁴ Trinity College Cambridge B 15 42 (*Commandment* MS 7)
- Th Thornton, Lincoln Cathedral 91 (*Desire and Delight* MS 2, Lyrics MS 4)
- Ti Cotton Titus C xix (*Meditation* A MS 2, *Meditation* B MS 3)
- Tr Trinity College Dublin 155 (*Form* MS 26, *Ego Dormio* MS 10, Lyrics MS 9)
- Tr² Trinity College Dublin 154 (*Form* MS 36)
- U University College Oxford 97 (*Form* MS 2)
- Up Upsala University C 494 (*Meditation* B MS 2)
- V Vernon, Bodl. eng. poet. a 1 (*Form* MS 6, *Ego Dormio* MS 4, *Commandment* MS 4, Lyrics MS 5)
- W Westminster School 3 (*Form* MS 7, *Ego Dormio* MS 5)
- Y Yale University 324 (*Commandment* MS 15)
- $\alpha$ The combination of MSS RGSVWT

## DESCRIPTION OF MANUSCRIPTS

### LONGLEAT 29 (Lt)

#### i) *External*

MS Longleat 29[1] is a vellum volume measuring 220 × 165 mm. Its nineteenth-century binding is of tan Russian leather, tooled in gold,

[1] The English contents of the manuscript, with the exception of Chaucer's *Parson's Tale*, were edited by me as a thesis for the degree of D.Phil. (Oxford, 1980), and a more detailed description of the MS, particularly of its provenance and language, will be found there.

and lettered on the spine with the title 'Ricardus Hampole de Amore Dei. Walterus de Hultone de Vita Activa. A Treatise on Penance etc. XV Cent.' Inside the front cover is a bookplate with the arms of the Right Hon. Lord Viscount Weymouth, Baron Thynne of Warminster, 1704. In its present binding the volume consists of the following leaves: i–ii, 1–169, iii–iv. The paper flyleaves are unmarked, except for a partial list of contents by a recent librarian. The average size of the pages is 205 × 146 mm; the measurements of the written material vary between 163 × 115 mm. and 155 × 105 mm. Marginal ruling occurs irregularly; where it exists, it consists of one vertical inner line and two vertical outer lines, with an upper and a lower horizontal line. No pricking is visible, and horizontal ruling for each line of text is rare. The present state of the manuscript is good, apart from discolouration and some staining. It is legible throughout, with the exception of two or three words obliterated at fol. 58$^{v}$. However at some period, probably during the last century, it has undergone extensive and skilful repairs, with fresh vellum being glued on to the existing pages.

ii) *Collation*

The binding holds four books. In the first (fols. 1–18) sewing is visible after fols. 3, 8, 13, and 17. Fols. 4 and 16 are of heavier vellum than the rest, and were possibly originally outer covers. If this is so, fols. 1–3, which are smaller, would appear to be odd leaves, and fols. 4 and 16 enclose two gatherings, fols. 5–12 and fols. 13–15, 15 being the odd leaf, and are followed by a pair of leaves, fols. 17–18. The collation of the second book (fols. 19–130) is 5–8$^{8}$, 9$^{9}$ (fol. 57 has been wrongly bound and probably belongs at the end of the eighteenth gathering), 10–17$^{8}$, 18$^{7}$. The middle sheet of the sixth quire (fols. 27–34) has been bound back to front, causing textual dislocation. The third book (fols. 131–46) consists of 19–20$^{8}$, and the fourth (fols. 147–69) of 21$^{8}$, 22$^{9}$, the first leaf being the extra one, and 23$^{6}$. Here the sewing comes after the second leaf, so the two final leaves are possibly loose; there is no break in the text to suggest missing leaves. Quire words are found on the verso of fols. 26, 34, 42, 50, 59, 67, 75, 83, 91, 99, 107, 115, 123, 138, and 163. The only signatures visible are 'a' on fols. 85 and 87, 'b' on fol. 92, 'b ii' on fol. 93, and the top loop of 'b' on fols. 94 and 95.

iii) *Scribes*

Three hands may be distinguished, but the contribution of the second and third is minimal. Hand A is for the most part a rounded Anglican formata, which towards the end of the manuscript becomes noticeably looser. Apparent changes within individual texts can be assigned to a renewal of pen or ink. Hand B, responsible for two lyrics on fols. $143^{v}$–$146^{v}$, is a loose and informal Anglicana of approximately the same date as hand A. Hand C, which is squarer and less cursive than the others, has inserted three short items as space fillers, a macaronic poem on fol. $3^{r}$, the Latin Pentecostal hymn 'Veni creator spiritus' on fol. $16^{v}$, and seven Latin maxims attributed to St Bernard on fol. $57^{r}$.

iv) *Lay-out, rubrication and punctuation*

Almost all the verse items are laid out as verse, the exceptions being the lyrics which form part of Rolle's prose epistles, and part of the second lyric of hand B. In lines of less than eight stresses the internal rhyme is ignored, and the poem written out in long lines, with the end rhyme usually indicated by concatenation in red. Poems with a regular 4:4 stress are written in short lines and laid out two columns to the page.

Capitalization is irregular. Each line of verse usually, but not invariably, starts with a majuscule initial. Proper names appear with both majuscule and minuscule initials. Majuscule initials denote a new sentence where there is no preceding punctuation. They also occur, but not with any regularity, after a punctus, whether that punctus is fulfilling the function of a modern comma or of a full stop. Sometimes each noun in a list is capitalized, if not preceded by an article. Capital 'C' and 'M' often appear in the middle of a sentence for no apparent reason; this is true to a lesser extent of 'S', 'B', 'R', and 'E'.

In the text written in the main hand, rubric initials are used to denote a new text, paragraph or stanza from fols. 19 to 143 and 155 to 169. Spaces are left for rubric initials at fols. 1–16 and 147–54. There is no rubrication at fols. 17–18. The most elaborate decoration occurs at fols. 68–132, where red is no longer the only colour used, and initials and flourishes are found in red interlined with mauve, blue interlined with red, and a combination of red, blue and mauve. Thin red strokes are drawn sporadically through initial letters, not necessarily majuscules, throughout the manuscript; underlining and some of the marginalia are also in red. Spaces at the end of lines are often filled with decorative penwork.

Rubrication occurs too in the punctuation. The sign which indicates the longest pause, ¢ , often used to introduce a new item or category in a list, is red, or occasionally blue, throughout the manuscript. Other forms of punctuation include a short dash, a dot, a dash in the shape of a tick, a sign like a modern 'Y', and occasionally one or two vertical lines. A peculiarity of hand A is a punctus formed by extending the loop of final -e, or less frequently final -t and final -n. The shorter pause or comma is denoted by a sign resembling a modern question mark. Hyphens are represented by one or two thin oblique strokes, and omissions by an inverted 'v'. Errors such as dittography, where marked, are either subpuncted or crossed out.

### v) *Provenance*

On fol. 2$^r$, beneath the manuscript list of contents, is written in green ink 'Constat Johni Thynne', followed by a paraph. This is repeated on fol. 166$^r$ as the final entry in the manuscript: 'Constat Johanni Thynne'. I have not found any examples of the paraph elsewhere, but the writing of Sir John Thynne, first knight of the name and builder of Longleat House, is well attested, and the signatures are undoubtedly his. There exists at Longleat a manusript list of the contents of the library there in 1577: 'The Cataloge of bookes taken in September 1577. S. John Thinnes bookes at longeleate'. These number a total of eighty-five, and the seventy-third and seventy-fourth entries read respectively 'A ladder to heauen in inglishe. An expositioun of the pater noster in lattin and inglishe. the forme of a confessioun in inglishe' and 'Tractatus'. The two entries are bracketed, and a marginal note in the same hand states 'albounde together in written hande'. This is beyond dispute the volume now known as MS 29.

On fol. 168$^r$ is just discernible the signature 'Goldewell', in a hand of the fifteenth century, following five lines of Latin verse of which only a few words remain legible. This could be the hand of a former owner of the manuscript. Letters dated 1548 and 1549[1] testify to a friendship between John Thynne and one Giles Pole, who until 1564 lived in the vicinity of Longleat at Warminster, and whose daughter was by 1567 married to the Longleat steward.[2] Giles Pole was the eldest grandson of Richard Pole (d. 1517). Richard Pole was the second husband of Elizabeth Goldwell, daughter of John Goldwell (d. 1466), citizen and mercer of London. Elizabeth appears to have been childless in both her marriages, and to have predeceased her second husband; in this way Goldwell property could have come into possession of the Pole

[1] *Thynne Papers*, vol. II, fols. 23 and 104.
[2] *Thynne Papers*, Book 149, fol. 16.

family, and the present volume have been given to John Thynne as a friendly contribution to the great new library at Longleat.

vi) *Date*

A probable *terminus a quo* of 1422 is provided by the last item in the manuscript, the revelation described as occurring in 'the ȝere of oure lord MCCCCXXII'. Internal evidence from the text of the exposition on the Lord's Prayer[1] indicates that this limit may be reduced to 1429. The palaeographic evidence suggests a *terminus ad quem* of not later than the middle of the century, or as much as a century after Rolle's death in 1349.

vii) *Contents*

| | |
|---|---|
| Fols. 1ʳ–1ᵛ | blank |
| Fol. 2ʳ | These tretises bene contened in this volume . . . þe peyne of purgatory shewed to a deuout womman solitary.<br>MS Index. |
| 1) Fols. 2ᵛ–3ʳ | Merita visionis corporis Cristi secundum Augustinum in libro de Ciuitate dei . . . sicut sintilla ignis in medio maris, sic omnis impietas viri ad misericordiam dei.<br>A Latin compilation on Corpus Christi, including quotations ascribed to Augustine, Gregory, Bernard, Peter of Ravenna, Anselm, Isidore and Jerome. |
| 2) Fol. 3ʳ | When þi hede quakes, Memento . . . Veni ad judicium.<br>A macaronic poem of eight lines on the Signs of Death (*IMEV Suppl.* 4035) in hand C. Also in ULC Ee iv 35 I, ULC Ff v 48, BL Royal 8 C xii, BL Sloane 747, Bodl. Tanner 407, Queen's Coll. Camb. 13, Trinity Coll. Camb. O 2 53. Printed[2] R. H. Robbins, *Medieval Studies* xxxii (1970), 282–99. |
| Fols. 3ᵛ–4ʳ | blank |

[1] Thesis, pp. 204–5.

[2] Printed refers throughout the list of contents to the text of Lt only.

Fol. 4$^{v}$ Here bygynneth a tretys that is called the laddre of heuyne . . . the ronges of this laddre ben these.

Title and introduction of next item.

3) Fols. 5$^{r}$–11$^{r}$ [T]he first ronge of þis ful holy laddyre is ryght feith with the workes of ryghtwisnesse . . . drawynge vp þis blessed `laddre′ to almyghty god, that ye mow ascende blessedly to his kyngedome.

An anonymous prose treatise in Englsh. Not known elsewhere.

4) Fols. 11$^{r}$–16$^{v}$ [O] thou soul myn whi art þou sorowful and why trowblest þou me. . . . Be pacient and stronge in hope of þe help of god, jn perseueraunce of prayere and of good dedes in aduersite. Amen.

Anonymous prose treatise in English, apparently directly translated by the Lt scribe. Not known elsewhere.

5) Fol. 16$^{v}$ Veni creator spiritus mentes tuorum visita. . . . Sit laus patri cum filio sancto simul paraclito nobisque mittat filius carisma sancti spiritus.

Latin Pentecostal hymn often ascribed to Rabanus Maurus. Hand C.

6) Fol. 17$^{r}$ Here bene contenet ix vertues þe whiche oure lord ihesu crist shewet to an holy man . . . so þat þy fleishe were kut al to peces.

Popular prose text in English, ascribed in many MSS to Albert of Cologne. Similar version found in Bodl. lat. liturg. e 17, BL Arundel 197, Royal 17 A xxvi, ULC Dd xiv 26 III, ULC Ff vi 33.

7) Fols. 17$^{r}$–18$^{v}$ Cur mali bonis habundant. D[iscipulus]: Cur mali diuiciis affluunt potencia florent sanitate vigent. . . . Sunt mali cum illis et non pro illorum sed pro suis malis dampnabuntur.

Latin questions and answers on the nature of good and evil, predestination, prelates, judges, the chosen, and the suffering of children.

8) Fol. 18$^{v}$ Gregorius. Qui cristi vestigia sequi dedignantur. . . . Celum ridet angeli gaudent mundus exultat demones fugiunt jnfernus contremiscit in salutacione angelica cum dicitur Aue Maria.

Latin sayings ascribed to Gregory, Isaiah, Daniel, Bernard, and Chrysostom.

9) Fol. 18$^{v}$ Hugo de sancto victore dicit Omnem creaturam audi quasi triplici voce loquentem. . . . Aqua in me submergeris terra a me absorberis aer in me venti laberis. Ideo Iob N. Interroga iumenta et doccbunt tc.

Passage ascribed to Hugh of St Victor. A similar hand has added 'ad uitam eternam amen' but this is not according to Job 12: 7.

10) Fols. 19$^{r}$–22$^{r}$ Pater noster qui es in celis sanctificetur nomen tuum. O almyghty O alwise and witty O al gracious and good euerlastynge heuenly fader . . . þat I may be j-sauet here and euerlestynge ioy deserue and haue amen. In nomine patris et filii et spiritus sancti amen.

Anonymous English meditation on the Lord's Prayer, combined with a litany naming several Irish saints. Not known elsewhere.

11) Fols. 22$^{r}$–24$^{v}$ O omnipotentissime O sapientissime O prudentissime O graciosissime et O benignissime eterne celestis pater . . . nos omnes introduc ad regnum glorie tue quod est sine fine amen.

Similar, but not identical, Latin version of the above item.

12) Fols. 24$^{v}$–29$^{v}$, 31$^{r}$ Confessio in anglicis. I knowleche and yeld me gilty to god almyghty and to holy chyrch and to þe gostly fader vnder god. . . . I cri god mercy and ask penaunce and absolucioun of god and of holy chirch and pray þe fadyr vnder god to pray to god of myght for me.

Anonymous form of confession in English. Also found in Laud misc. 210, Ashmole 1286 and Harley 4172 (imperfect).

13) Fols. 31$^{v}$, 30$^{r}$ Confiteor tibi pater Rex celi et terre tibique benignissime ihesu vna cum sancto spiritu coram sanctis angelis tuis et omnibus sanctis quia in peccatis sum natus . . . depelle a me queso tenebras tocius iniquitatis et perfidie et accende in

me lumen misericordie tue et ignem sanctissimi et suauissimi amoris tui qui viuis regnas deus etcetera.

Latin form of confession with prayers. No relation to the English item above.

14) Fols. $30^{r}$–$30^{v}$, $32^{r}$–$43^{v}$ Tractatus Ricardi heremite ad Margaretam de Kyrkby Reclusam de vita contemplatiua. In euery synful man and womman. . . . The grace of ihesu criste be with the and kepe the amen.

Rolle's *Form of Living.*

15) Fols. $43^{v}$–$47^{v}$ Ego dormio \`et´ cor meum vigilat. The þat lust loue. . . . In heuyn withouten endynge. Amen.

Rolle's *Ego Dormio.*

16) Fols. $47^{v}$–$50^{v}$ The comandement of god is þat we loue oure lord . . . to see hym in endles ioy þat thay haue loued.

Rolle's *The Commandment.*

17) Fols. $50^{v}$–$51^{r}$ Desyre and delit in ihesu criste . . . withouten gurchynge and heuynesse of thoght.

Rolle's *Desire and Delight.*

18) Fol. $51^{r}$ Gostly gladnesse in ihesu and ioy in hert . . . bot in gladnes in god euermore make þou þi glee.

Rolle's *Ghostly Gladness.*

19) Fols. $51^{v}$–$52^{r}$ Love is lif þat lesteth ay. . . . In loue lyve we and dye. Amen.

Lyric by Rolle (*IMEV* 2007). Printed S. J. Wilson, *RES* x (1959), 341–3.

20) Fols. $52^{r}$–$52^{v}$ Ihesu goddis son lord of mageste. . . . Gif al þi hert to crist þi quert and loue hym euermare. Amen.

Lyric by Rolle (*IMEV* 1715). Printed S. J. Wilson, *RES* x (1959), 344–5.

21) Fol. $53^{r}$ I sigh and sob both day and nyght . . . to loue without endynge. Amen.

Lyric by Rolle (*IMEV Suppl.* after 1364. 5). Printed S. J. Wilson, *RES* x (1959), 345–6.

22) Fols. $53^{r}$–$54^{v}$ Thy ioy be euery dele . . . I ioy withouten end. Amen.

Lyric by Rolle (*IMEV* 3730).

23) Fols. $54^{v}$–$55^{r}$ Al synnes shal þou hate . . . and so purgeth thyne. Amen.

Lyric by Rolle (*IMEV* 200).

24) Fols. $55^{r}$–$56^{v}$, $58^{r}$ Ihesu swet nowe wil I synge. . . . Swet ihesu þer to vs brynge. Amen.

Lyric, possibly the work of Rolle (*IMEV* 3238).

25) Fol. $57^{v}$ Almyghty god fadyre of heuyn . . . lord ihesu haue mercy on me.

Lyric (*IMEV* 241) also found in ULC Ii vi 43 (two versions), ULC Dd viii 2, Bodley 789, Harley 2406, and Lambeth 559. Printed S. J. Ogilvie-Thomson, *RES* xxv (1974), 390–1.

26) Fol. $57^{v}$ Mary of help both day and nyght . . . Mary mercy þou haue on me.

Lyric (*IMEV* 2121) also found in Lambeth 559. Printed S. J. Ogilvie-Thomson, *RES* xxv (1974), 391–2.

27) Fols. $57^{v}$, $57^{r}$ Mary modyre wel þe be . . . þat euer lesteth without mysshe. Amen.

Lyric (*IMEV* 2119), found in 31 MSS as part of the *Speculum Christiani* (ed. G. Holmstedt, EETS 182), and separately in 21 other MSS. Holmstedt mistakenly described the readings of Longleat 30 as those of Lt.

28) Fol. $57^{r}$ Bernardus dicit quod septem sunt si homo consideraret illa bene in eternum non peccaret. . . . Septima est consideracio gracie jneffabilis.

Latin list of seven points to consider, attributed to St Bernard. Hand C.

29) Fol. $58^{v}$ Omnipotens sempiterne deus qui dedisti famulis tuis. And þre pater noster and Auees And than kysse þe erthe and say . . . space and grace for thi mercy and pitte dere and swet ihesu etcetera. Explicit tractatus Ricardi heremite de hampolle ad Margaretam Reclusam de Kyrkby de amore dei.

Excerpt from a meditation on the Passion by Rolle.

30) Fols. $58^{v}$–$69^{r}$ Incipit tractatus Magistri Walteri de Hultone de

vita actiua et contemplatiua ad quemdam [*sic*]. Grace and þe goodnesse of our lord ihesu crist þat he hath shewed to the . . . Ransaker of þe myght of god and of his mageste without gret clennesse mekenesse shal be ouerleid and oppressed of hym self etcetera. Explicit tractatus Walteri de Hultone de vita actiua contemplatiua et mixta.

Shorter version of Hilton's *Mixed Life*, as found in Vernon, Chetham 6690, Rawl. A 355, Laud misc. 685, Plimpton 271, Simeon, Thornton, Harley 2254, and an unclassified Takamiya manuscript (ex Bradfer-Lawrence 10), the last four being imperfect.

31) Fols. 69[r]–73[v] Here may men lerne how thay shold suffre desaises gladly and nat dispeire be þay neuer so grete and also some of the gret and suttle temptaciouns of the fend and mannys fleysh agayns the sowle and of þe gracious remedies ayeyns ham. For as myche as the apostle seith that without feith no man may plese god . . . and graunt cristen mennys soules victory ouer þe fend to worshipe of þat lord. Amen. Explicit.

English version of Flete's *De Remediis contra Temptaciones*, as in Hunterian 520, Harley 6615, ULC Hh i 11, and BL Add. 37049.

32) Fols. 74[r]–78[r] Here begynneth þe lamentacioun of oure lady seynt Mary and al þe wordes þat were spok betwix hire sone ihesu and hyre in þe tyme of his passioune. Whan þat I Mary iesus modyr sat in Ierusalem . . . and þus endeth oure ladies lamentacioun with grete ioy of goddis ressurreccioun he graunt vs al his benysone. Amen. Expliciunt lamentaciones Marie in passione filii sui ihesu cristi.

Marian lament in English prose, also found in ULC Ii iv 9, Cotton Cleo. D vii, and Bodley 596.

33) Fols. 78[v]–80[v] Qualiter homo debet affici vel vti ad compaciendum cristo crucifixo. Ad compaciendum domino

nostro ihesu cristo crucifixo primo studeas quantum potes te vnire illi per feruentem amorem . . . non quiescat cor meum bone ihesu donec inueniat centrum suum ibi cubet ibi suum terminet appetitum. Amen.

Anonymous Latin treatise.

34) Fols. 81^r–128^v Prima pars penitencie. Oure swete lord god of heuyn þat no man wold perishe bot wol þat we al come to þe knowlech of hym and þe blisful lyf þat is perdurable. . . . This blisful regne may men purchace by pouerte spirituel and þe glorie by lownesse þe plente of ioy by hunger and þurst and þe rest by trauaille and þe lyf by deth and mortyficacioun of syn etcetera. Explicit deo gracias.

Chaucer's *Parson's Tale.*

Fols. 129^r–130^v blank

35) Fols. 131^r–143^r Loue of kynde and care me byndeth lady ȝow to lere with þe witte of wisemen. . . . Wisse vs in þe way of lyve To þe blisse þat hath none ende. Amen. Deo gracias.

Anonymous English prose treatise in three parts, ending in poem. Not known elsewhere.

36) Lower margins of fols. 131^r–144^r, 145^r–146^v Offe witte and wisedome þe begynnynge. . . . These bene prouerbes of Salomon þe wisest man þat euer was one.

Thirty-one proverbs in the form of rhyming couplets. Not known elsewhere.

37) Fols. 143^v, 145^r, 144^r Myghtffull mari y crownyd quene . . . helpe me lady ffull off grace. Amen ffor charite.

Lyric (*IMEV Suppl.* 2169) in hand B. Not known elsewhere.

Fol. 144^v blank

38) Fols. 145^v–146^v Timor mortis conturbat me þys is my song in my old age. . . . So þat whe neuer haue cause to say timor mortis conturbat me. Amen ffor charite.

Lyric (*IMEV* 3743) in hand B. Found also in Porkington 10.

39) Fols. 147$^{r}$–148$^{r}$ [I]n seiynge of þis orisone stynteth and bydeth at euery cros and þynketh whate ye haue seide ffor a more deuout prayere fond I neuer of the passioun who so wolde deuoutly say hitte. [I]hesu þat hast me dere j boght. . . . In ioy and blisse to lyue aye. Amen.

Lyric (*IMEV* 1761) found also in Bodl. e Museo 232, Bodl. Add. E 4, Bodl. 850, BL Add. 39574, Sloane 963, Egerton 3245, Huntington HM 142, Longleat 30, Pepys 2125, and Lambeth 559 (last two imperfect). Printed C. Brown, *RL XIV*, pp. 114–19.

40 Fols. 148$^{v}$–149$^{r}$ [O] Myghtful ihesu grete was þe peyne þat ȝe suffred . . . desyrynge perfitly and youre dyuyn wille. In wirship of þis wounde. Pater. Aue.

English prose meditation and prayers inspired by the cult of the Five Wounds. Found also in Bodl. e Museo 232.

41) Fols. 149$^{r}$–152$^{v}$ [A] womman recluse and solitarie coueitynge to know þe noumbre of þe woundes of oure lord ihesu crist . . . and kepe my soule in ioy þe whiche þat þou boghtest with þy precious blode. Amen for charite. Pater noster. Aue maria.

English prose version of the prayers known as the *Fifteen Ooes*, with prose introduction. English versions are found also in Harley 172, Lyell 30 (shortened introduction), Harley 2398 (shortened introduction), Tanner 407 (introduction), Bodley 850 (prayers), BL Add. 15216 (prayers), Royal 17 C xvii (prayers).

42) Fol. 152$^{v}$ A deuout orisone to our lord ihesu crist. [H]ayl ihesu crist word of þe ffadir . . . oure endles lif borne of þe virgyn Modyre haue mercy of vs. Amen.

English prose translation of the well-known 'Ave Iesu Criste verbum patris'. Similar translation found in BL Add. 39574.

43) Fols. 153$^{r}$–153$^{v}$ [O] Benigne ihesu þat woldest suffre so many greuous peynes and deth for mankynde . . . euer

ioyen in your goodnesse in blisse alwey lestynge amen.

English prose prayer, found also in Lyell 30.

44) Fols. 153v–154r O þanked be ye holy fadyr myȝtful god . . . glorye and praysynge with al reuerence be offred to yow of al good creatures withouten end amen.

English prose prayer, found also in Lyell 30.

45) Fol. 154r This meditacioun is good to sey euery day erly afor oþer prayeres. [A]lmyghty ihesu goddis son þrogh þe holygost conceyuet and borne of Mary virgyn þe I thank . . . al angelles patriarches prophetes apostles martires confessours virgynes wydews and al seyntes haue mynd and mercy of vs synful wreches. Amen.

English prose prayer, not known elsewhere.

Fol. 154v blank

46) Fols. 155r–165v Reuelacio notabilis. Al maner thynge þat is begone þat may turne to profite of mannys soule to god al only be þe wyrship ȝevyn. . . . Nomore fadyre at þis tyme bot god brynge vs to his kyngedome. Amen. Expliciunt Reuelaciones reuelate cuidam sancte Mulieri recluse.

A revelation of purgatory in English prose, found also in MSS Thornton and Bodl. Eng. th. c 58 (both imperfect).

Fol. 166r blank except for John Thynne's signature and paraph.

Fols. 166v–169v blank apart from scribbles, which include the signature 'Goldewell'.

viii) *Earlier descriptions*

Lt was first described in 1872 by the Historical Manuscripts Commission.[1] This report appears to have depended largely on the manuscript index, and is consequently very imperfect. English texts not noted are items 2, 4, 6, 15–18, 40, and 42–5. Item 12 is wrongly described as occupying eleven pages; items 19–23 and 25–7 are included in the description of 24, and the fact that the latter three are written on an intrusive leaf is not noted. Item 32 is wrongly described as occupying nine

[1] *Report* III, p. 181.

pages; *The Parson's Tale* takes up forty-eight leaves, not forty-nine; item 35 thirteen instead of twenty-five; item 46 is in prose, not verse.

Carleton Brown's notice in the *Register*[1] depended on this report, and consequently perpetrated the same errors.

Miss Allen[2] describes the Rolle texts in the manuscript. Her foliation is consistently out by two: f. 28 should read f. 30, etc. She incorrectly states *Ghostly Gladness* to be in the Thornton MS instead of ULC Dd v 64.

The faulty foliation in the *IMEV*[3] has been largely corrected in the *Supplement*; in the latter the only incorrect numbering is that of item 19 (f. $51^{v}$ not $51^{a}$), and the final page of item 24 (f. $58^{r}$ not $58^{b}$). Item 38 is oddly described in the *Supplement* as a lyric 'with a prose comment following which concludes with riming lines'.

The most complete description given hitherto is that of Manly and Rickert in their edition of *The Canterbury Tales*.[4] Their list of contents purports to single out the more important pieces for mention, but they have omitted items 15, 31, 40, and 42–5, and item 11 is inexplicably described as sixteenth-century Latin. Their foliation of items 3, 6, 12, and 19–27 is incorrect. Item 31 has been included in item 30, and items 40 and 42–5 in 41. The poem which concludes item 35 is not written in the margins of fols. 142–3 but as the main text; possibly this was confused with the proverbs (item 36) which are written in the bottom margins of fols. $131^{r}$–$144^{r}$ and $145^{r}$–$146^{v}$, and which are not mentioned at all. Item 37 is wrongly described as two poems. Their collation of the fourth book of the manuscript is inaccurate: $3^{4}$ should read $3^{6}$.

Manly and Rickert describe the manuscript as being in several different hands and styles. However this opinion is not upheld by palaeographers such as Neil Ker who have examined the manuscript, and whose judgement must invalidate the statement that the 'compilation was almost certainly made in a monastery, perhaps Christchurch, Canterbury, by a number of monks, one beginning the principal book, others adding smaller books that precede or follow, and still more filling in blank spaces with quotations etc.' Their collation showed the Lt text of *The Parsons's Tale* to be from an immediate common ancestor with the Ellesmere MS, but without the latter's editing, and so of high textual value, and it was for this reason that they were anxious to place

[1] *A Register of Middle English Religious and Didactic Verse* (Oxford, 1916–20), pp. 473–4.

[2] *Writings*, pp. 34–6.

[3] Entries 2007, 3730, 200, 3238, 241, 2121, 2119.

[4] J. M. Manly and E. Rickert, *The Text of the Canterbury Tales* (Chicago, 1940), i. 343–8.

the manuscript in the environs of Canterbury, and correctly identified members of the Goldwell family who held office in the priory there. However the manuscript shows none of the palaeographic characteristics of a Canterbury text, and although the link with the Goldwells remains valid, this is indication of ownership rather than composition. Moreover the contents of a volume such as Lt militate against monastic ownership, whereas there is every possibility that it would be the property of a devout lay family.

## BODLEY e Mus. 232 (Mu)

### i) *External*

Bodl. e Mus. 232 is a parchment volume of vii + 70 leaves, measuring 165 × 120 mm. It is still in its original binding of white leather, much worn, on bevelled boards. The second of the front flyleaves contains the inscription 'Ex dono Alex. Featherston Vicarij de Wolverton in Comitatu Bucks et Praebendarij de College in Cathedrali Ecclesia Lichfieldiensi A.D. 1680', and above it a contemporary hand has written 'Rich. Hampole–Meditations one the Passions of Christ', 'A Treatise of Edmond Archbishop of Canterbury', and the present shelf mark. On the seventh flyleaf a later hand adds 'See Bale ij for Richard Hampole p. 191.1'. The end flyleaves (fols. 67–70) originally formed part of a late thirteenth-century copy of the *Decretals* of Gregory IX, lib. 1, tit. 3, cc. 22–5. The average size of the manuscript pages is 160 × 113 mm., and of the written material 124 × 85 mm. Vertical ruling in the left hand margin and pricking are consistent, giving twenty-six lines to the page; there is some horizontal ruling. The manuscript has suffered some staining and cutting, but is legible throughout.

### ii) *Collation*

1–$7^{8}$, $8^{10}$, fols. 65 and 66 being a single sheet folded over and inserted at the end of the quire, $9^{4}$. Quire words occur regularly, and on fols. 10–11, 19–20, 25–8, 34–6, 43–4, and 50–2 respectively the signatures a ii–iii, b iii–iiii, c i–iiii, d ii–iiii, E iii–iiii, and F ii–iiii are visible.

### iii) *Scribes, lay-out, etc.*

The hand throughout the English text is that of the main hand of Lt, and the system of punctuation similar. Rubrication in red and blue is consistent until the last two items. The verse text is laid out as verse, but without concatenation.

iv) *Provenance*

The manuscript, together with several others volumes,[1] was presented to the Bodleian library in 1680 by Alexander Fetherston, vicar of Wolverton, Bucks, and prebendary of Lichfield Cathedral. Indications of earlier ownership are sparse; on fol. 69$^{v}$ a note in Tudor secretary, probably early sixteenth-century, reads 'Sspke to my nores for the krysneng shyt',[2] and on fol. 69$^{r}$ the signatures 'Annes hemperby', 'Annes helperby', 'Annes helperby', 'Elyȝabethe Stoughton', together with the opening phrases of the Hail Mary, all in contemporary late fifteenth-century hands, may testify to the manuscript's presence in a community of women. It is of interest that Helperby, in North Yorkshire, is only some ten miles from Kirkby Wiske, the probable birthplace of Rolle's disciple Margaret.

The text on fol. 62$^{r}$ concludes with the signature, in red, 'Jon Flemmyn', but I have it on Neil Ker's authority[3] that, although contemporary, this is not the hand of the Mu/Lt scribe. Possibly he was the rubricator, for it is at the point where his signature occurs that the manuscript rubrication ends. The same name occurs in a *Prick of Conscience* manuscript, Trinity College Dublin 156, where there are two marginal notes in a seventeenth-century hand 'Johannes Fleming hunc librum composuit'. This manuscript shows the same Anglo-Irish dialectal features as Mu,[4] and it would be tempting to presume a connection between the two, but this is not indicated palaeographically; differences in minim formation have convinced R. E. Alton that the Mu signature and the *Prick of Conscience* text are not in the same hand. If the late ascription to John Fleming is authoritative,[5] the similarity in names would thus seem to be coincidental.

[1] e Mus. MSS 15, 64, 66, 196, and probably 212.

[2] I am grateful to R. E. Alton for deciphering this.

[3] Confirmed by A. I. Doyle, *Survey* ii. 91.

[4] See below, p. xxxix.

[5] Most of the first page of the manuscript has been obliterated by gall stain, and the text supplied by the same hand as the ascription. Professors Lewis and McIntosh (pp. 51–2) take this writer to be John Fleming, but a page and a half of text scarcely seems to justify the description 'hunc librum'.

v) *Date*

There is no evidence, internal or external, for the date of Mu's composition, but it must be approximately that of Lt, i.e. 1430–50.

vi) *Contents*

1) Fols. $1^{r}$–$18^{r}$ Here begynneth a deuout meditacioun vp þe passioun of crist j made by Richard Rolle heremyt of hampolle. Lord as þou made me of noght . . . and ye abiden stil by þe rode fote.

Meditation on the Passion attributed to Rolle.

2) Fols. $18^{r}$–$23^{v}$ Seynt Gregory þe doctour seith þat without mekenes hit is vnleful to trust of foryeveness of þy syn. . . . For he wil noþer ete drynk ne slepe ne wak bot for more fortherynge of þe loue of god and what so euer he doth hit semeth in þe louyn of god. Expliciunt xii gradus humilitatis.

Treatise on humility and the twelve degrees of meekness, attributed to St Gregory and St Bernard. Also found in Rawl. C 894, Bodl. 220, Bodl. lat. th. e 26, Laud misc. 517, Harley 4011, Harley 4012, Royal 17 C xviii, Worcester Cath. F 172, and Coughton Court.

3) Fols. $24^{r}$–$62^{r}$ In þe name of oure swete lord ihesu crist here begynnen matires the wheche ben touched in þe tretis folwynge rudely endited to shon curiosite þat no man leve of inward holynesse for outward curiouse speche. . . . Here is endet þe tretice of seynt Edmond of pountney þat is called þe myrrour of holy chirche translated by Nicholas Bellew whose noun konnynge haue ye excused.

English version of St Edmund's *Mirror*. Other complete versions, without the translator's name, are found in Vernon, Simeon, Thornton, Bodl. 416, Douce 25, Peniarth 395, Huntington HM 502, BL Add. 10053, BL Add. 33995, Harley 4012, Westminster School 3, Madresfield Court (unclassified), and Coughton Court, Throckmorton MS. On fol. $23^{v}$ a seventeenth-century hand notes that the following matter was composed by St Edmund, Archbishop of Canterbury, in 1240.

4) Fols. 62$^{r}$–65$^{v}$ [I]n seiynge of þis orisone stynteth and bydeth at euery cros and thynketh whate ȝe haue seide ffor a more deuout prayere ffond I neuer of þe passioun who so wold deuoutly say hit as hit folweth. . . . In ioy and blisse to lyue ay. Amen.

See Lt, item 39.

5) Fols. 65$^{v}$–66$^{v}$ [O] Myghtful ihesu grete was þe peyne . . . pater noster aue.

See Lt, item 40.

vii) *Earlier descriptions*

*Summary Catalogue* 3657, with additional information in the annotated Bodleian copy which I have incorporated above. Item 5 is not mentioned.

Allen, *Writings*, p. 279, who wrongly identifies John Flemmyn as the scribe.

Doyle, ii. 90–1.

## LANGUAGE OF BASE MANUSCRIPTS

On linguistic evidence Professors McIntosh and Samuels[1] classify the dialect of Lt and Mu as Anglo-Irish. They list thirty distinguishing features of this dialect, any of which can and does appear in other dialects, but which cumulatively argue Anglo-Irish provenance. In Lt five of these features never occur; ten, predominantly of a phonological nature,[2] occur regularly; in the rest, predominantly morphological, the scribe shows such marked inconsistency that it appears he was prepared to adopt whatever forms he found in his copy.

The more significant characteristics of his language, showing both customary usage and flexibility, are as follows:

The reflex of OE *ā* normally appears as *o*, but *a* is found occasionally in texts of Northern origin, as Rolle: *haly*, and, particularly in rhyme, *lare*, *mare*, *sare*.

[1] 'Prolegomena to a study of medieval Anglo-Irish', *Medium Ævum* xxxvii (1968), 1–11.

[2] e.g. the forms *streynth*, *euche*, *þrogh*, *hyre* 'hear', *fale* 'many', *sylle* 'sell', *thegh*, *sigge* as against *segge*.

OE *ă* before a simple nasal is regularly *a*; before a lengthening group both *a* and *o* are found.

OE *y̆* normally appears as *y* or *i*, but *u* is found occasionally in *bury*, *thurst-*, *lust* v., *þurleden*, *cusset*, *clustre*, and *e* in *iberiet*, *mery*, *euel*, *besy-*.

The preferred vowel in unstressed inflexional syllables is *e*; *i/y* is frequent in the gen.sg., especially *Goddis*, *Cristis*, but very rare in the p.p.

The normal pr.2 sg.ind. ending is *-est*, but there are eleven occurrences of *-s* in the Rolle texts. Normal pr.3 sg.ind. is *-eth*, occasionally reduced to *-et*, with two occurrences of *-s* in Rolle texts.

Pr.pl.ind. shows both *-eth*, *-en* and no ending, the preference varying from text to text, although *-eth* predominates in the Rolle texts. Similar variation is seen in the use of *-n* in the strong p.p., it is preferred in the Rolle texts. Infinitives in *-n* are relatively infrequent.

Pr.p. is regularly *-ynge*, even when rhyming on *-and.*

The 3rd pl.nom.pron. is regularly *þay* (variously spelt); acc./dat. *ham*, less frequently *hem*, with only one occurrence of *thaym*; gen. *har(e)*, less frequently *her(e)*, and three occurrences of *þar.*

Initial *sh-* is always spelt as such. Medially it varies between *sh* and *ssh*, very rarely *sch.* Occasionally *s(s)h* is found for *ss*, as in *mysshe* 'miss' n. and v. rhyming on *-isse.*

The initial consonant in 'give' and related forms is predominantly *y*, but *g* occurs sporadically throughout.

Earlier *ht* is spelt both *ght* and *ȝt*, and initial [j] both *y* and *ȝ*; in both cases Mu prefers the *ȝ* forms. Items 39 and 40 in Lt correspond to items 4 and 5 in Mu, and here the scribe's spelling habits can be compared in detail. Small but significant variants in both manuscripts make it unlikely that one was copied from the other; whether they came from the same source or not, it is clear that he was prepared to interchange medial *i* and *y*, unstressed *e* and *y*, final *d* and *t*, and initial and final *þ* and *th*, and that final *-e* had no inflexional significance.

The sum of these features points to the standard fifteenth-century literary language based on the East Midland dialect(s), with a sprinkling of South-Eastern forms. The scribe's flexibility in all but a few of the Anglo-Irish criteria suggests that he had left his native country some time before, retaining only traces of his original linguistic habits.

## SUMMARY DESCRIPTION OF MANUSCRIPTS CONTAINING ROLLE TEXTS

### *The Form of Living*

1. Longleat 29 (Lt). Fols. 30$^{r}$–30$^{v}$, 32$^{r}$–43$^{v}$. Incipit 'Tractatus Ricardi heremite ad Margaretam de Kyrkby Reclusam de vita contemplatiua'. 'Hampolle' is written in the top margin of several pages, and once (fol. 42$^{v}$) 'Amor dei'.
2. University College Oxford 97 (U). Fols. 133$^{v}$–153$^{r}$. 'Heere bigynneth a trete þat Richard hermyte maade to a good ankeresse þat he louede.' 'Margaret' omitted in final paragraph. Other contents in common with S, W, G, P, Ld, B$^{2}$, La, Lt$^{2}$, Ff$^{2}$.

   Coxe 1852, i. 28–9; Doyle, ii. 148–161.
3. Bodl. Rawl. A 389 (R). Fols. 85$^{r}$–95$^{v}$. No incipit, Margaret's name omitted. Other contents include Rolle's *Incendium Amoris* and *Emendatio Vitae* in Latin, *The Commandment*, and two versions of *Ego Dormio*. There are three leaves missing before the start of the *Form*, and it is probable that these included a separate version of the passage on the Name of Jesus (*Form*, lines 610–25), as the opening lines of this passage 'If þou wilt be wel with god and haue grace to rewele þi lif wel right and come to þe ioye of luf þis name' occur just before the lacuna. The *Form* and the second version of *Ego Dormio* are separated by 'Amen', but have an explicit which possibly applies to both texts: 'Explicit quoddam notabile Ricardi Rolle heremite'. The Rolle texts evidently derive from a number of sources.

   Macray 1862, cols. 386–90; Doyle, ii. 143–7.
4. Paris Bibliothèque Ste-Geneviève 3390 (G). Fols. 57$^{v}$–95$^{v}$. 'Here bigynneþ a drawing of contemplacioun maad bi Richard hermite of hampole to an ancresse.' Also contains *Ego Dormio*, separated, as in R, S, V, only by 'Amen', and concluded 'Explicit Ricardus hampole'. Margaret's name omitted. Other contents in common with U, W, Ld, and Ld$^{2}$.

   *Catalogue Général des Manuscrits des Bibliothèques Publiques de France: Paris, Bibliothèque Sainte-Geneviève* (Paris, 1893–9); Doyle, ii. 38–9; W. P. Cummings, *PMLA* 42 (1927), 862–4.
5. BL Add. 22283 [Simeon] (S). Fols. 147$^{v}$–150$^{v}$. 'Her biginneþ þe fourme of perfyt liuinge þe whuche holi richard þe hermit of hampulle wrot to a recluse þat was i cleped Margrete.' Also contains

*Ego Dormio*, *The Commandment*, and the poem *Ihesu Swete*. As in R and G, the *Form* and *Ego Dormio* are separated only by 'Amen', and the two pieces concluded with a possibly common 'Explicit quoddam notabile Ricardi heremite'. It is of note that Rolle's surname is present only in R. However, unlike R and G, S gives Margaret's name in the final paragraph. Other contents in common with U, Ii, Ld, P, Ff$^2$, T$^3$, Ad$^2$, Th, and of course V.

*Additions Catalogue* 1854–1860, pp. 623–6; Doyle, ii. 162–72; Lewis and McIntosh, pp. 72–4; A. I. Doyle, 'The Shaping of the Vernon and Simeon Manuscripts', *Chaucer and Middle English Studies in honour of R. H. Robbins*, ed. B. Rowland (London, 1974).

6 Bodl. Eng. poet. a 1 [Vernon] (V). Fols. $334^{v}$–$338^{r}$ (corrected numbering). Incipit, explicit, format and Rolle contents as S. Other contents in common with Ad$^2$, Ld, Ii, T$^3$, P, and Th.

*SC* 3938–42; Doyle, ii. 162–72; Lewis and McIntosh, pp. 103–4; M. S. Serjeantson, *MLR* 32 (1937), 222–61.

7. Westminster School 3 (W). Fols. $205^{r}$-$225^{r}$. No incipit or explicit, but Margaret's name given. Also contains *Ego Dormio*, the two pieces written as one. The text has been corrected in several places. Other contents in common with U, G, Ld, B$^2$, Ld$^2$, T$^3$, Ff$^2$, Hh, Ii$^2$, Ha, and H.

Doyle, ii. 26–7; Ker, I. 422–4.

8. Trinity College Cambridge B 14 38 [322] (T). Fols. $127^{v}$–$148^{v}$. No incipit or explicit, but Margaret's name given. No other Rolle texts. A Wycliffite manuscript.

James, 1900–4, I. 437–48; Doyle, ii. 13–14.

9 ULC Dd v 64 III (Dd). Fols. 1–$22^{v}$. 'Incipit forma uiuendi scripta a beato Ricardo heremita ad Margaretam anachoritam suam dilectam discipulam.' 'Explicit forma uiuendi.' Margaret's name given. The *Form* is divided into chapters, the divisions occurring at lines 121, 232, 266, 309, 322, 488, 524, 609, 625, and 835 of the Lt text; a separate piece on the seven gifts of the Holy Ghost is inserted between lines 835 and 836 to form a twelfth chapter. The manuscript is in three sections, the first two containing Rolle's Latin works *Emendatio Vitae*, *Super Oracionem Dominicam*, *Incendium Amoris*, and probably originally the *Melum Contemplativorum* (Allen, *Writings*, p. 116). The third section contains the *Form*, *Ego Dormio*, *The Commandment*, thirteen lyrics, the authorship of some being considered by Miss Allen to be in doubt, and *Ghostly Gladness*, the penultimate item, which concludes 'Expliciunt cantica

diuini amoris secundum Ricardum Hampole'. The lyrics are followed by the beginning of a piece on the three workings in man's soul (*Writings*, p. 364, printed Horstman, i. 82), ascribed to Rolle in Trinity College Cambridge MS O 8 26, but in Dd the following leaves are missing, and there is no evidence that in this manuscript his name was ever attached. The same piece occurs anonymously in P.

*ULC Catalogue*, i. 278–80; Doyle, ii. 80.

10. Bodl. Rawl. C 285 (R$^2$). Fols. $40^r$–$57^v$. No incipit or explicit. 'Cecil' (? Cecily) substituted for Margaret. Also contains a separate version of lines 610–25 (fols. $59^r$–$59^v$, collated here as R$^3$) which merges without a break into a passage from the *Oleum Effusum*. All contents also found in Ff, with the exception of Book II of Hilton's *Scale*. Other contents in common with Dd$^2$ and H$^3$.

Macray, 1878, cols. 123–4; Doyle, ii. 115–16; Lewis and McIntosh, p. 157.

11. ULC Ff v 40 (Ff). Fols. $98^r$–$114^r$. No incipit or explicit. 'M' for Margaret. Also contains a separate version of lines 610–25 (Ff$^3$), as R$^2$, *The Commandment*, and an English version of *Emendatio Vitae*. Other contents common with R$^2$ and Dd$^2$.

*ULC Catalogue*, ii. 498–500; Doyle, ii. 116; Lewis and McIntosh, pp. 151–2.

12. BL Lansdowne 455 (L). Fols. $34^r$–$40^v$. No incipit. Last paragraph (lines 894 to end) omitted. *Form* ends 'Ardeat in nobis diuini feruor amoris', an explicit more commonly associated with *The Pistyl of Love*. The text of the *Form* is not all in the same hand, and there is a striking change of exemplar at l. 104. Also contains *Emendatio Vitae* in English, as Ff, C, D, Ad, Br, and Lt$^2$.

*Lansdowne Catalogue*, p. 126; Doyle, ii. 88.

13. Caius College Cambridge 669 (C). Fols. $75^v$–$106^r$. 'Now her bigynneþ anoþer good tretys of Richarde of hampole.' Original index entry reads 'Also an oþer tretis of Richard hampole þat is clepyd Amore langueo þat he made to a recluse'. *Form* ends 'Amen ihesu amen quod Iohn cok. Here endeþ þe tretys of Richarde hermyte of hampole þat ys clepid Amore langueo. Quod IX and III'. Margaret's name given. Long final variant shared with HeT$^3$BIiM. Also contains *Emendatio Vitae* in English.

James 1907–8, ii. 666–7; Doyle, ii. 201–2.

14. Hereford Cathedral Library P i 9 (He). Fols. $141^r$–$150^v$. Original index entry reads 'Vita inclusarum anglice'. Marginal heading

'Informacio sancti Ricardi de hampull scripta margarete incluse de hampull'. No explicit. 'M' for Margaret. Lines 595–609, including the lyric, omitted. Apparently a Franciscan volume (Doyle, i. 195).

*A Descriptive Catalogue of the Manuscripts in the Hereford Cathedral Library*, compiled by A. T. Bannister, with an Introduction by M. R. James (Hereford, 1927), pp. 105–6; Doyle, ii. 74–5.

15. Bodl. Digby 18 (D). Fols. 68v–93v. No incipit, rubric 'In alle þi doyingis þenke on þe ende'. Ends (l. 896) '. . . preie for richard heremite þat' whereupon the manuscript ends. This might suggest that D is descended from a copy bearing Rolle's own signature, but if this is so, it must have undergone several changes in transmission. The rest of its text is not outstanding, and Margaret's name is omitted. Also contains an English version of *Emendatio Vitae*, and an English text of the seven penitential psalms, here wrongly ascribed to 'Richard hampole heremyte'.

Macray 1883, col. 14; Doyle, ii. 88.

16. Trinity College Cambridge O 1 29 [1053] ($T^3$). Fols. 99v–117v. No incipit or explicit, ending 'amen par charite quod Jone ?Voulle. Finito libro reddeat gracia cristo god helpe now'. 'My deere freende in ihesu criste' substituted for Margaret. 'Amen' at l. 266. Text very verbose, full of pious ejaculations, doubled adjectives, etc., and these non-substantive variants are not recorded beyond l. 104. Miss Allen is incorrect in saying lines 1–121 are omitted. Also contains *The Commandment*. Other contents in common with S, V, W, Ii, P, Ld, $B^2$ $Ii^2$, and Th.

James 1900–4, III. 33–4; Doyle, ii. 87.

17. Bodley 110 (B). Fols. 134v–154r. No incipit or explicit. Margaret's name omitted. Text sometimes addressed to 'Frend'. Several hands, and frequent corrections, both right and wrong. Other contents mainly in Latin.

*SC* 1963; Doyle, ii. 272–3.

18. ULC Ii iv 9 (Ii). Fols. 190r–197v. Lines 1–282 and 765 to end only, lacuna being accidental. No incipit, Margaret's name omitted. Concludes 'Here endith the informacioun of Richerd the Ermyte þat he wrote to an Ankyr translate oute of Northern tunge in to Sutherne that it schulde the bettir be vnderstondyn of men that be of the Selve countre Amen'. Miss Allen read 'Selve' as 'Selbe', but Selby, Yorkshire, is hardly Southern and 'same' seems a more probable meaning. Other contents in common with $T^3$, S, V, Ld, P, and Lt.

*ULC Catalogue*, iii. 448–50; Doyle, ii. 55–7.

19. New York, Pierpont Morgan M 818 (M). Fols. 5$^{v}$–15$^{v}$. No incipit or explicit. 'Margery' for Margaret. Ex Ingilby (*Writings*, p. 262, XXXIII), ex Harmsworth 1945.

*Census Supplement*, p. 360; Doyle, ii. 57; Kane, pp. 8–9.

20. Magdalene College Cambridge Pepys 2125 (P). Fols. 84$^{r}$–85, 102$^{v}$–104$^{r}$, 108$^{r}$–116$^{v}$. Lines 1–121 are separated from the rest of the work and occur twice, in similar but not identical versions (collated as $P^1$ and $P^2$). The second extract begins 'Incipit tractatus Ricardi hampol heremite de conuersione ad deum et eius amore', breaking off at l. 121 with the note 'Quere residuum superioris istius tractatus in quinto folio subsequenti. Et incipit sic ffor þou hast forsake þe ioye and þe solas of þis worlde etcetera', recommencing on fol. 108$^{r}$ (not 109) with the heading 'For men and wymmen that beþ enclosed'. The whole concludes 'Richard of hampol made þis rewle of lyuyng'. 'Womman' substituted for Margaret. At l. 525 'Thre degrees of loue I shal tel þe', this manuscript adds 'shortly for y haue wryten of hem more pleynly byfore'. Also contains *The Commandment* and *Ego Dormio*. Other contents in common with Ld, U, S, V, Dd, $T^3$, Ii, $Ii^2$, $Ff^2$, and $Lt^2$.

James 1923, pp. 72–9; Doyle, ii. 128–9.

21. Beeleigh Abbey, Foyle MS (F). Fols. 131$^{v}$–146$^{r}$. 'Hic incipit liber Ricardi Hampole quem fecit vni anachorite.' No explicit. Margaret's name given. Ex Amherst (*Writings*, p. 262, XXXIV), ex Harmsworth 1945, ex Davis and Orioli. Other contents (*Prick of Conscience*) in common with S and V.

Lewis and McIntosh, 35–6.

22. Bodl. Laud misc. 210 (Ld). Fols. 1–19$^{v}$. No incipit. 'Explicit tractatus qui uocatur Forma viuendi compositus a Ricardo heremita de hampole qui obijt ibidem anno domini M CCC xl ix.' Margaret's name given. Other contents in common with Lt, P, U, W, S, V, $T^3$, Ii, $B^2$, Ro, Th.

*Quarto Catalogue* II, cols. 181–3; Doyle, ii. 39–40.

23. San Marino California Huntington HM 127 (H). Fols. 34$^{r}$–50$^{v}$. 'Incipit liber nuncupatus Amore langueo.' Margaret's name omitted. No explicit. *Form* immediately followed by a lyric (*IMEV* 611) as in $T^2$ below. Other contents in common with $Ii^2$, Ha, W.

*Census* I, 53; Hodgson, xvii; Doyle, ii. 86; *Handlist*, pp. 12–13.

24. Trinity College Cambridge B 15 17 [353] ($T^2$). Fols. 131$^{r}$–147$^{r}$. No

incipit or explicit, Margaret's name omitted. Text very similar to that of H. This manuscript was not known to Miss Allen.

James 1900–4, I. 480–1; Kane and Donaldson, 13–14.

25. Bodley 938 (B[2]). Fols. 209$^r$–236$^v$. 'Here bigynneþ a tretys whiche is clepid þe pricke of loue after Richard Hampol heremyte treting of iii degrees of loue.' No explicit, Margaret's name omitted. The text has undergone some correction. Miss Allen is wrong in stating that the lyrics are absent. Wycliffite texts, including an extract from the interpolated Rolle *Psalter*. Other contents in common with U, W, Ii[2], T[3], Ld, Ff[2], Hh.

*SC* 3054; Doyle, ii. 25–6.

26. Trinity College Dublin 155 (Tr). Fols. 11$^r$–34$^v$. No incipit or explicit, 'dere frend' substituted for Margaret. The order of the text is confused: it starts with lines 489–897, followed by 267–484, and finally 1–266 (at which point T[3] also has 'Amen'). The pronoun 'þou' is frequently replaced by the impersonal 'man', and there are many major and unique variants. Also contains *Ego Dormio*, the poem *Ihesu Swete*, and an aberrant version of the English *Oleum Effusum*. Other contents in common with H[3].

Abbott, p. 20; Doyle, ii. 86; Lewis and McIntosh, 159–60.

27. Manchester, Chetham 6690 (Ch). Fols. 116$^v$–130$^r$. 'Here begynneth a techynge þat Rychard hermyte made and sente it to ankres.' Explicit 'þis teching made Rychard hermyte and sent it to an Ankres þat was cleped Margarete'. Margaret's name also present in final paragraph, although lines 836–893 preceding this are inexplicably omitted. Other contents in common with S, V, Th, Ff.

Halliwell, p. 5; Doyle, ii. 70; Ker, III. 343.

28. BL Harley 1022 (Ha). Fols. 47$^r$–61$^v$. No incipit or explicit, Margaret's name omitted. Also contains an English version of *Oleum Effusum*, as Th. Other contents in common with W, H.

*Harleian Catalogue*, I. 510–11; Doyle, ii. 117–18; Hodgson, xi.

29. Bodl. Ashmole 1524 (A). Fols. 160$^r$–70$^v$ (Book VI, 1–10$^v$). Explicit 'Ricardus heremita exhibente gracia conditoris composuit istum librum ad salutem animarum', and a simple quatrain (*IMEV* 980). Margaret's name given. Lines 1–367 and 801–97 only, the lacuna probably being caused by the loss of some leaves before binding: the manuscript is a heterogeneous collection in many hands and folios of different size. A long variant partially shared with L at l. 244. Other contents (lyric) in common with La, Ti.

Black and Macray, 1845, cols. 1431–6.

30. BL Arundel 507 (Ar). Fols. 36r–38v, 43v, 45r–46v, 48r, 49r. Text consists of approximately lines 323–484, 836–76, 1–247, 877–93, and 255–309, in that order, in a very condensed style, but with several unique interpolations. All five extracts are interspersed with other texts, both Latin and English, including the *Seven Gifts*, *Ego Dormio* (incomplete), and a fragment of *Incendium Amoris*. There is no mention of Rolle, and the concluding passage with Margaret's name is lacking. Other contents in common with Th, H³, R².

*Arundel Catalogue*, pp. 143–5; Doyle, ii. 76; Arntz, x–xii.

31 BL Add. 37790 (Ad). Fols. 130v–132r. Contains approximately lines 526–835 and 489–510, in that order, in the same condensed style as Ar, and running straight into *Ego Dormio*. The first extract is entitled 'De triplici genera amoris spiritualis', a title which it also gives to *Ego Dormio*; the second is introduced 'Incipit tractatus de diligendo deo'. It is of interest that the abridged contents of Ad exactly complement those of Ar, suggesting that they were copied piecemeal from a single exemplar. Also contains the Misyn translation of *Incendium Amoris* and *Emendatio Vitae*. The manuscript is annotated by James Grenehalgh, the Sheen Carthusian.

*Additional Catalogue* 1906–10, pp. 153–6; Doyle, ii. 194–5; Colledge and Walsh, pp. 1–5.

32 ULC Ff v 45 (Ff²). Fols. 1–2v. Lines 1–129 only. Rubric 'God that is gracious and grounde of al goodenes ȝif vs myȝt and strengþe so to lerne this processe þat it may profite vs in virtue to oure soulis encres and bryng vs alle to þat joie þat neuere shal cees'. A poor text with many unique variants. Other contents in common with S, P, Lt², B², Hh, Ii², W.

*ULC Catalogue* ii, 501–3; Doyle, ii. 103.

33. ULC Ii vi 55 (Ii³). Fols. 3r–11r. Lines 664 to end only. No explicit, and Margaret's name omitted, but provides a good text. Other contents in common with Ld.

*ULC Catalogue* iii, 545–7; Doyle, ii. 84.

34. ULC Hh i 12 (Hh). Fols. 104v–114v. Contains only extracts. Lines 626–827 and 233–309 run consecutively in that order, and are reasonably close to other texts of the work. There are also short passages, intermingled with another text, comprising approximately lines 549–609, and including the lyric. The opening extract has the rubric 'ȝe þat wollen lerne to love god rede þis litill scripte'. Other contents (parts of *Pore Caitiff*) in common with B², Ff², Ii², W.

*ULC Catalogue* iii, 264–5; Doyle, ii. 110–11.

35. San Marino California, Huntington HM 502 (H²). Fols. 27ʳ–34ʳ. Lines 186–385 only. 'þou' usually replaced by the plural pronoun. Other contents in common with Ld.

*Census* I. 71; Doyle, ii. 39; *Handlist*, pp. 30–2.

36. Trinity College Dublin 154 (Tr²). Fols. 82ᵛ–105ʳ. Lines 610–835, headed 'Of dyuyne loue taken fourthe of a treatyss by þe sayd dewoute fader Richard Rolle hermyte mayd to a certan recluse'. There are also a few sentences from the *Form*, approximately lines 280–309, 184–97, and 436–60, at the start of Flete's treatise on remedies against temptation, which is here ascribed to Rolle. A poor text, despite the rare use of the author's surname in the colophon.

Abbott, p. 20; Doyle, ii. 89.

37. Edinburgh University 107 (E). Fols. 179ᵛ–182ʳ. Lines 610–25, 504–24, 721–2, 770–2, 819–35, and 875–93, running consecutively in that order, and described in the MS index as 'Five Meditations'.

Borland, pp. 168–70; Doyle, ii. 74.

38. Bodl. Laud misc. 524 (Ld²). Fols. 53ʳ–53ᵛ. Lines 489–549 only, breaking off in mid page in the middle of a word. Also contains *Emendatio Vitae.*

*Quarto Catalogue* II, cols. 378–80; Doyle, ii. 40–1.

39. Bodley 423 (B³). Fols. 241ᵛ–242ᵛ. Lines 280–309 only, as one of the extracts in Tr². Other contents in common with Ii², H, P, Ff², B², W. This extract not noted by Miss Allen.

*SC* 2322; Doyle, ii. 104; Lewis and McIntosh, pp. 141–2.

40. Bodl. Douce 302 (Do). Fol. 32ʳ–32ᵛ. Lines 329–98 only, occurring in the middle of poems by Audelay. Rubric 'De peccatis cordis'. Passage interrupted by a unique interpolation at l. 387. Extract not noted by Miss Allen.

*Catalogue of the Printed Books & MSS Bequeathed by Francis Douce, Esq., to the Bodleian Library* (Oxford, 1840), pp. 50–2.

41. Longleat 32 (Lt²). Fol. 28ʳ. Lines 610–25 only, joined on to the end of *The Commandment*, and ending 'Explicit tractatus nobilissimus'. Also contains *Emendatio Vitae* in English. Other contents in common with Br, Ii², S, V, U, Ff², P.

HMC III, 181; Doyle, ii. 90.

42. ULC Ii vi 40 (Ii²). Fol. 207ʳ–207ᵛ. Lines 610–25 only, joined on to the end of *The Commandment*. Wrongly ascribes a translation of St Edmund's *Speculum* to 'Ricardus Hampol'. Other contents in common with Lt², Br, B³, H, P, B², W, T³.

*ULC Catalogue* iii. 538–9; Doyle, ii. 90.

43. Bradfer-Lawrence 10 (Br), now in the possession of Professor Takamiya, Tokyo University. Fol. 33$^{v}$. Lines 610–25 only, joined on to *The Commandment* as Lt$^{2}$ and Ii$^{2}$. This is the manuscript referred to as Gurney by Miss Allen (*Writings*, pp. 241, 248, 252); she does not note this extract. Also contains *Ego Dormio* and *Emendatio Vitae* in English.

Doyle, ii. 89; P. M. Giles, *A Handlist of the Bradfer-Lawrence MSS deposited on loan at the Fitzwilliam Museum* (Transactions of the Cambridge Bibliographical Society 6, part 2, 1973), p. 89; M. G. Amassian, 'The Rolle Material in Bradfer-Lawrence MS 10', *Manuscripta* 23 (1979), 67–78.

44. Lambeth Palace 853 (La). Fols. 88$^{v}$–89$^{r}$. Lines 610–25 only. Extract not noted by Miss Allen. Also contains three of Rolle's lyrics, written as one.

James, 1930–2, v. 809–11.

*Ego Dormio*

1. Longleat 29 (Lt). Fols. 43$^{v}$–47$^{v}$. 'Hampole' and 'De amore dei' alternate in the top margins. No incipit or explicit.
2. Rawl. A 389 [see *Form* MS 3]. Two versions:

   R$^{1}$, fols. 77$^{r}$–81$^{r}$. Fol. 80, containing lines 201–87 is missing. A Northern text. No incipit or explicit.

   R, fols. 945$^{v}$–99$^{r}$.
3. BL Add. 22283 (S) [see *Form* MS 5]. Fols. 150$^{v}$–151$^{v}$.
4. Bodl. eng. poet. a 1 (V) [see *Form* MS 6]. Fols. 338$^{r}$–339$^{r}$.
5. Westminster School 3 (W) [see *Form* MS 7]. Fols. 225$^{r}$–231$^{r}$.
6. Bibl. Ste-Geneviève 3390 (G) [see *Form* MS 4]. Fols. 95$^{v}$–108$^{v}$. 'Explicit Ricardus Hampole'.
7. ULC Dd v 64 III (Dd) [see *Form* MS 9]. Fols. 22$^{v}$–29$^{r}$. 'Explicit tractatus Ricardi heremite de Hampole scriptus cuidam moniali de ȝedyngham.'
8. Bradfer-Lawrence 10 (Br) [see *Form* MS 43]. Fols. 24$^{r}$–28$^{r}$. 'And her begynnyth a tretis which tellith of þe nyne ordris of aungel and how men xuld be set in heuen as he wrot to an ankeresse.' This follows the translation of the *Emendatio Vitae* which has the incipit 'Heer begynnyth a tretise þat seynt rycharde of hampole made how synful men schuld amend her lyfis . . .'. There is a major textual dislocation in *Ego Dormio* covering lines 103–34.
9. Pepys 2125 (P) [see *Form* MS 20]. Fols. 99$^{r}$–102$^{r}$. 'Hic incipiunt tres gradus amoris secundum Ricardum de Hampol.' The first

lyric is considerably altered, and I print it separately in an appendix. Lines 267 to the end, including the second lyric, are omitted.

10. Trinity College Dublin 155 (Tr) [see *Form* MS 26]. Fols. 1–9$^{v}$. The first lyric (see appendix, p. 000) is divided into two, a new lyric is inserted at l. 235, and the second lyric omitted altogether, the text ending at l. 264.
11. BL Add. 37790 (Ad) [see *Form* MS 31]. Fols. 132$^{v}$–135$^{v}$. Line 510 of the *Form* '. . . praysynge of God' continues here 'thare are thre degrees of loue as is writtene nowe here aftyr', and the opening lines of *Ego Dormio* follow. At the conclusion of *Ego Dormio* the scribe continues 'The fyrste degree of luf is Insuperabill the secounde Inseperabill the thyrde Synguler', the same words with which he began the first *Form* extract on fol. 130$^{v}$.
12. BL Arundel 507 (Ar) [see *Form* MS 30]. Fol. 40$^{r}$–40$^{v}$. Lines 1–124 only (folio missing).

*Latin text*

Gonville and Caius College Cambridge MS 140/80 (Ca). Fols. 115$^{v}$–118$^{v}$.

*The Commandment*

1. Longleat 29 (Lt). Fols. 47$^{v}$–50$^{v}$. No incipit or explicit. 'Hampolle' and 'Amor dei' in some top margins.
2. Rawl. A 389 (R) [see *Form* MS 3]. Fols. 81$^{r}$–84$^{v}$. Text headed 'Richard hermit'. Lines 610–25 of the *Form* are appended to the end without a break, the whole concluding 'Deo gracias'.
3. BL Add. 22283 (S) [see *Form* MS 5]. Fols. 147$^{r}$–147$^{v}$. Incipit 'Here is a tretis þat techeþ to loue god wiþ al þin herte'. Lines 217–24 'set . . . loued' are replaced by 'loue ihesu with al þin herte with al þi soule with al þi þouȝt amen'.
4. Bodl. eng. poet. a 1 (V) [see *Form* MS 6]. Fols. 334$^{r}$–334$^{v}$. Incipit and conclusion as S.
5. ULC Dd v 64 III (Dd) [see *Form* MS 9]. Fols. 29$^{r}$–34$^{r}$. No incipit, 'Explicit tractatus Ricardi Hampole scriptus cuidam sorori de Hampole'.
6. ULC Ff v 40 (Ff) [see *Form* MS 11]. Fols. 88$^{v}$–92$^{r}$. Rubric 'De diuinis mandatis tractatus'. No explicit.
7. Trinity College Cambridge B 15 42 [374–6] (T$^{4}$). Fols. 2$^{r}$–5$^{r}$. No incipit. 'Explicit breuis tractatus perfeccio uite uocitatus.' Other contents in common with Ii$^{2}$, H, B$^{3}$.

James 1900–4 I. 510–13; Doyle, ii. 75.

8. Pepys 2125 (P) [see *Form* MS 20]. Fols. 85ᵛ–88ᵛ. 'A good rule for men þat desireþ to lyue perfit lif.' An extract (P[1]), containing lines 187–211, but apparently from a different exemplar, occurs at fol. 84ʳ, before the first passage of the *Form*, and concluding 'Epistola supra hortatur relinquere vana huius mundi et adherere celestibus'.
9. Huntington HM 148 (H[3]). Fols. 204ʳ–206ʳ. No incipit or explicit. Other contents in common with R[2], Th, Ar, Ff, Tr.

   *Census* I. 59; Doyle, ii. 126; Arntz, pp. ix–x; *Handlist*, pp. 21–4.
10. Longleat 32 (Lt[2]) [see *Form* MS 41]. Fols. 23ʳ–28ʳ. 'Here begynneþ a tretice how god comaundeþ vs for to loue him in alwise.' 'Explicit tractatus nobilissimus' (after lines 610–25 of the *Form*).
11. ULC Ii vi 40 (Ii[2]) [see *Form* MS 42]. Fols. 198ʳ–207ʳ. 'In þis tretis we are tauȝt how we schul loue god on al wise.' Concludes with lines 610–25 of the *Form*.
12. Bradfer-Lawrence 10 (Br) [see *Form* MS 43]. Fols. 28ʳ–33ᵛ. 'Her begynnyth a noble tretis of loue.' The text opens uniquely with a long excerpt from an English translation of chapter VIII of the *Emendatio Vitae*, which appears in its entirety at the start of this manuscript. The excerpt is partially printed by Miss Allen (*Writings*, pp. 252–3), but not considered by her to be Rolle's work. She states 'The appearance of a stray "sall" might show that it had a Northern prototype', but has misread MS *xal* as *sal. The Commandment* concludes as Lt[2] and Ii[2] with lines 610–25 of the *Form.*
13. Trinity College Cambridge O 1 29 (T[3]) [see *Form* MS 16]. Fols. 1–8ʳ. No incipit or explicit. The text is addressed to a man, and, as in the *Form*, is so expanded and verbose that I have not recorded its non-substantive variants beyond l. 41.
14. ULC Dd v 55 (Dd[2]). Fols. 90ʳ–91ᵛ. Lines 162 to end only. Two sentences (lines 187–93) occur separately (fol. 102ᵛ) together with a translation of a sentence from *Emendatio Vitae* ch. VIII; these are also found in R[2] (printed Horstman, i. 130–1; not the same sentence as in Br). Other contents in common with R[2] and Ff.

   *ULC Catalogue*, i. 275–6; Doyle, ii. 116; Lewis and McIntosh, pp. 150–1.
15. Yale University Library 324 (Y). Fol. iv. Lines 91–141 only, in a Northern dialect. The original folded leaf from a quire in a smaller manuscript has been smoothed out and bound sideways to form a single leaf. One half of each side contains the present text, and the remaining halves an excerpt from Hilton's *Mixed Life*. Extract not known to Miss Allen.

*Desire and Delight*

1. Longleat 29 (Lt). Fols. $50^{v}$–$51^{r}$. ‘hampole’ in top margins.
2. Lincoln Cathedral 91 [Thornton] (Th). Fol. $196^{v}$. ‘Item Idem de dilectacione in deo. Also of þe same delyte and ȝernyng of gode.’ ‘Explicit carmen qui scripsit sit benedictus Amen.’ It follows ‘A notabill tretys off the ten Comandementys Drawene by Richarde the hermyte off Hampull’ (printed Horstman, i. 195–6, and see *Writings*, pp. 276–7), and *Seven Gifts* (printed Horstman, i. 196–7, see *Writings*, pp. 274–5). Also contains one of the Lt lyrics, the short piece *The Bee* (*Writings*, pp. 269–71; printed Horstman, i. 193–4), an English version of *Oleum Effusum* as Ha and Tr, and a Latin prayer ‘þat þe same Richard hermet made þat es beried at Hampolle’. Other contents in common with Lt, Ar, $H^{3}$, S, V, Ld, Ii, $T^{3}$.

   *The Thornton Manuscript (Lincoln Cathedral MS 91)* 2nd ed. (London, the Scolar Press, 1977), vii–xx; *Writings, passim.*

*Ghostly Gladness*

1. Longleat 29 (Lt). Fol. $51^{r}$.
2. ULC Dd v 64 III (Dd) [see *Form* MS 9]. Fol. $41^{v}$.

*Lyrics*

1. Longleat 29 (Lt). Fols. $51^{v}$–$56^{v}$, $58^{r}$. Rubric (fol. $51^{r}$) ‘Cantalene amoris dei’. ‘Cantalene de amore dei’ is repeated in the top margins.

   (i) ‘Love is lif’, fols. $51^{v}$–$52^{r}$.

   (ii) ‘Ihesu Goddis son’, fols. $52^{r}$–$52^{v}$.

   (iii) ‘I sigh and sob’, fol. $52^{r}$.

   (iv) ‘Thy ioy be euery dele’, fols. $52^{r}$–$54^{v}$.

   (v) ‘Al synnes’, fols. $54^{v}$–$55^{r}$.

   (vi) ‘Ihesu swete’, fols. $55^{r}$–$56^{v}$, $58^{r}$. Written in double columns. The main text consists of 100 stanzas. In the lower and upper margins, in the same hand but darker ink, are seven further stanzas addressed to the Virgin, together with an introductory verse. In the side margins, against stanzas 16, 26, 38, and 48 respectively of the main text, is written ‘hora matutina’ ‘hora 1’ (prima), ‘hora 3’ (tertia), and ‘hora $6^{ta}$’ (sexta). These entries indicate that the text was being subdivided for liturgical use, although the task was not completed. It is impossible to tell whether they were added before or after the ‘Mary’ stanzas: possibly the 100 stanzas of the main text suggested the idea of a rosary, and indeed the text may have been deliberately reduced (see below, p. lxxxv) to 100 stanzas with a liturgical end in view.

2. ULC Dd v 64 III (Dd) [see *Form* MS 9]. Fols. 36$^{r}$–42$^{r}$.
   (v), fol. 36$^{r}$.
   (ii), fol. 37$^{r}$.
   (i) and (iii) written as one, fol. 38$^{r}$.
   (iv), fols. 42$^{r}$ and 40$^{v}$, written as two, with three stanzas omitted. At l. 48 the scribe adds 'Al vanites forsake if þou hys lufe wil fele etc vt supra' (l. 49 of the Lt text), indicating that the Lt format is correct. The stanzas on fol. 42$^{r}$ are headed 'Item secundum eundem Ricardum'.
3. Lambeth Palace 853 (La) [see *Form* MS 44]. Pp. 90–101.
   (i), (ii), and (iii), written as one.
4. Lincoln Cathedral 91 (Th) [see *Desire and Delight* MS 2]. Fol. 222.
   (iv), lines 89ff. missing.
5. Bodl. eng. poet. a 1 (V) [see *Form* MS 6]. Fol. 298$^{r}$.
   (vi) 110 stanzas, not including Lt's introductory verse, which here comes at the end of the poem. Of these 110, eight are 'Mary' verses, all of which occur at irregular intervals as part of the main text.
6. BL Add. 22283 (S) [see *Form* MS 5]. Fol. 89$^{r}$.
   (vi), length and format as V.
7. BL Add. 37787 (Ad$^{2}$). Fols. 146$^{v}$–156$^{v}$.
   (vi), 103 stanzas, including seven addressed to Mary. The introductory verse is lacking. Other contents in common with V, S, Lt.
   *Additional Catalogue* 1906–1910, 140–50; *Worcs. Misc.*, pp. 13–17.
8. BL Royal 17 B xvii (Ro). Fols. 13$^{v}$–18$^{v}$.
   (vi), 84 stanzas, four addressed to Mary. Introductory verse at the beginning of the poem. Also contains the *Emendatio Vitae* 'Explicit secundum R. h', and an unattributed fragment of *Incendium Amoris*. Other contents in common with Ld.
   Warner and Gilson, pp. 228–30; Doyle, ii. 77–8.
9. Trinity College Dublin 155 (Tr) [see *Form* MS 26]. Fols. 55$^{r}$–59$^{r}$.
   (vi), 69 stanzas. No 'Mary' verses, no introductory verse.
10. Huntington EL 34 B 7 (H$^{4}$). Fols. 83$^{v}$–85$^{v}$.
   (vi), 31 stanzas, including three to Mary. Introductory verse lacking.
   *Census* I, 134.

*Meditation* A

1. Longleat 29 (Lt). Fol. 58$^v$. Lines 159–69 only. 'Explicit tractatus Ricardi heremite de Hampolle ad Margaretam reclusam de kyrkby de amore dei.' It would appear that this meditation once formed part of a collection of Rolle's works made for Margaret of Kirkby under the general title 'De amore dei'. It is extant in only one other known manuscript, where it is again attributed to Rolle, and its presence in Lt, fragmentary though it is, must go far to confirm this ascription.
2. BL Cotton Titus C xix (Ti). Fols. 121$^r$–128$^r$. Incipit 'De passione secundum Ricardum'. This manuscript was not known to Miss Allen when *Writings* was published, but when it was brought to her attention, she told F. Wormald that she found nothing in it to preclude Rolle's authorship. She did not make the connection between it and the Lt fragment.

*Meditation* B

1. Bodl. e mus. 232 (Mu). Fols. 1–18$^r$. 'Here begynneth a deuout meditacioun vp þe passioun of crist, j-made by Richard Rolle heremyt of hampolle.'
2. Upsala University C 494 (Up). Fols. 1–32$^r$. Lines 1–13 missing.
3. BL Cotton Titus C xix (Ti) [see *Meditation* A, MS 2]. Fols. 92$^v$–117$^v$. 'Incipit quedam meditacio passionis ihesu cristi composita a Ricardo Rolle heremita qui obijt anno domini MCCCXLIX sancti moniales de hampul.'
4. ULC Add. 3042 (Add). Fols. 36$^r$–78$^v$. 'Here bigynneþ deuoute meditaciouns of þe passioun of crist whiche weren compiled of Richard Rolle hermyte of hampol þat diede in þe ȝeer of our lord MCCC & XLIX ȝeer.'

## PRINTED TEXTS

*The Form of Living*

C. Horstman, i. 3–49 [Dd, $R^2$, part of Ha].
H. E. Allen, *English Writings*, pp. 85–119 [Dd, collated with $R^2$].
K. Miyabe, *The Structure and History of the English Language in Honour of Prof. K. Miyabe*, ed. Y. Terasawa *et al.* (Tokyo, 1981), pp. 4–31 [diplomatic text of V].

G. E. Hodgson, *The Form of Perfect Living* (London, 1910). Modernized version.

G. C. Heseltine, pp. 15–51. Modernized version.

F. M. M. Comper, pp. 224–5 [lyric from S, spelling modernized].

M. Noetinger, *Le Feu de l'Amour, le Modèle de la Vie Parfaite, le Pater par Richard Rolle l'Ermite de Hampole* (Paris, 1928). French translation.

*Ego Dormio*

C. Horstman, i. 50–61 [Dd, R¹ with missing leaf supplied from V]; i. 415–15 [Ar].

H. E. Allen, *English Writings*, pp. 61–72 [Dd, with a few variants from R¹ and V].

G. E. Hodgson, *Some Minor Works of Richard Rolle* (London, 1923), pp. 63–77. Modernized version.

G. C. Heseltine, pp. 89–100. Modernized version.

E. Colledge, *The Medieval Mystics of England* (London, 1962), pp. 143–54. Modernized version.

F. M. M. Comper, pp. 228–34 [lyrics from Dd, spelling modernized].

'T', *British Magazine* ix (1836), 501–2 [lyrics from Tr].

M. G. Amassian and D. Lynch, 'The *Ego Dormio* of Richard Rolle in Gonville and Caius MS 140/80', *Medieval Studies* 43 (1981), 218–49 [Latin text of Ca].

*The Commandment*

C. Horstman, i. 61–71 [Dd and R].

H. E. Allen, *English Writings*, pp. 73–81 [Dd with some variants from R].

G. E. Hodgson, *Minor Works*, pp. 80–91. Modernized version.

G. C. Heseltine, pp. 3–11. Modernized version.

*Desire and Delight*

G. G. Perry, pp. 14–15 [Th].

C. Horstman, i. 197 [Th].

H. E. Allen, *Writings*, pp. 271–2 [Lt].

—, *English Writings*, pp. 57–8 [Th].

G. C. Heseltine, pp. 104–5. Modernized version.

*Ghostly Gladness*

C. Horstman, i. 81 [Dd].
H. E. Allen, *Writings*, p. 273 [Lt].
—, *English Writings*, pp. 51–2 [Dd].
G. C. Heseltine, p. 106. Modernized version.

*Lyrics*

F. J. Furnivall, *Hymns to the Virgin and Christ*, EETS 24 (1867), 22–31 [(i), (ii), (iii); La].
G. G. Perry, pp. 107–13 [(iv); Th].
J. Wickham Legg, *The Processional of the Nuns of Chester*, HBS xviii (1899), 30–3 [(vi); $H^4$].
F. J. Furnivall, *The Minor Poems of the Vernon Manuscript*, EETS 117 (1901), 449–62 [(vi); V].
C. Horstman, i. 75–8 [(ii), (i) & (iii); Dd]; i. 370–2 [(iv); Th]; i. 79–82 [(iv); Dd]; i. 74 [(v); Dd]; ii. 9–24 [(vi); V & Ro].
K. Sisam, *Fourteenth Century Verse and Prose* (Oxford, 1921), pp. 37–40 [(i) & (iii); Dd].
C. Brown, *RL XIV*, pp. 99–106 [(ii), (i) & (iii); Dd]; pp. 107–9 [(iv); Dd, lines 1–48 only].
H. E. Allen, *English Writings*, pp. 41–7 [(ii), (i) & (iii); Dd]; pp. 49–51, 52–3 [(iv); Dd]; p. 39 [(v); Dd].
N. S. Baugh, *Worcs. Misc.*, pp. 129–42 [(vi); $Ad^2$].
F. M. M. Comper, pp. 240–68 [(ii), (i) & (iii); Dd; (iv); Th with missing stanzas from Dd, spelling modernized].
S. J. Wilson, *RES* n.s. x (1959), 337–46 [(i), (ii), (iii); Lt].
C. and K. Sisam, *The Oxford Book of Medieval English Verse* (Oxford, 1970), pp. 177–82 [(i); Lt, spelling modernized].

*Meditation* A

H. E. Allen, *Writings*, p. 35 [Lt].
F. Wormald, *Laudate* 13 (1935), 37–48 [Ti, together with a description of the manuscript].

*Meditation* B

H. E. Allen, *English Writings*, pp. 27–36 [Mu, lines 18–250 only].

H. Lindkvist, *Skrifter utqifna af K. Humanistiska Vetenskaps-Samfundet i Uppsala* 19.3 (1917), 1–72 [Up, together with a description of the manuscript].

M. F. Madigan, *The Passio Domini Theme in the Works of Richard Rolle*, Elizabethan and Renaissance Studies 79 (Salzburg, 1978), appendix B, 236–77 [Ti].

C. Horstman, i. 92–103 [Add].

## MANUSCRIPT RELATIONSHIPS

### *Form of Living*

Scholarship over the past half century has shown the near impossibility of constructing a definitive stemma serviceable for recension, at least where a large number of manuscripts are concerned. Coincidental error, coincidental substitution and correction, and conflation all play their part in obscuring the picture, and the texts of the twenty-seven complete manuscripts of the *Form* have fully corroborated this. Nevertheless, it has been possible to discern certain regular groupings, albeit initially from sheer numerical persistence, and by examining the evidence of these to reach some conclusions, both about the validity of the text and the way in which it was transmitted.

The *Form* manuscripts show two main lines of descent, each branch containing one pre-eminent member, namely Lt and Dd. The agreement of two such unrelated versions goes far to authenticate such a reading; where they disagree, each can often reveal the other's deficiencies. Secondly, the variations between these textual groupings show Lt to be considerably closer to the original than Dd, which in turn is the closest within its group, while most manuscripts have gone through a dozen or more interim stages. It is evident that, within the course of a century, the *Form* was even more widely disseminated than the large number of extant copies testifies. Thirdly, certain discrepancies in textual relationships serve to illuminate the manner in which these texts were circulated and copied.

It is apparent from the description of manuscripts containing the *Form* that Lt and Dd must command special consideration on external grounds. They contain more of Rolle's English writings than any other manuscript. Both attribute these works to Richard of Hampole, and record the dedication of the *Form* to Margaret, Lt in addition, and uniquely, giving the place-name Kirkby. Dd has hitherto been the automatic choice for editors, but only by virtue of its Northern dialect; the validity of its text has never seriously been questioned. Horstman printed Dd with R$^2$ in parallel columns, but, as will be seen, these two manuscripts are closely related and their texts therefore similar; he collated from Ha, which is of the same family. Miss Allen, although purporting[1] to be collating from R (Rawl. A 389) had unfortunately confused her Rawlinson manuscripts, and was in fact also giving the readings of R$^2$ (Rawl. C 285). She was thus able to correct only minor errors at lines 23, 573, 591, 700, 768, and 856, and to supply omissions only at lines 209–10, 642–3, 672, and 799. Comparison with Lt reveals a considerable number of apparent further omissions:

33 'nat' *om.* DdCHeDT$^3$BIiMChHaA: Lt supported by (U)RG SVWTLR$^2$FfPFLdHT$^2$B$^2$TrFf$^2$.

33–4 'bot if he wend þat oþer he knew bettre or did better þan oþer' *om.* DdR$^2$FfCHeDIiMChHaA: Lt supported by PFLdHT$^2$B$^2$ Ff$^2$.

76 'þay make' *om.* Dd: Lt supported *alia.*

176 'body of' *om.* Dd: Lt supported *alia.*

182 'and mor perillous' *om.* SVDdR$^2$FfLCDT$^3$BIiMPFLdHT$^2$B$^2$ TrChHaA: Lt supported by URGWT.

189–90 'of oure body and for to make vs slowe and cold in Goddis loue' *om.* DdR$^2$FfLCHeDT$^3$BIiMPFLdHT$^2$B$^2$TrChA: Lt supported by URGSVWTH$^2$.

297 'shal' *om.* DdR$^2$FfLCHeDMChHaA: Lt supported by URG SVWTBPFLdHT$^2$B$^2$TrArH$^2$B$^3$Tr$^2$.

319–20 'as þou hast be ne of þe more merite þogh þou take þe to moor abstinence' *om.* WDdR$^2$FfLCHeDT$^3$BMB$^2$ChHaAHh: Lt supported by USVPFLdHT$^2$TrH$^2$, and partly by RGT.

333–4 'sorowe in har welfare' *om.* GDdR$^2$FfLCHeDT$^3$BMPFLdH T$^2$B$^2$ChHaAArH$^2$Hh: Lt supported by URSVWT.

551 'delite ne other' *om.* Dd: Lt supported *alia.*

592 'þe brighthede' *om.* DdR$^2$FfDTr: Lt supported by URGSV WTPFLdHT$^2$B$^2$HaHh.

610 'right' *om.* DdR$^2$FfLCHeDBMFB$^2$TrChHaELa: Lt supported by URGSVWTLt$^2$Ii$^2$BrTr$^2$Ad.

624 'done' *om.* DdR$^2$FfLCHeDT$^3$BMPFLdHT$^2$B$^2$TrChHaIi$^2$E LaTr$^2$: Lt supported by URGSVWLt$^2$Br.

[1] *English Writings*, p. 84.

687–8 ‘and maketh his hert clene of syn’ *om.* DdR$^{2}$FfLCHeDT$^{3}$BMTrHh: Lt supported by URGSVWTPFLdHT$^{2}$ChHaTr$^{2}$Ii$^{3}$Ad, partly by B$^{2}$.

697 ‘þan anoþer’ *om.* DdR$^{2}$FfLCHeDT$^{3}$BMPFLdHT$^{2}$B$^{2}$TrChHh: Lt supported by URGSVWTHaTr$^{2}$Ii$^{3}$.

698–9 ‘Than can non tel me if I loue God’ *om.* DdR$^{2}$FfLCHeDT$^{3}$BMPFLdHT$^{2}$B$^{2}$TrChHaHh: :Lt supported by URGWTTr$^{2}$Ii$^{3}$.

809–10 ‘he hath no ioy bot in God and al his hope is to cum to God’ *om.* DdR$^{2}$FfLHeDT$^{3}$BIiMTrChA: Lt supported by URSVWTPFLdHT$^{2}$B$^{2}$HaHhTr$^{2}$Ii$^{3}$, partly G.

812 ‘myche’ *om.* DdR$^{2}$FfLCHeBIiMPFLdHT$^{2}$B$^{2}$TrChHaA: Lt supported by URGWTTr$^{2}$Ii$^{3}$.

It is most unlikely that these seventeen omissions are instead additions of Lt and its supporting manuscripts. Those at lines 33–4 (where some manuscripts by retaining ‘nat’ have destroyed the sense), 189–90, 319–20, 333–4, 551, 687–8, 698–9 and 809–10 are clear cases of homoeoteleuton, though whether coincidental or transmitted is not always so apparent. At lines 297, 610, 624, 697, and 812 the Lt reading makes the better sense, and at l. 592 is supported by the Vulgate rendering of I Cor. 15: 41 ‘alia claritas solis . . .’. At lines 76, 176, and 551 Dd is unsupported. The reading at l. 182 could be an addition by the Lt manuscripts, but to prove this would necessitate proving a relationship between these manuscripts, and this we shall see is unlikely.

Four further variants between Lt and Dd do appear to be additions of Lt: l. 223 ‘þe deuyl’; l. 353 ‘and hire’; l. 370 ‘powere or’; l. 38 ‘or reprouen ham’. The last is merely a gloss on the Northern word ‘laken’: P has something similar with ‘or blameþ ham’, the others omit it. The other three are supported by no other manuscript; to suppose them original would be to admit a relationship between all the other texts, for which there is no further evidence. Similarly Dd’s reading at l. 129 ‘þat hegh es in heuen’ is unsupported, and therefore clearly an addition of Dd.

Lt has three major omissions, all of which are obvious cases of scribal error, occurring at lines 641, 655, and 723–4 (the last supposing a previous transposition of ‘peyn’ and ‘angre’). At l. 641 Lt is supported by TCChHh and originally B, at l. 655 by Tr, whose reading of the passage is substantially altered, and Hh, and at lines 723–4 the omission is unique. The support of the fragmentary Hh does not seem significant; it is a very poor text, and also supports Dd's omissions at lines 319–20, 333–4, 687–8, 697, and 698–9, while not sharing any other of Lt's provable errors. The agreement at l. 641 must be assumed coincidental; there is no further proof of relationship between Lt and T, C, B, or Ch. The manuscript punctuation of Lt suggests that the error had been perpetrated at an earlier stage of transmission. Lt has a further possible omission at l. 381, where it is supported by U. This might seem to indicate a relationship between Lt and U; on the other hand the omitted phrase is no more than a gloss on 'omyssioun', which is already sufficiently explained in the next phrase 'whan men leuen þe good þat þei shold done', and could therefore be as plausibly an addition in an ancestor of DdR$^2$FfLCHeDT$^3$BMPFLdHT$^2$B$^2$ChHa, manuscripts which elsewhere can be shown to be related.

In some further instances where the texts of Lt and Dd differ, there is no internal indication of whether this is due to addition or omission:

135 'in ihesu' DdR$^2$FfLCHeDT$^3$BIiMPFLdHT$^2$TrChHaA: *om.* Lt URGSVWT.

176 'als to hyr syght' DdR$^2$FfLCHeDT$^3$BIiMPFLdHT$^2$B$^2$TrChHaA: *om.* LtURGSVWTAr.

182 'þe forme of' DdR$^2$FfLCDBIiMPB$^2$A; 'þe liknesse of' FLd HT$^2$Ch; 'þe likenes and in þe forme of' T$^3$: *om.* LtURGSVW THa.

365 'goddes body' DdR$^2$FfLCHeDT$^3$BMPFLdHT$^2$B$^2$TrChHaAH$^2$: 'God' LtURGSVWTAr.

604 'His' LtDHh; 'is' UDdR$^2$FfHHa; 'My leues' RG; 'mi lyf is' SVWT; 'lorde þi' LCT$^3$BM; 'þe bond of' P; 'his is of' FLd; 'þis' T$^2$B$^2$; 'þe' Ch; 'of' Ha.

745 'thynk' DdR$^2$FfLCHeDT$^3$BMPFHT$^2$B$^2$TrChHaHh: *om.* LtUR GSVWTIi$^3$.

However a strong consistency of pattern is apparent, both in these readings and in the omissions of Dd already discussed. In the latter, where Dd has support, it is always of R$^2$FfD, usually of LCHeT$^3$BM TrCh, sometimes of PFLdHT$^2$B$^2$Ha, and occasionally, for reasons that will be explained shortly, of SV, W, or G. The evidence therefore suggests a vertical transmission of error among these Dd-group texts. As Lt gives the correct reading, its supporters here are of no significance in determining manuscript relationships. In the disputed readings, apart from the lyric (l. 604) where corruption is widespread, Lt is supported always by URGSVWT, once with the addition of Ha, and twice with the addition of Ar. The reading at l. 381 has already provided tenuous evidence for a relationship between Lt and U. If this can be substantiated, and if these two manuscripts can also be shown to be related to RGSVWT, the readings of this group could be common errors and the Dd text correct. If on the other hand there is no proven relationship between Lt, U, and RGSVWT, there is a much stronger case for accepting their readings as correct, and the related manuscripts of the Dd group in error.

It is beyond dispute that RGSVWT are all descended from a common ancestor. Their text of the *Form* is very poor. They share omissions at lines 61, 125, 155, 156, 204–5, 206, 217–18, 224–5, 227, 234, 237–8, 240, 244, 249, 268, 302, 304, 307, 308–9, 316–18, 326, 382–3, 390, 392, 403, 411, 421, 424–5, 489–90, 635, and 811, and this list is by no means comprehensive. They share major variants or additions at lines 106, 116–18, 137, 200–1, 211–14, 214, 223–4, 239, 245, 250–8, 292–3, 327–8, 370, 378–9, 381–2, 383, 392–8, 406–7, 410, 431, 446, 449, 470, 650, 684, 710, 728, 733, 743, 746, 771, 785, 785–7, 799, 811, 826, and 847. They also share omissions or variants with L at lines 19, 22–3, 33–4, 50–2, 59, 60, 67–9, 94–5, 96, 98, 99, and 100. None of these omissions or variants is found in Lt or U. However at l. 885 there is an omission shared by URGSVWT but not Lt, at l. 198 an omission partially shared by U but not Lt, and at lines 186, 330,[1] 492–3,[2], 657, and 697 there are variants shared by URGSVWT but not Lt. It would therefore seem that at an early stage of transmission a connection existed between U and RGS VWT.

Lt and U agree in six possible errors and a minor varient. At l. 361 they read 'mowe' against 'mowe makinge' of DdR²FfLCHeDT³BMP FLdHT²B²ChHaAH²Hh. This can only be regarded as an error if it can be proved that 'mowe' was not used as a verb at this period. It is first recorded as such *c.* 1430, whereas its use as a noun dates back to 1325. Thus although it is unlikely to have been used by Rolle himself in verbal function, it is perfectly possible that the scribes of the fifteenth-century Lt and U used it independently as such. At l. 507 Lt and U read 'thynge' against 'man' of all other manuscripts except SV who read 'non'. Here agreement of RGWT with the Dd group indicates that Lt and U are in error, but U also reads 'þei' for 'hym', thus changing the sense. If this pronominal substitution existed in a predecessor, the change from 'man' to 'thynge' could have been made deliberately by U, and so again is not necessarily a shared error. At

[1] Not G, see below. [2] Not T, see below.

l. 710 Lt and U read 'and' for 'in', but confusion of the ampersand with an abbreviated form of 'in' is too common to be significant; indeed the same error is found in Ha. At l. 103 Lt and U substitute 'lyght' for the majority 'cundle in'; this is an obvious synonym and could again be coincidental. However further agreements cannot be dismissed so lightly. At l. 596 both omit 'lord'. At l. 812, against the Dd group 'þis schewes' and RGSVWT 'þat is a greet tokenyng þat he sheweþ', Lt reads 'yit sheweth he', U 'it sheweth', and $Ii^3$, which is probably related to U (see below) 'yit sheweth'. Here the $Ii^3$ reading could show the original error, with Lt and U emending independently. At l. 601 both Lt and U omit 'for loue', which is found, although the textual placing varies, in all other manuscripts, and which is metrically preferable. The evidence is inconclusive, but may be regarded as cumulative; certainly the possibility of a relationship between Lt and U cannot be eliminated. However there is no evidence of a relationship between Lt and RGSVWT, and it therefore seems probable that in the disputed readings cited above, the demonstrably related manuscripts of the Dd group provide a revised text.

Before tracing further the textual history of the group URGSVWT, it is necessary to explain the position of L. This manuscript was seen to share an omission and a number of variants with (U)RGSVWT, but also the errors and omissions of the Dd group. With the sole exception of l. 13, L agrees consistently with RGSVWT from lines 1 to 104, where there is a natural break in the text. Here several manuscripts, including L, start a new chapter, and T has an 'Amen'. From that point on, apart from reading 'lord' for 'lady' at l. 130, and 'leryng' for 'lyuynge' at l. 265, L separates completely from RGSVWT and follows instead the readings of the Dd group. It is evident that it changed exemplars, and this is another indication, already seen in the complementary texts of Ad and Ar, that different sections of the *Form* were circulating separately. The readings of 'lord' and 'leryng' are more than simple textual aberrations; they are basic to a completely different concept of the work. If an intelligent scribe thought from the beginning that he was writing a form of learning for a lord, presumably he would continue to adjust his copy accordingly, regardless of the intrusion of ladies into his latest exemplar.

After U separates from RGSVWT, its development cannot be traced much further. It shares an omission with Ch and Ar at l. 35 which could be the independent abandoning of a gloss, an omission with $B^2$ at l. 284 and with F at l. 714, which are unimportant as so many manuscripts contract these passages in various ways, and an omission with GD at lines 142–3 which could be a case of independent scribal error. It shares several readings with the fragmentary Ii$^3$, as at lines 745, 833, 881, and 894. Apart from these, and its readings at those further points of variation between Lt and Dd which will be discussed later, it has a number of unique errors, and unique omissions at lines 82–3, 347–8, and 584–5. On the whole it provides a good text, and is probably not many removes from the original.

G appears to break away from RSVWT and follow a different exemplar for one brief passage, lines 329–48. RSVWT have omissions or variants at lines 330, 331, 333, 334–45, 346, and 347, none of which is shared by G. Indeed G now reflects the errors of the Dd group, notably at lines 333–4. Also in this part of the text it shares omissions or variants with Ld at lines 331 and 339, and with several manuscripts from the Dd group at l. 336. From l. 349 onwards it reverts to type, apart from individual errors. However it avoids the errors of RSVWT at lines 227, 414, 477–8, 490, and 882, and those of RSVW at l. 637. It also shares a further reading with Ld at lines 723–4. These differences could be the result of correction in an ancestor (there is almost no correction in G itself), possibly after conflation with an ancestor of Ld; they also indicate that G is closer to the original than RSVWT.

RGSVW share a large number of omissions or variants not found in T, and almost all of these occur between l. 493, just after what is often regarded as the second book or section of the *Form*, and l. 625, another natural break. It would appear that the scribe of T, as with L and G, has temporarily changed his exemplar. There is an agreement with DdR$^2$FfLCHeDT$^3$MChLd$^2$ at l. 521, and, in one brief section, a remarkable similarity to the readings of L: lines 509, 530, 539, 540, 543, 544, 557, 563, 564, 570, 580–1, 588, and 596. In the rest of the text T shares several readings with W, as at lines 14, 24–5, 70, 76, 86, 101, 108, 143–4, 207, 249–50, 354–63, 624, and 657. It also has individual omissions at lines 196, 295–6, 305–6, 421, 615, and 618–19.

W is one of the manuscripts of the *Form* where we can actually see that conflation has taken place. Its readings have been changed from those of T, or from those of one or more of RGSVT, at lines 21, 265, 310, 330, 389, 414, 482–4, 546, 564, 566, and 586, the original text being still faintly visible. At lines 74 and 181 it is corrected wrongly as B$^2$, at l. 272 wrongly as USVB$^2$, at l. 643 wrongly as T, at l. 597 wrongly as LtGFfB$^2$, and at l. 521 possibly correctly as LtURGSVPFLdHT$^2$B$^2$Tr Ha. There are also many changes of spelling and inflexional endings, as 'ȝ' for 'y', or 'eþ' for 'es'. These corrections are spread throughout the text, but apart from dialectal preference it is difficult to see the principle behind them. It appears that the corrector was usually working from a manuscript other than that of the RGSVWT family: possibly even conflating with the text of B², for B² has itself been emended to read as RGSVWT at lines 124, 410, and 802–3, and it contains other work in common with W. But why such minor and unsystematic corrections? W has unique errors and omissions at lines 153, 154, 161, 352, 366, and 531.

R has also been corrected, but very slightly and even more haphazardly, as at lines 134, 547, and 618. Only the last is correct or of any interest. It is noticeable that R shares many readings with G, as at lines 135, 186, 207, 209–10 (with Ld), 231, 234 (with He), 276, 360, 368, 378, 535–6 (G later corrected), 792–3 and 861, and a common ancestor for these two manuscripts is possible indicated, although this would entail G's immediate source having undergone later correction. R has unique omissions at lines 30–1, 106–7, 367–8, 736, 793–4, and 837–9.

As is to be expected, S and V share many readings not found elsewhere, approximately thirty. It is perhaps more valuable to record those places, however minor, where they differ:[1] lines 29, 94–5, 113–14, 161, 162, 203, 215, 221, 239, 264, 270, 312, 415, 518, 521, 546, 547, 573, 577, 585, 597, 609, 649, 713, 767, 775, 800, 808, 856, 875, and 887. There are errors on both sides; it is clear that neither manuscript has copied its text of the *Form* from the other, but that they derive from a common source. That source gives a very poor text, with numerous omissions for which there is no apparent reason. It is therefore probable that the agreement with DdR²FfLCDT³BIiMPFLdHT²B²TrChHaA at l. 182 is no more than coincidence.

Ignoring those places where L, G, and T change their exemplars, a tentative stemma emerges (Fig. 1). This reflects the general tendencies of these manuscripts, including their lack or otherwise of incipits, explicits, and Margaret's name. But it does not explain two inconsistencies: l. 227 'toucheth' Lt etc., 'þou chesest' RSV, 'þou sexte' T; l. 702 'hym' Lt etc., 'bodily' RT, 'boldli' GSVW; and it does not allow for agreements in error between Lt and U, excluding RGSVWT.

Such problems are multiplied in attempting a classification of the more numerous Dd type manuscripts. Certain persistent groupings recur: (L)CHeDT³BM, with Ii where relevant, (L)CHeD, T³BIiM,

[1] Further differences, too insignificant to record in the variants, occur at lines 37, 81, 155, 289, 305, 431, 446, 535, 541, 624, 693, 750, and 843.

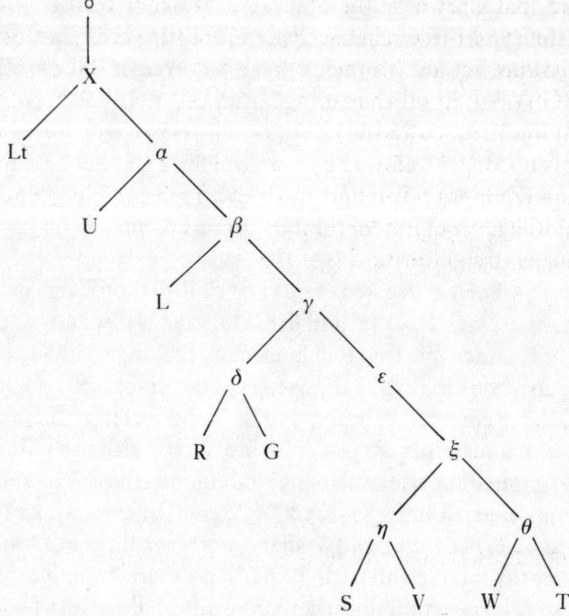


Fig. 1

PFLdHT$^2$B$^2$, PFLdHT$^2$, LdHT$^2$, HT$^2$, DdR$^2$Ff, R$^2$Ff. Tr, Ch, and Ha appear to follow no consistent pattern. But these groupings are frequently in conflict, and such unexpected agreements appear as T$^3$B MPFLdHT$^2$ or CHeDT$^3$BM combining with all or one of L, Tr, Ch, and Ha, or CHeT$^3$BM, CT$^3$BM, DT$^3$BM, T$^3$BMCh, HeBMHa, HeDTrCh, HePCh, CBCh, B$^2$ChHa, HT$^2$Ch, CCh, HeCh, DCh, BCh, B$^2$Ch, CB, DB, CD, DB$^2$, PHa, FTr, LdHa, R$^2$FfHe–the list could be extended almost indefinitely. An attempt to construct a stemma using as a basis only those seventeen omissions of Dd already discussed serves to illustrate the difficulty.

Dd's omissions at lines 182, 333–4, 624, 698–9, and 812 are shared by R$^2$FfLC(He)(D)T$^3$BMPFLdHT$^2$B$^2$(Tr)ChHa. The texts of He at l. 182, of Tr at lines 333–4 and of D at l. 812 are different, and therefore irrelevant to their ancestry. The occasional agreement of SV, W, or G will now be ignored. We may therefore assume that these nineteen manuscripts are all descended from a common source, Z with five errors (Z + 5e), or that only some of them are descended from that source and that elsewhere the omissions are coincidental. However the consistency of these manuscripts, not only in their agreement in these omissions but also in their agreement against the unrelated Lt and (U)RGSVWT in other readings, suggests the first hypothesis is correct. At lines 189–90 and 697 Z + 5e collects two more omissions (Z + 7e) but is no longer followed by Ha. At lines 809–10 an eighth omission occurs (Z + 8e) not found in PFLdHT$^{2}$B$^{2}$ or Ha, and at lines 687–8 a ninth (Z + 9e) not found in PFLdHT$^{2}$B$^{2}$ or Ha or Ch. So far the stemma is straightforward (see Fig. 2).

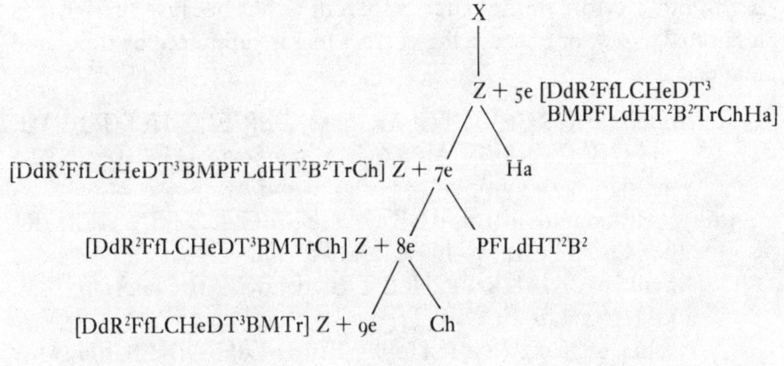


Fig. 2

But at l. 610 an omission is found shared by Z + 9e (T$^{3}$ providing a variant), Ha, Ch, F, and B$^{2}$; at lines 319–20 by Z + 9e, Ha, Ch, and B$^{2}$, but minus Tr; at l. 297 by Z + 9e, Ha, and Ch, but minus Tr, B, and B$^{2}$; and at lines 33–4 by Z + 9e, Ha, and Ch, but not by B$^{2}$, T$^{3}$, B, or because of its different exemplar, L. The remaining development is simpler. The omission at l. 592 is shared, anyway partially, by R$^{2}$FfD and Tr. The text of Tr is so corrupt that agreement here need not be significant. Dd, R$^{2}$Ff and D then divide further. Dd incorporates the individual readings which gives us its present text; R$^{2}$ and Ff share some further readings, and then they too divide. But the aberrancies of Ha, Ch, B$^{2}$, B, F, and Tr, whether due to coincidence, widespread conflation, or both, have clearly demonstrated the impossibility of establishing a definitive stemma.

Nevertheless, certain valuable facts have emerged from the attempt. Firstly, provided always that its omissions are genuine cases of vertical transmission, it is apparent that Dd could be as many as nine removes from the original, whereas, despite its later date of composition,[1] Lt could be as little as two. Secondly, the demonstrable changes in exemplar of L, T, and G, in conjunction with the formation of the text of Ad and Ar, the repetition in P, and the number of manuscripts containing brief extracts of the *Form*, often out of sequence, show that this work was in many instances being copied piecemeal, sometimes in sections smaller than a single quire. Finally, in a number of disputed readings, the existence of two main groups of unrelated manuscripts is frequently of assistance in determining the original text.

Further comparison between the texts of Lt and Dd reveals a number of other errors in the latter, apparent either because the sense is less satisfactory, or because the correct text is supported by unrelated manuscripts:[2]

15 'loueth' LtURGSVWTChAr; 'hase' DdR$^2$FfLCHeDT$^3$BIiMFLdHT$^2$B$^2$TrHaAFf$^2$. Although L supports Dd here, the Lt reading has the support of both Ch and Ar.

23 'world coueiteth' LtURGSVWTR$^2$FfLCHeDT$^3$BIiMPFLdHT$^2$B$^2$TrChHaAr; 'worldes couaytise' DdA.[3]

31 'thynken' LtUR$^2$FfCHeDT$^3$BMPLdHT$^2$B$^2$ChAAr; 'sai' DdHa; 'makiþ' F; 'doo' Tr.

92 'lecherie' LtUR$^2$FfCHeDT$^3$BIiMFLdHT$^2$B$^2$TrChHaAAr; 'lust' RGSVWT; 'thyng' Dd; 'boost' L; 'lecherie and a foul þyng' P$^1$P$^2$.

124 'reste and ioye in heuyn' LtURGSVWTR$^2$FfLCDT$^3$BIiMPFLdHT$^2$TrHaAFf$^2$; 'þat blys þat neuer mare blynnes' Dd; 'reste in heuyn' HeB$^2$Ch.

135–6 'God to queme' LtUR$^2$CHeDIiLdHT$^2$B$^2$Ha; 'pleysyng to god' RGW; 'quemyng to god' SVT; 'gode and wheme' DdFf;[3] 'hym to qweeme' LT$^3$; 'hem to worchyppe' B; 'gode to hym' MA; 'good and clene' P; 'hym to plesyng' Tr; 'good and queme to god' FCh.

153–4 'har ioye be' LtURGSVTR$^2$FfLCHeDT$^3$BIiMPFLdHT$^2$B$^2$TrChHaA; 'be þi ioy' W; 'þai ioy' Dd.

162 'þe lyknes of' DdR$^2$FfLCHeDT$^3$BIiMPFLdHT$^2$TrChA; *om.* LtUB$^2$Ha.

171 'he sayde' DdR$^2$FfLCDT$^3$BIiMFLdHT$^2$B$^2$ChHa; *om.* LtURGSVWTHePTrAAr.

[1] Lt is the younger MS by some fifty years.

[2] Minor variations in supporting MSS are here ignored.

[3] Noted by Miss Allen.

186 'vndre need' LtLCHeD$T^3$FLdH$T^2B^2$ChHaA; 'more þan nedeth' USVWT; 'þen nedeþ' RG; 'vndirnethe' Dd$R^2$FfM; 'under colour' BIi; 'under þe colour of nede' PTr$Tr^2$.

198 'abstinence' DdLCHeDChA; 'penaunce & abstynence' $R^2$Ff$T^3$ BIiMHa; 'penaunce' PFH$T^2B^2$Tr$H^2$; *om.* Lt.

233 'I' LtRGSVWTLCHeD$T^3$BIiMPFLdH$T^2B^2$ChHa; 'sithen it is' U; *om.* Dd$R^2$FfA. 'semeth' LtRGSVWT$R^2$FfLCHeDPLdH $T^2B^2$TrChHaA; 'is' UD$dT^3$BIiMF$H^2$.

243 'lyf' LtURGSV$R^2$LCHeDBIiMPFLdH$T^2B^2$TrChHaAr$H^2$ Hh; 'loue' WTDdFf$T^3$M.

276 'þat' URGSVWTDd$R^2$FfLCHe*D$T^3$BIiMPLdH$T^2B^2$TrHaA Ar$H^2$Hh; *om.* LtFCh (see note).

299 'hauynge' LtURGW$R^2$FfLCHeD$T^3$BMPFLdH$T^2B^2$TrCh; 'thankand' Dd.[1]

304 'and woo and' LtUPFLdH$T^2$Tr; 'and what' Dd$R^2$LCHeD$T^3$ M$B^2$ChAHh$B^3$; 'and' FfBHaAr.

328 'foule' LtU$R^2$FfLCHeD$T^3$BMPFH$T^2B^2$TrCh$H^2$; 'folowe' DdLd.

359 'fool' Lt$R^2$FfM; 'foul' UDdLCHe$T^3$PFHaArHh; 'for lesse' D; 'idyl' B; 'foly' $H^2$. See note.

376 'swelighynge' LtULCHe$T^3$MP$B^2$ChHa; 'swellyng' DdD; 'schewyng' $R^2$FfB.[1]

406 'al' LtU$R^2$FfLHeD$T^3$BMPFLdH$T^2B^2$Ch; 'þi schryft' Dd; 'al þi shrift' Ha.

423 'maner' LtURGSVLCHeD$T^3$BMFLdCh; 'man' WTDd$R^2$FfP H$T^2B^2$HaHh.

450 'forþi' LtRGW$R^2$Ff$T^3$Ha; 'therfor' UTLCHeBPFLdH$T^2$Tr; 'wherfore' SV; 'for' DdM$B^2$Ch; 'forwhi' D.

456 'neþer' LtU$R^2$FfHeD$T^3$BMPFLdH$T^2B^2$TrChHa; 'not heȝer' R; 'noȝt hier' G; 'not here' SVWT; 'noght al' Dd; 'not neþer' C; 'noght' ArHh.

518 'thynk ham' LtURGT$R^2$FfLCHeD$T^3$BMPFLdH$T^2$ChHa$Ld^2$ E; 'þenne' SV; 'þinke þanne' W; 'þynk' Dd;[1] 'thynk hem þen' $B^2$.

521 'eigh' LtURGSVW*PFLdH$T^2B^2$TrHa; 'loue' TDd$R^2$FfLC HeD$T^3$MCh$Ld^2$; 'þouȝt' B.

553 'and' U$B^2$TrCh; 'in' Dd$R^2$FfH$T^2$; 'and in' B; *om.* LtRGSVWT LCD$T^3$MPFLdHaAd.

[1] Noted by Miss Allen.

558 'seghynge' LtR$^2$FfT$^3$MHa; 'syngynge' UTLDdHeDB$^2$ChHh; 'seande' RGSVW; *om.* C.

573 'only' LtURGSVWTR$^2$FfLCHeDT$^3$MPFLdHT$^2$B$^2$TrHa; 'swa mykel' Dd;[1] *om.* B; 'myche' Ch.

586 'takeled' LtTHe; 'acombred' UP; 'fyled' RG; 'tangled' SVCD Ld; 'foulid' W; 'takked' DdLT$^3$MHa; 'taglede' R$^2$FfHT$^2$; 'towched' B; 'perseueraunt or costomable' F; 'smyttid' B$^2$; 'helden or defouled' Ch. See note.

646 'dedly' LtDT$^3$HT$^2$Ha; 'dedly syn(nes)' URGSVWTDdLCHe FLdB$^2$Ch; 'dedely luf' R$^2$Ff. See note.

664 'armes' LtURSVWTR$^2$FfDT$^3$BMPFLdHT$^2$B$^2$HaHhIi$^3$Tr$^2$; 'armer' GLCHe; 'mirynes' Dd.

803 'Casciodorus' LtRGSVWTCHeFLdHT$^2$B$^2$Ch; 'þe book of fasset' U; 'Austyne' Dd; 'Calcidor' R$^2$FfDT$^3$IiPIi$^3$; 'þe holy man' B; *om.* MTr; 'Saladur' Ha.

804 'þynge' LtCHeDT$^3$MPLdHT$^2$Ha; þat is *add.* URGSVB$^2$*Tr Ch; 'is' W; 'þat is' T; 'þat es farre' *add.* Dd; 'þat semeþ' *add.* B; *om.* R$^2$FfA.

805 'myght' LtRGSVWTR$^2$FfCHeDT$^3$BMPLdHT$^2$B$^2$Ha; *om.* UDdIiChTr$^2$; 'myȝtilich' FTr.

817 'only' LtURGSVWTIi$^3$; 'any' DdR$^2$FfLCHeDT$^3$BIiMPLdH T$^2$B$^2$ChHaA.

822 'day' LtURGSVWTR$^2$FfLCHeDT$^3$BIiMPFLdHT$^2$B$^2$HaA HhEIi$^3$; 'ioy' DdAd; 'blys' Ch.

831 'with me' LtURGSVWTR$^2$FfLCHeDT$^3$BIiMPFLdHT$^2$B$^2$Ch HaAAdIi$^3$; 'within þe' Dd.

886 'lighteth' LtURGSVWTHeBIiFAArIi$^3$; 'ligges' DdR$^2$FfLCD T$^3$MPLdHT$^2$B$^2$Ha.

Lt has errors[2] at lines 63, 95, 147, 231, 242, 277, 298, 357, 378, 436, 483, 507, 558, 597, 599, 601, 637, 645, 654, 664, 812, and 884. The reason for these, where apparent, is given in the textual notes. It is an indication of the manuscript's freedom from contamination that in all but five of these instances the Lt reading is unique.

Further variants between Lt and Dd are caused by minor syntactical differences, or the substitution of a synonym. Where these are for

[1] Noted by Miss Allen.

[2] I do not include here such minor errors as dittography (lines 291, 292, 630, 693), error in a single letter (63, 75, 79, 105, 162, 187, 203, 231, 382, 424, 477, 531, 564, 590, 661, 770, 881), or accidental omission of a single word (87, 129, 180, 310, 516, 596, 676, 742, 770).

dialectal reasons–prepositional variation, or 'praisynge' for 'louyng', 'euer' for 'ay', the Northern text is to be preferred, but elsewhere the original reading can only be conjectural. But here too the manuscript evidence can be significant, and often indicates Dd to be in error. The more interesting of these occur at the following lines: 38, 41, 52, 54, 55, 68, 80, 84, 103, 112, 117, 125, 130, 146, 171, 200, 204, 205, 221, 230, 231, 246, 287, 305, 309, 331, 340, 354, 361, 369, 389, 421, 424, 437–8, 454, 463, 473, 498, 499, 528, 540, 551, 556, 562, 573, 604, 620, 627, 629, 630, 650, 653, 656, 661, 668, 673, 676, 681, 703, 721, 725, 738, 757, 787, 788, 792, 805, 811, 814, 815, 845, 867, 894. The more problematical, especially where the punctuation of the text is affected, are discussed in the notes.

Finally there are a very few instances where both Lt and Dd appear to be in error. At l. 106 we have an example of widespread substitution of synonyms: 'vnstable and vnwise' Lt; 'bothe' U; 'unwitty' RGSVW; *om.* T; 'and whaynt' Dd; 'vnquaynt' R$^2$FfLT$^3$MChHa; 'vnsly' CHe; 'or slei3tes' D; 'many' BIi; 'meny vnwyse' P$^1$; 'unwarly' P$^2$; 'vnwyse' FLdHT$^2$TrFf$^2$; 'vnwar B$^2$; 'unredy' A. Here I would accept the R$^2$FfL T$^3$MChHa reading, three of which are Northern manuscripts, to be original. Dd's error is readily explicable, and Lt has substituted. At lines 273–4 the reading of the majority, including Lt and Dd, 'his grace enlumyneth þyn herte and forsaketh al vices' is unacceptable, and indeed most manuscripts, apart from LtDdLT$^3$MHa, have tried variously to emend. This could have been an error in the archetype. At l. 377 all relevant manuscripts read 'receyue', apart from Tr which has 'wiþ', and Ch 'to chargen nou3t'. This makes no sense in the context, and again suggests archetypal error. If my emendation to 'reteyne' is accepted, it is easy to see how the error occurred, but it is none the less surprising that it was allowed to stand in so many manuscripts. At l. 883 Lt reads 'fested', Dd 'fest', URGWFT$^2$B$^2$ArIi$^3$ 'fastneth hit', SVLd 'fastnen', TLCHeDT$^3$BIiMHaAE 'sette hit', R$^2$FfP 'fest þaim', and H 'susteneþ hit'. Contextually 'fest hit' is the most fitting reading. Possibly Lt's exemplar had 'fest it', which he took for one word (Northern 'festit'), and the exemplars of DdR$^2$Ff, SV, and PLd omitted 'hit' coincidentally.

### *Ego Dormio*

All the manuscripts containing *Ego Dormio* also contain all or part of the *Form*, and might therefore be expected to adhere to the same genetic pattern found there. But there are differences.

Again, Dd's text has always been regarded as the most authoritative. However comparison with the other manuscripts reveals it to be deficient in a number of respects. There are several omissions. Some of these are caused by straightforward scribal error, as in the following cases of homoeoteleuton:

21–2 'þe son. And as þou seest þe son'; 'And . . . son' *om.* Dd.

45 'to haue compassioun of þe passioun'; 'to . . . compassioun' *om.* Dd.

77–9 'fro God þat is lif of þe soule. And when a wreched man or a woman is departed fro God we seyn he is dede for he is slayn fro God'; 'þat . . . God(2)' *om.* Dd.

208–9 'here. When may I cum þe nere thi melody for to hire'; 'When . . . hire' *om.* Dd.

260 'þe peyn of helle and þe peyn'; 'of . . . peyn' *om.* Dd, and possibly l. 84, where the Lt reading 'men kan þynke in erth' ('men in hert kan þenke' RSVW) becomes in Dd 'we may here se or fele', with the following 'Al perisshethe and passeth þat we with eigh see' omitted.

Other omissions and variants of Dd are possibly of greater significance, and require to be discussed in greater detail. *Ego Dormio* is, in Dd alone, dedicated to a nun of Yedingham: 'Explicit tractatus Ricardi heremite de Hampole scriptus cuidam moniali de ȝedyngham'. But although Yedingham priory was near a manor held by Rolle's early patron John Dalton, and would thus have been familiar to him, the contents of *Ego Dormio* make such an ascription inappropriate. The author appears to be addressing one ignorant of any form of conventual life, and his object in writing is persuasion. The emptiness of earthly pleasures, which can lead only to damnation, is vividly contrasted to the joys of spiritual life with their ultimate reward. In the other epistles, one, according to Dd, also addressed to a nun, and the other to a recluse, the religious background is assumed, and the reader encouraged, indeed expected, to attain the higher degrees of spirituality. Here Rolle is writing for one who has yet to take the first step, and although the ideal is described he adds 'I say nat þat þou, or another þat redeth þis, shal do hit al'. His instructions are basic: where *The Commandment* speaks of the prime importance of loving God, *Ego Dormio* begins by stressing such humble necessities as keeping the ten commandments and being stable in the Catholic faith, and the recipient is exhorted no longer to desire riches but to give some of her clothes to the poor. Miss Allen admitted this difficulty, but attempted to overcome it by suggesting that *Ego Dormio* was written for a secular lady who did not take the veil until after its composition. I would agree that this text was written for a secular lady, but only the text of Dd gives us any reason to suppose that she was later connected with Yedingham. I would suggest instead that the text of Dd is descended from the copy of a later and non-authorial adaptation, a copy possibly made at the priory, where the dedication was appended. The Lt text includes the *Ego Dormio* among the pieces written for Margaret of Kirkby, who entered conventual life in 1343, the very date suggested by Miss Allen[1] for the composition of *Ego Dormio*. It is thus not beyond the bounds of possibility that she was the original recipient, and indeed that the epistle was influential in determining her future life.

Dd appears to have undergone a two-fold revision. Firstly a number of authorial references are eliminated. This is shown most strikingly in the first part:

2 'I fynd hit written'; 'it es writen' Dd.
2–3 'þat I haue set at þe begennynge of my writynge' *om.* Dd.
10–11 'Crist couaiteth þy fayrnesse in soule, þat þou gif holy þi herte, and I prech noght elles'; 'Criste couaytes noght els' Dd.
58 'I than writ hit'; 'þou þan wyt it' Dd.

It would then seem that the reviser's enthusiasm waned as he realized the magnitude of his task, and the only other alteration of this sort is the major omission at lines 169–70 of 'And thynke on me þat I be nat foryeten in þi praiers þat is aboutward þat þou ware dere with Crist whose mercy me nedeth', which could be achieved without materially altering the sense.

The second category of revisions, if they may be so termed, has the effect of making the work more general, and more suitable for a religious community:

1 'The þat lust loue, hold þyn ere'; 'þai þat lyste lufe, herken' Dd.
6 'Forþi þat I loue þe'; 'Forþi þat I lufe' Dd.
9 'He wil wed þe'; 'he wil with þe dwelle' Dd.
10 'and'; 'my dere syster in criste' *add.* Dd.
42–4 'The thynk nowe . . . hard to gif þi hert fro al erthly thynges . . . and go by one'; 'þe thynk . . . hard to gife þi hert fra al erthly thynges . . . and to be alane' Dd.

[1] *English Writings*, p. 60.

92–3 ‘when þou hast wel lyved in þe comandementȝ of God and straytly kept þe’; ‘when þai haue wele leued in þe ten comandementes of God and styfly put þam’ Dd.

143–4 ‘þou shalt be . . . Cristes dere mayden and spouse in heuyn’; ‘þou sal be . . . Criste dere seruande in heuen’ Dd.

The variants at lines 9 and 143–4 are particularly significant in the context of my argument, because of course a nun would already be the spiritual bride of Christ.

So far I have postulated my reviser as adapting his text to suit a conventual community. But, as with all Rolle’s work, the emphasis in *Ego Dormio* is individual and personal, and it must soon have become apparent that, short of rewriting the entire text, it was necessary to adhere to the particular. We therefore have the unique dedication ‘cuidam moniali’, but it is noticeable that, unlike Lt, no one nun is single out by name.

Dd has in addition a number of unique errors, which further devalue its text. They include l. 34 ‘says’ for ‘seest’, l. 37 ‘stabil þi’ for ‘stabilly’ and ‘be byrnande’ for ‘brennyngly’, l. 153 ‘intil’ for ‘in il’, l. 191 ‘alsso in þe blys of heuen es al þe aungels’ for ‘fouled as a fole in heuyn þe halowes’, which is not only unsupported but destroys the medial rhyme, l. 203 ‘and for it’ for ‘for þe I’, l. 214 ‘receyued’ for ‘reft’, lines 231–2 ‘þarfore’ for ‘þan for’ and ‘in’ for ‘þi’, l. 273 ‘lifand’ for ‘hauynge’, and l. 300 ‘hys’ for ‘my’. A few of these were noted by Miss Allen, collating from R$^1$ and V, but her main concern was to provide a readable text, and she drew no conclusions from them.

RSVWG, in all of which *Ego Dormio* follows immediately after the *Form*, still form the same closely related group. Examples are too numerous to cite in their entirety, but even a few will suffice to show the consistency with which these manuscripts agree amongst themselves and differ from the others:

14 ‘þi hert is’ LtR$^1$DdBrAdAr; ‘þou art’ RSVWG.

48 ‘solace’ LtR$^1$DdBrPAdAr; ‘bi a þousand part’ *add.* RSVWG.

55 ‘leue’ LtR$^1$DdBrPTr; ‘loue’ RSVWG.
‘fleisshely’ LtR$^1$Br; ‘litel is þe loue þat þou hast or felest in ihesu crist riȝt so if þou haue no flesshely lust ne lykyng in þese worldly þinges’ *add.* RSVWG.

78 ‘God’ LtR$^1$BrPTr; ‘þourȝe dedly synne’ *add.* RSVWG.

156–7 ‘in þoght and in dede’ LtR$^1$DdBrPAd; *om.* RSVWG.

219 ‘cheseth’ LtBrPTrAd; ‘sheweþ’ RSVWG.

'whom he wil' LtDdBrPTrAd; *om.* RSVWG.
280 'My hert peynteth þe palle þat stiddeth vs in stalle' LtDdBr; *om.* RSVWG.
300 'and yif my desyrynge' LtR$^{1}$DdBr; *om.* RSVWG.
308 'maistry' LtR$^{1}$DdBr; 'þouȝe I shulde neuer elde' *add.* RSVWG.

As in the *Form*, no single manuscript can be the exemplar of another. R, thought by both Horstman and Allen to be the source of SV, has unique errors at lines 10, 125, 138, 160, and 228, and a unique omission at l. 176. S and V differ at lines 18, 80, 82, 93, 109, 113, 164, 180, 188, 213, 288, and 299, and share a number of unique errors, as at lines 59, 83, and 130. W and G both have many individual readings, notably W at lines 32, 36, 38, 55, 56, 114, 143, 145, 154, 183–4, and 220, and G at lines 36, 84, 122, 132, 148, 156, and 157, and particularly in the lyrics, where several scribes apparently felt they had poetic licence to improve on their copy.

However in the *Form* RG were usually closer to each other than to SV or W, and SVW(T) shared some readings not found in RG. Here the pattern is different. R and SV appear to be more closely related to each other than they are to G or W. There are no obvious shared errors such as nonsensical omissions to prove this, but a comparison of variants shows that RSV share a number of presumably erroneous readings where WG follow the majority readings of the other manuscripts:

101 'spekynge' LtR$^{1}$WGPTr; 'speke' DdBrAdAr; 'spyande' RSV.
150 'enemyes' LtR$^{1}$WGDdPTrAdAr; 'þinges' RSV.
159 'felest' LtR$^{1}$WGDdBrPAdAr; 'fyndes' RSVTr.
191 'fouled' LtWGBr; 'folewed' RSV.
214 'abouen' LtWGDdBrPTrAd; 'fro' RSV.
224 'lif' LtWGDdBrPTrAd; 'loue' RSV.

Further variants show RSVG agreeing to the exclusion of W:

3 'þe' LtR$^{1}$WBrP; 'my' RSVG.
27 'loued' LtR$^{1}$WDdBrPTrAdAr; 'serued' RSVG.
47 'vset' LtR$^{1}$WDdBrPTrAdAr; 'brouȝt' RSVG.
49 'myrth' LtR$^{1}$WDdBrPTrAdAr; 'lust' RSVG.
51 'al' LtR$^{1}$WDdBrPTrAr; 'any' RSVG.
66 'þou' LtR$^{1}$WDdBrPTr; 'we' RSVG.
97 'degre' LtR$^{1}$WDdBrPTrAdAr; *om.* RSVG.
100 'al' LtR$^{1}$WDdBrPTr; *om.* RSVG.

124 'hert' LtR$^{1}$WDdBrPTrAd; 'þouȝte' RSVG.
'holy' LtR$^{1}$WDdBrPTrAd; 'only' RSVG.
128 'and' LtR$^{1}$WDdBrPTrAd; 'in' RSVG.
231 'lif' LtWDdPTrAd; 'loue' RSVG.

From these readings the stemma shown in Fig. 3 emerges and it would seem that, contrary to first expectations, R, G, and W did not copy the *Form* and *Ego Dormio* as a single entity and each from a single exemplar. This is further corroboration that Rolle's texts were often circulated and copied piecemeal.

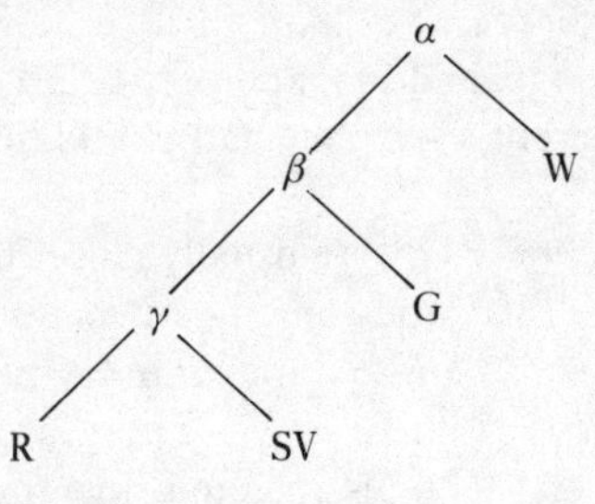


Fig. 3.

The text of Tr, as it did in the *Form*, abounds in variants and diffuse expansions, and also has some unique omissions, as for instance at lines 139–42. It divides the first lyric into two, and gives such an aberrant version that it is not collated here, but printed separately.[1] The second lyric is omitted altogether. A partial attempt has been made to adapt its text for a male recipient. There are many masculine pronouns in its expansions, and the details of women's clothing at lines 161–4, the references to wooing and marriage at lines 7–9, and to virginity at lines 155–6 are all either altered or eliminated. At l. 144 'mayden' is omitted, although 'spouse' remains.

P does not contain as interpolated a version as Tr, but nevertheless has enough expansions and variants to suggest that its text too has been adapted, as at lines 12–15, or 151–4. Here too the first lyric has too many variants to collate and is printed separately,[2] and the second is omitted in the manuscript, the text concluding with 'Amen' at l. 266. There are also a number of other omissions.

[1] See appendix, p. 000. [2] See appendix, p. 000.

Ad and Ar are closely related. They are not good texts; both share a very large number of identical omissions. However they agree in all but their most minor variants, matters of a single word or letter. Ar cannot always be read exactly as its leaves have been carelessly cut and bound, but in so far as it is legible even these small discrepancies occur only at the following: lines 28, 48, 93, 102, 106, 112, 118, and 124. At this point a folio is missing in Ar, and the text concludes at the start of the next sentence. However, despite their similarity, it does not seem that either manuscript can be a copy of the other. Ad presents *Ego Dormio* as if it were part of the *Form*. As noted in the description of manusripts, the Ad text of the *Form* is very condensed and fragmentary, and in a disjointed order, covering approximately only lines 526–835 and 489–510 of the Lt text. At l. 525, where Lt reads 'Three degrees of loue I shal tel þe', Ad has 'Thare ar thre degrees of loue as is writtene here aftyr', and then continues with the opening line of *Ego Dormio*. At the conclusion of *Ego Dormio*, after the second lyric, Ad reads 'Amen' and then goes straight on without a break repeating 'The fyrste degree of luf is insuperabill, the seconde inseperabill, the thyrde synguler', the same words with which it had commenced its first extract of the *Form*. It then suddenly breaks off, and starts a new work unrelated to Rolle. Interestingly, in Ar too *Ego Dormio* follows after chapters of the *Form*, but in Ar the arrangement is different. The Ar text of the *Form* consists of a similarly condensed rendering of lines 323–484, 836–876, 1–247, 877–93, and 255–309; in other words exactly those sections omitted by Ad. This, together with the disordered sequence in which both Ad and Ar present their fragments, suggests that a single exemplar containing both *Ego Dormio* and the *Form* was copied piecemeal and in separate places by the scribes of Ad and Ar. Presumably they were supposed to exchange sections of this exemplar as they completed copying, and this was duly done with the first text, but not with the *Form*. The scribe of Ar, having the larger part of the latter beside him, realized that it represented a separate work. The scribe of Ad mistakenly copied his three sections as a single text.

The Latin text Ca is a disappointment. Not itself a direct translation, but the copy of another Latin text,[1] it represents a textual tradition at many removes from the original. It does not derive from any extant English manuscript, but, like so many of them, has been adapted to suit a different audience; probably, as Dd, a conventual

[1] Shown by such errors as *capere* for *cupire*, *videns* for *vides*, *spem* for *speciem*, *sanctitate* for *sanitate*.

one, for Dd's reading at l. 10 is translated exactly 'mea cara soror in Christo'. Other echoes of Dd[1] include l. 1 *þai/illi*, 43 *al/omnimoda*, 55 *for þe luffe of god/ob amorem Iesu Christi*, the omission of *þis* at l. 33, 110 *þi/tuo*, 119 *grutchyng/murmure*, 138 *þe/te*, 145 *þis/istius*, 159 *þis/huius*, 204 *dere/care*, and 229 *euer mare and mare/semper magis et magis*. But it does not repeat Dd's omissions at lines 11, 21–2, 23, 77–9, and 208–9, nor Dd's reading at l. 84, where *aliquis valeat cogitare* is closest to G, and elsewhere, as will be seen, it reflects the readings of other manuscripts.[2] Moreover it has several interpolations of its own, notably after lines 91, 100, and 157, emphasizing the dangers of sin, particularly relapse into sin, and the joys of the heavenly banquet prepared for those who are able to resist; also some original omissions, as at lines 75–6, 86–7, 197–8, and 258–60.

The best texts of *Ego Dormio*, in so far as they are free from revision, are Br, R[1], and Lt. However Br in itself is a careless witness, with many slips and nonsensical variants, as at lines 14, 42, 66, 99, 115, 125, 134, 136, 150–1, 154, 171–2, 182, 185, 195, 202, 205, 207–8, 230–1, 240, 277, 287, 294, and 310. It also has a major textual dislocation: lines 103–34 ('wreth . . . suffrynge') are placed at l. 166 of the Lt text, with minor contextual adjustments made at the point of entry.

The Northern R[1] and Lt are very close, but it is for the most part an affinity of truth and not of error. They supply all the various omissions of Dd, P, Tr, AdAr, RSVWG and Br. However neither can be the exemplar of the other; R[1] has small errors at lines 62, 65, 75, 83, 153, and 194.[3] Lt omits a verb at lines 29 and 145, a noun at l. 89, possibly an adjective at l. 179, has faults of a single letter at lines 125 and 173, and has repeated 'swetnesse' for 'sekenesse' at l. 230. The extra relative pronoun at lines 54 and 89 looks like a scribal idiosyncrasy; it occurs elsewhere in the manuscript. On the evidence of the other texts, Lt has omitted 'melody al þe' at l. 51. 'and þe likynge' at l. 107, 'many kyrtels many' at l. 162, and 'in' at l. 234, and has further unique slips at lines 36, 67, 107, 181, and 196. At l. 125 LtRTr have variously converted the verb 'stele' of R[1]SVWGDdBrAd into an adverb 'stil'.

[1] Amassian and Lynch uncritically accept Dd as 'the best basis upon which Rolle's original text could be reconstructed' because 'in relation to the other manuscripts [it] has fewer problematical readings and has no obvious interpolation'. From this assumption they then interpret the support of the Latin text as giving authority to the readings of Dd. I hope to have shown that the reverse is true; that Dd and Ca both reflect a revised version.

[2] Including omitting the second lyric, as P and Tr.

[3] It should be remembered that R[1] lacks lines 201 to 287.

At lines 243–55 Lt has a passage which is absent from every other manuscript. Is this yet another example of scribal interpolation? On a priori grounds this seems unlikely. The Lt scribe is himself a faithful copier, and shows elsewhere no sign of tampering with his material, while the Rolle texts in this manuscript are so free from error and contamination that they cannot be many removes from the original. On stylistic grounds too the passage sounds authentic. The somewhat didactic manner used by Rolle in the early stages of all his English epistles dissolves in an emotional crescendo as he describes the final experience of mystic communion. And always the culminating bliss is death. In this the Lt passage is comparable to the conclusions of both the *Form* and *The Commandment*. Without it the final stage of his disciple's spiritual progress and, for a novice, her greatest incitement to persevere, is lacking. The vocabulary is that used elsewhere by Rolle. The phrase 'roust of syn' is found in *The Commandment*. The odd emphasis on sitting is explained in the *Form*: 'I haue loued for to sit . . . for I knewe þat I loued God more, and langer lested with me comfort of loue, þan goynge or standynge or knelynge. For syttynge am I in most rest and my hert most vpward.'

However these are mainly subjective criteria. For the passage to be authentic to Rolle must mean one of two things. Either all the other manuscripts, with the exception of $R^1$, must be descended from a common original, or Lt represents an authorial revision.

Relationship is unusually difficult to demonstrate. Dd, AdAr, Tr, P, and RSVWG have all in their different ways suffered a deliberate reworking, and partially shared omissions, even when the reason for them is not apparent, may therefore be coincidental. Two revisers working towards the same end may produce the same variant. But with these provisos, the evidence permits some tentative conclusions.

AdAr share two obvious errors with Dd at lines 16 and 45. After the text of Ar ends, Ad shares the omission of Dd at lines 169–70, a further omission at l. 256, and a variant at l. 263. These agreements would seem to indicate at least a distant relationship for these manuscripts. The readings at lines 16, 169–70, and 263 are also shared by the Latin text Ca. At l. 45 'to haue compassioun of þe passioun', where DdAdAr omit 'to . . . compassioun', Ca omits 'of þe passioun', reading simply 'conpaciendo'. At l. 256 Ca supports LtRSVWGBrPTr.

Dd and Tr agree in their readings at lines 9 and 62, and have partially shared variants at lines 10 (where the 'syster' of Dd becomes 'frend' in Tr in accordance with its general tendency to masculinize the text), 34, 44, 55, 64, 81, 134, and 221. Ca agrees with them only at lines 9, 10, 34, and 55. At l. 89 there is general confusion, and Lt's reading 'þer is al þe rabil' is opposed by 'þere wa es al þe rabil' R[1], 'her wo is al þe rebel' Br, 'ful woo is þat rabel' RSV and, with slight variations, W and G, 'where waa es euer stabel' Dd, and '... hem worþi to sorowȝ ay durable' Tr. P and AdAr omit the passage. This suggests that the original reading was that of R[1], from which Lt, accidentally or otherwise, has omitted 'wa'. Br has substituted the possessive 'her' for adverb 'þere', and RSV(WG) have substituted 'ful' for 'þere', 'þat' for 'þe' and omitted 'al'. It further suggests that Dd and Tr had a common ancestor which, not understanding the syntax of 'al þe rabil', changed it to 'ai durable'. Dd then substitutes 'whare' for 'þere', 'euer' for 'ai', and 'stabel' for 'durable'. Tr rewrites, but retains 'ay durable'. Here the Latin phrase 'suum placitum tristissimum in eis eternaliter firmandum' reflects the error of Dd and Tr.

P, Ad, and, where relevant, Ar agree, partially at least, in omissions at lines 6–7, 134–6, and 172–3, as well as a number of variants. None of these agreements is shared by the Latin. Dd, Tr, AdAr and Ca agree in a variant at l. 27; Dd, Tr, P, Ad and Br agree at l. 112, where Ca supports RSVWG. However these agreements are only significant if they are in error, and here the testimony of RSVWG becomes important. In all the above readings this group either sides with Lt and its supporting manuscripts, or else provides its own variant. But at l. 229 it is joined by P in the reading 'felyng þe loue of'. Here Dd has a similar 'feland lufe' and the Latin 'amoris ... leticiam sencies', but significantly the Lt reading 'fillynge þe ful of' is supported by Tr and Br. Similarly at lines 260–1 LtBrTr read 'helle and þe peyn of', which is omitted by DdRSVWGPAd and the Latin. Tr has been shown to be related to Dd, but never to Lt; its testimony therefore means that DdRSVWGP share a common ancestor which perpetrated the double error at l. 229, and further that there is a cross-relationship between this group, Ad, and Tr.

If this genealogy is accepted, the support of some members of this group indicates that LtR[1]SVBrPTr are correct to omit the 'and veyn' of RWGDdAdArCa at l. 43; that LtR[1]BrPTr are correct in reading 'whar hit wille' at lines 136–7, omitted by RSVWGDdCa; and that LtR[1]RWGBr are correct in reading 'and euer' at l. 152, omitted by SVDdTrCa. But, as always, some agreements are inexplicable. Thus at l. 7 both R[1] and Ca agree with WP in the apparently erroneous 'be comer and', of which the Latin 'Ego vellem esse veniens et nuncius' looks like an attempt at literal translation. At l. 54 R[1]BrP and in a different way RSVWG and Ca omit the preferable 'ioy' of LtDdTr. At l. 146 Lt is alone in reading 'rauyst' against the 'raysed' of R[1]BrPTrAd (Latin 'exultaberis'), 'receyued' RSVWDd, and 'rered' G, but as a difficilior lectio Lt is perhaps original, and it would only need the coincidental omission or overlooking of a suspension mark to result in the R[1]BrPTrAd reading.

Br is difficult to place. Its agreement with DdPTrAd at l. 112 has already been mentioned, but as this involves only a single letter, it could be coincidental. Equally inconclusive and sporadic are its agreements with DdAdAr at l. 28, with Dd(Tr) at l. 123, with Tr at lines 65 and 137, with Ad at l. 139, with RSVGDd at l. 58, with RSVGAd at l. 304, with RSVWG at l. 279, and with RSV(Ad) at l. 263. It cannot therefore be confidently assigned to a tradition which includes all these manuscripts, and whose representative originally omitted the Lt passage. But neither is it possible to demonstrate a relationship between it and Lt, a relationship which would effectively militate against the originality of the Lt passage. A possible relationship may be conceded between Br and R[1], from their agreements at lines 54 (but also P), 75, 120, 153, 176, and 291, but even this is built on the slenderest of evidence. Lt and R[1] share apparent errors at lines 31, 39, 165–6, and 311. Individually these are minor enough to be coincidental, but they are cumulative, and two of them (39 and 165) are half-shared by Br. Lt, Br and where relevant R[1] are in opposition to the other witnesses at lines 104, 224, 262, and 312. But although the readings of the latter group may sometimes be considered contextually preferable, they could equally well reflect transmitted error. In no case is it possible to assert that Lt and Br are united in error, and the authenticity of the Lt text cannot therefore be established or refuted stemmatically.

On the other hand, descent from an authorial revision cannot be discounted. Whether or not Margaret of Kirkby was the original recipient of this treatise, the Lt colophon suggests that at a later stage a careful collection had been made of Rolle's English writings especially for this favourite disciple. But between the composition of *Ego Dormio c.* 1343 and the *Form c.* 1348, she had progressed spiritually from the status of a laywoman to that of a recluse. Some of his early teaching would therefore be inadequate; what more natural than that the master himself, who in his more esoteric Latin writings yearned passionately for death, should rectify this by the insertion of this very personal passage.

*The Commandment*

S and V are still closely related, with only very minor differences at lines 1, 11, 32, 55, 57, 59, 76, 82, 111, 114, 123, 135, 189, 200, 207, 209, and 210. They present a poor text, with many major omissions, as at lines 5–6, 19–20, 37–41, 66–7, 85, 130–1, 137–8, 145, 160–6, 167–84, 188–9, and 211–13, and a six line textual dislocation at l. 202. None of these faults is shared by R, and it is clear that in this work SV and R no longer derive from a common source.

T$^3$ is also of little textual value. As in the *Form* its text, which is addressed to a man, is expanded and verbose, and I have not recorded its non-substantive variants beyond l. 41.

Lt$^2$, Ii$^2$, and Br are closely related, agreeing in many variants and omissions, and all concluding *The Commandment* with lines 610–25 of the *Form.* Of the three Lt$^2$ is perhaps to be preferred, having no unique omissions, while Ii$^2$ has omissions at lines 30, 94, 103, 197, and 211–12. Br has small omissions at lines 18–19, 21, 22, 49, 78, 101, 130–1, and 216, and all have unique errors.

No clear picture emerges of the relationship between the remaining manuscripts. T$^4$ appears to come from the same source as P. They share omissions at lines 25, 55, 66–72, 114, and 131, and agree in a major variant at lines 209–10. However the source cannot be immediate, because each manuscript individually shares an omission with Ff. Both also have unique errors, and T$^4$ tends to be expansive. Similarly H$^3$ and Ff must have had a common ancestor at one stage: they share an omission at lines 174–5 (with Dd$^2$) and a number of errors, as 'loue' for 'ful' at l. 23. But they too share omissions with other manuscripts and not with each other, as at lines 132–3 (FfT$^4$), 219 (FfPDd$^2$), 148–9 (H$^3$SV), and 189 (H$^3$LtRLt$^2$Ii$^2$Br), and again each has several unique errors. Ff no longer shows the close affinity to Dd that was found in the *Form.* The texts of Dd$^2$ and Y are too brief to evaluate.

The shared omissions at lines 107 and 189 confuse the issue further. At the former LtFfH$^3$ read 'þai shold nat haue two kyrtels: þat is þat oon shold nat haue as many cloþes as two myght be sustened with'. RDdT$^4$PLt$^2$Ii$^2$BrT$^3$Y omit 'two . . . haue'. This is obviously an early scribal slip which has gone undetected because it does not materially alter the sense, and it indicates that these eight manuscripts have a common ancestor, with LtFfH$^3$ alone preserving the original reading. But at l. 189 LtRH$^3$Lt$^2$Ii$^2$Br appear to share an omission. DdFfT$^4$PT$^3$

Dd$^{2}$ read 'to desyre þe ioy of heuen and to despyse þe vanitees of þis world'; LtRH$^{3}$Lt$^{2}$Ii$^{2}$Br omit 'of heuen'. There is no apparent reason for this, but the DdFfT$^{4}$PT$^{3}$Dd$^{2}$ reading is contextually preferable. But how did RLt$^{2}$Ii$^{2}$Br come to share the errors of two apparently unrelated groups? There are two possible explanations. Firstly, that the omission of 'of heuen' occurred at a very early stage of transmission, when the original and one of the first copies, $\beta$, were still in the same neighbourhood. $\beta$, from which RDdT$^{4}$PLt$^{2}$Ii$^{2}$BrT$^{3}$ all descend, and which originated the omission at l. 107, was then corrected from the prototype, possibly marginally, at l. 189. The ancestor of DdT$^{4}$PT$^{3}$ copied it after this correction, but the ancestor of RLt$^{2}$Ii$^{2}$Br either copied before the correction or overlooked it. Ff's inclusion of 'of heuen' does not rule out this possibility, as it is an obvious emendation to make, and could be the fortunate result of scribal ingenuity. However it is only partially satisfactory, as it does not explain how Ff shares an omission with T$^{4}$ at lines 132–3 and with PDd$^{2}$ at l. 219 while not omitting l. 107.

The alternative is to accept that all these manuscripts have been affected by widespread conflation, and indeed this is supported by the extant texts. Apart from SV and T$^{3}$, no one complete version of *The Commandment* is outstandingly good or bad. The variants, although large in number, are generally slight in significance. No manuscript is free from error or omission, but in comparison to Rolle's other English epistles they all present a fairly consistent text. This argues a relatively simple textual history, such as might occur if several copies were made from source, rather than one descending vertically from another. Moreover the nature of the work itself supports this theory. Its simplicity and didacticism makes it of less general appeal than Rolle's more mystical treatises, but possibly of more practical interest to its original recipients, the nuns of Hampole. It is easy to imagine such a text being in heavy demand as word spread round the nunneries of Yorkshire, and copies would proliferate, not only in a short period of time, but within a confined geographical area. In such circumstances conflation would have been inevitable, especially if the text was being copied piecemeal, as I have shown to have occurred with the *Form* and *Ego Dormio.*

Conflation too would explain the following textual groupings:

80 'may' LtDdSV; 'may be' RFfH$^{3}$T$^{4}$PLt$^{2}$Ii$^{2}$BrT$^{3}$.

91 'sechynge' LtDdT$^{4}$PT$^{3}$Y; 'schetyng & her sorowyng' R; 'serwynges' SV; 'and hir sorwynge' *add.* FfH$^{3}$Lt$^{2}$Ii$^{2}$Br.

164 'toure' LtDd; 'trone' RFfH$^3$T$^4$PLt$^2$Ii$^2$BrT$^3$Dd$^2$.
186 'bren' LtDd; 'brynge' RSVFfH$^3$T$^4$PLt$^2$Ii$^2$BrT$^3$Dd$^2$.
190 'mescheuous and greuous' LtDd; 'mysese & greuous' RLt$^2$; 'misese and of þe' FfT$^4$PDd$^2$; 'misese and þe' H$^3$; 'greuous' Br; 'misese and of þe hedous and wondurful' T$^3$; *om.* SVIi$^2$.

The authority of Lt and Dd with regard to Rolle texts, and their total lack of relationship hitherto, make it unlikely that in these instances they are agreeing in error. It may be assumed that the errors are in the other manuscripts, and are caused by the early contiguity of their prototypes.

Such widespread conflation makes it the more remarkable that Lt again provides a text which is on the whole free from contamination. The following errors are unique, and their nature is such that they may be attributed directly to the Lt scribe, here slightly less careful than in previous texts:

14 'þat þou' Lt; 'to' RSVDdFfH$^3$T$^4$PLt$^2$Ii$^2$BrT$^3$.
32–3 'bot ay (euer SV, alwey Lt$^2$Ii$^2$Br) þou (*om.* H$^3$Lt$^2$Ii$^2$Br) ⟨most SV⟩ þynkest (þenken SVT$^3$) on (in P) hym' RSVDdFfH$^3$T$^4$P Lt$^2$Ii$^2$BrT$^3$; *om.* Lt.
41 'to suffre' RDdFfH$^3$T$^4$PLt$^2$Ii$^2$BrT$^3$; *om.* Lt.
56 'þi' Lt; 'þe' RSVDdFfT$^4$PLt$^2$Ii$^2$Br; *om.* H$^3$; 'þo' T$^3$.
58 'þis' Lt; 'his' RSVDdFfH$^3$PLt$^2$Ii$^2$BrT$^3$; 'cristis' T$^4$.
140 'variytee' Lt; 'vnprofitable' R; 'vanites' SV; 'vnnayte' DdH$^3$; 'vanite' Ff; 'veyn' T$^4$PT$^3$; 'ydel' Lt$^2$Ii$^2$Br.
149 'feire' Lt; 'ferre' RDdFfT$^4$PLt$^2$Ii$^2$BrT$^3$.
152 'stynke and' Lt; 'stynkyng' RSVDdFfH$^3$T$^4$PLt$^2$Ii$^2$BrT$^3$.
178 'and' Lt; 'alle' RDdFfH$^3$T$^4$PLt$^2$Ii$^2$BrT$^3$Dd$^2$.
181 'kepeth' Lt; 'helpeth' RDdFfH$^3$PLt$^2$Ii$^2$BrT$^3$Dd$^2$; 'helpe' T$^4$.
183 'purge þe' Lt; 'purchace the þe' RDdFfH$^3$T$^4$PLt$^2$Ii$^2$BrT$^3$Dd$^2$.
192 'purgeth' Lt; 'purchace' RFfH$^3$T$^4$PLt$^2$Ii$^2$BrDd$^2$; 'purges' Dd. See note.
201 'loued' Lt; 'lifed' RDdFfH$^3$T$^4$PLt$^2$Ii$^2$BrDd$^2$P$^1$; 'liuen' SV.
212 'restyng' RDdFfH$^3$T$^4$PLt$^2$Ii$^2$BrT$^3$Dd$^2$; *om.* Lt.
221 'what' Lt; 'who' RDdFfH$^3$T$^4$PLt$^2$Ii$^2$BrT$^3$Dd$^2$.

Possible shared errors, apart from that at l. 189 already discussed, occur at the following:

11 'For' LtT$^3$; 'þarefore' RP; 'forwhi' SLt$^2$Ii$^2$Br; 'forþi' VDdFfSH$^3$T$^4$.
35 'fynd' LtRT$^4$P; 'fyndest' SVFfH$^3$Lt$^2$Ii$^2$Br; 'fyndes' Dd; 'felys'

T$^3$. Here the LtRT$^4$ form may represent a subjunctive; P adds 'may'.

45 'god' LtFfT$^3$; 'good' RSVDdH$^3$T$^4$PLt$^2$Ii$^2$Br. An unusual spelling for Lt if not an error.

97 'by' *om.* LtRDdFfH$^3$Lt$^2$Ii$^2$BrT$^3$; 'in ensample' SV; 'bytokenynge' T$^4$P. Possibly an original omission, with SV and T$^4$P variously trying to emend.

217 'his' RSVDdFfH$^3$PLt$^2$Ii$^2$Br; *om.* LtT$^4$.

Dd has fewer errors in this text than in *Ego Dormio*, and most of them have been exposed by Miss Allen through collation with R. Those that were not apparent include the omission at l. 107, and the omission of 'ne' at l. 72 and of 'and' at l. 190 which change the sense. Dd's reading 'cristes passyon' at l. 130 in place of 'Ihesu Crist' is supported by no other manuscript and may be a scribal emendation. At l. 55 the Lt reading 'shal' is contextually preferable to its omission in DdFfH$^3$; in minor variants at lines 28 and 143 the manuscripts are again divided.

Most manuscripts introduce or conclude *The Commandment* in general terms; only Dd and Lt are more specific. Dd concludes 'Explicit tractatus Ricardi Hampole scriptus cuidam sorori de Hampole'. Lt includes the work in a collection of texts all dedicated to Margaret of Kirkby. Internal evidence supports Dd's ascription. It indicates that *The Commandment* was almost certainly written for a nun rather than an anchoress: a nun moreover as yet unpractised in conventual life: 'If þi body be cled withouten as þyn ordre wille, loke þat þi soule be nat naked within', 'If þou can nat lyue withouten felewship', 'if þou faille and fal for temptaciouns or for angres or for ouer myche loue of þi frendes', 'bot perauentur þou wil say "I may nat despise þe world"'. Rolle's close association with Hampole makes it probable that this nun was indeed an inmate there. Moreover Hampole was notoriously lax in the matter of dress,[1] which would lend weight to the reference at lines 102–4. However the ascriptions of Dd and Lt are not mutually exclusive. Margaret of Kirkby was a nun at Hampole during Rolle's association with the convent. If the fifteenth-century prologue in MS Laud misc. 286[2] is to be believed, he wrote his English Psalter there at her request. On her enclosure at Layton in 1348, he dedicated the *Form* to her. If *The Commandment* was written for a nun at Hampole, it

[1] E. Power, *Medieval English Nunneries* (Cambridge, 1922), p. 329.
[2] Printed *Writings*, p. 174.

seems more likely that it would have been for this acknowledged favourite than for any other. Miss Allen objects to this on the grounds that 'each of Rolle's epistles gives a complete compendium of mystical piety and it is natural to suppose that each was directed to a different person'.[1] But the three epistles are only superficially alike, and it would be truer to say that each was written for a different purpose than for a different person. I have already suggested the possibility that *Ego Dormio* was written for the young Margaret, on the threshold of her spiritual life, and that the Lt text represents a later authorial revision for her. *The Commandment*, with its emphasis on practical instruction, could have been composed for her shortly after her entry into the convent *c.* 1343. It is true that there is some repetition in the three works, but in the *Form* such subjects as the mystical power of the Holy Name are greatly amplified. Possibly Rolle felt that he could only touch on them briefly when his disciple was young and inexperienced, but as she grew in spiritual understanding he was able to expand them more fully. The Lt ascription could be correct, not only with regard to the anthology of Rolle's writing made for Margaret which the manuscript contains, but also in its identification of the original recipient of *The Commandment.*

### *Desire and Delight*

Although Th has several other items in common with Lt, their versions of this piece do not seem related. There are a surprising number of variants for so short a text, and Th has an omission at l. 24. At l. 2 Lt has a possible omission, although this could be an addition on the part of Th, as there is no obvious reason for a scribe to omit it. Th's 'haly' at l. 2 certainly looks like an insertion as, unlike 'wondreful', 'pure', and 'fast', it is not expanded later. Although it shows signs of carelessness, as in the spellings at lines 9 and 13, the Lt text is superior. Its readings at lines 5, 8, 9 and 'heynesse' at l. 23 make better sense. 'Desyre' at l. 1 is preferable for its alliteration. Th's repetition of 'restreynynge' at l. 10 is an obvious scribal slip, as is its reading 'mekely' at l. 23, where the original was probably 'mekil'. Lt's 'affectuouse' at lines 3 and 17 and 'shorne' at l. 3 both sound genuine; both words are used by Rolle in his English *Psalter*. However Th's 'tagillynge' at l. 4 may well be correct, it is a word found only in works of Rolle; in the *Form* the same word is represented in Lt by 'takeled'.

[1] *Writings*, p. 256.

Th's 'etcetera' at the end of the piece led Miss Allen[1] to suggest that the work might be incomplete. However the fact that Lt stops at exactly the same place renders this unlikely.

## *Ghostly Gladness*

In Dd this strongly alliterative piece is included among the lyrics attributed to Rolle. Miss Allen sees[2] in it a reference to a vision which Rolle had on 2 February 1343, and consequently dates it around that year.

The two texts are very close, and as Dd and Lt have proved elsewhere to be unrelated, their readings here presumably give a faithful rendering of the original.

## *Lyrics*

The three lyrics[3] 'Love is lif' (i), 'Ihesu Goddis son' (ii), and 'I sigh and sob' (iii) are found elsewhere in La and Dd. In La they appear in the same sequence as in Lt, but as a single work written as prose. In Dd (ii) precedes (i) and (iii), and the two latter are presented as a single poem.

There can be little doubt that Lt's presentation of these lyrics as three separate works is correct. As Miss Allen has pointed out,[4] lines 1–60 and 67–8 of (i) are a close translation of Rolle's Latin treatise *Incendium Amoris*, chapters 40–1. It is precisely at the line where this source is abandoned that Lt concludes (i), and its reading 'The loue of hym ouercometh al þynge, in loue lyve we and dye', which is supported by La, makes an appropriate final line. It is also a direct rendering of the Latin source: 'cuius amor omnia uincit, et nos ergo in amore uiuamus et in quo eciam moriamur'. Here Dd reads 'þe lufe of hym ouercoms al thyng, þarto þou traiste trewly'. This version would appear to be a weakening of the conclusive original line in order to allow two poems, then distinct, to be joined together. The compiler of the Dd text may have been misled into linking the two poems by the fact that the closing stanza of (iii) closely echoes the opening stanza of (i). A similar, but more extensive, sophistication has taken place in La to allow the three poems of Lt to be written as one. The metre of (ii)

[1] *Writings*, p. 272.

[2] *Writings*, p. 273.

[3] Most of the following discussion is taken from an earlier article of mine: S. Wilson, 'The Longleat version of "Love is Life"', *RES* n.s. x (1959), 337–46. I am grateful to the editor of *RES* for permission to reproduce the material here.

[4] *MLR* xiv (1919), 320.

has been lengthened, and an attempt made to strengthen the sporadic internal rhyme, which made Furnivall print the poem in stanzas of eight short lines with three or four stresses in each, as against the four long lines of seven or eight stresses in Lt and Dd. To achieve this, the compiler of the La version frequently distorts the sense:

39–40 'þe Iues wold nat wand to pyne hym þat tyde;
As stremes doth on strand, his blode can doune glide.' LtDd.

'þe Iewis wolde not þan reste
To pyne him more in þat tide;
Al he suffride þat was wisest,
His blood to lete doun glide.' La.

41–2 'Blyndet ware his faire eyen, his fleisshe blody forbette;
His louesome lif was laid ful logh and sorowfully vmset.'
LtDd.

'Blyndid were hise faire yȝen,
And al his fleisch bloodi forbete;
Hise louesum lijf þat alle men siȝen,
Ful myldeli he out gan lete.' La.

Not only is Lt correct in its presentation of the three lyrics, but in (i) it provides a demonstrably superior text, many of its readings translating the Latin source more closely than the variants in Dd and La:

18 'Al þi þoght to hym thou yyve þat may hit kepe fro kare' Lt.
'mentem tribue illi qui eam ab eternis et temporalibus doloribus potest custodire' *Incendium.*
'All þi thoght til hym þou gyf þat may þe kepe fra kare' DdLa.

38 'And gif þi hert hym þat hit boght, þat he hit weld with wyn' Lt.
'et dederis cor tuum ipsi qui illud redemit, ut ille sit possessor tuus per graciam' *Incendium.*
'And gyf hym þi sawle þat it boght, þat he þe dwelle within' Dd.
'And ȝeue to him þat þee dere bouȝt þat he weelde þee withinne' La.

55 'In loue be our lyuynge, I wote no bettyre wone' Lt.
'In hoc amore . . . consistat uita nostra, meliorem nimirum mansionem et suauiorem nunquam inueni' *Incendium.*
'In lufe be owre lykyng, I ne wate na better wane' Dd.
'In loue, þerfore, be oure likinge, I knowe no betere won' La.

58 'And lestynge be no mare than hit ware bot a daye' Lt.
'et non erit amplius exultans et existens quam si non nisi per diem unum perduraret' *Incendium.*
'And lastand be na mare þan ane houre of a day' Dd.
'And schal be lastande na mare but as it were an hour of a day' La.

However, although Dd and La agree in some errors, their variants elsewhere as well as their format suggest that neither can be derived directly from the other:

20 'So þou may hym weld with wyn and loue hym euermare' Lt.
'quoniam sic eum cum gaudio ualebis possidere et ipsum sine fine diligere' *Incendium.*
'Sa þou may hym welde and wyn and luf hym euermare' Dd.
'So þou may weelde him withinne and loue him hertili euermore' La.
47 'In erthe þou hate no quede bot þat þi loue myght fel[l]e' Lt.
'In terra quidem non odias miseriam nisi que posset tuum purum amorem deicere et conturbare' *Incendium.*
'In erth þow hate, I rede, all þat þi lufe may fell' Dd.
'In erþe hate þou no maner qweed but loke þat þi loue may dwelle' La.

Sometimes Lt and La agree in a correct reading against Dd; l. 68 has already been cited, and minor instances include l. 2 'whan' LtLa, 'quando' *Incendium*, 'for' Dd; l. 45 'forþi' LtLa, 'igitur' *Incendium*, 'for now' Dd; and, allowing for dialectal differences, l. 15 'couereth' Lt, 'heliþ' La, 'facit nos conualescere' *Incendium*, 'comfortes' Dd. Thus although the Dd and La texts of (i) must go back to a common source which provided them with the errors which they share,[1] they would then seem to have developed independently. The Lt text descends from the original in a different line, and has errors of its own: l. 6 'is lickned', 'assimilo' *Incendium*, 'I lyken' DdLa; l. 12 'compileth', 'copulat' *Incendium*, 'copuls' DdLa; l. 19 'wandrynge', 'aduersitate et miseria' *Incendium*, 'wandreth' Dd, 'wandre' La; l. 44 'led', 'conuersatur' *Incendium*, 'lendes' Dd (La different). However these are minor scribal slips; in general the Lt text is markedly superior.

The textual value of the Lt version of (ii) and (iii) is harder to determine, as there is no known source with which to compare these

[1] Dd and La agree in major variants at lines 61 and 66, but as Rolle here departs from his source, there is no way of telling whether it is they or Lt that are in error.

poems. However the uniform excellence of the Rolle texts in this manuscript lends weight to its variant readings, and it seems probable that, as the three poems are found together in the three manuscripts in which they occur, they had the same textual history. Agreement between Dd and La in the following instances could therefore be agreement in error:

(ii) 6 'me' Lt; 'men' DdLa.
10 'haue' Lt; 'hate' DdLa.
45 'anoon' Lt; 'agayne' DdLa.
(iii) 16 'vs' Lt; 'me' DdLa.

Lt is sometimes supported by La against Dd:

(ii) 3 'world' LtLa; 'land' Dd.
24 'in lif' LtLa; 'and lyfe' Dd.
29 'brest' LtLa; 'hert' Dd.
47 'he þat' LtLa; 'on hym þat' Dd.
(iii) 4 'langynge' LtLa; 'sang' Dd.
11 'forlete' LtLa; 'forgete' Dd.

All three manuscripts are at variance in the following:

(ii) 4 'way' Lt; 'hand' Dd; 'ward' La.
8 'wene' Lt; 'wane' Dd; 'wexe' La.
36 'naked' Lt; 'nayled' Dd; 'doon' La.
(iii) 26 'ebbynge' Lt; 'dawyng' Dd; 'derknes' La.

Lt is clearly in error in reading 'aye' for 'maye' at l. 23 of (ii), and in confusing 'loue' and 'lif' at lines 21 and 24 of (iii). At l. 8 of (iii) Lt reads 'so stabil he is a childe' against 'fra euel he wil hym schylde' DdLa. Here 'childe' is obviously an error for 'shilde', but it is impossible to tell if the rest of the line is at fault. The Lt reading 'boweth' at l. 13 of the same lyric is probably a misreading of a Northern contracted form of 'behove' (see note). Finally the Lt variant 'slynge' at l. 34 of (ii) against DdLa 'swyng', although the difficilior lectio, does appear suspect. In the required sense of 'beat', the only example in the *OED*, recorded for 1450, is with reference to eggs.

The fourth Lt lyric 'Thy ioy be euery dele' is also found in Th, where a leaf containing lines 89–108 is missing, and Dd. In the latter it is presented as two poems, the first containing lines 49–108, and the second lines 1–8, 13–16, 21–32, and 37–48. The scribe of Dd was apparently aware that these two poems were intended as a single work:

at the end of his second poem he copied the opening line of the first, and added 'vt supra'.

There is no obvious relationship between the three manuscripts; all have minor individual variants, and it is thus a reasonable assumption that, when two texts agree against a third, it is the third which is in error. This presumes Lt to be at fault at lines 2, 5, 14, 16, 22, 27, 40, 48, 63, 69, and 78, although I have only emended when the sense is affected. Further variants at lines 2 and 3 appear to be dialectal substitutions, as is the use of 'euery' and 'euer' for 'ilk a' and 'ay'. Where the text of either Dd or Th is deficient, Lt has obvious errors of sense at lines 10, 35, 91, and 108. The only shared errors that are apparent occur at lines 24 and 45, where Lt and Th both read 'lyf' for 'luf' and 'lyuynge' for 'louynge', but this is common enough to be coincidental. There are only two occasions where all three texts differ: l. 44 'wisse' Lt, 'bryng' Dd, 'rayse' Th, and l. 62 'þat' Lt, 'þai' Dd, 'þan' Th.

The fifth lyric is found elsewhere only in Dd. The two texts are very similar, containing only a few minor variants, and most of these, as at lines 2, 9, and 23, are deliberate Southernizations by Lt or a predecessor. The Lt reading 'purgeth' for 'purchase' at l. 24 must derive from a form 'purges' as in Dd, here carelessly mistaken for the 3rd sg. present indicative. This form is not recorded in the *OED*, but a similar error occurs in both the Dd and Lt texts of *The Commandment* (l. 192), and it would thus appear to be a genuine, if idiosyncratic, spelling.

(vi) *'Ihesu swet'*. It was seen in the description of manuscripts containing this poem that its length in them varied considerably. VS have the longest text, including three stanzas absent in Lt. Of these, one is shared by Ad² and Ro, occurring as stanza 15 in all four manuscripts, one is shared by Ad², Ro, and Tr, occurring as stanza 26 in VSAd²Ro and as stanza 20 in Tr, and the third, a 'Mary' verse, is shared by Ad² and H⁴. This occurs as stanza 97 in VS, 90 in Ad², and 30 in H⁴. The fact that these stanzas are not unique to VS suggests that they formed part of an early text of the poem, and were deliberately omitted by a predecessor of Lt, possibly to achieve the round one hundred stanzas which would identify with a rosary. Tr has a further stanza (68), which is not found elsewhere, and which may therefore be an addition. Similarly varied is the stanzaic sequence.[1] VSAd²RoH⁴, apart from the verses omitted by the three latter manuscripts, tend to follow the same sequence. It is only when the 'Mary' verses occur, written marginally

[1] The different order is shown in the textual variants.

in Lt, that the pattern is broken. This, together with the total lack of 'Mary' verses in Tr, lends support to the evidence of the Lt manuscript that these verses were not originally part of 'Ihesu swet', but had a separate existence.

The poem 'Ihesu swet' is itself a combination and expansion[1] of two separate lyrics, 'Suete Iesu king of blysse' and 'Iesu suete is þe loue of þe'. The longest version of both these lyrics is contained in the early fourteenth-century MS Harley 2253, at fols. $75^r$ and $77^v$ respectively, which I shall take as a base text for these poems, and refer to as $Ha^1$ and $Ha^2$.[2] $Ha^1$ contains 15 stanzas, and $Ha^2$ 50. Lt, V, S and $Ad^2$ have incorporated all but two of these stanzas, although sometimes in a very approximate form. As it is inconceivable that two or more revisers would have independently adapted and expanded the same two lyrics, which do not even run consecutively in any extant manuscript, LtVS $Ad^2RoTrH^4$ must all then derive from a single source, which we may call X.

As VS contain the longest text, and as their stanzaic sequence, apart from the new verses, reflects that of $Ha^1$ and $Ha^2$ in consecutive order, it may be further assumed that these two manuscripts represent most faithfully the original format of X. However the evidence of the 'Mary' stanzas indicates that X, unlike VS, was a poem addressed to Christ alone. The manuscripts of 'Ihesu swet' must therefore differ in their lines of descent. Lt and Tr, lacking the 'Mary' stanzas, descend directly, although independently, from X. Both retain the opening 'Ihesu swet' with the emphasis in every verse on the name of Jesus, but transposed in $VSAd^2RoH^4$. $VSAd^2RoH^4$ descend from an intermediate stage, $\alpha$. $\alpha$ copies X, and then, either immediately after, or on an adjacent leaf, copies an eight stanza intercessionary prayer to Mary. Influenced possibly by the increasing popularity of Marian literature in the fourteenth century, it occurs to him that the two texts might well be combined. He therefore marks the 'Mary' stanzas for insertion at intervals into the text of 'Ihesu swet', but his notations are insufficiently clear, and the intended order of insertion is variously confused by the predecessors of VS, $Ad^2$, Ro, and $H^4$. One immediate objection

[1] New stanzas are as following in the Lt numbering: 1, 8–13, 28–33, 42, 48–55, 57–61, 64–5, 68–70, 76, 82–3, 85–7, 91, 95, 100, and the 'Mary' stanzas 16, 27, 41, 56, 72, 98.

[2] $Ha^1$ printed T. Wright, *Specimens of Lyric Poetry composed in England in the Reign of Edward I*, Percy Society, iv (1842), 57–9; K. Böddeker, *Altenglische Dichtungen des MS. Harl. 2253* (Berlin, 1878), pp. 191–3; C. Horstman, ii. 9–11; C. Brown, *RL XIV*, pp. 7–9; G. L. Brook, *The Harley Lyrics* (Manchester, 1948), p. 51. $Ha^2$ printed T. Wright, *op. cit.*, pp. 68–76; K. Böddeker, *op. cit.*, pp. 198–205; C. Horstman, ii. 11–24.

can be raised to this hypothesis: the version of Ha² contained in MS Harley 2253 itself includes a 'Mary' stanza similar to one found in V, S, Ad² and the margin of Lt. If X has incorporated Ha², how can it then be a poem devoid of 'Mary' stanzas? However this difficulty is not insuperable. It is obvious that the lyrics in MS Harley 2253 are not themselves the source of X. They have manifest errors, and in some stanzas lacunae which do not occur in 'Ihesu swet'. Their textual evidence indicates that a certain amount of conflation has taken place. Moreover neither of the other two extant versions of 'Iesu suete is þe loue of þe' contains any 'Mary' verses. It may therefore still be accepted that Lt and Tr derive from X, which was a poem to Christ alone, and that VSAd²RoH⁴ derive from $\alpha$ where the 'Mary' stanzas were first introduced and the opening words of each stanza changed. That the subsequent transmission of Lt, Tr, VS, Ad², Ro and H⁴ is independent may be deduced from the textual evidence of these manuscripts.

As already noted, Lt may have at some stage deliberately dropped two stanzas, but no such liturgical explanation can account for the extensive omissions of Ad², Ro, H⁴, and Tr. Ad² omits stanzas 28–33 of the Lt text; Ro omits stanzas 55, 62–6, 68–84, 92, and the 'Mary' stanzas 56, 67, and 72; H⁴ omits stanzas 2, 5–6, 8–14, 17, 19–25, 30–1, 34–5, 37–8, 42–3, 48–55, 57–61, 64–5, 68, 71, 73–84, 87, 90–7, 99–103, 105–7, and the 'Mary' stanzas 16, 41, 67, 72, and 98; Tr omits stanzas 9, 12–14, 29–33, 42–4, 57–61, 64–5, 71, 73, 79, 84, 90–4, 102–3, and 106. There is some slight overlapping in these omissions, but no exact correspondence, and they are unlikely to have been transmitted vertically. They are too widespread to be simple errors of transcription, except possibly in the case of Ad², which might alternatively have had a page missing in its exemplar. I would therefore suggest that, although the reason for them is not apparent, they are deliberate and independent revisions.

The only clear relationship which emerges is, foreseeably, that between V and S. It is once again evident that neither has copied from the other; they differ at the following lines: 56, 72, 116, 174, 218, 327, 329, 335, 342, 346, 392, and 400. However their texts are still close enough for them to share a single source. This source is probably in error in the following readings, if only because VS error seems more likely than agreement in error between manuscripts whose relationship is not otherwise indicated:

41 'Ihesu' LtAd$^{2}$RoTr; 'to him' VS.
130 'curious' LtRoH$^{4}$; 'disirrous' VS.
258 'þat' LtAd$^{2}$; *om.* VS.
'ground' LtAd$^{2}$; 'þat' VS.
289 'se' LtAd$^{2}$Ha$^{2}$; 'þe' VS.
335 'techynge' LtAd$^{2}$; 'knowyng' VS.

The other five manuscripts all have a number of individual errors, and there are many readings where they are variously grouped, but where the true reading cannot be positively determined. Some examples of these are:

84 'wicked engyne' LtVS; 'þe fundus engyn' Ad$^{2}$; 'wicked pyn' Ro; 'helle pyne' Tr; 'fendes engyn' Ha$^{1}$.
86 'þi hert' Lt; 'þi blessed' VS; 'þi swete' Ad$^{2}$Tr; 'al þi' Ro; 'þi' Ha$^{1}$.
108 'be my help' LtRo; 'prey for me' VS; 'pray for us' H$^{4}$.
115 'þat I did' Lt; 'and gult' VS; 'I gilte' Ro; 'I dyd' H$^{4}$.
137 'my lemon' LtVSRoHa$^{2}$; 'my lord' Ad$^{2}$; 'lord' Tr.
143 'hert in loue' LtH$^{4}$; 'loue and herte' VSAd$^{2}$Tr; 'luf in al' Ro; 'loue and eke' Ha$^{2}$.
208 'dampned' LtVSAd$^{2}$; 'synful' RoTr.
266 'Crist' LtHa$^{2}$; 'loue' Ad$^{2}$; *om.* VS.
296 'besoght' Lt; 'of þouȝt' VS; 'i douȝth' Ad$^{2}$; 'brouȝt' Tr; 'y wroht' Ha$^{2}$.
337 'me' LtVSAd$^{2}$Ro; 'me grace' TrH$^{4}$.
355 'to þe fle' LtVSAd$^{2}$Ha$^{2}$; 'turne to þe' Ro; 'flee to þe' Tr; 'turne to me' H$^{4}$.
381 'hote' LtTr; 'swete' VSAd$^{2}$RoHa$^{2}$.
388 'þou' Lt; 'þou my swete' VS; 'þou my lord' Ad$^{2}$; 'þou my god' Ro; 'alle my helpe' Tr; 'my lif' Ha$^{2}$.
395 'hit' LtVSAd$^{2}$Ha$^{2}$; 'I' RoTr.

N. S. Baugh[1] has discussed the possibility of a relationship between VS and Ad$^{2}$, and this might account for the agreement between VAd$^{2}$ already noted at lines 218 and 327, and that between VSAd$^{2}$ at l. 96: 'hert' LtRoTr, 'swete' VSAd$^{2}$, *om.* Ha$^{1}$, and at l. 367: 'vayn' Lt, 'þing non' VSAd$^{2}$.[2] However the many divergent readings of VS and Ad$^{2}$ show that, in this text at least, the relationship must be distant.

Lt and Ro have an apparent partial agreement in error at l. 68, where the readings are 'no witnes' Lt, 'wetenes' Ro, 'swetnesse' VS,

[1] *Worcs. Misc.*, pp. 37–9. [2] See note to l. 367.

'no swetnus' Ad$^2$TrHa$^2$, the last being presumably correct. However this is more likely to be an independent slip on the part of Ro's scribe, for he makes the same mistake at l. 384, although this time it is corrected. The only other slight indications of a relationship between Lt and Ro occur at l. 97 'sheld' Lt, 'child' Ro, 'barne' VSAd$^2$Ha$^1$, which could as well be a Lt misreading of any Southernized text; at l. 47, where they both read 'blame' for 'blan', but where Ro has in addition revised the whole line; and in their agreement in the placing and readings of stanza 27, which is a 'Mary' stanza, and so does not affect the relationship of Lt's main text. It is therefore probable that there is no close relationship between Lt and Ro. However the picture is complicated by the readings of Ha in both its lyrics. Ro and Ha have several agreements against all the other manuscripts, notably at lines 133, 144, 151, 173, 184, 408, 409, 425, and 427. If these are true readings, this would entail agreement in error between Lt, VS, and, where applicable, Ad$^2$, Tr, and H$^4$, thus effectively destroying my earlier suggestion of separate descents from X and $\alpha$. However Ha's agreements are not confined to Ro. It also shares readings on occasion with Ad$^2$, excluding Ro, as at lines 84, 88, and 138, and this must indicate conflation at an early stage of the $\alpha$ line of descent. Moreover Ha has two interesting agreements with Lt. At l. 99 they agree against VSAd$^2$Ro, while Tr's reading is different and the line is omitted by H$^4$, and again at l. 375 they agree against VSAd$^2$Ro, the line this time being omitted by Tr and H$^4$. Both of these agreements represent the *difficilior lectio* and are therefore probably correct. If this is so, they serve to strengthen my theory of transmission: the VSAd$^2$Ro errors occurred at the $\alpha$ stage.

'Ihesu swet' is attributed to Rolle in Lt alone, occurring as part of the whole collection of works dedicated to Margaret of Kirkby. Horstman, who did not know of the Longleat manuscript, pointed out in his edition of the Vernon text of the poem that some stanzas were strongly reminiscent of Rolle. Miss Allen agreed with this, saying of Ha$^2$ 'this lyric held in germ the English mysticism of the fourteenth century: it would be very probable that it was known to Rolle, and used in his own devotions, and, if it were so used, he would be very likely to add some stanzas of his own and copy the whole for a disciple'.[1] But she then weakened her own case by a misstatement: 'The authority of the Longleat MS. in . . . ascribing the whole lyric to Rolle is weakened by the fact that . . . [the stanzas cited by Horstman] are only added in the

[1] *Writings*, p. 303.

Longleat copy after the ascription has been made.' This is not so; these lines form part of the main Lt text, and come before the ascription. Misled by her own mistake, she then concluded that as 'Ihesu swet' was included among the works of Rolle in Lt, it was clear that Rolle knew and loved the poem, and that some of it should be assigned to his *Dubia*.

It is tempting now to take Miss Allen's argument a stage further and suggest that, although Rolle was not responsible for the original lyrics found separately in Ha and elsewhere, or for the text of 'Swete Ihesu' as it is found in V and the other $\alpha$ group manuscripts, he may well have been the compiler of the original X. Other factors beside the Lt ascription lend weight to this suggestion. In its devotion to the name of Jesus, its emphasis on Christ's suffering, its reiteration of such adjectives as 'swete' and 'hote', this poem is indeed typical of Rolle. Another interesting point is the original lack of 'Mary' stanzas: Rolle's English work is conspicuously devoid of Marian worship. Moreover, although none of the extant manuscripts is Northern, there are several Northern elements in the poem. Thus we find the rhyme word 'grete' at l. 71 in LtAd$^{2}$RoHa$^{1}$, Southernized to 'wepe' in VSTrH$^{4}$, and again at l. 185 in LtAd$^{2}$RoH$^{4}$Ha$^{2}$, Southernized in VSTr. At l. 59 the rhyme word 'blo' is Norse-derived. At lines 2 and 316 Lt has uncharacteristically retained 'langynge' which all other texts give as 'longynge'. At lines 11, 71, 257, and 337 Lt and others use the form 'gyf', and at l. 407 'forgyf'. At l. 97 'barne' VSAd$^{2}$Ha$^{1}$ has already been noted. At l. 313 LtVS read 'ȝernynge' ('desiryng' Ad$^{2}$). At l. 57 Ro has 'dree' ('soffrest' LtVSAd$^{2}$TrH$^{4}$), and at l. 119 'ay' ('euer' LtVS). The rhyme words in stanza 65 are revealing: all the manuscripts containing this verse have been forced to rhyme the Southern adverbial suffix '-liche' with the verb 'stik'. The rhymes at lines 33–6, 109–12, 117–20, and 205–8 are Northern, as are 'blyn' at l. 276 and 'dede' at l. 196. The past participle 'sene' rhyming on 'quene' at l. 92 is primarily a Northern form, as is 'sekynge' (sighing) at l. 120. These Northern features appear to have been superimposed on an originally non-Northern text, whose Southern elements are retained in occasional rhyme words, as lines 52, 248 and 251, while a further indication of Southern origin is seen in the metre. This often depends on the pronunciation of historical final -e, either grammatical or etymological, whereas a Northern composition would have been unlikely to feature it much after 1300. However, this need not have worried Rolle unduly if he were adapting the poem: he is not elsewhere noted for metrical accuracy. It is interesting too that the 'Mary' stanzas contain no Northern features, but have some non-Northern elements, as in the rhyme at lines 61–4 and 221–4.

All this is not, of course, conclusive proof that Rolle compiled X, but it is suggestive, and I can find no counter evidence. The fact that it is only in Lt that the poem is ascribed to him is not significant; if $VSAd^2RoH^4$ derive from $\alpha$, and $\alpha$ omitted the ascription, it would be irretrievably lost. The omission in Tr is also explicable. Tr contains two other Rolle texts, the *Form* and *Ego Dormio*. Both have undergone extensive alteration, as has its text of 'Ihesu swet', and neither are attributed to Rolle; indeed in places they are hardly recognizable as his work. Lt has undoubted authority where Rolle's writings are concerned, and its ascription here deserves serious consideration.

However the Lt text of 'Ihesu swet' appears to have been considerably revised, and cannot be claimed to represent closely the original X. The probable omission of two stanzas, the later insertion of the 'Mary' stanzas, the liturgical notation and the changed verse order have already been noted. These are all deliberate changes: they could not have existed in X. There are also many textual variants. Some of these are clearly errors; they include the inversion of lines 126 and 127, and instances at the following lines: 6, 23, 39, 47, 50, 51, 60, 68, 76, 80, 97, 145, 152, 195, 209, 222, 233, 244, 263, 289, 302, 306, 319, 320, 321, 323, 360, 362, 367, 372, and 414. In these the sense is deficient, and where possible they have been emended according to the evidence of the other texts. A further extensive group of variants exists where Lt disagrees with all the other manuscripts, but where its readings make sense and where there is no obvious cause for error. These may be cases of deliberate substitution: 15, 40, 56, 58, 75, 95, 110, 168, 172, 179, 226, 227, 240, 249, 268, 283, 310, 325, 339, 358, 363, 376, 422, and 427.

These considerable and seemingly unnecessary changes are unlikely to have been the work of the Lt scribe. He may have been responsible for the obvious errors, although he is not usually so careless; he was probably responsible for the substitution of dialectal synonyms; he was certainly responsible for the insertion of the 'Mary' stanzas, which he must have found by consultation with other manuscripts. But the evidence of the other texts in this manuscript shows that he was a reliable copier, not a drastic innovator. There must have been at least one intermediate stage between Lt and X.

### *Meditation* A

The collection of Rolle works in Lt concludes with a short passage of prose before the final all-embracing dedication to Margaret of Kirkby. This passage is part of a second meditation on the passion found in MS Titus C xix, and there too it is attributed to Rolle: 'De passione secundum Ricardum'. Ti is written in a Southern dialect, but traces of Northernisms indicate that this text was copied from a Northern prototype. From the number of variants present in the few lines where the two manuscripts can be compared, it does not seem as if they were closely related. I print the text of Ti within square brackets.

### *Meditation* B

The text of the second meditation has affiliations elsewhere. A shorter English text in ULC MS Ll i 8 (Ll)[1] is occasionally verbally close, although often completely divergent. This too is attributed to Rolle: 'Explicit quedam meditacio Ricardi heremite de hampole de passione domini. Qui obijt anno domini m°xl°viij et cetera.' An early fourteenth-century Book of Hours, ULC MS Ee vi 16 (E), contains a series of Anglo-Norman prayers on the Passion which in subject matter bear a strong resemblance to the longer English meditation. Finally, translations of several sections of the text are included in a fifteenth-century Latin compilation found in two independent manuscripts, BL Royal 8 C xv (R) and Bodley 417 (S). M. M. Morgan[2] has examined the relationship of these four versions, and concluded that E, or a hypothetical original version, Latin or French, was the source of Ll, and that MuUpTiAdd descend from E through an intermediate version similar to Ll. Ll represents a more personal adaptation of E, probably for the writer's own use; the text of MuUpTiAdd has been further altered for general devotional use. The Latin texts quote translations of MuUpTiAdd.

It has proved difficult to establish the validity of this text by recension. In some thirty instances MuAdd are found in agreement against UpTi, but in none is the correct reading self evident, and judgement must remain subjective. Thus at lines 52, 76, 108, 213, 291, 313, 336, 379, and 381 there seems nothing to choose between their readings. At lines 125, 194, 197, 234, 399, and 421 the UpTi variants appear preferable

[1] Printed J. Ullmann, *Englische Studien* vii (1884), 454–68; Horstman, i. 83–91.
[2] *Medium Ævum* 22 (1953), 93–103.

stylistically and contextually, while at lines 152, 226, 246, 336, 338, 372, 390, 398, 440, 504, 525, 533, and 542 those of MuAdd may be preferred. The support of Ll cannot be regarded as decisive if it and MuUpTi Add are independent reworkings, and its text is rarely close enough verbally for comparison. However in a few instances it lends weight to the readings of one group or the other, supporting MuAdd at l. 336

'aggregged gretly and manyfold' MuAdd; 'greued þee gretly and many folde encreside' UpTi; 'agreggyd many fold' Ll;

372–3 'and þey leid þe flatte þeron' MuAdd; 'and þere þei leide þe flatte þeron' UpTi; 'and layde þe þere onne' Ll;

398 'if a man may no feruour fynd, þynk hym' MuAdd; 'ȝif a man may no feruour fynde þan late him þenke him' UpTi; 'ȝef a man no sauowre fynde thenk hym' Ll;

525–6 'Oo sparcle of loue, oo reuth of þy passioun kyndel in myn hert' MuAdd; 'O sparcle of loue O good ihesu late þe rewþe of þi passioun kyndel in myn hert' UpTi; 'a sparkle of þi passyoun of loue and of reuthe kyndele in myn herte' Ll;

and UpTi at l. 399 'and hold hym self vnworthy' MuAdd; 'and rebuke him silf and holde him silf vnworþi' UpTi; 'and rebukynge and reuylynge and seyng hys weykenesse and ȝeldyng hym self vnworthy' Ll; and thus the genetic relationships of both MuAdd and UpTi may be tentatively assumed.

Certainly conflicting agreements across such a stemma are rare. MuTi may be in error against UpAdd at lines 221 and 378, and UpAdd against MuTi at l. 40. At l. 253, where the manuscripts divide MuTi, Add, Up, the latter's reading is preferable; at l. 353 Add seems correct against MuTi and Up. The MuUp reading at l. 467 may represent a shared error which Ti and Add have tried variously to emend, but the use of the verb in this context is just conceivable. However at lines 411 and 470 the MuUp reading seems indefensible. Such agreements must be attributable to coincidence or conflation. The partially shared error of Mu, Up, and Ti at lines 349–50, which Add has avoided by transposition, suggests that none of these manuscripts descends directly from the original.

Add presents a very poor text, with frequent transpositions and changes of tense, and, on the evidence of the other manuscripts, has omissions at lines 14, 49, 73–4, 94, 103–4, 108, 126–7, 155, 157, 185, 202–3, 216–17, 218, 243, 301, 316, 332–3, 347–9, 366–7, 438–9, 452, 508–9, 520–2, 551–2, and 556, and further errors at lines 42, 58, 69, 91, 105, 204,

208, 257, 277, 295, 317, 375, 379, 409, 489, and 515. It provides a long and unique addition at l. 84. Although at lines 200–1 and 214 its readings appear contextually preferable, the agreement of the other manuscripts against them renders them suspect.

The text of Ti is marred by carelessness. There are four instances of dittography, ten of letter(s) omitted from a word, over thirty of the omission of a single word, and further omissions at lines 252, 307, 369, 380, and 522–3, as well as a number of minor variants.

The best text, in so far as freedom from obvious errors is concerned, is Up, with minor omissions only at lines 301, 335, and 526, minor errors at 33, 114, and 221, and variants which are probably deliberate substitutions at 97, 163, 252, 377, and 381.

It was decided to include the Mu text of this meditation in this edition in the expectation, or at least the hope, that the scribe had obtained his copy from the same excellent source that he used in Lt. This is manifestly not the case, despite the retention of an occasional Northernism. Collation shows Mu to have omissions at lines 137 (the Latin prayers), 162, 190, 362, and 411 (the result of eye-skip), and 81, 334, and 399; more minor omissions of a single word or letter occur at lines 18, 21, 55, 76, 82, 106, 125, 131, 148, 270, 295, 483, and 510. Variants, although not greatly affecting the sense, are found at lines 148, 152, 182, 210, 212, 380, 383, 416, 479, 494, 503, and 511. The scribe has shown himself in Lt to be a careful copyist, and it would therefore seem probable that most of these errors are transmitted.

Rolle's authorship of this text has already been questioned. Miss Allen accepts it on external evidence, and argues a case of sorts for its style and content. But many scribal ascriptions have proved spurious, and she is forced to admit,[1] both of this and Ll, that they 'are singularly barren of passages unmistakably characteristic of Rolle'.[2] Morgan's findings on the genesis of the text, if accepted, accentuate these doubts. She is unwilling to commit herself on authorship, but considers that, while Rolle could have been responsible for Ll, the longer text is more probably the work of a reviser. The absence of this work from such comprehensive collections of Rolle's writing as Lt and Dd, the presence of another meditation on the same subject authenticated by the scribe of Lt, and the disappointing quality of Mu's text, further combine to suggest its exclusion from the canon.

[1] *Writings*, p. 281.

[2] Madigan, *op. cit.* disagrees strongly with this, and would assign it to Rolle on stylistic grounds alone. But she acknowledges that this approach may be overly subjective, an admission reinforced by the different reactions the piece has aroused in readers.

## EDITORIAL PROCEDURE

The aim of this edition has been to restore Rolle's original text as nearly as is possible in an alien dialect. To this end emendation is made wherever the evidence of variant manuscripts shows conclusively that the base text is in error, even when the manuscript reading appears to make sense. Where corruption is obvious, but no satisfactory variant is available, I have exercised my critical judgement. All such corrections are given in square brackets in a spelling consistent with scribal usage, the manuscript reading being shown in the footnotes. However manuscript readings which appear to be the result of deliberate choice on the part of the scribe or a predecessor, as the substitution of dialectal synonyms, or minor syntactical differences, are retained if they do not affect the meaning of the text.

Letters which are obscured by the binding or obliterated by physical damage are restored in square brackets without comment. Punctuation, capitalization, and word division are all editorial.

In accordance with current EETS practice, abbreviations are silently expanded. Most of these are standard, but a few require special mention. Endings in -cōn I have expanded as -cioun, and endings in-iōn as -ioun. A possible alternative would have been -cione and -ione, but the manuscripts gave no guidance. However endings in-sōn are expanded as -sone, and endings in-ōn ('glotōn', 'habergeōn') as -one, as these spellings are occasionally written in full. A bar over 'p', which occurs frequently, is expanded as '-pe': 'slepe', 'helpe', 'shipe' etc.; the single instance of 'hōpe' is tentatively rendered 'hoope'. A peculiarity of the LtMu hand is to cross final -ll; where this occurs in an obviously plural context, it is expanded '-lles', and where singular as '-lle'. Final -r with a flourish, another regular feature, is expanded '-re', but the occasional flourish through final '-gh' is ignored. 'Ihū' is expanded 'Ihesu', and 'ihc̄' as 'Iesus'. Manuscript marginal or interlinear insertions are marked ` ´.

Variant readings, apart from orthographical or inflexional differences, are given in full for all texts apart from the *Form*, where the large number of manuscripts involved made such a treatment impractical, and the variants shown consequently represent only about a third of those extant. Evidence of manuscript relationship is often shown by the accumulation of minor agreements, and there is a very real danger that such drastic editorial selectivity might present a distorted or misleading picture. This is particularly true of the aberrant manuscripts T[3] and Tr, and the fragmentary texts Ff[2], Hh, Tr[2], H[2], and Ld[2], whose unique variants I have been forced to ignore. Thus it must be stressed that if their testimony is not cited, it does not necessarily mean that they are in agreement with Lt. However, draconian measures here gave me more flexibility elsewhere, and with the remaining thirty-five manuscripts I have worked on the general principle that only those variants which do not materially alter the sense are unrecorded. These include the omission or addition of articles, of repeated possessives and conjunctions, of variant prepositions, conjunctions, and adverbs, and differences in number (man/men, or he/they used as generalizations), word order, and syntax. The use of synonyms, usually dialectal in origin, is also largely disregarded; examples include 'gar'/'do'/'make', 'ȝerne'/'desire'/'wil'/'couait', 'tyne'/'lese', 'ay'/'euer', 'fandynge'/'temptacioun', 'louynge'/'praisynge'/'worshipynge'/'heriinge' (but not 'love' in its modern sense), 'forþi'/'therefore'/'wherefor', 'ill'/'euil'/'bad'/'wicked', 'lare'/'lernynge'/'techynge', 'fend'/'deuyl', 'apert'/'oppyn', 'stalworth'/'strong'/'streynthful'/'myghty', 'trow'/'leue'/'hope', 'als tyte'/'anon'/'sone'/'hastylyche', 'soth'/'trew'. But in all cases, if manuscript preference seems to be particularly indicative of manuscript relationship, some examples have been retained. If several manuscripts agree substantially in a variant, the version of the leading siglum is given, and minor internal differences passed silently over. Elsewhere differences within a variant are noted as follows: '*om.*' or a variant in round brackets refers only to the word it immediately follows; diamond brackets denote an addition. A siglum followed by an asterisk (W*) shows a corrected reading; where the manuscript has been corrected to read as the lemma, the siglum is followed by '*corr.*' (W *corr.*).

# INTRODUCTION

# I
# THE FORM OF LIVING

## Tractatus Ricardi heremite ad Margaretam de Kyrkby, reclusam, de Vita Contemplatiua f. 30r

In euery synful man and womman þat is bounden in dedely syn ben þre wrechednesse, þe which bryngeth ham vnto þe deth of helle. The first is defaut of gostly streynth, þat þei ben so woke within in hare hert þat þei may nether stond ayeyns temptacioun of þe fend, ne þei mow nat lifte vp har wille for to desire þe loue of God and folow þerto. That oþer is vse of fleisshely desires: for þei haue no wil ne myght to withstond, þay fallen in lustes and lykynge of þis world, and for þey þynken ham swete, þei dwellen in ham stille, many vnto har lyves end. And so þei comen in to þe þrid wrechednesse, þat ˋis´ chaungynge of lestynge good for a passynge delyte: þat is to sey, þey yeven endlees ioy for a litel ioy of þis lif. If þei wil turne ham and rise to penaunce, God | wol f. 30v ordeyn har wonnynge with angels and holy men. Bot for þei chesen þe vile syn of þis world, and haue more delite in þe filth of har fleissh þan in þe fairhede of heuyn, þei lesyn both þe world and heuyn. For he þat loueth nat Ihesu Crist, he leseth al þat he hath and al þat he is and al þat he myght get; he nys nat worth þe lif, ne to be fed with swynes met. Al creatures shal ben stirred in to his vengeaunce in þe day of dome.

These wrechednes þat I of told ben nat only in worldisshe men and wommen that vsen glotony or lecherie and other oppyn synnes, bot þei ben also in sum men þat semen in penaunce and in good lif. For þe deuyl, þat is enemy vnto al mankynd, whan he seth a man or a womman amonge a þousand turne ham holy to God, and forsake al þe vanite and þe richesse þat men þat loueth þe world coueiteth, and seche þe ioy lestynge, a thousand wiles he hath in what manere he may deceyue ham. And whan he may nat brynge ham in to sych synnes þe which myght make al wondre on ham þat knewe ham, he begileth many so priuely þat þai can nat oft tymes fele þe trape þat hath take ham.

Sum men he taketh with errour þat he putteth ham in; sum with synguler witte, whan he maketh ham wend þat þe thynge þat þei thynken or done is beste, and forþi thei wol no consail haue of othre þat ben bettre and connyngre þan þei. And þis is a foul stynkynge

pride, for he wold nat set his witte befor al othre bot if he wend þat oþer he knew bettre or did better þan oþer. Sum þe deuyl deceyueth þrogh vaynglorie, þat is ydel ioy, when any hath pride and delite in ham self of þe penaunce þat þei suffren, of good deedes þat þei doon, of any vertu þat þei haue; ben glad þat men preisen ham, sory whan men laken ham or reprouen ham, haue enuy to ham that ben spoken more good of þan of ham; þei holden ham self so glorious and so ferre passynge þe lif þat oþer men leden þat ham þynken þat no man shold reproue ham in any thynge þat þei done or sey, and dyspisen synful men and oþer þat wil nat done as þei bidden ham. How may þou fynd a synfuller wreche þan such on? And in so mych is he þe wors þat he wot nat þat he is ille, and is holden and honoured of men as wise and holy. Sum ben deceyued with ouer mych lust and lykynge in mete and drynke, whan þei passen mesure and comyn in to outrage, and haue delite þerin, and weneth þat þei synneth nat, and forþi amend ham
f. 32r nat, and so þei destruen vertues of soule. Sum ben begiled | with ouer mych abstynence of mete and drynk and sleepe; that is temptacioun of þe deuyl for to make ham faille in myddes har worke, so þat þei brynge hit til non endynge as þei shold haue done if þai had know skylle and hadden discrecioun, and so þei lesen har merite for har frowardenesse.

These giles leith our enemy for to take vs with whan we begynneth for to haat wrechednesse and turne vs to God. Than many begynneth þe worke þat þei neuer more mowen for to brynge to an end. Than þey weneth þat þei mowen do what so her hert is set on, bot oft þei fallen ar þei comen in myddes þe wey, and þat þynge þat þei wend was for ham is lettynge for ham. For we haue a longe way to heuyn, and as many good dedes as we done, as many priers as we make, and as many good thoghtes as we þynken in trouth and hoope and charite, so many pases go we to heuynward. Than if we make vs so woke and so feble þat we may noþer worch ne pray as we shol[d]en do, n[e] þyn[k]e, be we nat gretly to blame, þat faillen whan we had moost need for to be stalworth? Ande wel I wote þat hit nys nat Goddis wille þat we so do, for the prophet seith 'Lord, I shal kep my streynth to þe', so þat he myght sustene Goddis seruice in to his deeth day, nat in a litel and a short tyme waste hit, and seteþen ligge waillynge and gronynge by þe wogh. And hit is mych more perille þan men weneth, for Seynt Ierom seith þat he maketh of ravyn offrynge þat outrageouslye turmenteth his body in ouer litel mete or sleepe; and Seynte Bernard seith fastynge and wakynge letteth nat goostly goodes bot helpeth, if þei be done with discrecioun; withouten þat þei ben vices. Forþi hit is nat good to peyne vs so mych, and seþyn haue vnþanke for our dede. Thar haue ben many, and ben, þat weneth þat hi[t i]s nat al þat þay don, bot if þat þai ben in so myche abstinence and fastynge þat þey make al to speke of ham þat knowen ham. Bot oft syth hit befalleth þat euer þe moor ioy and wondrynge þai haue withouten of þe preysynge of men, euer þe lasse ioye þei haue within of þe loue of God. At my dome þe[i] shol[d]en plese Criste mich moore if þei toke, for his loue an in thanke and praysynge of hym, for to susten har body in his seruice, and for hold ham fro mych speche of men, what so God sent for þe tyme and þe stidde, and yeven ham seþen entierly and perfitly to þe loue and preisynge of Ihesu Crist, har lord, þat wol stalworthly be loued and lestyngly be serued, so þat har holynesse were more sene in Goddis eigh þan in mannys | egh. f. 32v

For euer þe bettre þat þou art, and þe lasse speche þou [hast] of men, þe mor is þi ioy afor God. A, whate `hit´ is mych to ben worþi preisynge and be nat preiset, and whate wrechednesse hit is for to haue þe name and þe habite of holynesse and be nat so, bot couer pride, wreth or envy vndre þe cloþes of Cristes childhode. A foul lecherie hit is to haue lykynge and delite in mennes wordes, þat can no more deme whate we bene in our soule þan þei wote whate we thynke. For oft sith þei seith þat he or sho is in þe hegher degre þat is in þe lower, and þat þei seith is in þe lower is in þe hegher; forþi I hold hit bot wodenesse to be gladdir or sorier wheþer þei sigge good or yville. If we be about to hide vs fro speche or preisynge of þe world, God wol shewe vs to his praysynge and oure ioy. For þat is his ioye, whan we ben streynthful to stond ayeyns þe priue and þe oppyn temptaciouns of þe deuyl, and sechen no thynge bot þe preisynge and þe honour of hym, and þat we myght entierly loue hym; and þat oweth to be oure desyre, oure prayer and our entent nyght and day, þat þe fyre of his loue lyght oure hert, and þe swetnesse of his grace be our comfort and our solace in wel and in woo.

Thou hast herd nowe a partie how þe deuyl deceyueth with hi[s] sutil craftes vnstable and vnwise men and wommen. And if þou wilt do good consaille and folowe holy lernynge as I hope thou wolt, þou shalt destroy his trappes, and brand in þe fire of loue al þe bondes þat he wol bynd þe with, and al his malice shal turne þe to ioy and hym to moor sorowe. God suffreth hym for to tempte good men for har profite, that þei may be þe hegher coroned whan þei haue þrogh his helpe ouercome so cruel an enemy, that ofte syth hath in body and soul confounden many men. In thre maners he hath power to be in a man. On a maner: hurtynge þe goodes þat þei haue of kynd, as in doumb men and in other, blemesshynge har thoght. On anoþer maner: berevynge þe goodes the whiche þei haue of grace, an so is he in synful men whan he deceyuet þrogh delite of þe world and of har fleisshe, and ledeth ham with hym in to helle. In þe þrid maner: tourmentynge a mannes body, as we rede he was in Iob. Bot wit þou wel, if he begil þe nat within, þe dar nat dreed what he may do without, for he may do no moor þan God yeueth hym leue for to done.

For þat þou hast forsaken þe solace and þe ioy of þis world, and take þe to solitarie life for Goddis loue, to suffre tribulaciouns and anguysshes here, and aftre to cum to reste and ioye in heuyn, I trow f.33r stidfastly þat þe confort of Ihesu Criste and | swetnesse of his loue, with þe fyre of þe Holy Goste þat purgeth al syn, shal be in þe and with þe, ledynge and lernynge þe how þou shalt þynke, how þou shalt prey, what þou shalt worche, so þat in a few yers þou shalt haue more delite to be by þyn on and spek to þi loue [and] þi spouse Ihesu, þan if þou were lady of a thousand worldes. Men weneth þat we haue peyn and penaunce, bot we haue more ioy and verrey delite in oon day þan þei haue in þe world al har lyfe. Thei seen our body, bot þei seth nat oure herte wher our solace is. If þei saw þat, many of ham wold forsake al þat þei haue for to folow vs. Forþi be comforted and stalwarth, and dreed no noy ne anguysshe, bot fast al þyn entent þat þi lif be God to queme, and þat þer be no thynge in þe þat shold be myspaynge to hym þat þou ne sone amend hit.

The state þat þou art in, þat is solitude, þat is most able of al othre to reuelaciouns of þe Holy Goste. For whan Seynt Iohn was in þe Ile of Pathmos, þan God shewed to hym his pryuetees. The goodnesse of God hit is, þat he conforteth ham wondrefully þat hath no confort of þe world. If þei yeuen her herte entierly to hym, and coueiteth ne secheth nat bot hym, than he yeueth hym self to ham in swetnesse and delyte, in brandynge of loue and in ioy and melody, and dwelleth euer with ham in har sowle, so þat þe confort of hym departeth neuer fro ham; and if þei oght begynne to erre þrogh ignorance or freelte, sone he sheweth ham þe right way, and al þat þei haue need of he [ler]eth ham. No man cometh to such reuelaciouns and grace þe first day, bot þrogh longe trauaille and bisynesse to loue Ihesu Criste, as þou shalt hire aftreward.

Natforþi he suffreth ham to be tempted in dyuers maners, both wakynge and slepynge, for euer þe more temptacioun and þe greuouser þei stonden agayne and ouercomen, þe moor shal har ioye be in his loue whan þei ben passed. Wakynge þei ben oþerwhile tempted with foul thoghtes, vile lustes, wiked delites, with pride, jre, enuy, dispaire, presumpcioun and oþer many, bot har remedy shal be prier, gretynge, fastynge, wakynge. These þynges, yf þei be done with discrecioun, þei putteth away synne and filthed fro þe soule, and maketh hit clene for to receyve þe loue of Ihesu, þat may nat be loued bot in clennesse.

Also þe fend oþerwhile tempteth men or wommen þat ben solitarie, bi ham on, in a quaynt manere and sutile. He transfigure[th] hym in an angel of light, and appereth to ham and seith þat he is oon of Goddis angels comen to confort ham, and so he desceyueth foles. Bot ham þat ben wise, and | wol nat anoon trow to al spirites, bot asketh consaille of f. 33v conynge men, he may nat begile ham. As I fynd of a recluse written, that was a good womman, to þe whiche þe yuel angel oft tymes appered in þe fourme of a good angel, and seid þat he was comen to brynge hir to heuyn. Wherfor sho was right glaad and ioyful, bot neuerþelatre sho told hit to hir shrift-fadyre, and he, as a wise man and quaynt, yave hir þis consail: 'Whan he cometh, bid hym þat he shewe þe oure lady Seynt Marie. Whan he hath don so, sey "Aue Marie".' Sho did so, and þe fend seyd 'þou hast no need to se hir; my presens suffiseth to þe', and sho seid jn al maneres sho wold se hir. He saw þat hym behoued oþer do hyr wille, or sho wold dispise hym. Anoon he broght forth þe fairest body of womman þat myght be, and shewed hit to hir, and `anon she´ set hir on hir knees and said 'Aue Maria', and al vansshed awey, and for shame sethen he came neuer aye to hyre. This I sei, nat for I hoop þat he shal haue leue to tempt þe in þis maner, bot I wol þat þou be warre, if any such temptacioun befalle [þe], slepynge or wakynge, that þou trow nat ouer sone til þou knowe þe soth.

Moor priuely he transfigureth hym, and mor perillous, in an angel of lighte, þat comynly al men ben tempted with, whan he hideth yuel vndre þe liknesse of good, and þat is in two maners. Oon, whan he eggeth vs to ouer mych eese and reste of body and softhed to oure fleisshe, vndre need to sustene our kynd; for such thoghtes he putteth in vs: bot yf [w]e et wel and d[r]ynke wel and sleep wel and ligge soft and sit warme, [w]e may nat serue God, ne leste in þe trauaille þat [w]e haue begune. Bot he þynketh to brynge vs to ouer mych luste of oure body, and for to make vs slowe and cold in Goddis loue. Another is whan, vndre the liknes of goostly good, he entisseth vs to ouer sharpe and ouer mych penaunce for to destrue oure self, and seith thus: 'Thou wost wel þat he þat suffreth most penaunce for Goddes loue, he shal haue most mede. And þerfor et litel and feble mete, and drynk lasse: þe thynnest drynk is good jnogh for þe. Rek nat of sleep. Werre þe heere and þe habergeone. Al þynge þat is affliccioun for þy fleisshe, do hit, so þat þer be noon þat may passe þe in penaunce.' He þat seith þe þus, he is about to slee þe with ouer mych, als he þat seid þe þe toþer wild sle the with ouer litelle. Forþi, if we wil be right disposed, vs bihoueth set vs in a good meen, so þat we may destroy oure vices and hold our fleisshe vndre, and neuerþelatre þat hit be stalworth in þe seruice of Ihesu Criste. |

f.34r A[l]so our enemy wol nat suffre vs to be in reste whan we slep, bot þan he is about to begile vs in many maneres: orwhiles with grisful ymages for to make vs ferd, and mak vs loth with our state; otherwhile with faire ymages, faire syghtes and þat semen confortable, for to make vs glad in vayne, and make vs wene þat we ben bettre þan we ben; othrewhile telleth vs þat we bene holy and good for to brynge vs to pride; othrewhile he seith þat we ben wicked and synful for to make vs fal in dispaire. Bot he þat is ordeynour of al þynge suffreth nat þat oure sleep be without meed to vs, if we adresse oure lif at his wille. And witte þou welle þat þou synnest nat slepynge, if þou be euermore wakynge withouten outrage of mete and drynke, and without yuel thoghtes. Bot many hath þe deuyl desceyuet þrogh dremes, whan he hath maked ham set har hert on ham, for he hath shewed ham sum soth, and sethen begiled with oon þat was fals. Forþi seith þe wise man that many bisynesse foloweth dremes, and þei fel þat hopped in ham.

Wherfor, þat þou be nat begilet with ham, I wil þat þou witte þat þer ben vj maners of dremes. Two ben, neþer holy man ne other may eschape: þey bene if har womb be ouer lere or ouer ful; than many vanitees in dyuers maneres befalleth ham slepynge. The þrid is of illusioun of þe deuyl, oure enemy. The ferth is of thoght before and illusioun folwynge. The fyfte þrogh reuelacioun of þe Holy Goste, þat is done in many maneres. The vj is of thoghtes before þat falleth to Criste or holy chirche, reuelacioun comynge aftre. In thus many maners toucheth þe ymage of dremes men whan þei slepen; bot so mych þe lattre we shal yeue feith to any dreme þat we may nat sone witte whiche is soth, which is fals, which of oure enemy, which of þe Holy Gooste. For wher so many dremes ben, þer ben many vanytees, and many þei make to erre, for þei [hegh]en vnstable me[n], and so deceyueth ham.

I know þat þi lif semeth yeuen to þe seruice of God. Þan is hit sham to þe, bot if þou be as good, or bettre, within in þi soule, as þou art semynge at þe syght of men. Therfor turne þi þoȝt perfitly to God, as hit semeth þat þou hast þi body. For I wold nat þat þou wene þat al ben holy þat haue þe habite of holynesse and be nat occupied with þe world, ne þat al bene il þat ocupien ham with erthly bisynesse. Bot þei ben oonly holy, what estate or | degree þei bene in, þe which despiseth f. 34v al erthly thynges, þat is to sey loueth hit nat, and brandyn in þe loue of Ihesu Criste, and al har desire is sette to þe ioies of heuyn, and hatyn al syn, and cessen nat of good workes, and felen [a] swettnesse in har herte of þe lyf withouten end; and neuerþelattre þei thynken ham self vilest of al, and holden ham wrochedest, leest and loweste. This is holy mennys lyf; folow hit and be holy.

And if þou wilt be in mede with þe apostle, þynke nat what þou forsakes, bot what þou despisest. For as mych þey forsaken þat folowen Ihesu Criste in wilful pouerte and in mekenes and charite and pacience, as þei may coueite þat folowen hym nat. And þynke with how mych and how good wille þou presentes þy vowes befor hym, for to þat he hath his egh. And if þou with gret desire offre þi priers, with gret feruour coueit to se hym, and sek non erthly comfort bot þe sauour of heuyn, and in contemplacioun þerof haue þi delite, wondrefully Ihesu worcheth in his louers, þe which he reueth fro þe luste of fleisshe and blood þrogh tendre loue. He maketh ham to wil non erthly thynge, and doth ham rise in to solace of hym, and to foryet vanyteeȝ and fleishly loue of þe world, and to dreed no sorowe þat may falle, to loth ouer mych bodili aise. To suffre for his loue ham þynken hyt ioy, and to be solitarie þei haue gret confort, þat þei be nat letted in þat deuocioun.

Now maist þou see þat many ben wors þan þei semen, and many ben bettre þan þei semen, and nameli amonge thaym þat haue þe habite of holynesse. And þerfor enforce þe al þat þou may, þat þou be nat wors þan þou semest. And if þou wilt do as I teche the in þis short fourme of lyvynge, I hope þrogh þe grace of God þat, if men hold þe good, þou shalt be wel bettre.

Atte þe begynnynge turne þe entierly to þi lord Ihesu Crist. That turnynge to Ihesu is nat els bot turnynge fro al þe couaitise and þe lykynge and þe occupaciouns and bisynes of worldly thynges and of fleishely luste and vayne loue, so that þi þoght, þat was euer downward modelynge in þe erth whil þou was in þe world, now be euer vpward as fyre, sechynge þe heghest place in heuyn, right to þi spouse þere he sitteth in his blysse. To hym þou art turned whan his grace enlumyneth þyn herte, and [hit] forsaketh al vices, and confourmeth hit to vertuȝ and good thewes, and to al manere of debonerte and mekenesse, and þou maist laste and wix in goodenesse þat þou hast begunne, without slownes or sorynes or irkynge of þi [ly]f.

Foure þynges shal þou haue in þi þoght tyl þou be in perfite loue, f. 35r for whan | þou art comen þerto, þi ioy and þi desire wol euer be brendynge in Crist. On is þe mesure of þi lif here, þat so short is þat vnnethe is oght; for we lyve bot in a poynt, þat is þe lest þynge þat may be, and sothly oure lif is lasse þan a poynt if we likene hit to þe lif þat lesteth euer. Anoþer is vncerteyntee of oure endynge; for we wot neuer whan we shal dey, ne whare we shal dey, ne howe we shal dey, ne whodre we shal go whan we ben dede; and þat God wol, þat þis be vncerteyne til vs, for he wol þat we be euer redy to dey. The þrid is þat we shal answare before þe rightuous juge of al þe tyme þat we han had here: how we haue lyved, whate oure occupacioun hath bene and whi, and what good we myght haue done whan we haue ben ydul. Therfor seith þe prophete: 'He hath callet þe tyme ayeyns me.' That same tyme þat he hath lent vs here for to dispend in good oops and in penauns in his seruice, if we wast hit in erthly loue and in vanyteeȝ, ful greuously most we ben punshed and demed. Forthy þat is on of þe most sorowe þat may be, bot if we afforce vs manly in þe loue of God, and do good to al þat we may do while our short tyme lesteth. And euery tyme þat we thynketh nat on God, we may accompt hit as þe þynge þat we haue losten. The fourth is þat we þynke how mych þe ioy is þat þay shal haue, þe which lesteth in Go[ddis] loue to har endynge. For þei shal ben breþere and felewes with angels and holy men, louynge and hauynge, praisynge and seynge þe kynge of ioy in þe fairheed and shynynge of his mageste; þe whoch sight shal be meed and mete and al delytes þat any creature may thynke, and moor þan any man may tel, to al his louers withouten end: hit is myche lightre to cum to þat blisse þan to tel hit. Also þynke what sorow and woo and peyn and tourment þai shal haue, þe whoch loued nat God ouer al þese thynges þat men seen in þis world, bot fileth har body and har soul in luste and lechurie of þis lif, in pride and coueitise and oþer synnes. þei shal brand in þe fire of helle with þe deuil whom þei serued, as longe as God is in heuyn with his seruauntȝ euermore.

I wil þat þou be [euer] clymynge to Ihesuward, and echynge þi loue and þi seruice in hym; nat as fools doon: þei begynnen in þe heghest degree and comen doune to þe loghest. I sei nat, for I wol þat, if þou haue begunne vnskylful abstynence, þat þou hold; bot for many þat weren brendynge at þe begynnynge and able to þe loue of Ihesu Criste, for ouer mych penaunce þei haue letted ham | self, and maked f. 35v ham so feble þat þei may nat loue God as þei sholden do. In þe whiche loue þat þou wix euer more and more is my coueitynge and myn amonestynge. I hold þe neuer of þe lasse merite if þou be nat in so mych abstinence as þou hast be, ne of þe more merite þogh þou take þe to moor abstinence, bot if þou set al þy þoght how þou maist loue þi spouse Ihesu Criste mor þan þou hast don; þan dar I sey þat þy meed is wyxynge and nat wanynge.

Wherfore, þat þou be right disposed, both for þi soule and þi body, þou shalt vndrestond foure þynges. The first is what thynge fileth a man. That other, what maketh hym clene. The þrid, what holdeth hym in clennesse. The fourth, what þynge draweth hym for ordeyne his wille al to Goddis wille. For þe first, witte þou þat we synneth in þre thynges þat maken vs foule: þat is with herte, mouth, and dede.

The synnes of oure herte bene þese: il thoghtis, il delites, assent to syn, desire of il, wikked wille, il suspeccioun, vndeuocioun (if þou let þi hert any tyme be ydel without occupacioun of þe loue and þe praysynge of God), il dreed, il loue, errour, fleishly affeccioun to þi frendes or to others þat þou louest, ioy in any mannys ilfare, sorowe in har welfare (whethre þai ben enemys or no), despit of pouer or of synful men, honour riche men for har richesse, vncouenable ioy of any worldis vanytee, sorow of þe world, vntholmodnesse, perplexite (þat is dout what is to do, what nat, for euery man oweth to be sikyre what he shal do and what he shal leue), obstinacioun in il, noy to do good, angre to serue God, sorow þat he did no more ille, or þat he did nat þat luste or þat lykynge of his fleishe þe which he myght haue done, vnstablenesse of thoght, pyne of penaunce, ypocrisi, loue to plese men, dred to displese ham, sham of good deed, ioy of il dedes, singulere witte, coueitise of honour or of dignite or to ben holden bettre than othre, or richer, or faire, or to be more dreded, vaynglorie of any good of kynd or of happe or of grace, shame with pouer frendes, pride of ryche kyn or of gentil (for al we ben like fre bifore Goddis face, bot if our dedes make any bettre or wors þan oþre), dispite of good consaille and of good techynge.

Synnes of þe mouth ben these: to swere oft sithes, forswerynge, sklaundrynge of Criste or of any of his halowes, neune his name without reuerence, gaynsigge and stryue ayeyns sothfastnes, | gruch ayayns f. 36r God for any anguys or noy or tribulacioun þat may befalle in erth, vndeuoutly and without reuerence sei and hire Godis seruice, bacbitynge, flattrynge, lesynge, myssiggynge, wreyynge, disfamynge, cursynge, manacynge, sowynge of discord, tresone, fals witnes, il consail, scornynge, vnbuxomnes with word, turne good deedes to il for to make ham be holden il þat don ham (we owen for to lap oure neghbors dedes in þe best and nat in þe worst), exite any man to jre, reproue in anoþer þat he dothe hym selfe, vayne speche, moche speche, fool speche, speke idel wordes or wordes þat ben nat need, roosynge, polisshynge of wordes, defense of syn, cryinge [and] laghtre, mowe on any man, synge seculere songes and loue ham, preise il dedes, more synge for preisynge of men þan of God.

Synnes in deede ben these: glotony, lechurie, dronkenes, symony, wichecraft, brekynge of haly daies, sacrilege, receyue God in dedly syn, brekynge of voues, apostasie, dissolucioun in Goddis seruice, yeue ensample of yuel dedes, hurt any man in his body or in his goodes or in his fame, thefte, rauyn, vsure, deceyte, syllynge of rightwisnesse, herknynge of il, yeve to harlotes, withhold necessaries fro þe body or yeve hit outrage, begyn a thynge þat is aboue oure powere or myght, custume to syn, fallynge eft in syn, feynynge of moore good þan we haue for to seme holier or connynger or wiser þan we bene, hold þe office þat we suffice nat to, or þat may nat be holden without syn, led karolles, brynge vpe newe gyses, rebelle to his suffrayne, defoul ham þat ben lasse, syn in syght, in hyrynge, in smellynge, touchynge, handlynge, swelighynge, in giftes, waies, signes, biddynges, writynges; re[t]ey[n]e þe circumstances, þe which ben tyme, stidde, maner, noumbre, persone, dwellynge, connynge, eld ([þ]e[s]e maketh þe syn moor or lasse), to coueit to syn ar he be tempted, constreyne hym to syn.

Oþre many synnes bene þer of omyssioun, whan men leuen þe good þat þei shold done, [n]at þynkynge of God, ne dredynge ne louynge hym, ne thankynge hym of his benfaites, doth nat al þat he doth for f. 36v Goddis loue, sorow nat for | his syn as he shold done, dispose hym nat to receyue grace, and, if he haue taken grace, vse hit nat as hym oweth ne kepe hit nat, turne nat at þe inspiracioun of God, confourme nat his wille to Goddis wil, yeue nat entent to his priers, bot rabble on and rek neuer bot that þei ben seide, do negligently that he is holden to þrogh a vowe or comandement or enyoynte in penaunce, and drawe aleynth þat is to do sone, hauynge no ioy of his neghbors profite as of his owne, sorowynge nat for his ilfare, standynge nat agayns temptacioun, foryeuen nat ham þat heth done hym harme, kepynge nat trouth to his neghbore as he willed he did to hym, and yeldynge nat to hym a good deed for anothre if he may, amendynge nat ham that synnen befor his eighen, pesynge nat striffes, techynge nat ham þat bene vnconynge, confortynge nat ham þat beth in sorowe or in sekenesse or in pouerte or in penaunce and in prisone. These synnes and many other maken men foule.

The thynges þat clenseth vs of þat filthede ben þre, ayeyns þay þre manere of synnes. Þe first is sorowe of hert ayeyns þe synnes of thoght; and þat behoueth to be perfite, þat þou wolt neuer syn moor, and þat þou haue sorow of al þi synnes, and þat al ioy and solace bot of God and in God be put out of thy herte. The tother is shrift of mouth agayn þe syn of mouth; and þat shal be hasted withouten delayynge, naked withouten excusynge, and entier without departynge, as for to tel a syn to oon prest and anoþer to anothre: sey al þat þou wost to oon, or al is nat worth. The þrid is satisfaccioun, þat hath þre parties, fastynge, prier, and almysdede; nat only to gyf pouer men met or drynke, bot for to foryeve ham þat doth þe wronge and pray for ham, and enfourme ham how þay shal do þat ben in poynt to perisshe.

For þe þrid þynge, þou shalt witte þat clennesse behoueth be kept in hert, in mouth, and in werke. Clennesse of herte þre þynges kepeth. Oon is wakynge thoght and stabil of God. Anoþer, bisynes to kepe þi fyve wittes, so þat al þe stirrynges wickid of ham be closed out of þi fleisshe. The þrid is honest occupacioun and profitable. Also clennesse of mouth kepeth þre þynges. Oon is that þou bethynke þe befoor ar þou speeke. Anoþer, þat þou be nat of mych speche bot of litelle, and namely euer tyl þi hert be stablet in þe loue of Ihesu, so þat þe þynke þat þou lokest euer on hym, wheþer þou spek or noȝt. Bot such a grace may | þou nat haue in þe first day, bot with longe trauaille and f. 37r
gret bisinesse to loue, and with custume, þat þe egh of þyn hert is euer vpward, shal þou cum þerto. The þrid, þat þou for no thynge ne for no mekenesse ly on any maner, for euery lesynge is syn and il and nat at Goddis wille. [Þ]e dar nat say þe soth euer bot if þou wille, bot al lyynge hate. If þou say a thynge of þi self þat semeth þi louynge, and þou say hit to þe louynge of God and help of oþer, þou dost nat vnwisely, for þou spekest sothfastnesse. Bot if þou wil haue any pryue, tel hit to none bot to such one that þou ware siker þat hit shold nat be shewed bot only to þe louynge of God, of whom is al goodnesse, and þat maketh sum better þan oþer and giffeth ham special grace, nat only for ham self, bot also for ham þat wil do wel to har ensample.

Clennesse of werke þre thynges kepeth. Oon is assiduel þoght of þe deeth, for þe wise man seith 'Bethynk þe on þi last endynge, and þou shal nat syn.' Anoþer is, fle fro il felewshipe þat yeueth more ensample to loue þe world þan God, erth þan heuyn, filth of body þan clennesse of soule. Þe þrid is temperaunce [and] discrecioun in mete and drynke, þat hit be neþer to outrage ne byneth skylwise sustenaunce of þe body. For both cometh to on endynge, outrage and ouer myche abstinence, for noþer is Goddis wille, and þat many wil nat wene, for nat þat man may say. If þou take þe sustenaunce of such good as God sendeth for þe tyme and þe day, what hit be, I outtake no maner of mete þat Cristen men vseth, with discrecioun and mesure, þou dost wel, for so did Crist hym self and his apostles. If þou leue many mettis þat men hath, noght dispisynge þe mete þat God haþ made to mennys help, bot for þe þynke þat þou hast no need þerof, þou dost wel, if þou see þat þou art as stalworth to serue God, and þat hit breketh nat þi stamake. For if þou haue broken hit with ouer mych abstinence, þe is reft appetit of mete, and oft shal þou be in quathis as þou ware redy to gif þe gooste; and wit þou wel, þou synned in þat dede. And þou may nat witte sone wheþer þyn abstinence be agayn [þ]e or with þe; forþi, whils þou art yonge, I rede þat þou ete and drynke bettre and wirre als hit cometh, þat þou be nat begilet. And aftreward, whan þou haste prouet many þynges and ouercomen many temptaciouns, and knowest þi self and God better þan þou dost now, þan, if þou se þat hit be to do, þou may take þe to more abstinence, and whils þou may do priue penaunce þat al men dar nat witte. Rightwisnesse is neþer in fastynge | f. 37v ne in etynge, bot þou art rightwise if al ilike be to þe, dispite as praysynge, pouert as richesse, hungre and need as delites or dayntees. If þou take þese with a praisynge of God, I hold þe blessed and hegh bifore Ihesu. Men þat comen to þe, praise þe, for þei see þi gret abstinence, and for þay se þe enclosed. Bot I may nat praise þe so lightly, for oght þat I se þe do withouten, bot if þi wil be confourmed entierly to do Goddis wille. And set noght by har praysynge ne har lakynge, and gif þou neuer tale if þei speke lasse good of þe þan þai did, bot þat þou be brennynger in Goddis loue þan þou was. For of a thynge warne I the, I hoop þat God hath noon perfite seruaunt in erthe withouten enemyes of sum men, for only wrechednesse hath non enemye.

For to draw vs þat we confourme our wille to Goddis wille, þer ben þre þynges. On is ensample of holy men and wommen, þe which was ententif nyght and day to serue God and dred hym and loue hym; and if we folow ham in erth, we mowe be with ham in heuyn. Anoþer, þe goodnesse of our lord God, þat despiseth none bot gladly receyueth al þat wil cum to his mercy, and is homelier to ham þan broþer or sustre or any frend þat þai most loued or most trusteth on. The þrid is þe wondre ioy of þe kyngdome of heuyn, þat is more þan tonge can tel or hert may thynke or eygh may see or eere may hire. Hi[t] is so mych þat, as in helle myght no thynge lyve for mych peyne bot þat þe myght of God suffreth ham nat to dey, so þe ioy in þe syght of Ihesu in his godheed is so mych þat þei most dey for ioy, if hit ne ware his goodnesse þat wil þat his louers be lyvynge euer in blisse, as his rightwisnesse wil þat al þat louet hym nat be euer lyvynge in fyre, þat is horrible to any man to þynke. Look þan what hit is to fele; bot þa[i] þat wil nat dred hit ne thynke hyt now, þei shal suffre hit euermoore.

Now as þou herd how þou may dispose þi lyf, and reul hit to Goddis wille. Bot I wot wel þat þou desirest to hyre sum special poynt of þe loue of Ihesu Criste, and of contemplatif lif þe which þou hast taken þe to at mennys syȝt. As I haue grace and connynge, I wil lere þe.

Amore langueo. These two wordes ben written in þe boke of loue þat is called þe songe of loue, or þe songe of songes. For he þat mych loueth, hym lust oft to synge of his loue, for ioy þat he or sho hath when þay þynke on þat þat | þay loue, namely if har louer be trewe and f. 38r louynge. And is to þe Englisshe of þese two wordes 'I languysshe for loue.' Dyuers men in erth haue dyuers yiftes and graces of God, bot þe special yift of þo þat ledeth solitary lif is for to loue Ihesu Criste. Thou saist to me 'Al men loueth hym þat holdeth his commaundementȝ.' Soth hit is, bot al men þat kepeth his biddynge kepeth nat also his consail, and al þat doth his consail is nat as fulfilled of þe swetnesse of his loue, ne feleth nat þe fyre of loue brennynge his herte. Forþi the dyuersite of loue maketh þe dyuersite of holynesse and of mede. In heuyn þe angels þat ben most brennynge in loue ben next God. Also men and wommen þat most hath of Goddis loue, wheþer þei don penaunce or none, þei shal be in þe heghest degre in heuyn; þei þat loue hym lasse, in þe lower ordre. If þou loue hym myche, miche ioy and swetnesse and brennynge thou felest in his loue, þat is þi confort and streynth nyght and day. If þi loue be nat brennynge in hym, litel is þi delite, for hym may no [man] fele in ioy and in swetnesse bot if þai be clene and fild with his loue. And þerto shalt þou come with grete trauaille in praynge and in þynkynge, hauynge suche meditaciouns þat ben al in þe loue and in þe praysynge of God. And whan þou art at þi mete, preise euer God in þi thoght at euery morsel, and say þus in þi herte: 'Praised be þou, Kynge, and þanked be þou, Kynge, and blessed be þou, Kynge. Ihesu, al my ioynge, of al þi yiftes good, þat for me spilet þi blood, and deyed on þe rood, thou gif me grace to synge þe songe of þi praisynge.' And þynke hit nat only whils þou etest, bot bothe bifore and aftre, euer bot when [þou] praiest or spekest. Or if þou haue oþer þoghtes þat þou hast more swetnesse in and deuocioun þan in þo þat I lere þe, þou may thynk ham, for I hope þat God wil do suche þoghtes in þyn hert as he is paied of, and as þou art ordeyned fore. When þou praiest, loke nat how mych þou saist, bot how welle, þat þe eigh of þy hert be euer vpward, and þi thoght on þat þat þou seist, as mych as þou may. If þou be in praier and in meditaciouns al þe day, I wot wel þat þou mow wax gretly in þe loue of Ihesu Criste, and myche fele of delite, and within short tyme.

Thre degrees of loue I shal tel þe, for I wold þat þou myȝt wyn to þe heghest. The first degre is insuperabile, þe toþer is cald inseperabile, the þrid is synguler. Thi loue is insuperabile when no thynge that is f.38v contrarie to Goddis | loue may ouercum hit, bot hit is stalworth agayns al fandynges, and stable, wheþer þou be in ese or in anguys, in heel or in sekenesse, so þat þe þynke þat þou wil nat for al þe world, to haue hit withouten end, wreth God oo tyme; and þe ware leuer, if au[þ]er shold be, to suffre al þe peyne and woo þat myght cum to any creature, ar þou wold do þe þynge þat myght myspay hym. On þis maner shal þi loue be insuperabile, þat no þynge may brynge hit doun, bot spryngynge on heght. Blesset is he or sho þat is in þis degre, bot yet ware þai blesseder þat myght hold þis degre and wyn in to þe toþer, þat is inseperabile.

Inseperabil is þi loue when al þi hert and þi þoght and þi myght is so hooly, so entierly and so perfitly fasted, set and stablet in Ihesu Criste þat þi þoght cometh neuer of hym, neuer departeth fro hym, outtaken slepynge; and als son as þou wakest, þi hert is on hym, seiynge 'Aue Maria. Gloria tibi, domine', or 'Pater noster', or 'Miserere mei deus', if þou haue ben tempted in þi slepe, or thynkynge his loue and his praisynge as þou did wakynge. Whan þou may no tyme foryit hym, what so þou dost or seist, þan is þi loue inseperabil. Ful mych grace haue þay þat ben in þis degre of loue, and me thynke þou, þat hast nat elles to do bot for to loue God, may cum þerto, if any may get hit.

The þrid degre is heghest, and most ferly to wyn; þat is cald synguler, for hit hath no pere. Synguler loue is when al confort and solace is closet out of þe herte, bot of Ihesu Crist only. Oþer delite ne other ioy list hit nat, for þe swetnesse of hym in þis degre is so confortable and lestynge, his loue so brennynge and gladynge, þat he or sho þat is in þis degre may as wel feele þe fyre of loue brennynge in har soule as þou may fele þi fynger bren if þou put hit in þe fyre. Bot þat fyre, if hit be hoot, is so delitable and wonderful þat I can nat tel hit. Þan þe sowl is Ihesu louynge, Ihesu thynkynge, Ihesu desyrynge, only in coueitys of hym [ondynge], to hym seghynge, of hym brennynge, in hym restynge. Than þe songe of preisynge and of loue is comen. Þan þi þoght turneth in to songe and in to melody. Þan þe behoueth synge þe psalmes þat þou before said; than þou mow be longe about fewe psalmes. Than þe wil þynke þe deth swetter þan hony, for þan þou art siker to see hym þat þou louest. Þan þou may hardily say 'I langu[y]sshe for loue'; þan may þou say 'I sleep and my hert waketh.'

In þe first degre men may say 'I langwisshe for loue', or 'Me langeth in loue', and in þe | toþer degre also, for languysshynge is whan men f. 39r failleth for sekenesse. And þat ben in þese two degrees faillen fro al þe couaitise of þis world, and fro lust and lykynge of synful lif, and setteth har entent and har hert to loue of God; forþi þei may say 'I languysshe for loue', and myche more þat ben in þe secunde degree þan in þe first. Bot þe soul þat is in þe þrid degre is as a brennynge fyre, and as þe nyghtgalle, þat loueth songe and melody, and failleth for mykel loue; so þat soul is only conforted in praisynge and louynge of God, and til þe deth cum is syngynge gostly to Ihesu and in Ihesu. And 'Ihesu' nat bodily cryinge with þe mouth: of þat maner of syngynge speke I nat of, for þat songe hath both good and il, and þis maner of songe hath none bot if þai be in þis þrid degre of loue, to þe which degree hit is impossibil to cum bot in a greet multitude of loue. Forþi, if þou wil witte what kyn ioy þat songe hath, I say þe þat no man wote bot he or sho þat feleth hit, þat hath hit, and þat prayseth God syngynge þerwith. O thynge tel I the: hit is of heuyn, and God yeueth hit to whom he wil, bot nat withouten grete grace comynge bifore. Who-so hath hit, hym thynke al þe songe and þe mynstralcie of erth nat bot sorowe and woo þerto. In souereyn rest shal þay be þat mow get hit. Gangerels and janglers and kepers of comers and goers arly and late, nyght and day, or any þat takeled is with any syn wilfully and wittyngely, or þat hath any delite in any erthly thynges, þei ben as ferre þerfro as is fro heuyn to erth. In þe first degre ben many; in þe toþer degre ben ful fewe; bot in þe þrid degre vnnethes ben any, for euer þe more þat þe perfeccioun is, þe fewer folwers hit hath. In þe fi[r]st degre ben men likned to þe sterres, in þat oþer degre to þe mone, in þe þrid degre to þe son; forþi seith Seynt Poule 'Oþer ben þe brighthede of þe son, oþer of þe mone, oþer of þe sterres.' So is hit of þe louers of God. In þis þrid degre, if þou may wyn therto, þou shalt wit of more ioy þan I haue told þe yet, and amonge oþer affecciouns and songes þou may in þi longynge synge this in þyn herte to thy [lord] Ihesu, wh[en] þou coueiteste his comynge and [thy] goynge:

When wil þou cum to comfort me, and brynge me out of care,
And gyf me þe, þat I m[ay] se, hauynge for euermare?
Thy loue is euer swettest of al þat euer ware;
My hert [for loue] when shal hit brest, þan languyssh I no mare. |
f. 39v For loue my thoght hath fest, and I am fayn to fare.
I stand in stil mournynge of al loueli este lare;
His loue-langynge, hit draweth me to my day,
The band of swet brennynge, for hit holdeth me ay
Fro place and fro playnge, til þat I get hit may,
The syght of my swetynge, þat wendeth neuer away.
In welth beth our walkynge, withouten noy or nyght;
My loue is in lastynge, and longeth to þat syght.

If þou wil be wel with God, and haue grace to reul þi lif right, and cum to þe ioy of loue, þis name Iesus, fest hit so faste in þi herte þat hit cum neuer out of þi þoght. And whan þou spekest to hym, and seist 'Ihesu' þrogh custume, hit shal be in þyn ere ioy, in þi mouth hony, and in þyn hert melody, for þe shal þynke ioy to hyre þat name be nempned, swetnesse to spek hit, myrth and songe to thynk hit. If þou thynk Ihesu continuely, and hold hit stably, hit purgeth þi syn and kyndels thyn hert, hit clarifieth þi soule, hit remoueth anger, hit doth away slownesse, hit woundeth in loue, fulfilleth in charite, hit chaseth þe deuyl and putteth out drede, hit openeth heuyn and maketh a contemplatif man. Haue in memorie Ihesu, for al vices and fantasies hit putteth fro þe louer. And haille oft Mary, boþ day and nyght; mych loue and ioy shal þou fele if þou wil do after þis lare. The dar nat gretly couait many bokes; hold loue in hert and in werke, and þou hast al done þat we may say or write. For fulnes of þe lawe is charite; in þat hongeth al.

Bot now may þou ask me and say: 'þou spekest so mych of loue; tel me what loue is, and whare hit is, and how I shal loue God verrayly, and how I may knowe þat I loue hym, and in what state I may most loue hym.' These bene hard questions to louse to a febel man and a fleisshely as I am, bot neuerþelatter þerfor I shal nat leue þat I ne shal shewe my wit, and as me thynke þat hit may be, for I hope in þe help of Ihesu, þat is wel of loue and pees and swetnesse.

The firste askynge is: what is loue? And I answare: loue is a brennynge desire in God, with a wonderful delite and sikernesse. God is light and brennynge. Light clarifieth oure skyl; brendynge kyndyls oure couaitise, þat we | desire nat bot hym. Loue is a lif coupelynge togiddre f. 40r
þe louynge to þe loued, for mekenes maketh vs s[wete] to God, purtee ioyneth vs to God, loue maketh vs on with God. Loue is fairhede of al vertuȝ. Loue is a thynge þrogh which God loueth vs, and we loueth God, and euery of vs other. Loue is desire of þe herte euer thynkynge to þat þat hit loueth, [and whan hit hath þat hit loueth], than hit ioyeth, and no thynge may make hit sory. Loue is a desire betwix two, with lestyngnesse of thoghtes. Loue is a stirrynge of þe soule for to loue God for hym self, and al other thynge for God; the whiche loue, when hit is ordeyned in God, hit doth away al vnordeynt loue in any [þynge] þat is noght good. Bot al dedly is vnordynat loue in a thynge þat is nat good; þan loue putteth out al dedly syn. Loue is a vertue þat is þe reghtest affeccioun of mannes soule. Trouth may be withouten loue, bot hit may nat helpe withouten hit. Loue is perfeccioun of lettres, vertu of prophecie, froyt of trouth, heel of sacrementȝ, stabilynge of witte and conynge, riches of pouer men, lyf of deiynge men.

See how good loue is. If we suffre to be slayne, if we gif al þat we haue to begger staf, if we can as mych as men may can in erth, to al þis withouten loue is noght bot sorowe orde[yned] and torment. If þou wil ask how good is he or sho, [ask how mych loueth he or sho], and þat can no man tel þe; forþi I hold hit bot foly to deme of a mannys herte, þat noon knoweth bot God. Loue is a rightwise turnynge fro al erthly thynges, and ioyned to God withouten departynge, and kyndled with þe fyre of þe Holy Goost, fer fro fylynge, fer fro corrupcioun, obleged to no vice of þis lif, hegh abouen al fleisshlye lustes, euer redy and gnedy to contemplacioun of God, in al þynges vnouercomen, þe su[m] of al good affecciouns, heel of good maneres, end of þe comandementȝ of God, deth of synnes, lif of vertuȝ, vertu whils fightynge lesteth, [corone] of ouercomers, armes to holy thoghtes; withouten þat, no man may pay God; with þat, no man synneth, for if we loue God in al oure hert, þer is no þynge in vs þrogh þe which we serue to syn. Verray loue clenseth þe soule, and delyuereth hit fro þe peyn of hel, and of þe foul seruice of syn, and of þe orrible feleweshipe of deuelys; and of þe fendes son maketh Goddis son, | and parsonel in þe heritage of heuyn. f. 40v
We shal afforce vs to cloth vs in loue, as þe jren or þe cole doth þe fyre, as þe aire doth þe son, and þe wol doth þe hewe. Þe cool so cloth hit in fyre þat al is fyre; þe aire so cloth hit in þe son þat al is light; and þe

wole so substanciali taketh þe hewe þat hit is al like hit. In þis maner shal a trewe louer of Ihesu Crist do: his hert shal so bren in loue þat hit shal be turned in to fire of loue, and be as hit ware al fyre, and he shal be so shynynge in vertuȝ þat in no partie of hym [he] be durke in vices.

The toþer askynge is: whare is loue? And I answare: loue is in þe hert and in þe wil of þe man, nat in his hand ne in his mouth; þat is to say nat in his werke bot in his soule. For many speketh good and doth good, and loueth nat God, as ypocrites, þe whiche suffreth gret penaunce and semeth holy to mennys sight, bot for þay secheeth praysynge and honour of men and fauour, þay hath lost hare me[de], and in þe sight of God ben þe deuels sonnes and rauysshynge wolfes. Bot if a man gif almusdede and take hym to pouert and do penaunce, hit is a signe þat he loueth God; bot þerfor loueth he hym nat but when he forsaketh þe world only for Goddis loue, and maketh his hert clene of syn, and setteth al his thoght on God, and loueth al men as hym self, and al þe good dedes þat he may do, he doth ham in entent for to pay Ihesu Criste and to cum to þe reste of heuyn. Þan he loueth God, and þat loue is in his soule, and so his dedes sheweth withouten. If þou do þe good and speke þe good, men supposeth þat þou louest God. Forþi loke wel þat þi þoght be in God, or els þou dampnest þi self and deceyuest þo men. No thynge þat I do withouten proueth þat I loue God, for a wikked man myght do as myche penaunce in body, als myche wake and fast as I do. Howe may I þan wene þat I loue, or hold me bettre þan anoþer, for þat þat euery man may do? Certes my hert, whether hit loue my God or nat, wot no man bot God. Than can non tel me if I loue God, for noght þat þay may se me do. Wherfor loue is in þe wil verraili, nat in werke bot as signe of loue. For he þat saith he loueth God, and wil nat do in dede þat in hym is to shewe loue, say hym þat he lieth. Loue wil nat be ydel: hit is wirchynge sum good euermoor. If hit cesse of worchynge, wit þou þat hit keleth and vansheth away.

The þrid askynge is: how shal I verraily loue God? I answar: verray loue is to loue hym with al þi myght stalworthly, in al þi hert wisely, in al þi soule deuoutly and swetly. Stalworthly may no man loue hym bot if he be stalworth. He is stalworth þat is meke, for al gostly streynth cometh of mekenesse. On whom resteth þe Holy Goste? In a meke
f.41r soule. Mekenes gouerneth vs, and kepeth vs [in] al our temp|taciouns so þat þay ouercum vs nat. Bot þe deuyl deceyueth many þat ben meke þrogh tribulaciouns and reproues and bacbytynges; bot if þou be

wroth for any anguys of þis world, or for any word þat men seith of þe, or for oght þat men saith to þe, þou art nat meke, ne þou may so loue God stalwarthly. For loue is stalworth as deth, þat sleth al lyuynge þynge in erth, and hard as helle, þat spareth nat to ham þat ben dede; and he þat loueth God perfitly, he greueth hym nat what sham or anguys þat he suffreth, bot he hath delite, and coueiteth þat he ware worþi to suffre torment and peynt for Cristis loue, and he hath ioy þat men reproue hym and spek il of hym, as a dede man, what so men doth or seith, answareth nat. Right so, who-so loueth God perfitly, þai ben nat stirred for any word þat men may say. For he or sho kan nat loue þat may nat suffre peyn and angre [for har frendes loue, for who-so loueth, þai hath no peyn]. Prout man or womman loueth nat stalwarthly, for þay ben so feble þat þay falle at euery stirrynge of þe wynd þat is temptacioun. Þei secheth hegher stid þan Crist, for þai wil haue har wille done, wheþer hit be with right or with wronge, and Crist wil þat no þynge be done bot wel, and withouten harme of other men. Bot who-so is verray meke, þai wil nat haue hare wille in þis world, þat þay may haue hit plenerly in þe toþer. In no þynge may men soner ouercum þe deuyl þan in mekenesse. Þat he mych hateth, for he may wake and faste and suffre peyne more þan any creature may, bot mekenesse and loue may he nat haue.

Also þe behoueth loue God wisely, and þat may þou nat do bot if þou be wise. Thou art wise when þou art pouer withouten coueitise of þis world, and despisest þi selfe for þe loue of Ihesu Crist, and dispendest al þi witte and þi myght in his seruice. For sum þat semeth most wisest ben most foles, for al har wisedom þai spend in coueitise and bisynesse about þe world. If þou saw a man haue precious stones, þat he myght by a kyngedome with, if he yaue ham for an appil as a child wold do, right myght þou say þat he ware nat wise, bot a greet fool. Also, if we wil, [we] haue precious stones, pouerte and penaunce and gostly trauaille, with þe which we may by þe kyngdome of heuyn. For if þat þou loue pouerte, and despisest richesse and delites of þis world, and hold þi self vile and pouer, and þat þou hast noght of þi self bot syn, for þis pouert þou shalt haue richesse withouten end. And if þou haue sorowe for þi synnes, and for þou art so longe in exile out of þi contre, and | forsake þe solace of þis lif, þou shalt haue for þis sorow f.41v þe ioy of heuyn. And if þou be in trauaille, and punysshe þi body skylwisly and wisely in wakynges, fastynges, in prayers and in meditaciouns, and suffre heete and cold, hungre and þurste, mysaise and anguysshe for þe loue of Ihesu Criste, for þis trauaille þou shalt cum to reste þat lesteth euer, and sit in a seet of ioy with angels. Bot sum ben þat loueth nat wisely, like to children þat loueth more an appille þan a castelle. So doth many; þay gyf þe ioy of heuyn for a litel delite of har fleisshe, þat is noght worth a ploumbe. Now may þou se þat, who-so loueth wisely, hym bihoueth loue lestynge þynge lestyngly, passynge þynge passyngely, so þat his hert be set and fested in no þynge bot in God.

And if þou wil loue Ihesu verraily, þou shal nat only loue hym stalwarthly and wisely, bot also deuoutly and swetly. Swet loue is when þi body is chaste and þi þoght clene. Deuout loue is when þou offres þi praiers and þi þoghtes to God with gostly ioy and brennynge hert in þe hete of þe Holy Goste, so þat þe þynke þat þi soule is as hit were dronken for delite and solace of þe swetnes of Ihesu, and þi hert conceyueth so mych of Goddis helpe þat þe þynke þat þou may neuer be departed fro hym. And þan þou comest in to such rest and pees in soule, and quyet withouten þoghtes of vanytees or of vices, as þou ware in silence and sleepe, and set in Noe shipe, þat no þynge may let [þe] of deuocioun and brennynge of swet loue. F[ro] þou hast getten þis loue, al þi lif til deth cum is ioy and confort, and þou art verraily Cristis louer, and he resteth in þe, whose stid is maked in pees.

The ferth askynge was, how þou myght knowe þat þou ware in loue and charite. I answare þat no man wot in erth þat þai ben in charite, bot if hit be þrogh any priuelege or special grace þat God hath geven to any man or womman, þat al oþer may nat take ensample bi. Holy men and wommen troweth þat þei hath trouth and hoope and charite, and in þat doth as wel as þei may, and hopeth certeynly þat þei shal be sauf. Þay wot hit nat anon, for if þay wist, har merit ware þe lasse. And Salomon seith þat þer ben rightuouse men and wise men, and har werkes ben in Godis hond. And natforþi man wot nat wheþer he be worþy hatreden or loue, bot al is reserued vncerteyne til anoþer world. Neuerþelatter, if any had grace þat he myght wyn in to þe þrid degre f.42r of loue, þat is cald synguler, he wold knowe þat he ware in loue; bot | in þat maner his knowynge is, þat he myght neuer ber hym þe hegher, ne be in þe lasse bisynesse to loue God, bo`t´ so mych þe more þat he is sikyre of loue wold he be bisy to loue hym and dred hym þat hath made hym such, and done þat goodenesse. And he þat is so hegh, he wold nat hold hym selfe worþier þan þe synfullest man that gooth on þe erthe.

Also vij experimentȝ ben, that a man be in charite. The first is when al coueitise of erthly thynge is quenched in hym. For whare so coueitise is, þer is no loue of Criste; þan if he haue no coueitise, signe is þat he hath loue. The secunde is brennynge desyre of heuyn. For when men hath felet oght of þat sauour, þe more þei haue, þe more þai couait; and he þat noght hath felet, noght he desireth. Forþy, when any is so myche gyffen to þe loue þerof þat he can fynd no ioy in þis lif, token he hath þat he is in charite. The þrid is if his tonge be chaunget: þat was wonet to speke of þe erth now speketh of God and of þe lif þat lesteth euer. The iiij is exercise of gostly profite, as if any man or womman gif ham entierly to Godis seruice, and entremetteth ham of no erthly bisynesse. The v is when þe þynges þat ben herd in ham self semeth light for to do; þat loue maketh. For as Casciodorus `s´eith, louereden is þat bryngeth þat þynge negh impossible to possible myght, apertly. The vj is hardynes of thoght to suffre al angres and noyes þat cometh; withouten þis, al þe oþer suffiseth nat. For hit shal nat make a rightwise man sory what so bifalleth hym, for he þat is rightwise, he hateth nat bot syn, he loueth nat bot God and for God, he dredeth nat bot to wreth God, he hath no ioy bot in God, and al his hope is to cum to God. The vij is delitabilite in soule when he is in tribulacioun, and praysynge of God in euery angyre þat he suffreth; and [þ]i[s] sheweth wel þat he loueth God myche, when no wo may brynge hym downe. For many preisen God whils þay ben in ese, and in aduersite þai gurch, and falleth downe in to so mych sorynesse þat vnnethes may any man comfort ham, and so sklaundre þai God, chydynge and fyghtynge agayns his domys. And þat is a kaitif praysynge, þat only welth of þe world maketh; bot þat praisynge is of myche price þat no violence of sorowe may do away.

The vt askynge was in what state men | may moste loue God in. I f.42v
answare: in what state so hit be þat men ben in most reste of body and soule, and leste is occupied with any nedes or bisynesse of þis world. For þe þoght of þe loue of Ihesu Criste, and of þe day þat lesteth euer, secheth reste withouten, þat hit be nat letted with comers and goers and occupaciouns of worldes þynges; and hit secheth withjnnen grete silence fro þe noyes of couetise and vanytees and erthly thoghtis. And namely al þat loueth contemplatif lif, þai seke rest in body and soule. For a gret doctour seith þat þay ben Goddis trone þat dwellen stille in a stid, and ben nat about rennynge, bot in swetnesse of Cristis loue ben stabled. And I haue loued for to sit, for no penaunce ne for no fantasie `þat´ I wold men spake of me, ne for no such þynge, bot only for I knewe þat I loued God more, and langer lested with me comfort of loue, þan goynge or standynge or knelynge. For syttynge am I in

most reste, and my hert most vpward. Bot þerfor peraduenture is hit nat þe best to anoþer to sit as I haue done, and wil do to my deth, bot if he were disposed as I was in his soule.

Two lifes ben þat Cristen men lyuen in. On is cald actif lif, for hit is in more werke bodily. Anoþer, contemplatif, for hit is in more swetnesse gostly. Actif lif is mych outward, and in more trauaille, and in more peril for temptaciouns þat ben in þe world. Contemplatif lif is myche inward, and forþi hit is lestynger and sykerer, restfuller, delitabeller, louelier and more medeful, for hit hath ioy in Goddis loue, and sauour in þe lif þat lesteth euer, in þis present tyme if hit be right led. And þat felynge of ioy in þe loue of Ihesu passeth al oþer merites in erth, for hit is so herd to cum to for þe freelte of oure fleisshe, and þe many temptaciouns þat we ben beset with and letteth vs nyght and day. Al oþer þynges ben light to cum to in regard þerof, for þat may no man deserue, bot only hit is gyfen of Goddis godenes to ham þat verrayli yeueth ham to contemplacioun and to quyet for Cristis loue.

To me[n] or wommen þat taketh ham to actif lif, two þynges falleth. On is to ordeyn hare meyne in þe drede and in þe loue of God, and fynd ham har necessaries, and ham self kepe entierly þe commaundementȝ of God, doynge with har neghbore as þai wold as þai do to ham. Anoþer is þat þai do by har powere þe vij werkes of mercy, þe which ben fede þe hungri, yif þe þursty to drynk, clothe þe naked, herbrow hym | f.43r þat hath no housynge, visite þe seke, comfort ham þat ben in prisone, and bury dede men. Al þat may and hath cost, þai may nat be quyt with on or two of þese, bot ham behoueth do ham al, if þai wil haue þe benysone on domesday þat Ihesu Crist shal yeve to al þat doth ham; or elles may þai drede þat malisone þat al most haue þat wil nat do ham whan þay had goodes to do ham with.

Contemplatif lif hath two parties, a lower and a hegher. The lower partie is in meditacioun of holy writynge, þat is Goddis word, and in other good thoghtes and swete þat men hath of þe grace of God about þe loue of Ihesu Crist, and also in praysynge of God in psalmes and ympnys, or in praiers. The hegher partie of contemplacioun is biholdynge and desyre of þe þynges of heuyn, and ioy in þe Holy Goost, þat men hath oft, þogh hit so be þat þai be nat praiynge with þe mouth, bot only thynkynge of God, and of þe fairheed of angels and holy soules. Þan may I say þat contemplacioun is a wonderful ioy of Goddis loue, þe which ioy is a praysynge of God þat may nat be told. And þat wondreful praisynge is in þe soule, and for aboundance of ioy and swetnesse hit ascendeth in to þe mouth, so þat þe hert and þe tonge accordeth in on, and body and soule ioyeth in God lyuynge.

A man or a womman þat is ordeynet to contemplatif lif, first God inspireth ham to forsaake þis world, and al þe vanyte and þe couaitise and þe vile luste þerof. Sethen he ledeth ham by ham on, and speketh to her herte, and, as þe prophet seith, he yeueth ham to souke þe swetnesse of þe begynnynge of loue. And þan he setteth ham in wil to gif ham holy to praiers and meditaciouns and teris. Sethen, when þei han suffre[d] many temptaciouns, and þe foul noyes of thoghtes þat ben ydel, and of vanytees þe which wil comber ham þat can nat destroi ham, is passynge away, he maketh ham gaddre to ham har hert and fest [hit] only in hym; and openeth to þe eigh of har soule þe yate of heuyn, so þat þat eigh loke in to heuyn. And þan þe fire of loue verrailye lighteth in to har hert, and brenneth þerin, and maketh clene of al erthly filth; and seþen forward þei ben contemplatif men, and rauist in loue, for contemplacioun is a sight, and þai seth in to heuyn with har gostly eigh. Bot þou shalt witte þat no man hath perfite sight of heuyn whils þei ben in body lyvynge here, bot as sone as þai dey, þai ben broght bifor God, and | seth hym face to face and egh to eigh, and f.43v
wonneth with hym withouten end, for hym þai soght, and hym þai couaited, and hym þai loued in al har myght.

Lo, Margaret, I haue shortly seid þe fourme of lyuynge, and how þou may cum to perfeccioun, and to loue hym þat þou hast taken þe to. If hit doth þe good and profite to þe, thanke God and pray for me. The grace of Ihesu Criste be with the and kepe the. Amen.

# II
# EGO DORMIO

Ego dormio ˋetˊ cor meum vigilat. The þat lust loue, hold þyn ere and hyre of loue. In þe songe of loue I fynd hit written þat I haue set at þe begennynge of my writynge: ‘I slepe and my hert waketh.’ Mich loue he sheweth þat neuer is wery to loue, bot euer, standynge, sittynge, goynge, or any oþer dede doynge, is euer his loue þynkynge, and oft sithe þerof dremynge. Forþi þat I loue þe, I wowe þe, þat I myght haue þe as I wold, nat to me, bot to my Lord. I wil becum a messager to brynge þe to his bed þat hath mad þe and boght þe, Crist, þe kynges son of heuyn, for he wil wed þe if þou wil loue hym. He asketh þe no more bot þi loue, and my wil þou dost, if þou loue hym. Crist couaiteth þy fayrnesse in soule, þat þou gif holy þi herte, and I prech noght elles bot þat þou do his wille, and afforce þe day and nyght to leue al fleisshely loue, and al lykynge þat letteth the to loue Ihesu Crist verraily. For whils þi hert is holdynge to loue of any bodily thynge, þou may nat perfitly be cowpled with God.

In heuyn ben ix ordres of angels, þat ben contened in þre gerarchies. Þe lowest gerarchi conteneth angels, archangels, virtus. The mydel gerarchi, potestates, principatis, dominaciones. Þe heghest gerarchi, þat next is to God, conteneth thronus, cherubin and seraphyn. The lowest ordre is angels, the heghest seraphyn; and þat ordre þat lest is bright is sevyn so bryȝt as þe son. And as þou seest þe son brighter þan þe candel, þe candel brighter þan þe mone, þe mone brighter þan þe sterris, also ben þe ordres of angels in heuyn euery brighter þan oþer, fro angels to seraphyn. This I say to kyndel þi herte to coueit þe felewshipe of angels; for al þat ben good and holy, whan þai passe out of þis world, shal be taken in to þese ordres: sum in to þe lowest, þat han loued God mych; sum in þe myddis, þat han loued God more; oþer to þe heghest, þat most loueth God and most brennynge [ben] in his loue. Seraphyn, þat is to say brennynge; to þe f.44r whiche ordre þai ben recey|ued þat lest couaiteth in þis world, and most swetnesse feleth in God, and [most] brennynge hertes hath in loue.

To þe I writ þis speciali, for I hope in þe more goodnes þan in anoþer, þat þou wil gif þi þoght to fulfil in dede þat þou seest is profitable for þi soule, and þat lif gif þe to in þe whoch þou may holyest offre þi [hert] to Ihesu Criste, and lest be in besynesse of þis world. For if þou stabilly loue God and brennyngly whils þou lyvest here, withouten dout þi sete is ordeyned for þe ful hegh and ioiful bifore þe face of God amonge [his] holy angels. For in þe self degrees þer proud deuelys felle doun ben meke men and wommen, Cristes doves, set in, to haue rest and ioy withouten end, for a litel short penaunce and trauaille þat þai han suffred for Goddis loue. The thynk nowe peraduenture hard to gif þi hert fro al erthly thynges, fro ydel spech, fro al fleisshly loue, and go by one to wake and pray and þynke þe ioy of heuyn, and to haue compassioun of þe passioun of Ihesu Criste, and to ymagyn þe peyn of helle þat is ordeyned for synful men. Bot witterly, fro þat þou be vset þerin, þe wil thynke hit lighter and swetter þan euer þe did any erthly solace. Also sone as þi hert is touched with þe swetnesse of heuyn, þe wil litel luste þe myrth of þis world; and when þou felest ioy in Cristes loue, þe wil loth with þe ioy and þe comfort of ertly games. For al þe [melody, al þe] richesse, al þe delites þat al þe men of þis world can ordeyne or thynke, semeth and is bot noy and angre to a mannes herte þat verraily is brennynge in þe loue of God, for he hath mirth and melody and ioy in angels songe, as þou may wel witte. If þou leue al thynge þat þe lust fleisshely, and haue no þoght of þi sib frendes, bot forsaak al for Goddis loue, and only gif þi hert to couait Goddis loue and to pay hym, more ioy þou shalt fynd in hym þan I can þynke. How myght I than writ hit? I wot neuer jf many men be in suche loue, for euer þe hegher þat þe lif is, þe fewer folowers hit hath here, for many thynges draweth men fro Goddis loue. Þat þou may hire and se, þat God conforteth his louers more þan þay wene þat loueth hym nat, for thogh we seme in penaunce withouten, we shal haue ful mych ioy withjn, jf we ordeyn vs wisely to Goddis seruice, and set in hym al our thoghtes, and forsake vanyte.

Gif al þyn entent | to vndrestond þis writynge; and if þou haue set þi desyre to loue God, h[i]re [þese] þre degrees of loue, so þat þou may ry[s]e fro on to anoþer til þat þou be at þe heghest. For I ne wil nat helle fro þe þat I hop may turne þe to holynesse. The first degre of loue is when a man holdeth þe ten commandementȝ, and kepeth hym fro þe vij deedly synns, and is stabil in þe trouth of holy chirch; and when a man wil nat for any erthly þynge wreth God, bot trewely standith in his seruice, and lesteth þerin til his lyves end. This degre of loue behoueth euery man haue þat wil be saued, for no man may cum to heuyn bot he loue God and his neghbore, withouten pride, jr and enuy, bacbitynge, and withouten al oþer venymous synnes, as slownes,

f. 44v

glotony and lecherie and couaitise. For þese vices sleeth þe soule, and maketh hit depart fro God þat is lif of þe soule; and when a wreched man or a womman is departed fro God, we seyn he is dede, for he is slayn fro God, withouten whom no creature may lyve. As a man poysoned in a swet morsel taketh venym þat sleeth his body, so doth a synful wrech in lykynge and luste: destroieth his soule, and bryngeth hit to deth withouten end. Men thynke hit swet to syn, bot har hire þat is ordeyned for ham is bitterer þan galle, sowrer þan attyre, wors þan al þe woo þat men kan þynke in erth. Al perisshethe and passeth þat we with eigh see; hit vansheth in to wrechednesse þe wel of þis world. Robes and richesses roteth in þe diche; pride and peyntynge slak shal in sorowe. Delites and dreries stynke shal ful sone; har gold and har tresour draweth ham to deth. Al þe wiked of þis world dryueth to a dale þat þay may se har sorowynge; þer [wo] is al þe rabil. Bot he may synge of solace þat loued Ihesu Crist, when al þe wreches fro wel falleth in to helle.

Bot when þou hast wel lyved in þe comandementȝ of God, and straytly kept þe fro al deddly synnes, and paied to Crist in þat degre, bethynke þe þat þou wil more loue God, and do better with þi soule, and bicum perfite. And þan entres þou in to þe toþer degre of loue, þat is to forsake al þe world, and þi fadyre and þi modyre and al þi kyn, and folow Crist in pouert. In þis degre þou shalt study how clene þou may be in herte, and how chaste in body, and gyf þe to mekenesse, suffrynge and buxumnesse. And loke how faire þou may
f.45r make þi | soule in vertuȝ, and hate al vices, so þat þi lif be gostly, nat fleishly, neuer more spekynge il of þi neghbore, ne gefynge an il word for anoþer, bot al þat men seith, il or good, suffre hit debonerly in þi hert withouten styrrynge of wreth. And þan shal þou be in rest within, and lightly cum to gostly lif, þat þou shalt fynd swetter þan eny erthly þynge. Perfit lif and gostly is to despise þe erth, couait þe ioy of heuyn, and destroy þrogh Goddis grace al wicked desires of þ[e] fleishe, and foryet þe solace [and þe likynge] of þi kynreden, and loue ham nat bot in God: wheþer þei lyve or dey, be pouer or riche, be hole or seke, in woo or in wel, þank þou euer God and blesse hym in al his werkes. For his domes ben so priue þat no creature may comprehend ham, and oft sith sum men hath har lykynge and har wel in þis world and helle in þe toþer, and sum men ben in pyne and persecucioun an anguys in þis lif and hath heuyn to har mede. Forþi, if þi frendes be euer in ese and hele and in welth of þis world, þou and þai bothe may þe more drede þat [y]e lese nat þe

ioy withouten end. If þai be in penaunce, in sekenesse, or if þai life rightwisly, þei may trist in God to cum to his blisse.

Forþi in þis degre of loue þou shalt so be fild in grace of þe Holy Gost þat þou shal nat haue sorowe ne gretynge bot for gostly thynge, as for þi synnes and oþer mennys, and aftre þe loue of Ihesu Crist, and in þynkynge of his passioun; and þat I wille þat þou myche mynd of, for hit wil kyndil þi hert to set at noght al þe goodes of þis world and al þe ioy, and to desyre brennyngly þe light of heuyn with angels and halowes. And when þyn hert is ordeyned holy to þe seruys of God, and al worldis thoghtis put out, þan wil [þ]e lust st[e]ll bi þi on to þynke of Crist, and to be in mych prayng, for þrogh good þoghtes and holy praiers þi hert shal be mad brennynge in þe loue of Ihesu Crist, and þan shal þou fele swetnesse and gostly ioy, both in praynge and þynkynge. And when þou art by þyn on, gyf þe myche to say psalmes of þe psauter and pater noster and auees, and take nat entent þat þou say many, bot þat þou say ham wel, and in al þe deuocioun þat þou may, liftynge vp þi þoght to heuyn. Better hit is to say seven psalmes in desire of Cristes loue, hauynge þi hert on þi praynge, þan seuen hundred suffrynge þi þoght to passe in vanytees of bodily thynges. What good hopis þou may come þerof, if þou let þi tonge blaber on þe boke, and þi hert ren about | in dyuers steddes in þe world, whar hit f.45v wille? Forþi set þi þoght in Crist, and he shal reue hit to hym, and hold hit fro þe venym of worldis besynesse.

And I pray þe, as þou couaitist be Goddis louer, þat þou loue þis name Ihesu, and þynke hit in þi hert so þat þou foryet neuer hit, whar-so þou be. And witterly I hete þe, þou shalt fynd mych ioy and comfort þerin, and for þe loue þat þou louest Ihesu so tenderly and so specialy, þou shalt be fild ful of grace in erth, and be Cristes dere mayden and spouse in heuyn. For no thynge so mych payeth God as verray loue of his name Ihesu. If þou [loue] hit right and lestyngly, and neuer let for no thynge þat men may say or do, þou shalt be rauyst in to a hegher lif þan þou can couait. His goodnesse is so myche þat, þer we inwardly ask hym of oon, he wil yif vs þre, so wel paied he is when we set al oure hert to loue hym.

In þis degree of loue þou shalt ouercum þi þre enemyes, þe world, þe deuyl, and þy fleishe, bot neuerþelatter þou shalt haue euer fightynge whils þou leuest, and euer, til þou dey, behoueth þe be bisy to stand, þat þou fal nat in il delite ne in il thoght or in il word and in il werke; forþi gret oght þi desyre to be þat þou loue Crist verrayli. Thi fleishe shal þou ouercum throgh holdynge of þi maydenhede for Goddis loue only, or, if þou be noght mayden, þrogh chaste lyuynge in þoght and in dede, and þrogh discrete abstinence and resonable seruice. The world shal þou ouercum þrogh couaitynge of Cristes loue and þynkynge of his swete name and desyre to heuyn. For also sone as þou felest sauoure in Ihesu, þe wil þynke al þe world noght bot vanyte and noy for mennys soules. Þou wil nat couait þan to be riche, ne to haue many clothes and faire, [many kirtils, many] dreries, bot al þou wil set at noght, and dispise al, and take no more þan þe nedeth. The wil þynke two clothes or on ynogh, þat nowe hath fyue or six; forthy gif sum to Crist, þat goth naked and pore, and hold nat to þe al, þat wot nat [if þou] li[ue] til þai be half gone. The deuylle is ouercomen when þou standis stabilly agayne al hys fandynges in sothfaste charite and mekenes.

f. 46r And thynke on me, þat I be nat foryeten in þi praiers, þat | is aboutward þat þou ware dere with Crist, whose mercy me nedeth. I wil þat þou neuer be ydel; for be euer other spekynge of God, or wirchynge some notable werke, or thynkynge in hym, and principaly þat þi thoght be euer hauynge hym in mynde. And thynke of[t] þis of his passione:

My kynge þe watyre grete, and þe blod he swete;
Sethen ful sore bet, so þat his blood hym wette,
When har scourges met.
Ful fast þay can hym dinge, and at þe piller swynge,
His [faire] face fouled with spetynge.
The þorne crowneth þe kynge; ful sore is þat prickynge.
Alas, my ioy and my swetynge is d[em]ed for to henge.
Naillet was his hand and naillet was his feet,
And þurlet is his side, so semly and so swete.
Naked his white brest, and rede his blody side,
Wan was his faire hewe, his woundes depe and wide.
In fyve stiddes of his fleisshe þe blode kan doun glide
As stremes done on þe stron[d]e; this peyn is nat to hide.
To þynke is gret pitte, how demed he is to deth,
And nailled on þe tre, þe bright angels brede.
Dryvyn he is to dele, þat is oure gostly good,
And fouled as a fole, in heuyn þe [halowes] food.
A wonder hit is to se, who-som vndrestood,
How God of mageste was deynge on þe roode.
Bot soth þan is hit said þat loue ledeth þe rynge:
Þat hym so low hath leyd bot loue hit was no thynge.

Ihesu, receyue my hert, and to þi [loue] me brynge;
Al my desire þou art, I couait þi comynge.
Thou mak me clene of syn, and let vs neuer twin.
Kyndel me fyre within, þat I þi loue may wyn,
And se þi face, Ihesu, in blis þat neuer may blyn.
Ihesu, my soule þou mend; þi loue in to me send,
þat I may with þe lend in ioy withouten end.
In loue þou wound my thoght, and lift my hert to þe;
þe soul þat þou haste boght, þi louer make to be.
Bot þe I couait nat; þis world for þ[e] I fle.
þou art þat I haue soght; thy face when may I se?
Thou make my soule clere, for loue þat chaungeth chere.
How longe shal I be here? When may I cum þe nere
Thi melody for to hire?
Of loue to hyre þe songe þat is lestynge so longe?
Wil thou be my louynge, þat I þi loue may synge?

If þou wil þynke þis euery day, þou shalt fynd gret swetnesse, | þat shal draw þi hert vp, and mak þe fal in wepynge and in grete langynge to Ihesu; and þi þoght shal be reft abouen al erthly þynges, abouen þe sky and þe sterres, so þat þe egh of þi hert may loke in to heuyn. f. 46v

And þan entres þou in to þe þrid degre of loue, in þe whiche þou shalt be in gret delite and confort, if þou may get grace to cum þerto. For I say nat þat þou, or another þat redeth þis, shal do hit al, for þat is in Goddis wille, þat cheseth whom he wil to do þat here is said, or other thynge in oþer maner, as he gifeth men grace to har hele. For dyuers men taketh dyuers yiftes of our lord Ihesu Criste; and al þei shal be set in þe ioy of heuyn þat endeth in charite. Who-so is in þis degre, wisdome he hath, and discrecioun, to lyve at Goddis wille.

This degre of loue is cald contemplatif lif, þat loueth to be [onely] withouten ryngen or dyn and syngynge and criynge. At þe begynnynge, when þou comest thereto, þi goostly egh is taken vp in to þe light of heuyn, and þare enlumyned in grace and kyndlet of þe fyre of Cristes loue, so þat þou shal feel verraily þe brennynge of loue in þi herte, euermore lyftynge þi thoght to God, and fillynge þe ful of ioy and swetnesse, so myche þat no s[eke]nesse ne shame ne anguys ne penaunce may gref þe, bot al þi lif shal turne in to ioy. And þan for heynesse of þi hert, þi praiers turneth in to ioyful songe and þi þoghtes to melodi. þan Ihesu is al þi desire, al þi delit, al þi ioy, al þi solace, al þi comfort, so þat on hym wil euer be þi songe, and [in] hym al þi rest. þan may þou say 'I slepe and my hert waketh. Who shal to my leman say, for his loue me longeth ay?' Al þat loueth vanyteeȝ and specials of þis world, and setteth har hert on any other þynge þan on God, in to þis degre may þay nat cum, ne in to þe toþer degre of loue bifore named. Forþi al worldes solace þe behoueth forsake, þat þi hert be holdynge to no loue of any creature ne to any bisinesse of erth, þat þou may in silence be euer stabilly, and stalworthly in hert and mouth loue God.

Ful entierly þe behoueth gif þi hert to Ihesu, if þou wil cum to þis degre of loue. Fro þou be þerin, þou hast no nede afterward of no lykynge, of no liggynge, ne of bed, ne of worldes solace, bot euer þe wil list sit, þat þou be euer louynge thy Lord. In þis degre of loue þou wil
f.47r couait þe deth, and be ioyful when þou hirest | men name deth, for þat loue maketh þe as siker of heuyn when þou deyest as þou now art of deile, for þe fyre of loue hath brent away al þe roust of syn. And I wene, fro þou or I or anoþer be broght in to þis ioy of loue, we mow nat lyue longe after as oþer men doth, bot as we lyue in loue, also we shal dey in ioy, and passe to hym þat we haue loued. In þis degre of loue al drede, al sorow, al wo, al ydel ioy and al wicked delites is put fro vs, and we lyve in swetnesse of heuyn. Thynk euer to lest, and to be bettyr and better, and þat wil gif þe grace to loue hym as he doth another. Oure Lord yeueth nat to men and wommen fairhede, richesse and delites for to set har hertes þeron and dispend ham in syn, bot for þay shold knowe hym and loue hym and þanke hym of al his yiftes. Þe more is þar shame if þai wreth hym, þat he hath gyffen to ham many yiftes in body or in soule. Forþi, if we couait to fle þe peyn of helle and þe peyn of purgatorie, vs bihoueth restreyne vs perfitly fro þe lustes and þe lykynges and fro þe il delites and þe wicked drede of þis lif, and þat worldis sorowe be nat in vs, bot þat we hold al oure herte fast on Ihesu Criste, and stand manly agayns temptaciouns.

Now I write a songe of loue þat þou shalt haue delite jn w[hen] þou art louynge Ihesu Criste.

My songe is in seghynge, my lif is in langynge,
Til I þe se, my kynge, so faire in þi shynynge.
So faire in þi fairhede, in to þi light me lede,
And in þi loue me fede; in loue make me spede,
That þou be euer my mede.
When wil þou cum, Ihesu my ioy, and keuer me of kare,
And gyf me þe, þat I may se, hauynge for euer more?
Al my coueitynge ware comen, if I myght to þe fare;
I wil no þynge bot only þe, þat al my wilnes ware.

Ihesu my sauyour, Ihesu my confortour, of fairnesse þe floure,
My helpe and my sokour, when may I se þi toure?
When wil þou me kalle? Me langeth in to þi halle
To se þe and þyn alle. Thi loue let hit nat falle;
My hert peynteth þe palle þat stiddeth vs in stalle.
Now wax I pale and wan for loue of my leman.
Ihesu, both God and man, thi loue þou lered me þan
When I to þe fast ran; forþi now loue I can.
I sit and synge of| loue langynge þat in my brest is bred. f. 47v
Ihesu, Ihesu, Ihesu, why n[e] ware I til þe ledde?
Ful wel I wot þou sest my state; in loue my þoght is stedde;
When I þe se and dwel with þe, þan am I fild and fedde.
Ihesu, þi loue is feste, and me to loue þynketh best.
My hert, when may hit brest, to cum to þe, my rest?
Ihesu, Ihesu, Ihesu, to þe is þat I mourne;
Forþi, my lif and my lykynge, when may I hethen tourne?
Ihesu, my dere and my drery, delites art þou to synge;
Ihesu, my myrth, my melody, when wil þou cum, my kynge?
Ihesu, my hele and my hony, my quert, my confortynge,
Ihesu, I couait for to dey when hit is þi paynge.
Langynge is in me lent, þat my loue hath me sent.
Al wo fro me is went, sethen þat my hert is brent
In Criste loue so swete, þat neuer I wil lete,
Bot euer to loue I hete, for loue my bale may bete,
And to my blisse me brynge, and yif my desyrynge.
Ihesu, my loue swetynge,
Langynge is in me light, þat byndeth me day and nyght,
Til I hit haue in sight, his face so fay`e´re and bryght.
Ihesu, my hope and hele, my ioy euer euery dele,
þi loue let hit nat kele, þat I þi loue may fele,
And won with þe in wele.
Ihesu, with þe I bigge and belde; leuer me ware to deye
þan al þis world to weld and haue hit in maistry.
When wil þou rewe on me, Ihesu, þat I myght with þe be,
To loue and loke on þe? My sete ordayn for me,
And set þou me þerin, for þan [may] we neuer twyn,
And I þi loue shal synge þrogh syght in þy shynynge
In heuyn withouten endynge. Amen.

# III
# THE COMMANDMENT

The comandement of God is þat we loue oure Lord in al our hert, in al oure soule, in al oure thoght. In al oure hert: þat is in al our vndrestondynge, witouten errynge. In al our soule: þat is in al oure wille, withouten syggynge ayeyne. In al oure thoght: þat is þat we thynke on hym withouten foryetynge. In þis maner is verray loue and trewe, þat is werk of mannys wil; for loue is a wylful styrrynge of oure thoght in to God, so þat hit receyue no thynge þat is agayne þe loue of Ihesu Criste, and þerwith þat hit be lestynge in swetnesse of deuocioun. And þis is perfeccioun of þis lif, to þe whiche al dedly synnes ben contrarie and enemy, bot nat venyal synnes, for venyal syn doth nat away charite, bot only letteth þe vse and þe brennynge þerof. For[þi] al þat wil loue God perfitly, ham behoueth nat alonly flee al dedly synnes,
f.48r bot | also, as myche as þay may, al venyal synnes, in þoght, in word and dede, and namely [to] be of litel speche. And þat silence be in occupacioun of good thoghtes, hit helpeth gretly to Goddis loue; for ianglers and bacbiters, þat appeireth other mennes lif with wicked wordes, and al þat loueth har owne state bifor al oþer, or þat despiseth any state in þe which a man may be safe, þai haue no more sight of þe loue of God in har soule þan þe eigh of a bak hath of þe son. For vayn speche and il wordes ben signe of a veyn herte and il, þat is withouten grace of God; and he þat speketh euer þe good, and holdeth euery man better þan hym self, he sheweth wel þat he is stabile in goodnesse in his hert, and ful of charite to God and his neghbore.

And þat þou may wyn to þe swetnesse of Goddis loue, I set here þre degrees of loue, in þe which þou be euer wyxynge. The first degre is cald insuperabile, the toþer inseperabile, þe þrid synguler. Thi loue is insuperabile when no þynge may ouercum hyt; þat is neþer wel ne wo, ese ne anguys, loue of fleishe ne lykynge of þis world, bot euer hit lesteth in good thoght, if hit ware tempted gretly, and hit hateth al syn, so þat no thynge may quenche þat loue. Thi loue is inseperabile when al þi þoghtes and willes ben gedered togeddre and festned holely in Ihesu Criste, so þat þou may no tyme foryet hym, [bot euer þou þynkest on hym], and forþi hit is cald inseperabile, for hit may nat be departed fro þe þoght of Ihesu Crist. Thi loue is synguler when al þi delite is in Ihesu Crist, and in non oþer thynge fynd[eth] ioy and comfort. In þis degre is loue stalwarth as deth and hard as helle; for as deth sleth al lyvynge thynge in þis world, so perfit loue sleeth in a mannys soule al fleishly desyres and erthly coueitynge; and as helle spareth nat to dede men, bot tormenteth al þat cometh þerto, also a man þat is in þis degre of loue, nat only he forsaketh þe wreched solace of þis lif, bot also coueiteth [to suffre] pyne for Goddis loue.

Therfor, if þe list loue any þynge, loue Ihesu Criste, þat is þe fairest, rychest and wisest, whose loue lesteth in ioy endles. For al erthly loue is passynge, and witeth sone away; noght þat falleth þerto is dwellynge bot pyne þat hit deserueth. If þou be coueitouse after go[o]d, loue hym, and þou shalt haue al good. Desyre hym trewely, and þe shal want no thynge. If delites like þe, loue hym, for he yeueth delites to his louers þat | neuer may perisshe. Bot al þe delites of þis world ben feynt f.48v and fals and fallynge in most nede; þai begyn in swetnesse, and har endynge is bitterer þan galle. If þou can nat lyue withouten felewship, lift þi þoght to heuyn, þat þou may fele confort with angels and halowes, þe which wil helpe þe to God, and nat let þe as þi fleishly frendes dothe. Restreyne þi wille a while fro al lust and lykynge of syn, and þou shal haue aftreward al þi wille, for hit shal be clensed and mad so fre þat þe shal lust do no thynge bot þat is paynge to God. If þe list speke, forber hit as þ[e] begynnynge for Goddis loue, for when þi herte feleth delite in Crist, þe wil nat lust to spek ne iangle bot of Crist. If þou may nat dure to sit bi þin on, vse þe stalwarthly in [h]is loue, and he shal so stabilly set þe þat al þe solace of þis world shal nat mowe remeve þe, for þe wil nat list þerof.

When þou art by þyn on, be euer, til slepe cum, oþer in praier oþer in gode meditaciouns; and ordeyn þi praiynge and þi wakynge and þi fastynge þat hit be in discreccioun, nat ouer mych ne ouer litel. Bot þynke euer þat of al þynge most coueiteth God loue of mannys harte, and forþi seke more to loue hym þan to do any penaunce, for vnskylful penaunce is litel worth or noght, bot loue is euer þe best, wheþer þou do penaunce litel or mych. Be aboutward in þi myght þat þou ware so jnwardly gyfen to þe loue of Ihesu Crist þat, for gostly ioy of þi soule, noght þat men myght say or do mak þe sory, so þat þy þoght within be fed only in swetnesse of Cristes loue, nat in delite of erthly ese, in praysynge of men, if þay begyn to speke good of þe, ne in ydel ioy. Trist in God, þat he wil gif to þe þat þou praiest hym for skylfully. Skylful praier is, to Cristen mannys soule, to seche and aske nyght and day þe loue of Ihesu Criste, þat hit may loue hym verrayly, felynge comfort and delit in hym, outcastynge worldes þoghtes and il bisynesse. And syker be þou, if þou couait his loue trewly and lestyngly, so þat no loue of þi fleishe ne anguys of þe world ne speche ne hatreden of men draw þe agayn and cast þe nat in bisynesse of bodily þynges, þou shal haue his loue, and fynd and fele þat hit is delitabiler in an houre þan al welth þat we here se may til domys day.

And if þou faille and fal for temptaciouns or for angres or for ouer | [f.49r] myche loue of þi frendes, hit is no wonder if he hold fro þe þynge þat þou couaitest nat trewly. He saith þat he loueth ham þat loueth hym, and þay þat erly waketh to hym shal fynd hym. Thou art erly wakynge oft sithes: whi þan fyndes þou hym nat? Certes, if þou seke hym right, þou shalt fynd hym; bot euer whils þou sechest erthly ioy, þogh þou wake neuer so erly, Crist may þou nat fynd, for he is nat founden in har land þat lyveth in fleishly lustes. His moder, when he was willet fro hir, soght gretynge erly and late amonges his kynreden and hirs, bot sho fand hym nat, for al hir sechynge, til at þe last she come in to þe temple, and þer she fond hym sittynge amonges þe maistres, hyrynge and answarynge. So behoueth þe do if þou wil fynd hym: sek inwardly in trouth and hope and charite of holy chirche, castynge out al syn and hatynge hit in al þi hert, for þat holdeth hym fro þe, and letteth þe þat þou may nat fynd hym. The herdes þat soght hym fand hym liggynge in a crib bitwix two bestes; [by] þat þou knowe if þou seke hym verraily, þe behoueth go in to þe way of pouert and nat of riches. The sterre led þe þre kynges in to Bedleem; þer þay fond Crist swedled in cloutes sympilly as a pouer barne. Therby vndrestond, whils þou art in pride and vanyte, þou fyndest hym nat. How may þou for shame, þat art bot seruaunt, with many cloþes and riche folow þi spouse and þi lord, þat yed in a kyrtel, and þou trail as myche behynd þe as al þat he had on? Forþi I rede þat þou part with hym ar þou and he mete, þat he reproue þe nat of outrage, for he wil þat þou haue þat þou hast mestier of, and no more. He seid to his disciplesse þat þai shold nat haue two kyrtels: þat is þat oon shold nat haue as many cloþes as two myght be sustened with. For to trauaille þerabout is outrageous bisynesse þat he forbedeth.

The loue of Ihesu Crist is ful dere tresoure, ful delitable ioy, and ful syker to trust a man on. Forþi he wil nat gif hit to folis, þat can nat hold hit and kepe hit tendrely, bot to ham he gyfeth hit þe which, neþer for wel ne for wo, wil let hit passe fro ham, bot ar þay wold dey or þei wold wrath Ihesu Criste. And no wise man doth precious licour in a stynkynge vessel, bot in a clene; as Crist doth nat his loue in a foul herte in syn and bounden in vile lust of fleishe, bot in a hert þat is clene and faire in vertuȝ. Natforþi a foul vessel may be made clene, `so´ þat a ful der thynge sauely may be done þerin; and Ihesu Crist oft sith purgeth many synful mannys soul, and maketh hit abile, | þrogh his grace, to f.49v receyue þe delitable swetnesse of his loue, and to be his wonnyngested in holynesse. And euer þe clenner hit wixeth, þe mor ioy and solace of heuyn Crist setteth þerin; forþi, at þe first tyme when a man is turned to God, he may nat fele þat swet licour til he haue bene wel vsed in þe seruice of God, and his hert be purget þrogh prayers and penaunce and good thoghtes in God. For he þat is slowe in Goddis seruice may nat be brennynge in loue bot if he do al his myght and trauail, nyght and day, to fulfil Goddis wil. And whan þat blessed loue is in a mannys herte, hit wil nat suffre hym to be ydel, bot euer hit stirreth hym to do sum good þat myght be lykynge to God, as in prayinge, or in worchynge profitable þynge, or in spekynge of Ihesu Crist, and principali in þoght, þat þe mynd of Ihesu Criste passe neuer fro his thoght. For if þou loue hym trewly, þou wil glad þe in hym and nat in other þynge, and þou wil thynk on hym, kastynge away al other thoghtes. Bot if þou be fals, and tak oþer þan hym, and delite þe in erthly thynge agayns hys wil, witte þou wel, he wil forsake þe as þou dost hym, and dampne þe for þy syn.

Wherfor, þat þou may loue hym trewly, vndrestond þat his loue is proued in þre þynges: in thynkynge, in spekynge, and worchynge. Chaunge thy thoght fro þe world and cast hit holy on hym, and he shal nurisshe þe. Chaunge þi mouth fro [vnnayte] and wordys speche and spek of hym, and he shal confort the. Chaunge þi hand fro workes of vanytees and lift ham in his name, and wirche only for his loue, and he shal receyue þe. Do þus, and so þou louest trewly, and þou gost in þe way of perfitnes. Delit þe so in hym þat þi hert receyue noþer worldis ioy ne worldes sorowe, and dred nat anguys or noy þat may bifal bodily on þe or on any of þi frendes, bot bitake al in to Goddis wille, and thanke hym euer of al his sondes, so þat þou may haue reste and sauour in his loue. For if þi hert be led, oþer with worldes drede or worldis solace, þou art ful fe[r]re fro þe swettnesse of Cristes loue. And loke wel þat þou seme nat on withouten and be anoþer within, as ypocrites done, þe which ben like to a sepulcre þat is peynted richely withouten, and within reten stynk[ynge] bones. If þou haue delite in þe name of religioun, loke þat þou haue more delite in þe dede þat falleth to religioun. Þi habit seith þat þou hast forsaken þe world, þat þou art gyffen to Goddis seruyce, þat þou delite þe nat in erthly thynge. Loke þan þat hit be in þi hert as hit semeth in mennys sight, for no þynge may make þe religious bot vertuȝ and clennesse of soule in charitee. If þi body be cled withouten as þyn ordre wille, loke þat þi f. 50r soule | be nat naked within, þat þyn ordre forbedeth. Bot naked be þi soule fro al vices, and warm lapped in loue and mekenesse. Drede þe domes of God, so þat þou wreth hym nat. Stabil þi þoght in his loue, and hel out of þe al synnes. Kast away slownes. Vse þe manly in goodnesse. Be debonair and meke to al men. Let no þynge brynge þe in to ir or enuy. Dight þi soule faire; make þerin a toure of loue to Goddis sun, and mak þi wil be couaitous to receyue hym as gladly as þou wold be at þe comynge of a thynge þat þou loued most of al thynge. Wesshe þi þoght clene with loue teres and brennynge desire, þat he fynd no thynge foul in þe, for his ioy is when þou art faire and louesom in his eghen. Fairhede of þe soule, þat he couaiteth, that is to be chaste and meke and myld and suffrynge, neuer gurche to do his wille, euer hatynge al wikednesse. In al þat þou dost, thynke euer to cum to syght of his fairhede, and set al þyn entent þerin, þat þou may cum þerto at þyn endynge. For þat oght to be end of al our trauaille, þat we euermore, whils we lyve here, desyre þat sight in al oure hert, and þat vs þynke euer lange þerto. Also festyn in þi hert þe mynd of his passioun and of his woundes; gret delite and swetnesse shal þou fele if þou hold þi þoght in mynd of þe pyne þat Crist suffred for þe.

If þou trauaille right in his loue, and desyre hym brennyngly, a[lle] temptaciouns and dredes of il þou shalt ouercum and defoul vndre þi fete þrogh his grace. For al þat he seth in good wil to loue hym, he [hel]peth ham agayn al har enemys, and rereth har thoght abouen al erthly þynge, so þat þai may haue sauour and solace in þe swetnesse of heuyn. Pur[chace the] þe wel of gretynge, and sese nat til þou haue hym, for in þe hert where terys spryngeth, þer wil þe fyre of þe Holy Gost be kyndled; and seþen þe fyre of loue þat shal bren in þi hert wil bren to noght al þe roust of syn, and purge þi soule of al filth, as clene as þe gold þat is proued in þe fourneys. I wot no thynge þat so jnwardly shal take þi hert to couait Goddis loue, and to desyre þe ioy [of heuyn], and to despise þe vanytees of þis world, as stidfast þynkynge of þe mescheuous and greuous woundes and of þe deth of Ihesu Crist. Hit wil rer þi thoght abouen erthly lykynge, and make þi hert brennynge in Cristis loue, and pur[chace] in þi soule delitabilte and sauour of heuyn.

f. 50v Bot perauentur þou wil say 'I | may nat despise þe world. I may nat fynd in myn hert to pyne my body; and me behoueth loue my fleishly frendes, and take ease when hit cometh.' If þou be tempted with such þoghtes, I pray þe þat þou bethynke þe, fro þe begynnynge of þis world, whare þe worldes louers ben now, and whar þe louers ben of God. Certes, þei wer men and wommen as we ben, and ete and dranke and laghet; and þe wreches þat loued þis world toke ese to har body, and l[y]ued as ham lust in lykynge of har wicked wille, and lad har dayes in lust and delites; and in a poynt þai fel in to helle. Now þou may se þat þay ware greet folys and foul glotones, þat in a fewe yers wasted endles ioy þat was ordeyned for ham, if þai wold haue done penaunce for har synnes. Thou sest þat al þe richesse of þis world and delites passeth away and cometh to noght. Sothly, so doth al har louers, for no þynge may stand stabilly on a fals ground. Har bodies ben gefen to wormes in erthe, and har sowles to þe deuelys of helle. Bot al þat forsaketh þe pompe and þe vanyte of þis lif, and stond stalworthly agayns al temptaciouns, and ende[th] in þe loue of God, þai ben nowe in ioy, and hath þe heritage of heuyn, þare to won withouten end [restynge] in þe delites of Goddis syght, for here þay soght no more reste ne ese to har body þan þai had nede of.

O þynge I rede the, þat þou foryet nat his name Iesus, bo[t] þynke hit in þi hert, nyght and day, as þi special and þi dere tresour. Loue hit more þan þi lif. Rot hit in þi mynd. Loue Ihesu, for he made þe and boght þe ful dere. Gif þi hert to hym, for hit is [his] dette. Forþi set þi loue on his name Ihesu, þat is hele. Þer may no il þynge haue dwellynge in þe hert þer Ihesu is holdyn in mynd trewly, for hit chaseth deuylles, hit destrueth temptaciouns, and putteth away wicked dredes and vices, and clenseth þe þoght. Wh[o]-so loueth hit verrayly is ful of Goddis grace and vertuȝ, in gostly comfort in þis lif, and, when þei dey, þei ben taken vp in to þe ordres of angels, to see hym in endles ioy þat thay haue loued.

# IV
# DESIRE AND DELIGHT

Desyre and delit in Ihesu Criste, þat hath no thynge of worldis thoght, is wondreful, pure and fast. And þan is a man circumcised gostly, when al other bisynesse and effectuous thoghtes ben shorne away out f. 51r of his soule, þat he may haue | reste in Goddis loue, withouten taryynge of oþer þynge. The delite is wondreful when hit is so hegh that no þoght may reche thereto to brynge hit doune. Hit is pure when hit is blyndet with no thynge þat is contrarie þerto. And hit is faste when hit is certeyn and stabile, delitynge bi hit self.

Thre þynges make þe delite in God hegh. On is restregnynge of flesshly lust in compleccioun. Anoþer, destruynge or repressynge of il styrrynge and of temptacioun in wille. Þe þrid is kepynge of heighynge of þe hert in lightnynge of þe Holy Gost: þat he hold his hert vp fro al erthly thoght, þat he set non obstakle at þe comynge of Criste in to hym. Euery man þat coueiteth endles hele, be he bisi nyght and day to fulfil þis lare, or elles to Cristes loue may he nat wyn, for hit is heigh, and al þat hit dwelleth in hit lifteth aboue layry lustis and vile couaitise, and aboue al affectuouse thoghtys of any bodily thynge.

Two þynges maketh our delite pure. On is turnynge of þe sensualite to þe skylle, for when any is turned to delit of his fyve wittes, alson vnclennesse entreth in to his soule. Another is þat þe skyl mekely be vsed in gostly þynges, as in meditacioun and orisone and lokynge in holy bokes. Forþi þe delit þat noght hath of vnordynat styrrynge, and myche hath of heynesse in Crist, and in whiche þe sensualite is al turned to þe skyl, and þe skyl al set and vset to God, maketh a mannes soule in reste and sikernesse, and euer to dwelle in good hoope, and to be payed of al Goddis sondes withouten gurchynge and heuynesse of thoght.

# V
# GHOSTLY GLADNESS

Gostly gladnesse in Ihesu, and ioy in hert, with swetnesse in soule of þe sauour of heuyn in hope, is helth in to hele, and my lyf lendeth in loue, and lightsomnes vmlappeth my thoght. I dred nat þat me may wirch wo, so myche I wot of wele. Hit ware no wonder if dethe ware dere, þat I myght se hym þat I seke; bot now hit lengthes fro me, and me behoueth to lyve here til he wil me lese. List and lere of þis lare, and þe shal nat myslike. Loue maketh me to melle, and ioy maketh me jangle. Loke þou lede þi life in lightsomnes; and heuynesse, hold hit away. Sorynesse let nat sit with the, bot in gladnes in God euermore make þou þi glee.

# VI
# LYRICS

## (i)

Love is lif þat lesteth ay, þer hit in Crist is feste; f. 51v
Whan wel ne wo hit chaunge may, as written hath men wisest;
The nyght is turned in to day, the trauaille in to reste;
If þou wil loue as I þe say, thou may be with þe beste.

Love is þoght with gret desyre of a faire louynge;
Loue [I lyḳene] to a fyre, þat quenchen may no þynge;
Loue vs clenseth of our syn, loue our bot shal brynge,
Loue þe kynges hert may wyn, loue of ioy may synge.

The sete of loue is set ful hegh, for in to heuyn hit ran;
Me thynke þat hit in erth is slegh, þat maketh man pale and wan;
The bed of blisse hit goth ful negh, I tel þe as I can;
þegh vs þynke þe wey be dregh, loue co[u]pileth God and man.

Love is hottyre þan þe colle, love may non beswyke;
The flaume of loue who myght þolle, if hit ware euer ylike?
Loue vs couereth and maketh in quert and lifteth to heuyn-rike;
Loue rauyssheth Crist in to oure hert; I wot no lust hit lyke.

Lere to loue, if þou wil lyve when þou shal hethen fare.
Al þi þoght to hym thou yyve þat may hit kepe fro kare.
Loke þi hert fro hym nat twyn, þogh þou in wandr[eth] ware,
So þou may hym weld with wyn, and loue hym euermare.

Ihesu, þat me lif hath lent, in to þi loue me brynge;
Tak to þe al myn entent, þat þou be my desyrynge.
Wo fro me away ware went, and comyn my coueitynge,
If þat my soul had herd and hent þe songe of þi praysynge.

Thi loue is euer lestynge, fro þat we may hit fele;
Therin me make brennynge, þat no þynge may me kele.
My þoght take in þi hand and stabil hit euery dele,
That I be nat holdynge to loue þis worldis wele.

If I loue an erthly þynge, þat payeth to my wille,
And set my ioy and my likynge when hit may cum me tille,
I may me drede of departynge, þat wil be hote and ille,
For al my welth is bot wepynge when pyne my soul shal spil[le].

The ioy þat men hath sene is likened to þe haye,
That now is faire and grene, and now witynge away.
Such is þis world, I wene, and shal be to domys daye,
In trauaille and in tene, for fle no man hit may.

If þou loue in al þi þoght, and hate þe filth of syn,
And gif þi hert hym þat hit boght, þat he hit weld with wyn, f. 52r
As þi soul Crist hath soght, and þerof wold nat blyn,
So þou shal to blisse be broght, and heuyn won withjn.

The kynd of loue þis is, ther hit is trusty and trewe,
To stond in stablenesse and chaunge for no newe.
The lif þat loue myght fynd, or euer in hert hit knewe,
Fro kare turneth þat kynd, and le[n]d[eth] in myrth and glewe.

For þi loue þou, I rede, Crist, as I þe telle.
With aungels take þi stede; þat ioy loke þou nat sylle.
In erthe þou hate no quede bot þat þi loue myght fel[l]e;
For loue is stalwarth as dede, loue is hard as helle.

Love is a light birthyn, loue gladdeth yonge and olde;
Loue is withoutyn pyne, as louers haue me tolde;
Loue is a gostly wyne, þat maketh bigge and bolde;
Of loue no thynge shal tyne þat hit in hert wil holde.

Loue is þe swetest þynge þat man in erth hath tane;
Loue is Goddis derlynge; loue byndeth blode and bone.
In loue be our lyuynge, I wote no bettyre wone;
For me and my louynge, loue maketh both be one.

Bot flesshely loue shal fare as doth þe floure in Maye,
And lestynge be no mare than hit ware bot a daye;
And soroweth sethen ful sare har proudhede and har playe,
When þei ben casten in care til pyne þat lesteth aye.

When erth and ayre shal bren, þan may þay quake and drede,
And vp shal rise al men to answare for hare dede.

If þay ben seyn in syn, as now har lyf þai lede,
þay shal sit helle within, and derkenesse haue to mede.

Rich men har hand shal wrynge, and wicked werkes bye;
In flaume of fyre knyght and kynge with sorow and shame shal lye.
If þou wil loue, þan may þou synge to Crist in melodye;
The loue of hym ouercometh al þynge; in loue lyve we and dye.

Amen.

(ii)

Ihesu, Goddis son, Lord of mageste,
Send wil in to my hert only to couait þe;
Ref me likynge of þis world, my loue þat þou may be;
Take my hert in to þi way; set me in stabilte.

Ihesu, þe Maiden son, þat with þi blode me boghte,
Thirle my soule with þi spere, þat loue in me hath wroght.
Me langeth led me to þi light and festyn in þe my thoght;
In þi swetnesse fil my hert, my wo make wene to noght. f. 52v

Ihesu, my God, my Kynge, forsake nat my desyre;
My thoght make hit be meke, I haue bothe pride and jre.
Thi wil is my desyrynge, of loue kyndel þe fyre,
That I in swet louynge with angels tak my hyre.

Wownd my hert within, and weld hit at þi wille;
On blis þat neuer shal blyn þou make me fest my skylle.
That I þi loue may wyn, of grace my thoght þou fille,
And make me clene of syn, þat I may cum þe tille.

Root hit in my hert, þe memorie of þy pyne;
In sekenes and in quert þi loue be euer myne.
My ioy is al of þe, my soule tak hit as thyne;
My loue wixynge euer be, so þat hit neuer dwyne.

My songe is in sighynge, whils I dwel in þis waye;
My lif is in langynge, þat byndeth me nyght and daye
Til I cum to my kynge, þat I won with hym [m]aye,
And se his fayre shynynge in lif þat lesteth aye.

Langynge is in me lent, for loue þat I ne can lete;
My loue hit hath me sent, þat euery bale may bete.
Sethen þat my hert was brent in Cristis loue so swete,
Al wo fro me is went, and we shal neuer mete.

I sit and synge of loue-langynge, þat in my brest is bredde;
Ihesu, my kynge and my ioynge, why n[e] ware I til þe ledde?
Ful wel I wote in al my state in ioy I shold be fedde;
Ihesu, me brynge in to þi wonnynge, for blode þat þou shadde.

Demed was to henge þe faire angels foode;
Ful sore þei kan hym s[w]ynge when þat he bounden stoode;
His bake was in betynge, and spild his blessed bloode;
The þorne crowned þe kynge þat naked was on roode.

White was his naked breste, and reed his blody syde;
Wan was his faire face, his woundes depe and wyde.
Þe Iues wold nat wand to pyne hym þat tyde;
As stremes doth on strand, his blode can doune glide.

Blyndet ware his faire eyen, his fleisshe blody forbette;
His louesome lif was laid ful logh and sorowfully vmset.
Deth and lyf bigan to stryve wheþer myght maistry mare,
When aungels bred was dampned to deth to saue oure soules sare.

Lyf was slayn and risen anoon; in fairhed may we fare;
And deth broght to litel or noon, and kasten in endles kare.
He þat þe boght haue al þi þoght, and led þe in his lare;
Gif al þi hert to Crist, þi quert, and loue hym euermare.
Amen.

(iii)

I sigh and sob both day and nyght for on so faire of hewe. f. 53r
Ther is no thynge my hert may light, bot loue þat euer is newe.
Who-so had hym in his syght, or in his hert hym knewe,
His mournynge were turned in to bryght, his langynge in to glewe.

In myrth he lyveth nyght and day, þat loueth þat swet childe:
Hit is Ihesu, forsoth I say, of al mekest and mylde.

Wreth fro hym wil al away, þogh he ware neuer so wylde,
That in hert hym loued þat day, so stabil he is a [s]hilde.

Of Ihesu þan moste list me speke, þat al my bale may bete.
Me thynke my hert wil al to-breke when I þynke on þat swete.
In loue lacid he hath my thoght, þat I shal neuer forlete;
Ful dere me thynke he hath me boght with blody hond and feete.

For loue my hert b[ehou]eth to brest when I þat faire biholde.
Loue is faire þer hit is feste, þat neuer wil be colde.
Loue vs reveth þe nyghtes reste; in grace hit maketh vs bolde;
Of al werkes loue is þe beste, as holy men vs tolde.

No wonder þegh I seghynge be, and seþen in sorow be sette;
Ihesu was nayled vpon þe tre and al blody forbette.
To þynke on hym is grete pitte, how tendrely he grette;
This hath he suffred, man, for þe, if þat þou syn wil lette.

Thar is no l[if] in erth may telle of loue þe lest swetnesse;
That stidfastly in loue can dwelle, his ioy is endles.
God shild þat he shold euer to helle, þat loueth and langynge is,
Or euer his enemys hym shold quelle, or mak his l[oue] be lasse.

Ihesu is loue þat lesteth ay, to hym is our langynge.
Ihesu þe nyght turneth to day, þe ebbynge in to sprynge.
Ihesu, þynke on vs nowe and ay, for þe we hold oure kynge.
Ihesu, gif vs grace, as þou wel may, to loue without endynge.
Amen.

(iv)

Thy ioy be euery dele to serue þi God to paye;
For al [þis] worldis wele, þou sest hit wendeth awaye.
þou besy þe his loue to fele, þat lest wil with þe aye,
And þan þi care shal kele, and pyne turne þe to playe.

In Crist [þou] cast þi thoght, hate al wreth and pride,
And þynke how he þe boght with woundes depe and wide.
When þou hym self hast soght, wel þe shal betyde;
Of riches rech þou noght, fro helle þat he þe hyde.

Thay turne har day to nyght, þat loueth þis erthly syn,
And slayn ben in þat fyght þa[r] we our lyf shal wyn;
For þat þay loue vnryght, and þerof can nat blyn,
þay lese þe lond of light, and helle sytteth within. f. 53v

Thou do as I þe rede, liftynge vp þi hart,
And say to hym þat was dede: 'Crist, my hele þou art.'
Syn synketh as lede, an ferre falleth fro quert;
Forþi stabil þi stidde þa[r] smytynge may nat smert.

Lerne to loue þi kynge, wose loue euer wil leste;
Haue hym in þi þynkynge, and fest his loue so feste
That for non erthly thynge no quayntise may hit caste;
Thy songe and þi swetynge he wil be at þe laste.

In Crist couait solace, his loue chaungeth þi chere;
With ioy thou take his trace, and seigh to s[it] hym nere.
Euer sechynge his face, thou make þi soul clere;
He ordeyneth hegh þi place, if þou his l[oue] wil lere.

Thou kepe his biddynges ten; hold þe fro dedly syn;
Forsak þe ioy of men, þat þou his loue may wyn.
Thy hert of hym shal bren, your l[oue] shal neuer twyn;
Langynge he wil þe len to won heuyn within.

Thou þynke on his mekenes, how pouer þat he was borne;
Bihold his blody fleisshe: his heed priketh þe þorne.
Thi loue, let hit nat lesse; he saued þe forlorne;
To serue hym in swetnesse al þan haue we sworne.

Festyn þi hert to fle al þi worldis care,
That þou in rest may be; þou saue þi soul sare.
[His] loue take in to þe, and loue hym more and mare,
His face þat þou may se when þou shal hethen fare.

If þou be in fandynge, of loue þou hast grete nede
To stid þe in stabilynge, and gif þe grace to spede.
Thou dwel euer with þi kynge, and in his loue þe fede,
F[or] litel I haue connynge to tel of his fairhede.

Bot loue hym to þi myght, whils þou art lyvynge here,
And loke vp to that sight, þat non be þe so dere.

Say to hym day and nyght: 'When may I negh þe nere?
Wisse me to þi right, thi melody for to hire.'

In þat lif þe sted, þat þou be euer l[y]uynge,
And gif hym loue to wedde þat þou wil with hym stand.
Ioy in þi brest is brede, when þou art hym louynge;
Thi soul þa[n] he hath fedde, in swet loue brennynge.

Alle vanytees forsake, if þou his loue wil fele;
Thi hert þou hym bitake, he can hit kepe so welle; f. 54r
Thy myrth may no man make, of God is euery dele;
Thi þoght let hit nat quake; thi loue let hit nat kele.

Of syn þe bitternesse, þou fle euer fast þerfroo;
This worldis wickednesse, lok hit nat with þe goo;
This erthly bisynesse, that hath men wirched woo,
Thi loue hit wil make lasse, if þou hit til the too.

Al we loue sum þynge, þat knowynge hath of skylle,
And hath þerin lykynge, when hit may cum vs tille;
Forþi do Cristis biddynge, and loue hym as he wille,
Whose loue hath non endynge, in ioy withouten ille.

Thay þat louen fleishely ben likned to þe swyne
In filth þat let ham ly; thar fairhede wil þay tyne;
Har loue parteth porely, and put hit i[s] to pyne;
Swetter is loue gostely, that neuer more may dwyne.

If þou loue, whils þou may, the kynge of mageste,
Thi woo wendeth away, thi hele hegheth to þe,
Thi nyght turneth to day, þi blisse mow euer be;
When þou art as I say, I pray þe thynke on me.

Our þoght shal [w]e sette togedyre in heuyn to dwelle,
For þer þe good ben mett, that Crist holdeth fro helle.
When we our syn han grette, þe tythynge may we telle
That we fro ferre hath fette the loue þat non shal felle.

The world, cast hit behynd, and say 'Ihesu, my swete,
Fast in þi loue me bynd, and gyf me grace to grete.
To loue þe turne my kynd, for euer to loue I hete,
That I þi loue may fynd, that wel my bale may bete.

Of loue wound me within, and to þi light me lede.
Thou make me clene of syn, that I þe deth [n]a[t] drede.
Als þou to saue mankynde suffered þi side to blede,
Gif me wit to wyn the sight of þe to mede.'

His loue is tristy and trewe, who-so hym louynge ware.
Sen first þat I hit knewe, hyt keped me fro kare.
I fond hit euer newe to ler me Goddis lare,
And now dar me nat rewe þat I had suffred sare.

In loue þi hert þou hegh, and fight to fel þe fende;
Thi day shal be vndregh, that þe no sorow shende.
When þi deth negheth negh, and þou shalt hethen wende,
Thou shal se hym with eigh, and cum to Crist, þi frende. f. 54v

Afforce þe for to feste in Crist þi couaitynge;
Thou chese hym for þe beste, he is þi wedded kynge.
For ioy þi hert bo[s] breste to haue such a swetynge;
Of al I hold hit worst to loue another thynge.

His loue is lif of al that wel lyuynge may be;
Thou stid hym in þi stalle, let hym nat fro þe fle.
For sone he wil þe calle, thi sete is make to þe,
And haue þe in his halle, euer his face to se.

This mede for þi I say, þat þou kyndel þi þoght,
And make þi loue verray in hym þat þe hath wroght.
For al `þat´ loue hym may, bot þat þay wil hit noght,
To pyne turneth her play: that sorow ham self hath soght.

Syn, þat is so sowir, gif hit in þe no grith.
Of loue take þe þe floure, þat þou may laike þe with;
Swetter is þe sauour than of þe feld or frith.
Set hym in þi sokour that lecheth þe lym and lyth.

Tak Ihesu in þi þynkynge, his loue he wil þe send;
Thy loue and þi lykynge, in hym þou let hit lend.
Avise þe in praynge, tharin þou may þe mend,
And þou shal loue þi kynge i[n] ioy withouten end.

Amen.

(v)

Al synnes shal þou hate throgh kastynge of skylle,
And desyre to go in þe gate þat is withouten ille.
Toumble nat fro þe state þat þou hast tane þe tille;
Hit ledeth to þe kynges yate, thar þou may layke þi fille.

Here if þou punysshe þe, welth shal þou wyn.
No wondre hit is if þou be in sorowe for þi syn.
Sum seith þay may se, and blynd beth withjn;
And if þay nowe be set fre, the deth shal ham twyn.

Deth beteth al so sore þat non may defend,
And maketh many il to fare, when þay nat wend.
I wot non þat he wil spare; with al wil he lend.
Forþi of syn make þe bare; þou knowest nat þi end.

Now may we quake tremblynge, for dred to low lye.
The beme bloweth at our hand, the dome is fast bye.
The kynge cometh with his hoste for to fel his enemye,
And al þe proud with har boste he demeth to deye.

Me þynke hit ryngeth in myn ere: 'Ded men, rise to be demed!'
Bot hym þe deuyl may nothynge dere, that here hath Crist quem[ed].
Al þe wicked in þat were to helle fyre is flemed; f. 55r
The kynge hym self shot þe spere, for hym hit best semed.

That day our ioy shal bigyn, that here suffreth pyne;
Our fleisshe witte of mychel wyn, and bryght as sone shyne.
Our setys heuyn ben wythin, me list sit in myn;
Loue Crist and hate syn, and so pur[chace] thyne.
Amen.

(vi)

Who-so seith þis with good wille
Shal fynd grace his loue to fille;
The Holy Gost his hert shal tille,
From synn hym brynge, and fendis ille.

st. 1 Ihesu swet, nowe wil I synge
To the a songe of loue-langynge.

Do `in´ my hert a wel to sprynge,
The to loue ouer al thynge.

2 Ihesu swet, kynge of blisse,
My hert loue, my hert lysse,
In loue, Lord, þou me wisse,
And let me neuer þi loue to mysse.

3 Ihesu swet, my hert light,
þou art day withouten nyght;
Gyf me both grace and myght
For to loue þe aright.

4 Ihesu swet, my sowl bote,
In my hert þou set a rote
Of þi loue þat is so [sw]ote,
And wet hit þat hit grow mote.

5 Ihesu swete, my herte gleme,
Brighter þan þe son-beme,
As þou was borne in Bethleeme,
þou make in me þi loue dreme.

6 Ihesu, no songe may be swetter,
Ne thoght in hert blestfuller,
Noght may be f[e]led lightfuller
Than þou, so swete a louer.

7 Ihesu, þi loue was vs so fre
þat hit fro heuyn broght the;
For loue þou dere boght me,
For loue thou honge on rod tre.

8 Ihesu, to thi disciples dere
þou seidest with ful drery chere,
Als þei setten al in fere
A while or thou taken were,

9 Ihesu, þou saidest þat þou were
Ful of sorowe and of hert sore,
And bad ham dwel a while þore
Whil þou besoghtest þi fader ore.

10 Ihesu, þou went vpon þi fete
To þe mount of Olyuete,
And to þi fadyr or [þou] lete
þou mad a prayer with hert swete.

11 Ihesu, þou saidest 'If hit may be,
Dere fader, I pray to the,
þis peyn passe away fro me;
As þou wil, so mot hit be.'

12 Ihesu, þou torn[ed]est to hem than,
And fond ham slepynge, euery man.
þou bad ham wake or þou bla[n];
Anon ayeyn þe `way´ þou name.

13 Ihesu, after, þe self bone
þat þou w[e]nt for to done,
And als þ[e] þrid tyme sone
þou madest, with a myld mone.

14 Ihesu, for loue þou suffr[ed]est wronge,
Woundes sore and peynes stronge;
þi peyn rewful was full longe,
Ne may hit telle tunge nor songe.

15 Ihesu, þou soffr[ed]est for loue so wo
þat blody stremys yow [ran] fro;
þi white body was blak and blo,
Our synnes hit made, w[ailaw]o.

16 Mary modyre, myld quene,
Send grace syn to fleen,
That we may þy son seen
And euer with hym in blys to bene.

17 Ihesu, swet is þe loue of þe,
þer may no thynge so swet be;
Noght þat man may þynke or se,
þay hath no [s]w[e]tnes agayns þe.

18 Ihesu lord, þi loue is swete,
Wo is hym þat hit shal lete;

Gyf me grace for to grete
For my synnes teres wete.

19 Ihesu swet, kynge of londe,
Make me to vndrestonde,
þat I may with hert fonde
Howe swete [is þ]i loue bond.

20 Ihesu dere, me reweth sore f. 55v
Of my mysdedes I haue done yore;
Foryeve me, Lord, I wil no more,
Bot I þe aske m[ercy] and ore.

21 Ihesu good, lord myne,
My l[if], my soule, is al thyne;
Vndo myn hert and lyth þerjnne
And saue me fro wicked engyne.

22 Ihesu swete, lord goode,
For me þou shedest þi hert blode;
Out of þi hert come a flode,
Thi modyr hit sawe with drery mode.

23 Ihesu swete, bryght and shene,
Hyre me, Lord, for I me mene
For Mary praier, myld quene,
þat þi loue be on me sene.

24 Ihesu swete, my soule fode,
Al þi werkes ben ful goode;
Thou boght vs on þe roode
And sheddest þeron þi hert bloode.

25 Ihesu lord, [c]h[i]ld beste,
þi loue in my hert feste;
Whan I go south or weste
In þe alon fynd I reste.

26 Ihesu swet, wel may hym be
þat þe shal in þi ioy se;
With loue cordes draw þou me
þat I may come and be with the.

27 Mary modyre, lady bright,
þou darest, þou wilt, þou art of myght;
My hert loue, my lif, my light,
þou be my help both day and nyȝt.

28 Ihesu, þi corone sat ful sore,
The scornynge when þou betten wore;
Hit was for me, Ihesu, þin ore,
þe peynes þat þou soffr[ed]est þore.

29 Ihesu swete, þou henge on tre,
Nat for þi gilt bot for me,
For synnes þat I did agayns þe:
Swet Ihesu, foryeve þou me.

30 Ihesu, when þou streyned wore,
Thy peynes wexed more and more;
Thy modyr euer with þe was thore
With sorowful sekynge and hert sore.

31 Ihesu, whi were þou peyned so
And neuer wroghtest wronge ne wo?
Hit was for me and many moo
þat þou so herd were begoo.

32 Ihesu, what sawe þou in me
Of oght þat nedeful was to þe,
þat þou so herd on rode tre
Woldest for me peyned be?

33 Ihesu, whi were þou so gelus,
So feruent and so curious,
To by with price so precious
Wreched man so vicious?

34 Ihesu, for vs þou hange on rode,
For loue þou yaue þi herte blode;
Loue the made oure sowle fode;
þi loue vs broght to al goode.

35 Ihesu, my leman, þou art so fre
þat al þou did for loue of me.

What shal I for that yeld þe?
Noght bot loue thou kepest of me.

36 Ihesu, my god, my lord, my kynge,
þou me askest non other thynge
Bot trew hert in loue-longynge
And loue teris with stil mournynge.

37 Ihesu dere, my loue, my [light],
I wil þe loue and þat is right;
Do me the loue with al my myght,
And for þe mourne both day and nyght.

38 Ihesu, do me so loue the
þat my þoght euer on þe be;
With þy eighen loke on me
And [mildely my nede þou] se.

39 Ihesu, þi loue is al my thoght;
Of oþer þynge reche I noght
Bot þat I haue agayn þe wroght,
And þat þou hast me so dere j-boght.

40 Ihesu, þogh I synful be,
Full longe hast þou spared me;
þe more owe I to loue the
þat þou with me hast ben so fre.

41 Mary myld, fre and gent,
Pray for me, þou art present,
þat whan my soul is fro me we[nt]
þat hit haue good jugement.

42 Ihesu, forsoth, now is no thynge
In al þis world of such lykynge,
þat can so myche of loue-longynge,
As þou, Ihesu, my dere kynge.

43 Ihesu, wel ow I to loue the, f. 56r
For þou shewedest þi rod tre,
þi corone of þorne and naylles þre,
þe sharp speer þat to hert stonge þe.

44 Ihesu, of loue I se tokenynge,
þi armes spred to loue clippynge,
Thi hede bowed to swet kyssynge,
þi side al open to loue showynge.

45 Ihesu, euer when I þynke on the
And lok vpon þi rode tre,
þi swet ymage blody I se:
Lord, do þat sith to wound me.

46 Ihesu, þi modyr, þat bi þe stoode,
Of loue teres she lete a flode;
Thy woundes and þi holy bloode
Hyre made a ful drery mode.

47 Ihesu, loue þe dede to grete,
Loue þe dede þi blode to swete;
For loue þou were sore bete,
Loue þe dede lyf to lete.

48 Ihesu, þi loue þou teched me
With swet wordes of hert fre
þat þou spake on rode tre:
So ful of loue may non be.

49 Ihesu, þe first was, as I rede,
That þou þi dere fader bede
þat [he] foryeve ham har mysdede,
Al þat deden þe to dede.

50 Ihesu, þat oþer was, j-wisse,
þat þou saidest, as written is,
þat þe thef shold haue blisse
With þe þat day in paradisse.

51 Ihesu, þe þrid was of mone
Whan þi moder shold fro þe gone;
A sone þou betoke hir one,
And seid 'Womman, take here Iohn.'

52 Ihesu, as þou were peyned more,
þe firth word þou seidest þore:

'A' quod þou 'me þursteth sore':
Hit was for ham þat dampned wore.

53 Ihesu, þe fift rewe[th] me
þat þou saidest on rode tre:
'My God, my God, how may þis be
þat þou hast forsaken me?'

54 Ihesu, þe six word was
Whan þou seidest 'In manus tuas.'
þou betoke þi fadyre in þat place
þi soule, as his wil was.

55 Ihesu, in þi peyne meste
Neuer was so meke a beste;
þou saidest 'Consummatum est.'
þi hede fel doun, þou yelded þe goste.

56 Mary, þat slakest al wo,
[He]l peyns þou shild me fro,
And yif me grace here so to do
þat I fro hen to heuyn mot go.

57 Ihesu, þou saidest 'Al ye
þat gone in þe way by me,
Abide, and cum and se
If any peyn be like me.'

58 Ihesu, þou seidest 'Tel me,
Mi dere folke, what may hit be,
What haue I gilt agayns þe
þat þou so bitter art to me?'

59 Ihesu, [þou] saidest þan more:
'My dere folk, tel me yore,
Haue I with my holy lore
And with good dedes hert yow sore?'

60 Ihesu, þou saidest after yite:
'My dere vynyard I þe sete;
My fader blisse I þe hete,
And I my self; what wil þou bette?'

61 Ihesu, þou saidest 'How is þis?
My swete, what haue I do amisse
þat þou, withouten any lisse,
Yeldest me [peyn] ayeyn blisse?'

62 Ihesu, fyve wellys fynd I in the
þat to loue sprynge drawen me;
Of rede blode þi stremes be:
My soule euer wosshen he.

63 Ihesu, my soule euer draw þe to,
Make my hert wyde vndo;
Yif hit þi loue to drynke so
þat fleishely lustes be fordo.

64 Ihesu, mych I owe to þe; f. 56v
Who shal hit yeld wold I se;
Me behoueth my self to be,
As þou peynes suffred for me.

65 Ihesu, þi loue gif me fullyche
þat in my hert ground hit stik;
My soule hit pershe jnwardliche
þat I be þyn entierlyche.

66 Ihesu, do me loue þe so
þat whar I be and what I do
þat [I] for wel ne for wo
Neuer let my hert turne þe fro.

67 Mary swete, mayden fre,
For Ihesu Crist besech I the:
Thy swet sone do loue me,
And mak me with hym to be.

68 Ihesu, my lord swetynge,
Hold me euer in þi kepynge;
Make of me þi derlynge
þat I þe loue ouer al þynge.

69 Ihesu, my wel and al my wynne,
Al my ioy is þe withjnne;

Nowe and euer kepe me fro syn;
To do þi wille let me nat blyn.

70 Ihesu, myghtful heuyn kynge,
þi loue be al my lykynge,
My mournynge and my longynge,
With swet teres to þe gretynge.

71 Ihesu, yeve me for þi name
Paciens in peyne and shame,
þat to my soule hit be as game,
And make my hert myld and tame.

72 Mary, I pray þe as þou art fre,
Of þy sorowes part with me,
þat I may sorow here with þe,
And a partener of þy blis to be.

73 Ihesu, al þ[at] is fair to se,
þat to fleisshly likynge may be,
Al worldis blisse, do me fle,
And al my tent yeve to þe.

74 Ihesu, in þe be al my thoght,
Of oþer þynge ne rech I noght;
When I of þe may fele oght
þan is my soul wel besoght.

75 Ihesu, if þou forlet me,
What may I lyke of þat I se?
Blisse ne may with me be
Til þou cum ayayn to me.

76 Ihesu, þou hast me dere boght;
Al þat [to] syn draweth oght
I holy put hit out of my þoght,
So þat I wrath þe noght.

77 Ihesu, my soule is spoused to þe,
With right [h]i[t] owet þyn owen to be;
þogh I haue synned agayns þe,
þi mercy is euer redy to me.

78 Ihesu, þi mercy by leue I craue;
Me behoueth þe to haue;
The dewe of grace vpon me laue
And worþi me make þi loue to haue.

79 Ihesu, þou be al my yernynge;
In þe, Lord, be al my lykynge,
My þoght, my dede and my mournynge,
To haue þe euer in loue-langynge.

80 Ihesu, my loue, of myld mode,
My soul hath nede of þi good;
Mak hit clene and [þ]ol[e]mode
And f[u]lled of þi loue blode.

81 Ihesu, my soul pr[ay]eth þe,
Let hit nat vncloþet be,
Cloth [hit] with þi loue so fre,
With good werkes þat liken þe.

82 Ihesu, fairnes ask I noght,
Ne proud cloþes nobily wroght,
Broches ne rynges dere j-boght,
Bot hert loue and clene þoght.

83 Ihesu, whan so hit liketh þe,
Loue sparkles þou send me;
Make my hert al hote to be,
Brennynge in þe loue of þe.

84 Ihesu almyghty, heuyn kynge,
Thy loue is a ful derne þynge;
May no man hit fele þrogh techyng[e]
Bot if he hit fele þrogh þynkynge.

85 Ihesu, gif me þat I may se
þe gret godnes þou hast done me,
And I vnkynd agayn the:
Foryeve me, Lord, þat art so fre.

86 Ihesu, þi loue and flesshly þoght
Won togeddre þay may noght; f. 58r

As hony and galle togeddre broght
Swet and bittyr accorden noght.

87 Ihesu, with hert I thanke þe;
þogh I wreched and synful be,
In trew hope I pray to the
þi blisse and mercy þou graunt to me.

88 Ihesu, þogh I be vnworþi
The to loue, Lord almyghty,
þi godenes me make hardy
My soule to do in þi mercy.

89 Ihesu, þy mercy conforteth me,
For non may so synful be
þat syn wil leue and to þe fle,
þat mercy ne fyndeth he.

90 Ihesu, for synful, as written is,
þou come out of þi hegh blisse
In to Mary wombe, j-wisse,
To yif vs al rest and lisse.

91 Ihesu, þogh I synful be,
[I] haue euer truste in the;
Der Lord, I pray the
þat of my synnys þou mend me.

92 Ihesu, þat art so good a man,
þi loue desyr I as I can;
Me to let, suffre [n]an,
Swet Ihesu, my dere leman.

93 Ihesu, euer beseche I the
þi jnward loue þou graunt me;
þogh I þerto vnworthi be,
þou mak me [worthy], þou art so fre.

94 Ihesu swet, þou art so good,
Do þi loue drynk my hert blode;
þi loue me make swith wood
þat wonder blesful is my food.

95 Ihesu, mak me do þi wille
Now and euer, loud and stylle;
With þi loue my soul fulfille
And suffre þat I do nat ille.

96 Ihesu, þi loue is hote and stronge,
My lif is al þeron longe;
Tech me, Lord, þi loue songe
With swet teris euer amonge.

97 Ihesu, if þou fro me go,
My hert is ful of sorow and wo;
What may I say bot 'Wailawo'
Whan þou art gone me fro?

98 Mary, þy son pray hertily
For me, wreche and vnworþy,
þat he þynk on me j[n]wardly;
Graunt me to come to his mercy.

99 Ihesu, þyn ore, þou rew on me;
Whan shal my soul cum to þe?
How longe shal hit here be,
þer I ne may þe, my lemman, se?

100 Ihesu, þi lore þou teche me
With al my hert to loue þe;
With þi myght mak hit so be,
And þerto, Lord, constrayn þou me.

101 Ihesu, my lef, my lord, my kynge,
To þe my soule hath gret longynge;
þou hast hit weddit with þi rynge;
Whan þi wil is, to þe hit brynge.

102 Ihesu, þat dere boghtest me,
Make me worthy to cum to þe;
Al my synnes forgyf þou me
þat I may come and dwel with þe.

103 Ihesu fayre, my lemmon bryght,
I þe pray with hert of myght:

Brynge my sowle in to þi light
Þer is day withouten nyght.

104 Ihesu, þi help at my endynge;
Take my soul at myn [dei]ynge;
Send hit socour and confortynge
Þat hit drede no wicked þynge.

105 Ihesu, for þi mercy fre,
In siker h[o]pe þou help me
To scap peyn and bid with þe,
And euer in blisse with þe to be.

106 Ihesu, Ihesu, blessed is he
Þat in þi ioy þe shal se,
And haue fully þe loue of þe:
Swet Ihesu, þou graunt me.

107 Ihesu, þi blisse hath no endynge;
Þer is no sorow nor gretynge,
Bot pitte and ioy with gret lykynge:
Swet Ihesu, þerto vs brynge.

Amen.

# VII
# MEDITATION A

[f. 121r] [In the honour of the gloriouse passioun of oure lord Ihesu Crist, and his blissede moder Seint Marie, and Seint Iohn the euaungeliste, and Seint Marie Magdalene, Seint Michael, and of my holy aungel, and of alle the halowes of heuene, Pater noster, Aue Maria.

Umbithinke the of the grete loue of oure lord Ihesu Crist, how he wolde comme doun from heuene til erthe, and take flesche and blode in oure lady, Seinte Marie, for the and for al mankynde. Domine, non secundum peccata nostra facias nobis, neque secundum iniquitates | f. 121v nostras retribuas nobis. Adiuua nos, deus salutaris noster, et propter gloriam nominis tui libera nos, et propicius esto peccatis nostris propter nomen tuum. Te laudo, te adoro, te glorifico, tibi gracias ago, domine Ihesu criste, qui me precioso sanguine tuo redimere voluisti. Pater noster.

Thinke than of the grete louyng that holy chirche made at his birthe, that is at Ȝoole. Sithen of New Ȝere day, when his flesche was schorene away for loue of man. Sithen of Twelftday, how the kynges with grete worschipe made thaire offryng. Also on Candelmesday what worschipe was doun vntil hym, and how mekeli he wolde ben offred in to þe temple. Sithen how he satte among the doctours and preched and teche[d] commandementis. Sethen how mekely he wolde be baptisede f. 122r of his disciple. Sithen how mercy|fulli he prechede mercy and ȝaue til alle hem that wolde aske it. Sythen how mercyfully he helid alle that wolde be hole, bothe blynde, halt, and lame. Sithen what meschief he suffred, that is hungur, thriste and colde, and many hooge reproeues, so many that no tounge may telle ne hert thinke. [A]ue Ihesu, rex celorum, fili regis angelorum. O Ihesu, flos omnium salus in te sperancium, sume preces petencium, Ihesu redemptor omnium.

Lifte vp thin hert and thinke on that feste that he made to his disciples bifore his passioun. Sithen how mekely he wisshe his disciples feete and kissed hem. Sithen of the grete loue that he schewed when he lefte his precious body in erthe in tokenyng that we f. 122v schulde be in him and he in vs. Sithen how he tauȝt his disciples | to be in loue and charite and kepe commandementis; that was when he saide 'In that schalle alle men knowe that ȝe er my disciples, ȝif ȝe kepe my commaundementis and ilkone of ȝow loue other.' Sithen how mekel[i] and how lowly Iesus prayde to his fader. Sithen how efte he prayed and bitauȝte his moder and his disciples to his [fader] for to kepe. Sithen how he come to his disciples and fonde hem slepyng, and asked hem ȝif thay miȝt nouȝt wake an houre with him. Sithen how efte he praide, and than, for anguisse of the payn that he wist that he schulde suffre, þe blode dropped doun to erthe as swete doth on men for grete trauaile. And than Seint Michel comme from his fader and saide 'Lord Ihesu, I and al the fayre felauschepe of aungels haue offerd ȝoure swete blode to ȝoure fader | and praied for ȝow, and he sayde f. 123r "My sone Iesus [w]ote wele that mannes soule bihoueth to be bouȝt with schedyng of blode, and ȝif he wille the hele of mannes soule that we haue ay tendrely louede, him behoueth to dye."' Than this der-worthi lord answered, and saide a worde of grete loue that was 'Hele of mannes soule wille I on al wise, therfore I shal titter chese for to dye in that mannes soule be sauede, than I shal chese for to eschape it and mannes soule be perist. And therfore nouȝt my wille but my fadris be done.' Than Michel comforted oure lord and saide 'Be of goode com-fort, dere lord Ihesu,' he sayde, 'for it falleth to him that is grete to suffre gret thinges, but soone thilke gret peynes schal be gone, and after shal ioye comme withowten ende.'

Sythen how mekeli he toke þis | comfort of his disciple, and sithen f. 123v how he come to his disciples and bad hem slepe and rest, and sithen how he come to hem and bad hem rise and wake, and sithen how he met Iudas þat traitour, and sayde 'Frende, warto commes thou?' and mekely kissed him. And sithen how he met the grete oste of Iewis and asked hem whom þei souȝte, and thei saide 'Ihesu of Nazareth', and he sayde 'I am he', and thei for ferde felle alle adoun to the grounde. Here may thou wele see that thei miȝt not do til him but his owne wille. And sithen after, when it was his wille, thei toke him and bonde his hondis behinde him tille the blode out brast at ilka fynger ende. Sethen how þei ledde him to Anna house, and of this byndyng wi[ss]e the first. When his hondis were ybounden, thei fest a rope a|boute his f. 124r neke and an othere aboute his myddel, and so thei led him, and sum come bifore, and sum behynde and donge him, and sum for hurtyng of here hondes toke stones in here hondes and smote him on the heued and on the bake and where thei miȝt hitte him. And sithen how thei spitten in his face so that thei made [him] like a lepre. And sithen how thei lede him to Caifas house, and sethen how thei hid his eiȝen, and smote him vpon the hede that it was bolned as an ouene kake, and tugge[d] vp þe heer bi the rootes. Sithen how Iesus bihilde Petir

denyande him, and Petir than ȝede forthe and wepte ful sore. Sithen
how thai drouȝe him to prisone. I wille telle the how þei prisoned him.
Thei brouȝt him in to an house that was paued with stone, and bonde
f. 124v him by the nek and by the myddel, | for Iudas bad hem lede him warly
'For ȝif he wille' he saide 'he may go from ȝow.' And also thei lefte
thefes to turment him and bete him in the prisone. Than say this
psalme 'Miserere mei, deus, secundum magnam misericordiam
tuam', and say to the ende, and this orisoun 'Absolue, quesumus
domine, animas famulorum famularumque tuarum.'

Umbethinke the than how [thei] toke him oute [fro] prisone, and
bonde his hondes behinde him that the blode brest oute at the nales,
and sithen how thei led him to Pilat, and sethen how thei accused him
bifore Pilat, and he stode as a lombe and answered no worde. Sithen
how thei sente him to Herode. Sithen how mekeli he stode tofore
H[e]rode. Sithen how Herode sente aȝein and saide he was but a
foole. Sithen how thei naked him. Sithen how thei led him to a piler
f. 125r and bonde | him. Sithen how thei scourged him that fro the hede to the
feete thei lefte nouȝt hole on him. Sithen how thei corouned him with
thornes, that on ilka side of the skynne the blode oute brest. Sithen
how thei led him and kest doune a roughe clothe, and bad him done it
vpon him, and mekely as a lombe he toke it up and dide it upon him.
Sithen how thai demed him vnto the deth. Sithen how mekeli he bare
the crosse. Sithen what sorowe comme to his herte when he sawe his
moder; what for sorowe and what for angwise of his peyne he felle
doun, and the crosse upon him, that it was wondre that he was nouȝt
bresed vnto deth. Sithen he turned him aȝeyne, and saide to thilke
holy creatures that folowed him wepynge 'Wepeth not for me but for
f. 125v ȝour sy[lu]es.' Sit|hen how thay led him to the mount of Caluarie, and
than thai rof of that clothe that was done vpon him, and al the skynne
and al the hide come withal. And than when he was naked oure lady
toke a couerchief that was on hire hede, and bonde aboute his myddel
to couere his membris with. Sithen how thei leide done the crosse and
kest him doun thereon, and nayled him with a grete nayle thourȝ the
riȝt honde. Sithen how thei festned a rope by the lifte honde and
drouȝe it oute whiles any synuȝ or skynne wolde last hole. And also a
thefe satte on his riȝt arme ay possyng him with his fote for to make þe
synewes to seiȝe oute that it was wonder that he ne had ben ded with
that peyne. Than thei nayled throuȝt the tother honde. Sithen how
f. 126r thei fest a rope to his riȝt fote and drowe him | oute to it come to the
hole, and than thai toke a nayle and stroke thourȝ the fote, and when it

was thourȝ one of the thefe[s] toke the tone ende aboue the fote, and the other benethen, and rowed aboute among the synewes to eke his peyne. Sithe how thei fest a rope by þe tother fote and drourȝe it to it come at the hole, and than thei set the tother fote on that and nayled hem bothe on to the harde tree. Sithen how thei lifte up the crosse and swapped it doun in to the erthe that al his woundis brest oute and blede. Sithen biholde how blody his blisful bodi was, hongyng on the rode. Sithen how mekeli he praiede for his enemyes. Sithen how he bitauȝte his moder to Iohn and Iohn to his moder. Sithen how mercifulli he forȝaf the thef, and saide he schulde that day be with him | in (f. 126v) blisse. Sithen how he saide to his fader 'Fader, whi hastou forsaken me?' Sithen how he saide 'Me thristes', and thei ȝaue him galle and eiselle menged to drinke. And than when he had tasted, he saide 'It is ended tha[t] bifore was profecied of me', and so ȝeldid vp the spirit and suffred harde dethe for vs. Sithen how dulefulli he honge on the rode. Sithen how Longeus stong him to the herte with a sp[er]e. In honore gloriose passionis domini nostri Ihesu Cristi, et beatissime Marie virginis genitricis eius, beati Iohannis euaungeliste, beati Iohannis baptiste, Sancti Michaelis, et sancti angeli mei, et omnium sanctorum et sanctarum, passio Ihesu conforta me. This is the Latyn that is saide bifore at the bigynnyng on Engglische; chese whethere the thinke better. Pater noster.

Thinke than how dulefulli thi derworthi lord honge on | the roode al (f. 127r) the longe day. Sithen how he was stonggede to his hert roote. Sithen how thei toke him doun of the crosse and what sorowe there was. Sithen what sorowe there was when thei laide his precious body in graue. Sithen how he whente to helle and brouȝte oute alle that bifore loued him. Sithen when he rose from deth to life on the thridde day. Sithen how graciously he whente up to heuene. Sithen how he sente witte and wisdome in to erthe. Sithen how at the day of dome thou schalt ȝeue rekenyng of al thi life to the leste thouȝt. Sithen efter Pater noster, Aue Maria. I say, thou wrecched caitife, sithen thou schalt ȝiue a rekenyng of the leste thouȝte, vmbithinke the how thou hast spended this day, whiche is ordened to the to spende to the loouynge of thi lord and helthe | of thi soule. Bethinke the, and begynne at (f. 127v) morne, and so from houre to houre and frome tyme to tyme til thou comme at euene, and than of that thou hast trespassed aske mercy. And also soon as thou mayist, comme to thi confessioun, and rise oute þereof and than say 'Lord, I haue this day and al my life falsly and wickedly despended aȝeyns thi louynge and the helthe of my soule.

I aske mercy and forȝyuenesse for thi mercy and thi pitte. And Ihesu, ȝif there be ouȝte that hath ben to thi louyng, to the of whom al grace and alle goodenes commeth be louyng, honour and worschip, and in f. 58v honour of the holy trinite] 'Omnipotens sempiterne deus qui dedisti famulis tuis.' And þre pater noster and auees, and than kysse þe erthe and say 'Bethynke the, thou wreched kaytif, how hit shal be of þe when þou shalt be cast in a pitte vndre þe erthe, whan todis, w[or]mys, snakys and other venymous bestes shal ete þi eighen, [thy nose], þi mouth, thy lippes, thi tonge, thy hede, thy hondes, thy [fete], and al þi body. Who shal þan be thy helpe, thy comfort and thy refuyt? Than, þou wreche, shal þer non be the for to comfort bot þat derward lord Iesus. Therfor, þou wreched kaytif, now, whan tyme is of mercy and `of' pite, ren to þat derward lord Ihesu, and say "Mercy, der Ihesu, space and grace for thi mercy and pitte, dere and swet Ihesu."'

[f. 128r] [And than I go to rest, and when I haue blissed me I say 'Te passion of Ihesu comforte me' v tymes, and haue mynde of the v woundes in the hondes, feete, and herte. Now, dere brothere in Ihesu, ȝif this in soule ouȝte profite the, I praye the for the loue of almiȝti Ihesu, praye for me that oure lord Ihesu kepe me to his louynge.]

Explicit tractatus Ricardi, heremite de Hampolle, ad Margaretam, reclusam de Kyrkby, de amore dei.

# VIII
# MEDITATION B

## Here begynneth a deuout meditacioun vp þe passioun of Crist, j-made by Richard Rolle, heremyt of Hampolle

Lord, as þou made me of noght, I beseche þe, yeue me grace to serue þe with al my hert, with al my myȝt, with al my streynth, with al my konnynge, with al myn entencioun, with al myn vndrestondynge, with al þe myȝt of my soule, with al my þoȝt, with al my speche, with al my wittes, with al my werkes, with al my occupaciouns, with al my bysynesse, with al my reste.

Lord, þat madest me lyk to þe, I besech þe, yeve me grace to loue þe with al my wil, with al my luste, with al my soule, with al my loue, with al my lykynge, with al my mynd, with al my wysshe, with al my desyre, with al my deuocioun, with al my longynge, with amendynge of my lyf, with lestynge in goodnes, with verray contricioun and shryft and penaunce for my synnys.

Lord, þat mad me and al my lymmys, I beseche þe, yeve me graeȝ to serue þe with al my lymmys, so þat my lemmys be þy lemys and al occupied in þy seruice, and euer bowe to þy biddynge, euer redy to meve or to rest at þy wille, and euer lame | to þe dedes of syn, and euer f. 1v
fresshe and redy to þy biddynge.

Lord, þat made [me] and hast yeven me many yiftis, gostly, bodily, and worldly, I beseche þe, graunt me grace to vse ham al in þy seruice, and to þat end þe whoche þou yaf ham to me, þat I euer wyrship þe in þy yiftes; and graunt me grace euer to be meke in þy yifte[s], to hold me apaid and neuer to be proud ne presumptuouse of þy yiftes, bot euer to know me for such as I am, a synful wreche.

Lord, þat lyghted fro heuyn to erth for loue of mankynd, fro so heigh to so low, fro so heigh lordship to so low pouerte, fro so heigh nobeley to so low meschief, fro so heygh wel to so low wo, fro so heigh blys to so low peyne, fro so heigh myrth to so low sorow, fro so lykynge a lyf to so peynful deth, now, lord, for al þy loue þat þou shewedist to mankynd in þyn incarnacioun and in þy passioun, I beseche þe of mercy and helpe.

Swet Ihesu, I thank þe, lord, with al my hert for þou profered þe to þat place where þou wist þy deth ordeyned; and I þank þe, lord, for þer þou shewedest wel þat þou was willy to dey for vs, and so I f. 2r beleue, lord, þat þou | chese þe day and þe tyme when þou woldest dey, and euery poynt of þy passioun was done at þy ordynaunce, and I beleue, lord, þat þou laide þy soule when þou wold, and, when þou woldest, tak hit ayeyne. Now here, swete Ihesu, I beseche þe, graunt me grace to profite to þe with good wille and sorow of hert for my synnys, and criynge mercy and wil to amend me in shrift and penaunce for my synnys, in good continuance of good lyvynge, in hool loue to þe þat made me; and graunt me to turne to þe in oft shrift in euche temptacioun and tribulacioun of my fleishe, world, or enmy; and graunt me grace þat euch þoȝt of me, word or werk, shew þat I am turned to þe; and yeve me grace fayne to turne to þo dedes with ful wille þat þou hast ordeyned for me. Swete Ihesu, lord, I beseche þe, hyre my prayere. Pater noster. Aue Marie. Et ne nos. Adoramus te Criste. Oracio. Domine Ihesu Criste, fili dei viui, pone passionem, etcetera.

Swete dere lord, Ihesu Crist, I þank þe with al my hert and connynge of þat swet prayer and þat holy orisone þat þou made before f. 2v þy holy passioun for vs on þe Mount of Olyvet; | and lord, I thank þe for þer þou taghtest vs to pray whan þou saidest 'Fadyr, nat my wille bot þy wille be fulfilled.' For þy wil, lord Ihesu, and þy faderes wil bene al one wille. þan þou prayed nat for þy self bot for vs, to teche vs þat haue contrarious wille to þe fadyr of heuyn fo[r] to leue oure wille and to pray þat þe faderes wil of vs be fulfilled. Now here, swete Ihesu, I beseche þe þat I be euer at þy wille, and put out my wille bot when my wille accordeth with þyne, and graunt me grace to seche what is þy wil and turne þerto. Pater noster. Aue. Adoramus te. Domine Ihesu Criste, fil[i] de[i] viui.

Swet lord Ihesu, I thank þe as I can of al þat ferdnesse and angwishe þat þou suffred for vs when an angel of heuyn come to comfort þe, and when þou swettest blode for anguysshe. Swet Ihesu, I beseche þe for þy swet mercy þat þou be my help and comfort in al temptacioun, anguysh or tribulacioun, þat I may þrogh þy swet comfort turne out of al meschief of soule and of body in to helth of vertue and of meknes. Pater noster, etcetera.

Swet Ihesu, I þank þe of þy deseses þat þou haddest when Iudas f. 3r betraied þe; | þou told hym biforne and warned hym, þerfore hit was oon of þe grettest syn þat euer was. Now, lord Ihesu, I beseche þe, kepe me of gret synnys, as ouerhope, wanhope, and al maner of synnes ayeyns kynde, and yeve me grace to þynk euery syn grete þat on any manere wise may greue þe, lord Ihesu, for no gilt is litel þat greueth þe. Pater noster. Aue, etcetera.

Swet Ihesu, I þank þe for al þe desaises þat þou suffredest when þou was takyn of þe Iewes, for some pulled [þe], some shoven þe, drowen þe, despised þe, skorned þe, tugged þe, and toren þe. And, swet Ihesu, I þank þe for al þat meknes þat þou sheweddeste þer when thou lete hem do as þay wold. Now, swet Ihesu, I besech þe, tak me to þe and make me al þyne, and yif I fle to any syn of þe world, my fleishe, or þe fend, swet Ihesu, fet me sone home ayeyne as [a lord doth his] bondman, and dryve me with tribulacioun [sone] to penaunce. Yit, swet Ihesu, in þe is al souereyne medicyne, and I, lord, am al sek in synnes; þerfor, swet Ihesu, tak me to þe, and set me vndyr þy cure. Yit, swet lord Ihesu, þis lif is ful of fondynges and enemyes, and þer is no socoure | bot in þe, swete Ihesu; þerfor, swet Ihesu, take me to þe f. 3v within þy gouernance and shildynge, and let neuer þy hondwerk be fordone. Yit, swet Ihesu, þou art al good, and to þe longeth al loue; þan tak to þe myn hert hooly, þat al my loue lyȝt on the þat al boghtest, so þat my hert neuer turne fro þe for no temptacioun, bot euer cleue fast vpon þe. To loue þe, swete Ihesu, is most medeful, moste spedeful, and most nedefulle. Pater noster. Aue Maria. Adoramus, etcetera.

Swet Ihesu, I yeld to þe þankynges and graces for þat tresone and shame þat þou hadde when þay bonden þe to a tre as a thef. Now, swet Ihesu, I beseche þe, bynd me to þe so þat neuer tribulacioun ne temptacioun depart vs atwyn. Bynd me to þe, swete Ihesu, in byleve, hope, and charite. In bileue fest me to þe, swet Ihesu, þat neuer il lore ne errour ne heresy turne me fro my beleue; and graunt me, swete Ihesu, þat my beleue be in mesure, nat to large, belevynge þat shold nat be beleued, ne to strait, leuynge þat shold be beleued, and, swet Ihesu, make me to beleue in to al þe sacre|mentes of holy chirche and al þe f. 4r ordinaunces, and trist to God of my saluacioun. Swet Ihesu, bynd me to þe in hope, so þat al my hope, trist, comfort, solace, and gladnes be in þe; in euche wel or wo myn hope and triste be only in þe. Let neuer my hope be to streite, lest I falle in wanhop, ne to large, lest I trist in ouerhope; and graunt me grace, [swete] Ihesu, to continue in good werkes and in þy seruys with discrecioun, þat I may wilfully hope and trist to þe and in þe. Swet Ihesu, bynd me to þe in charite, þat al my loue hool be to þe in wille, worde, or werk, and let me loue no þynge bot þe, or for þe, as þou dost, frend or foo; and let none vnskylful wreth ne hate ne enuy brek þe bond of my charite, and let me, lord, loue þe euer þe lenger, þe bettyre, þe more kunnyngely, þe more besyly, þe more stidfast, and let me loue þat þou louest, and hate þat þou hatis. Pater noster. Aue, etcetera.

Swete Ihesu, I yeld þe þankynge and gracis for al þe steppis and pacis þat þou yede toward þyn owne peyne and þyn owen deth. I f. 4v beseche þe, swet Ihesu, þat þou reule al my goynge and al þe | affeccioūns of my hert. Pater noster. Aue, etcetera, prius.

Swet Ihesu, I þank þe for al þe shame, anguyshe, and felonyes þat þou suffredest before Anne and Cayphas, Pilate and Herode, and namly I thank þe, swet Ihesu, for þat mercyfulle lokynge þat þou, turnynge ayayne, beheld vpon Peter, þy disciple þat forsoke þe, and yit in myche angwishe þou sheweddest þy loue opynly to hym, so þat neuer shame ne peyn myȝt draw þy hert fro hym. Now, swet Ihesu, turne þe eygh of [þy] mercy toward vs synfulle, so þat þrogh þy mercy and grace we mow repente of oure trespas and mysdedes, so þat we may come with Seynt Peter to þy mercy. Pater noster. Aue vt prius.

Swet Ihesu, I þanke þe for þat meke and stille stondynge afore Pilate and al þe fals accusours of þe Iewes. Nowe, swet Ihesu, here I beseche þe, graunt me grace faithfully to haue in mynd in euche temptacioun þat I stond byfore [þe] my domysman; and graunt me grace paciently [to] suffre accusacioūns, snybbynge, and al euyl wordes of foes for þy loue; and graunt me to know euch man bettyr þan me, and f. 5r to meke me euer and hold me low. And, swet | Ihesu, when I shal be demed, haue mercy on me, and let þy mekenes and þat dome þat þou vnskylfully suffred excuse me fro þat dome þat I skylfully shold haue. [Pater noster, etcetera.]

Swet Ihesu, I yeld þe þankynge for al þat shame and anguyshe þat þou suffred when þay spitten in to þy face, þat swete myrroure and bodilye blis of heuyn, vpon whiche angels and seyntes haue deynte to loke. Nowe, swete Ihesu, yeve me grace to haue most deynte to þe inwardly loke and þynk vpon þat blessed face, and, swet Ihesu, restore þe lyknesse of þy face and in my soule þat foule synnes haue fadyd; and, leue lorde, let me neuer haue lykynge in þe face of syn in temptacioun, and graunt me grace neuer to assent to lust of syn; and graunt me grace to wyrship the in euch creature, and let me neuer haue pride of chere of my face, ne lust to syn for semblant of any othyr face. And, [swete] Ihesu, graunt me grace to se þy blessed face in heuyn. Pater noster. Aue, etcetera.

Swet Ihesu, I yeld þe þankynge as I can of al þe evil wordes, sclaundres, scornynges, blasphemes, mowes, and shamys þat þe Iewes f. 5v seid to þe in al | tyme of þy precious passioun, and of al þe holdes and prisons þat þay helden þe in when þou was drawen and harred to Anne and Cayfas, now to Herode and Pilate, and closed withjn har places. Now, swete Ihesu, here I þank þe, and I beseche þe, graunt me suffraunce and streynthe to stond stidfastly and paciently to suffre wordes of despite and rebukynge for þy loue, and neuyr to gurch for tribulacioun and angyr or sekenesse of þy sond; and graunt me grace, swet Ihesu, stidfastly to stond in al þe assaillynge and temptaciouns of my foos, bodily and gostly. Pater. Aue.

Swet Ihesu, I thank þe for al þe stappis and pacis þat þou yede hiddreward [and þederward] in the tyme of þy passioun, and I beseche þe, graunt me grace in al my wayes and gatys þat þay be ordeyned to þy worshipe and saluacioun of my soule; and graunt me grace wilfully to go to þy seruice, and spare for no peyne ne penaunce, and mak me loth to meve, swet Ihesu, to any lust ayayn þy wille. Pater noster, etcetera.

Swete Ihesu, I yeld þe þankynge for þat dispitous blyndfellynge þat þe Iewes did to þe, and here I pray the, swete lord Ihesu, shild me fro blyndynge of syn in custume, | f. 6r in longe vnshrift, in ouerhope and ouertrist to my self, and shild me fro perpetuel blyndynge of dampnacioun and excludynge fro þe blisful syȝt of þy glorious face, and let me clerly se in to þe face of my conscience; and yeve me grace, swet Ihesu, to kepe myn eyeghen fro al euyl syghtes þat eggen to synne, and graunt me to se þy blessed presence endlesly. Pater noster. Aue, etcetera, vt supra.

Swet Ihesu, I thank þe euermore for þat sham and shendshipe þat þou suffreddeste in þy buffetynge, for many a sore stroke þou suffreddest þan, for euche of ham strof to smyte bifore othyre. Now, swete Ihesu, graunt me here wilfully to suffre deseises and tribulaciouns for þy sake, and neuyr to gurche for sekenesse ne for wronges of man, bot euer to þank þe of al þy sondes. And graunt me, lord Ihesu, purgatory for my synnes er I deye, and hertely, lord, continuely hit to pray, and when hit cometh, lord, yif me pacience and hert hooly to þank þe of þy blesful and gracious sond. Pater noster. Aue, etcetera.

Swet Ihesu, I yeld þe graces and þankynge for al þat sore and longe and egre payne | f. 6v þat þou suffreddest for vs, and for al þat preciouse blode þat þou bledde when þou was naked, bound fast to a pillere and scourged ful sore, for þat was a bittyr peyne. For þe to scourgen weren [chosen men þat weren] stronge and stalwarth and willy to slee þe, and hit was longe or þey was wery, and þe scourges weren made ful stronge and smert, so þat al þy body was bot woundes, and many woundes in oon wou[n]de, for þe knottes smytten oft in oon place, and at euch strok smot hit þe deppyr. And þat was, swet Ihesu, a large yift and a plenteuous she[w]ynge of þy loue. þan was þy body lyk to hevyn, for as heuyn is ful of sterris, so was þy body ful of woundes. Bot, lord, þy woundes bene bettyr þan sterris, for sterres shynen bot by nyght, and þy woundes bene ful of vertu day and nyght. Al þe sterris by nyȝt lygheten bot litel, and oon cloud may hide ham alle, bot oon of þy woundes, swete Ihesu, was and is inogh to do away þe cloudes of al synful men, and to clere þe conscience of al synful men. Here, swete Ihesu, I besech þe þat þese woundes be my meditacioun nyght and f. 7r day, for | in þy woundes is hool medicyne for euche desaise of soule. Also, swet Ihesu, þe sterres ben cause of euche þynge þat is grene or groweth or bereth fruyt. Now, swet Ihesu, mak me grene in my beleue, growynge in grace, berynge fruyt of good workes. Also sterris ben cause of mynys metailles, and of precious stonys. Now, swet Ihesu, mak me togh as metaille ayeyns temptaciouns, and precious as perle in to þe heigh degre of charite. Pater, etcetera.

And yit, lord, swet Ihesu, þy body is lyk to þe nette, for as a nette is ful of holys, so is þy body ful of woundes. Here, swet Ihesu, I beseche þe, cache me in to þis net of þy scourgynge, þat al my hert and loue be to þe, and drawe me euyr to þe and with þe as a net draweth fyshe, til hit come to þe bank of deth, þat neuyr temptacioun, tribulacioun ne prosperite pul me fro þe, and as a nette draweth fyshe to þe lond, so, swet Ihesu, brynge me to þy blisse. Cache me, lord, in to þe nette of þy mercy þat is holy chirche, and kep me þat I neuyr brek out of þe bondis of charite. Cache me, swet Ihesu, in þe net of þy comaunde- f. 7v mentis, þat neuyr syn haue me | out of þe close of þy vertues. Pater noster. Aue, etcetera.

Efte, swet Ihesu, þy body is like to a dufhouse, for a dufhouse is ful of holys: so is þy body ful of woundes. And as a doue pursued of an hauk, yf she mow cache an hool of hir hous she is siker ynowe, so, swete Ihesu, in temptacioun þy woundes ben best refuyt to vs. Now, swet Ihesu, I beseche þe, in euche temptacioun graunt me grace of some hoole of þy woundes, and lykynge to abide in mynd of þy passioun. Also, swete Ihesu, þy body is like to a hony combe, for hit is in euche a way ful of cellis, and euch celle ful of hony, so þat hit may nat be touched without yeld of swetnesse; so, swet Ihesu, þy body is ful of cellys of deuocioun, þat hit may nat be touched of a clene soule without swetnesse of lykynge. Now, swet Ihesu, graunt me grace to touche þe with criynge mercy for my synnes, with desyre to gostly contemplacioun, with amendynge of my lyf and contynuynge in goodnes, in stody to fulfille þy hestes and deli[t]a[b]ly to abyde in mynd of þy passioun. Pater noster. Aue.

More yit, swet Ihesu, þy body is lyke a | boke written al with rede f. 8r ynke: so is þy body al written with rede woundes. Now, swete Ihesu, graunt me to rede vpon þy boke, and somwhate to vndrestond þe swetnes of þat writynge, and to haue likynge in studious abydynge of þat redynge, and yeve me grace to conceyue somwhate of þe perles loue of Ihesu Crist, and to lerne by þat ensample to loue God agaynward as I shold. And, swete Ihesu, graunt me þis study in euche tyde of þe day, and let me vpon þis boke study at my matyns and hours and euynsonge and complyne, and euyre to be my meditacioun, my speche, and my dalyaunce. Pater noster. Aue Maria.

And yit, swet Ihesu, þy body is lyk to a medew ful of swete flours and holsome herbes: so is þy body fulle of woundes swet sauorynge to a deuout soule, and holsome as herbes to euch synful man. Now, swet Ihesu, I besech þe, graunt me swete sauoure of mercy [and] þe holsom resseit of grace. Pater noster. Aue.

Swete Ihesu, I yeld þe þankynge of al þe peynes and shames þat þou suffred for þy swet wille for vs | whan þou was cloþed in purpur for to f. 8v shame þe, and corowned with þornes for to peyn þy swete hede, and þay on knees knelynge scornynge þe, and cleped þe lord and maistyr, and spit in þy face and buffeted þe, and as myche shame as þay couth þay said to þe. Here, swete Ihesu, I beseche þe, for al þo shamfulle turnes, foryeve vs al þe shame and peyn þat we haue deserued by oure syn, and graunt vs grace to worship þe in als many wise and as hertely as þe Iewes shamed þe in þy passioun. And, swete Ihesu, graunt vs grace of suche cloþynge and array as most pleseth þe, and neuer to desyre disgysynge ne pride of atyre, and, swete Ihesu, graunt me grace to ber my hede lowe and neuer to shewe pryde in semblant ne chere, and, swet Ihesu, let me kepe my v wittis to þe worship of þe, and let me neuyre desyr state ne degre ferþer þan þou hast ordeyned for me. Pater noster. Aue Maria.

Swet Ihesu, I þank þe with al my hert for al þat blode þat þou so plenteuously bled in þy coronynge before al folke, when þy swet face was al on blode, and on euche syde þou was forcried and des|pised to f. 9r þat stronge [and foul] deth, and demed so wrongfully þerto. Blessed and þanked be þou, [swete] Ihesu, and loved of al þy creaturs. Here, swete Ihesu, I beseche þe, weshe my soule with þat blode, and enoynt and depeynt my soule and my mynd with þat preciouse blode, and graunt me grace for þy myche mercy to jugge my self wilfully and deme to saluacioun of my soule. Pater noster.

Swet Ihesu, I yeld to þe þankynges and graces for al þe peynes and shamful turnes þat þou soffred when þou bare þyn owne cros and jugement vpon þyn naked bak, for þay drowen and pulled þe so felly, þay putted þe and smot þe shamfully, as hit were a thef þat bare his owne galows. A, der lord, swete Ihesu, what þou was woobigone when at þe begynnynge of Herodes comaundement þy kyrtil was take fro þe, þat cleued so fast to þy body with blode of þy scourgynge, when þou was so rased and rent, and bette so sore and so longe til al þy vttyr blode was bled, and þy skyn vnneth hanget togyddre. Þan, when þay drewe of þy cloth þat cleued to þe with dried blode, and þou so tendyr f. 9v and so yonge and freshe of age, | þay toke no reward how sore hit greuet þe, þat pitevous strypynge, when many a pece of þy tender skyn folowed; þan was hit reuth to se þy body al stremed on blode. A, lord, swete Ihesu, me þynketh I se þe rede blode ren doun by þy chekes, stremes aftyr euche stroke of þy coronynge and scorgynge; byfore and behynd and on euche syde þe skyn of þy hede þe þornes al to-renten, for euche þorne prikked to þe brayne pan. Allas, swete Ihesu, how may a Cristen soule se his Lord soffre so myche peyne þat neuer trespased; þy gryntynge and þy gronynge, þy sorowynge and seghynge, þe reuth of þy chere persheth myn hert. Þe croune of al blisse, þat coroned þe blessed, [þe] kynge of al kynges, þe lord of al lordes, is of helle houndes corowned with þornes. Þe worshipe of hevyn is despised and defouled. He þat shope son and alle creatures, and al þynge is of his yifte, he ne had nat where he myght hide his hede, and he was so pouer þat he goth al naked in syȝt of al folke. Here, swet Ihesu, I besech þe, f. 10r yeve me | grace to ber with þe þe cros of penaunce for þy loue and for my synnes as þou didde for me and for my synnys, and let me ber hitte in to my deth tyme as þou dede, and let me neuer be wery ne gurchynge for þat I suffre for þy loue. And yeve me grace to do penaunce in þis lif for my synnes, and graunt me my purgatory here, and yeve me grace to suffre esely wordes of despite for þy loue. Pater noster. Aue, etcetera.

Swet Ihesu, I yeld þe þankynges for al þe angyr and sorow þat þou suffred when þou bare þe cros toward þy deth, and me þynketh, lord, I se how þey led þe forth naked as a worme, turmentours about þe and armed kneghtes. Þe prese of þe peple was wondyr mych; þey harried þe shamfully, and spurned þe with har fete as þou haddist be a dogge. A, þis is a reuthful syȝt: þy hede is ful of þornes, þy heere ful of blode, þy face is al wan, þy lokynge is mournynge, þy chekes and hede al bolned with buffetys, þy visage is defowled with spittynge. þe Iewes haue so besene þe þat þou art lyker a mysel | f. 10v þan a clene man. þe cros was heuy and hegh, and so hard trussed on þy bake þat was bare þat þou art crushed and shrynkes þervndre. A, swet Ihesu, þou groned ful hard whan hit sate so sore to þy naked body þat is so seke, so ful fright of peynes, so febyl and so wery, what by longe and gret fastynge bifore, what with wakynge al þe nyȝt without rest, what with betynge and biffetynge and shameful wordes and dedes byfore. þy fleishe þer þe cros sitteth is skynles and ouer-ron with blode rewes. þe peyne of þy birthen greveth þe so sore þat euche fote þat þou gost styngeth to þy hert. þus þou gost, swet Ihesu, in to Ierusalem toward þy deth. Al þe pepil comyn and folwen and gawren vpon þe and wondreth; with suche processioun was neuer thef led to his deth. Here, swet Ihesu, I prey þe to graunt me grace to folow þe in mynd of þy passioun, and in suffrynge somwhate for þy loue, and in hauynge compassioun of þe. Pater noster, etcetera.

Swet Ihesu, what sorow fel to þy hert when þou keste þy eyen vpon þy dere modyr. þou saw hyr folow þe amonge þat grete pres as a womman out of hir self mynd for inderly sorow, þe whiche passed | f. 11r al sorowes. Now she wronge hir hondes, wepynge and seighynge; now she cast hir armes [abrode]; þe watyr of hir eyghne dropped at hir fete; she fel in dede swowne oft tymes for peynes and sorowe. Hir sorowe, swet Ihesu, [and] hir dele, aggregged gretly and manyfold al þyn oþer peynes, and when she knewe þat hir sorow greved þe so sore, þan was hir wel wors, and so sorow of ether for oþer wexeth manyfold. þe heigh loue of youre hertes euery til othyr, þat was perles, brennynge kyndly, made your sorow euery for other vnlyke to any oþer sorowe or woo on erth. As youre loue was makles, so was your sorowe perles; hit stikked at youre hertes as hit were deth. A, lady, mercy; how was þou so bold amonge so many kene foos to folow so nere? How was hit þat arghnes of wommanes kynd or shamynge of maydenhede ne hadde withdrawe þe? And hit was nat semely to þe to folow such a rowt, bot þou had no reward to mannys drede, ne to noȝt elles þat shold þe lette, for as out of þy self þou were for sorow of þyn owne sone, and so on hym was al þy hert sette. þy | f. 11v loue was so kene sette in þy hert to þy sone, þy sighynges were so fer fette, þy dele and sorow so ful [in þy breste], þy chere so drery for dedly woo, þat hit bereft þe rekkynge of bodily drede, and of worldly shame, and of al manere lettynge. Now, lady, þat peyne and passioun shold haue be myne, for I had deserued hitte and was cause þerof; þerfor, swete lady, as þ[o] woundes and peynes weren myne owne by ryȝt, get me of þy mercy oon of ham al, þat hit may abyde as a prike at my hert. Get me, swete lady, a drop of þat reuth þat þou hadde, to folow hym with as þou dede. Al þat woo is myne by ryght. Set me on myn owne, ne be þou nat so wrongful to withhold alle. Þogh al þy wo be þe lefe, þou art ful large; þan part with þe pouer þat litel hath, and yeve me of þy syghynge þat seighed so sore, and let me sygh with the, sethen I began al þis woo. I ask, derworth lady, neþer castelles ne tours ne oþer[e] worldes welle, ne son [ne mone] ne none of þe bodies of hevyn, ne no þynge bot woundes of reuth, peyne, and compassioun of swet Ihesu. My lordes f. 12r passioun is alle | my desyre. I haue appetite to peyne, to beseche my lord a drope of his rede blode to make my soule blody, and a drop watyre to weshe with my soule. A, modyr of mercy and of compassioun, socour of al sorow and bote of al bale, modyr of al wreches and deelful, visite my soule, and set in my hert þy son with his woundes. Send me a sparcle of compassioun in to my hert þat is hard as stone, and a drope of þat passioun to suple hit with. Pater noster. Aue.

Swete Ihesu, I þank þe with al my hert for al þe peyne þat þou soffred when þe cros was cast doun on þe ground, and þey leid þe flatte þeron, and with cordes drow þy hondes and fete to þe holys, and nayled first þat oon hand, and streyned þat oþer to þe oþer hole, and þan drowen alle þy body, swet Ihesu, doun, to þe holys raght þy fete, and þe naylles, lord, weren blont, for þey shold terre þe skyn and bruys þe fleishe. Now, swete Ihesu, me þynketh I se þy body on þe rode al blody, and streyned þat þe ioyntes twynnen; þe woundes now opyn, þy skyn al to-drawen recheth so brode, þy hede corowned | f. 12v with þornes, þy body al woundes, nailles in þy handes and fete so tendyr, and in þe synwes þer as is most peynful felynge. Þer is no lennynge for þy hede; þy body is streyned as a parchemyn skyn vpon a rake; þy face is bolned þat first was so fayre; þy ioyntes vndone; þou stondest and hongest on nayllys; stremes of blode ren doun by þe rode; þe syȝt of þy modyr encresceth þy peyne. A, lord, swete Ihesu, þat woldest vnmythty become to make me myghty in mendynge my syn, I spek, lord, of þy passioun and of [hey] deuocioun. I fynd no swetnesse, bot spek as a iay, and nat wot what I mene. I stody in passioun, and fynd no tast, for my synnys bene so many and so dym þat þey haue shot out deuocioun and stopped al þe sauour of swetnesse fro my soule, and þerfore I speke and blondre forth as a blynd man, and spek without wisdome and connynge of so deuout matier. Bot þou, swete Ihesu, þat quykkest þe dede and turnes to good lyf fro deth of syn, quyken me, lord, swete Ihesu, and yeve me grace to fele some of þat swetnesse of swete sauoure and gostly deuocioun; lene me þe lyȝt of grace to | haue sum insyght in soule. Bot lord, I wot wel þat who-so f. 13r desyreth and secheth aryȝt, þogh he fele nat, he hath þat he wot nat, þ[e] loue of þy godhede; and if a man may no feruour fynd, þynk hym self ⌊feble and outcast⌋, and hold hym self vnworthy to haue deuocioun or eny suche specialte of oure lord, and so he shal get sonest þe yifte of his grace. Pater noster, etcetera.

Swete Ihesu, when þe Iewes heved vp þe cros and made hit falle sore in to þe hole þat was made þerfore, and þan brosten þy woundes and al to-shaked þy body þat honged so sore, lord, swete Ihesu, woo was þe þan when þe sore woundes of handes and of fete bare al þe peyns of þy body. Swete Ihesu, þan þy modyr was woo ynow þat saw þis; she seighed and wronge hir handes, she wept teres ynogh, and al þat, lord, was echynge of þy woo, and þat plas was wlatsome with stynk of carions many. And þus were al þy fyve wittes occupied with peyne to bote þe trespas of oure v wittis. In þy syght þou were blyndfeled, and for þou sawe [þy modyr so wo, and for þou sawe] [h]a[m] þy foes þat were most holden to be þy frendes, as þe Iewes. In þi smel|lynge of stynch of carions þat were so many, for þou was, lord, f. 13v done to þe deth in þe foulest place of Ierusalem, þer al þe carions of þe toun weren outcast, and þat smel, swete Ihesu, was ful greuous to þe. In þy tast, lord, greved þe þe galle aftyr þyrst, for, swet Ihesu, myche plente of peyne causeth þurst and drynes, and þat is bittyr in taste, and þe Iewes yaf þerto galle to eche thy bittyr tast. In hyrynge, swete Ihesu, þou was agreved with fals accusynge and scornys when þey seid 'Hail, kynge' and spitted in þy face, with hyrynge of foul cry when þay cried to haue swete Ihesu on þe rode, and when þay cried 'He kouth oþer men saue, now let hym saue hym self if he may.' In felynge, swet Ihesu, þou was pyned in þy byndynge, harrynge, buffetynge, blyndfellynge, scourgynge, coronynge, in berynge of þe cros, in drawynge of cordis on þe cros, and naylynge fete and handes to þe cros. Þer hanged þou pore, swet Ihesu, and woobigone, so þat of al þe goodes on erth þou had nat bot a litel cloth to helle þy lendys. And yit þou art kynge of al kynges and lord of al lordes, and hevyn and erth and helle is þyne. And yit, lord, þou | woldest be so pouer þat tyme þat f. 14r þou had none erth to dey vpon bot on þe cros in þe eyre, and þerfor, swete Iesus, on þe was seid 'foxes haue dennes and byrdes haue nestes', bot þou at þy deth tyme had nat to rest þy hede vpon. A, swete Ihesu, þat was a reuthful word whan þou said 'Al ye þat passe by þe way, abyde and behold if þer be eny sorow lyk to my sorow þat I suffre for man.' And, swete Ihesu, yit þou prayed to þy fadyre foryeve ham þe gilte of þy deth, so mych, lord, is þy mercy. And, swet Ihesu, nat withstondynge al þy grete peyne, yit þou toke hede to þe þeff vpon þy ryȝt hand when he asked mercy, and, swete Ihesu, nat withstandynge al þy gret peyne, þou graunted to hym bettyr þan he asked. Now, swete Ihesu, sethen þou art in blisse and nat in peyne, be nat now to daungerous ne to straunge of þy mercy, for seldome is a man more gracious in wo þan in blis. A, lord, woo was þe for þy modyr when þou þy leve toke of hir, and wold dey, and bitok hyr to Seynt Iohn to comforte and to kepe. Here, swete Ihesu, I besech þe, þat am ful of synnys, now, lord in blisse, haue mercy on me, and graunt me grace when hit is f. 14v þy wille | to be with þe in paradise. Pater noster. Aue Maria, etcetera.

Swete lady, mayd and modyr, woo was þe bygone whan Crist had take his leve at þe and bitoke þe to Iohn. þat sorow myght haue be þy deth, and at þat leue-takynge þe teres of þyn eighen ran doun faste. Seighynges and sorowes saten ful ney þyn hert; þou fel adoun on swowne; þy hede henged doun; þy armes fellen þe by; þy coloure wox al wan; þy face waxed al pale; the swerd of sorow of þy sones deth smote þrugh þy hert. þat chaungynge, lady, when þou haddest Iohn for Criste, was ful deleful, and as a þrow of deth to þyn hert. A, swete lady, why had I nat þan haue bene by þe, and herd þat þou herd, and seen þat syȝt with þe, and of þat moche sorow haue take my parte if I myȝt haue in cas slaked þy woo, for men seien hit is solace to haue company in peynes? Now, swet Ihesu, sethen I myght nat be þere at þy deth, graunt me grace to haue þat deth continualy in mynd, in deuocioun, and in dalyaunce, and graunt me mynd of my deth ofte, and to f. 15r amend my lyf, and to haue sorow in hert for my mys|dedes. Pater noster. Aue Maria, etcetera.

Swete Ihesu, þan cried þou deelfully on þe rode, and swetly seid þou were aþurst, and þat was no wondyr, for peyn is þirstlew, and þay, lord, yaven þe galle and eysel. Swet Ihesu, þat was no kelynge of þyrst, bot echynge. A, swete Ihesu, þey yoven þe poyso[n]e to kele þy þurst, and þou yave ham þy hert blode to quenche har synnys and to kele har soules. Bot, swet Iesus, þis þurst was manyfold: in body for peyne, and in soule þou þursted amendement of har synnys þat didden þe to deth, and þou þursted d[e]ly[uer]aunce of soules in helle þat here in lyf had kepte þy lawes. Here, swete Ihesu, I beseche þe, graunt me grace for þy sake to suffre þurst and hungyr for þy loue, and withstond lustis and temptaciouns of euche fondynge of fleyshe, of þe worlde, or of þe fende, and yeve me grace in suffraunce to folow þe shadow of þy cros, and to þurst þy seruice, and loue þy presence to my hert in desyre and yernynge of þi charite. Pater noster.

Swet Ihesu, I þank þe with al my soule for þat deelful word þat þou said to þy fadyr on heigh afor þy deþ: | f. 15v 'Dere God, whi hast þou forsak me, þat no þynge þou sparest me?' Swet Ihesu, þy manhede was for vs forsaken; so foul deth and so peynful suffred neuyre man. Þer is no bodily peyne lyke þyne. Þy manhede was tendyrly, þy dignite was excellent; þe fadyr son of heuyn betwix two theues, and amyd al þe world, for al men [shold] hit witte, and on þe hegh holy day when al men comyn to þe cite, and so hit was no priue shame. Þou henge al naked, þy skyn al to-rente, euch lyth from other, with cordes drawen, coroned with þornes, woundes wyde, many and grisly. Þe sorow of þy modyr was þe more peyne þan al þy other wo; þe losse of mannys soule þat pyned þe sore. Swete Ihesu, þy moche mercy, þy endles loue and reuth may no man beþynke, seþen þou suffred so sore for ham þat þer were þy focs. Pater noster. Aue Maria, etcetera.

Swete Ihesu, I wille in my þoȝt lay me flatte on þe erth, and [neþer] if I myȝt, for I am cause and gilty of al þy peynful deth. I wil take þe rode fote in my armys flat on þe | f. 16r ground, as þou lay, swete Ihesu, amonge þe stynkynge bonys þat lay þer wlatfully. No þynge shal hit greve me, bot hit shal be loue and lykynge to me, so mych þat I wil nat vpward cast myn eighen to þat gloriouse syȝt of þy woundes, for I þat am cause of ham alle, and vnworþy to loke hem vpon, þus wil I ligge to kepe of þy blode. Swet Ihesu, þens wil I nat flitte til I be with þy precious blode becomyn al rede; til I be mad with þy blode as oon of þyn owne, and my soule softe in þat swete bath, and so may [hit] fal, swete Ihesu, þat my hert may opyn þat is now herd as stone, and bicome nesshe þat dede was by syn, and quyk toward þe by vertue. Swet Ihesu, þy preciouse passioun rered dede men out of har gravis, hit opened hevyn, hit brast helles yatis, þe erth trembled þerwith, þe son loste his lyȝt, and my sory hert, þat is of þe fendes kynde, is harder þan any stonys, for þay cleued in þy passioun, and my hert may nat fele of þy passioun a litel poynte, ne rise with þe dede in reuth þerof. Now is þe malice of my hert, þat is so wikked, more þan is þy | f. 16v passioun, þat is þy precious deth, þat wroght such wondres and manyfold more, [and þe] mynd þerof stirreth nat my hert. Bot, swet lord, a drop of [þy] blode droped vpon my soul in mynd of þy passioun may suple and soft my soule in þy grace, þat is so hard. I wot wel, swet Ihesu, þat my hert is nat worþy þat þou sholdest come þerto and þerin alyȝt. I ask hit nat of þe dignite of þy sepulcre, bot, swete Ihesu, þou lyȝted in to helle to visite þer and ryghtyn, and in þat manere I ask þy comynge in to my soule. Swete Ihesu, I know wel also þat I was nevyr worþy to be þy moderes felew, to stond at þy passioun with hir and with Iohn, bot, swete Ihesu, if I may nat be þer in þat manere for my grete vnworþynesse, I hold me worþy for my gret trespas to honge besyde þe as oon of þe þefes. And also, swete Ihesu, if I may nat be þer in þat manere for my grete vnworþynesse, I hold me worthy for my grete trespas to haue parte of þy deth, and so, þogh I be nat worthy þerby to be lyghted in hert, me nedeth, lord, [and] wikkednesse asketh to be f. 17r ryȝted. | Come þ[an], swete Ihesu, at þy wille, and lyȝt in to my soule as þou for best knowest. Oo sparcle of loue, oo reuth of þy passioun kyndel in myn hert, and quyken me þerwith þat I be brennynge in þy loue ouer al þynge, and bath me in þy blode so þat I foryet alle worldly welle and fleishely lykynge. Þan I may blesse þe tyme þat I fele me stirred to þe of þy grace, so þat noon oþer welle lyk me bot þy deth. Pater noster. Aue, etcetera.

Swet Ihesu, þan þou said 'Fadyr, in to þy handis I betake my soule.' Here, swet Ihesu, I beseche þe, haue and hold in þy hondes my soule, þat hit neuer desyre with hool purpos fully ony þynge bot þe or for þe, and let neuyre wel ne wo turne my soule out of þy gouernaunce, and at my last end, swet Ihesu, receyue my soule in to þy hondes, þat no fend let me fro þy b[l]isse. Pater noster.

Swet Ihesu, þan þou said last 'Alle is endet.' Þan fel þy hede doun, and þy spirit passed fro þe. Þe erth trembled, þe son lost his lyȝt, dede men rissen out of har grauys, þe temple cleue, stones al to-revyn: þo f. 17v weren witnesse of þy godhede. Swet Ihesu, þan þe sharp | spere persed þy syde, and blode and watyre ran out. A, swet Ihesu, þan were v grete flodes of blode in handis and fete and in syde. Þy chyn hangeth vpon þy brest, þe white of þy eyghen is cast vpward, þy lippes shrynken, þy white tethe shewen, þy louely face is become al pale, þy here clotred al with blode; þe mynde of þis matier I wold were my deth. A, swete Ihesu, þan was þy modyr ful woo. Now sho loked vpon þy hede and vpon þe croun, now on þy face, now on þy hondes with nailles, now vpon þe wyde wounde on þy syde, now vpon þy fete nailled on þe rode, now vpon al þy body scourget, and at euery tyme she fond a newe sorow. She wept, she wronge hir hondis, she seighed, she sobbed, she falleth doun. Iohn on þat oþer half is ful of sorow. Þey wrynge har handes and maken myche dele when þey loken vpward; þe syȝt of þe

crucifix so stykketh in har hartys as hit were þe deth. Now, swet lady,
for thy mercy, sethen I am cause of al þat woo and peyne, graunt me of
þy gret | grace a poynte of þy peyne, a syȝt of þy sorow, to seigh and to f. 18r
sorow with þe, þat I may somwhate fele parte of þat sorow þat al hath
made. Graunt me, swet lady, to haue and to hold þis passion in mynd
as hertely, as studiously, in al my lif, as þou, lady, and Iohn hadden in
mynd when þe peple was gone, and ye abiden stil by þe rode fote.

Explicit.

# VARIANTS

# *The Form of Living*

1 synful] *om.* BIiP$^{2}$ and womman] *om.* Ar

2 which] whhich Lt ham] men A of helle] *om.* Ch

3–4 ben . . . þei$^{1}$] *om.* A 3 so] *om.* U, to B woke] feble URGTLP$^{1}$P$^{2}$FLdHT$^{2}$Tr, feynte SV, leþi CHe

4 fend] oþer temptaciouns of her fles *add.* He 4–5 þei . . . nat] *om.* P$^{1}$ mow . . . for] lest not B, lustyn Ii

5 har] hertis noþer *add.* T wille] hertes G desire] geten Ff þe] to RG of] *om.* RG and . . . þerto] *om.* T$^{3}$IiM

6 vse] *om.* M, ful Ch fleisshely] lustes & *add.* B, *om.* Ar desires] delites U, likynge F to withstond] but U, to stond *alia*

7 þay] but liȝtliche F, lyghtly þey Ld lykynge] desires F for] *om.* RGSVT þey] *om.* G, hyt BIi

8 ham] so *add.* $\alpha$, it FfIiCh swete] þat *add.* $\alpha$ þei] þeer U, þe A dwellen] ful menye *add.* U in ham] with hym T stille many] *om.* U$\alpha$ stille] ful *add.* Ar

8–9 And . . . to] *om.* Ii

9 comen] turnen $\alpha$ þe þrid] þre U þat] þe thred wrechednes DdR$^{2}$FfLCDT$^{3}$BFLdHT$^{2}$B$^{2}$HaAAr, *om.* Ii chaungynge] thankynge Ii of] euer *add.* TLCHeBIi, ay *add.* DdT$^{3}$MTr, a *add.* WP$^{1}$P$^{2}$, *om.* B$^{2}$

10 a$^{1}$] as U, litele *add.* T þat . . . sey] as who seiþ UDdR$^{2}$FfLCDT$^{3}$BIiMP$^{2}$FLdHT$^{2}$B$^{2}$HaAFf$^{2}$Ar, & so $\alpha$, also He, for P$^{1}$ endlees] lastande RG ioy] blis $\alpha$

11 litel] passyng *add.* M of . . . lif] here LCHeDT$^{3}$BIiMChHaA lif] world TrFf$^{2}$Ar ham] to god(e) *add.* $\alpha$CBF rise] *om.* $\alpha$Ar, vp *add.* FLdHT$^{2}$ to] do $\alpha$Ar, do *add.* LBIiM, and do CT$^{3}$ penaunce] for her synne *add.* RGSVW, and wold ordeyn to do penaunce *add.* B[*subpuncted*]

12 ordeyn] hem *add.* BIi, þat B$^{2}$ har wonnynge] for hem to wone $\alpha$, be *add.* B$^{2}$ har] the þe Ii and . . . men] *om.* Ii holy men] halugs Ar holy] gode Ff men] in heuen *add.* $\alpha$TrAr chesen] raþer *add.* RG, heere *add.* SV, ay *add.* W, alway *add.* T

12–13 þe . . . syn] at be in lust Ar

13 haue . . . þe] *om.* Ar delite] likyng $\alpha$TrFf$^{2}$ in . . . fleissh] þerinne $\alpha$ þe] vyle *add.* Ch 13–14 þan . . . heuyn$^{1}$] *om.* Ar

14 heuyn$^{1}$] ihesu passiþ out of her herte & ⟨at þe laste LB*⟩ *add.* LCT$^{3}$BIiM þei . . . heuyn] *om.* WTT$^{3}$BIiM[*W and B corr. in later hands*] lesyn] fote siþes *add.* F heuyn$^{2}$] and ihesu passeth out of here hertus *add.* Ld 14–17 For . . . dome] *om.* P$^{1}$P$^{2}$ þat] *om.* Ar

15 loueth] hase DdR$^{2}$FfLCHeDT$^{3}$BIiMFLdHT$^{2}$B$^{2}$TrHaAFf$^{2}$ leseth] lest He and$^{1}$ . . . is] *om.* $\alpha$L 15–16 and$^{2}$ . . . nys] *om.* He

16 get] haue WT ne] but U swynes] swete T, swetnesse H, *om.* A met] me A

17 dome] But *add.* $\alpha$L, which dome schal be ful dredeful to alle synweris *add.* F

18 These] iii *add.* CHeT$^{3}$BIiMFB$^{2}$TrAr þat . . . told] *om.* Ar I] haue *add.* UDdR$^{2}$FfCHeDT$^{3}$BIiMP$^{1}$P$^{2}$FLdHT$^{2}$B$^{2}$ChHaAFf$^{2}$ of] ȝow He, here B, don y A told] speek $\alpha$LLd, seyd Ch, And *add.* Ha only] *om.* F worldisshe] wrecchid D

19 wommen] *om.* Ar glotony . . . other] *om.* Ch oppyn] *om.* $\alpha$LAr synnes] and wrecchednesses *add.* $\alpha$L

20 in$^{1}$] *om.* H sum] hem $\alpha$LFf$^{2}$, other Dd semen] holy *add.* B, vsen Ch in$^{2}$] men of He, *om.* Ch penaunce . . . in] *om.* Ar in$^{3}$] semen to lyven Ch

21 þat . . . mankynd] *om.* Ar  þat] *om.* TBHa  is] haþ RSVTL, *om.* GHa enemy] enuye RGSVTLD, enuyous HeA  21–2 or . . . þousand] *om.* Ar

22 a] two F  ham] al *add.* C$T^3$BIiM  holy] only RFLdH$T^2$  God] sekyng þe ioye euer lastyng *add.* $P^1P^2$  22–3 al . . . richesse] lykynges and þe vanytees of þis world *α*L  al] vtterly B, *om.* Ar

23 and . . . richesse] of þe wordle as richesse delites and oþer suche $P^1$  men] þay $P^1$  þat loueth] of *α*LF$f^2$ Ar  þat$^2$] *om.* CHe$T^3$BIiMFTr  loueth] noȝt *add.* A, in *add.* CHe$T^3$BIiMF  world] worldes DdA, and *add.* CHe$T^3$BIiMFF$f^2$  coueiteth] and folwen *add.* *α*L, couaytise DdA, *om.* Ar  23–4 and$^2$ . . . lestynge] *om.* *α*L$P^1P^2$Ch  and$^2$] ⟨moore $T^2$⟩ þan H$T^2$

24 ioy] euer *add.* UCHeBIiFLdH$T^2B^2$F$f^2$, þat is *add.* Ff, ay *add.* $T^3$MTrAr  24–5 a . . . ham] þanne he casteþ (chacyþ T) him (hem T) by wrenches and wyles for to ouercome hem ⟨as he þat haþ a þousande wyles for to deceyue men wiþ RGSVL⟩ ⟨wyth hys gynnes (synne T) WT⟩ *α*L  a . . . hath] þen he castiþ with wyles and wrenchis F in . . . may] til Ar

25–7 And . . . ham] *trs. to l. 29* B  25 And . . . synnes] *om.* WT  And] For RGSVL  whan] he seeþ þat *add.* RGSVL$T^3$  brynge . . . sych] ⟨ouercomen ne SV⟩ bigyle hem wiþ þo RGSVL  sych] ⟨grete and Ar⟩ open BIiAr  25–6 þe . . . ham$^2$] *om.* Ar  25–6 þe . . . myght] to BIiF, þat $B^2$  þe] þorough $T^3$M

26 which] he *add.* T$T^3$MHa, þei *add.* L  make] *om.* $B^2$  ham$^1$] hym A  þat . . . ham] *om.* *α* $R^2$FfLCh  ham$^2$] þanne *add.* *α*L$T^3B^2$Tr  begileth] bigyled R, þen *add.* $P^1P^2$

27 many . . . priuely] þaim with so priuei synnes Ar  many so] *trs.* FfH$T^2$, hem so CHeD$T^3$BIiMChA  þai] *om.* D, þe H  can] knowe HeF  27–8 oft . . . ham] perceyue his wilis Ar  tymes] wite and *add.* Ld  fele þe] þe felle He  trape] ne þe snare *add.* BIi, snare $P^2$, trayne Ha  27–8 hath . . . ham] þai ben taken inne *α*L$P^1$FCh, he haþ takin hem in CDBIiLd$B^2$TrHaAF$f^2$

29 Sum . . . in] *om.* D$T^3$BIiM  he taketh] beo taken S  þat . . . in] *om.* Ch ham in] *trs.* C  sum with] *om.* *α*, *trs.* $T^3$BIiM, and F  with] *om.* U

30 witte] and is *add.* BIi, als *add.* A  30–1 whan . . . beste] *om.* R, þat þei wene þat no man may þenke ne do better þan þei GSVWTL  whan . . . ham] so þat þei Ar whan he] And $P^1$  30–1 maketh . . . is] thynkyth what thyng that he doth it were for Ii  ham] *om.* $T^2$  wend] wynne A  30–1 þe . . . done] þaire doing and conseil Ar

31 thynken] sai DdHa, makiþ F  or done] *om.* Ff  and] þat is *add.* C  forþi] siþen RGSVL, syche W, *om.* T, for $R^2$FfCHeF$f^2$  thei] suche U  no . . . of] not be counsailete oþer F  no . . . haue] noght do after conseil Ar  consail] take ne *add.* CHe  haue] take *α*LBIi

32 ben . . . connyngre] can mare and better Ar  bettre . . . connyngre] wisere F and connyngre] *om.* T  connyngre] wysere RGSVIiH$T^2$TrChF$f^2$  þei] and moor of kunnynge *add.* T  þis . . . stynkynge] þat comis of Ar  is] *om.* Ii  stynkynge] *om.* WH, stenche of CHe

33–4 for . . . oþer] *om.* Ar  33–4 he$^1$ . . . oþer] but ȝef þei wenden þat þei deden muche bettere þan outhere þei wolden not sette so muche by here owene wittes and U 33 nat] *om.* DdCHeD$T^3$BIiMChHaA, ells *add.* $R^2$Tr  33–4 set . . . oþer] worche by counsail but triste on his owne witte *α*L  witte] wylle M  33–4 bot . . . oþer] *om.* Dd$R^2$FfCHeD$T^3$IiMChHaA  33–4 bot . . . did] and so wyl they not do but ȝyf he wened þat hys were B

34 oþer$^1$] *om.* $P^1$FLd$B^2$F$f^2$  bettre] *om.* $P^1$  þan] any *add.* B, alle *add.* F$B^2$F$f^2$ þe deuyl] he Ar

35 þat . . . ioy] *om.* UChAr  is] *om.* $T^3$F  ioy] and is *add.* $T^3$BIi  when any] þat Ar  hath] greet *add.* U  35–6 and . . . self] *om.* Ar

36 ham] hym GSVWTLCT$^{3}$P$^{1}$P$^{2}$F[*R corr.*] of$^{1}$] þat G þat . . . suffren] *om.* Ar suffren . . . þei] *om.* Ch good deedes] goodes B good] god and Ar

37 haue] suche *add.* Ii ben] or Ff þat] when *alia ex.* Ar men . . . ham] þei ben preysed of men BIi whan] if Ar

38 laken] put faute on T, blame LCHeFLdHT$^{2}$, hateþ P$^{1}$P$^{2}$ or . . . ham] or blameþ ham P$^{1}$P$^{2}$, *om. alia* 38–9 haue . . . ham$^{2}$] *om.* Ch ham$^{2}$] oþere αLFf$^{2}$ ben spoken] men speken UFf$^{2}$

39 good] *om.* Ff þan . . . ham] or holden bettur þan þai RGSVL, *add.* WT glorious] holy A, gode Ar 39–40 and . . . leden] *om.* Ar so$^{2}$] do A ferre] faire T[*W corr.*], muche B, inoh Ii, ferþe A

40 passynge] al oþure and *add.* SV lif] of oþer *add.* Ch þat . . . leden] of oþere men B$^{2}$TrAFf$^{2}$ leden] latin H shold] vndernyme hem or *add.* P$^{1}$, reprehende hem ne *add.* P$^{2}$

41 reproue] reprehende UWDdR$^{2}$HeDT$^{3}$MB$^{2}$ChHaA, undurnymen RGL, vndertaken FfBIi, blame TrAr ham] no man R[*subpuncted*]

42 as . . . hym] at his byddyng T as] and Ii þei] wyl ne as thei *add.* B ham] do *add.* T$^{3}$P$^{2}$, *om.* BFf$^{2}$Ar How . . . fynd] *om.* Ar

43 synfuller] fouler Ha wreche] *om.* Ii, man Ch, mai noght be *add.* Ar in . . . mych] *om.* Ar he$^{2}$] men A

44 wot] seeþ αLF, weneþ B$^{2}$ ille] but weneth þat he be good *add.* U, inne SV and$^{1}$] for he U, naþerles (thowe Ii) he *add.* BIi holden and] *om.* Ar holden] good *add.* αLBMFLdHT$^{2}$A, hooly *add.* D and$^{2}$] muchel *add.* U honoured . . . men] þer beeth an hundred Ld honoured] honours R of . . . as] *om.* U 44–5 and holy] *om.* D

45 Sum] oþere *add.* α ben deceyued] he disseyueþ CAr and lykynge] *om.* Ar

46–7 whan . . . þerin] *om.* Ar 46 and . . . outrage] *om.* αL comyn . . . to] don BIi

47 weneth] not *add.* αL nat] *om.* αL 47–8 and$^{2}$ . . . nat] *om.* R$^{2}$FfHe forþi] for D ham] *om.* W, ȝow T

48 nat] nowþe T and . . . soule] *om.* Ar of soule] ofte T[*W corr.*] Sum] oþere *add.* α ben] he Ar begiled] desceyued αLTr, bigilis Ar

49 and sleepe] *om.* P$^{2}$ 49–50 that . . . deuyl] *om.* Ar is] comeþ of Ch

50 deuyl] of helle *add.* He faille] fall DdR$^{2}$FfIiFCh, abide CHeA 50–2 in . . . frowardenesse] of her gode dedes þat shulde be to goddes praysing and mede of her soules αL 50–2 so . . . frowardenesse] *om.* Ar

51 hit] *om.* CHe, them Ii non] gode *add.* T$^{3}$F as] that Ii had] *om.* B$^{2}$, do *add.* D know] holden B$^{2}$ skylle] resoun FLdHT$^{2}$

52 hadden] halden DdR$^{2}$FfCHeDT$^{3}$MP$^{1}$P$^{2}$FLdHT$^{2}$TrHaAFf$^{2}$, *om.* IiCh, knowen B$^{2}$ and . . . frowardenesse] *om.* He so] for vnþryft *add.* P$^{1}$, *om.* F merite] mede UCP$^{1}$P$^{2}$ for . . . frowardenesse] *om.* P$^{1}$ frowardenesse] foly BIi

54 These . . . with] Thus oure enemy bigyleth vs U, þis bygyler oure enemye þus takiþ vs CHeT$^{3}$BIiMA giles] wyles RGWT, gylder DdR$^{2}$FfAr, bigilingis L, grynne DLd, snare ⟨or gryn P$^{2}$⟩ P$^{1}$P$^{2}$ChHaFf$^{2}$, panter HT$^{2}$, gilt B$^{2}$ leith] techiþ vs B$^{2}$ enemy] ⟨þe fend G⟩ bifore vs *add.* αL for . . . with] til vs Ar for to] *om.* A take] tempte αL

55 haat] oure *add.* B$^{2}$ wrechednesse] wikkednesse UDdR$^{2}$FfCHeT$^{3}$BIiMP$^{1}$P$^{2}$FLdHT$^{2}$B$^{2}$ChHaAFf$^{2}$Ar, synne αL, synne and wickednes Tr God] goode SVFfCT$^{3}$IiP$^{2}$B$^{2}$TrAr, goodnesse HT$^{2}$A Than . . . begynneth] and so he makuth vs to bygynne BIi Than] and so UT, *om.* SV, and L many] some Ar

56 þe worke] hit of þynk F worke] to þenke P$^{1}$, *om.* HT$^{2}$A, þinge(s) *alia* þei] we BIi mowen] *om.* He brynge to] *om.* HaAr Than] and ȝet U, for SVAr, þouȝ L þey] suche BIi

57 þat . . . mowen] for to FfBIi what] al B so] euere hem likeþ or ellus *add.* G hert] hare H is set] setteþ G oft] *om.* T$^{3}$BIiMB$^{2}$ fallen] failen U$\alpha$LHeDT$^{3}$BIiMP$^{1}$P$^{2}$LdHT$^{2}$B$^{2}$TrChAArFf$^{2}$

58 ar] where H þe . . . and] *om.* T þe] of here UB wey] gate SVWDdR$^{2}$FfHaAr, werk B 58–9 and . . . ham$^{2}$] *om.* Ar þat þynge] *om.* M þat þei] þe G wend] wenen UTR$^{2}$FfLCHeBIiMFB$^{2}$Ff$^{2}$ was for] sholde helpe P$^{1}$P$^{2}$ was] best *add.* BB$^{2}$

59 lettynge] and hyndryng *add.* $\alpha$L For] *om.* ChAr and] *om.* DTr

60 good] *om.* $\alpha$L done] in loue and charite to þe worshepe of god and helpe (loue SV) of oure euen cristen *add.* $\alpha$L as$^{2}$ . . . make] *om.* $\alpha$L many$^{2}$] gode *add.* T$^{3}$FTrChA

61 þynken] haue He trouth . . . and$^{2}$] *om.* $\alpha$ trouth] fayþ *add.* P$^{1}$P$^{2}$ hoope] good loue L and$^{2}$] in FHa, of H charite] I trowe and hope þat *add.* RGWTL many] gode *add.* A

62 pases] pathes Ld, fre *add.* Ch vs] *om.* Ar so$^{1}$] to HeIi, *om.* Ld woke] feble UWTCHeP$^{1}$FLdHT$^{2}$B$^{2}$Tr, feynt SV, megre L, leþy P$^{2}$ and . . . feble] *om.* UWTP$^{1}$FLdHT$^{2}$B$^{2}$TrA feble] leþi CHe

63 noþer] neuer C ne] *om.* B pray] ne thynken *add.* Ii as . . . do] *om.* Ar sholden] shollen Lt ne þynke] no þynge Lt, *om.* UT$^{3}$IiB$^{2}$Ch, thynk þe A 63–4 be . . . nat] we are Ar

64 gretly] *om.* Ld 64–5 þat . . . do] *om.* Ar faillen] fallen SVTLFf, so *add.* Ii be] stonde $\alpha$L

65 I] we $\alpha$L þat we] *om.* L, for to B$^{2}$ so do] so to do L, be so B

66 for] Dauid *add.* AFf$^{2}$Ar seith] fortitudinem meam ad te custodiam þat is *add.* Ar Lord] *om.* TAr to þe] *om.* G, and þus schuld a man do *add.* Ar he] I HeBFB$^{2}$Ff$^{2}$Ar

67 sustene] contynue in B Goddis] þi Ar his] my HeBFB$^{2}$Ff$^{2}$Ar deeth] laste LB day] eende L 67–9 nat . . . weneth] *om.* Ar 67–9 nat . . . wogh] and þerfore waste we not oure tyme in a litill whyle ne lye we ⟨noȝt grocchyng and T⟩ grennande (gronyng SVWTL) by þe walles and (*om.* WT) so lete (þat WT) oure lorde be mysserued þourȝe febulnes and mysreuled (mysrulyng GSVWTL) of oure self $\alpha$L nat] nowe *add.* Ii in$^{2}$] *om.* M litel] *om.* Ii and a] *om.* HeIiTr

68 short] *om.* HeFf$^{2}$ waste hit] ⟨and a Ii⟩ lyuen (litil Ii) streyt BIi, wasted awey Ch hit] al *add.* He, *om.* M, my myȝt F waillynge and] *om.* CHeA waillynge] wastynge U, wanand DdR$^{2}$T$^{3}$MB$^{2}$TrHa, wonend Ff, wauerynge D, don syk BIi, tremblynge P$^{1}$, quakyng P$^{2}$, tornynge Ld, wending HT$^{2}$, monande Ch and] *om.* Ii gronynge] grone B

69 wogh] way P$^{1}$P$^{2}$A mych] *om.* $\alpha$LLdTrChFf$^{2}$ þan] many *add.* $\alpha$L men] we C

70 þat he] *trs.* Ii he] man B of ravyn] his *add.* T$^{3}$TrHa, noutȝ wel hys B, of a vyne his Ii, sacrifyce [*subpuncted*] his *add.* M, a rauenows P$^{1}$, a raveyn LdFf$^{2}$, of rauynge Ch offrynge] to god *add.* A 70–1 outrageouslye . . . body] wastis his strinth Ar outrageouslye] tristely R, vnriȝtfulliche or vnþristiliche G, untreweliche SV, vndestrely T[*W corr.*], bi outrage gouernynge (vnslyly Ld) FLd

71 body] lord SV litel] mychel abstinence of $\alpha$L mete] and drynke *add.* $\alpha$L sleepe] or ony oþer penaunce *add.* A and] But BB$^{2}$ Bernard] Austen WT

72 and wakynge] *om.* T$^{3}$BIiM, and werchyng Ch, or oþer penaunce *add.* A letteth . . .bot] *om.* Ar nat] *om.* He goodes] dedys Ff, vertues Ch helpeth] muche *add.* He, gasteli godis *add.* Ar

73 with] wisdom and *add.* TTr withouten] with BIi þat] discreciun SVF þei] þe fastyng BIi ben] turne in (not BIiM) to T$^{3}$BIiMTr 73–9 Forþi . . . God] *om.* Ar Forþi] For $\alpha$LFf$^{2}$

74 vs] þe bodi G so] to BP$^1$LdFf$^2$, *om.* Ii and seþyn] þat we W*B$^2$, and T vnþanke] maugre FLdHT$^2$, of god *add.* A our] ȝoure G dede] trauayll AFf$^2$

75 haue ben] beþ TL many] men and wymmen *add.* G, *om.* Ha and ben] *om.* αLC, ȝit *add.* T$^3$BIiP$^1$P$^2$TrFf$^2$, nowe *add.* Ch hit is] his Lt hit] all T$^3$BIiP$^1$P$^2$Tr nat] euel *add.* HT$^2$ al] *om.* BIiMP$^1$P$^2$FLdHT$^2$Tr þay] *om.* R$^2$, he Ii

76 myche] penaunce and *add.* M and fastynge] *om.* RGSVLB$^2$, of mette or drynke WT and] in DT$^3$M þey make] *om.* Dd

77 speke of] wonder on Ha þat$^1$ . . . ham] *om.* HeP$^1$P$^2$Ch euer] *om.* RGDLd ChFf$^2$

78 ioy and] *om.* Ha and wondrynge] *om.* αL þai haue] *om.* M withouten] outwiþ RW, vnto wit G of$^1$] *om.* WIi, with T, and Ch þe$^1$] loueyng of *add.* A preysynge . . . men] world αL preysynge] leuynge Ff

79 euer] *om.* αLHeP$^1$FChHaFf$^2$ ioye] *om.* IiTr þei haue] is He within] in here soule B of$^1$] *om.* Ch loue] louynge T$^3$MFf$^2$, preysyng IiB$^2$Ch God] gode W, and þe loue of him *add.* Ch þei$^2$] þe Lt, men Ar

80 sholden] shollen LtRGFfCFFf$^2$ mich] *om.* αFfLdFTrChHaAr moore] *om.* DAr, bettre LdTr, beter *add.* F toke] met and drynk *add.* BIi 80–1 an . . . hym] resonably U an] *om.* DdChAr, a resonable sustynaunce Ld

81 and praysynge] *om.* HeCh hym] comoun dyete *add.* He for to] as þai myȝt F in] wiþ in RGWTB, with to F seruice] what þat god sende in þankynge and preisynge of hym *add.* U for$^2$] þerwiþ αL

82 hold] kepen Ch men] and take ⟨pacientlich F⟩ *add.* LFB$^2$Tr, takyng *add.* BIi 82–3 what . . . stidde] *om.* U what] which mete G sent] hem *add.* RGTR$^2$Ff, sendeþ ⟨hem WLHa⟩ WLB$^2$TrHa 82–3 and . . . stidde] *om.* SV

83 seþen] *om.* DBP$^2$FLd and perfitly] *om.* αL loue] louyng RGBIi, heriȝinge SV, worschip L, of god *add.* CP$^1$Ch, seruyse Ha 83–4 and preisynge] *om.* αL

84 preisynge] longyng BIi of] and P$^1$, her god and *add.* P$^2$ Ihesu Crist] *om.* Ar har lord] *om.* αLTrHa har] þat Dd, our R$^2$FfBFLd 84–5 þat . . . serued] *om.* Ar be loued] *om.* F

85 lestyngly] wiþ meke herte *add.* He, strongeliche F holynesse] loue G, penaunce He

86 eigh] siȝte αLBT$^2$TrCh þan . . . egh] *om.* WT egh] siȝte RGSVLT$^2$Tr, *om.* DdIiAr

87–8 For . . . God] Forþi sais þe hali man Ar 87 euer] *om.* BCh art] in þe syght of god *add.* T$^3$Ch 87–8 þou . . . men] is of the B hast] *om.* Lt, hold Ii of men] *om.* T

88 is . . . afor] ioye hast þow in U hit . . . mych] ioye is hit P$^1$ hit is] *trs.* SVC HeT$^3$P$^2$, is DA, is hit worth B, *om.* Ii 88–9 mych . . . for] *om.* CHeDT$^3$BIi MCh HaA mych] ⟨more L⟩ worþ *add.* αLTr, ioye P$^1$, *om.* P$^2$, gret FLd worþi] *om.* F

89 preisynge] loue P$^2$, worschipful F be] *om.* P$^1$P$^2$ whate] *om.* F wrechednesse] worthinesse T, se *add.* H

90 þe . . . and$^1$] *om.* αLP$^2$ name] of *add.* C and$^1$ . . . habite] *om.* B$^2$ and$^1$] of Ch holynesse] hinesse H and$^2$] it *add.* Ch so] holy P$^1$FTrFf$^2$Ar 90–1 bot . . . childhode] *om.* Ar couer] turne to R$^2$Ff, coueryd ⟨with M⟩ MHa, hely P$^1$, holi F

91 pride] proude F, under holynes *add.* Ch wreth . . . envy] and synne B$^2$ Cristes] crist αL, crist hit is a barhudynge of F, relygyoun Ch childhode] *om.* αLCh, conuersacioun CHeBA

92 lecherie] lust α, thyng Dd, boost L, and a foul þyng *add.* P$^1$P$^2$ is] gostely *add.* A lykynge and] *om.* B lykynge] lust SV and delite] *om.* αLHeFf$^2$Ar delite] lust U wordes] louyng RW, loue G, preisynge SVTL, and delite in ham *add.* Ha, or any likyng *add.* B, rosynge Ar no] *om.* D

93 we$^{1}$] ȝe He, *om.* Ha our] ȝoure He, *om.* Ar thynke] in oure herte *add.* αLT$^{3}$Tr

94–6 For . . . yville] *om.* Ar 94 oft] som Ch þei] he Ii, þat *add.* A he . . . sho] *om.* He 94–5 is$^{1}$ . . . hegher] ben (*om.* L) better lyuande (lyuen L) þan þei ben (do L) ⟨and of sum oþere þat þei are wers þan þai ben RGVWTL⟩ αL þat$^{2}$] *om.* HeA, and Ii

95 and . . . hegher] *om.* D, and also þei seyn on þe contrarye manere Ch and . . . lowere] *om.* A seith] þat he or sho *add.* Lt, *om.* F

96 bot . . . sorier] nouȝt (*om.* L) worþ (*om.* WTL) but a wickednes (wrecchednesse SVTL) to haue veyn (idel SV) ioye or sorwe of her speche αL wodenesse] folye Ch wheþer] when F þei] þe P$^{2}$, me F sigge] speke αLHe, seme B good . . . yville] on or oþer P$^{1}$

97 be . . . to] wyllen BIi, *om.* Ar speche] iangelynge Ha 97–8 of . . . praysynge] *om.* B$^{2}$ of] men or of *add.* P$^{1}$ þe world] wordes W, men HeFf$^{2}$, þan *add.* αLBIi 97–8 God . . . ioy] *om.* He

98 shewe] strengþe αL vs to] *trs.* FfCT$^{3}$ vs] þynges *add.* P$^{1}$P$^{2}$ to . . . ioy] ⟨and make vs RGSVWL⟩ to be loued of him αL oure] owne *add.* B$^{2}$ For . . . ioye] *om.* H For . . . is] and He þat] it L his] *om.* αLIiLd, oure FfHe, þe B$^{2}$, goddis Ar ioye] to god *add.* αL, be *add.* He, loueynge T$^{3}$BIiM, of god *add.* B$^{2}$ whan] þat BAr

99 ben . . . stond] stonde stalwerþly αL to stond] *om.* Ar to] and B ayeyns . . . oppyn] priuyly and apert þe T oppyn] fondyngys of þe dewell and *add.* A temptaciouns] stondyng B

100 of . . . and$^{1}$] *om.* A deuyl] and his werkes *add.* αL and$^{1}$] þat we *add.* Ar preisynge] loue αLB honour] praisyng Ii

101 hym$^{1}$] god αLDT$^{3}$BIiMP$^{1}$ChFf$^{2}$, ⟨ihesu C⟩ crist CHeA and$^{1}$ . . . hym] *om.* Ld þat$^{1}$] *om.* U we] *om.* R$^{2}$Ff hym$^{2}$] hem A and$^{2}$ . . . oweth] and euer RG, *om.* SVL, boþe WT þat$^{2}$] he Ch to be] bisie we vs in L

102 oure prayer] *om.* HeIiB$^{2}$ oure] and Ar and . . . entent] *om.* IiAr, to ben herd Ch and] *om.* RG, to *add.* L entent] boþe *add.* SVT$^{3}$Ii day] and our praier and our intent *add.* Ii þat] forto Ld fyre] desyre T his] *om.* R$^{2}$FfCHe DT$^{3}$BIiMChHaAFf$^{2}$

103 lyght] quyken in R, quenche not in G, cundle ⟨in WLR$^{2}$FfCh⟩ SVWDdR$^{2}$FfLC DBIiMTrHaAFf$^{2}$Ar, brenne yn T, tende HeP$^{1}$P$^{2}$, myght kyndell T$^{3}$B$^{2}$, alyghte LdHT$^{2}$ and$^{1}$] in BIi grace] and he *add.* BIi 103–4 and$^{2}$ . . . solace] *om.* B$^{2}$ and$^{2}$] *om.* C

104 solace] boþe *add.* C wel] hele He and$^{1}$] eke *add.* L woo] amen *add.* T

105–10 Thou . . . sorowe] *om.* Ar 105 nowe] *om.* Ff a partie] opynlych T, *om.* CHeA how] þat A deceyueth] desayuede F his] hit Lt, *om.* SV

106 sutil] foule He craftes] whiles T, castes R$^{2}$Ff vnstable and vnwise] bothe U, unwitty RGSVW, *om.* T, and whaynt Dd, vnquaynt R$^{2}$FfLT$^{3}$MChHa, vnsly CHe, or sleiȝtes D, many ⟨vnwyse P$^{1}$⟩ BIiP$^{1}$, unwarly P$^{2}$, vnwyse FLdHT$^{2}$TrFf$^{2}$, vnwar B$^{2}$, unredy Ar wommen] þat wole not worche wiþ þe counsel of wysere þen þei ben *add.* α And] þerfore *add.* αT$^{3}$, wherfor Ii, now P$^{1}$, *om.* P$^{2}$ if] *om.* Ha 106–7 do . . . wolt] *om.* R do] folew GSVWT

107 folowe] *om.* GSVWT as . . . wolt] *om.* P$^{1}$Tr as] *om.* SV hope] ȝif þat *add.* SV þou] and F

108 destroy] alle *add.* FfT$^{3}$BF, and breke *add.* L his] gynnes and *add.* C, þees B$^{2}$ trappes] deceytes ⟨and his wyles RGSV⟩ α brand] hem *add.* UCIiFFf$^{2}$, breke GT in . . . loue] *om.* α loue] and breke *add.* CBIiMA al] and Ld þe$^{2}$] hise L

109 bynd] trappe α with] in þe fyre of loue (lust SV) *add.* α al] also He, *om.* Ch to$^{1}$] muche *add.* U, more *add.* Ch to$^{2}$] *om.* Ha

110 moor] muche UTF, *om.* BIi God] good G hym] heom SV, þe fend HeAr good] *om.* Ar men] and wommen *add.* LT$^{3}$FTrFf$^{2}$

111 profite] mede α, *om.* A hegher] in heuen *add.* α T$^{3}$BIiTrChFf$^{2}$

112 so . . . an] her α cruel] fel Ch 112–13 that . . . men] *om.* Ar that] þe whiche enemy RGWT ofte syth] *om.* α hath] bothe UDdR$^{2}$FfLHeDT$^{3}$BIiMP$^{1}$P$^{2}$FLdHT$^{2}$TrHaAFf$^{2}$, *om.* α CCh

113 confounden] schendeþ B, deseseth Ch, confoundeth *alia* men] a man and womman α 113–14 In . . . man] *om.* S thre] this U he] þe deuell DdR$^{2}$Ff LCHeDT$^{3}$BIiMP$^{2}$TrChHaAAr to . . . a] of Ch

114 man] by suffraunce of god *add.* L On . . . maner] first Ch hurtynge] huydyng U, desyryng Ff, harmyng BIi þe] hise B$^{2}$ þat . . . haue] of Ch as] summe tyme *add.* BIi in] of LHe

115 men] and wymmen *add.* SVWT and . . . other] and wode men RGSVW, *om.* T other] on [*deleted*] *add.* W, in *add.* T blemesshynge] enblemysshynge RG, vnblemissching SV, blemescheþ He, defoulyng P$^{1}$, blemysched Ch har] in B, *om.* Ch thoght] as in wood men *add.* C, *om.* Ch On . . . maner] *om.* B$^{2}$

116 berevynge] by uengynge T, rewarde Ch 116–18 an . . . helle] þat he makeþ (let SV) hem lese þourȝe werkes of synne α is . . . in] he hath power on U he] sene R$^{2}$Ff

117 whan] þe whilk DdBFLdHT$^{2}$B$^{2}$Ar, wham R$^{2}$FfDT$^{3}$IiP$^{1}$P$^{2}$HaFf$^{2}$ he] hath *add.* UDdR$^{2}$FfLCHeDT$^{3}$BIiMP$^{1}$P$^{2}$FLdHT$^{2}$B$^{2}$ChHaAAr deceyuet] hem *add.* ULCHe MChA

118 and] so he *add.* LCT$^{3}$BIiMTrHa, after *add.* Ar ledeth] led R$^{2}$FfHe ham] *om.* R$^{2}$FfFf$^{2}$ maner] he *add.* UDdB$^{2}$Ar, as *add.* P$^{1}$ tourmentynge] turmenteth UDdFB$^{2}$, aneintis Ar

119 a . . . body] *om.* GF a mannes] her RSVWT, a Ar body] withinne *add.* Ar we rede] *om.* SVAr he$^{1}$] *om.* U was in] of U, dide withe the holy man α, has done Dd wit . . . wel] *om.* Ar þou] *om.* BIi, now Ch

120 nat . . . nat] *om.* He nat$^{1}$] here *add.* Ar within] þi soule *add.* α, in þin herte *add.* LCT$^{3}$BIiMFTr þe . . . dreed] drede þee nought Ch dreed] douten SV, nouȝth *add.* He, him *add.* Ar what] for þat Ar may do] doþ B$^{2}$ do$^{1}$] þe *add.* DdR$^{2}$FfLDT$^{3}$BIiMA without] to þi body *add.* α LCT$^{3}$BIiMFTr

121 God . . . hym] he haues Ar God] he Ld yeueth] haþ ȝyue WT for . . . done] *om.* SVFf$^{2}$, Bot *add.* R$^{2}$Ff, Freende *add.* LCT$^{3}$BIiM

122 For . . . forsaken] Wha so forsakis Ar forsaken . . . and$^{2}$] *om.* B forsaken] *om.* Ld and . . . ioy] *om.* C þis] lyf and of þis *add.* Ld

123 take] ȝeue FLdH, takis Ar þe] him Ar life] and to leuy alone *add.* T Goddis] sake and *add.* He loue] to forsake þe ioye and þe solace of þys world *add.* B, sake Ch tribulaciouns] passiounes G, angers Ar and anguysshes] *om.* α D

124 anguysshes] noyes Ar here . . . heuyn] *om.* Ar here] in þis lyf *add.* α B$^{2}$* I] þi A

125 stidfastly] *om.* α, treuly DdAr

126 purgeth] clenseþ RGCh 126–7 in . . . þe$^{1}$] *om.* Ar in . . . and] *om.* RG 126–7 and . . . þe$^{1}$] þat woll be T

127 ledynge and] *om.* T$^{3}$BIiM ledynge] þee *add.* URGSVWDdR$^{2}$FfLCHeDF LdHT$^{2}$B$^{2}$TrCh, louynge þe T, him *add.* Ar þou$^{1}$] he Ar 127–8 þynke . . . shalt$^{1}$] *om.* A þynke . . . shalt] *om.* H how$^{2}$ . . . shalt] and UAr, *om.* B how$^{2}$] whan T

128 prey . . . shalt$^{1}$] *om.* Ch what . . . shalt$^{1}$] and BAr a . . . yers] o fey here HT$^{2}$ þou$^{2}$] he Ar

129 þi$^{1}$] his Ar loue] lord TAr and$^{2}$] *om.* Lt Ihesu] crist ⟨þat hegh es in heuen Dd⟩ *add.* DdR$^{2}$FfLCHeDT$^{3}$BIiMFLdHT$^{2}$TrChHaA 129–30 if . . . were] to be a C

130 þou] he Ar lady] lord α LBAr, here *add.* Dd a thousand] londes or *add.* R, al þis He we] þat leue by vs selven alone *add.* B, þe solitari Ar haue] been in Uα DdR$^{2}$FfLCHeDPFLdHT$^{2}$B$^{2}$TrChHaAAr

131 penaunce] grete *add.* Dd, when þei se vs *add.* B$^2$ bot] wyte þey wel þe soþe *add.* B we] he Ar haue] *om.* C more] verrey *add.* RWTTr ioy and] *om.* C and] moore *add.* UDdR$^2$FfLDT$^3$IiMPFLdHT$^2$B$^2$ChHaAAr verrey] *om.* RWTTr

132 þei . . . in] men of Ar world] haues *add.* Ar body] wyþoute *add.* BAr

133 wher] al *add.* B$^2$HaAr our] ioye is and oure *add.* He solace] and oure ioie *add.* L, delite Ha þat] we seon *add.* SV, it LT$^3$, oure solace Ch of ham] men B wold] leuen and *add.* RGSV

134 vs] in pouerte *add.* LCHeT$^3$BIiMTrA 134–7 Forþi . . . hit] *om.* Ar Forþi] for þei RFf, for we B$^2$ comforted . . . stalworth] strong and of good ⟨hart and Ii⟩ comfort BIi, in good counfort and myȝti Ch and$^1$] *om.* F stalworth] in god *add.* αT$^3$, stalworþliche F and$^2$] to G

135 dreed] suffre RG no] *om.* G noy ne] *om.* α, eiȝe ne He anguysshe] diseses W*, anger B bot] and G, now *add.* B$^2$ fast] sette UTBFLdHT$^2$ al] þin herte and *add.* LD entent] þouȝt SV, in ihesu *add.* DdR$^2$FfLCHeDT$^3$BIiMPFLd HT$^2$B$^2$TrChHaA lif] loue Ch be] good and *add.* FCh 135–6 God . . . queme] pleysyng to god RGW, quemyng to god SVT, gode and wheme DdFf, him to qweeme LT$^3$, hem to worchyppe and plesyng B, gode to hym MA, good and clene P

136 and] loke *add.* D þat$^1$] lete L hym] god SVCh

137 þat] ȝyf BIi sone] fonde to WT hit] wiþ shrifte and forþinkyng (*om.* R, forȝyuynge T) for I do þe to witen *add.* αF

138 The . . . solitude] þa þat are solitari Ar The . . . in] þou þat art in þat degre Ha þou] we BIi art in] hast Ch þat$^2$ . . . solitude] *om.* HT$^2$ þat is$^1$] *om.* α þat$^2$] *om.* BIiMFLdB$^2$ solitude] solitary ⟨lyf SVTr⟩ RGSVWLCTrA, þenkyng alone T, so littel He þat is$^2$] are Ar þat$^3$] *om.* UαDdR$^2$FfLCHeDPHaTrA, and it T$^3$BIiM most able] best P of . . . othre] *om.* LTrA

139 to] þorou G, haue *add.* F 139–40 For . . . pryuetees] *om.* Ar Seynt] *om.* SV þe$^2$] a WT Ile] hulle F

140 Pathmos] onlynes RG, alle lyues SV shewed] sende α to hym] *om.* U his] *om.* α

141 hit] *om.* αCHeDT$^3$BIiMFLdB$^2$TrChHaA, þat L is] so mykel *add.* αLCHe T$^3$BIiMFLdTrHa, *om.* Ch he] *om.* TPChAr wondrefully] wordly B

142 If] *om.* WTHe þei] but THe her] *om.* W herte] entent α, *om.* H hym] god TFCh 142–3 and . . . hym] *om.* UGD ne secheth] to seken RSV, *om.* TF

143 bot] oonly *add.* LCBIiM 143–4 than . . . delyte] for þe godnes of god is so mich and deliteþ WT he] þai F 143–5 ham . . . in] if þai coueitiþ no þynge but him þen he makeþ hem haue vertues F ham] him H and] *om.* BP

144 brandynge] beyngyng A of] *om.* BIi, his *add.* A loue] and charite *add.* F and in] of Ch and melody] *om.* HaA and$^3$] schal L, *om.* Ii, which F euer] here BIi

145 har] melodye of B, *om.* Ii sowle] hertes HeP 145–6 so . . . ham] *om.* T

146 and] *om.* R$^2$Ff þei] þe C oght . . . to] *om.* Ar oght] *om.* RGSVCHe, any tym DdB$^2$ erre] here R$^2$Ff or freelte] *om.* RGSVWA, vnkunnyng T or] of FfCIiFLdHT$^2$Ha

147 sheweth] wysses Dd al] *om.* Ch need of] *om.* Ch lereth] sheweth Lt, heeriþ DB$^2$Ch, releues MLd, schewiþ and releueþ F

148 ham] and ledes þam in luf *add.* Ha cometh] may kom Dd and grace] *om.* DT$^3$Ar

149 longe] gret SV, *om.* D trauaille and] greet *add.* αT$^3$, *om.* Ha bisynesse] and seching *add.* B$^2$, and *add.* Ha 149–50 as . . . aftreward] *om.* TrAr shalt] I hope *add.* He

150 hire aftreward] herafterward He

151 Natforþi] þan *add.* DdR$^2$FfLHeMLdHB$^2$A, ȝyt *add.* BIi be] turmentid and *add.* He both] *om.* HT$^2$Ar

152–4 for ... passed] *om.* Ar 152 euer] *om.* Ch more] and greuous be þe *add.* F temptacioun] þat þei han *add.* U 152–3 and ... greuouser] *om.* WF

153 greuouser] hardore SV, greuaunce sere M, greuaunces PCh, and *add.* FHT$^{2}$ þei ... agayne] ȝef þei withstondyn hem U þei] þow W, ȝe F stonden agayne] *om.* W, hem *add.* HT$^{2}$ and] *om.* W, vn BB$^{2}$ ouercomen] hem *add.* URGSV TIiHT$^{2}$B$^{2}$Ha, hit *add.* F 153–4 har ... be] be þi ioy W, þai ioy Dd har] ȝoure F

154 in ... loue] *om.* αFHa þei] ȝe F ben] *om.* BF passed] hem *add.* LCHe DMA, passen hennys BF, hens *add.* Ii 154–5 þei$^{2}$ ... tempted] *om.* Ar þei$^{2}$] *om.* F oþerwhile] *om.* α

155 wiked delites] *om.* α with$^{2}$] of Ch jre] with F

156 enuy ... har] *om.* P dispaire] *om.* TFLdHT$^{2}$B$^{2}$ presumpcioun] *om.* α many] temptacions *add.* LCT$^{3}$BIiMTr, synnes *add.* F har] þer is Ch remedy] þer aȝens *add.* L shal] þat schulde Ch be] holy *add.* He

157 wakynge] *om.* He These þynges] *om.* Ar þynges] foure SVWT, werkes Ch yf ... be] i SV 157–66 þei ... As] *om.* Ar

158 þei ... and$^{2}$] *om.* SV þei putteth] þat doþ HT$^{2}$, may put Ha away] *om.* T and filthed] *om.* T$^{3}$BIiMHa filthed] slewþe T, fiȝtiþ LCHeA, foly F fro] for LCHe

159 hit] a mannes herte α, her F for] fro A of] *om.* Ch loued] seruyd B

161 oþerwhile] *om.* BIiHa tempteth] tempted V, gode *add.* LCHeT$^{3}$BIiM 161–2 þat ... on] *om.* Ha

162 bi ... on] *om.* W, i lone by hem self T, leuyng al one BIi a] anoþer G and sutile] *om.* Ii, and solilyche Ch He] *om.* Ch transfigureth ... in] makeþ him liche to α transfigureth] transfigured Lt, formeþ Ch in$^{2}$] þe lyknes of *add.* DdR$^{2}$FfLC HeDT$^{3}$BIiMPFLdHT$^{2}$TrChA an] *om.* SFA

163 of] and Ii light] in liknesse *add.* P 163–4 oon ... angels] *om.* Ch oon] an angel B$^{2}$ Goddis] þe gode L

164 comen] sent P to] him for to *add.* F so he] suche T desceyueth] hem þat beþ *add.* α, þem *add.* M foles] him Ch

165 and] *om.* P anoon] *om.* αCD, leeue ne *add.* BIi trow] hem neþer *add.* L, ne triste *add.* P to all] *trs.* B al] here Ff, yuele *add.* D, *om.* Ld bot] and α, *om.* A asketh] takeþ S, *om.* V 165–6 of ... ham] þat þei bigyle hem nat P 165–6 of ... men] *om.* LdHT$^{2}$

166 conynge] wise(r) USVDTr, kunne T, witty LCHeT$^{3}$BIiMFChA men] for *add.* Ii I] a A a] anker þat was *add.* α recluse] reclusid and schut T, ankere BIi written] *om.* Ha

167 that ... womman] *om.* Ar was] *om.* G good] blessed C yuel angel] deuel α oft ... angel] *add. later hand* B oft tymes] *om.* αAr

168 a good] goddis CA

169 Wherfor ... bot] *om.* Ch was] *om.* Ar right] *om.* SVTIiPLdHT$^{2}$ bot] and Ar

170 neuerþelatre] *om.* BAr told] sayde α, schewide LCHeDT$^{3}$BIiMFLdTrA hit] *om.* WT hir ... fadyre] a wise counceyllour C as] was H and quaynt] *om.* αAr

171 quaynt] redy U, war DdA, sutil L, sly CD, gode Ha þis] to RGSVAr, *om.* WTCh, his P counsail] and seyde *add.* P Whan ... cometh] *om.* R, þat sche scholde G, he sayde *add.* DdR$^{2}$FfLCDT$^{3}$BIiMFLdHT$^{2}$B$^{2}$ChHa, next *add.* P bid] preie U, *om.* R, comand B hym] hem B

172 þe] hire G Seynt Marie] gods moder *add.* B, *om.* Ha Whan ... so] and þenne SV hath don] doþ PTrCh don so] schewid hire Ar sey] youre *add.* Ii

173 Sho ... so] *om.* W, aftyr his conseyl *add.* T, als he bad so scho did Ha and] þo *add.* U, *om.* DdR$^{2}$FfHeDTrChHa no] *om.* A hir] here *add.* Ar my] *om.* B

174 sho$^{1}$] *om.* R$^{2}$Ff seid] þenne *add.* SVWT sho$^{2}$] I Ar He . . . þat] *om.* Ar He] and þe fend LPF, and He saw] sayde He, seyþ B þat] on alle maneres *add.* α

175 hym . . . wille] she wold nedys se hure and fulfille hur desir P wold] *om.* SV Anoon] riȝt *add.* U, and Ar

176 forth] beforn hire syȝt (*om.* A) ChA body of] *om.* Dd body] lady He be] als to hyr syght *add.* DdR$^{2}$FfLCHeDT$^{3}$BIiMPFLdHT$^{2}$B$^{2}$TrChHaA shewed hit] sche wente B$^{2}$ hit] *om.* GDdMFChAr, hir L

177 anon] *om.* UαDdR$^{2}$FfLCDBIiMPFLdHT$^{2}$B$^{2}$TrChHaAAr hir$^{1}$] doun *add.* BIiMF hir$^{2}$] *om.* RGSVHeHaAr knees] ryth deuoutlych supposyng hyt hadde be oure lady *add.* B said] byganne to sey hire Ii and$^{3}$] als tyte *add.* DdR$^{2}$T$^{3}$MHaA, anon *add.* FfLCHePFLdB$^{2}$TrCh, as soone *add.* D, sodenly *add.* BIi, also swiþe *add.* HT$^{2}$ al] *om.* He

178 for shame] *om.* SVT sethen] *om.* HeCh he] *om.* FfDBLd neuer . . . hyre] nomore þere Ch aye] *om.* UαDdR$^{2}$FfLCDBIiMPFLdHT$^{2}$Tr, more after (so Ha) HeHa, þere B$^{2}$, agayn Ar to] *om.* TChAr, so to tempte CHeTr hyre] þer T, so to tempte hir *add.* LIiA, *om.* ChAr 178–202 This . . . Crist] *om.* Ar

179 for . . . hoop] *om.* FfF for I] in B, I Ha shal haue] haþ B$^{2}$ þe] so *add.* Ch in . . . maner] *om.* P bot] for *add.* UαDdFfLdHT$^{2}$B$^{2}$, for Ch

180 be] ay *add.* Ha if] of W such] wyk Dd, *om.* Ld þe] *om.* LtB

181 or wakynge] *om.* L that þou] and B trow] hem *add.* URGW*FB$^{2}$, hit *add.* SVCh, þan *add.* T nat] *om.* F sone] þeron *add.* He, to þam *add.* Ha 181–3 til . . . lighte] *om.* He

182 Moor priuely] and ȝitt (if T) anoþer maner α, yet *add.* Ii and . . . perillous] *om.* SVDdR$^{2}$FfLCDT$^{3}$BIiMPFLdHT$^{2}$B$^{2}$TrChHaA and] þat is WT in] þe forme (liknesse FLdHT$^{2}$Ch) of *add.* DdR$^{2}$FfLCDBIiMPFLdHT$^{2}$B$^{2}$ChA, þe likenes and in þe forme of *add.* T$^{3}$ an] *om.* UR$^{2}$DB, to S

183 lighte] of *add.* WT þat . . . with] *om.* Ch þat] and He with] as *add.* L, in þis manere He, and is *add.* BIi he] þei He, hym *add.* B hideth] holdiþ his F yuel] al BIi

184 vndre þe] in F þe . . . of] *om.* DCh liknesse] colour Ld good] god B Oon] and is RG, is *add. alia* whan] *om.* Ch

185 eggeth] styres WPTr, temptiþ L eese and] *om.* Ch 185–6 and$^{2}$ . . . fleisshe] *om.* WTrCh softhed] sustynaunce F, softe H oure] *om.* Ff

186 vndre need] moore (*om.* RG) þan nedeth Uα, vndirnethe DdR$^{2}$FfM need] þe colour ⟨of nede PTrTr$^{2}$⟩ BIiPTrTr$^{2}$ sustene . . . kynd] oure sustenaunce α such] whuche SV, soþe T thoghtes] þowe T he] þei He putteth] put ese SV

187 in vs] *om.* Ha vs] oure hertes αBH, to oure mynde that Ii bot yf] boþe G we] ye Lt and . . . wel] *om.* A drynke] dynke Lt wel$^{2}$] *om.* IiTrH$^{2}$ and$^{2}$] *om.* Ii sleep . . . and] *om.* RG ligge] wel and *add.* HeP, and go *add.* F

188 warme] or elles *add.* GF we] ye Lt, he Tr nat] *om.* H God] to pay *add.* M

189 we] ye Lt, he DTr haue] *om.* Ii Bot . . . to] and so he wolde P Bot] Boþe G, þus *add.* L ⟨beware for Ii⟩ þerby *add.* BIi, and þus F, by þis mene *add.* Ch, *om.* A þynketh] þan *add.* B$^{2}$ vs] *om.* Ch ouer] done *add.* Ch mych] ese and *add.* RGB$^{2}$ luste] and ese *add.* SVWTH$^{2}$, lufe Ii 189–90 of . . . loue] *om.* DdR$^{2}$FfLCHeDT$^{3}$BIiMPFLdHT$^{2}$B$^{2}$TrChA, and so vse vs in vyses Ha

190 Goddis loue] godenes T

191 whan] he *add.* SV, he hides ille *add.* R$^{2}$Ff, *om.* B$^{2}$, þat Ha liknes] and *add.* T good] godes GLP he] *om.* Ld entisseth] styrs W 191–2 ouer . . . and] *om.* αDPH$^{2}$, appreue B$^{2}$ ouer] *om.* DdR$^{2}$FfCT$^{3}$BIiMFLdHT$^{2}$ChHaA

192 penaunce] and hardnesse *add.* P self] soule U, slepe A seith] wyl sey B

193 thus] if T, *om.* Ld he] or scho *add.* HaH$^{2}$ suffreth] doþ TT$^{3}$ 193–4 for . . . loue] *om.* SV

194 shal haue] is worþi SV    et] wel and drynke *add.* Ld    and . . . mete] *om.* αBIi    and feble] of þo feblest Ha

195 þe$^1$] and Ch    thynnest] meneste α    Rek] ryȝt T    of] *om.* T    sleep] to *add.* Ch

196 þe$^1$ . . . habergeone] *om.* T    and] *om.* UR$^2$FfCBIiMPB$^2$HaA, of D    habergeone] þat *add.* L    Al] *om.* F    affliccioun] noyande α, torment FLdT$^2$Tr, turnement H

197 hit] for goddes loue *add.* αH$^2$, *om.* TrCh    þer be] *om.* αBH$^2$    be] may T$^3$IiB$^2$    þat may] *om.* αT$^3$BIiMB$^2$H$^2$    may] *om.* LHeF    penaunce] and abstynence *add.* LCT$^3$    197–9 He . . . litelle] *om.* Ld    197–8 He . . . þus] Somme saiþ to þe F

198 þe$^1$] *om.* SV    about] warde to begyle þe and *add.* Ha    þe$^2$] body and soule *add.* UαH$^2$    198–9 with . . . litelle] *om.* α    with . . . mych] *om.* U    mych] ⟨penaunce and R$^2$FfT$^3$BIiMHa⟩ abstinence *add.* DdR$^2$FfLCHeDT$^3$BIiMChHaA, penaunce *add.* PFHT$^2$B$^2$TrH$^2$    198–9 als . . . litelle] *om.* BIiFHT$^2$    seid] seiþ He

199 wild] ⟨is aboute L⟩ to DdR$^2$FfLCDT$^3$MPB$^2$ChHaAH$^2$, *om.* He    litelle] penaunce *add.* UPH$^2$, abstynence *add.* L    Forþi] but RGWT, for A    we] þou F    wil] *om.* Ha    be . . . disposed] plese god α    right] wel F

200 vs . . . meen] as good men schulde we most WT    vs bihoueth] þou moste F    bihoueth] behouid H    set . . . in] *om.* RGSV    vs] þe F    200–1 so . . . vndre] nouþer ⟨take W*⟩ to litel ny to mychel ⟨do penaunce T⟩ but þat þe flesshe be vndur þe spirit α    so] and DdR$^2$FfLDMPFLdHT$^2$Ha    we] þou F    oure] oþer He, *om.* BFB$^2$Tr

201 our] þi F    vndre] but *add.* B, foot *add.* P    and] *om.* C    neuerþelatre] loke *add.* U, also α, *om.* CTr    hit] þow U, heo SV

202 in . . . Criste] to serue god α    of . . . Criste *om.* C

203 Also] Aso Lt    203–4 our . . . maneres] slepand he temptis vs Ar    whan] whil S    we] *om.* A

204 þan] þat Ld    he . . . about] is his besynesse Ch    he is] *om.* Ff    is] *om.* R$^2$    204–5 orwhiles . . . state] *om.* α    with] *om.* F    grisful] foule liknesses of U, vggly DdR$^2$FfT$^3$IiMHaAArH$^2$, ferdlich L, ferli CHe, ferful DTr, oryble BHT$^2$, grisly PCh, gastful FLd, foule B$^2$

205 ymages] thingis Ar    make . . . and] *om.* Ha    ferd] radde DdR$^2$Ar, a dredde Ff IiMPB$^2$A, agast LCHe, aferde and drad T$^3$, dredful FLdHT$^2$    and . . . state] *om.* Ar    loth] full A    our] owen *add.* U

206 with] liknesses of *add.* U    206–7 faire . . . vayne] *om.* Ha    faire . . . confortable] *om.* α    faire syghtes] *om.* T$^3$BIiM    faire] *om.* A, and Ar    and . . . confortable] *om.* TrAr    and] *om.* UFB$^2$Ch, oþer thyngs *add.* A    þat] *om.* Ld

207 vs . . . make] *om.* CAr    glad] and ioyous *add.* B    in vayne] and fayne RG    vayne] glory *add.* WTF, vanyte BIi    make] ȝeueth Ff    207–8 we$^1$ . . . þat] *om.* Ar    ben$^1$] holy and goode and *add.* BIi    ben$^2$] and thurgh þo fayre syghtes gare vs ioy en veyn and wene þat we are qware we are noght *add.* Ha

208 othrewhile . . . for] *om.* B    telleth vs] *om.* α    telleth] maketh U    vs$^1$] weene *add.* U    holy and] *om.* Ii    and good] *om.* Ar    for to] and so Ar

209–10 othrewhile . . . dispaire] *om.* Dd    209 he seith] *om.* T    seith] maketh vs to weene U    we] *om.* A    and synful] *om.* Ld    209–10 make . . . fal] brynge vs RGLd

210 in] and D    210–11 he . . . And] *om.* Ar    he] *om.* G    suffreth] sufficeþ T, vs noght to be temped hardur þan we myght agayn stande *add.* Ha    nat] ne ȝit Ha    oure sleep] þis lettyng αL

211 be] don to vs *add.* SVT    to vs] *om.* SVTr, as þus H    if] but SV    we] schul *add.* SV    211–14 adresse . . . thoghtes] suffre al ⟨paciently and RGWT⟩ mekely for

his loue and ȝyue no faiþ to hem (him SV) ⟨þat þat is ur enemi SV⟩ but stalworþely (studefastliche SVT) triste in ihesu crist $\alpha$ adresse] ordeyne LCTrH$^2$, wole dresse D, rewle P, redresse FLd

212 welle . . . þou] *om.* Ld euermore] whanne þou art *add.* L

213 wakynge] *om.* C outrage] and excesse *add.* P of] *om.* H without] oþer Ar yuel] foule F

214–19 Bot . . . þat[3]] *om.* Ar 214 Bot] of o þing I warne þe þat *add.* $\alpha$ many] a man and womman *add.* $\alpha$T$^3$ hath] *om.* TrCh desceyuet] deceyues TrCh 214–15 he . . . ham[1]] þei Ch

215 hath] *om.* M maked] schewid hem summe soþe to make B$^2$ ham[1]] and *add.* V[*S corr.*] set . . . ham[2]] *om.* F ham[2]] and *add.* V, hym Ff, dremes Ch he] þe deuyl Ch shewed] wente RSVWT, saide G ham[3]] *om.* GHeCh

216 begiled] hem *add.* UDdR$^2$FfHeDT$^3$MPFLdHT$^2$B$^2$HaAH$^2$, bigyleþ hem (*om.* G) $\alpha$LCBIi oon] anoþer SV, summe T$^3$IiM, synne B, *om.* P þat was] *om.* Ch was] is SVTL, arn BIiTr Forþi] for as SV

217 many] muche SVH$^2$, *om.* A bisynesse foloweth] a man bileueth his foule U bisynesse] oþer synnes Ch 217–18 and . . . ham] *om.* $\alpha$H$^2$, and þere as buþ manie dremes beþ manie vanites He and] whan U þei] he F fel] fallyn FfIiB$^2$TrCh, ben begiled C, ben (is F) deceyuyd BF, felow M þat] as he U, and LM hopped] hopen FfB$^2$, trowen CBIiMTr, truste F, leuyn Ch

218 ham] þat many war *add.* A

219 Wherfor] loke *add.* T, be ware *add.* LCHe, for lok A þat[1]] *om.* T begilet] deceyued $\alpha$TrH$^2$ with ham] And *add.* U, *om.* P þou[2]] *om.* R$^2$

220 vj] fiue L, þre B, sere Ch Two ben] þe whyche B neþer . . . other] na man Ar

221 eschape] or eskape *add.* P þey bene] *om.* WTL þey] þeose hit S, þulke V if] whanne BIi womb] *om.* S lere] empty URGDBIiHT$^2$B$^2$TrH$^2$, voyde SVTLC He, tome WDdR$^2$FfT$^3$MLdHaAAr, come FCh or . . . ful] oþer with mete oþer with drynk F many] may TFfP

222 in . . . maneres] *om.* Ar in] and A ham] *om.* LCHeDTrA þrid] oþer B

223 enemy] þat fereth vs ofte beforn and illusioune folwende of oure enemy *add.* Ff ferth] þridde B of] þe T 223–4 before . . . folwynge] þat a man þenkeþ er he slepe and $\alpha$

224 fyfte] fyrþe B þrogh] þiuȝt L 224–5 þat . . . maneres] *om.* $\alpha$Ch

225 done] *om.* B$^2$ many] sexe Ld, sere Ar maneres] þat bifalliþ hem slepinge *add.* F vj] fyfþe B thoghtes] þat fallen (are Ar) *add.* CIiMAr before] *om.* T, þat ⟨þei He⟩ falliþ *add.* LHe þat . . . to] of ihesu $\alpha$ falleth] touchiþ LCHeT$^3$B IiM

226 Criste] *om.* RHa chirche] by *add.* UT, of *add.* B, with *add.* IiPB$^2$, and *add.* FLd, or *add.* Ha 226–7 In . . . slepen] *om.* Ar thus] þis SVFLd many] *om.* SVBF

227 toucheth] þou chesest RSV, þou sexte T, þouȝtes P of] *om.* Ha dremes] of *add.* ChHa men . . . slepen] *om.* $\alpha$ men] and wommen *add.* LT$^3$, *om.* A so] *om.* L

228 þe lattre] þe lothere LdT$^2$, þe othere H, *om.* Ha yeue] oure *add.* B$^2$, ony trowyng *add.* A feith] or credence *add.* G, to hym *add.* C to] hem or to *add.* T, *om.* C any dreme] þam Ha any] dede *add.* C sone] *om.* $\alpha$FH$^2$, wel L, ȝeue [*subpuncted*] *add.* D

229 soth . . . which[2]] *om.* Ar soth . . . is] *om.* A soth] ne to summe *add.* G fals] sum tyme *add.* SVWT, lees D þe] our P

230 so] *om.* DdHeAr, þat LC vanytees] forþi sais salomon mani bisynes folows dremes and þai felle þat trowid in þaim *add.* Ar

231–6 and . . . body] *om.* Ar 231 and[1]] *om.* C þei[1]] may *add.* DdFfHa

231–2 for . . . ham] *om.* HeDTrCh for] and so L heghen . . . men] make men proude BIi heghen] ben LtHT², eggen UCA, bitriflen RG, ⟨be WTH²⟩ doten SVWTH², ⟨temptiþ and stiriþ and so þei L⟩ enpriden LT³MLd, entir and F vnstable] vnwise UH², *om.* α, ⟨manye L⟩ vnwhaynt DdR²FfLT³MLdHT²B²A, vnsly C, quently P, quoynte F, vnwhayne Ha men] me Lt[*subpuncted*] so] *om.* GSVPF, queyntly *add.* BIi

232 ham] many C, þat tristiþ on hem *add.* F

233 I] sithen it is U, *om.* DdR²FfHeFA know] woot weel L þi] self and þyn *add.* T, þer A semeth] is UDdT³BIiMFH², be *add.* HT² ycuen] quemen A þe . . . of] *om.* TH² seruice] loue B² God] semende *add.* BIiM þan] þat it *add.* B hit] mychil *add.* L

234 to þe] *om.* Ch if þou] þi lyf RGHe, it Ch or bettre] *om.* α in . . . soule] *om.* αF art semynge] semest wiþouten αF, outewarde *add.* T³BChHh

235 at . . . men] *om.* Ch at . . . of] to oþer F Therfor] *om.* RSVHaA turne] þe and *add.* A þoȝt] ȝouȝþe T perfitly] profitablich L to God] *om.* F

236 hast] do *add.* UαDdR²LCHeDT³MPLdHT²B²HaAH²Hh, dost FfF, don withouten (*om.* Ii) in *add.* BIi nat] *om.* MFAAr al] siche *add.* LCHe

237 ben] not *add.* M*FAArH² haue] were Ii þe¹] name and þe *add.* F habite] siȝt L 237–8 and . . . world] *om.* αAr

238 ocupien] medlyn *alia* ham] *om.* USVTBIiPHh erthly bisynesse] þe world ⟨and bysynes þerof B⟩ αB erthly] werldly MFB²Ch bisynesse] thyngys Ii

239 oonly] *om.* ST³BIiMFTrA, outliche He, holy B² holy] *om.* Ld what . . . in] *om.* Ar bene] stande D, set *add.* T³BIiM despiseth] desiren α, loues Ar

240 al] noon α, noght Ar thynges] more þen hem nedeþ *add.* RGSV, mor þan need is *add.* WT, in her hertes *add.* Ch þat . . . nat] *om.* αAr loueth] loue ȝe C hit] þe werld Ch and] but UT³BIiMFH² brandyn] bene moost brennande α, bringes D, only *add.* BIiM, brennynge F

241 is] *om.* UB al²] *om.* T

242 syn] in her hertes *add.* Ch and¹ . . . workes] *om.* He cessen nat] settiþ hem F good] godys TM and²] folewiþ and *add.* He felen] falleth Ld a] and Lt[*subpuncted*], alle UHe, grete *add.* F

243 lyf] loue WTDdFfT³M ham self] þe T

244 vilest] foulest UCPB², worste RGW and . . . loweste] *om.* αIiTrH² holden] *om.* Ch ham] þo mast *add.* Ha wrochedest] of alle *add.* CF, wreccis DT³BMHa leest] *om.* UHa, last *add.* He, last D, in þe sight of god *add.* Ch loweste] of alle oþere and þoruȝ mynde þat þei haue of her owne wreccidnes (defautes A) þei deme not oþer boldlich for hem silf beþ in drede a good trist þei haue alwey to god þat he wole do mercy to þilke þat drediþ for to do synne for loue of goddis goodnes more þan for drede of peyne and vpon siche god is apaied þat nyle not agilte (greue A) him for loue (*om.* A) þat he is so good and on her riȝtwisnes þei triste not but al on his mercy *add.* LA, of alle oþer *add.* CMHa, loþest of alle oþer B,loþest H, laste B² is] *om.* Ch 244–5 holy . . . and] to folwen holy mennes lyf and to B holy mennys] holynesse of R²Ff

245 and . . . holy] if þou may αH² and] þou sal *add.* Ar holy] and ellys schall we neuer be saued for so god byndet *add.* A

246 And] þenke *add.* RWT in mede] meded α mede] mend B, mynde Ii with] of HT² nat] onlyche *add.* A forsakes] hast lefte α, forsoke DdAr

247 despisest] deest SV, hast despised G as . . . þat] ihesu cristes loue and αH² mych] as *add.* C forsaken] forsoke Ar 247–9 folowen . . . pacience] *om.* WT folowen] louen Ch

248 Ihesu Criste] him RGH², hem SV wilful] *om.* A and pacience] and chastite L, and penaunce He, *om.* B²Tr

249 as . . . nat] *om.* αH² may] *om.* F coueite] couaitiþ F, *om.* Ld þat] and P hym] *om.* He nat] *om.* A 249–50 And . . . wille] *om.* W, whan T

250 mych . . . how] *om.* BIiTrHa  and . . . wille] loue RGSVH$^{2}$  and how] *om.* Ch  wille] and deuocioun *add.* Ar  presentes] offerest RSVWTTrH$^{2}$, hast offred G  vowes] herte and þi prayers αH$^{2}$, preiers LCHeT$^{3}$BIiMTrAAr, wordis B$^{2}$, body Ha  befor] to αTrHaH$^{2}$  hym] ihesu Ii, god Ar  250–8 for . . . aise] and þenke on þat word þat he to þe saiþ ⟨þere he saiþ RG⟩ fili da michi cor tuum ⟨et sufficit T⟩ þat is sone (*om.* W) ȝyue me þin herte and saye þus to him in þi soule lord ihesu if I hadde an herte þat al loue were in þat euer was of aungels and mankynde I wolde biseche þe to receyue hit lord ihesu and ⟨ȝut T⟩ hit were not to suche a lord as þou art þat ȝaf þi self for him (me GTH$^{2}$) to deȝe on þe croys ⟨and ouer þat þou ȝaue me alle þat I haue to body and to soule to siche gostly speche he takeþ good kepe RGSVH$^{2}$⟩ and siþen he (þou T) seendeþ (semeþ R, takeþ soo he scheweþ G) to þat soule þat dwelleþ (longeþ SVWTH$^{2}$) þus in loue and leteþ hit fele of his swetnes þat fedeþ alle aungels and þanne whenne þat sely (self W) soule feleþ þat swetnes þat god to hit bryngeþ (sendeþ SV, birles W, dyȝeyþ T, huldeþ oute þerto H$^{2}$) þan wol hit kepe no bodily ese ne lustes of þe flesshe but forȝeteþ (forȝyuyþ T) alle ⟨fals SV⟩ vanytees of þis false (cursede SV) world and to drede no sorwes ne angres þat may falle to þe flesshe αH$^{2}$

251 to . . . egh] þat he haþ hit is for þe He  he] ihesu P  his egh] reward Ch  his] *om.* BIi  251–3 And . . . delite] *om.* Ar

252 feruour] dreede U, sauour ⟨he heres hem A⟩ LCHePFLdA, fauour T$^{3}$MHT$^{2}$, longyng BIi, of luf *add.* Ha  coueit] sone coueytande Ch  non] oþer *add.* L, in no manere of Ch  bot] him and in *add.* B$^{2}$  252–3 þe . . . of] oure sauyour U  þe sauour] þy sauyour B

253 in] *om.* FA  þi] he LF  253–5 wondrefully . . . and] god reuis fra his lofers þe lust of flesh and of Ar  wondrefully] wonderful werkyis M, when durfullich F

254 worcheþ] werreþ D  þe . . . reueth] *om.* L  reueth] bynemeth U, takiþ CPHT$^{2}$, nemeþ He  luste] loue LPTr, of þe lust *add.* F

255 and blood] *om.* BIi  and] þoruȝ H  blood] for *add.* Ii, and *add.* Ch  þrogh . . . loue] *om.* ArHh  He] and TrHaAr  to] haf *add.* R$^{2}$Ff  wil] to *add.* R$^{2}$Ff, desire L, louen Ch

256 rise] *om.* B  in to] to haue T$^{3}$BIiM  foryet] alle *add.* F

257 and$^{1}$] of P, al *add.* F  loue] lustis LCHeA  of . . . world] *om.* Ar  dreed] grutche with Ha  no] werldly *add.* M  may] *om.* B

258 falle] to laghte þat may fallen *add.* Ff, to hem ⟨and makith hem L⟩ *add.* LBCh to . . . aise] ⟨to loth Ii⟩ and bodyly desese BIi  loth . . . mych] lodeli Ff  loth] hente hem U, laghte R$^{2}$, loue H  bodili] *om.* FfP  To suffre] anger *add.* αH$^{2}$, *om.* B, angwysch and trybulacyoun *add.* Ch  his] goddes αH$^{2}$  loue] þenne *add.* SV, þat *add.* T, angers and tribulacyons *add.* M  ham] to T$^{3}$Ii, *om.* BM

259 hyt] deynte and *add.* B  ioy] swete αH$^{2}$, and mirthe *add.* Ld  and] *om.* TT$^{3}$LdCh, so *add.* C  solitarie] ⟨bi WT⟩ hemself *add.* RGWT, heo alone SV  þei . . . gret] hem (him LC) þinketh LCHeDChA, to þinke it T$^{3}$BIiMTr, *om.* Ar  gret] delitite and ioy with grete *add.* Ha  confort] and *add.* CHeT$^{3}$M  259–60 þat . . . deuocioun] *om.* BIi  þat] *om.* H, for þan A  þei$^{2}$] beþ by hem self and *add.* T letted] but He

260 þat] here URSVWTR$^{2}$FfLFLdB$^{2}$ChHaArH$^{2}$, *om.* GCHeA  deuocioun] and her prayers *add.* αH$^{2}$

261–5 Now . . . bettre] *om.* Ar  261 ben] *om.* A  261–2 wors . . . ben] *om.* H  261–2 and . . . semen] *om.* WTC[*B corr. in margin*]ChH$^{2}$.

262 ben] *om.* A  þan . . . semen] *om.* He  amonge] alle *add.* C  þat] *om.* A haue] nat *add.* Ii

263 of] relygyoun and *add.* Ch  enforce] strength WTBIiFLdHT$^{2}$  þe] *om.* BP þat . . . may] þy myght Ld

264 nat] so SB  wors] wiþinne *add.* αH$^{2}$  semest] wiþouten *add.* αH$^{2}$  do] soo *add.* WT  as . . . the] *om.* W  I] sal *add.* Ha  þis] *om.* P  short] *om.* U

265 of lyvynge] *om.* Ch lyvynge] leryng RGSVTLH$^{2}$[*W corr.*], lufyng A þe$^{1}$] helpe and *add.* F

266 wel] *om.* WTCh bettre] þan þou art holdene *add.* W, in tyme comynge amen *add.* T$^{3}$

267 Atte . . . begynnynge] *om.* Ar entierly] *om.* FLdHT$^{2}$ to] god *add.* BH$^{2}$
267–8 That . . . fro] and leue Ar

268 to Ihesu] *om.* $\alpha$HeBIiHaH$^{2}$ nat . . . turnynge] *om.* WT 268–70 bot . . . þoght] *om.* C turnynge$^{2}$] *om.* SV, turne þe B al þe] *om.* GSV 268–9 and . . . bisynes] *om.* Ld 268–9 and .. occupaciouns] *om.* B and þe] *om.* SV and] of WL

269 and$^{1}$] of LCh occupaciouns and] *om.* $\alpha$ and$^{2}$] *om.* SV, of M of$^{1}$] þe warlde and *add.* T$^{3}$Ch worldly thynges] þe (þis Ff) werld R$^{2}$FfAr worldly] werthly W

270 luste] luffis Ha and . . . loue] *om.* T$^{3}$BIiMPLdHT$^{2}$TrH$^{2}$ vayne] idel SV loue] spech Ha so . . . was] and be noght Ar þoght] entente $\alpha$ was] *om.* F euer] er S, *om.* LTrHa, beforn Ch downward] *om.* Ar

271 modelynge] pouryng U, *om.* $\alpha$LHeBIi, moldand R$^{2}$, mellende Ff, wrotynge D, medlyng PTrCh, grobbynge FLdHT$^{2}$ whil . . . world] *om.* C whil] as Ar world] þat hit be *add.* RGSVW, late it *add.* T now] bot Ar be] it *add.* U, *om.* RGSVW euer] *om.* $\alpha$He

272 vpward . . . fyre] *om.* C fyre] fer USVWB$^{2}$ sechynge] to *add.* RW, to SV, schynyng to T right] *om.* $\alpha$, so *add.* H spouse] ihesu *add.* $\alpha$T$^{3}$TrH$^{2}$

273 his] *om.* C hym] whom FLdH$^{2}$, *om.* HT$^{2}$ art turned] turne þe Ha

274 enlumyneth] lyȝteneþ ⟨in TIi⟩ RGTLIiTr, lihteþ ⟨in F⟩ SVWCHeFAr, schetteþ in B, alyghteþ Ld and$^{1}$] for to $\alpha$PB$^{2}$H$^{2}$, so þat R$^{2}$Ff hit] *om.* LtU$\alpha$DdLCHeD T$^{3}$MPFLdHT$^{2}$B$^{2}$HaAH$^{2}$, þou BIiTrChAr forsaketh] forsakest UCHeDBIiFLdH T$^{2}$TrChAr, forsake $\alpha$PB$^{2}$H$^{2}$ al] *om.* P and$^{2}$] *om.* A confourmeth] confourmest ULCHeDBIiPB$^{2}$TrCh, conferme T, acordest FLdT$^{2}$, accordeþ H

275 hit] him SV, þee LBIiLdCh, *om.* F, þi wille Ar to$^{1}$] goode *add.* BTr and . . . thewes] *om.* B thewes] þouȝtes $\alpha$Ch, condiciouns P and$^{2}$ . . . debonerte] *om.* $\alpha$ debonerte] pouerte MF, þat þow hast bygunne withouten slownesse and wyrynesse *add.* A and mekenesse] *om.* C

276 and$^{1}$] þat *add.* U$\alpha$DdR$^{2}$FfLCHe*DT$^{3}$BIiMPLdHT$^{2}$TrHaAArH$^{2}$Hh, þat B$^{2}$ maist] alway *add.* G, *om.* Ar laste and] *om.* Ha and$^{2}$ . . . goodenesse] in goodenes and wexe in verte C and wix] alwey R, *om.* G, and way A 276–7 þat . . . lyf] and in ekyng of loue A hast begunne] bigynne UW

277 without] eny *add.* HeB$^{2}$ slownes] slaught Ii or sorynesse] in seruice W, *om.* TC or$^{2}$ . . . of] ouerþynkyng on B irkynge] werynesse URGTLCHeDLdH T$^{2}$TrHh, owenyng SV, weeryȝyng PH$^{2}$, wickidnesse F þi] þis SV, þe Ff lyf] self Lt, and ⟨þerfore SVWT⟩ þese (*om.* SV) *add.* $\alpha$

278 þi þoght] mynde $\alpha$ 278–80 tyl . . . Crist] *om.* Ar in perfite] *trs.* C perfite] perfiȝtnes and L loue] lyf UTr

280 is$^{1}$] þys *add.* B, this Ii þi] þis Lt 280–1 here . . . oght] þat short is RGT, þat schorteþ SV, þat schortis W here] *om.* DT$^{3}$BIiMTrA so] *om.* HAr 280–1 þat$^{1}$ . . . oght] *om.* ArH$^{2}$ þat$^{1}$ . . . is] yt P vnnethe] unese T$^{3}$IiM

281 we . . . in] sothe þis lyfe is bot Ha bot] *om.* RB$^{3}$, as *add.* TrAr in] *om.* T poynt] if we lickyn it to þe lyue bot in a poynte *add.* M 281–2 þat$^{1}$ . . . poynt] *om.* HaAr

282 if we] *om.* Ar likene . . . to] take (in Ar) reward of BAr lesteth] schal last BFB$^{2}$

283 Anoþer] but þer P vncerteyntee] vncerteyn WFfCTr$^{2}$, vnsykernesse FLd oure] lyues *add.* Ch endynge] deȝing RGWT we wot] wetyn U

284 we$^{1}$ . . . dey$^{1}$] *om.* αAr  ne$^{1}$ . . . dey$^{2}$] *om.* CHePCh  ne$^{1}$ . . . dey$^{1}$] *om.* R$^{2}$Ff T$^{3}$BMTrB$^{3}$  we$^{2}$ . . . dey$^{2}$] *om.* αH$^{2}$  we$^{3}$ . . . dey$^{3}$] *om.* Ar  ne$^{2}$ . . . dey] *om.* UB$^{2}$ we$^{3}$ . . . dey] *om.* BM  dey$^{3}$] ende RGW, deynen S*, ordeynen V  ne$^{3}$] whare ne *add.* R$^{2}$Ff

285 go] *om.* Ar  whan . . . ben] after oure Ar  þat$^{1}$] þerfore UH$^{2}$, *om.* αHe TrArHh  285–6 þat$^{2}$ . . . dey] noght þat we witte for we suld be ai redi Ar 285–6 þat$^{2}$ . . . wol] *om.* PA  þat þis] *om.* BB$^{2}$, it M  þis] hit SVT$^{3}$FChH$^{2}$B$^{3}$Tr$^{2}$, deþ THa  be] certeyn and oure tyme *add.* Ha  vncerteyne] vnknowen SV, certayne R$^{2}$FfD, and vnknowen *add.* LHe  til vs] *om.* UChTr$^{2}$

286 for . . . wol] *om.* SV  euer] *om.* DM  to dey] *om.* Ld  þrid] secunde P

287 we] *om.* A  had] lyued UαM, bene DdLCHePLdHB$^{2}$ChAH$^{2}$B$^{3}$Tr$^{2}$, *om.* R$^{2}$Ff DBFT$^{2}$HaHh, mysspendid T$^{3}$  here] *om.* α

288 how . . . bene] *om.* P  we . . . lyved] *om.* M  haue] here *add.* CHeTrB$^{3}$ lyved . . . whi] despended hit (*om.* W) αAr  whate] wan B  and whi] *om.* LCHe TrAH$^{2}$Tr$^{2}$, it has ben *add.* Ha

289 whan] while B$^{2}$B$^{3}$  haue ben] were αArH$^{2}$, ben B  Therfor] for þis RG, for so SV, for þus WT, for He  289–94 seith . . . we] *om.* Ar  seith] sayde DdR$^{2}$ FfLCDT$^{3}$BMPHT$^{2}$B$^{2}$HaAB$^{3}$Tr$^{2}$

290 He] ho T  callet] i tayled SV, causyde TTr$^{2}$  þe tyme] þee W, þer T ayeyns me] *om.* B$^{2}$  me] vs αH$^{2}$  That . . . þat] þe whiche URGSV  That] es *add.* R$^{2}$FfLdB$^{3}$Tr$^{2}$, for L  same] ewyrch WTHeBFLdChTr$^{2}$, ilk DdR$^{2}$FfT$^{3}$MHT$^{2}$ HaA, ech LCDB$^{2}$HhB$^{3}$  tyme$^{2}$] day WTDdR$^{2}$FfLCHeDT$^{3}$BMPFLdHT$^{2}$B$^{2}$ChHa AHhTr$^{2}$  þat he] *om.* T

291 he] he *add.* Lt[*subpuncted*]  lent] ileuyd F, sent ChA  vs] *om.* F  here] *om.* T$^{3}$BM, tyme *add.* P, houer B$^{2}$  dispend] it *add.* LHeBH$^{2}$, spend siluer F  oops] vse UDdR$^{2}$FfLHeDT$^{3}$BMPFHT$^{2}$B$^{2}$TrChHaAHhB$^{3}$Tr$^{2}$, werkes αC, þewes Ld  and] *om.* TBFCh  penauns] and *add.* WTDdR$^{2}$FfLCHeDT$^{3}$BMPLdHT$^{2}$B$^{2}$TrChHaAB$^{3}$ Tr$^{2}$  his] gods DdR$^{2}$FfCHeDT$^{3}$BMPFLdHT$^{2}$B$^{2}$TrChHaAB$^{3}$Tr$^{2}$, good L

292 seruice] for *add.* α, þan *add.* T$^{3}$B  we] þanne *add.* U, lese hit or *add.* He hit] our tyme P  in erthly] in erthly *add.* Lt[*first subpuncted*]  ful] wel SVHT$^{2}$ 292–3 greuously . . . demed] dere mon we abigge hit α

293 punshed] þerfor *add.* B  Forthy] For SVWTDdMCh  is] *om.* G  on of] *om.* B

294 bot] *om.* αLHeDT$^{3}$HT$^{2}$AH$^{2}$Hh  if] *om.* DdCHeDHaB$^{3}$  afforce] strength WTBFLdHT$^{2}$  vs] not *add.* α, in al manere *add.* Ch  manly . . . and] to Ar manly] namly TLCHeDT$^{3}$MPFLdHT$^{2}$ChHaAB$^{3}$, bysyly B  God] good B  and . . . good] *om.* THeDCh  do] *om.* C, al þe *add.* FB$^{2}$

295 to al] *om.* αFB$^{2}$Ar  to] *om.* CHeCh, wiþ D  we . . . euery] lastud and eche tyme we may þe whyles oure short A  do] *om.* UDdFfLCHeDT$^{3}$BPFLdHT$^{2}$B$^{2}$Ha ArH$^{2}$HhB$^{3}$, now RWT, now *add.* G, to R$^{2}$M  while our] in þis α  our . . . lesteth] we are here Ar  tyme] lyf Ch  lesteth . . . tyme] *om.* SV  lesteth] þat we dwellen here RGWT, duriþ LLd  295–6 And . . . may] *om.* T  And] in R  euery] for He, al þe ChH$^{2}$

296 God] good B  accompt] holde α, rekne P  hit] þat ⟨tyme GT⟩ RGSVT, *om.* TrArHh  as] *om.* Ch  þe . . . haue] *om.* SVWBTrChAr  þynge] tyme CDFHaB$^{3}$ Tr$^{2}$  we haue] is RGT, we A

297 losten] tynt WDdR$^{2}$FfT$^{3}$MHa, forlost B, or lorne *add.* P, lorn LdH, lefte A fourth] þridde P  þat we] to C, schul *add.* T$^{3}$BM  is] *om.* CAr  shal] *om.* Dd R$^{2}$FfLCHeDMChHaA

298 lesteth] and lyueþ *add.* P, duriþ FLd, and enduren *add.* B$^{3}$  Goddis] good LtB$^{2}$Hh, *om.* αChH$^{2}$Tr$^{2}$  loue] of god *add.* αChH$^{2}$Tr$^{2}$  endynge] dai *add.* LTr

299 ben] as *add.* α  breþere] briht as feire (fyer WT) SVWT, *om.* B  and$^{1}$ . . . angels] with aungelis and felawes Ff  and$^{1}$ . . . with] in felouschipe of T  and$^{1}$] *om.*

B and$^{2}$ . . . men] *om.* *α*H$^{2}$ holy men] halughs Ar men] *om.* L louynge] heryinge SVTH$^{2}$, lyuyng CPH, *om.* He, worschiping B$^{2}$ hauynge] *om.* SVTHaH$^{2}$, thankand Dd

300 praisynge] *om.* *α*LCT$^{3}$BMPFLdHT$^{2}$TrH$^{2}$ seynge] seo S þe kynge] *om.* Ld ioy] blis HT$^{2}$Ch in] and Ch þe$^{2}$] his RSVWTHeH$^{2}$Tr$^{2}$, *om.* GTr and shynynge] *om.* T$^{3}$BM

301 of] in SVTHeF his] lufe A sight] *om.* WDBTr$^{2}$ be] mast *add.* R$^{2}$Ff meed and] *om.* CBChB$^{3}$ mete . . . al] *om.* R$^{2}$Ff mete] fode *α*H$^{2}$ and$^{2}$] drynke and *add.* BCh al] þe ⟨most G⟩ RGH$^{2}$, *om.* SVWH, manere *add.* B

302 and . . . tel] *om.* *α* and . . . may] or tonge B man] tunge UFLdChA, *om.* DdLCHeDMPHT$^{2}$HaAr may] *om.* Ha tel] hit *add.* F

303–4 to . . . hit] *om.* M 303 is] so *add.* G 303–4 lightre . . . hit] þat blisse þat tunge ne may hit telle ne eiȝe see ne ere here ne herte þenke G þat] þis TAr, þe Ff, hys B, ilk *add.* A

304 þan] it es *add.* Ha to] þenke hit or *add.* He, *om.* CH$^{2}$ tel hit] for hit is so mychel þat herte ne may þenke hit ne tunge telle hit *add.* RSVTH$^{2}$, helle D Also] The ferthe is to P sorow] pyne Dd and$^{1}$ . . . tourment] *om.* *α*H$^{2}$ and woo] *om.* FfBHaAr woo] what DdR$^{2}$LCHeDT$^{3}$MB$^{2}$ChAHhB$^{3}$ and$^{2}$] *om.* DdR$^{2}$LCHeD T$^{3}$BMPFLdHT$^{2}$B$^{2}$TrChAB$^{3}$ and$^{3}$] what *add.* LCHeT$^{3}$B$^{2}$B$^{3}$, with diuerse Ha

305 þai] ȝe R shal] *om.* PLdHT$^{2}$ loued] louyn U*α*DdR$^{2}$FfHeBPFLdHT$^{2}$B$^{2}$ TrChH$^{2}$Tr$^{2}$, wil luf Ar 305–6 þat . . . world] *om.* T 305–6 þat . . . seen] þat ben RGSVW, but settiþ herre wille F, *om.* Ar

306 seen] may see UTr$^{2}$ in] of Ar bot] and F fileth] folowyþ TB, feles A har . . . and$^{1}$] *om.* R$^{2}$Ff har$^{1}$] in þis A and$^{1}$] nowt *add.* B luste and] *om.* D and lechurie] *om.* B and$^{2}$] of Ha lechurie] likinges *α* CH$^{2}$B$^{3}$

307 of þis] in her F lif] world *α*H$^{2}$ in$^{1}$ . . . synnes] *om.* *α* in$^{1}$] of Ff

308–9 of . . . seruauntȝ] *om.* *α* 308 of helle] *om.* P 308–9 with . . . seruauntȝ] *om.* T$^{3}$BMFAr with . . . deuil] withouten ende C serued] serueþ F

309 seruauntȝ] þe whiche is *add.* UDdR$^{2}$FfLCHeDT$^{3}$BMPFLdHT$^{2}$B$^{2}$TrChHaAAr HhB$^{3}$Tr$^{2}$, sergeantis R$^{2}$, lordschip B, *om.* P euermore] wiþouten ende *α*BTrTr$^{2}$, *add.* F, God for his mikil grace kepis alle fra helle and bring vs til his blisse amen *add.* Ar

310 I] *om.* Dd, My P wil] is *add.* P euer] *om.* LtFf clymynge] enclinande ⟨and takyng þi loue SV⟩ RGSVB, cleuyng T[*W corr.*], schynynge DT$^{3}$M, vpward *add.* F and . . . loue] *om.* SV echynge] euere synge U, encresynge LCHePB$^{2}$Ch, techinge D, doyng B, settynge F, seking HT$^{2}$ loue] liif CHe

311 in$^{1}$] to *α*B

312 degree] *om.* GSVWT[*R corr.*] doune] *om.* C to] in S, at W loghest] þis *add.* L sei] is *add.* L nat] þat *add.* C for . . . þat] *om.* UP for] þat SV, for *add.* C, þys *add.* B, if *add.* M, *om.* F I wol] *om.* B þat] noȝt T, if R$^{2}$, *om.* Ld if] *om.* RGW, þat TR$^{2}$

313 haue begunne] vse *α* vnskylful] *om.* M, suche P abstynence] but *add.* P, penaunce HT$^{2}$ þat þou] and also T hold] it *add.* U*α*DdR$^{2}$FfDT$^{3}$MPFLdHT$^{2}$ B$^{2}$HaAHh, it nat *add.* L, it oute *add.* C, on hit *add.* He, kepe hyt stylle BCh bot] *om.* BCh, y sey hit *add.* PTr for] *om.* H þat$^{2}$] *om.* DHa

314 weren] are Ha at . . . begynnynge] *om.* SVC and] is F, as LdHT$^{2}$ able] alle L, abel HT$^{2}$

315 ouer] so *add.* A penaunce] abstynense B, vsynge *add.* P þei] þat F, þe A haue] hadde P, *om.* A 315–16 letted . . . loue] not þe loue of C letted . . . and] *om.* P letted] alledgede R$^{2}$Ff

316 ham] *om.* B so] to RG, *om.* B$^{2}$H$^{2}$ loue] seruen SV God] ne seruy hym *add.* B sholden] haue *add.* BTr do] *om.* DdR$^{2}$FfLCHeDMPChHaAHh 316–18 In . . . amonestynge] *om.* *α* þe whiche] whos B

317 loue] *om.* T$^3$M wix] be LCHeDT$^3$BMHaA, encresse Ch euer] *om.* FCh and more] *om.* UPT$^2$ and$^1$] *om.* D 317–18 is . . . amonestynge] as y consayl and amonest B is] as F coueitynge] and ȝernynge *add.* Ch 317–18 and$^2$ . . . amonestynge] *om.* DH$^2$

318 amonestynge] is *add.* F 318–19 lasse . . . þe] *om.* SV 318–19 if . . . merite] *om.* B$^2$ if] þat B be in$^1$] do M

319–20 as . . . abstinence] *om.* WDdR$^2$FfCHeDT$^3$BMChHaAHh 319 as . . . be] *om.* RGT hast] *om.* H

320 moor] *om.* RG if . . . þoght] loke *α* þoght] hert TrCh how] mykel *add.* *α* maist] most Ha loue] þi lord ihesu cryste and *add.* Ch

321 þi spouse] *om.* Ld spouse] lord *α* I] wel *add.* SVB$^2$

323 Wherfore . . . þou] Foure thinges nedes man til knowe if he sal Ar Wherfore] and for *α* þou] shalt *add.* *α*Ld right] þe better *α* both] *om.* *α*T$^3$BMArH$^2$ and . . . body] *om.* T$^3$BM

324 þou . . . þynges] *om.* Ar fileth] maketh foule T, defouled H a man] him Ar

325 hym$^1$] *om.* M, a man Ld holdeth] helpyth Ch hym$^2$] clene and *add.* G

326 draweth] ordeineþ C, makyth BH$^2$ hym . . . ordeyne] *om.* *α* hym] *om.* R$^2$Ff ordeyne] conforme C

327 wille] and hys lyfe *add.* B al . . . wille] *om.* C al] *om.* *α*PFTrArH$^2$Hh For . . . first] And I answar to þo fyrst and say þat synne fyles a man and Ha For] *om.* Ff 327–8 witte . . . foule] þou shalt undurstonde þat al þe synne þat man synneþ is in þre *α* þou] wel *add.* LCHeT$^3$BMPFLdHT$^2$B$^2$TrChH$^2$ þre] *om.* R$^2$Ff

328 thynges] is *add.* A vs] all *add.* A foule] folowe DdLd, before god *add.* Ha þat . . . with] in RGSVT

329 þese] *om.* BMH$^2$ to syn] or Ar

330 syn] *om.* URSVT[*W corr.*] desire . . . il] *in margin W* desire] wilnen SV of il] *om.* T of] *om.* SV il$^1$] *om.* Ch wikked wille] *om.* RSVWT wikked] *om.* PTr il$^2$] *om.* RSV suspeccioun] presumpcioun U vndeuocioun] yuel deuocioun T, *om.* LdChA 330–1 let . . . hert] *om.* Ar let] þi thoght of *add.* Ha

331 be] *om.* UCHe, ly L ydel] uncouetouse R, vnocupyed SVWT without . . . of] in RSVWT occupacioun] of delite *add.* Ff 331–2 of . . . God] *om.* B$^2$ il dreed] *om.* Do of . . . loue] *om.* GLd loue] of god *add.* FfHa and] of DdC praysynge] longynge TB

332 God] hym FfHa il$^2$] foul U, *om.* Ha loue] *om.* UHHa errour] *om.* RSVWTTrCh affeccioun] loue Ch þi] *om.* GR$^2$FfHT$^2$ frendes] kyn B

333 or . . . louest] *om.* RSVWT or to] *om.* UHe others . . . louest] *om.* Ch þat . . . louest] *om.* Ar any mannys] *om.* RSVWT any] oþer Ch ilfare] of þyne enemyes *add.* RSVWT 333–4 sorowe . . . welfare] *om.* GDdR$^2$FfLCHeDT$^3$BMPFLdHT$^2$B$^2$ChHaAArH$^2$HhDo

334–5 whethre . . . frendes] *om.* RSVWT 334 whethre . . . no] *om.* Ar enemys . . .no] þin frendes or þin enemys Ch of$^1$] or D synful] symple P

335 honour] to holde wel of B$^2$ riche] *om.* Ar richesse] and worship hem *add.* B$^2$ vncouenable] vnable G, vnconabyll DdFfT$^3$MHaADo, vncouenabli C, vnskylful B worldis] wordis of R$^2$FfHh, godes or *add.* M

336 þe world] ⟨losse of GHeBDo⟩ þe worldes catel GLCHeT$^3$BMFLdT$^2$ADo, other mens welefare R$^2$Ff, worldliche Ch vntholmodnesse . . . is] *om.* CHeT$^3$BM vntholmodnesse] unbuxom U, *om.* LA, vnsuffrable D, ilost F, myshap Ch is] to *add.* UCh dout] dreden Ch

337 is] best *add.* Ld to] þat it Ff what nat] *om.* A what] woot D 337–8 nat . . . what] *om.* F nat] is to leue P 337–8 for . . . leue] *om.* Ar euery] eny H man] *om.* Ha oweth . . . sikyre] knowiþ C, shold wyte P oweth] is holde U he shal] is to P

338 do . . . shal] *om.* G and] *om.* LdHT$^2$ he shal] not UB, to CPCh, *om.* M he] *om.* A leue] *om.* UB obstinacioun] hardnes Ch il] wyk is B, euel dede doyngus F, yuel heuynes and Ch noy] loth UB, enuye L, ioie D, anyede F, noȝt HB$^2$ good] when he may *add.* B$^2$ 338–9 to . . . God] and F

339 serue] do GLd, suffre D, *om.* Do God] good GLd he$^1$] we L did no] nad Ha no] *om.* A ille] wel Do 339–40 or . . . lykynge] of fulfillynge Ch

340 lykynge] *om.* U, wil DdR$^2$FfLCHeDT$^3$BMPLdHT$^2$B$^2$HaAH$^2$HhDo fleishe] fleschelych wil Ch þe which] when Ar done] it *add.* Ar vnstablenesse] vnstedfastnesse HT$^2$

341 of$^2$] and B loue] sone U, lef F men] þe poeple U, for praising *add.* F, or coueyten to ben loued oþer wyse þan for god *add.* Ch

342 ham] for loste of catel *add.* F ioy . . . dedes] *om.* A il] ydul He

343 honour] or of ryches *add.* Ha dignite] or of name *add.* Ch bettre] or wisere *add.* Ar than] þat A or richer] *om.* LCHeDT$^3$BMHaA

344 richer] wyser Ch faire] or semelycher *add.* Ch, or worthiere *add.* Ar dreded] adred or rewarded Ch vaynglorie] vein ioye C, vayn likyng Ch of] or Ch any] *om.* LdAr kynd] kynne Ar

345 happe] fortune DB or$^2$] *om.* B$^2$ shame] to be schamed F pouer] good D frendes] or of ony bodilyche vnschapyliche hede *add.* Ch of$^3$] þi *add.* Dd kyn] kynde Ld

346 fre] *om.* T Goddis face] god RSVWTT$^3$ our] goode *add.* He

347 make] vs *add.* LHeDT$^3$BMPA any] of vs *add.* RSVW, us GTFLdChArDo, oþer B bettre] worse or bettir þan oþer C or wors] *om.* RSVWT þan oþre] haue U 347–8 consaille . . . techynge] *om.* P 347–8 consaille . . . good] *om.* U

348 techynge] and many oþere *add.* RSVWT, and of ony oþer steryng of loue or of drede or ioye or of sorwe mysrewled sette in ony oþer þing þan god oþer in goodnes or elles for god it is synne of herte or begynnyng of synne *add.* Ch

349 ben these] *om.* Ha these] *om.* A oft sithes] when no nede is αH$^2$, and of tyme B forsweryngel] is *add.* RTHa

350 sklaundrynge] *om.* SV or . . . halowes] þat es Ha of his] *om.* T halowes] is to *add.* G, *om.* DCh, holy B his name] hym W* his$^2$] goddis Ar without] his *add.* Ld

351–3 gaynsigge . . . seruice] *om.* ChDo 351 sothfastnes] trouþe DBTr gruch] weping D ayayns] soþfast *add.* G

352 God . . . or$^2$] *om.* W anguys] aȝe *add.* G, angris DBPAr noy or] any RGL, *om.* SVTDT$^3$BMTrAr, eny oþer Ff noy] tene F may] *om.* Ha in erth] *om.* RSVWTBAr, mirthe LCA, in herte Ff

353 vndeuoutly] wyþowten ony deuocion B and hire] *om. alia* seruice] office He bacbitynge] *om.* LCHe

354–5 flattrynge . . . manacynge] glosynge stryuinge þretinge FLdDo 354 flattrynge . . . wreyynge] *om.* A lesynge . . . wreyynge] cursynge (*om.* He) desceyuynge and bacbiting LCHe, *om.* HT$^2$ lesynge] mysansweryng *add.* P wreyynge] corsynge UPTrH$^2$, warying RGSVWDdR$^2$FfDT$^3$MB$^2$ChHaArHh, trasyng T, bannynge B disfamynge] *om.* CHT$^2$ 354–63 cursynge . . . God] ony man to ire to spek foul wordes þat wer no nede glosyng plesyng or for loue of men or drede and of oþer many mor þan her (I T) be (can T) tolde (telle þe þridde is of T) WT cursynge] chidyng URGSVLCHeBPTrCh, flytyng DdR$^2$FfT$^3$T$^2$B$^2$HaAArH$^2$Hh, fiȝtyng D, *om.* MH

355 manacynge . . . discord] mannes RG manacynge] *om.* HeCh sowynge] makyng SV, spekynge wordes B discord] as *add.* SV tresone] makyng ⟨of discorde R⟩ *add.* RG witnes] ȝeuynge *add.* B 355–6 il . . . word] *om.* RGSV

356 scornynge] hethyng DdR$^2$FfT$^3$MHaArHh, *om.* PCh word] innoyes Ha deedes] *om.* SVT$^3$BMHArH$^2$ 356–8 for . . . worst] *om.* RGSV for to] and M

357 don] louen Ff, greuen C, mysdo B ham$^2$] woo *add.* LtD, any gref *add.* L, noy *add.* He, but *add.* B, gode *add.* MPChDo, wel *add.* F, yuel *add.* Ld, euel HAr, it B$^2$, greuaunce *add.* A lap] turne ULCHeDBFLdChADo, wyndde T$^3$M, couere PHT$^2$, take B$^2$

358 dedes] *om.* D exite] entysyng SV, steryng ⟨or exitynge B⟩ BCh, eggyng A man] or womman *add.* B jre] wreche F 358–60 reproue . . . speche] *om.* RGSV reproue] vndernyme UHeP, reprehende DdR$^2$FfLCT$^3$MB$^2$ChHaAAr, or ellis to undertake B

359 þat] such a þing as U, þen F he] þou Ar dothe] wel do B hym] þe Ar 359–60 vayne . . . speche] *om.* B$^2$ vayne] idel U, venym B 359–60 fool speche] *om.* LdHT$^2$TrChDo fool] foul UDdLCHeT$^3$PFHaArHh, for lesse D, idyl B

360 speke . . . need] venemouse speche Ar speke] and He, foule *add.* F idel] foule RGSV or . . . need] *om.* F or wordes] *om.* RGSVC nat need] noyande RG roosynge] bostynge USVDBPFLdB$^2$ChADo, preysynge LC, rasynge M

361 polisshynge of] plesyng RGSV, glosinge LCF, praysing of glosinge He, likyng in fayre Ch, closyng of *add.* A wordes] to men for þanke to haue *add.* RG, to haue þonkes *add.* SV of syn] *om.* Ha cryinge . . . laghtre] *om.* F cryinge] erryng U, grennyng B, scornyng A and] in LtUSVR$^2$FfLCHeDT$^3$LdHT$^2$B$^2$ChHaAArHhDo, of DdM, *om.* B 361–2 laghtre . . . synge] syngynge G laghtre] liȝing R, lewed SV 361–2 mowe . . . synge] *om.* RSV 361–2 mowe . . . man] and to make mowes in scorne of þyn euen cristene B mowe] makyng *add.* DdR$^2$FfLCHeDT$^3$B MPFLdHT$^2$ChHaAH$^2$HhDo, skorne or make þe mowe Ar

362 man] for sekenes or mayne or vnkonyng or ani oþer defaute *add.* Ar synge] any *add.* F seculere] wordly B$^2$Tr, *om.* A and . . . ham] *om.* RGSVTr loue] til here *add.* Ar ham] seculere mirþes L, to Ch 362–3 preise . . . synge] as karoles and oþer songes þat ben mad of paramours and lecherye and of al oþer songes more B

363 for] to RGSV preisynge] plesyng or for loue RGSV, loue B, luf loueyng A men] or drede *add.* RGSV God] and many oþere moo þan here ben rekened (nempned SV) *add.* RGSV

364 deede] and *add.* T these] *om.* M glotony lechurie] *see notes for Ar* symony] *om.* WTr

365 wichecraft] *om.* F daies] *om.* F God] goddes body DdR$^2$FfLCHeDT$^3$BM PFLdHT$^2$B$^2$TrHaAH$^2$, goddis Ch, or of any sacramentis *add.* Ar

366 voues] broken *add.* W*, lawefully made *add.* C apostasie] *om.* $\alpha$ dissolucioun] unstudefastnesse SV, necligence FLdDo

367 yeue] ȝifte of euel $\alpha$, euyl *add.* B$^2$Do, il Ar of . . . dedes] *om.* W of] to GFfBP, in SV, any *add.* B$^2$, in ani Ar 367–8 dedes . . . his] *om.* R dedes] schewynge *add.* SV, *om.* He hurt] thorogh M body] or in soul WFf 367–8 his$^2$ . . . fame] name B[*subpuncted*]

368 fame] gode los SV, name T$^3$M thefte] ȝefte Ld rauyn] *om.* B vsure] gouel Ch 368–9 deceyte . . . harlotes] *om.* M 368–9 deceyte . . . il] *om.* T$^3$B deceyte] *om.* $\alpha$C, lesynge and sellyng oþer in oþir manere F syllynge] shewyng RG rightwisnesse] vnriȝtwisnes RG

369 herknynge . . . il] *om.* $\alpha$H$^2$ herknynge of] to hure LCHeDB$^2$, to listyn Ch yeve] ȝiftes *add.* L, good *add.* Ch harlotes] for here iapes *add.* $\alpha$H$^2$, mysleuyng men Ch þe] a mannes $\alpha$H$^2$, þi DdR$^2$HeT$^3$BMFB$^2$

370 hit outrage] more þen mestier were $\alpha$ hit] þy body to B, hym F, to Ch outrage] outragely H aboue] ouer LCHeDT$^3$BHa, our M, out of Ld, ouer *add.* B$^2$ oure] ȝor SV, *om.* LCHeDHaH$^2$, þy T$^3$BMB$^2$ powere or] witte and T, *om.* *alia* myght] powere Ld

371 custume . . . syn$^1$] to falle in synne ⟨or T⟩ by custome $\alpha$H$^2$ to] don *add.* B

fallynge . . . syn] *om.* SVDB$^2$H$^2$, recidiuacion Ar eft] ofte URWTDdR$^2$FfLCHeT$^3$ BMPFTrCh, *om.* Ld feynynge] desire LCHe

372 haue] ned of *add.* He 372–3 for . . . to] nouʒt sufficiaunt to vs ne degre F seme] be halden Ar holier] hali Ar or connynger] *om.* αTrArH$^2$, þan we ben *add.* C, betterer B or wiser] *om.* Ch, or wise Ar þan . . . bene] *om.* Ar hold] kepe BCh

373 we] haue *add.* D, ben *add.* B$^2$ suffice] suffisant B$^2$ to] do WH$^2$, do *add.* TCLdTr, *om.* D 373–4 or . . . karolles] *om.* LCHeDT$^3$BMChHa or] holden *add.* SVWTF, þat office *add.* B$^2$ þat] we *add.* R$^2$Ff, *om.* Ar may . . . be] men (use W) mow not α syn] *om.* T$^3$T$^2$ 373–4 led karolles] *om.* αTrH$^2$Hh, or daunses *add.* B$^2$

374 gyses] to be *add.* DdR$^2$FfLCHeDT$^3$BMPLdT$^2$B$^2$TrChHaH$^2$Do to . . . suffrayne] *om.* C his] here USVL, mennes RG, a man WT, *om.* HeAr, oure T$^3$BFCh, sure M, þi B$^2$ suffrayne] souerence M 374–5 defoul . . . lasse] ⟨and unbuxum G⟩ and many oþere synnes αH$^2$ defoul] doumbe to U, do fowle B, despyse F ham] sogettis B$^2$

375 ben] han DDo lasse] erelees U, þan we (he PHa, þei B$^2$) *add.* LCHeBMPF B$^2$Ha syn in] as αH$^2$, in He syght] *om.* αH$^2$, seyng He in hyrynge] *om.* RGWT in$^2$] feirlek SV in smellynge] *om.* B$^2$ 375–7 smellynge . . . reteyne] tastyng heryng seyng handelyng seyinge (*om.* G) euel (many W) wordes and RGWT, tastynge speche hondelyng siʒt and SV 375–6 touchynge . . . swelighynge] *om.* Ar touchynge] tastynge Ld

376 handlynge] *om.* LFCh swelighynge] swellyng DdD, schewyng R$^2$FfB, *om.* FLdHT$^2$TrDo 376–7 giftes . . . reteyne] *om.* C, vois and B giftes] wiʒtes He, ʒeuynge *add.* Ch, wyʒtis *add.* Do waies] in mesouris *add.* F, in metyng *add.* B$^2$ signes] *om.* D, in tokens *add.* Ha biddynges writynges] *om.* LCHeT$^3$M, in herkenynges Ch biddynges] bekenyng PLdHT$^2$B$^2$Do writynges] *om.* DHa

377 reteyne . . . ben] *om.* Ar reteyne] wiþ Tr, to chargen nouʒt Ch, *om.* Do, receyue Lt *and alia* circumstances] þat maken þe synnes more *add.* αH$^2$, of synnes *add.* HeBFCh þe$^2$ . . . ben] as ⟨what RG⟩ RGWTCh, also SV, þat is ⟨for to seye LCHeT$^3$Ha⟩ þe LCHeT$^3$BHa, beþ þese F

378 noumbre] how ofte wiþ what RG persone] cause *add.* Ar connynge] *om.* αFLdHT$^2$TrH$^2$Do eld] *om.* αH$^2$ 378–9 þese . . . lasse] also αH$^2$ þese] yere Lt, þat D, þei þat B$^2$, ben þat *add.* Ch, circumstances *add.* Ar

379 lasse] and euere *add.* F to$^1$] *om.* UFHT$^2$, þe RSV ar he] or þan Ff, or to CHeCh he] a man α, *om.* Ha 379–80 constreyne . . . syn] *om.* ChH$^2$ constreyne] conformyng WT hym] *om.* T, any He, hem F

381–2 Oþre . . . done] And as hit is synne ⟨forte do þis riht so hit is synne SVWTH$^2$⟩ to leue þe gode dedes þat a man is holden to done to þe worshepe of god αH$^2$ 381 Oþre] þus Ld 381–2 synnes . . . done] *om.* Do synnes] þat *add.* BC, mo *add.* M þer] as *add.* L, *om.* CBAr, synnes *add.* Ha of] as T$^3$Ar omyssioun] þat es of levyng of gude vndone (dede B) *add.* DdR$^2$FfLCHeDT$^3$BMPFLdHT$^2$B$^2$HaHh, þat is ⟨of leuyng and forsakyng of goodnes Ch⟩ *add.* ChAr whan . . . good] *om.* HeT$^3$BMHaCh good] vndo *add.* LCD

382 þei shold] scholde be HeT$^3$M done] þat is *add.* LCHe nat . . . of] as þese þat a man loue RGSVW, and ʒif a man loue noʒt T nat] þat Lt God] ne doande þo loouyng to god *add.* Ha ne dredynge] and drede ⟨not T⟩ god α, *om.* FfH$^2$ 382–3 ne$^2$ . . . hym] *om.* α

383 ne thankynge] and þanke ⟨hym noʒt T⟩ α his benfaites] al goodnes þat he haþ done him (hem G, þe T) to body and to soule αH$^2$ his] *om.* B 383–4 doth$^1$ . . . loue] and þat a man make α al] þe gode *add.* Ar he] schulde *add.* LCHeDT$^3$MF, scholde be B doth$^2$] do LCHeDT$^3$BMF

384 loue] sake Ha sorow nat] not do sorwe B nat$^2$] *om.* RGSVW his] *om.*

HeBCh done] and he also sungeþ in dede þat *add.* SV, *om.* BAr dispose] disposeþ SVH$^2$, ordeine HT$^2$

385–6 and . . . God] as he shulde do RGWT, *om.* SV 385 and . . . grace] *om.* CLdB$^2$Hh if] *om.* M taken] resayued FDo nat] *om.* C oweth] to do *add.* LCHeBMT$^2$B$^2$

386 ne . . . nat$^1$] *om.* Ch ne] to HeM hit] *om.* B nat$^1$] as he schulde *add.* F turne] his *add.* LdCh, trowis Ar nat$^2$] *om.* BB$^2$ God] þe holy gost T$^3$F his] þi He

387 Goddis wil] him B$^2$ yeue] Also to take RGWT, ne takeþ SV nat] his *add.* LCDMFLdHChDo, þin *add.* He entent] kepe RG rabble] rebell Ha on] it oute faste LCHe, fast *add.* BM, *om.* ChHa and] but H rek] þenke B

388 bot] hou SVHaDo, so TB$^2$, be L ben] *om.* L, sone *add.* B negligently] rechelesliche SVB, neglygence T, þe avowe *add.* B$^2$ that] þo þinges *α* holden] bownden DdT$^3$Ar to] done *add.* *α*LCHeT$^3$BPLdT$^2$ChDo, *om.* FfF 388–9 þrogh . . . penaunce] *om.* B 388–9 þrogh . . . vowe] *om.* B$^2$

389 a . . . or] goddis C comandement] elles þourȝe biddyng of soueryn *α*, comawnded DdB$^2$ or$^2$ . . . penaunce] and tarieþ to turne to his god C or$^2$] *om.* R enyoynte] of ioynyng T, any þynge iȝeue him F in] of RGWT, *om.* SV and] do *add.* SV, in T drawe] drawyng T aleynth] on litel (long G) þing RG, a long ⟨þing SVB⟩ SVTLCHeBPFLdHT$^2$, thing *add.* W

390 to] be *add.* P do] seid B sone] hastily *α*, rundli B profite] ioie B as . . . owne] *om.* *α*, as him oweth LdDo as] he owȝt *add.* HT$^2$

391 sorowynge nat] ne no sorwe RGSV his] neiȝboures *add.* LP ilfare] disese P standynge nat] ne wyþstonde B nat$^2$] *om.* HT$^2$ agayns] euyl *add.* B temptacioun] as we scholde *add.* B

392 ham . . . heth] trespaces RGWT, *om.* SV ham] *om.* D þat . . . hym] *om.* HT$^2$ heth] *om.* BB$^2$ hym] wrong and *add.* Ch harme] *om.* *α* 392–8 kepynge . . . foule] and many oþere synnes ⟨mo þan I haue witte to telle here G⟩ *α*

393 neghbore] euen cristen B$^2$ yeldynge] ȝeuynge D nat to] *om.* C to hym$^2$] *om.* BP

394 may] amende him and *add.* B$^2$ amendynge nat] also yf he ne reprehendiþ F ham . . . synnen] þe senne þat we seen don B ham] *om.* Ha synnen] he synnes Ha 394–5 befor . . . eighen] *om.* Ha his eighen] him Ar his] oure T$^3$B

395 pesynge] lettynge B, also susposynge F ham . . . bene] *om.* Ha, þe Ar

396 ham . . . beth] þe Ar in sorowe] sorowful Ha, sary Ar or$^1$] þa þat are *add.* Ar in$^1$] sikyng or *add.* He 396–7 or$^2$ . . . prisone] *om.* LdHT$^2$Do

397–8 and . . . foule] *see notes for Ar* 397 synnes] þingis B$^2$

398 foule] in þe siȝt of god *add.* ChDo

399–400 The . . . synnes] Aȝeynes þese synnes þat fylen (folewen WT) us þen are þese þre þat clensen vs *α*, and þre þynges make men clene of þat filthe for ageyn þre maner of synnes arn þre remedies B 399 The] Thre Ar þat$^1$] *om.* Ar of . . . filthede] *om.* He þat$^2$] *om.* FLdT$^2$Ch, siche B$^2$, þis Ar filthede] folie H, synnis and filthis Ar 399–400 ben . . . synnes] *om.* Ar þre$^1$] these Ld, remedyes *add.* Ch 399–400 ayeyns . . . synnes] *om.* Ld þre$^2$] *om.* L

401 to] þat þou (it Ch) FCh be] so *add.* R$^2$FfBAr perfite] on þis wyse *α* þou$^1$] we RG wolt] be neuer (*om.* USVR$^2$Ff) in ⟨ful R$^2$Ff⟩ wil to U*α*R$^2$FfB, haue in wille He neuer] *om.* URGWCB, so *add.* V syn] no *add.* UC 401–2 moor . . . synnes] *om.* B moor] efte RGSVT, oft W 401–2 and$^2$ . . . synnes] *om.* CCh and$^2$] *om.* WT

402 haue] hertly *add.* U, ai *add.* Ar al$^1$] *om.* *α*Ha 402–3 þat . . . herte] na ioie ne solace but in god Ar þat] of D ioy and] *om.* Ch and solace] *om.* W, be set on noþing *add.* C, ⟨þat þou Ld⟩ haue *add.* LdHT$^2$, be *add.* Ch bot] be ⟨onliche LHeT$^3$BMF⟩ *α*LHeT$^3$BMF, onli *add.* CHa, god and *add.* Ch of$^2$] *om.* D

403 and . . . God] *om.* PFHa and] *om.* H God . . . herte] goodnes C be . . . herte] *om.* *α* God] and al euel *add.* U, ⟨ne B⟩ þat he ⟨neuer F⟩ *add.* LHeT$^3$BMF, and þat oþer *add.* Ch be] nouȝt *add.* LHeT$^3$M, clene *add.* Ch put] *om.* F thy] *om.* B, hys Ha 403–4 agayn . . . mouth] *om.* *α*FB$^2$Hh, to þi god C

404 and . . . be] *om.* Ha þat] *om.* RGLdCh shal be] don B$^2$ 404–7 hasted . . . worth] *see notes for Ar* hasted] done hastily for mony pereles *α*, *om.* C, do *add.* P, after þi trespas *add.* F 404–5 withouten . . . excusynge] also soþfastly þat is to telle þe synne as hit was done and how (whanne SV) and where and wiþ whom for a synne may be more in o degre þan in anoþer *α* withouten] with Ld delayynge] or lettynge *add.* Ch naked] and C

405–7 and . . . worth] for noþing may be hid to god and þan counceile þou wiþ good prestis þat louen þi soule and not þi goodis C 405 and] also shrifte shal be *α* without departynge] and not departed (disparclyde T) *α* 405–6 as . . . anothre] holliche to o mon schewyng þi sunnus and not sum to on and sum to anoþer SV as] nouȝt T$^3$P tel] say F

406 prest] *om.* RG, man WTTr anoþer] a synne RGW 406–7 sey . . . worth] ⟨but holly to oon man ⟨⟨þou shalt tellen alle þi synnes RG⟩⟩ RGWT⟩ and þou shalt loke þat he be (haue SVT) kunnynge and haue powere of þi bisshop or of þi parsone þat haþ powere (charge SV, rewle T) of þi soule *α* þat . . . wost] *om.* B al] þi schryft Dd, *add.* Ha

407 worth] *om.* HeB þrid] þat clensis vs *add.* Ar

408 and] *om.* Ar gyf] forgyff M drynke] and clathis *add.* Ar bot] and T

409 foryeve] ȝeuen UFf þe] ham Ff and$^1$ . . . ham] *om.* Ha and$^2$] to Ch

410 how . . . do] *om.* Ar þat . . . perisshe] if þou kanst better þan þai ⟨also þou schalt undirstonde þat clennesse bihoueþ to be kept in hert and in mouth and in werke B$^2$⟩ *α*B$^2$ to] spyllen and *add.* Ch perisshe] what þei shulden do *add.* U

411 For . . . kept] þe iii what haldis men in clenesse iii thingis clenesse Ar For . . . þynge] *om.* *α*, and þus B, *deleted* B$^2$ shalt] wel *add.* LCHe 411–12 behoueth . . . Clennesse] *om.* LB$^2$ behoueth] *om.* P

412 þre þynges] *om.* Ar

413 Oon is] *om.* Ar wakynge] waker of U, stabel LdHa and stabil] *om.* Ha and] to be *add.* U stabil] stabilnes CF, stedfast B, waker Ld Anoþer . . . kepe] and kepes Ar bisynes] *om.* B

414–15 so . . . profitable] fra alle þe wike of þe flesh and be ocupid in honeste and profetable ocupacion Ar 414 stirrynges] strengþes RSVTB[*W corr.*], strines M of ham] *om.* R$^2$Ff closed] clensid T, spered Ch

415 Also] *om.* SAr

416 þre . . . þou] *om.* Ar befoor] *om.* SVFfB$^2$

417 ar] or U, þan *add.* Ff, þat B, what F speeke] bifore *add.* U of$^1$] ouer *add.* Ld, to *add.* B$^2$Ch bot . . . litelle] *om.* BChAr

418 and . . . þe$^2$] bot Ar namely] semliche He euer] *om.* *α*BFB$^2$Ch tyl] þat T stablet] stable U, stedfast ⟨and stable P⟩ BP 418–19 þe þynke] þou seme L

419 þou lokest] þyn loue be F hym] ihesu Ar 419–22 Bot . . . þrid] *om.* Ar

420 may . . . nat] no man M haue] come to Ch bot with] wiþoute F longe] gret *α*Ch trauaille] grace SV

421 gret] *om.* *α*BChHa to] of GSVPLdHT$^2$Ha, *om.* Ch loue] hym *add.* Dd, ihesu cryst *add.* LCHeT$^3$BMFTr, *om.* Ch, ihesu Ha and . . . custume] *om.* *α* and] *om.* DdT$^2$ with] þat be B, withoute F, gret Ch þat] of Ha þe . . . hert] þin eghe T$^3$BM þe . . . of] *om.* T

422 vpward] and þan (so *α*B$^2$Ha) *add.* U*α*R$^2$FfPLdB$^2$ChHaHh, and þine herte also and þus *add.* LCHeT$^3$BM, to ihesu and þus *add.* F þou$^1$] sone *add.* F þerto] to ⟨þat RG⟩ grace *α* for$^1$ . . . ne] *om.* Ha 422–3 ne . . . mekenesse] make no *α*, *om.* FTrAr

423 ly] make lesynge F maner] man WTDdR$^2$FfPHT$^2$HaHh and il] *om.* αFTrHaAr nat] aȝenst R$^2$PTrAr at] *om.* SVDdR$^2$BMPT$^2$TrAr, pay to T

424 þe . . . wille] *om.* Ff[*corr. later hand*] þe] ye Lt, þou HT$^2$ nat] *om.* R say] al *add.* UDdR$^2$FfLCHeDT$^3$LdB$^2$ChHaArHh euer] *om.* Ch 424–5 bot$^1$ . . . hate] *om.* Ar bot$^1$] *om.* LCHeP 424–5 bot$^2$ . . . hate] *om.* α al] weyis *add.* B, *om.* HB$^2$

425 lyynge hate] loke þou hate synne for ȝyf þou lye þou sennest B hate] þou owest to flee Ch say] se H a thynge] *om.* Ch 425–6 semeth . . . hit] be F 425–6 þi$^1$ . . . hit] *om.* B$^2$ þi$^2$] þe UH, *om.* RGWLAr, to SVT louynge] of god *add.* W*

426 þou$^1$] *om.* D, þine entent is for to Ch and . . . oþer] *om.* Ar help] hele RGSV, helþ W, ensaumple or profit F 426–30 nat . . . þat] wele for god Ar nat] but F

427 vnwisely] euel B, wel F, vnskilfully B$^2$ for] but SV spekest] nouȝt (*om.* Ch) but *add.* FCh if . . . pryue] neuerþeles B wil] *om.* F any] a RG, þinge *add.* LHePF, it T$^3$MCh pryue] þing *add.* αT$^2$, loouyng *add.* R$^2$Ff

428 hit . . . none] not BCh þou ware] is B siker] of *add.* RGW þat] *om.* SV

429 shewed] ne diskeuered *add.* F, discouered B$^2$ only] *om.* TBB$^2$ to] telle D þe] þy B 429–30 of$^2$ . . . maketh] þat makeþ of his godnesse SV is] comen UGWTT$^3$BF, *om.* R

430 maketh] to He sum] oon α, *om.* B, hem PHa þan oþer] sum wers B ham] a RG, a *add.* WT, *om.* DT$^3$BMCh, his *add.* B$^2$ special] mare Ar

431 only] al α ham] for hem *add.* Ch also] *om.* αAr ham . . . ensample] ensampil til oþer Ar ham$^2$] oþer α wil . . . ensample] haue wille to done wel α

432 þre thynges] *om.* Ar kepeth] helpiþ L Oon is] *om.* Ar is] busy and *add.* P assiduel] bisy RGSVDdBFLdHT$^2$Tr, often Ch þe] þi R$^2$FfLCBB$^2$

433 deeth] deede USV, ende B$^2$ 433–4 for . . . is] and Ar wise] which H seith] sone *add.* T, first *add.* B$^2$ last] *om.* He

434 il] oþer F felewshipe] *om.* He yeueth . . . ensample] hyt stere þe not B yeueth] wol B$^2$ ensample] þee *add.* B$^2$

435 to] do yuele and to *add.* Ld þan$^1$] to loue of *add.* P erth . . . heuyn] and loue more RGWT, *om.* SV erth] or F 435–6 of . . . of] þen clennesse more þe body þen þe B

436 þe . . . is] alswa Ar temperaunce] a mesure RGSVW, *om.* T and discrecioun] *om.* U and$^1$] of Lt, in SV, *om.* T discrecioun] destruccioun W

437–8 þat . . . body] *om.* Ar 437 outrage] outrages GB$^2$, outragously take B ne] to lytel *add.* Ch 437–8 byneth . . . body] to scarse α, till ouer mekill fastynge T$^3$BM byneth . . . sustenaunce] vnskilful abstynence F byneth skylwise] þat it be to litel ⟨to þe L⟩ LCHe, by unskilful Ld sustenaunce] substaunce CHe 437–8 of þe] for þi Dd

438–9 For . . . abstinence] *om.* T$^3$BM 438 cometh] gon Ch endynge] of *add.* F, *om.* Ar 438–9 outrage . . . abstinence] *om.* C

439 abstinence] fastynge *alia* for$^1$] and Ar noþer is] boþe byn aȝeyne TrAr 439–40 and . . . say] *om.* TrAr and þat] þougȝ B þat] *om.* SVHa wene] yt *add.* B

440 may] *om.* L say] hem I seye þe forsoþe *add.* α, but I seie *add.* B, I say forsoþe *add.* F of . . . as] whuche SV, suche as B good] *om.* RGWTHeT$^3$MLdTr

441 sendeth] þe *add.* Ha and] in HT$^2$ day] stede He, þai F what . . . be] *om.* Ar I outtake] þou ouȝtest forsake SV, and take T I] *om.* L no] *om.* R$^2$Ff

442 mete] and drynke *add.* HePCh þat . . . vseth] *om.* Ar Cristen] *om.* T, mete *add.* H with] withouten T and mesure] þat *add.* U, þan T

443 for] *om.* M Crist . . . his] þe Ch hym self] *om.* WTCBTrArHh, ihesu Ff, many tymes *add.* L his] discyples þe *add.* B apostles] Nat forþi (for þen SV) *add.*

RGSVWF, neuerþelatre *add.* TCh, also *add.* L, but *add.* B, deciples Ld leue] loue RFfHHh 443–5 many . . . help] somme in na despite Ar many] any LB

444 þat . . . mete] *om.* SV hath] vsen RGWTLHeFCh dispisynge] ordeinynge HT$^2$

445 þat . . . þerof] þe nedis þaim noght Ar no] *om.* HT$^2$ þerof] bot *add.* C þou$^1$ . . . wel] *om.* SV wel] also *add.* U, or *add.* F 445–56 if . . . witte] *om.* Ar

446 see] saist F as] *om. alia* stalworth] anow *add.* T$^3$BFTrCh serue] þy *add.* B God] wiþ þe (þi SVW) sustenaunce þat þou hast or (eer R) usest (vsed RW) *add.* $\alpha$ 446–8 and . . . mete] but of a þing be war þat þi stomak be not broken þourȝe ouer mykel abstinence for so may hit liȝtly be and if hit so be þen hastou leste þe (a SV, *om.* WT) apetide (pece SV) of mete and drynke $\alpha$

447 þou] *om.* Ch hit] þat R$^2$FfLCDT$^3$MFHT$^2$B$^2$Ha, þi stomake P with] *om.* F 447–8 þe . . . reft] þanne hastow lore B, is take fro þe P þe] þan C is] þan *add.* M

448 reft] bynome LCHe, kyndeliche *add.* Ch and] *om.* He oft . . . quathis] þat shal make þe to be ofte in feyntnes $\alpha$ oft] *om.* B$^2$ be] falle B, hauen Ch in] *om.* P, many Ch quathis] feyntise U, coþes to ȝyue vp L, cowȝis CB, þouȝtis F, *om.* P ware . . . to] schuldest SVB, wery to D redy] *om.* Ha 448–9 to gif] *om.* L

449 gif] vp *add.* URWTBPHT$^2$, ȝelde ⟨vp FLd⟩ HeFLdB$^2$ChHa synned] synnest U$\alpha$DBFLdHT$^2$B$^2$TrCh dede] of abstinence *add.* $\alpha$ And] I warne þe *add.* $\alpha$, for *add.* HeB 449–50 þou . . . nat] *om.* T

450 sone] liȝtly B$^2$ þe$^1$] 'þ' *obliterated Lt, om.* R$^2$ forþi] I rede þe þat þe *add.* SV, for DdMB$^2$Ch

451 whils] þe tyme DdCh yonge] in ȝouþe W, in bigynnyng D I . . . þou] *om.* SV rede] drede D and drynke] *om.* Ch wirre] mar R$^2$Ff

452 hit cometh] god sendeþ hit (*om.* SVWT) þe and vsen hem in mesure and in tyme $\alpha$ hit] þat B, þey Ld cometh] to þee *add.* B$^2$ þou . . . begilet] þin enemy bigyle þe not for he is more sotele and queynte þen alle þe men þat euer were ⟨outaken ihesu crist RGSVW⟩ $\alpha$ And] but C

453 prouet] sayd He and$^1$] *om.* V

454 and God] bothe *add.* U, *om.* M dost now] dudest ⟨beforne M⟩ SVDdM þan$^2$] for Ff, *om.* F, þat Ld

455 þou$^1$ . . . priue] oþer peyne Ch þe] þan *add.* T, *om.* DdLHeDMLdHT$^2$HaHh do] more *add.* L priue] more $\alpha$

456 þat] þen $\alpha$ dar] shullen UCh nat] *om.* $\alpha$ witte] for þenne hit (he T) is lesse to charge for *add.* $\alpha$, þou myȝt wel don it *add.* Ch neþer] not heȝer R, noȝt hier G, not here SVWT, noght al Dd, mete ne drynke þat is *add.* B, noght ArHh

457 etynge] ne in drinking *add.* C bot] *om.* Ch if] in R, þou takest *add.* F al] boþe BCh, *om.* Ar ilike] likyng G, he like R$^2$Ff, likynglich F þe] þat is to say *add.* GF

458 as$^1$] alle *add.* DT$^3$M as$^2$] *om.* RGSV, and C, alle DT$^3$M

459 take] al *add.* $\alpha$Ch þese] al U, þe H, þer B$^2$, gladlyche *add.* Ch praisynge] loue SV, þankinge LCHe of] beforn Ff God] and holde þe wel payed þenne *add.* $\alpha$ þe] wel *add.* SV blessed] in erþe *add.* B 459–60 and . . . Ihesu] in þe siȝte of god $\alpha$

460 bifore] god and *add.* P 460–2 Men . . . lightly] and noght Ar praise] *om.* P þei see] *om.* BCh see] or here speke of *add.* RSVWT, here speke of G 460–1 þi . . . se] *om.* He þi] þe in so F, *om.* H

461 and] *om.* LdHT$^2$ þay] men L, þe H enclosed] holdeþ þe holy and hyȝe and þat passyng oþer and preyseþ þe and wurshepiþ þe þerof P 461–2 I . . . lightly] þat may I not do RGS*WT, þou maiȝt hit nat do V may] schal F praise þe] *om.* Ha

462 lightly] withoute *add.* F for oght] *om.* F I . . . do] þou dose Ar 462–3 þi . . . do] þou wilt enterly comforme þe to B þi . . . be] þou wult be PF, þou be wel Ch wil] sal *add.* Ar confourmed] enformed Ff, wel *add.* F

463 entierly] *om.* TAr do] *om.* αDdR$^2$FfLT$^3$MLdB$^2$HaArHh set] rekke ULCHe by] of ULCHe har$^1$] mennes UBAr, *om.* Ch 463–4 ne . . . lakynge] *om.* TDT$^3$BM

464 lakynge] blamynge SVLCHePFLdHT$^2$ gif] recche TFLdHT$^2$, take LCHe, if þou ȝeue Ch take] recche U, hede LCHe, how F if] *om.* F þei] þou T, men Ar 464–5 of . . . did] or more F of þe] *om.* B

465 did] bifore *add.* RGSVW, were wonte byfore T, of oþer more *add.* Ch þat] þan Ha be] þe R$^2$ brennynger . . . loue] more louande god α Goddis] *om.* B$^2$ was] bifore *add.* α 465–6 For . . . the] *om.* Ar

466 warne] telle D I$^1$ . . . þat] *om.* B perfite] *om.* Ha in erthe] *om.* SVHa

467–8 of . . . enemye] *om.* α 467 for] þe book seyþ *add.* P, saue F

468 enemye] enuy Ch, sola miseria caret inuidia *add.* Ar

469 For . . . we] To α For to] and þerfore U, þe iiii what Ar draw] we *add.* U vs] oure wille F confourme] acorde FLd þer ben] *om.* RSVWT

470 þre] oþere *add.* L, *om.* F þynges] are gode to haue in mynde *add.* α, þat we moste folwe *add.* F is] þe holy *add.* α ensample] and (of WT) þe good lyuynge (louynge T) þat *add.* α of] *om.* RGSVW, goude and T and wommen] *om.* Ar and] haly *add.* DdR$^2$FfLCDT$^3$MFLdHT$^2$ChHh wommen] han lyued (be in T) bifor vs *add.* α was] busy and *add.* LCHe, arn B

471 ententif] bisye UαBPTr, diligent DF, in besinesse HT$^2$ nyght . . . day] *om.* T$^3$BM to . . . God] in goddes seruyse α God] in to here lyues ende *add.* B and$^2$ . . . hym$^2$] *om.* α and$^2$] þat *add.* U and$^3$ . . . hym] *om.* T$^3$BMPFLdHT$^2$Ha loue] loueden UHe, preise D and$^4$] for B

472 if] *om.* DdHe ham$^1$] him CBH be] wone M ham$^2$] him CBH þe] in H

473 God] *om.* UαDdR$^2$CHeDMPFLdHT$^2$B$^2$ChHaAr, ihesu Ff þat] *om.* B receyueth] he takeþ B

474 wil cum] comes DdR$^2$FfLCHeDMPLdHT$^2$B$^2$Ha, comyn to hym Ch 474–5 and . . . on] *om.* Ar is] more *add.* LF homelier] only T, himul F ham] raþer *add.* T or] to F

475 any] oþer *add.* Ch þai] he F most$^1$] myȝten U loued . . . most] *om.* F loued] loue *alia* most$^2$] *om.* URGWTCBTr on] is til other *add.* M þe] most *add.* L

476 wondre] vntelland Ar þe . . . of] *om.* Ar kyngdome] blis C 476–7 more . . . is] *om.* Ar þan] any *add.* WTFfD 476–7 or . . . hire] *om.* He

477–8 or$^1$ . . . as] *om.* RSVWT 477 or$^1$ . . . see] *om.* TrHa Hit] his Lt so mych] soþ B, also M mych] *om.* CHeDCh þat] *om.* He

478 as] *om.* BMCh, also HT$^2$ myght$^1$] leue *add.* Ff thynge] man U lyve] *om.* H mych] *om.* FfB myght$^2$] muche strengþe T

479 God] is so miche and *add.* G ham] hit He þe$^1$ . . . in$^1$] *om.* HT$^2$, in þe blysse of heuen in Ch in$^1$] and of T in$^2$] of B

480 mych] ioye *add.* Ch dey] þat þer be *add.* B if hit] *om.* BFB$^2$ if] of SVW hit . . . goodnesse] his goodnesse ne were so muche U

481 þat$^1$] he *add.* LCHeMFTr wil] while FfB lyvynge] louende Ff, *om.* Ha in] his *add.* SVHh blisse] and *add.* U, ioye and gladnesse B as] also B, And T$^2$ wil] while B

482–4 þat$^1$ . . . euermoore] *om.* RGSV, þat schrewis schulle dey in helle but if þey mend hem here T 482 al] þo W*Ar louet] louen UW*R$^2$FfLHeDFHB$^2$Tr, louen is louers be liuyng euer in blis as his riȝtwisnes wole þat alle þat louen C lyvynge] togidere *add.* U fyre] peyne UW*, and torment *add.* B 482–4 is . . . euermoore] haþ noon ende W* is] so *add.* B$^2$, *om.* Ch

483 to$^1$] þat FfD Look . . . wil] *om.* Ch Look . . . fele] *om.* Ar þan] for goddes loue *add.* P, now F hit] *om.* R$^2$FfDT$^2$, þat fir P fele] hit contynuel *add.* F bot] for *add.* He þai] þat Lt 483–4 nat . . . now] and drede it nouȝt Ch

484 now] heere UAr, *om.* CB, nouȝt H  shal] fele hit þenne and *add.* P  suffre] fele Ld  hit] elleswhere *add.* UT$^3$, þare *add.* Ar  euermoore] withoute ende *add.* LCHeT$^3$BM, in helle *add.* F, and suffre hit *add.* Ld

485 how] what manere SV  dispose] reule *α*  and . . . hit] *om.* *α*B$^2$  hit] þe M

486 wille Bot] þaye F  to hyre] *om.* TM  486–7 of . . . loue] *om.* Ha

487 lif] *om.* B  taken] ȝeue FLdHT$^2$

488 at . . . syȝt] *om.* BCh  at] as ⟨hit seemeþ SV⟩ to RGSVT, in a W, *om.* F  I$^1$ . . . connynge] god wole ȝyue me grace RGSVW, I kan Ch  grace] *om.* Ld  connynge] Amore Langueo *add.* D  wil] gladliche *add.* U  lere] telle TPCh

489–90 Amore . . . þat] þe wordes in þe book of loue wel ȝe wyte is nempned amore langueo and it B  489 Amore langueo] *om.* TD  These] *om.* D  ben] *om.* D  written] *om.* T$^3$M  489–90 þe . . . called] *om.* *α*

490 þat . . . loue] *om.* R$^2$FfPFLdHT$^2$Tr  or . . . songes] *om.* RSVWTB  songes] languysshyng U  he] *om.* M  mych] *om.* FB$^2$

491 loueth] ihesu *add.* *α*, loued H, him myche *add.* B$^2$  hym] muche *add.* F  lust] wel *add.* Ch  oft] *om.* RGT$^3$H  his] *om.* UB$^2$Ad, þis T  or sho] *om.* *α*HeAd, or suche F

492 when . . . þynke] *om.* Ad  þay$^1$] he *α*He  on þat] *om.* Ff  þat$^1$ . . . þay] *om.* *α*  þay] he HeAd  if] of L  har] his *α*HeAd  louer] loue *α*HeBFLd$^2$  492–3 and louynge] and lastyng URGSVW, and leuyng He, *om.* B

493 to] teld D  þe] in *add.* FfD  two] *om.* CHe  languysshe] dwelle RG, longe SVWF, angwische He, longe or y morne Ld, am seke HT$^2$, mourne B$^2$  for] in GSVW[*R corr.*]

494 loue] or elles I morne in loue *add.* G, or I longe for loue *add.* TLCHeCh  Dyuers] for soþe SV  in . . . graces] louen dyuersely (lousliche SV) as þat þei haue dyuerse (heore SV) ȝiftes RGSVW  in erth] *om.* HeAd  and graces] *om.* B  of God] *om.* Ad  of] þat Ch  God] þe holy gost B, ȝeueth *add.* Ch  þe] moost *add.* *α*LCHeT$^3$BMFCh

495 yift] grace He, *om.* B  ledeth] liuen CHe  loue] oure lord *add.* Ch

496 to me] perauenture þat RGSVW, þus *add.* P, *om.* B$^2$AdLd$^2$  hym] god Ad  holdeth] kepen GCT$^3$FB$^2$ChAd

497–8 biddynge . . . his$^1$] *om.* L  497 biddynge] and comaundementis *add.* F  also] al RGWTHAd, *om.* SVCMFTrChHaLd$^2$

498 and] ȝitt ouer *add.* RGSVW  doth] not *add.* UCHeT$^3$BLd$^2$, kepen WDB$^2$Ha Ad  as] *om.* UT$^3$PTrHaLd$^2$, alle (*om.* W) iliche *α*LF, also DdCHeBLdHT$^2$B$^2$Ch, alle DM  498–9 fulfilled . . . herte] brennande in his loue RGSVW

499 fyre] brenninge *add.* HT$^2$  of] *om.* UTLd  loue . . . his] brennynge here U, ⟨þe HT$^2$⟩ brennyng loue (*om.* Ld) in TDdR$^2$FfLCHeDT$^3$BPFLdHT$^2$B$^2$TrChHaLd$^2$ his] in Ad  499–500 Forþi . . . of$^3$] but aftir þat þou louest þou shal haue þi RGSVW  Forþi] for D

500 of$^2$] *om.* D  and of] of Ha, in Ad  mede] in heuene *add.* B  500–8 In . . . loue] *om.* Ad  500–1 In . . . God] *om.* RGSVW

501 God] in heuen *add.* F, hym Ch  501–2 Also . . . loue] who so moost him (*om.* RW) loueþ in erþe RGSVW

502 and wommen] *om.* F  Goddis] good He  don] be in Ha

503 or] ar M  none] don D  þei$^1$ . . . degre] heȝest shal ben RGSVW  be] dwellyng *add.* F  degre in] *om.* Ch  degre] endeles *add.* F  503–4 þei$^2$ . . . ordre] *om.* RGSVW

504 hym$^1$] *om.* FfT$^3$Ch  lasse] shullen be *add.* U, noght M  lower] degre and in lower *add.* F  hym$^2$] *om.* RGSVW, ihesu ChE  myche] *om.* TLCHeDBMLd$^2$ miche] in B, *om.* M  504–5 ioy and] is þe ⟨þe G, þat SV⟩ RGSVW

505 and brennynge] *om.* RGSVR$^2$Ff  and$^2$] *om.* W  felest] brennande *add.* RG, fyndes Ha  his] þat RGSVW  loue] and fels hym *add.* Ha  505–6 þat . . . day] *om.* RGSVW  þi] *om.* T

506 and$^{1}$] þi ioy and þi *add.* Ha  streynth] both *add.* UR$^{2}$Ff

507 delite] loue He  hym] þei U, *om.* B  man] thynge LtU  fele] fle T  in$^{1}$] perfit *add.* B  ioy . . . in] *om.* RGSVW  swetnesse] suauyte U

508 clene] of synne and of vice *add.* RGSVW  fild] fulfilde UGTFfFHT$^{2}$B$^{2}$E, ful LTr, thyrlede T$^{3}$BM  þerto] þerfor T, tille loue god entierly Ad  þou] þei B  grete] and hard *add.* Ff, grace Ad

509 in$^{1}$ . . . þynkynge] and bisinesse and preyere wiþ good þouȝt B  in$^{1}$] and GDT$^{3}$MPFLdHT$^{2}$HaAd  in$^{2}$ . . . hauynge] þenke to haue TL  þynkynge] thankyng R$^{2}$  hauynge] haue F, *om.* M  suche] þouȝtes or *add.* G, swete SV, *om.* ChAd

510 al in] *trs.* T  al] *om.* ChAdLd$^{2}$  God] ihesu crist Ch, there are thre degrees of loue as is writtene nowe here aftyre *add.* Ad

511 preise . . . thoght] to haue þyn herte on god and B  preise] ⟨loke þou TL⟩ þonke TLCCh  euer] *om.* HeCh, þi *add.* B$^{2}$  God] in þi herte and *add.* Ha  in . . . thoght] and þenk alwei in þin herte He  thoght] herte Ch  and] *om.* B

512 herte] þouȝt He  Praised . . . and$^{1}$] *om.* Ch  and$^{1}$ . . . Kynge] *om.* UTLCHeDT$^{3}$BMLd$^{2}$, þonked F  þou$^{2}$] my *add.* Ha  512–13 Kynge$^{2}$ . . . ioynge] *om.* SV  Kynge$^{2}$] lord G  512–13 and$^{2}$ . . . ioynge] *om.* RGWTr

513 be] *om.* T  Kynge] lord *add.* Ch  al$^{1}$ . . . ioynge] ioye F  my] *om.* He  ioynge] weldyng HeLd$^{2}$, ioy B$^{2}$Ch  al$^{2}$] *om.* B  þi] *om.* D  good] god RSV  þat] þou *add.* Ch

514 spilet] scheddyst WTLFLdChE  þi] herte *add.* G  blood] bodi SV  and] for me *add.* Ld  deyed] for me *add.* SV, dedist þe naile B  þe] *om.* ULd  rood] tre *add.* G  thou] *om.* RGSVWFf  me$^{2}$] *om.* T$^{2}$  grace] ioye Ld

515 þe] *om.* Ff, a C  praisynge] loue ⟨sweteli G⟩ RGSVW, loouyng my lof to þe ay spryng withouten any feynyng Ha  þynke hit] þenkest Ff  hit nat] *om.* G  hit] *om.* MTrLd$^{2}$  whils . . . etest] at mete RGSVWLdHa  515–16 bot . . . praiest] *om.* H

516 bothe] *om.* GChE  bifore] mete *add.* RGW  euer] *om.* GD  bot] *om.* GT  þou$^{1}$] *om.* Lt  spekest] do hit deuouteli *add.* G  Or] but TLCT$^{3}$M, *om.* Ha  if] *om.* SVFf, bote HeFE, þat B

517 þou haue] any *add.* G, *om.* D  þoghtes] þyngus B  hast] any *add.* G  more] delit in and *add.* Ha  swetnesse] likyng RGSVW, in god *add.* F  and deuocioun] *om.* RGWDB, so þat þei ben holy SV  and] a Ch, in Ha

518 þan] þou hast *add.* RG  in þo] *om.* SDB$^{2}$, in V  þat . . . þe] here P  þe] *om.* U  þou may] *om.* T$^{3}$BM  thynk] *om.* SV  ham] þenne SVW, *om.* Dd, wel *add.* F, þen *add.* B$^{2}$  do] haue B, putte PFTr

519 is] schal beo SV, *om.* F, most *add.* TrCh  519–20 þou . . . fore] ben ordeyned for þe RGSVW  ordeyned] disposed HT$^{2}$

520 fore] For *add.* M, to be F  praiest] shalt preye RGSVW  þou saist] *om.* Ch  saist] preyest] RGSVWFLdB$^{2}$Ha  how welle] *om.* U  welle] þou sayest *add.* RGSVW, myche D, þat þou myȝt seyn and *add.* Ch, it is sayde Ha

521 þat$^{1}$] *om.* BLdH  þe] þyn SLd  eigh] loue TDdR$^{2}$FfLCHeDT$^{3}$MChLd$^{2}$, þouȝt B  vpward] to god *add.* F  and] hauande ⟨in R, þin G⟩ RGSVW, also þat B  thoght] be *add.* B, studefastlich *add.* F  on] and T$^{2}$  þou] preyest or *add.* G

522 mych . . . may] þou myȝt U  may] saist R, for hit is better to saye fyue wordes wiþ a good (*om.* G) deuocioun in þi herte þen fyue þousande letyng (lete SV) þi þouȝte (herte SV) go þenkyng (wauerynge SV, walterand W) on dyuerse þinges in þe world and *add.* RGSVW  be in] ȝyue (ocupi W) þe to RGSVW  in$^{2}$] gret *add.* W

523 I . . . Criste] *om.* RGSVW  wel] *om.* D  þe] lust of þo *add.* Ha

524 and . . . and] greet shal be þy swetenes þat þou shalt fele RGSVW  and$^{1}$] leue *add.* F  fele] *om.* M, felþe F  delite] and wexe in þe swetnesse of god *add.* F

525 Thre . . . þe$^{1}$] knowe þe degrees of loue and I schal telle þe how F  Thre] þe He  I . . . þe$^{1}$] þer ben RGSVW  þe$^{1}$] shortly for y haue wryten of hem more

pleynly byfore *add.* P 525–6 for . . . heghest] *om.* He wold] desire and wilne F wyn] come TLCBMPHT$^{2}$Ch, wende FLd$^{2}$

526 degre] of loue *add.* T$^{3}$Ad 526–7 þe . . . synguler] *om.* P

527 Thi] þe HeF

528 loue] wille RGSVWT$^{3}$BMF may ouercum] ouercomyþ TDdR$^{2}$FfLCHeDT$^{3}$BMPFLdHT$^{2}$B$^{2}$TrHaLd$^{2}$ hit$^{2}$ . . . stalworth] ⟨with U⟩ stondeth ⟨euer RGSVW⟩ stalworthly URGSVW hit$^{2}$] *om.* DdR$^{2}$FfBMPLdHT$^{2}$B$^{2}$Ha is] so *add.* TLTr, euer *add.* F stalworth] to suffren and standyn *add.* Ch 528–9 agayns . . . stable] *om.* D

529 al] þe Ff, *om.* Ad fandynges] of þy enemy *add.* B and . . . or$^{1}$] *om.* Ad and stable] *om.* RGSVW, þat TL stable] stabely U, it is myȝti Ch þou] þei R, þi G ese] wele RGSVWB anguys] wo RGSVW

530 so . . . þynke] *om.* TL þe . . . þat] *om.* Ad hit] *om.* F

531 withouten end] for evyre Ad withouten] with Ld and . . . leuer] *om.* W þe] ȝe Ad 531–2 if . . . be] *om.* GAd auþer] auyer Lt, ouȝte D

532 be] don *add.* He al þe] *om.* HaLd$^{2}$ peyne] þat *add.* G woo] who G myght . . . creature] any creature miȝte suffre and þe deþ B

533 þou] þo D wold do] dyd Ad hym] on any wyse *add.* RGSVWB, god ChAd On . . . maner] and thus Ad 533–4 shal . . . be] is thy lyfe Ad

534 þat] when UAd 534–5 þynge . . . heght] affeccyon ne loue ne drede of no þing þat is made may brynge it doun from ihesu þat is sette upon Ch may] breke ne *add.* B hit] *om.* DdR$^{2}$DBMPLdHT$^{2}$Ld$^{2}$ 534–5 bot . . . heght] *om.* B bot] þat hit be euer *add.* UαL, more *add.* C, alwey *add.* F, ⟨it is Ad⟩ ay *add.* HaAd spryngynge] springe ⟨and be D⟩ GDP, springeþ ⟨allway T$^{3}$M⟩ HeT$^{3}$M

535 heght] him L, to wende to þi lordis blis *add.* F 535–7 Blesset . . . inseperabile] *om.* Ad Blesset] Blessset Lt is . . . sho] ben þei CF 535–6 bot . . . degre] *om.* RG[*corr. later*]T$^{3}$BM yet] *om.* SV

536 blesseder] in *add.* Ch þat$^{1}$] þei *add.* Ch myght hold] ben in G* hold] kepyn Ch degre] *om.* Ch and] may *add.* G*T$^{3}$B wyn] come BPFLdHT$^{2}$TrChHaLd$^{2}$, may *add.* M þat$^{2}$] þis THeLd$^{2}$

538 þi . . . when] when þi loue B$^{2}$ loue] þouȝt SV when] *om.* M al] *om.* B þi$^{3}$] loue *add.* G þoght] and mynde *add.* G and$^{2}$ . . . myght] *om.* RB$^{2}$ þi$^{4}$] þe Ch myght] with alle þi wille *add.* F, myghtis of þine soule Ch

539 so entierly] *om.* SVTr and$^{1}$ . . . perfitly] *om.* TL set] *om.* Ad and stablet] *om.* B$^{2}$

540 neuer . . . hym$^{1}$] *om.* TLHeBTrLd$^{2}$ neuer] ne F of . . . departeth] *om.* CAd neuer$^{2}$ . . . hym$^{2}$] *om.* ChAd neuer$^{2}$] is *add.* RGSVWTr, *om.* BF departeth] departed UαDdR$^{2}$FfLHeLdTrHaLd$^{2}$, *om.* B, departi F

541 als son] also U wakest] art wakid lete B seiynge] ihesu mercy or *add.* B$^{2}$

542 Aue Maria] *om.* Ad

543 if . . . slepe] *om.* He haue] *om.* B$^{2}$ ben] nouȝt *add.* TL 543–4 or . . . wakynge] *om.* Ad 543–4 or . . . praisynge] and þanne þou þenkest on him Ch or thynkynge] and þouȝt nouȝt B or] but TL

544 his$^{2}$ . . . wakynge] *om.* Ld as] þat B wakynge] loke þou crie hym mercy *add.* B Whan] so þat TL, for B, ȝyf Ad may . . . tyme] nouȝt Ad

545 hym] þanne *add.* Ch seist] and ȝif þou do þus *add.* B þan] *om.* Ch inseperabil] ⟨þat is L⟩ undepartid *add.* TL, for *add.* He 545–8 Ful . . . hit] *om.* Ad Ful] of *add.* D, for F

546 grace] ioye SVLd þay] of loue *add.* G þat$^{1}$] þan C of loue] *om.* SV þat$^{2}$] *om.* RGSLCDT$^{3}$HCh[*W corr.*]

547 to do] *om.* D bot] *om.* R$^{2}$ loue] herie SV God] þou *add.* R*SWTLDBMCh, and so *add.* G may] þou *add.* G, almiȝt H 547–8 þerto . . . hit] to Ch may] *om.* CHe

549 degre] of luf *add.* WC, *om.* H, þat *add.* Ch is heghest] *om.* C is$^1$] singulere for it is *add.* Ha heghest . . . is] *om.* Ad ferly] wonderful UGFLdHT$^2$ChHh, wonder R, of alle *add.* SV, staunge T [*sic*], mastry B, merueyllous PTr wyn] getynge F, gete Ld 549–50 þat . . . hit] and Ha

550 pere] forþi it hat so *add.* Ha loue] lif R$^2$ when] *om.* Ld al] þin Ch solace] ioye G

551 closet] spered BAd, schut Ld þe] þi RGSVWDdMB$^2$TrChAd, *om.* B herte] outerly *add.* F only] thanne *add.* U, *om.* T delite . . . other] *om.* Dd delite] *om.* Ch ne] *om.* SV

552 ioy] þine herte *add.* Ch list hit] or lust is G, kepest þou S, leste I V, lykeþ hym (hit F) BFHh nat] haue *add.* U, to hem *add.* Ch for] but B þe] *om.* GSVW[*R corr.*] hym] ihesu crist B, hem LdTr in] *om.* GSVWBB$^2$[*R corr.*] so] *om.* Ha 552–3 confortable . . . so] muche loue He confortable] comfortyng *alia*

553 and$^1$] *om.* B lestynge] and ⟨in B⟩ *add.* UBB$^2$TrCh, in *add.* DdR$^2$FfHT$^2$ his] þis RGSVW, *om.* BF loue] is *add.* αDMLdChHa so] is P 553–4 and$^2$ . . . brennynge] *om.* P he . . . sho] who so F or sho] *om.* CAd

554 degre] of loue *add.* GT$^3$Ha as wel] *om.* Ad of] *om.* T, goddys *add.* Ad brennynge] and gladynge *add.* F, and lastande in hym *add.* Ad 554–9 in . . . comen] *om.* Ad har] his C soule] þat is in þis degre *add.* P

555 bren] brennande RGFf Bot . . . fyre] and Ch þat] þe RGW fyre$^2$] of loue *add.* UB, *om.* Ha 555–6 if . . . hoot] *om.* B

556 be] noȝt *add.* TL so] *om.* GCh, swete *add.* D þan] þou hast hit whanne *add.* B 556–7 þe . . . is] is loue Ld þe] þi DdBPB$^2$

557 Ihesu$^1$] *om.* PTr, þankande and *add.* Ch louynge] on *add.* U, heryinge SV, preisyng CHeCh Ihesu thynkynge] *om.* SVCh Ihesu$^2$] crist in *add.* P thynkynge] preysing ihesu þonking TL, þankynge FLdT$^2$B$^2$ desyrynge] and coueitynge *add.* F 557–8 only . . . seghynge] *om.* PLdHT$^2$ 557–8 in . . . restynge] and to loue hym brennyng in hym lastyng in hym B 557–8 in . . . hym$^2$] of F in] þe *add.* SVDd, *om.* Ch

558 ondynge] and Lt, dwellyng URGSVWHa, hauyng TLCHeDB$^{2*}$Ch, anedande Dd, hangand R$^2$Ff, ȝhernande T$^3$M, *om.* Tr, brennynge Hh to] *om.* CT$^3$MB$^2$TrHh hym$^2$] *om.* CTr seghynge] syngynge UTDdLHeDFB$^2$ChHh, seande RGSVW, *om.* CTr, vnto him *add.* T$^3$M of . . . brennynge] and euer Tr, *om.* Hh of hym] in his loue Ch restynge] and ioyande *add.* RGSVW, lesting HT$^2$

559 Than . . . and] and whanne þe song of preisyng lesteþ in þin herte and þe song B Than] þat RGT preisynge] ioye PFLdHT$^2$TrHa and] *om.* T comen] into þe soule (herte Ch) *add.* TrCh þoght] songe F

560 turneth] beþ turned P, schal turne F and . . . synge] *om.* PHT$^2$ and . . . melody] *om.* F and] of S þe$^1$] *om.* B

561 psalmes] song BCh 561–2 þat . . . psalmes] *om.* SVW 561–2 þou$^1$ . . . Than] *om.* M before said] herst songe B said] *om.* H than] þat B$^2$ 561–2 mow . . . þe$^1$] *om.* Ld be longe] *om.* L about] in seying of a B 561–2 fewe psalmes] hem P fewe] þo UFfHT$^2$

562 psalmes] in þine preyinge *add.* Ch Than] þouȝe R deth . . . hony] syker of loue PHT$^2$Ha deth] betere and *add.* Ff, praier B hony] þanne þe wole þinke þe syker of loue *add.* Ld, the life Ad for] and B, *om.* FB$^2$ art] ful *add.* UTDdR$^2$Ff LCHeDT$^3$BPFLdHT$^2$B$^2$TrChHaAd

563 see] haue TL þat] þan L þou$^1$] most *add.* Ff þou$^2$] *om.* F hardily] hertely W, *om.* BAd say] amore langueo that is *add.* Ad 563–4 I . . . say] *om.* B I] longe for loue or I *add.* TL

564 languysshe] langusshe Lt, longe RGSVLdHT$^2$[*W corr.*], or I longe *add.* He, mourne B$^2$Hh loue] or y longe for loue *add.* C, or y morne for loue or y am syk for loue *add.* Ld 564–5 þan . . . loue] *om.* SVB say] ego dormio et cor meum vigilat that is *add.* Ad sleep] for luf *add.* W waketh] for luf *add.* W

565 degre] and in the seconde *add.* Ad men may] þan maistou RGW langwisshe] langure RG, longe LdHT$^2$, mourne B$^2$ 565–6 or . . . also] *om.* Ad langeth] langwyssches FfPHa

566 and] *om.* RGSVWLd also for] *trs.* M also] as W, *om.* Ad for] *om.* RGB$^2$ languysshynge] longyng I syng þis W*, longinge LdHT$^2$, mournyng B$^2$ is] for sikenesse *add.* B

567 failleth] fallen RSVWR$^2$FfL for] from SVF faillen] lakken U, fallen RGSVTR$^2$FfLH al] *om.* C

568 lust] loue P synful] cursed SV lif] þat is sikenesse of soule *add.* F and] þen þai *add.* F 568–9 setteth . . . and] streche þe weynes of B$^2$ setteth] of *add.* TL, alle *add.* F

569 har$^1$ . . . and] *om.* Ff and] in F hert] holly *add.* U, only *add.* He of] *om.* RGSVWHe forþi] for W þei] eche of hem B languysshe] langure RGB, longe SVWLdHT$^2$, mourne B$^2$

570 and] *om.* FLdHT$^2$Ha more] mowe þey ⟨sey so TL⟩ *add.* TLP in$^1$] *om.* L 570–1 þan . . . first] *om.* P þan] and R$^2$Ff

571 Bot] in *add.* D þe soul] he Ad is$^2$] all *add.* M, as mychel (*om.* Ha) brennyng ⟨in loue PHT$^2$Ha⟩ *add.* PFLdHT$^2$Ha as a] al TLCHeT$^3$BCh, *om.* Ad as$^1$] *om.* U a] *om.* RGSVWDdR$^2$FfDMFTr brennynge] as *add.* RGSVWT$^3$Ad, *om.* LdTr and] but B

572 and$^2$] *om.* U, in so myche þat it B failleth] falleþ SVR$^2$Ff, as kynde seiþ *add.* B, neuer *add.* F for] sor G mykel] for in *add.* G, *om.* P

573 loue] *om.* L, þat it haþ in singyng and riȝt *add.* B 573–95 so . . . yet] *om.* Ad þat] þe RGTDdR$^2$FfLHeDT$^3$MPFLdHT$^2$B$^2$Ch, þe *add.* SWHa, þi B soul] þat is so brennyng *add.* U, þat *add.* He only] ⟨swa Dd⟩ mykel DdCh, *om.* B conforted] in comfort in þe þridde degre F praisynge] *om.* GFf, loue W and$^1$] *om.* GSVFf louynge] *om.* SV, lykynge W, preisyng P, worschipynge FLdHT$^2$ of God] *om.* PHT$^2$Ha

574 cum] he *add.* UCh, for euere hit *add.* B, sche *add.* B$^2$ is] euere *add.* U, *om.* GSV, his L, sesses nouȝt of Ch syngynge] is *add.* L gostly] *om.* DTrCh 574–5 and . . . Ihesu] *om.* RGSVWBH and$^2$ . . . Ihesu$^2$] *om.* D 574–5 And Ihesu] *om.* PFLdT$^2$TrCh And] of *add.* TLCHeT$^3$MB$^2$Ha

575 bodily] *om.* B$^2$ cryinge] cry W with] *om.* D mouth] myrþe D syngynge] song RGSVWHeLdCh

576 for] *om.* Ff songe] *om.* B hath] is B both] *om.* B$^2$ and] but TLBCh

577 songe] þat is pryncypaliche in þe herte *add.* Ch none] yuel *add.* LCHe, no maner of wyk B bot . . . loue] *om.* B bot] buþ S, *om.* L þai] þat *add.* SP þrid] *om.* S 577–8 of . . . degree] *om.* Ch to . . . which] Tho þis B

578 degree] *om.* ULdTr, of loue *add.* B impossibil] possible B$^2$ cum] no *add.* B$^2$ bot . . . loue] þerto with ony werching of man for it is a free specyal ȝifte of god ȝouen to hem þat he wille and in wel myche loue muste þee herte ben filled or he schulde felyn þis song Ch in . . . Forþi] *om.* HT$^2$ Forþi] for PCh, But FLd

579 if] *om.* H wil] wit Ff songe] of loue *add.* B I] answare and *add.* U

580 bot] loke B or sho] *om.* CHe feleth . . . þat$^3$] is þerinne for to B þat$^2$ . . . God] and loueþ good He 580–1 and . . . þerwith] in her loue þey beþ seyngyng TL, sauynge Ch God] and in her loue þai buþ *add.* F

581 þerwith] in herte but *add.* B, *om.* F tel . . . the]knowe wel B is of] comeþ fro B of . . . and] an heuenlyche song þat Ch and] þat W hit] *om.* T$^3$Ch

582 grete] *om.* T$^3$HTr grace] *om.* SV

583 þe songe] menstralye Ch mynstralcie] melodye FfCh of] þis *add.* B erth] world BFB$^2$

584 woo] and *add.* U þerto] and moreouer (euere SVW) *add.* RGSVW, *om.* TLCHeT$^3$B 584–5 In . . . and$^1$] *om.* U rest] ioye F, and pes *add.* Ch mow]

*om.* Ha  get] haue He, wiþ goddes grace come B  hit] But *add.* TCHeM$B^2$Ch, *om.* D, þerto B

585–6 Gangerels . . . day] *om.* B  585 Gangerels . . . and$^2$] and þat schal no ianglers gete ne no F  Gangelers] gagelers RG, *om.* SVCHeH$T^2$, Goars WDCh, iongelours T, ianleres Ld, tangelers $B^2$  janglers] swerers *add.* He  and$^2$ . . . goers] *om.* D$T^3$M  and$^2$ . . . of] ofte $B^2$  kepers] leperes L  of] and SPH$T^2$, gestys and *add.* C  585–6 and$^3$ . . . day] *om.* HeCh  and goers] to þe nale *add.* L, *om.* $B^2$

586 or] but B, þat Ch  any$^1$] man or womman B  takeled] acombred UP, fyled RG, tangled SVCDLd, foulid W*, takked DdL$T^3$MHa, taglede $R^2$FfH$T^2$, towched B, perseueraunt or costomable F, smyttid $B^2$, helden or defouled Ch  any$^2$] *om.* $T^3$MCh, foul *add.* F

587 any$^1$] *om.* UαDd$R^2$FfLCHeD$T^3$MPFLdH$T^2$$B^2$ChHa  delite] and loue *add.* Ch  any$^2$] synne or in any *add.* G  erthly] worldli G

588 þerfro] þe fro Ff, from þis degree TrCh  is] *om.* CLd$B^2$Tr  to erth] *om.* T 588–9 degre . . . degre$^1$] *om.* D  many] few TL

589 ful] but SVTr, *om.* TLHe$B^2$ChHh  fewe] fewer TL  bot] *om.* W  euer] *om.* RGSVWCh

590 perfeccioun] persecucion H$T^2$  folwers . . . hath] comes þar to Ha  first] fist Lt

591 men] many DdPF, and wommen *add.* B  in$^1$] *om.* W  to$^2$] *om.* F

592 to] *om.* F  Oþer] On þer P  ben . . . brighthede] *om.* Dd  brighthede] liȝt TLCHe$T^3$BM, *om.* $R^2$FfDTr, clerte Ch

593 oþer$^1$] or RGSVWPF$B^2$TrHa, *om.* L  of$^2$] *om.* H  oþer$^2$] or SVWBPF$B^2$Tr Ha  þe] trewe *add.* F

594 In . . . degre] *om.* $B^2$  þis . . . degre] þese þre degrees F  þrid] *om.* C$T^3$ wyn] come CHeBPFLdH$T^2$Ch  therto] in to þe þridde degre $B^2$  shalt] haue and *add.* F

595 ioy] *om.* SV  þe] *om.* $B^2$  595–609 and$^1$ . . . syght] *om.* He  595–6 oþer . . . longynge] his langynges may Ad  oþer] þine Ch  and songes] *om.* RGSVWCh  songes] ioies B, and longynges *add.* F

596 in . . . longynge] *om.* BF  longynge] syngynge U, langure RG, languissching SVWD, louenge T  this] songe *add.* TL  þyn] his Ad  thy] ly F, oure Ch, *om.* Ad  lord] *om.* LtUAd

597 when . . . goynge] *om.* BAd  when] whombe Lt[*Cd illegible*]  and . . . goynge] *om.* Ch  thy] his LtGW*Ff$B^2$  goynge] song S, hennyes *add.* TL, hens and sayst þus in longyng *add.* F

598 me$^1$] *om.* MHh  of] þis *add.* F

599 gyf] ȝeuyng F  me] þe SV, þou Ff, to *add.* D  þe] to me SVHh, *om.* TLCB $B^2$Tr, me Ff, ioye *add.* Ch  may] me Lt, þe *add.* TC$B^2$, *om.* M  se] þee *add.* LPHh, þy *add.* F  hauynge] and haue ⟨þe G⟩ α, lestand Ch  for] þee UTL$T^3$BM$B^2$Ha, *om.* Dd$R^2$FfCDPFLdH$T^2$ChAd

600 loue] to me *add.* $T^3$B  euer] to me *add.* TLCM, most C, *om.* B, loue þat is þe Ch  swettest] to me *add.* RGWF, swetnesse to me SV, swetnesse D  al] eny G, oþere *add.* Ad

601 for loue] *om.* LtUTDd$R^2$FfLCD$T^3$MPFLdH$T^2$$B^2$ChHaHh  hit] þou Ff brest] for loue *add.* TDd$R^2$FfLCD$T^3$PFLdChHa, breke ⟨for luf MH$T^2$⟩ WMH$T^2$Hh þan] þat RGSVWMAdHh, *om.* $T^3$PLdH$T^2$, ne F  languyssh] langure RG, langisching SV, longe WTLLdH$T^2$, mourne $B^2$  I] hit mai SV, for loue *add.* $B^2$, it Ha  no] *om.* P

602 For . . . fare] *om.* Ad  For] al on *add.* α  thoght] herte SVT$T^3$  hath] is αPFLdH$T^2$Ch  fest] fasted U, set SVT, made festnynge L$T^3$M, made myn herte festinge Ch, mad seynyng B, fette $B^2$, festned Ch  and] *om.* T, þat Ch  I am] is V am] *om.* BF  fare] gone SV

603 stand] astoneyed *add.* α, stif *add.* B in] *om.* H stil] gret F of] for TLC T³BMFB²ChHh, *om.* LdHT² al] oon RGSVWHh, *om.* TDLdHT²Ch, ane þe R²FfBB², þe LCT³MF louelieste] of *add.* RWDdR²FfCDT³MPLdHT²B²Ha, on *add.* G, louelokes of S, louelokest of VL, louest of T, loue hest of B, louenesse F, in *add.* Ch lare] laale T

604 His . . . langynge] *om.* Ad His] is UDdR²FfHHa, My leues RG, mi lyf is SVWT, lorde þi LCT³BM, þe bond of P, hit is of FLd, þis T²B², þe Ch, of Ha loue] long SV langynge] of him *add.* Ch, fandyng Ha hit] þat TFLd, *om.* DT³ChHh my] deth *add.* Ch day] For *add.* Ch

605 band] lond D, fyr P, bronde F swet] loue ⟨is euer T⟩ α Ad, hoot P brennynge] lufyng Ha, langynge Ad for] *om.* CMChHh hit] þat T, *om.* ChHh holdeth me] haþ me drawe T, euer and *add.* M ay] euere UD, away B

606 place] solace T fro] *om.* GFHh, al B² til] for LC þat] *om.* B²Hh get . . . may] may gete U hit] *om.* GDdR²FfLCDT³BMPFLdHT²B²Ch

607 syght] song T swetynge] for *add.* C wendeth] schal wende B²Hh

608 In . . . nyght] *om.* Ch beth] shal be RGLCT³BM walkynge] wakynge RGSVWDdR²FfB²HaAd 608–9 withouten . . . syght] *om.* Ad or] of SVB², and F nyght] myȝte T

609 loue] soule T in] *om.* S, euere TB, þe F, ay B² and] ofte I L, ay CT³M, me B, euer *add.* Ld longeth] in *add.* G, longyng T, longe sore L, me *add.* T³M to] see *add.* B, *om.* Ld þat] þi F, *om.* Ld syght] liȝt T, siþ D, þer I schal ben euere in ioye withouten noye or nyght *add.* Ch

610 wel] *om.* FfCh, dere Ad with] in B 610–11 God . . . name] *om.* PLdHT² reul] þenke He, wel *add.* F lif] loue α, self B² right] *om.* DdR²FfLCHeDBMF B²TrChHaELa, vnto his plesynge T³

611 þe] his Ad loue] knyt *add.* F fest hit] shal be festnede T, *om.* F hit] *om.* FfCHeBTr²Ff³, him HT² so] *om.* FfAd faste] sadliche U herte] mynde Ii² 611–13 þat . . . custume] for Ad hit] he HT²

612 of . . . þoght] þerof CHeB þoght] herte LIi² to] of B² and seist] sayande ⟨his name B⟩ T³BM

613 Ihesu] *om.* Ch shal be] is Ch ere] herte GE ioy] ioyen SV, and in þyn herte ioye and *add.* LdHT² mouth] waxen swete as *add.* SV

614 hert] ere G 614–16 for . . . stably] *om.* Ad for] and C þe] he T² shal] schulde Ch ioy] mirþe G name] of ihesu *add.* TrLaTr²

615 nempned] red B hit¹] *om.* LdHT² myrth . . . hit] *om.* T myrth . . . to] or B myrth] ioye G songe] blisse G, ioye SVFCh thynk] singe C

616 thynk¹] þis name *add.* U, singe C, speke Ld continuely] *om.* P hit¹] in ⟨þin SVW⟩ herte *add.* α, him L, *om.* R³ stably] in þi thoght (herte ChE) *add.* MChE 616–17 hit² . . . hert] *om.* Ch purgeth . . . and] *om.* M purgeth þi] distroith Ff

617 kyndels] tendeþ SVLHe, luf in *add.* M, tendriþ P, tent F, alyghteþ LdHT² hert] with fyre of luf and *add.* Ha 617–18 hit² . . . slownesse] and putteþ oute angyr and sorwe and slewþe Ch remoueth] rennuþ F anger] *om.* He 617–18 hit³ . . . slownesse] *om.* H

618 away] al *add.* He slownesse] slouþe CT²Br hit woundeth] *om.* B² woundeth] woneþ GSVWTBr[*R corr.*], wyndeþ þee LLa, þe *add.* CBMLd, wendeþ þe HeF, þo herte *add.* Ha, is wounded Lt²Ii² 618–19 fulfilleth . . . drede] *om.* T fulfilleth] fulfild UChLt²Ii²BrLa, þe *add.* SVLCHeT³MFLdT²TrE, it *add.* Ha, it is fulfyllynge Ad in²] *om.* RGWB²Ff³ chaseth] awey *add.* BMTrETr² schameþ Lt²Ii²

619 putteth] þe *add.* B out] of *add.* B, our B², pryde and *add.* Ha heuyn] ȝates *add.* Ha a] it T

620–6 Haue . . . me] *om.* Ad 620 Haue . . . Ihesu] and glad to hure of god L in] *om.* DP memorie] muynde SVDdFLdHT²B²ChELt²Ii²Br, *om.* D, mynde on (ofte La) PLa al] of Ii² fantasies] defautes UM hit] he RW, *om.* T

621 putteth] away *add.* *α*, owte *add.* Dd fro] to B, out and wysses and ledes Ha louer] of him (ihesu ChE) *add.* LCHeMFChE, alle þe oþere louerid D, *om.* BTr$^2$ 621–5 And . . . al] *om.* R$^3$Ff$^3$ And . . . nyght] *om.* BCh haille] hailleth LtD, greteth UFHT$^2$, calle *α*, grete LLdEIi$^2$, saluteþ C, also P, *om.* Ha oft] on *α*Ha, of PF Mary] man U, also *add.* RGT boþ] *om.* SV nyght] and *add.* GSVWTBr[*R corr.*], with aue maria *add.* LCHeMFE

622 loue and] *om.* Ch loue] ioie Lt$^2$Ii$^2$BrLa ioy] blisse Lt$^2$Ii$^2$Br, loue La fele] fynde *α* þis] is B lare] greet ofte owre lady boþe day and nyȝt with aue maria *add.* B The] hit SV dar] nedeth USVLt$^2$La gretly] *om.* GDB$^2$Tr

623 bokes] þat *add.* RW, but *add.* GSVTT$^3$BFTrE hold] haldes W in$^1$] þin *add.* TTrChEBr in$^2$] þi *add.* TChBr, *om.* D werke] worde F, dede Ii$^2$ and] for þenne *α* hast] dost TIi$^2$Tr$^2$, sal haue R$^2$Ff

624 done] *om.* TDdR$^2$FfLCHeDT$^3$BMPFLdHT$^2$B$^2$TrChHaEIi$^2$LaTr$^2$ þat$^1$] al *add.* Ii$^2$ we] I He write] wite R fulnes] fulfillyng LBChTr$^2$, louenesse P of] *om.* LB lawe] bagge U, loue WT 624–5 in . . . al] and þerinne is þe lawe comprehended B

625 hongeth] þing SV al] and þat es luf to god and to þi neghburgh *add.* Ha, þe lawe ⟨etcetera explicit tractatus nobilissimus Lt$^2$⟩ *add.* Lt$^2$Ii$^2$, both lawe and prophesie explicit amen *add.* Br

626 now] *om.* SVF, þanne B may . . . say] seist þou to me þus P ask . . . and] *om.* T me] *om.* T$^2$B$^2$, what is loue Ch say] what is loue syþþe *add.* B, syn *add.* Ch so] *om.* LCHe of loue] þerof B

627 hit is] es lufe DdAd, *om.* B God] *om.* B$^2$

628 and how] þat P hym] ihesu B$^2$, god Ad 628–9 and . . . hym] *om.* MCh

629–32 These . . . swetnesse] *om.* Ad 629 to louse] *om.* TrCh louse] assoyle UM, lere RGWTDdR$^2$FfT$^3$BHa, onswere to SV, teche LCHeLdHT$^2$B$^2$Hh, lerne D, knowe P, aske F, expownde Tr$^2$ febel] fleschely Ch 629–30 and . . . fleisshely] to answeren to Ch a$^2$] as B

630 as I am] as I am *add.* Lt [*subpuncted*] þerfor] *om.* Ld nat] *om.* Ff leue] lette DdLChHaTr$^2$, spare B þat . . . shal] to B$^2$Tr$^2$

631 shewe . . . and] seyn Ch wit] as god wil ȝiue me grace *add.* B þat . . . be] *om.* He hit] *om.* TrCh be] by resun *add.* U, I sal sey *add.* M 631–2 for . . . is] troste in ihesu þat is helpande Ch hope] in ihesu and *add.* G 631–2 in . . . Ihesu] þat in þe ihesu is help SV

632 is] art SV loue] wit L and$^1$ . . . swetnesse] *om.* B and$^1$] of L pees] loue L and$^2$] of SVR$^2$FfF, *om.* CHe swetnesse] pees L, *om.* CHe, I sal solue þies questyons *add.* M

633 loue$^1$] and swettenes *add.* CF And . . . answare] *om.* FfTr I] þan H answare] and seie þat *add.* L, þus *add.* B, swete H

634 desire] *om.* D in God] *om.* HT$^2$ 634–5 with . . . brennynge] *om.* LdHT$^2$ delite] and swetnes *add.* Ha and sikernesse] in god He, of god for *add.* F

635 and] in P, *om.* Ch Light] þat *add.* RB clarifieth] clarifide F oure skyl] *om.* *α* oure$^1$] *om.* F skyl] in as moche as it is *add.* B brendynge] and *add.* RWTF, and G, hyt *add.* B kyndyls] quyketh U, cuyndeliche SVT, tendeþ LHe, liȝtneþ C, tiendreþ P, tendyng F, alyȝteth LdHT$^2$, kyndeþ B$^2$ 635–6 oure couaitise] vs Ad

636 couaitise] wille TrCh we] nouȝt coueyten nouȝt *add.* Ch desire] luf Ha hym] god Ha is] as F lif] þing B coupelynge] coupled B

637 louynge] luf T$^3$M for] loue and *add.* Ff, in *add.* B vs] hit P swete] subiect LtAdTr$^2$, swifte RSVW, suget swetnesse P, redy Ch 637–8 purtee . . . God$^2$] *om.* SV 637–8 purtee . . . God$^1$] *om.* B$^2$ 637–8 purtee ioyneth] purgeþ D purtee] clennes RGLCHePHT$^2$Ch, powert WTT$^3$MFLdHh, in pouert and B

638 God$^1$] hym in loue B, bote *add.* HeCh loue . . . God] *om.* T vs$^2$] *om.* MAd fairhede] faderhede H al] *om.* Ff

639 vertuȝ] loue is a þinge of alle vertues *add.* HT$^2$ thynge] turned *add.* RGWT, turnyng *add.* SV þrogh] þouȝt to god þe SV which] þing *add.* C 639–40 and . . . other] or LdHT$^2$ and] yf F

640 and] *om.* Ha 640–77 Loue . . . vices] *om.* Ad thynkynge] kynge D

641 þat$^2$ . . . loueth$^1$] is loued Ch and . . . loueth] *om.* LtTCB[*corr. later*]Ch 641–2 hit$^3$ . . . and] *om.* Ha hit$^3$] he He ioyeth] þanne it lyketh *add.* Ch

642 sory] bot it ioyes hertly *add.* Ha 642–3 Loue . . . thoghtes] *om.* DdHe betwix . . . with] to knowe P two] *om.* B

643 a] strenghte *add.* F stirrynge] strengþe W*, streng T, myght Ch to] þe H loue] of *add.* H 643–4 for$^2$ . . . God] *om.* B$^2$ for$^2$] biforen SV

644 al] *om.* He loue] *om.* GB$^2$ is] sette and *add.* Ch

645 al] *om.* GLdHT$^2$ vnordeynt] defourmed D 645–6 in$^2$ . . . thynge] *om.* BM in$^2$] of LCHe, and B$^2$ any] al TF þynge] loue Lt 645–6 þat . . . good$^1$] *om.* DCh

646 good$^1$] ⟨in F⟩ god GWMFLdHaHh Bot . . . good] *om.* MP al] *om.* B$^2$Ch dedly] syn *add.* U$\alpha$DdLCHeFLdB$^2$Ch, luf *add.* R$^2$FfTr$^2$ is] vs F vnordynat] ordeynde T$^3$F good] god GFLdHHaHh, *om.* DdR$^2$FfLCHeD

647 a . . . is] *om.* B reghtest] riccheste SVWTB$^2$Ha, rygth R$^2$FfT$^3$

648 of] þat is in (*om.* L) LCHe, to H soule] þat suffereþ nouȝt hym be witout þat he loueþ FTr Trouth] þouȝt SV, nogth *add.* R$^2$Ff 648–9 may$^2$ . . . helpe] is not helplych B

649 nat] *om.* R$^2$FfHHa hit] *om.* S, loue VLChHaTr$^2$, him HeF perfeccioun] and *add.* B, affeccion F lettres] *om.* B, alle holy writte TrCh vertu] vertues and B of$^2$] is a C

650 heel] help DdHh, helthe ChTr$^2$ sacrementȝ] sacrifise $\alpha$

651 lyf . . . men] *om.* LdHT$^2$ deiynge] ded WD

652 good . . . is] god lufs R$^2$FfM suffre] weore i suffred SV

653 to$^1$] for L begger staf] ⟨been at U⟩ beggers astaat URGWTP, beggers SVB, þe loue of god L, pouer men FB$^2$Tr$^2$ can$^1$] haue WD, come F as . . . as] þat C as$^2$] al *add.* DdMP, any *add.* LCHeF men] we B may] *om.* DdPF can$^2$] gan oþer may cumme F in erth] *om.* T, or angeles in heuen *add.* Ch to$^2$] do U, *om.* GSVTHePT$^2$B$^2$TrHh[*W corr.*], for B, do *add.* FHa þis] wit *add.* B$^2$

654 loue] and charyte *add.* B noght] *om.* BF, ordeyned *add.* T$^3$BMCh sorowe . . . and] *om.* D sorowe] and *add.* WT, and wo *add.* Ff ordeyned] or deeth Lt, *om.* T$^3$BMB$^2$Ch, or dying LdT$^2$ and] *om.* WT, to C

655 ask$^1$] wetyn Ch or sho$^1$] *om.* CHe ask . . . sho] *om.* LtTr mych] þei *add.* L loueth . . . sho] he loueþ þe C loueth] loue SVP he$^2$ . . . sho] *om.* L or sho$^2$] *om.* He sho] is in *add.* SV, god *add.* T$^3$Ch, haþ *add.* P þat] þan M

656 forþi] for URSVWTDdPHT$^2$HaHhTr$^2$ bot] *om.* CHeDT$^3$MB$^2$

657 rightwise] riȝt wil URGSVTr$^2$, riche wylle WT, ryȝtwisnes L turnynge] turned U$\alpha$Tr$^2$

658 and] es *add.* DdR$^2$FfLCDT$^3$BMPFHT$^2$TrChHa ioyned] ioying SV, ȝiue B, enioyned Ld, oned Ch and] or T kyndled] queked U, kyndely T, ytende LHe, y lyȝtned C, tiendred P, aliȝteþ F, alyhted LdHT$^2$, kyndelyth Ch

659 fer$^1$] for F fylynge] filthe ULCh, felynge T$^3$Ha, defoulynge FHT$^2$ corrupcioun] ne bunde *add.* B obleged] ibounde UHePHT$^2$Ch, oblysed WDd, bowand F

660 no . . . lif] non of þis passyng þynges but euere to þat þat an F of . . . lif] þis loue is SV, free and Ch þis] þi U, þe He lif] world He al] werldlyche and *add.* Ch fleisshlye] þinges and alle oþer loues and *add.* Ch redy] to diȝe *add.* G and] ay W, *om.* TB, alwey *add.* Ch

661 gnedy] willy ULHe, gredy RGSVWDdR$^2$FfDT$^3$MFLdHT$^2$B$^2$ChHaHhTr$^2$, *om.* TB, willeful CTr, desiryng P contemplacioun] syght Ch God] in whom it is sette *add.* Ch in] and R al . . . vnouercomen] loue is comfort to men þat þei be nouȝt

ouercome loue is L vnouercomen] *om.* αCHeT³BM, ouer comyng of syne loue is F 661–2 þe . . . affecciouns] *om.* He sum] sun LtTR²FfLDT³T²B²Hh, sowle B, ground Ch

662 of¹] in B al] *om.* B² affecciouns] unouercome *add.* CT³M, haþ ouercomyng *add.* B heel . . . maneres] *om.* Ch heel] heleþ F end] and D, haldyng F

663 vertu . . . lesteth] *om.* M vertu] strengþe SV, *om.* L whils . . . lesteth] wel fayreng B

664 corone] sorow Lt armes . . . thoghtes] *om.* Ch armes] armer GLCHe, mirynes Dd withouten] wiþ He þat] loue ChTr² no] *om.* He

665 pay] loue α, plese PHT²ChTr², haue Ld with] wiþouten T² þat] loue weel rewled Ch synneth] dedli *add.* He if] *om.* SV God] *om.* B

666 in vs] *om.* LCHeDBMCh vs . . . we] ure þouȝt þe while þat wol SV þrogh . . . serue] þat acordeþ F þrogh] *om.* CD, til Ha þe . . . we] *om.* H [*space left*] we serue] serueþ D we] mowe *add.* LHeT³M, may C

667 clenseþ] chaungyþ T hit] *om.* B, here F 667–8 and² . . . syn] *om.* LCHeDT³BMCh

668 orrible] *om.* U, vnsemely RG, foule SV, huge WT, vgly DdR²FfT³MHaTr²Ii³, gastliche LCHeF, ferdful D, dredful B, grisliche PCh, gastful LdHh, hidouse HT² 668–9 of² . . . son²] sone makeȝ vs (*om.* BM) goddes seruauntes T³BM, sone makeþ here F of²] *om.* B²

669 fendes] fende WT, and *add.* Ld son¹] *om.* G, soone WLd, seþen he T, scisme T², it *add.* B² maketh] hym *add.* WTLd Goddis] þe T son²] sones G and] *om.* BMF parsonel] partynere UGTR²FfLCT³BMPFHT²B²ChHaHhIi³, parcener RWHeLd, perceþ SV, parcenel Dd, perseyuour D, partaker Tr² heritage] blisse GFfHa heuyn] alle oþer ȝiftes of þe holy gost wicked men mown han sauyng loue for loue only scedeþ schedeth þe reprouyd from goddis chosen þanne *add.* Ch

670 afforce . . . to] *om.* B afforce] strenþe HT² vs¹] *om.* DdHh to . . . vs] *om.* CCh to] and D cloth] close G as . . . fyre] *om.* Ch jren . . . þe¹] *om.* MF or] of RT cole] stele TC 670–1 þe³ . . . þe³] *om.* T

671 and . . . hewe] *om.* B 671–2 wol . . . þe²] *om.* W doth²] *om.* U, takyþ T, in takyng of *add.* F hewe] of *add.* T, lytte fatte (*om.* M) T³M, for þe iren or *add.* B, þat it es alle elykked *add.* Ha 671–2 þe⁵ . . . fyre²] *om.* Ch cool] is *add.* BTr² so] *om.* F cloth¹] closeþ GSVHB², cloþide TTr², glad B hit¹] is T, *om.* BB²Tr² in¹] þe T²

672 al¹] he F, it Ha þe¹ . . . light] *om.* Dd aire] sunne eri eyr G, erþe is B, is *add.* Ch cloth] closeþ GSVFHB², cloþid T, glad B, enclosed Ch hit] *om.* SVTBB²Ch þat . . . light] *om.* Ch al²] hit SVTBHa, *om.* W, he F is²] al *add.* SVWBFHa light] fyrliȝt G, sunne T 672–3 and . . . hit²] *om.* T³BM

673 so] doþ þe W, *om.* DIi³ substanciali] fully TFLd taketh . . . hewe] in þe coloure Ch þe . . . hit²] it þat it is al hewe C þe] *om.* SVLd, his T hit¹] *om.* ChTr²Ii³ al . . . hit] lykest Ch al] *om.* DdR²FfLHeDHhTr² hit²] to þe colour T, þo hew Ha

674 shal] *om.* F a] þe LCHe of] in Ff hert] *om.* Ld so] *om.* FCh loue] of ihesu cryste *add.* Ch hit] al Ch

675 be¹] al *add.* α turned] als *add.* Ha and . . . ware] þat it schal be B² be²] *om.* F al] *om.* L, a Ch fyre] loue LdHT², of luf *add.* Ha 675–7 and² . . . vices] *om.* P, and so schal a man boþen brenne and schynen now haue I tolde þe somwhat what loue is Ch he shal] *om.* Ha he] *om.* R²Ff

676 be¹] *om.* DdR²FfLCHeDT³BMFLdHT²B²HaHh so] al WT, *om.* FfMB² shynynge] schyne DdR²LCHeDT³BMFLdHT²B²HaHh, owakene Ff þat] þer shal be *add.* αTr² in²] *om.* T³ BMB²Tr² he] *om.* LtαLMB²Tr², shal UT³BF, schal *add.* FHT², may *add.* Ha be²] *om.* αLd, found *add.* F durke] eny derkenesse (þyng F) UαF in] of α, þat toucheþ F

677 vices] or (*om.* W) of synne *add.* α Ha

678 is$^1$] *om.* D And . . . answare] *om.* RTr answare] and say *add.* Ff, answered L, þee þat *add.* Ch þe] his R, *om.* G, mannes TrHa

679 of . . . man] *om.* Ha nat . . . mouth] *om.* T$^3$BM nat] is *add.* L to say] *om.* Ad

680 nat] oonliche *add.* U his$^1$] so *add.* Ld, wordes (speche Ad) ne in his *add.* TrAdHh many] man D, *om.* Ha speketh] sein C

681 and] many *add.* Dd, ȝit *add.* BTrTr$^2$, *om.* B$^2$ God] good RF þe whiche] þei C, þe Ld suffreth] done TrAd gret] *om.* Ad

682 and] *om.* LDMCh to . . . sight] *om.* Ad þay] þe GFf secheeth] speke R$^2$Ff, þenkiþ B$^2$

683 praysynge] loue WT and honour] *om.* Ad and fauour] *om.* Ad and] *om.* G

684 in] *om.* D þe$^2$] as B, þei B$^2$ rauysshynge] rauynge He, wormes F wolfes] cloþed vndur cristes cloþing *add.* α, mete F

685–6 Bot . . . nat] *om.* Ad 685–6 if . . . bot] *om.* B$^2$ 685 if] *om.* F a] good *add.* α gif] do THePFLdHT$^2$Tr take] ȝeue Ch do] to GTCB, *om.* SV, vse Ff

686 a] greet *add.* D loueth$^1$] nouȝt *add.* F bot] nouȝt onliche *add.* L loueth$^2$ . . . nat] *om.* L he$^2$] þei Ch hym] hem B$^2$ when] ȝif B, *om.* Ad

687 he] þei B$^2$Ch, þat *add.* Ad only] *om.* CTr$^2$ Goddis] sake and *add.* Ff loue] sake LCHe, and ȝiueþ almesdede and takiþ hem to pouert and penaunce it is a signe þat þei louiþ god *add.* B$^2$ 687–8 and . . . syn] *om.* DdR$^2$FfLCHeDT$^3$BM TrHh and] but if he B$^2$ maketh] purgeþ α PHT$^2$B$^2$Ha, clenseþ FLdCh his] her Ch

688 setteth] secheþ SV his] loue and *add.* F, *om.* H, herte and *add.* T$^2$, her Ch thoght] herte SV 688–9 God . . . þe] *om.* SV God] hym Ff and$^2$] doþ *add.* F al$^2$] *om.* ChAd

689 dedes] *om.* Ad he$^1$] þei Ch, *om.* Ad do] *om.* Ad he$^2$ . . . ham] *om.* F he doth] do GAd he$^2$] þei Ch ham] þen SV, *om.* FfPB$^2$ in . . . for] *om.* Ad to] þat he may B$^2$TrHa pay] ples WLT$^3$PLdHT$^2$TrCh, and plesyn *add.* Ff, queme F

690 and] so *add.* C reste] blisse LT$^3$FTr of] oure lord ihesu and to com to þo rest of *add.* W þan] *om.* Ad loueth] haþ F God] and ellis nouȝt *add.* L 690–1 and$^2$ . . . is] *om.* FAd and$^2$] *om.* C

691 þat] þan TC in] *om.* Ch his$^1$] *om.* CBMF, þe B$^2$ so . . . withouten] þat schewes he in his dedes Ad so] þat F his$^2$] þe good (*om.* He) GHe sheweth] it *add.* Ch 691–704 If . . . away] *om.* Ad þou] he L 691–2 do . . . and] *om.* LdHT$^2$Ch

692 good$^2$] þe goode *add.* Ld, it doth *add.* Ch men] *om.* W, þou T supposeth] supposen Ch, wil suppose Ha Forþi] *om.* T

693 loke] loue R wel] wel *add.* Lt [*subpuncted*], wol R, *om.* GSVLCHeT$^3$BMLd, þan T þat] al G, al *add.* Ff þoght] herte SV, entencioun L, thanke M

694 þo] oother UBPFTrTr$^2$, *om.* CB$^2$ChHh men] but *add.* α LHeT$^3$ I do] þou dost P I$^2$] þou P

695 God] withinne *add.* Ha 695–6 do . . . and] *om.* B as myche] more C 695–6 penaunce . . . myche] *om.* DT$^3$M penaunce] as I *add.* ChHa in] *om.* SV, his *add.* Ch body] *om.* SV

696 wake and] wakende Ff and] as muche SVTr as . . . do] *om.* Ha as] moche as *add.* B I do] eny man T, þou dost or y P, a good F I$^2$] *om.* FfT$^3$, men He, þou B þan] *om.* F wene] *om.* T$^2$ I loue] he loueþ F 696–7 loue . . . me] be Ch loue] god *add.* α FfLCHeDT$^3$BMFTrHh, lyue better P

697 me] hym F þan anoþer] *om.* DdR$^2$FfLCHeDT$^3$BMPFLdHT$^2$B$^2$TrChHh for þat] whan U þat$^1$ . . . euery] þulke SV do] as ferforth to alle mannes siȝt as I

doo *add.* U$\alpha$Ii$^{3}$ hert] wotes *add.* T$^{3}$BMLd, wate and na man elles bot god *add.* Ha

698 hit] I GSVWTR$^{2}$FfDB$^{2}$TrCh my] *om.* GFfCHePB$^{2}$TrChHaHh, gode *add.* B, his F nat] þat *add.* LCHeT$^{3}$M, þer ne may no man *add.* F wot] noȝt ne *add.* WT, and elles B bot God] *om.* F 698–9 Than . . . do] SV 698–9 Than . . . God] *om.* DdR$^{2}$FfLCHeDT$^{3}$BMPFLdHT$^{2}$B$^{2}$TrChHaHh Than] þat T

699 if] þingþe T loue$^{1}$] my *add.* WT for noght] *om.* D, no þyng F se me] seyn or B se] *om.* D Wherfor] for SV, wheþer for H loue$^{2}$] *om.* T

700 þe] his D nat] al on *add.* F bot . . . loue] *om.* Ch bot] only *add.* P as] a URSVWTHeBHa, in a *add.* G, in a Dd, hit is a F he . . . he] ho C

701 God] *om.* Ch wil . . . do] doth nouȝt Ch do] schewe it U, it *add.* B, folwe F dede] and *add.* B þat . . . loue] as him owede to doo U, *om.* Ch

702 hym] bodily RT, boldli GSVW he] *om.* Ii$^{3}$ hit] he He is] euer *add.* WTLT$^{3}$, ay *add.* MHa sum] *om.* SV, in F good] goodnesse F, warke *add.* Ha

703 hit$^{1}$] he HeH cesse] is wery (sadde Ii$^{3}$) UIi$^{3}$ wit . . . and] þan it T, he H wit . . . þat] *om.* SVCh þou] wel *add.* URGWR$^{2}$FfLCT$^{3}$MPFLdHT$^{2}$B$^{2}$Tr, wel B keleth] weweþ B

704 vansheth] wereth U, dwyneþ RG, slydeþ SV, wites WDdR$^{2}$HT$^{2}$ HaHh, wastyþ TCT$^{3}$BMPLd, wendeth FfFB$^{2}$Ch, bowis D, wit is Ii$^{3}$

705 askynge] of loue *add.* T I$^{1}$] þou WTC verraily] *om.* WT God] *om.* UIi$^{3}$ 705–6 verray . . . to] *om.* G verray] verrayly Ad

706 loue$^{2}$] *om.* F hym] god UFB$^{2}$, *om.* PCh hert] stalworthly and *add.* G

707 þi] þouȝt or in al þi *add.* $\alpha$ soule] seyinges U, herte Ff and swetly] *om.* C 707–35 may . . . wise$^{1}$] þou loves ȝif þou be meke and suffre stalwordly and mekely alle angers and hardnes for goddys sake Ad 707–8 Stalworthly . . . stalworth] *om.* B loue] *om.* U hym] *om.* ULdTr, god B$^{2}$Ch

708 stalworth$^{1}$ . . . is] *om.* F He . . . stalworth] *om.* B$^{2}$ChHa meke] stalworþly may no man loue hem but he be stalworþe *add.* B al] a B$^{2}$

709 cometh . . . mekenesse] *om.* C Goste] but *add.* $\alpha$HeT$^{3}$BMFLdChHaTr$^{2}$ meke] mans *add.* Ff

710 soule] man T Mekenes] kepeþ vs and *add.* F, mekely B$^{2}$ gouerneth vs] coueryþe woo T kepeth] helpeþ B, ledes Ha vs$^{2}$] and defendeþ vs *add.* $\alpha$ in] and LtUHa, aȝens Ch

711 so . . . nat] ouercomes so þat þai cast vs noght doune Ha deuyl] oure enemy *add.* He, *om.* Ld deceyueth] vs ⟨and Ch⟩ *add.* LdCh many] men B$^{2}$ þat . . . meke] *om.* Ha ben] semeþ L

712 tribulaciouns] and angwys of þis werd *add.* Ff and reproues] stryuenges B, *om.* Ch, þam qwilk are halden meke *add.* Ha and$^{2}$] *om.* L bacbytynges] and suche oþer *add.* L

713 wroth] worþ S anguys . . . any] *om.* Ch world] þat men seyn of þe *add.* T, þou lufs not god *add.* Ha or . . . word] *om.* W seith] speken BF 713–14 of$^{2}$ . . . to] to þe or ellis of He 713–14 of$^{2}$ . . . saith] *om.* T$^{3}$BMCh of þe] *om.* H

714 or . . . þe] *om.* CD for . . . saith] *om.* UF saith] dose Ha nat] verreyle *add.* $\alpha$ ne . . . so] þou muste Ch so] *om.* WTFfFHaTr$^{2}$ loue] serue Ha

715 God] so *add.* FfHa stalwarthly] ne luf hym lastandely *add.* Ha 715–16 sleth . . . erth] spares no erthly thyng to sla it Ha sleth] slowe D al] men lyfand and all *add.* M lyuynge] louynge FfH, *om.* BPTr

716 þynge] *om.* Ch in] þis world and in *add.* Ff as] is T spareth] riȝt *add.* HT$^{2}$ to . . . dede] þat euer is or was so is hardnes of hert RSVWT dede] is or euere was so is hardnesse of herte G

717 and] for $\alpha$Tr$^{2}$, þarefoor R$^{2}$Ff þat] *om.* M he$^{2}$] it UCHeBFTrChHh, *om.* RWT greueth hym] dredeþ SV nat] *om.* HTr$^{2}$ what] harme *add.* T

718 hath delite] deliteþ C, and ioy *add.* Ha and] þat SV coueiteth] coueytise FfDBPHa þat$^{2}$] þe R$^{2}$, þeigh Ff

719 suffre] þat *add.* T, more *add.* FCh  and peynt] *om.* T  Cristis loue] ihesu crist Ha  he] þat *add.* F  hath] but *add.* L

720 and . . . hym] *om.* B$^2$  hym] and *add.* αTr, for he wote wel þat he is worþi for to suffre wel more for his synnes þat he hath ydo and *add.* L, and is *add.* F  as] *om.* R, of *add.* PLd  dede] sad R  man] þat *add.* U, þat wote noȝt *add.* FTr

721 seith] he *add.* UDdBTrChHh, and *add.* D, to hym and *add.* P  answareth] riȝt *add.* WTTr$^2$  nat] þerto *add.* α, aȝen *add.* L  Right] *om.* R$^2$FfCHeDBMChHhE who-so] *om.* F

722 stirred] greued SV, in wreth *add.* Ch  word] wo LdHT$^2$  men] sayn or *add.* RGWT  may] *om.* SVCh  say] of hem *add.* α, of him *add.* L  or sho] *om.* CHe kan nat] behoueþ no B

723 peyn . . . angre] a worde Ha  peyn] penaunce Ch  angre] anguische SVT$^3$ 723–4 for . . . peyn] *om.* Lt  for . . . loue] *om.* Ha  for] of H  har] his C  for] crist seiþ *add.* GLd, or T

724 loueth] me *add.* GLd, stalworthliche hem þenkeþ *add.* L  hath] feliþ He, suffur Ha  womman] þat *add.* D  nat] god *add.* TrCh

725 for] *om.* W  so] *om.* SV  feble] weyke RGWDdR$^2$FfDT$^3$BMB$^2$HaIi$^3$Tr$^2$, feynte SV, leþi LCHeP  þat þay] and SV  falle] fayleþ F  at] in W  stirrynge] meuyng F

726 þat is] of T$^3$BMHa  is] atte eche *add.* LTr  þei] suche folke L  secheth] sette M  hegher] þeyr *add.* M  stid] place UChTr$^2$, *om.* TCFLdHT$^2$  Crist] stiȝede *add.* C

727 wille] *om.* R  727–8 done . . . þat] *om.* Ch  done] forþ ⟨riȝt G⟩ RGSV wheþer . . . be] be hit α  with[1]] *om.* αCDBPFTr$^2$  or] *om.* R  with[2]] be hit RGWT, *om.* SVCDBPFHTr$^2$  and[1]] *om.* C, ower lord ihesu *add.* B

728 be done] *om.* Ch  wel] al ryȝtfulnesse F, welthe Ch  men] and ⟨þei do nouȝt T⟩ so ⟨ne T⟩ þei (*om.* T) folwe (feleþ W) not ⟨ne do not RGSVW⟩ þat þat is þe wille of crist but ben rebel þerto and seken more maistry here in erþe þen euer dude he for he seiþ himself ⟨in þe gospel SVWT⟩ I coom not to do my wille but þe wille of him þat sent me *add.* α  728–9 Bot . . . verray] and þerfore þei þat wolen be verreyly α  Bot] and so UTr

729 meke] *om.* F  wil nat] shul not wilne to α  haue] *om.* LCDT$^3$BM  hare] owyne *add.* LTr  wille] ⟨to be B⟩ done here *add.* αB, here *add.* HeT$^3$FTr, be done *add.* MLd  world] bot *add.* Dd  729–30 þat . . . may] by cause to F  þay] *om.* C

730 hit] fulfilled more *add.* RG, heore wil more SV, more *add.* WT  plenerly] priueliche folfuld SV, done and fulfild *add.* WT, priuely F, *om.* TrCh  in . . . toþer] elleswhere U  toþer] haue mynde þat *add.* WT, lif *add.* L, world *add.* F  730–1 men . . . deuyl] þe deuyl sunner be ouercome B  men] liȝtlyer ne *add.* α

731 þat . . . hateth] ne þer is no þing þat he hateþ more α  mych] *om.* DM, souerently B  731–2 may . . . more] doþ more penaunce T  may wake] make D

732 and[1]] *om.* B  suffre] penaunce and *add.* W  peyne] penaunce CBCh  any] oother *add.* UDdR$^2$FfLCHeDT$^3$MPFChHa  creature] or man *add.* T  may] *om.* CBFCh, do *add.* TTr$^2$

733 haue] and þerfore to shewe openly ⟨to alle men RGWT⟩ þat þou art goddes sone and not þe deueles sone haue and holde mekenes and loue and charite for charite as seynt austyn telleþ makeþ vs knowen whiche beþ goddes sones and whiche þe deueles sones *add.* α

734 þou] do D  do] *om.* C

735 Thou . . . wise] *om.* BFHT$^2$  art . . . when] loues wisely ȝif Ad  pouer] pure iste] him RGH

$^2$, hem SV  wilful] *om.* A  and pacience] and chastite L, and penaunce He, *om.* B$^2$Tr

249 as . . . nat] *om.* αH$^2$  may] *om.* F  coueite] couaitiþ F, *om.* Ld  þat] and P hym] *om.* He  nat] *om.* A  249–50 And . . . wille] *om.* W, whan T

wisedome] and her w *add.* F, wyt Ha spend] spillen UDdR$^2$FfLDT$^3$BMPFHT$^2$B$^2$ Ii$^3$ 738–9 in . . . and] about þo Ha in] vanytes and *add.* Ch

739 and bisynesse] *om.* C about] of UCHeDT$^3$BMTrHa a . . . haue] *om.* B haue] all *add.* WT

740 he$^2$] þanne *add.* U, *om.* SV, þei Ff ham] alle *add.* LHeCh

741 wold . . . right] *om.* SV do] *om.* UM right] wysly *add.* Dd, wel LHe, *om.* BTrCh, wel *add.* F, fully *add.* H nat . . . bot] *om.* SVCh nat] *om.* H greet] *om.* Ch

742 Also] in þe same wise *add.* U, riȝt so goostly ⟨to speke RGSVT⟩ α, wharfoor R$^2$Ff, now B, and Ch if . . . haue] we ȝif we haue wollen He if] syþ B wil] *om.* αB, þat *add.* Ff we] *om.* LtUαLCDT$^3$BPTrChHaHhIi$^3$ stones] we mosten take vs to *add.* U, þat is *add.* GLFLdTrTr$^2$, as *add.* P pouerte] and paciens *add.* G and penaunce] pacience P

743 and] *om.* SV may] *om.* F heuyn] and þou coueite þerfore any louyng or worshepe or fauour of men or (*om.* W) of þe world þou ȝyuest þese noble vertues for þat þat nouȝte is to helpe or profite to þi soule and vtterly þou lesest þe mede þat þou schuldes haue for þe gode dedes if þai were done only for þe honour and louyng (þe loue T) ⟨and þe loue RW⟩ of god as þei shulde be *add.* α

744 loue] traueil and *add.* P despisest] alle *add.* Ld richesse] honouris T

745 vile . . . self] *om.* Ld and pouer] *om.* UIi$^3$ and$^2$] thynk *add.* DdR$^2$FfLCHe DT$^3$BMPFHT$^2$B$^2$TrChHaHhTr$^2$ noght] *om.* M

746 syn] and wrecchednes *add.* αTr$^2$, and *add.* M, and heldest þee in þin owen syght wers þan ony other *add.* Ch for . . . pouert] if þou suffrest þis pouert godely (mekely WT) for þe loue of god α haue] *om.* G richesse . . . end] þe kyngdam of heuen Ch 746–9 And . . . heuyn] *om.* Ha 746–8 if . . . lif] *om.* Ch if] *om.* Ii$^3$

747 sorowe] swo now Ff þou . . . in] þin lange Ff þou art] þi herte is B$^2$ þou] *om.* H in exile] *om.* F in] þis *add.* LCHeT$^3$BMLd of] *om.* T

748 þi] þis RFf þe] þi L þis$^1$] þe G, þi F lif] world G þis$^2$] þi GPFLd HT$^2$ sorow] here *add.* ChTr$^2$

749 þe] gret *add.* L ioy] blisse Ld, kyngdam Ch of heuyn] withowten ende B þou] *om.* R$^2$ punysshe] pynest SV, puttes W, oft *add.* T$^2$ body] *om.* F

750 and$^1$] *om.* CDT$^3$BMHh wisely] *om.* CDT$^3$BM wakynges] and trauayle *add.* Ha

751 mysaise] mescheef α

752 anguysshe] angres α for . . . trauaille] *om.* U cum to] haue He

753 reste . . . euer] þe euerlastynge rest D lesteth] schal lesten Ch, is Ha euer] *om.* W a] *om.* LCF, þe HeB$^2$ seet] setys LC of ioy] an higȝ B, *om.* Ld angels] bryȝt *add.* F ben] *om.* T$^3$BM

754 loueth$^1$] are Ha wisely] and (bot W) been *add.* URGSVW, but *add.* LCHeTr Tr$^2$, are *add.* T$^3$BMIi$^3$, wyse Ha like] ylykened F children] ȝynge *add.* Ff loueth$^2$] and leten *add.* RGW, tellen SV, and setteþ *add.* T more] of *add.* RSVWT, by *add.* G þan] ⟨þai do WT⟩ of *add.* α

755 So . . . many] þat beþ B many] ⟨nowe L⟩ for *add.* UL þay] and R, þat GSVWTCHeT$^3$MTrChTr$^2$, of þo þat Ff, þat *add.* B gyf] chaungen R, and chaungen *add.* GSVW, and þangyþ *add.* T ioy] blisse Ch delite] lust B har] þe SVPH, fowle *add.* B

756 þat . . . ploumbe] *om.* Ch þat$^1$] and SV ploumbe] appel LCHeFTr

757 loueth] wole loue UDdR$^2$FfLCHeDT$^3$MPFLdHT$^2$B$^2$TrChHaHhIi$^3$Tr$^2$ wisely] willi T lestynge þynge] *om.* F þynge] and þat *add.* B 757–8 lestyngly . . . þynge] *om.* HT$^2$ 757–8 passynge . . . passyngely] *om.* B 757–8 passynge þynge] and let passe þyngis þat is F

758 þynge$^1$] *om.* R his] þyn Ld, þe TrCh set] *om.* Ch and] *om.* ChHaTr$^2$ fested] *om.* HaTr$^2$ bot] onliche *add.* L

759 God] him SV

760 And] bot He wil] *om.* T

761 and$^{1}$] but Ff also] als Ha and swetly] *om.* C and$^{2}$] als Ha 761–2 Swet . . . chaste] þowe loves deuoutly and swetly ȝif þou be chaste in bodye Ad

762 is$^{1}$] *om.* F þoght] soule SV, tunge LCHe 762–72 Deuout . . . pees] *om.* Ad is$^{2}$] *om.* CD 762–3 þi$^{2}$ . . . and$^{1}$] all Ch

763 and$^{1}$ . . . þoghtes] *om.* P þoghtes] þouȝtest S to God] *om.* Ch with] *om.* B hert] and *add.* WT 763–4 þe . . . of] *om.* T$^{3}$BM

764 hete] herte P, worschip F, hest HT$^{2}$ 764–5 is . . . for] be fulfilled of ful F is . . . hit] *om.* Ch

765 and$^{1}$] of M solace . . . þe] *om.* GDFHh of$^{1}$] and B þe . . . of] swete P Ihesu] and of þe swetnesse of hym *add.* P, þat þe þenkeþ *add.* F and$^{2}$] þanne *add.* B conceyueth] coueyteþ Ch

766 þe þynke] he þenkeþ BIi þou] he Ii, I Ch

767–72 And . . . pees] *om.* He 767 And] *om.* S þan] *om.* SR$^{2}$FfCDMPCh Hh, þat TL, ȝif BIi comest] to this þou schalt haue *add.* Ii in to] *om.* Ii and] in G

768 and quyet] *om.* PTr withouten] ydel *add.* Ch of$^{1}$] and G, or BCh or] *om.* SVDd vices] þanne art þou *add.* B

769 in silence] *om.* R and$^{1}$] a R sleepe] sleptest U and$^{2}$ . . . shipe] *om.* Ch and$^{2}$] *om.* BM set] sitte SV, as þou sat L, *om.* M, þe *add.* F Noe shipe] suche a stedefastenesse F, noyshepe T$^{2}$ Noe] an esy T, a LC, on H þat] þanne BLd

770 þe] *om.* LtR$^{2}$FfLCHeB$^{2}$ChIi$^{3}$, hit LdHT$^{2}$ of$^{1}$] þin Ch brennynge . . . loue] swete luf in brynnyng in ihesu Ha brennynge] ȝernyng B loue] or *add.* G, þat þou felest *add.* Ch Fro] For Lt, þat tyme þat *add.* LT$^{3}$IiHT$^{2}$Ch, for þe tyme þat B, when PFLd getten] sette C, the *add.* B, *om.* F

771 loue] and *add.* W is] *om.* PE confort] of ihesu crist and of þe holy goost *add.* α and$^{2}$ . . . verraily] als verray R$^{2}$, as ihesu Ff, and verray F and$^{2}$] þanne *add.* URGSV, þan WT, þat C, þan most þat þou schalt han it ful þanne *add.* Ch 771–2 þou . . . louer] verey crist þat is loue of alle goode louers P þou art] *om.* DdHT$^{2}$B$^{2}$HaHhIi$^{3}$Tr$^{2}$ þou] *om.* Ii art] *om.* Ld 771–2 verraily Cristis] a verrey α

772 louer] of god *add.* RGWT, lore F, *om.* B$^{2}$ and . . . þe] *om.* D he] þanne *add.* α resteth] schal rest (lestyn Ii) T$^{3}$BIiM whose] and þan (*om.* B) has þou ane T$^{3}$BIiM, for his Ch stid] þat *add.* T$^{3}$M, place BChTr$^{2}$ is] *om.* BIi in pees] wiþ god and his angell B pees] and reste *add.* U, with god and his aungels *add.* T$^{3}$IiM

773 ferth] petitioun or (of our WT) *add.* RGWT þat] whan URGLBPAd

774 and charite] *om.* Ff I . . . charite] *om.* B no] *om.* G wot] witturly *add.* RW, utterly *add.* G, rediliche *add.* SV, may know TTr$^{2}$, sikerliche *add.* L in$^{1}$ . . . charite] þis T erth] herte P þat$^{2}$] wheþer RGSVWTr in$^{2}$] perfite *add.* RGSVW, loue and *add.* Ld charite] or not *add.* RGSVWT$^{3}$Tr

775 any] *om.* B$^{2}$Ch priuelege . . . þat] specyalte of Ad or] of RGSVR$^{2}$FfCPCh Tr$^{2}$ grace] of god *add.* RGSVW God] he RGVW, *om.* SHe, go F, that he *add.* Ad

776 any] a T man . . . womman] *om.* Ad or womman] *om.* T womman] so *add.* RSVWT, and *add.* F al] *om.* Ch oþer] *om.* WT nat] *om.* FfDTrCh, haue *add.* He bi] but *add.* αIi 776–90 Holy . . . erthe] *om.* Ad

777 wommen] *om.* He troweth] *om.* αCB, stedefastly *add.* Ch þei] *om.* αCB hath] studfaste *add.* α trouth] in god *add.* RGT, þouȝt ⟨in god W⟩ SVW and charite] in god SV

778 þei$^{1}$] þe P may] for þe tyme *add.* α

779 sauf] ȝet *add.* URGSV, it wot þat *add.* WT, but *add.* LBIiFTrCh hit] *om.*

GTT$^3$Ch  þay$^2$] þou L  wist] hit *add.* RSVWT, it on and on *add.* Ch  merit] mede SVHa

780 þer] þei RGSVTD, it DdR$^2$FfMLdHT$^2$HaIi$^3$, *om.* F  men$^1$] and wemmen *add.* TLCHeIiMB$^2$Ha  and$^1$ . . . men] *om.* RSVTHeIiMLdHT$^2$B$^2$Hh  wise] *om.* GLCB  men$^2$] wemmen WFfLCB, wym G, and wymmen *add.* T$^3$, *om.* FTr  and$^2$] *om.* G, þat SV, in *add.* T$^2$

781 werkes] hertis B$^2$  natforþi] þerfore UB$^2$Tr$^2$, forþi GIiTr, þowh no Ch  nat] noþer B, *om.* Ch

782 reserued] keped α IiCh, receyued LD  vncerteyne] certayne F

783 any] þou B  had . . . he] *om.* HeCh  þat . . . myght] to BTr  þat] *om.* Ha  wyn . . . to] within T  wyn] come BIiPFLdHT$^2$Ch  þrid] ferþe HT$^2$

784 of] *om.* Ld  loue$^1$] *om.* LdHa  is] I ⟨haue R⟩ RSVR$^2$FfT$^3$MT$^2$HaIi$^3$Tr$^2$  cald] calle SVTr$^2$  he$^1$] þou B  he$^2$] þou B  loue] and charyte *add.* B, charyte and þat he schulde neuere lefyn Ch  784–5 in$^2$ . . . he] he þat hath þis knowyng Ch

785 his . . . he] of knowynge men B  his] is D, *om.* MP  is] schulde be UαLT$^3$TrTr$^2$, *om.* DM  þat$^2$] *om.* M  myght] *om.* UCIi  neuer] *om.* MB$^2$  ber] here H  hym] hem B  hegher] þerfore but þe lower *add.* α, in herte *add.* Ch  785–7 ne . . . bisy] for þe more siker þat he were of þe loue ⟨of god RGSV⟩ þe more bisy shulde he be α

786 to] godes loue or to *add.* Ld, in þe Ch  loue] serue F, of *add.* Ch  786–7 þat . . . to] *om.* B  786–7 is sikyre] is full Ii, sechiþ B$^2$

787–90 wold . . . erthe] *om.* He  787 wold] wil Dd, *om.* IiCh  he] and Ii  be] is more Ch  hym$^1$] *om.* SV  hym$^2$] hem Ii$^3$  787–8 hath . . . goodenesse] he wolde nought for all þe werlde ne for no þing dysplesen him Ch

788 made . . . and$^1$] *om.* B  hym such] *om.* T$^3$IiM  hym] *om.* R$^2$FfLCDHhIi$^3$  such] bisynes *add.* R$^2$FfCDHh  þat$^1$] so many α  goodenesse] to (for CT$^3$BIiM Ha) him *add.* UαDdLCT$^3$BIiMPFHT$^2$B$^2$TrHa  And . . . is] þough he be neuer so parfit and U  And] knowe þat *add.* R$^2$Ff  he þat] þouȝ he L  he] *om.* SV  þat$^2$] *om.* R$^2$Ff  is] þis RGWT, be L  so hegh] grace ⟨of loue RGSVT⟩ ⟨þat he SV⟩ haþ geten (ȝyuen RG) of god worþily α  so] *om.* F  hegh] in þat degre *add.* B  788–9 he$^2$ . . . worþier] *om.* T

789 hold] *om.* F  hym] hem F  selfe] better ne *add.* G, þerfore þe SV, *om.* WM  þan] affor Ii  synfullest] foulest C  that] *om.* TrCh  gooth] walkeþ α, is Ff

790 þe erthe] fote B

791 Also] by *add.* P, neuerþeles Ch  experimentȝ] proueues UIiHT$^2$, þinges TT$^3$, experiensus LCPChHh, toknes B  ben] to knowe *add.* ULAd, *om.* P, to wit *add.* Ha  that] shewen ⟨men G⟩ wheþer *add.* α, if LAd, werby B, *om.* P, techen þat *add.* B$^2$  a man] þei G, may *add.* C, may knowe ⟨by FLdHT$^2$Tr⟩ if he *add.* DT$^3$BPFLdHT$^2$TrCh Tr$^2$, þou B$^2$  in] perfyt *add.* SV  charite] or he ne is *add.* RT, or not *add.* GSVWT$^3$

792 al] erþely ⟨þing and G⟩ *add.* α, þe B  of] and T, al *add.* B  erthly] worldly α  thynge] godes α  is] *om.* IiTr$^2$  quenched] dede GFLdHT$^2$, slokkend DdR$^2$FfD MB$^2$TrHaAdIi$^3$Tr$^2$, aqueynt He, slekenynge B, slakyth Ii  792–4 For . . . loue] *om.* Ad  792–3 whare . . . is$^1$] who so coueiteþ þese RG

793 is$^2$] *om.* H  793–4 þan . . . loue] *om.* R  he] a man SVWTTr, we C  no] *om.* U  coueitise] of þe world *add.* SVWT

794 he] *om.* Ch  hath] no *add.* U  loue] of crist *add.* SVWT, to god *add.* Ff  brennynge] myȝti Ch  desyre] *om.* SVB  of] þe blysse of *add.* Ch  794–8 For . . . charite] *om.* Ad  794–5 For . . . oght] þe more þat þei han felte Ch

795 when] *om.* D, what B  men] he α, man or womman B  felet] *om.* L  oght . . . sauour] sauour ogth of þat Ff  oght] *om.* B  þat] *om.* C  sauour] of þat blysse of heuen *add.* Ch  þe$^1$ . . . haue] *om.* T$^3$BIiMCh  þei] he α  haue] þerof *add.* RWT, þerfore offe *add.* G, feleþ þerof SV  þai] he α T$^3$Ii, *om.* F

796 couait] and schal couet it *add.* W he$^{1}$] þat L, or sche *add.* B hath felet] feliþ CB$^{2}$ felet] þerof *add.* α noght$^{2}$] ne noght *add.* F Forþy] for IiTr$^{2}$

797 any] a mannes hert R, a man G, a man haþ þat he SV, a man þat has it he WT, þing *add.* D þerof] of god LT$^{3}$TrChTr$^{2}$, of ihesu D þat] þan T he] *om.* RFH, þey B no] *om.* D ioy] ne sauoure *add.* Ch in . . . lif] worldliche SV þis] erþely B, werldlyche *add.* Ch lif] loue Ld

798 token . . . is$^{1}$] so is he taken SV he hath] it is LChTr$^{2}$ he$^{2}$] *om.* Ii is in] loueth Ch, has Ha charite] god Ch if] of F 798–9 his . . . now] he Ad his] þine Ch chaunget] chaungyng Ff

799 þat$^{1}$] is to saye if he *add.* α wonet] bifore *add.* RG, *om.* Dd, moche B þe erth] erþely þinges and worldliche (wonderly R) and flesshely (*om.* W) and now he haþ lefte suche maner of speche and α, and þe world *add.* L, worldly þynges and erþelich F, erþeliche þingis ChTr$^{2}$ þe$^{1}$] *om.* CBPB$^{2}$ 799–800 now . . . euer] *om.* P speketh] oft *add.* Ad God] and gostly þinges *add.* α

800 lesteth] *om.* F, schal lestyn or elles he holdeþ his pes Ch is] in *add.* RG, of *add.* M exercise] hauntinge HT$^{2}$ gostly] *om.* WT profite] seruyse L, werkes FTr 800–1 as . . . to] and Ad as] and GS, þat B

801 ham$^{1}$] *om.* P entremetteth . . . no] leue Ad entremetteth] entermelleþ B

802 erthly] oþur SV, þyng ne erthly *add.* P bisynesse] thingis LB$^{2}$ when] a man þinkeþ þat *add.* αB$^{2*}$ þe] no R, þo GBPB$^{2}$, þeos SVWT, *om.* LCHeTrAdATr$^{2}$ þynges] þat Ad ben] þei bere He in . . . self] *om.* Ad ham] it Dd

803 semeth] to him *add.* α, *om.* B$^{2}$ þat . . . maketh] for greet loue þat he haþ to god and a greet lykyng þat he feleþ in his loue αB$^{2*}$, for loue makeþ alle harde þinges lyghte Ch 803–5 For . . . apertly] *om.* LAd For] and BIiMLdCh as] *om.* SVBTr ChHa, also Ii Casciodorus] þe book of fasset U, Austyne Dd, calcidor ⟨a clerk Ii⟩ R$^{2}$FfDT$^{3}$IiP, þe holy man B, *om.* MTr, saladur Ha, calcid Ii$^{3}$ seith] seide PHT$^{2}$

804 louereden is] lorde es he T$^{3}$, he is a lord B, a dere louerede is he M, louerd is F, *om.* Ch is] þat þing *add.* RGSVB$^{2*}$, a þing *add.* WTA, þe thyng *add.* R$^{2}$Ff, a *add.* Ii he *add.* T$^{2}$ þat$^{1}$] þat *add.* U, loue *add.* Ch þat þynge] *om.* R$^{2}$FfFA þat$^{2}$] þe UDdDLdHT$^{2}$Ii$^{3}$Tr$^{2}$, *om.* CHeT$^{3}$IiM, a PB$^{2}$Ch, þe for Ha þynge] þat is *add.* URGSVB$^{2*}$TrCh, is W, þat is T, þat es farre *add.* Dd, þat semeþ *add.* B negh] nerhande ⟨and Dd⟩ RGSVWDdFfB$^{2*}$Tr, oure hand T, wele nyȝe C, neer and DPLdHT$^{2}$HaIi$^{3}$, nou T$^{3}$, *om.* BMA, nere Ii, nyand Ch impossible] in possible TB$^{2}$A to] mowe be *add.* U

805 myght apertly] apartylich and myȝtilich F myght] *om.* UDdIiChTr$^{2}$, to *add.* He apertly] *om.* αCHeBChTr$^{2}$, to saye *add.* T$^{3}$IiM, to see *add.* A of] in Ch thoght] þat is for *add.* U to] þat RG suffre] pacientliche *add.* UTr$^{2}$, suffreþ RG al] *om.* B$^{2}$ angres] hardnesse A, anguyssches *alia* and] of He

806 noyes] disses W þat cometh] *om.* T cometh] to a man and *add.* U, þolemodly (*om.* T) and mekely and stalworþly for þe loue of crist *add.* α, wiþouteforþ *add.* TrA 806–8 withouten . . . God$^{2}$] *om.* Ad þis] *om.* F oþer] vertues *add.* αA

807 what so] what so *add.* Lt hym] *om.* WT for] *om.* B

808 God$^{1}$] good RVLMFCh 808–10 and . . . God] *om.* C 808–9 and . . . God$^{2}$] *om.* G and . . . God] *om.* SVDdR$^{2}$FfHeT$^{3}$BIiMFLd and] *om.* LDHT$^{2}$B$^{2}$ Ch God$^{2}$] *om.* D

809–10 nat . . . God] and his trewthe L 809 bot . . . God$^{1}$] forte worche good SV, but to werke wyk Ii 809–10 he . . . God] *om.* DdR$^{2}$FfLHeDT$^{3}$BIiMTrChA

810 delitabilite] delitable GWLLdIi$^{3}$Tr$^{2}$, delyt SVCBHT$^{2}$, delectable gladnes FTrA

811 and] ȝet *add.* U, makes *add.* DdR$^{2}$FfLCHeDT$^{3}$BIiMPB$^{2}$HaA, doþ *add.* FLdHT$^{2}$ praysynge . . . God] *om.* α praysynge] loueth UAd, thanking LIiPHT$^{2}$, and þonking *add.* He, preyseth Ch of] *om.* ULdChAdIi$^{3}$ God] with ioye *add.* Ch in] and IiFTr$^{2}$ euery] *om.* SV, euel T, al P angyre] þyng F 811–18 þat$^{1}$ . . . away] *om.* Ad suffreth] þankeþ god and loueþ god þerfore *add.* α

812–13 and . . . downne] *om.* D  812 and] in *add.* T$^{3}$  þis . . . wel] þat is a greet tokenyng þat he sheweþ α  þis] yit LtIi$^{3}$, it U, thus L  sheweth] he *add.* LtT$^{3}$, semeþ F  wel] *om.* C  loueth] his *add.* GSVWT  myche] mekeliche SV, *om.* DdR$^{2}$FfLCHeBIiMPFLdHT$^{2}$B$^{2}$TrChHaA, most T$^{3}$  812–13 when . . . downe] *om.* T$^{3}$BIiM  no] desese ne *add.* L  wo] ne sorwe ne angre may kele his loue þat he haþ to ihesu crist ne lowen (slaken SVWT) hit ne *add.* α, sorow Dd  may] *om.* α

813 hym] hit α  downe] fro loue L, from god *add.* Ch  For] þere beþ *add.* α, But DT$^{3}$BIiM  many] men and wymmen *add.* α, summe ben þat D  preisen . . . ese] þat alle whyles þei haue her ese and her likyng in þe world ⟨and in þe welþes RGSVT⟩ ⟨þat beþ þerin T⟩ þei loue ⟨not W*⟩ god ⟨and (ne W) lovnen (herien SV, leue W) him RGSVW⟩ α  ese] and prosperite *add.* B, of herte *add.* Ch  and] but α Tr$^{2}$, when thay be *add.* L

814 in$^{1}$] whenne þei fele any α  aduersite] of þis world as soone *add.* α, desese L gurch and] *om.* WT  gurch] anon *add.* L, grunteþ F  falleth] *om.* R$^{2}$FfCHeDChA, they be þan broughte L  downe] *om. alia*  so] *om.* RGT$^{3}$BMTr  mych] sorwe and *add.* RGSV  sorynesse] þai falle *add.* R$^{2}$Ff, ⟨þat T$^{3}$BIiM⟩ þei ben brouȝt ⟨doun so T$^{3}$BIiM⟩ *add.* CHeDT$^{3}$BIiMChA, harm P

815 ham] hym W  and so] *om.* SV, and L  chydynge] flytande RGWDdR$^{2}$FfT$^{3}$ IiMChHaIi$^{3}$, gruching T, stryuynge FLdHT$^{2}$, flightans A

816 and] *om.* WA  fyghtynge] *om.* WA, stryuyng T, chidand Ch  And] *om.* CTr$^{2}$ þat] suche α, þis Ch  kaitif] wrecchede URGTCHePFLdHT$^{2}$Tr$^{2}$, carfull L, feble Ch  praysynge] and loue *add.* RGW, and loueþ *add.* SV, þis is loue *add.* T, honouryng and louyng P, lyuyng FTr, þankinge HT$^{2}$

817 þat . . . maketh] *om.* F  þat only] *trs.* T  only] any DdR$^{2}$FfLCHeDT$^{3}$BIiM PLdHT$^{2}$B$^{2}$ChHaA  of . . . maketh] or aduersite makiþ him to grucche aȝens goddis wille CHeT$^{3}$BIiM  praisynge] loue UFfCHeT$^{3}$BIiMCh, loue and þat louyng α Tr$^{2}$, other loue and louynge L, honourynge and wurshepyng P, þankinge HT$^{2}$  of$^{2}$] so *add.* TDFIi$^{3}$, so L, to preysen Ch  myche] of *add.* L, more C, suche A

818 þat] non angur letteþ ⟨ne abateþ G⟩ ne slakeþ ne *add.* α  of] ne RGSVWHCh, non *add.* T, or B  do away] lette B  do] it *add.* WL, it adoun ne put it *add.* T

819 v$^{t}$] firste LDLdH, eyghtand Ch  men] we B$^{2}$  may] *om.* Ff, plesen god and *add.* Ch  moste] beste CB  loue] loueden Ff, serue B  God] and loue him *add.* B, him Ch  I] the Ad

820 in$^{1}$] þat BCh  what] swilk Dd, þat Ad  so . . . be] *om.* Ad  þat] þan H ben in] haue M  most] *om.* Ii, best F  reste] boþe *add.* D  820–1 and soule] *om.* Ha

821 any] *om.* Ad  nedes] ledis HT$^{2}$  or bisynesse] *om.* Ld  or] of F

822 þe . . . of$^{1}$] *om.* HT$^{2}$  þe$^{2}$ . . . of$^{1}$] *om.* Ii  day] ioy DdAd, blys Ch  þat] *om.* H  euer] withouten ende Ch

823 secheth] suche C, sekeriste H, lovys Ad  reste] and *add.* T, *om.* H  withouten . . . letted] þat it be not ouercome wiþoute ne lette C  withouten] *om.* He, wiþ T$^{2}$  þat . . . with] lette of SV  hit] he LD  letted] cumbred HeT$^{3}$BIiM  goers] iangelers L, angris D

824 þynges] thoghtis AE  hit . . . withjnnen] þat it be in Ch  withjnnen] to be in α, with M, in *add.* F  grete] myche α, grace L, *om.* Ld

825 silence] and *add.* D  fro] for SV  noyes] voys U  of] and þe WIiF, *om.* T couetise] of the word *add.* Ii  and$^{2}$] of α BTrETr$^{2}$, in He  erthly] thyngis and *add.* Ff, worldly B, ydill Ii, occupacyouns and *add.* Ch  thoghtis] þinges GTr  825–6 And namely] *om.* M

826 namely] for *add.* Ld  þat] seken and *add.* α  loueth] lyueth LdE  lif] for *add.* TAE  þai] *om.* Ch  seke] sulde M  rest] boþe *add.* TF

827 gret] *om.* L  þay] þat *add.* α, ye LHeA  trone] trewe seruauntes α, þat are *add.* M  þat$^{2}$] þei shulen α, euere *add.* Ii  dwellen] stably *add.* α  stille] *om.* TCh

828 a] *om.* Ff, here B about] remeuyng ne *add.* F rennynge] remewynge UFfH T$^{2}$Ch, flyted B, flyttyng Ii 828–9 in . . . stabled] beþ stedfast and stabel in cristes loue P swetnesse . . . loue] þe loue of crist $\alpha$ Cristis loue] criste F

829 ben] *om.* L stabled] mad (*om.* H) stable BH And] I sey as for me *add.* U haue loued] haued D, loued F sit] but *add.* LB, when I prayede *add.* Ad ne] *om.* DF no$^{2}$] feyntise ne *add.* Ch

830 fantasie] feyntyse SVWCB men] me T me] *om.* A ne . . . þynge] *om.* Ch þynge] doynge B

831 for] þat SVWTDT$^{3}$T$^{2}$IIaE knewe] knowe RGSVWCBHT$^{2}$AETr$^{2}$, felte Ch loued] loue RGSVWBE more] so *add.* G lested] lastande endured (endureþ SV) RGSVW, lasting TLCATr$^{2}$, laste He, lasteþ B with] within Dd me] þe *add.* $\alpha$L, þe Dd comfort] of þinkyng *add.* $\alpha$

832 of] his *add.* $\alpha$ loue] sittand *add.* $\alpha$HeBAdE, so *add.* A þan] it dede (doþ B) *add.* UB For] or T syttynge] *om.* C

833 most$^{1}$] more T reste] of herte *add.* C, *om.* Ii my] in UIi$^{3}$ most$^{2}$] *om.* H vpward] to god to (and WT) þenke (þinking T) on him *add.* $\alpha$, to god *add.* FTr$^{2}$, eesid B þerfor] *om.* SVF

834 þe] so W anoþer] þe my dere freende T$^{3}$, *om.* M haue done] did Dd done . . . wil] *om.* C wil] wilne to SVW, go *add.* P to$^{2}$] *om.* SVW deth] dede SV, day *add.* BP, come *add.* F, lyues ende Ch

835 was] and ȝitt am *add.* RGSV, am and als I was W, am in myn T, disposed *add.* C, am FCh in . . . soule] *om.* W his] my BTr$^{2}$

836–93 Two . . . myght] *om.* Ch 836 Two] manere of *add.* $\alpha$ ben] to *add.* F men] vsen for to *add.* $\alpha$, þat þai *add.* F 836–8 On . . . gostly] actiue and contemplatiue Ad is$^{2}$] *om.* G

837 in$^{1}$] *om.* R$^{2}$FfH more$^{1}$] myche RSVWTF, *om.* T$^{3}$BIiM werke] trauail $\alpha$FTr bodily] *om.* G 837–9 for . . . lif] þat R in$^{2}$] *om.* P, inward B 837–8 more$^{2}$ . . . outward] *om.* B$^{2}$ 837–8 more$^{2}$ . . . gostly] muche bodily swetnesse SV more$^{2}$] moch WT swetnesse] and it is *add.* L, and *add.* DTr

838 gostly] *om.* GFLd mych] more GLdTr 838–9 and$^{2}$ . . . for] more of C

839 peril] peyne Ff þat ben] *om.* L world] but *add.* G, and *add.* WT lif] *om.* C

840 mych] mor *add.* WT inward] outward CDLd forþi] for R$^{2}$FfIi lestynger] miche *add.* G, *om.* W, lastyng F and$^{2}$] mor W sykerer] more *add.* SV, seker F restfuller] and L delitabeller] more *add.* L

841 louelier] *om.* $\alpha$FTr, fullare Ar medeful] nedful W for] forþi R$^{2}$Ff, ther for Ii hath] is HTr in] and LDT$^{3}$M Goddis] good B$^{2}$A

842 sauour] fauour RSV, schineþ D, ai sorugh Ar in$^{1}$ . . . euer] *om.* Ar euer] and *add.* TIi, *om.* DT$^{3}$ in$^{2}$ . . . tyme] whils we be here L present tyme] lif here Ar hit] *om.* A right] not D led] *om.* RSV, sadde T, left D

843 And] for Ii of$^{1}$] on *add.* He ioy] þat hit haþ *add.* B in] and Ar þe . . . Ihesu] goddes loue P Ihesu] ioye HT$^{2}$ oþer] *om.* W merites] merþis TLCT$^{3}$ BIiM 843–4 in erth] *om.* LP

844 for$^{1}$] but LBIiTr so] *om.* LIiTr, wel B cum to] cunne telle Ff, ouercome Ii to$^{2}$] *om.* M for$^{2}$] *om.* Ii, fro M*, þat Ar þe] fylthe and *add.* A freelte] fylthe M oure] *om.* RGSVT, þe W and þe] haþ B, in Ii þe] so FLd

845 we . . . and] *om.* LDBIi ben . . . with] bet ynne beþ ysette F ben] inne *add.* LdHT$^{2}$, *om.* A beset] temptede RGT, lapped SV, schent W, ocupied B$^{2}$ and . . . vs] *om.* SV and] *om.* GAr, þat DdR$^{2}$FfCHeT$^{3}$MLdHT$^{2}$B$^{2}$TrHaA, whiche L, to F letteth] lette F vs] boþ *add.* WFf, *om.* CB$^{2}$

846 day] þe whiche we ben bisett wiþ *add.* DIi þynges] thoghtis L, *om.* B in] hauyng L, *om.* HeDHa þerof] and why *add.* B for] *om.* G

847 deserue] ne come to *add.* P bot . . . godenes] *om.* C bot] for FfLHeDT$^{3}$Ii MTrHaA only] *om.* LHeDT$^{3}$BIiMTrHaA is] frely *add.* Ii of] *om.* H godenes] and fre grace *add.* $\alpha$ verrayli] holliche SV, þerto *add.* W

848 contemplacioun] contemplatif lif Ff, *om.* Ar and] *om.* Ar quyet] lyf *add.* RGSVT, and rest lyif *add.* W, reste P for] in C, of B loue] lyif Ii[3]

849 men . . . wommen] þa Ar taketh] ȝeueth BFLdHT[2]Tr 849–50 two . . . is] hem behouyth haue tway thingis L falleth] longen B, are necessarie Ld

850 On is] hem falleth for Ld hare] a L meyne] men Ii drede] degre Ii

851 har] *om.* F and] þat *add.* RGSVW ham self] *om.* LTr ham] hym WT entierly] only T, *om.* LTr

852 God] and of gode *add.* F doynge] on is that þey do L þai[2]] men U

853 Anoþer] and ouere W, and noþer F is] þis W þat] if W by . . . powere] here to þe pore F

854 clothe . . . naked] *om.* Ff

855 hym . . . housynge] þe howsles LB[2] comfort] visite LCHeA, and DT[3]BIiM TrHa þat ben] *om.* T

856 and[1] . . . men] *om.* F bury] graue WTDdR[2]FfArIi[3] dede men] men þat beþ dede *α* may[1] and] *om.* Ar may[1]] hase Dd and] don SV hath] þe SV, mai Dd cost] wheerof ULCHeB[2]TrAr, to done hit wiþ B, goodes Ii, wherwith PF 856–7 þai . . . ham[1]] *om.* Ar 856–7 þai . . . with] and hit suffiseþ not ⟨to hem þat ben of pouwer SV⟩ to don *α* þai] þat Ff, ne B, *om.* LdTr nat] excuse hem or *add.* LDBIiA, be excused ne *add.* CHe 856–7 be quyt] excuse hem T[3]M

857 quyt] *om.* He, excused PFTr of þese] or þre FfD þese] werkes ⟨of mercy RGSV⟩ ⟨þo þat beþ of power and may wel done hem RGW⟩ *add.* RGSVW, werkes to hem þat beþ of pouere and haþ where of to do hem *add.* T bot] *om.* T behoueth] bihouede D do] to F ham[2]] *om.* FfCB, þire Ar al] *om.* P

858 þe] goddes F benysone] of god *add.* SVLDMP on] of CT[3]LdHT[2] þat[1]] whiche blessyng L, þere D Ihesu Crist] god Ar

859 ham] þes werkes of charite F þai] alle *add.* PLdHT[2], *om.* A al] þei UPTrAr, þey *add.* B most] *om.* W 859–60 wil . . . ham[1]] don hem nouȝt and namely B

860 whan . . . with] *om.* LdHT[2], and haue whare with Ar whan þay] þat RG whan] sithen Ii þay had] he findeþ hem and leneþ hem C, he sent (lent Ha) hem FHa had] han RG ham[2]] þer Ff with] al *add.* He

861 Contemplatif] þis Ar lif] *om.* C hath] is in F two] *om.* L lower[1]] lenger B and . . . lower] *om.* RG lower[2]] lenger B

862 of] and in U is . . . word] oþer is goddis C is] in *add.* G, of *add.* FfLHeDT[3]BIiMFHaA Goddis word] gode wordis Ii in[2]] all *add.* Ff

863 other] oure F good] swete *add.* G and swete] *om.* GL, and swetnesse FHT[2]TrA men] *om.* G God] þe holy goste F

864 about . . . Crist] *om.* LCHeDT[3]BIiMHaA, and in his luf Ar loue] lif Ff in[1] . . . God] *om.* LCHeDT[3]BIiMTrHaA in[1]] to þe *α* praysynge] loue RG of God] *om.* Ar of[2]] *om.* G

865 ympnys . . . in] *om.* L in] oþere ⟨deuocioun and W⟩ deuoute *add.* *α*, holi *add.* He, oþer ⟨goode B⟩ BH[2]B[2] partie . . . contemplacioun] *om.* Ar

866 biholdynge] of heuen *add.* *α* and[1]] of Ff, *om.* LIi desyre] *om.* LIi, þenkinge Ld of[1]] *om.* Ii þe . . . heuyn] heuenly þynges P þe[1]] þis W, hygh L of[2]] þat beþ in (þerin SV) *α* heuyn] *om.* SVT and[2]] to haue L in] of FfB[2]

867 þat . . . oft] *om.* L, and Ii hath] han hadde D, had A oft] of grace R[2]Ff, of P þogh] whan T, and if DdR[2]Ff, al be it þat L hit . . . þat] *om.* TLCHeDBIiMTrHa ArA

868 þe[1]] her B bot] *om.* A only] *om.* D þe[2]] holy *add.* M fairheed] companey T, briȝtnesse HT[2] of[3]] heuene and of þe *add.* B

869 holy] *om.* Ff þan . . . þat] *om.* Ar I] *om.* A þat] þat *add.* Ii[3]

870 of Goddis] and C of] *om.* M 870–1 þe . . . told] *om.* G þe . . . God] *om.* C 870–1 ioy . . . þat[1]] *om.* B is] and LHe, *om.* D, in IiM a] in U praysynge] loue IiM

871 þat$^1$] ys so myche that it L, *om.* HeDIiM þat$^2$] þanne R praisynge] ioie C and$^2$] *om.* C

872 aboundance] ⟨in B⟩ plente LCHeBHT$^2$ of] and B, in F and] of þe He, *om.* B swetnesse] þeer of *add.* U, *om.* BLd hit] þat CDT$^3$IiMHa, *om.* Ld ascendeth] stiȝeþ vp SVB, vp *add.* P, fro þe herte *add.* F, comeþ vp HT$^2$

873 so . . . on] acorde B so . . . tonge] *om.* M þe$^1$] þyn T, *om.* P hert . . . tonge] tonge and þe mouth LCHeDT$^3$IiA hert] ye Ha þe$^2$] þy T accordeth] bothe *add.* UFfP, alle *add.* RGWF on] *om.* A 873–4 and$^2$ . . . lyuynge] *om.* LdHT$^2$ and$^2$] *om.* W soule] in to on and þe bodi and þe soule *add.* C ioyeth] ioyn bothen Ff

874 in] on *add.* G, to W God] good UHePF lyuynge] ⟨inwardly holdande and louande (leuande GW, lyuyng T) as hit were to god RGWT⟩ for greet swetnes and louyng to be wiþ him *α*, louende FfB, *om.* L, in *add.* D

875 or . . . womman] *om.* Ar to] contemplacioun or to *add.* Ha God] *inserted* S, *om.* V

876 forsaake] al *add.* RG 876–7 vanyte . . . luste] lustes and vanitees and vyle couetyse F and$^2$ . . . couaitise] *om.* Ar and þe] *om.* U, of SV and$^2$] al *add.* He

877 and$^1$ . . . luste] *om.* BIi and$^1$] all *add.* WT vile] *om.* URGTrIi$^3$, foul WTP luste] and lykyng *add.* *α*, of the flesshe *add.* LAE, luf Ha þerof] þer oft Lt, al utturly *add.* *α*, *om.* He, and þe fowle lust of her flesch *add.* B ledeth . . . on] goth by hym silf L ledeth] lete HT$^2$ by] be T$^2$

878 her] ȝar D and] *om.* C as . . . he] *om.* Ar as] also G seith] spekeþ F ham . . . souke] and sowkith L ham] it D, *om.* A to] in B, a M, *om.* Ha souke] fele T, sowle B, songe M, *om.* Ha

879 begynnynge] brennynge SVWTCHeTr of$^2$] *om.* TCTr þan] *om.* TPF he] *om.* PLd, þe F ham in] þeir T$^3$BIiM ham] hym ⟨hoolyche L⟩ TLE in] a *add.* RG, þe *add.* LCHe 879–80 to . . . ham] in B

880 ham] to *add.* FfT$^3$IiM holy] only GT, *om.* L, and holyly *add.* P to] *om.* FfT$^3$BIiM 880–1 and$^2$ . . . temptaciouns] *om.* LIi teris] of eyȝe *add.* F when] þat Ff þei] he F

881 suffred] suffren Lt foul noyes] fulnesse U foul] ful Ii$^3$ of] and P

882 ydel] ydelnesse P of vanytees] veyn LCHeDT$^3$BIiMTrHaAE wil] *om.* USV comber] come to RSVWT, ouercome C ham] hym TLE destroi] fele B

883 ham$^1$] and her herte *add.* B$^2$ is . . . away] and þey þat distroy hem T, *om.* LAr, þanne He, but þat he haue hem passynglich and such oure lord F is] and whan þilke þouȝtes ben U, þat beþ RGA, by C, and when þat þei are T$^3$BIiM passynge] passed UT$^3$BIiMLd away] *om.* LdHT$^2$ he] god TE ham$^2$] *om.* SV gaddre] togidere *add.* DLdHa to ham] *om.* T to] *om.* HeD ham$^2$] him SVAE fest] fested Lt, fastneth URGWFT$^2$B$^2$ArIi$^3$, fastnen SVLd, sette TLCHeDT$^3$BIiMHaAE, susteneþ H

884 hit] *om.* LtSVDdLd, þaim R$^2$FfP only] holliche SVR$^2$PF, *om.* LCHeDBIiM HaA, to hym and *add.* F and] then he *add.* L of$^1$] *om.* Ii har] þat L soule] þat *add.* F yate] grace F of heuyn] *om.* Ii of$^2$] to V

885 so . . . heuyn] *om.* U*α*Ar loke] se F þan] þat UCHeT$^3$Ii$^3$, *om.* B, when B$^2$ fire] stye R$^2$Ff loue] lyf G

886 lighteth] ligges DdR$^2$FfLCDT$^3$MPLdHT$^2$B$^2$HaA in . . . hert] *om.* WT to] *om.* URSVDdR$^2$FfLCHeDT$^3$BIiMPFLdHT$^2$B$^2$HaAEIi$^3$ har] þe P þerin] them within in ther hert Ii maketh] hem *add.* B$^2$ clene] out *add.* Ff of] *om.* H al] *om.* R$^2$Ff

887 erthly] þing and *add.* Ff and$^1$] so *add.* *α* seþen] *om.* W, sechen B$^2$ ben] *om.* G and$^2$] are G rauist] ravissching S, reuled B in] þe *add.* CHeT$^3$BIiM

888 loue] of god *add.* CHeT$^3$BIiM, of loue of ihesu criste *add.* F for] to F and . . . seth] to make men seon SV, to se B$^2$ and] þat RGTP, *om.* R$^2$Ff þai] þat be

contemplatif *add.* LB, *om.* F seth] þat haueþ hit *add.* HeT³ heuyn] þat han it *add.* CIiM

889 witte] wele *add.* CHeT³BIiM

890 ben¹] in flesch ne while he is *add.* F lyvynge] *om.* Ar here] in erth *add.* L þai dey] *om.* CIi þai¹] þe Ff þai²] þe T 890–1 ben . . . and³] *om.* B²

891 and²] *om.* UHT²

892 wonneth] dwellyn ULP soght] seeþ He

893 couaited] coueiten CHeH loued] loueþ He, desireden B al] *om.* Ha

894–7 Lo . . . Amen] *om.* L 894–6 Lo . . . me] *om.* Ar 894 Lo] nou *add.* SVWT Margaret] heere UIi³, now RGIi, Cecil R², M FfHe, *om.* DBHT²B²Ha, my dere freend T³Tr, Margery M, woman P haue] nou *add.* SV shortly . . . and] teld þe somdel Ch shortly] *om.* T³, worschipyd H þe] þee *add.* URGSVWDdT³B LdB², a *add.* CF, a D fourme] for me T, formyng Ff, enfourme HeT³MA lyuynge] louyng URSVTR²FfIiFHa and] *om.* M how] *om.* B²

895 þou¹] men D to¹] þe loue of god and *add.* Ch 895–6 and . . . to¹] *om.* Ch and] *om.* B² loue] of *add.* FfCHeT³BIiM hym] god D þou hast] han D taken] ȝeue FLd 895–6 þe to] hem þerto D

896–7 If . . . Amen] *om.* Tr 896 doth þe] be T and . . . þe] *om.* DF to þe] also U, *om.* GSVR²FfHeBIiChHa, þerof P me] richard heremite þat D[*MS ends*]

897 The . . . Amen] *om.* W of] oure alþer (*om.* SVT) lord *add.* RGSVT, almyȝti *add.* CHeT³BIiMF, god *add.* Ar Ihesu Criste] god SV Criste] verry (*om.* M) god and man verrayly (þat is verry CHeT³BIiF) loue and comforte of his louers CHeT³BIi MF, *om.* ChArA with] *om.* A the . . . the] vs euere (*om.* Ar) TAr the¹] amen *add.* R and . . . the] *om.* Ch the²] and me also *add.* U, worþily to him *add.* RGSV, from alle yuel and bringe þe to þi spouse ⟨of ihesu B⟩ þat þou hast take þe to þe whiche is euer lyuynge ⟨god HeIiMF, and B⟩ wiþouten ende *add.* CHeT³BIiMF

## *Ego Dormio*

1 Ego . . . vigilat] *om.* RSVWGTrAdAr    1–2 The . . . loue[1]] *om.* Tr    The] þow RSVWGBrPAdAr, þai Dd    lust] desyrest SV, for to *add.* Br, lustest to P    loue] god *add.* Br    hold . . . ere] herken Dd    hold] heder *add.* G, bowe down P    ere] eeren WG, herte Br

2 songe] boke Tr    I . . . hit] it es Dd    hit] *om.* RSVWGTrAd(Ar *cut off*)    2–3 þat . . . writynge] *om.* Dd, þes wordes Tr, ego dormio et cor meum vigilat that is AdAr    haue] *om.* RSVWG    at] in Br    þe] my RSVG

3 my writynge] þis book P    my[1]] *om.* Br    loue] *om.* Tr

4 he sheweth] is schewid of hym Br, or she *add.* P    wery] irke R[1]DdBrAdAr    to] of RSVWGP    euer] ay R[1]WDdAdAr    standynge] lastyng [d]wel P

5 or] in *add.* Br, as P    any . . . doynge] wirkand Dd    any] *om.* AdAr    oþer] good *add.* Br    dede] þing Tr    is . . . loue] and haþ alwey loue in his myn[de] P    is] hath Br    euer] ay R[1]DdAdAr, of *add.* Tr    his] of RSVWGAdAr, *om.* Br    and] when he slepes *add.* Tr    5–6 oft . . . þerof] in slepe AdAr    5–6 oft sithe] many tymes G

6 þerof] es *add.* Dd    dremynge] and metyng *add.* P, metynge Tr    6–8 Forþi . . . þe[2]] *om.* AdAr    Forþi þat] And for SVTr    I[1]] muche *add.* Tr    þe[1]] *om.* Dd    wowe þe] wolde SVTr    6–7 þat[2] . . . bot] *om.* P    þat[2]] *om.* Tr

7 Lord] ihesu crist *add.* Tr    7–8 I . . . bed] *om.* Tr    wil] wolde SVBr    becum a] be comer and R[1]WP    a] *om.* RG, þat Dd

8 his] þis Br    þat . . . þe[2]] for he has bouȝt þe with a grete pris ȝee with þe inwarde blode of his herte Tr    Crist] ihesu *add.* P

9 heuyn] that made vs and bought vs *add.* AdAr    for . . . hym] *om.* AdAr    wil[1]] wolde Br    wed þe] with þe dwelle DdTr    þe[1]] *om.* Br    9–10 He . . . hym] *om.* RSVWGP    hym] and *add.* Tr    9–10 þe . . . more] *om.* AdAr    asketh] of *add.* Tr

10 þi . . . hym] only þi loue nowþer landes ne riches ne golde ne siluer ne no þing elles bot onely þi loue þat þou wolt trewly loue hym and my der frende in criste I conseyle þe þat þou [. .] þe deceyuable luf and þe fals of þis wreched world and onely loue hym and þat þou [. .] þe nyȝt and day how þou may plese hym and be feyrest in his siȝt Tr    þi] oure AdAr    and . . . hym] *om.* AdAr    and] my dere syster in criste *add.* Dd    Crist] cristes P, he Tr    couaiteth] coueited R, loue is P

11 þy . . . prech] *om.* Dd    þy] þe Tr, oure AdAr    in] on R, of þi Tr    soule] þat hit be feyre areyede wiþ gode vertues and clene *add.* Tr, and *add.* RSVWGAdAr    þat þou] þerfore P    þou] we AdAr    gif] hym *add.* R[1]RWBrPAdAr, sette Tr    þi] oure AdAr    herte] to him *add.* SVGTr    11–12 I . . . þou] *om.* AdAr    11–12 I . . . wille] of þi body no rewarde þou hit be cloþed in an sacke Tr    I] *om.* R    prech] preye SV, þe *add.* P

12 þat] þat *add.* W    12–15 and[1] . . . God] This y wryte to rembraunce for peraventure we be nat alwey togider in þis lif for þen þou se me nat þou maist haue mynde of my wordes and do hem in dede an þen sikerly we shal be togiders in blisse withowte ende P    and[1]] þerfore Tr    afforce] enforce RSVGDdAdAr, enforme Br    þe] vs AdAr    nyght] to doo his wille *add.* Tr    to] þat þou Dd, and Tr    leue] forsake Tr

13 loue] wille Tr    13–15 al . . . God] bodyle affecoun of fleschly frendes or any oþer erþely þing for þou may nouȝt parfytly luf but ȝif þou so doo Tr    al] *om.* RSVGBr    lykynge] lustes AdAr    the] vs AdAr    Ihesu] hym AdAr    Crist] *om.* WAdAr

14 For] I *add.* R[1], ay *add.* DdAdAr    whils] if þi will and Br    þi . . . is] þou art

RSVWG þi] oure AdAr is] be Br holdynge] bowynge SV, holdyn Br to] þe *add.* RSVWG of] *om.* DdBrAdAr bodily] erthely AdAr

15 þou] we AdAr nat] verily and *add.* Br with] to Br

16 heuyn] wham DdAdAr, þer *add.* P contened] conteyd R$^1$ þre] there Br gerarchies] In *add.* SV

17 gerarchi] *om.* SV conteneth] beoþ SV, conteþ Br archangels] and *add.* RSVWGDdPAdAr virtus] In *add.* SV

18 gerarchi] contenys *add.* R$^1$RWGDdBrPTr, conteneþ SVAdAr potestates] principates Dd principatis] et *add.* SV, and *add.* WGP, and potestates Dd dominaciones] In *add.* S heghest] þridde G

19 gerarchi] *om.* AdAr þat . . . God] *om.* RSVWG is to] est Dd to] *om.* PTrAdAr

20 seraphyn] and þat jerarchie is next to god *add.* RSVWG The . . . seraphyn] *om.* AdAr ordre] *om.* WDd angels] and *add.* RSVWG heghest] is *add.* WDdBrP, order is *add.* Tr

21 þat . . . bright] *om.* P þat] lowest is and *add.* Tr sevyn] sythe *add.* DdTrAdAr, tymys *add.* Br so bryȝt] bryghter TrAdAr as$^1$] is *add.* R$^1$, þan is Tr, then AdAr þe$^1$] þis R$^1$ 21–2 And . . . son] es Dd And] Riȝt G

22 þan$^1$] is *add.* Tr þe$^1$] a DdP þe candel$^2$] or P brighter$^2$] *om.* G þan$^2$] is *add.* Tr mone$^1$] or *add.* P

23 brighter] *om.* G þan] is *add.* Tr þe$^1$] a Dd sterris] sterne DdTrAdAr also] riht so SVTr, so all Br, so P þe$^2$] euery P, *om.* TrAdAr ordres] ordre P of angels] *om.* Dd of] þe *add.* P in . . . euery] *om.* P euery] ilk ane R$^1$DdAdAr, is *add.* SV, ichon WGBrTr

24–5 fro . . . angels] *om.* AdAr 24 fro] þe first þat beþ *add.* P to$^1$] into þe hiȝest ordre þat is P seraphyn] and *add.* P I . . . to] shuld Tr say] to þee for *add.* W kyndel] styre P þi herte] and W þi] mannes Tr herte] þouȝt P

25 coueit] to be wiþ *add.* Tr þe . . . of] þat þow may be felow with W for] and AdAr holy] byse hem to kepe goddis lawe Tr

26 out] *om.* R$^1$ world] þei *add.* Br, lif P in$^1$] *om.* RSVWG þese] her Br, þe P ordres] of angels *add.* P in$^2$] *om.* R$^1$RSVWGBrAdAr

27 han loued$^1$] loueþ P loued$^1$] serued RSV, *om.* G God] *om.* DdTrAdAr mych] serued *add.* G in] to R$^1$RSVWGBrAdAr, intil DdPTr han loued$^2$] loueþ P

28 God$^1$] him RWG, *om.* DdTrAdAr oþer] summe SVBrPAdAr to] intil DdP þat] and Ad loueth God] parfyteliche keped goddis loue Tr loueth] lufed DdAdAr, han louyd Br God$^2$] *om.* P 28–9 and . . . loue] *om.* AdAr most brennynge] brennandest R$^1$DdBrP, brennynge W

29 ben] *om.* Lt 29–30 Seraphyn . . . receyued] *om.* Tr þat] *om.* R$^1$RSVWGDdBrPAdAr to$^1$] at DdAdAr 29–30 þe whiche] suche RSVWG

30 ordre] ordirs G þat] and Tr couaiteth] coueytid PTr in] of AdAr world] of worldes godes *add.* G, worshippes or riches *add.* Tr and] wyche *add.* Br

31 most$^1$] likynge and *add.* Tr God . . . in] his Tr most$^2$] *om.* LtDdBr brennynge] brynandest DdBr, thayre *add.* AdAr hertes] *om.* P hath] beþ P in] his *add.* DdBr, goddis *add.* PAdAr

32 loue] god W

33–6 To . . . world] *om.* AdAr 33 To] *om.* G þis] *om.* Dd speciali] *om.* P þe] þi P more] *om.* P 33–4 þan . . . anoþer] *om.* P

34 anoþer] any other R$^1$RWBr, mony oþere SVGTr þat$^1$] and þat RSVWGTr, and Dd, if P seest] says Dd is] *om.* G, maste *add.* Dd, most plesinge to þi lorde god and most *add.* Tr profitable] profit P

35 and . . . þe$^2$] To þat lyfe þou ȝeue Tr lif] þou RSVWG, loue P þe to] to þe suche desir P to] þat *add.* RSVWG in] *om.* Dd may] most and *add.* Tr holyest] holliche SV

36 hert] wille Lt, selfe and alle þe strengþes and loue of þi herte to þi lorde and þi sauuioure Tr of] in Br þis] þe G 36–7 For . . . brennyngly] Wha sa loues brennandly and stabily AdAr For if] forȝyue W

37 þou[1]] wille *add.* R[1]Br stabilly . . . brennyngly] stable þi hert in þe brennynge loue of god Tr stabilly] stabil Dd, stedfastly P loue] lyue G, þi lufe Dd God] *om.* RSVGDd, hym W brennyngly] hertly W, be byrnande Dd þou lyvest] he is AdAr lyvest] art Br 37–8 withouten dout] *om.* AdAr withouten] eny *add.* P

38 dout] ende Tr þi] his AdAr sete] settyll R[1]Dd, sege SV, place W is] schalle be AdAr ordeyned] dygth W for þe] *om.* WDdTrAdAr hegh] in heuen *add.* Dd and ioiful] *om.* AdAr ioiful] in heuene *add.* P 38–9 þe . . . God] goddes face DdAdAr þe[2]] glorious *add.* Tr

39 his] *om.* LtR[1], þe Br holy] *om.* GP þe] þat AdAr self] same Br, *om.* AdAr degrees] degre RSVWGDdBrPAdAr, ioye Tr þer] þat þe RSVG, þat WBr, þeir Dd, þe *add.* P, fra whilke the AdAr 39–40 proud deuelys] þe fendes þat were his angelys for her pride Tr

40 deuelys] aungels RSVWG doun] fra *add.* Dd, wer ynne þer *add.* P, froo Tr, *om.* AdAr ben] *om.* RSVWG, schalle AdAr Cristes . . . in] þat kepen goddis comandementes biþ ordeyned Tr Cristes] crist RSVWG, *om.* P doves] granteþ R, graunted SV, dowes W, granteþ hem G, *om.* P set] (to) ben set RSVGAdAr, heer setes W in] for RSVWG, *om.* DdPAdAr

41 to] and AdAr haue] *om.* W rest . . . ioy] *om.* Tr and[2]] in W

42 trauaille] here in þis lif *add.* Br han] *om.* WAdAr suffred] here *add.* RSVWGTrAdAr The thynk] þou þinkest Br nowe] *om.* Dd

43 hard] and heuy *add.* P gif þi] *om.* W (*corr. in margin*) thynges] thyng R[1]WP, as *add.* Tr fro[2]] and fro W, al *add.* Dd spech] and veyn *add.* RWGDdAdAr, murþes and pleyes of þis vanitees and fro yuel speche and ydel tales and Tr fro[3]] and SV, and fro WDdAdAr al] *om.* P

44 go] goos W, to be DdTr by] þine *add.* R[1]RSVWGBrPTr, *om.* Dd, the *add.* AdAr one] self RSVGTr, alane Dd wake] walk DdBr and[3]] hertly to *add.* Tr þynke] of *add.* RSVWGDdAdAr, on *add.* PTr ioy] ioyes GTr

45 and] *om.* AdAr to . . . compassioun] *om.* DdAdAr haue] pyte and *add.* Tr of[1]] on Tr passioun] peynes RWG, peyne SV, oft *add.* P (*crossed out*), peynes and þe harde deþ þat ihesu crist suffurd for vs and for oure synne Tr, compassioun Ad(*corr.*)Ar Ihesu] *om.* P 45–6 and . . . ymagyn] *om.* AdAr

46 ymagyn] of *add.* RSVWGAdAr þe] *om.* G, grete *add.* Tr peyn] peynes RSVWGPTr men] man Dd, þat wollen nouȝt forsake her synne and þe lustes and þe false likynges of þis wreched world Tr witterly] soþliche SV, trwly WP, vttirly Br, certeynly Tr

47 fro . . . be] beo þou SV fro] þe tyme *add.* P þat] *om.* RWGDdAdAr vset] brouȝt RSVG þerin] to serue god Tr þe] þou Br lighter and] *om.* Tr

48 euer] *om.* DdAdAr þe[1]] *om.* W, þou DdBr, ȝe Ad did] dedist Br, þouȝte P any] *om.* W erthly] thyng or *add.* Dd solace] bi a þousand part *add.* RSVWG, or murþe of þis world *add.* Tr

49 þe[1]] þou RSVGBr, for þan *add.* Tr wil] haue *add.* Br, ful *add.* P luste] lyke RSVGAdAr, to *add.* Br, þen *add.* P, of *add.* Tr þe[2]] any RSVWG myrth] lust RSVG, myrthes AdAr 49–51 and . . . games] *om.* AdAr

50 in] of SV þe[1]] þou RSVGBr wil] þinke *add.* RSVG, be ful *add.* Tr loth] lette W with] of SV, al W, *om.* Br þe[2] . . . þe[3]] any Tr and] wiþ *add.* G þe[3]] *om.* BrP of] al *add.* RSVW, þis worlde and *add.* Dd

51 games] game WGP, solace Br, pleyes Tr þe[1]] *om.* Dd melody al þe] *om.* Lt melody] and *add.* Dd, melodyes and alle þe myrþes Tr al[2]] and WBrAdAr þe[2]] *om.* DdBrAdAr richesse] and *add.* RSVWGDdBrAdAr al þe[3]] *om.* WDdBrAdAr

delites] delite RSVG, and game *add.* AdAr   al[4]] any RSVG, a AdAr   þe[4]] *om.* RSVWGDdAdAr

52 men] man GAdAr   of] in R[1]RSVWGDdBrPTrAdAr   semeth . . . is] beþ RSVWG, sownes Dd   and[1]] þat it Br   noy and] *om.* W   noy] noyous Br

53 angre] and disses *add.* W   a] *om.* BrAdAr   verraily] treweliche SV, swetely Tr   is brennynge] brennes Tr   þe . . . God] goddis loue AdAr

54–5 for . . . witte] *om.* AdAr   54 he] þat *add.* Lt   and[1]] *om.* Tr   melody] joy Dd   and ioy] *om.* R[1]BrP   ioy in] *om.* RSVWG   ioy] melody Dd   in] of R[1]Br   angels songe] þe delites of heuene Tr   as] *om.* P

55 witte . . . þou] and þou wult P   leue] loue RSVWG   55–6 thynge . . . þi] fleschly loue and AdAr   thynge . . . fleisshely] þi flesshly lustes and haue no mynde of hem P   þe . . . fleisshely] þi fleschly lufe list for þe lufe of god Dd, haue letted þi loue fro þe loue of god Tr   lust] to loue *add.* G   fleisshely] litel is þe (þi WG) loue þat þou hast or felest in ihesu crist riȝt so if þou haue (*om.* RSV) no flesshely lust ne lykyng in þese (þe G) worldly þinges *add.* RSVWG   and] ne RSVWG   haue no] *om.* W   of] on GDdTr

56 þi] *om.* DdTr   sib] fleshly P   frendes] ne fremmed Tr   bot . . . loue] *om.* AdAr   forsaak] hem *add.* RSVWG   al] holy *add.* Tr   56–7 and . . . hym[1]] pay and plese þou þi swet lord ihesu crist and P, in þat þat þei byn lettynge to þe for to luf hym and coueytes wiþ alle þi herte for to hold his loue Tr   gif] him *add.* W

57 Goddis loue] þe loue of god W   and . . . hym] *om.* W   pay] preyse Br hym[1]] god SV, and *add.* Br   shalt] haue and *add.* Dd   fynd] þan *add.* Tr

58 I[1]] þi herte Tr   can] on *add.* DdAdAr   þynke] telle of RSVWG, *om.* P How . . . hit] or write AdAr   How] Whoo Tr   I[2]] þou Dd, *om.* Tr   than] *om.* SV writ] wyt Dd   hit] *om.* W   58–9 I[3] . . . loue] certeyne I ne wote bot ful fewe wolen bysy hem to suche maner of lyfynge Tr   58–9 I[3] . . . in] Fewe men þou shalt fynde to telle þe of P   I[3]] and W   wot] *om.* Br   neuer] not RSVWGBrAdAr many] any RSVGDdBr   men] man DdBr, *om.* AdAr

59 euer] ay R[1]WDd   þat] *om.* WGDd   þe[1] . . . is] þou louest P   þe[1]] þi R[1] lif] lust SV, loue G   59–60 folowers . . . here] comeþ þerto P   59–60 hit . . . here] þer byn Tr

60–8 here . . . holynesse] *om.* AdAr   60 here for] wherfor SV   60–4 for . . . vanyte] *om.* P   men] man Dd   þat] and Dd, as Tr

61 God] *om.* RSVWG   conforteth] conforten W   his] goddes RSVWG, muche *add.* Tr   wene] he doth *add.* Br, trowe Tr

62 for] forþi DdTr   thogh] if R[1]Tr   withouten] in mannes syȝt *add.* Tr   shal] *om.* G

63 ful] *om.* WDdBrTr   withjn] þat worldly men can nouȝt se ne knowe Tr wisely] bisily RSVWG, trewly and bysyle Tr   Goddis seruice] fulfille þe wille of god Tr

64 forsake] al *add.* Dd   vanyte] vanytees RG, of þis worlde *add.* Dd, vanitees and synne and veyne worschippes of þe world and Tr, lok þow *add.* W, and *add.* Br

65 Gif] þenne *add.* RSVWG   al] *om.* Dd   þyn] oure BrTr   entent] y pray þe *add.* P   þis writynge] and kepe his comaundementes Tr   þis] *om.* Br   and] *om.* R[1]Br   set] *om.* G, al *add.* RSVGDdTr

66 desyre] deserte Br   loue] of *add.* R   God] *om.* Br   hyre þese] here ben LtRSVWG, here þere R[1]DdTr, herkne and y shal telle þe herof P   þou] we RSVG

67 ryse] ryve Lt   67–8 til . . . holynesse] *om.* Tr   þat] *om.* R[1]RSVWGDdBrP at] in DdP   þe] best and þe *add.* RSVG, best and at þe degree of þe *add.* W 67–8 For . . . holynesse] *om.* P   ne] *om.* SVWDdBr   nat] no þing SV

68 helle] layne Dd, hide Br   I hop] *om.* RSVWG

69 a] *om.* AdAr   holdeth] kepeth G   ten] *om.* G   commandementȝ] of god *add.* G   hym] hem R[1]

70 fro] owt of P þe[1]] *om.* G vii] *om.* SV is] stedfast and *add.* P stabil] stabled G, trewely Tr þe[2]] *om.* RSVG, feith and P trouth] bileeue SV

71 a] *om.* AdAr any] no WP þynge] þinges ne for no peyne þat falles to his body Tr God] any tyme *add.* Tr

72 his[1]] goddes PTr

73 behoueth] owthe Br, nedes AdAr euery] ilk R[1]DdAdAr, iche WGBrTr man[1]] to add WGBrPTrAdAr

74 bot] if *add.* R[1]DdBrPTr God] aboue alle þinge *add.* Tr neghbore] as hym selue *add.* Tr pride] or *add.* SVW Ir] wraþþe SVTr and[2]] or RSVW, *om.* GDdPTrAdAr

75 enuy] any R[1], and *add.* RSVW, or *add.* Dd, *om.* Br and . . . as] *om.* AdAr and] *om.* W venymous] venome Br, deedely Tr synnes] synne Dd as] *om.* Dd, and Br slownes] *om.* Dd, slauȝþe SVBrPAdAr

76 and[1]] *om.* RSVWGDdBrPTrAdAr þese] þis W vices] synnes RSVG, vice W, *om.* Tr

77 hit] to *add.* R[1]DdBrPAdAr depart] part W 77–9 þat . . . God] *om.* Dd 77–9 and . . . lyve] *om.* AdAr a] *om.* RWG, þe SV

78 or] and R a] *om.* R[1]RSVWGPTr God] þourȝe dedly synne *add.* RSVWG seyn] þat *add.* RSVWG 78–9 he[2] . . . slayn] his synne haþ departed hym Tr

79 withouten . . . lyve] þat is verrey lyfe Tr lyve] for *add.* DdTr man] þat is a *add.* P

80 poysoned] *om.* TrAdAr in] of Dd taketh] may take Tr venym] or poysen *add.* Tr, poyson AdAr þat] and S his] þe RSVWGBrAdAr

81 wrech] man Tr in] a *add.* AdAr and[1]] or AdAr luste] of hys flesch *add.* Dd, of synne þat is swete to þe flesche takes venym and poysen þat *add.* Tr destroieth] slees Tr his] þe Tr

82 hit[1]] hym Tr to[1]] þe *add.* W deth] peyne Tr Men] Many Tr hit[2] . . . syn] syn swete PAdAr hit[2]] is *add.* RV to[2]] *om.* Tr 82–4 har . . . erth] þe raunsen þerfore is sorwoȝe and peyne wiþouten ende wors þan eny man may þenke onne for ȝif man wolde haue mynde on þe peyne þat is ordeyned for sinnes þei shul haue litel delite in synne Tr hire] mede RSVWGDdAdAr þat] *om.* W

83 for ham] *om.* SV ham] hit *add.* R, þanne hit W, synne P bitterer] bitter R[1]SV þan[1]] and R[1], þe *add.* RSVWGDd galle] and *add.* W þan[2]] þe *add.* GDd attyre] and *add.* RSVWG

84 þe . . . þat] *om.* G þat . . . passeth] *om.* AdAr men . . . erth] man in hert kan þenke RSVW, men kan þynke G, we may here se or fele Dd men] man R[1]BrP in] on P 84–5 Al . . . see] *om.* Dd, al þyng þat we se with eiȝe wereþ and passeþ P passeth] vanisscheþ G, awey *add.* Tr

85 with eigh] may here Tr eigh] eighen SV see] or with herte may thynke *add.* AdAr 85–9 hit . . . rabil] *om.* AdAr hit . . . world] and þat we wiþ dele and alle þe riches and welþes of þis worlde warpes to wrecchednes Tr hit] and SVW vansheth] wanys R[1]RDdBrP, wendeþ W wel] weoleþe SVWDdP

86 and[1]] alle *add.* Tr þe] *om.* Dd diche] her *add.* Tr pride and] prowde Dd peyntynge] her deyntes Tr 86–7 slak . . . dreries] *om.* Tr slak shal] slakes Dd

87 in] into Dd, with P dreries] deyntees P stynke] cesse P har[2]] *om.* W

88 to] þe *add.* G 88–9 Al . . . rabil] *om.* P þe] *om.* RSVG wiked] wrecches G þis] þe G dryueth] worþe driuen G, drawes Dd 88–9 a . . . rabil] nouȝt and bringeþ hem byfore þe iuge þat þei may see her dome and hem selfe worþi to sorowȝ ay durable Tr

89 þer . . . rabil] þere wa es al þe rabil R[1], ful woo is þat rabel RSV, ful of wo it is þat rable W, ful who is þe rabel G, whare waa es euer stabel Dd, her wois al þe rebel Br wo] *om.* Lt Bot . . . may] þenne mow þai RSVWG 89–90 he . . . solace] þan schul be solace and ioy to hem Tr he] þat *add.* Lt

90 loued] han *add.* RSVGTr, lufes DdBrPAdAr when al] *om.* Dd al] *om.* Tr þe] oþere RSVWG fro] for her Tr wel] welthe PTr

91 falleth] schul falle Tr

92 þou] þai Dd wel] kepid þe and *add.* P þe] ten *add.* Dd of God] *om.* AdAr

93 straytly] styffely R[1]DdBr, clene RSVWG, stalwardly P, [. .]aly Tr, wele AdAr kept] kepest SV, put Dd þe] þam Dd al] *om.* RSVWGAd, þe Ar synnes] synne RSVWG, and byn deuoute in prayers in godly ocupacyones *add.* Tr and . . . degre] *om.* P paied] payest RSDd, plesyd W, trewely serued Tr to Crist] oure lord RSVWG, god DdTrAdAr to] *om.* Br degre] and *add.* RSV, and þou *add.* G, þan *add.* Tr

94 þe] *om.* RG þat . . . wil] to AdAr þat] how Tr wil] þe *add.* Br, may Tr loue] plese Dd

95 bicum] sumwhat mor *add.* Tr perfite] and ferre fro þe worlde *add.* Tr And] *om.* SVGDd in to] *om.* RSV, in W, to G þe] þat SVG toþer] secunde BrAdAr

96 þat] Thys (The AdAr) secunde degre of loue PAdAr world] in als muche as it lettes þe to loue god *add.* Tr and[1]] *om.* RSVWGDdTrAdAr þi[1]] þe Br, *om.* TrAdAr þi[2]] *om.* RSVPTrAdAr, þe Br

97 kyn] and wordely hauynge *add.* Tr and] to P in] wilful *add.* Tr pouert] boþe in body and in spiryte and *add.* Tr degre] *om.* RSVG shalt] looke and *add.* W

98 may] *om.* Dd be in] kepe þi Tr herte] from unleful desyres *add.* Tr and[1]] *om.* AdAr chaste] þou maiȝt beo *add.* SV in[2]] þi Tr and[2] . . . to] howe AdAr

99 mekenesse] and *add.* WGTr, meke AdAr suffrynge] suffraunce P buxumnesse] to god and to man for þe loue of god and charite *add.* Tr, buxome AdAr, besynesse Br loke] *om.* AdAr faire] clene RSVWG may] *om.* WTr

100 in] with Tr hate] hatynge AdAr al] *om.* RSVG, of AdAr vices] vice W, synnes Tr be] al *add.* Tr gostly] and *add.* GDdBrPAdAr

101 fleishly] also *add.* Br, and *add.* AdAr neuer] noȝt Tr spekynge] spyande RSV, speke DdBrAdAr il[1] . . . an] *om.* P il[1] . . . neghbore] yuel wordes ne wraþful ne angrely Tr il[1]] euel RSVGDdAdAr, harme Br ne] neuermore *add.* RSVWG gefynge] gyf R[1]RSVWGDdBrAdAr an] any GDd il[2]] euel RSVWGDdBrTr AdAr

102 men] man RGP seith] to þe *add.* Tr il . . . good] be it good or euyl Br, *om.* AdAr il] euel RSVGDdPTr good] here hit and *add.* RSVWG debonerly] mekely RSVGDdPTrAr, goodly *add.* Ad

103 wreth] wreche R, or of wreche *add.* SVG

104 within] and wiþoute *add.* RSVWGDdPTrAdAr and] so *add.* Dd lightly] sal þou *add.* Dd cum] in *add.* R[1] to] þe *add.* Dd, into P swetter] and more delectable *add.* Tr þan] euer was *add.* Tr

105 erth] world wiþ his desires and to RSVWG, worlde and DdAdAr, and to *add.* P, worlde and make hit fully dede in hem þat Tr couait] virtuuous lyfynge and *add.* Tr

106 ioy] ioyes WAd destroy] *om.* P, þo puttyng awey Tr þrogh] wiþ RSV wicked desires] wickednes and lust RSVWG wicked] euyll AdAr

107 þe] þi Lt, *om.* RSVWG fleishe] to slake and lose *add.* P þe[1]] ioye and þe *add.* P, likyng and þe *add.* Tr and þe likynge] *om.* Lt, þe worlde and Tr þe[2]] *om.* RBr of] al *add.* RSVG, *om.* Br þi] *om.* SV

108 and . . . God] *om.* Tr loue . . . God] *om.* AdAr ham] *om.* Dd lyve . . . dey] *om.* TrAdAr dey] or *add.* GDd be] þei *add.* SVP

109 be] *om.* RSVWGDdPTrAdAr hole] *om.* Dd or[1]] of Br seke] or *add.* Dd in[1] . . . wel] deede or quyk AdAr or[2]] and Br in[2]] *om.* G wel] hele VDd, deede or on lyue *add.* Tr þou] *om.* AdAr euer] ay R[1]WDdAdAr

110 his[1]] þi Dd domes] workes P so] *om.* Br

111 creature] man P and] for RSVWGAdAr sith] tym W men] *om.* DdAdAr hath] here *add.* RSVWG

112 har] *om.* WTrAdAr wel] welþe RSVW, welþe and myrþe G, wil DdBrPTrAd and . . . toþer] *om.* Tr toþer] worlde *add.* Br men] *om.* RAdAr

113 ben . . . pyne] pyneþ P pyne and] *om.* Tr and[1]] *om.* RVG, in SP persecucioun] and reproue *add.* Tr an anguys] *om.* WAdAr an] in *add.* SV lif] worlde P hath] ioy and reste wiþouten ende in *add.* Tr heuyn] in þat oþer *add.* G to] for Tr

114 mede] And *add.* SVTr 114–17 Forþi . . . blisse] *om.* AdAr Forþi] þerfore SVPTr, for WBr frendes] frend RSVG euer] ay R[1]WDd, alwey P in[1]] þaire *add.* Dd and[1]] in *add.* RSVWG and[2] . . . welth] *om.* W in[2]] *om.* DdPTr of] in W

115 bothe] ȝe P may] haue *add.* RSVWGDdTr, be *add.* Br þe[1]] *om.* WP more] in *add.* Br þat . . . nat] to cum to Br þat] leste RSVWG ye] þe Lt, þai RSVWGDd lese] loueþ P nat] *om.* RSVWG

116 ioy] of heuen *add.* Dd, hele and lyfe Tr end] And *add.* SV be] lyfe Tr penaunce] oþer persecucion *add.* P in[2]] or RSVGP, and WDdTr, or in Br sekenesse] and tribulacioun and suffur it mekeliche *add.* Tr 116–17 or . . . rightwisly] and lede ryȝtwis lyfe in loue and charite Tr or] *om.* P if þai] *om.* G

117 rightwisly] forsoþe *add.* P in God] wel RSVWG, *om.* Dd, to god BrTr his] þe RSVGDd, *om.* W

118 Forþi] And þerfore SV, for BrP so] *om.* RSVWGDdTrAdAr fild] fulfilled GDdP in] wiþ þe RSVWDdPAd, wiþ GTrAr grace of] *om.* G

119 þat] þanne RSVWG, swa þat AdAr nat] *om.* GDdBrPAdAr 119–20 haue . . . mennys] morne for þi fleschely frendes ne for none erþely þing þat may falle but for synne and losynge of virtues Tr haue] na *add.* DdBrPAdAr ne] and RSVWG gretynge] wepyng RSVWGBrP, grutchyng Dd 119–20 gostly . . . for] *om.* AdAr

120 as] and R[1]Br oþer mennys] nat for a wordly frend P mennys] men synnes W aftre] offre þe for P and] be *add.* G, to be *add.* Tr

121 in þynkynge] þinke ofte W, bithenk þe P in] swete *add.* Tr of[1]] often on P and] *om.* AdAr þat[1] . . . of] haue þat muche in þi mynde Tr þat[1]] *om.* RSVWGDd 121–2 I . . . hit] *om.* AdAr wille] chulle SV, pray þe W, þou do *add.* P þou] hafe *add.* R[1]RSVWGBrP, haue it *add.* Dd myche] in *add.* Dd of] þerof RW, þere onne G, *om.* Dd, of it Br, and often þeron P

122 hit] I G kyndil] stire P hert] and make þe *add.* P 122–3 set . . . to] *om.* AdAr 122–3 goodes . . . ioy] vanitees and þe ydel ioy of þis world Tr þis] þe SVG al] *om.* RSVWGDdTr

123 ioy] ioyes R*SVWG, þarof *add.* DdBr, of þis world *add.* Tr to] þe SV brennyngly þe] þe brennyng P light] lif PTr, dwellynge AdAr of] in TrAdAr

124 halowes] seyntes P, holy seyntes Tr, and sette alle the worlde atte noght *add.* Ad, set all þe godes of þe werld at noght *add.* Ar(*Ar ends*) þyn] þe Br hert] þouȝte RSVG holy] only RSVG þe . . . of] serue P

125 al worldis] wickede RSVG, ill W thoghtis] thoght is R[1], þouȝte RSVG, werkis Br, beþ *add.* P, and desyres *add.* Tr out] of þi soule *add.* Tr wil] xal Br þe] ye Lt, þou SVGAd, þou haue Br lust] to be *add.* R, *om.* SVAd, to *add.* WGBr, þing mery to be Tr stel] stil LtRTr, þe *add.* SV, to go allone P bi . . . on] *om.* R þi] þe DdAd on] self SVGPTr, alane Dd þynke] depely *add.* Tr of] on SVWGDdTrAd, on ihesu P

126 and[1]] *om.* Tr to] *om.* G prayngе] prayer P, preyer and to þenke holy meditacciounes Tr þrogh] *om.* RSVWG 126–7 good . . . praiers] þat Tr 126–7 holy praiers] mykille prayinge Ad holy] goode P

127 þi . . . mad] shulen make þin herte to be RSVWG Crist] *om.* W, an vse þe to be michel prayng *add.* P

128 and[1]] in RSVG gostly] comforte and *add.* Tr both] but Br and[2]] in *add.* R[1]WDdBrPTrAd

129 þyn] þe DdAd on] self RSVGPTr, alane Dd gyf . . . to] haue muchel in þi mynde to Tr, *om.* Ad gyf] vse P say] þe *add.* R[1]RSVWGBrPAd

130 and[1]] þe *add.* RSVGBr auees] ⟨þe R⟩ aue maria ofte siþes (tymes W) RSVWG, aue maria DdTr nat] no SVWDdBrPTrAd entent] kepe RSV, tent DdBrAd, hede PTr þat þou] to Ad þat] þauh SV

131 say] not *add.* SV many] psalmes *add.* G bot] þoo *add.* WG 131–2 þat[1] . . . may] take hede how weel and how deuoutely þou may sey hem Tr þat[1]] *om.* Ad þou[1]] shalt *add.* RSV say] for þe tyme ⟨loke þat W⟩ þou say *add.* RSVWG ham] *om.* W, be wel seyde G and] *om.* WDd in] wiþ RSVWGDdAd þe] *om.* WBr, þi P

132 liftynge] castyng SV, hauynge G, lefte BrP, reysynge Tr vp] *om.* SVGP þoght] hert GBrPAd heuyn] for *add.* RSVWPTr, heuenward for G hit] *om.* G seven psalmes] fyue wordes in ful deuocioun Tr psalmes] *om.* P in] wyth DdAd

133 þi[1]] the Ad on þi prayngе] þeron Tr on] of Dd prayngе] prayer ⟨þat þou seyst G⟩ RSVWGBrP seuen] fyue Tr

134 hundred] þousande GTr, thowsand *add.* Dd suffrynge] not thynkynge þeron Br þi] hert and þi *add.* Tr þoght] þouȝtes SVAd to . . . of] fleying aboute and varying in þe world and aboute Tr to] *om.* RSVDd in] into P vanytees] vanite RSVWG 134–6 bodily . . . in[2]] *om.* P bodily] worldly G thynges] thyng R[1], For *add.* RSVWGTr

135–7 What . . . wille] *om.* Ad 135 hopis] trowes RSVW þou] þe V may come] comes Br may] to Tr þou let] *om.* W let] suffur Tr on] in W þe] þi G

136 boke] neuer so longe fast *add.* Tr hert] mynde G ren] be rennande and goande (raykand W) RSVW, be rennynge G, riotiþ Br dyuers] sere R[1]Dd steddes] places and vanitees Tr in[2]] of RSVWG 136–7 whar . . . wille] *om.* RSVWGDd

137 wille] I sey þe forsoþe noo more þan a man þat greued þoȝ he chide or speke to an hard stone *add.* Tr Forþi] And (*om.* W) þerfore SVWBr þi] herte and þi *add.* Br þoght] and þi hert *add.* Tr in] on G, ihesu *add.* Br Crist] stedfastly *add.* Br and[1]] as Br reue] reule RSVWGDdBr, rere P, drawe Tr, take Ad hit] vp *add.* P hym] þe Br

138 hit] þe Dd þe] *om.* RSV venym] venyms RSV, venemus W of . . . besynesse] and þe veyne bysynesse of þis wreched world Tr of] *om.* W, þe *add.* Dd worldis] hertly R, eorþliche SVWG

139–42 And . . . þerin] *om.* Tr 139 I . . . as] *om.* Ad þou[1]] desirest and *add.* P, that *add.* Ad couaitist] to *add.* R[1]RSVWGDdBrPAd þat þou] *om.* RSVAd þis] his BrAd

140 þynke] write Ad

141 so] þat *add.* G, þat Br, euere *add.* P And] *om.* W, for Ad witterly] soþeli GDdAd, sikerly P hete] say Dd þe] þat *add.* DdPAd fynd] haue G

142–3 for . . . specialy] ȝif þou loue ihesu crist trewly in þis lyue Tr 142 and[1]] *om.* Ad þe . . . louest] swha so loues Ad þou] *om.* P louest] louedest RSVW so[1]] *om.* Ad and[2]] *om.* W so[2]] *om.* Ad

143 þou] he Ad fild ful] fulfilled GDd ful of] with Ad in erth] within W in] hert and in soule and mynde in *add.* Tr be] *om.* RSV

144 mayden] servande DdP, *om.* Tr, frende Ad and] *om.* SVDdTrAd, his *add.* WP spouse] *om.* SVDdTrAd in] þe ioyful blisse of *add.* Tr For] Forþi Tr so mych] *om.* PAd payeth] plesys WBrP as] doþ *add.* P

145 loue] þouȝt W his . . . Ihesu] god Tr his] þis Dd Ihesu] And *add.* SV, for *add.* Tr þou] wolt *add.* RSV loue] *om.* Lt hit] *om.* RSVP, hym TrAd right and] *om.* W, trewly and Tr

146 let] leue to loue hit G, leeue þe loue of þat name P no] *om.* Ad men] man RSVWG say] do Dd do] and (*om.* SV, in erþe G) þenne *add.* RSVWG, say Dd, to þee *add.* Tr rauyst] raysed R[1]PTrAd, receyued RSVWDd, rered G, reysyd vp Br to] *om.* SVW

147 a] *om.* RSVW lif] loue P þan] þat Tr þou] with hert *add.* Tr can couait] coueitede RSVWG, for *add.* Tr þat] *om.* Dd, wat Tr þer] what W, if Br, euere Tr we] hertly and *add.* W

148 inwardly] *om.* G, in þis worlde Tr ask] of *add.* W of oon] any þing deuoutely with loue and trust of hert Tr of] *om.* RSVWGDd yif] graunte Tr vs þre] fyfe Dd þre] þrefold better þan we euere axe Tr we] wil *add.* Dd

149 al] *om.* W hert] fully *add.* Tr

150 loue] euer *add.* W, euermore *add.* G shalt] euermore *add.* RSV þi] þese RSVG, *om.* W 150–1 þre . . . þy] *om.* Br þre] *om.* Dd enemyes] þinges RSV

151 þy] þe R 151–4 bot . . . Crist] and þen art þou wurþi and perfit to be crowned in lif withowten ende and þen hast þou þe dignite þat crist ȝaf to his apostelis þat þou maist sitte with hem on þe day of dome for to iugge oþer boþe goode and euele for þe gret loue and desir þat þou hast to loue god P þou . . . haue] the byhoues to be in Ad euer] more *add.* RSVWG fightynge] and temptaciouns *add.* Tr

152 leuest] her *add.* Br and . . . stand] *om.* Ad and euer] *om.* DdTr euer] *om.* SV, ay W til . . . dey] þerfore Tr til] whiles W behoueth þe] þou most W, to *add.* DdBrTr be bisy] bisily RSV, *om.* G, and *add.* Br, euer *add.* Tr stand] wiþstond temptaciouns Tr

153 þat . . . nat] and not to falle Br þat þou] and to R[1] in il[1]] intil Dd il[1]] euel RSVBrTr, foule lustes yuel G delite] delites RSVWGDdTr ne in] *om.* Tr il[2]] euel RSVGDdBr, foule Tr thoght] þoghtes RSVWGDdTr or] ne RSVGDdTr, no W il[3]] euele RSVGDdBrTr word] wordes RSVWGDdTr and] or R[1], ne RSVGDdBr, no W, nor Ad il[4]] euel RSVGDdBr, foule Tr werke] werkes RSVWGTr

154 forþi . . . verrayli] *om.* Ad forþi . . . þou] for alle þi desyre þou schuldest ordeyne Tr forþi . . . desyre] for þe gret loue and þe gret desyre auȝte Br forþi] and (*om.* G) þerfore SVG, in *add.* W gret . . . desyre] þi grete disirynge ouȝte SV oght] drede fell W desyre] gernynge R[1]RWGDd to] *om.* GDd loue] ihesu *add.* RSVWG

155–6 throgh . . . and] *om.* Tr 155 throgh] with DdAd holdynge] kepyng Br

156 only] *om.* Br or] and PAd noght] na R[1]DdBrPAd, vn RSV, a G mayden] þou shalt ouercome þi flesh *add.* P þrogh] with Ad lyuynge] afturward *add.* RSV, hennes (*om.* W) forward *add.* WG, and resonabel *add.* Dd 156–7 in . . . dede] *om.* RSVWG in[2]] *om.* DdTrAd

157 þrogh] with TrAd discrete] grete RSV, þe grette W, *om.* G, thy grete Ad abstinence] penaunce Tr and . . . seruice] *om.* Dd and[2]] of W, in P seruice] abstinence and clene and chaste lyfynge in þouȝt and dede and deuoute preyers and honest ocupacioun Tr

158–9 þrogh . . . to] wiþ holdyng of wilful pouerte puttyng awey alle coueytise of erþely þinges desyringe after cristes loue and þenkyng on his blessed name and on þe grete ioyes þat byn in Tr 158 þrogh] with Ad of[2]] on DdP

159 his] þis Dd name] ihesu *add.* WGDdAd felest] fyndes RSVTr

160 in] þe loue of *add.* Tr þe wil] þat while R, þou wil Br þe[2]] þis WG noght] *om.* GPTrAd bot] a *add.* P 160–1 noy . . . soules] also for no mannes seyȝyng P noy] dises W, noyous Br

161 for] to WTr þou . . . þan] coueyte þou nat for P wil] shal RSVWG þan] *om.* SVWAd riche] ne to ocupye þe aboute many worldly goodes ne haue gold ne siluer *add.* Tr ne] *om.* R[1]RSVWGDdAd to haue] *om.* Tr

162 clothes] mantils R[1]DdBr, mantels or gownes (coules SVW) RSVW, mantels and many gownes G, garnementȝ P 162–4 and . . . six] moo þanne þe nedes to kepe þe fro colde ne none oþer þing more þan euere nedeful to þi body ne take no more of þe world þan scharpe nede askes and ȝif þou hast more þan nedys Tr and . . . dreries] ne mychel cloþyng to þi bodi P and faire] *om.* W and] to *add.* G faire] and *add.* RSV, or *add.* W, couerchefs and *add.* G many kirtils many] *om.* Lt many kirtils] and Ad many[2]] and RSVWGDd 162–3 al . . . and[2]] *om.* Ad al . . . set] set þou al þis wordles richesse and aray P wil] shalt RSVWG

163 and[1] . . . al] *om.* P al] *om.* RSVW, hit G, it als noght it ware Dd take] hafe Ad 163–4 The . . . ynogh] *om.* Ad The] for þan þou Br þynke] herafter when þou art comen to þe swetnesse of þe loue of ihesu crist *add.* P

164 clothes] mantils R[1]DdBr, mantels or two gownes (coules VW) RVWG, coules or two mantels S, garnementes P on] riȝt *add.* WG ynogh] þanne þou *add.* RSVW, þan ȝif þou *add.* G, þow *add.* Dd, þere þou *add.* P, ȝyf þou *add.* Ad þat] *om.* GPAd nowe] *om.* RSVWGDdAd fyue or six] þre or foure RSVWG six] clathes *add.* Ad forthy] *om.* RSVWGDdTrAd, for whi Br, therfor P gif] þou *add.* Br sum] it Tr

165 Crist] god Br goth] as *add.* Ad naked] þat is to seyȝe to nedy men *add.* P and pore] in a pore wede RSVWGDdAd, and hongree Tr and[1]] or Br and[2]] ne Tr hold] hit *add.* SV nat] þe goodis *add.* Tr to þe] *om.* Dd þe] þi self PTr al] *om.* Tr 165–6 þat . . . gone] *om.* P þat] for þou DdTrAd 165–6 if þou] þi LtR[1], to GTr, þine Br, schalle *add.* Ad

166 liue] lif LtR[1], *om.* Br þai] it Br, þoo Tr half gone] spended þat þou haste Tr half] halfyndele Br gone] spent RSV, don W, wend G The] The *add.* Lt deuylle] fende Tr is] þou schal Tr 166–7 when . . . stabilly] wiþ strongly standynge Tr

167 al] *om.* RSVWGTr fandynges] fondynge WG, temptaciouns PTr sothfaste] parfyte Tr and] *om.* Tr

168–70 mekenes . . . with] meke preyer and deuoute as holy writte wittenes Resistite diabolo et fugiet a vobis for myche helpe þe bysy preyer of an ryȝtwisse man to ihesu Tr

169–70 And . . . nedeth] *om.* DdAd 169 And] þanne *add.* RSVWG is] am WP aboutward] so faste abowte P

170 ware] lef and *add.* P me] þee W, moche *add.* G nedeth] and me both *add.* W I wil] and Tr þat] *om.* Ad

171 be[1]] were Br for] and (*om.* P) þerfore RSVWGP, but DdAd, but for to Br, but þat þou Tr be[2]] þou *add.* RSVWGP, *om.* DdAd euer] neuermore W, ay Dd other] *om.* RSVBrPAd, withouten W, more G spekynge] speke Dd God] or prayande *add.* Ad 171–2 or . . . werke] *om.* Br wirchynge] wirke Dd

172 notable] nobel P, goode TrAd werke] *om.* Ad or . . . hym] and profytable Tr or] elles þat þi mynde be *add.* P thynkynge] thynk Dd in] on RSVWGDdBrPAd hym] ⟨ihesu G⟩ or praying hym *add.* RSVWG, god PAd 172–3 and . . . mynde] *om.* Ad and] *om.* Dd principaly] namly P þat] in *add.* RSVWG 172–3 þi thoght] þou PTr

173 be . . . And] *om.* P be . . . hym] þou (*om.* Tr) haue him euer (ay WTr) RSVWGTr euer] ay Dd in] þi *add.* Tr 173–4 thynke . . . passione] þenkyng on his harde passyon þat he suffurd for mankynd how he þat was kynge of alle kynges weped water with sore teres and [. .] for þe harde peyne þat he schuld goo vnto and suffur and for þe noye and þe sorowȝ þat he schuld haue alle hys body swette water and blode and so dude neuer creature in þis world safe onely he for neuer man myȝt suffur so muche peyne as he dude for þe loue of mannes soule and þat grete loue schulde stur vs to haue grete sorowȝ and mynde of his passyon syngyng þis mournynge

songe Tr  thynke] *om.* Ad  oft] of Lt, many times G, *om.* BrAd  þis] siþes RSVW, *om.* GDdBrPAd  of] on RSVGDdPAd

175–211 My . . . synge] *see appendix for versions of P and Tr*  175 My kynge] howe he Ad  My] how þi RSVWG  þe[1]] he RSV, *om.* WG, þat Dd  watyre] he *add.* Br  grete] wepte RSVGBr  þe[2]] *om.* RWDd, he SVG  he] *om.* RSVWGDdAd  swete] and *add.* SVWGBr

176 Sethen . . . wette] *om.* R  Sethen] was *add.* SVWG, aftyr Ad  sore] him *add.* R[1]Br, was he *add.* Ad  so þat] tille Ad  his] he with Ad  blood] was *add.* Ad

177 When . . . met] *om.* Ad  hat] þe W, his Br

178 can] gun R[1]RSVWDdAd, begun Br  hym] to *add.* Br  and] *om.* Br  piller] pileres RSV  swynge] bynde G, and *add.* Dd

179 faire] *om.* Lt  fouled] defowlyng Dd, defoulyd Ad  with] thar *add.* Ad

180 The] and wiþ G, his Ad  þorne] kẏng RSVW, kene *add.* G, heede thay Ad  crowneth] crowned ⟨was G⟩ RSVWGBrAd  þe] wiþ RSVWAd, þi G  kynge] þorn RSVWAd  ful . . . prickynge] *om.* G  ful] *om.* WAd  sore] scharp W  is þat] he is RV, *om.* SAd, he was W  prickynge] prikked VW

181 Alas . . . henge] *om.* Ad  Alas] Al G  swetynge] he *add.* RSVWG  demed] dampned Lt  for] *om.* Dd

182 was[1]] were RSVWG  hand] hende R[1], hondes RSVWGDdAd, hed Br  and] *om.* Dd  was[2]] were RSVWG  feet] Naylid was is handis *add.* Br

183 þurlet] persyd Br  is] was RSVGDdBr  183–4 so[1] . . . side] *om.* W  so[2]] *om.* Br

184 Naked] was *add.* RSVG, es *add.* DdAd, al *add.* Br  white] swete RSVG  rede] es *add.* Dd, blody es Ad  his blody] *trs.* RSVG  blody] *om.* Ad

185 Wan] Than Br  hewe] face Ad

186 blode] hit *add.* RSVWG  kan] gan RSVWGDd

187 As] þe *add.* R[1]Br  stremes] streme R[1]RWGBrAd  done] doþ RSVWGBr, *om.* Dd  on] of R[1]RSVWDdBrAd  stronde] strone Lt  this . . . is] is hit R, hit is SV  this] his WGDdBrAd  is] *om.* W

188 To þynke] þis to see Dd  þynke] hertly (inwardly W) on (opon W) certes (*om.* S) hit (*om.* VG) *add.* RSVWG, it *add.* Br, this *add.* Ad  is] ful *add.* S  he] *om.* R[1]  is] was RSV  to] þe *add.* R[1]RSVGDd

189 on] vpon RSVWG  þe[1]] a WG, rode *add.* DdAd, *om.* Br  þe[2] . . . brede] þat is oure alrer heed RSV, þow (he G) þat art (is G) owr alder (alles G) hed WG

190–1 Dryvyn . . . food] *om.* Ad  190 is[1]] was RSVDd  dele] þole and he G  good] breed RSVWG

191 And] i SV, is G  fouled . . . halowes] alsso in þe blys of heuen es al þe aungels Dd  fouled] folewed RSV  halowes] holiest Lt, aungels RSVWG

192 A] and SV  who-som] hose SV  som] so RWGDdAd

193 deynge] done RSVW, nayled G, put Br  on] opon RSVWGBr  roode] wiþ þeues as þeof were he who wolde (*om.* SV) haue mynde of þis for crist of synne sese he *add.* RSVW, wiþ þeues as þeef were he þat greet deel was to see whoso þis wold haue in mynde to seese of synne mater schulde he fynde *add.* G

194 þan] is RSVW, it is G  is hit] is R[1], þat is RSV, þat I WG, is to Br  said] seye Br  þat] *om.* G  loue] loueþ SV, þou Ad

195 hym . . . hath] in him so loue was Br  hath] *om.* G  was] is W

196 loue] ioy Lt

197 art] bot *add.* Dd

199 me] my RSVBr, *om.* W, þi G  fyre] me *add.* WG, herte Ad  wyn] fynde W

200 And . . . blyn] *om.* Ad  blis] ioy Dd  neuer] more *add.* G  may] schal SVWDd, *om.* Br

201 in to] þou in SV  201–87 send . . . þe[2]] *lacking in R[1]*  me] þou *add.* Br

202 lend] wende Br  in] to *add.* Br

203 In] þi *add.* W wound] wende RSV, wynne W, wynde G

204 þe] my DdAd þat] *om.* DdAd þou] *om.* G, dere *add.* Dd hast] dere *add.* GAd þi louer] bifore þe RSVWG to] hit RSVG, it to WDdBrAd

205 Bot] I coueyte *add.* SV, For G, *om.* Dd þe] I leue and *add.* G I couait] *om.* SV nat] *om.* SVDd þis] þe G world] noght and *add.* Dd for þe] forþi Lt, for Dd, fro þe Br I] it Dd hit] *om.* RSVWGBr, I Dd

206 when . . . I] þou gar me Ad may I] *trs.* Br se] þee *add.* W

207–8 for . . . nere] *om.* Ad 207–8 for . . . here] *om.* Br 207 for] þi RSVWG þat] *om.* RSVWGDd chaungeth] my *add.* RSVWGDd

208–9 When . . . hire] *om.* Dd 208 may I] *trs.* Br cum] neȝe RSVWG

209 for . . . hire] *om.* W for] *om.* RSVGBrAd

210 Of loue] ofte RSVWGDd, euer Ad þe] þi WAd, *om.* DdBr

211 Wil . . . synge] *om.* Ad Wil] *om.* Dd louynge] longinge G þi] *om.* Dd

212 wil] *om.* Ad euery] ilk a WDd fynd] þerinne *add.* RSVG, haue Tr gret] *om.* DdPAd, delite and *add.* Tr swetnesse] þerin *add.* W þat] it *add.* W

213 and[1]] þat sal Dd mak] gar Dd in[1]] to *add.* SVWGP wepynge] gretyng DdAd, grete lykynge of heuenly þinges Tr in[2]] *om.* RSVWGTr, to *add.* P grete] *om.* TrAd langynge] haue *add.* RS, louynge haue VG, lowyng Tr to] of Tr

214 Ihesu] crist and longyng to dwelle wiþ hym *add.* Tr shal] al be on ihesu and so *add.* Dd reft] rauyssched GBr, receyued Dd, reisid ⟨vp Tr⟩ PTrAd abouen[1]] fro RSV al] *om.* G þynges] and *add.* RSV, þinge WDd 214–15 abouen[2] . . . sterres] and fleschely desyres Tr

215 sky] firmament DdPAd and] alle *add.* P þe[2]] þo W þi] þe Br

216 And] *om.* P

217 be in] haue Dd in] ful *add.* Tr delite] swetnesse Tr get . . . þerto] *om.* Ad get] wynne Tr þerto] þere P

218 For] and P I . . . or] *om.* Ad another] any oþer RSVWGBrPTr, ylke man Ad þat[2] . . . þis] *om.* RSVWG þis] litel boke *add.* Tr shal] nouȝte *add.* Ad al] as þei rede it or see it writen Tr þat[3]] hit GDdP

219 in] at Dd, *om.* P þat cheseth] to chese Dd cheseth] sheweþ RSVWG whom . . . wil] *om.* RSVWG 219–20 to . . . maner] *om.* Ad do] it *add.* Tr or] els *add.* Dd

220 other þynge] *om.* P in] of RSVWG, on DdBrTr as he] and Ad men] mon SV, hem WAd, in þis world diuers *add.* Tr grace] graces Tr to] haue *add.* Dd har hele] *om.* W, her soules helthe P, hele of her soules Tr, do the beste Ad

221 dyuers[1]] sere DdAd men] in þis world *add.* Tr taketh] han Tr dyuers[2]] sere DdAd yiftes] grace Dd, and graces *add.* Tr Ihesu Criste] god to reule hem wiþ in þis lyfe Tr, *om.* Ad Criste] *om.* W 221–2 al . . . in] afterwarde to haue diuersyle Tr þei] *om.* RSVWGDdPAd

222 þe . . . of] *om.* Ad ioy] ioyes GTr of] in Tr þat . . . charite] aftur þat þei doo in þis lyfe for diuers wonynge places byn þe blisse of heuene to hem þat schul come þider as crist seiþ him selfe multe mansiones in domo patris mei sunt Tr

223 degre] of loue *add.* Tr he] schul *add.* Tr lyve] loue RSVWDdAd at] after BrTr, as P Goddis] god P

224 This . . . cald] and so come into verrey Tr This] The thridde PAd of loue] *om.* Dd lif] loue RSV þat] and þan schal he Tr loueth] `is´ loue W, only *add.* Br, loue Tr onely] *om.* LtBr, by hymself P

225 withouten . . . and[1]] þenkynge and to ihesu hertely W* withouten] fro RSVG ryngen] *om.* P, noyse Tr or] and RSVGBr, *om.* P dyn . . . and[2]] *om.* Tr dyn] noys GP, *om.* Ad and[1]] *om.* SVAd, or DdP and[2]] or DdPAd criynge] or ydel tales of þis world *add.* Tr At . . . begynnynge] *om.* Ad

226 is] schul be Tr 226–7 in . . . heuyn] þurȝ stirynge of þe holy goste Tr

227 light] blis RSVWGDdPAd and] *om.* W þare] ⟨it WG⟩ is RSVWG

enlumyned] li3ted WDdP, schul be ly3ttened and clarified Tr  in] wiþ RSVWGDd TrAd, with þe P  grace] of god *add.* P  kyndlet] comforted P  of[1]] wiþ RSVW GDdPTrAd  þe] *om.* Dd

228–30 þou . . . þat] *om.* Ad  228 feel] haue RSVWG  brennynge] bigynnyng R  in] at P

229 euermore] lastinge and *add.* RSVWTr, lastynge in þin (*om.* P) *add.* GP, and mare *add.* Dd  lyftynge] *om.* RSVWGP, reysyng vp Tr  thoght] euermore (ay W) vpwarde *add.* RSVW, schal be euere vpward *add.* G, studefastly *add.* Tr  to] þe mynde of P  and] *om.* RSVP  fllynge . . . of] felynge þe loue of RSVWGP, feland lufe Dd

230–1 and . . . ioy] *om.* Br  230 and] so muche *add.* RSVWG, so mich and also of *add.* P  swetnesse] in delyte of heuenly þinges *add.* Tr  so myche] *om.* RSVWGP  sekenesse] swetnesse Lt  ne[1]] no W, *om.* DdAd  shame] anguys Dd anguys] schame Dd  ne[3]] no W

231 penaunce] shal *add.* RG, þat *add.* SV  may] schal ⟨non W⟩ SVW  lif] loue RSVG  in] *om.* RSV  þan for] þarfore Dd

232 hert] in loue *add.* Tr  þi[2]] in Dd  turneth] shul turne RSVWGTr þoghtes] þoght W

233 to] into SVP  Ihesu] criste *add.* W  is] shal be RSVWGTr  al[2]] *om.* Ad al[3]] *om.* Ad  al[4]] *om.* Ad  solace] and *add.* BrPAd  al[5]] and Tr

234 so] al I wate Dd  on] of RSVTr, in GPAd  wil] *om.* Dd, schal Tr  euer] more *add.* RSVWG, *om.* Ad  be] alle *add.* Ad  songe] in desyrable longyng of soule *add.* Tr, reste Ad  and] *om.* DdP  in] *om.* Lt, ioyful þou3tes of *add.* Tr, of Ad rest] sange Ad

235 say] synge G, safely *add.* Tr  235–6 Who . . . ay] and synge þis songe of loue ihesu for þe mourne I may / As turtel þat longeþ boþe ny3t and day / For her loue is gone hyr froo / For after þe lorde me longeþ ay / And þat is al my myrþe and pley / Where I sitte or goo / þerfore lord þou rewe on me / And helpe me sone þat I may see / þe feyerhe[d] of þi face / with angelys þat byn bry3t and clere / And holy soules þat þou bou3tes dere / into holy place Tr  to] telle P  leman] and *add.* P

236 say] þat *add.* RSVWGP  ay] euere P  Al þat] wha so Ad  Al] þo *add.* P vanytee3] vanyte P  specials] speciali WBrP, frenscheppe Tr

237 hert] hertes RSVWG  on[1]] in WP  other] erþely Tr, *om.* Ad  þynge] þinges WGDd  þan] bot onely (*om.* Ad) Tr Ad  on[2]] in WP, of DdBr

238 degre[1]] þanne *add.* W  þay] *om.* GAd  to] *om.* W  þe] þat SVWGP, *om.* Dd  degre[2]] *om.* TrAd  of loue] *om.* WGTrAd, þat *add.* SV  bifore] is *add.* SV

239 named] sayed BrPTr  Forþi] And (*om.* PTr) þerfore SVGDdPTr, For Br worldes solace] the solace of the worlde Ad, and ydel tales and veyne speches or wordes wiþ bysye and kepyng of þi þou3t *add.* Tr  þe] hem RSVWG  behoueth] moste P 239–40 þat . . . no] and Ad  þi] her RSVWG  hert] ne þi loue *add.* Tr  239–40 be holdynge] beholdith not Br  be] not *add.* RSVWG

240 holdynge] bowynde SVTr, cleuyng P  no] *om.* Br  240–2 loue . . . God] erþe loue ne fleschely frenschyppe and þat þou kepe þi hert strongly in goddis loue and his drede with scylence and stablenes in his servyce Tr  any[1]] ilke worldely Ad  ne . . . erth] and alle worldly besynesse Ad  any[2]] no RSVWGDd, *om.* P  of] in Dd þat þou] and Ad  þou] þei RSVWG

241 may] euer (*om.* WDdP) be *add.* RSVWDdP, be Ad  be euer] *om.* RSV, euer W, and Ad  euer] ay Dd, *om.* P  stabilly] stable WBrAd  and] *om.* Ad  stalworthly] strongliche G, stalworth Br, *om.* Ad  241–2 in . . . God] with (*om.* Ad) þi hert in goddes lufe and hys drede DdAd, in goddes loue and his drede P  in] wiþ RSVWG  mouth] to *add.* WG

243–55 Ful . . . another] *om.* RSVWGDdBrPTrAd

255–6 Oure Lord] god P

256 yeueth] ȝeue Br to] *om.* TrAd and wommen] *om.* DdAd

257 þeron] holly on hem RSVWG, on Dd, on (in P) hem BrPTrAd dispend] dispendeþ SV in] on W shold] loue god þe better *add.* Tr

258 and . . . hym[1]] *om.* Tr yiftes] and þerfore *add.* RSVWG 258–9 þe . . . shame] muche is her schame þe more Tr, and nowe þen Ad

259 he] *om.* RSVDdPAd, so kyndely Tr to] *om.* RSVWGDdPAd ham] so *add.* TrAd many] *om.* Dd, riche *add.* Tr

260 or] and GDdPTrAd in] *om.* G soule] the mare is thare schame *add.* Ad Forþi] For Br, And þerfore P, *om.* Ad peyn[1]] euerlastyng peynes and tormentes Tr of] in Tr 260–1 helle . . . of] *om.* DdPAd 260–1 and . . . of] *om.* RSV 260–1 þe . . . of] *om.* WG peyn[2]] harde peynes Tr

261 restreyne] reste RSVWG, refreyne PTrAd vs[2]] in perfite loue and (*om.* G) *add.* RG perfitly] in perfyt loue *add.* SV, in perfytte loue and wisely fle W þe[1]] *om.* G lustes] loue W, lust Dd þe[2]] *om.* GBr Ad

262 lykynges] likyng WDd fro] *om.* GTrAd, al *add.* Dd þe[1]] *om.* GAd, alle P il] euel RSVGBrP, *om.* TrAd 262–4 and[2] . . . agayns] here in þis world and regne with god in ioy in þe toþer world and haue we oure truste and oure delyte on ihesu crist strongly standyng ayens alle Tr þe[2]] *om.* DdAd wicked] wrechid Br drede] dedis P lif] worlde RSVWGDdPAd and[3]] *om.* W þat] þo *add.* W, þe *add.* G, no *add.* P

263 worldis . . . þat] *om.* Ad worldis] world W bot] and P al . . . fast] euere faste hoope P al] euer RSVBr, *om.* WGDd, ay Ad oure] more R herte] hope DdAd on] in WDdBrPAd

264 manly] myȝtili P agayns] al *add.* DdPAd

265–313 Now . . . endynge] *om.* Tr 265–6 Now . . . Criste] *om.* Ad 265 I write] haf y writen here P haue] *om.* SVGDd when] wom Lt, whom RSV

266 Criste] þat loue iesus vs graunte amen *add.* P (*ends*)

267 seghynge] sittyng R, syngyng SVG, (W *corr.*), syhtyng Dd lif] loue GBr

268 Til] þat *add.* RW þe] *om.* RWG kynge] derlyng RSVG, swetynge W 268–9 so . . . fairhede] *om.* Ad faire] is *add.* R, he is *add.* W þi] his RSVWG

269 þi[1]] his SV, þe Br in] on W þi[2]] þe Br light] þou *add.* RSVWGBr

270 in[1]] wiþ RSVWG þi loue] þou *add.* RSVWG, þe Br in[2]] þi Br me[2]] to *add.* RSVWGDdBrAd

271 That] and RSVWG

272 wil] schalt G my ioy] *om.* Ad keuer] couer WGDdAd of] from Br kare] sore SV

273 me þe] *om.* Ad may] þe *add.* Ad se] þe *add.* Br hauynge] and haue RSVWG, lifand Dd, and hafe the Ad for] *om.* DdBrAd

274–5 Al . . . ware] *om.* Ad 274 coueitynge] þan *add.* W

275 þat] þou G al] *om.* Br wilnes] willes G, will DdBr

276 sauyour] sauour Br confortour] comforth WBr of] al *add.* RSVWGBrAd al my *add.* Dd þe] *om.* Dd, þou Ad

277 helpe] herte Br 277–81 when . . . leman] *om.* Ad se] þe in *add.* RSVWG

278 in] *om.* RSVWDd

279 and] *om.* Dd þyn] hem RSVWGBr, þan Dd

280 My . . . stalle] *om.* RSVWG stiddeth] stondith Br

282 loue] lore R, *om.* Br lered] tautest G

283 to þe] *om.* RSVWG fast] to þee *add.* RSVWG forþi] for þe S

284 langynge] *om.* Ad in] *om.* W brest] hert RSVWG

285 why ne ware] whyn ware Lt, whi neore SV, when war WDdAd 285–6 ledde Ful] leful W

286 Ful . . . sest] ihesu Ad Ful] for SV state] I praye þou see *add.* Ad þoght] herte G stedde] ledde Br

287 I . . . dwel] my herte dwellys Ad þe[1]] *om.* Br and[1]] I Br

288–9 Ihesu . . . rest] *om.* Ad 288 and] in RWG, to SV loue] þe ⟨me G⟩ *add.* RSVWG þynketh] me *add.* R, þink me SW, þink I me V, thynk Dd

289 My . . . brest] whenne myȝte I deȝe RSVWG may hit] *trs.* Br to[1]] and WG my[2]] and haue wiþ þe ioye and RSVW, and dwelle in ioye and G

290 to] for SV þe] it *add.* DdBr

291 Forþi] to þe RSVWG, for Dd lif] loue RSVWG, lefe Ad and my] *om.* Ad lykynge] lyfynge R[1]Dd when] why ne R[1] Br hethen] hennes RSVGBr, till the Ad

292 and my] *om.* Ad my drery] derne RSVWG delites] delite R[1]GDdBrAd art þou] *trs.* RSVWG to] of whom I RSVWG

293 my myrth] *om.* Ad myrth] and *add.* Br my[2]] and RSVWGDd

294 and my hony] *om.* Ad and] *om.* SV hony] holy Br my quert] keper G quert] and *add.* WDd, herte and Br, and alle *add.* Ad

295 I couait] my wille were RSVWG couait] desyre Ad for] *om.* SVGAd paynge] likynge RSVWG

296 Langynge . . . sent] *om.* Ad my] þi G, gret Br sent] schent W

297 þat] *om.* R is[2]] was RSV

299–300 Bot . . . desyrynge] *om.* Ad 299 to . . . hete] loue hym in myn herte G for] his G may] he he S, he V

300 And] *om.* G my[1]] *om.* SV, þi G, hys Dd and[2] . . . desyrynge] *om.* RSVWG yif] me *add.* R[1]DdBr desyrynge] ȝernynge R[1]DdBr

301 loue] my *add.* Dd, lefe Ad

302 me] both *add.* W day . . . nyght] straytely Ad

303 Til] þat *add.* RSVG hit] *om.* RSVWG, of the Ad in] *om.* Ad his . . . bryght] *om.* Ad so] *om.* G

304 and] myn GDd euer] *om.* RSVGBrAd euery] ilk a R[1]DdAd, ich W

305–6 þat . . . in] til y be in thy Ad 305 I] *om.* Br þi[2]] þe W

306 þe] me Br

307–11 Ihesu . . . twyn] *om.* Ad 307 Ihesu] my ioye fully *add.* RSVWG bigge] begge RSV, lyge W ware] me *add.* Br

308 maistry] þouȝe I shulde neuer (noȝt WG) elde *add.* RSVWG

309 þou] on me *add.* RSVW on me] *om.* RSVW Ihesu] *om.* G myght] ihesu *add.* G with . . . be] be wiþ þe RSVWG

310 To . . . þe] to loke on þe and to loue þe (*om.* W) RSVW, mekely for to loke on þe and sweteli for to loue þe G sete] setell WDd ordayn . . . me] ordeynyd before Br for me] redy RSVG

311 may] *om.* LtR[1], shul RSVWGBr, moun Dd

312 And . . . shal] of loue þenne shul we RSVWG And] þat Ad shal] maye Ad þrogh . . . shynynge] *om.* Ad in] of RSVWGDd

313 heuyn] blysse Ad endynge] ende Br, ende and fra the neuer twynne botte ay be in thy louynge Ad Amen] so be it good ihesu *add.* W

## *The Commandment*

1 comandement] commawnde H$^3$ God] oure lorde ihesu omnipotent *add.* T$^3$ is] þis *add.* BrT$^3$ oure Lord] hym as our dere and souereyne makere and agayne byar with his preciouse blode on þe rode tree on þe mounte of caluarre on þe gode fryday with hedouse peynes and stronge enterly abouen alle oþer þynge and in alle oþer þynge T$^3$ Lord] ihesu *add.* V, god *add.* T$^4$PBr hert] hertis Br

2 soule] and *add.* T$^4$P oure$^2$] mynde and *add.* P thoght] herte þorwout SV oure$^3$] *om.* T$^3$ is] *om.* T$^4$, to saye *add.* T$^3$

3 witouten] any maner of *add.* T$^3$ errynge] heryng H$^3$, erys Ii$^2$ is] to saye *add.* T$^3$ in] *om.* Lt$^2$

4 withouten] eny *add.* PT$^3$ oure] mynde or *add.* P is þat] *om.* H$^3$, is to saye T$^3$ we] *om.* Br, vnkynde wrecches of adam kynd suld *add.* T$^3$

5 hym] besily nyght and day *add.* T$^3$ withouten] any *add.* T$^3$ maner] of loue *add.* T$^3$ trewe] and *add.* T$^3$ 5–6 þat . . . wil] *om.* SV

6 is$^1$] non elles bot *add.* T$^3$ for] whi *add.* T$^3$ wylful] wonder H$^3$ of . . . thoght] *om.* H$^3$ oure] hert in som gode *add.* T$^3$ in] *om.* T$^3$

7 hit] *om.* T$^4$, þan *add.* T$^3$ receyue] rayse H$^3$, receyvith T$^4$ loue] and þe likynge *add.* T$^3$ of] suet *add.* T$^3$

8 Criste] godde son off heuyn *add.* T$^3$ and] so þat it be T$^3$ þerwith] þer þorugh Ff þat . . . be] ay T$^3$ in] þe *add.* Br of] and P

9 is] þe *add.* RSVDdFfH$^3$T$^4$Lt$^2$Ii$^2$Br þis] *om.* H$^3$, ilke *add.* T$^3$ lif] loue T$^4$P to] into T$^3$ whiche] lyffe *add.* T$^3$ al] maner of *add.* T$^3$ synnes] syn RSVDdFfT$^4$PLt$^2$Ii$^2$Br ben] is RSVDdFfT$^4$PLt$^2$Ii$^2$Br 9–10 contrarie and] *om.* SV

10 and] *om.* Br synnes] syn RSVDdFfH$^3$T$^4$PLt$^2$Ii$^2$Br, synne þat es in mannes freelte T$^3$ for] whi *add.* T$^3$ doth] driueþ SV

11 only] bot ȝit it T$^3$ þe vse] us SV, as T$^4$P, deuocion Lt$^2$Ii$^2$Br þe$^1$] *om.* Ff and] yn T$^4$PT$^3$ þe$^2$] *om.* T$^4$Lt$^2$Ii$^2$BrT$^3$ þerof] in þat tyme þat þou art out of it *add.* T$^3$ Forþi] For LtT$^3$, ⟨and P⟩ þarefore RP, forwhi SLt$^2$Ii$^2$Br al] þo *add.* T$^3$

12 wil] perfytliche *add.* SV, we Ii$^2$ God] *om.* H$^3$ perfitly] *om.* SV alonly] to *add.* FfLt$^2$Ii$^2$Br al] *om.* SVFf synnes] synne SVFfH$^3$T$^4$PIi$^2$Br

13 also] *om.* SVBr, in T$^3$ þay] he SVPIi$^2$ may] be grace of god gyffen vnto þeme *add.* T$^3$ al] *om.* SVH$^3$, maner *add.* T$^3$ synnes] synne RSVDdFfH$^3$Lt$^2$Ii$^2$Br, and þat es to seye as *add.* T$^3$ in$^2$] and RDd, *om.* FfH$^3$PLt$^2$Ii$^2$BrT$^3$ word] worth R and] in SVT$^4$

14 namely] name Br, also anoþer þinge for *add.* T$^3$ to] þat þou Lt speche] in congregacioun of pepull *add.* T$^3$ þat] is *add.* T$^4$, suche *add.* P, þat *add.* Ii$^2$T$^3$ be$^2$] þat tyme *add.* T$^3$ occupacioun] doyng T$^4$

15 good] and trewe *add.* T$^3$ thoghtes] þought FfH$^3$BrT$^3$, for *add.* T$^4$P, werkis Ii$^2$ hit] þe whuche SV, for ⟨surely T$^3$⟩ þat FfIi$^2$T$^3$, *om.* H$^3$ gretly] mykell H$^3$T$^3$

16 and] also *add.* T$^3$ þat] þei FfBr, falsely with þeir wykked and cursed tunges *add.* T$^3$ appeireth] and dispise *add.* T$^3$ lif] beynge T$^3$ wicked] and wharped *add.* T$^3$ wordes] of þe mouth *add.* T$^3$

17 al] men SV, *om.* T$^4$PT$^3$ þat$^1$] *om.* T$^3$ loueth] roses Dd bifor] forby FfLt$^2$Br al$^2$] *om.* P, ony Ii$^2$ oþer] oþeres stat P, mennes *add.* T$^3$ or þat] and SV or] elles þei *add.* T$^3$ despiseth] folily *add.* T$^3$ 17–18 any . . . safe] oþer mennes astat SV state] aste Br

18 þe$^1$] *om.* PIi$^2$T$^3$ may] *om.* T$^3$ safe] faste T$^4$, and some what able towarde his

god forsoth *add.* T$^3$ of$^1$] in Ii$^2$Br þe . . . of] our lord Ff 18–19 in . . . soule] *om.* Br

19 þe$^1$ . . . bak] a blynde man T$^4$ þe$^1$] þei Ff eigh] eiȝen SV a] þe H$^3$ bak] reremows P of$^2$] in PIi$^2$ son] when it bryghtli schynes vpon þe firmament *add.* T$^3$ For] whi *add.* T$^3$ speche] wordes Ff 19–20 and . . . wordes] *om.* SV il] idell T$^4$PLt$^2$Ii$^2$, evyl BrT$^3$

20 wordes] speche Ff ben] is þe SV, a *add.* Ff, is Ii$^2$, verrey *add.* T$^3$ signe] tokenyng T$^4$P, tokene Ii$^2$, and tokyn *add.* T$^3$ and] þat con SV, yn any T$^4$, an *add.* PIi$^2$, also *add.* T$^3$ il] euel SVT$^4$PLt$^2$Ii$^2$BrT$^3$, wickede Ff, *om.* H$^3$ þat] it *add.* H$^3$ withouten] þe *add.* RFfH$^3$T$^4$PLt$^2$Ii$^2$Br God] his makere *add.* T$^3$

21 speketh] þe *add.* Ff euer] ay RDdH$^3$, alwey Lt$^2$Ii$^2$BrT$^3$ þe] *om.* FfT$^4$Ii$^2$BrT$^3$ good] *om.* Br, of all his euen cristen wher euer so he sitteþ or standeȝ *add.* T$^3$ holdeth] hodyth Br euery] uche SVFfLt$^2$Ii$^2$Br, ilk a Dd better] in þair lyfynge *add.* T$^3$ þan] he is in his lyfe *add.* T$^3$

22 self] sothely *add.* T$^3$ wel] in þat *add.* T$^3$ he$^2$ . . . goodnesse] godenes is stablid Ii$^2$ he] *om.* H$^3$T$^4$ is . . . in$^1$] hath stablyd Br is] full sadde and *add.* T$^3$ in$^1$] and T$^4$, of gret T$^3$ in his] of T$^4$ his] *om.* PT$^3$ and] þat (also T$^3$) he is *add.* Ii$^2$T$^3$, is *add.* Br

23 ful] loue FfH$^3$ of] in Ff to] of Ii$^2$, his *add.* T$^3$ and] to *add.* SVDdH$^3$PIi$^2$ Br, to all *add.* T$^3$ neghbore] besyde hym lyfynge *add.* T$^3$

24 may] *om.* P wyn] come RP, beo SV, þe soner *add.* T$^3$ to þe] in SV, þe *add.* Br swetnesse] swetnesses T$^4$ Goddis] ihesu SV I] haue *add.* Br set] vnto þe *add.* T$^3$ here] *om.* Lt$^2$Ii$^2$

25 of loue] *om.* SV loue] lastande *add.* T$^3$ in . . . wyxynge] *om.* T$^4$P in] *om.* Ii$^2$ which] loke þat *add.* Lt$^2$Ii$^2$Br, thre *add.* T$^3$ þou] mai *add.* SVFf euer] *om.* RSVFfH$^3$Lt$^2$Ii$^2$Br, ay Dd, þorugh grace faste T$^3$ wyxynge] euer more and more *add.* SV, wysse and H$^3$, encresing Ii$^2$, in to þe plesynge and louynge of suet ihesu *add.* T$^3$ degre] *om.* SVT$^4$, loue Ff, of alle *add.* T$^3$

26 toþer] is cleped *add.* SV, secunde ⟨is T$^4$⟩ DdT$^4$PIi$^2$T$^3$ inseperabile] and *add.* T$^4$PT$^3$ þrid] is ⟨callede T$^3$⟩ *add.* SVT$^4$T$^3$ synguler] and þerfore þou salte undirstande on þis maner þat *add.* T$^3$ is] þat tyme *add.* T$^3$

27 þynge] þat is *add.* T$^3$ þat is] *om.* SV, as T$^4$P, at say *add.* H$^3$, to saye openly *add.* T$^3$ wel] welth T$^3$

28 ese] *om.* T$^4$ anguys] ne *add.* T$^4$ loue . . . fleishe] fleschly loue SV loue] lust DdT$^4$PLt$^2$Br of$^1$] þe *add.* Ii$^2$, þe foule and freel *add.* T$^3$ lykynge] lefyng H$^3$ þis] þe SV, wikked *add.* T$^3$ euer] ay RDdH$^3$T$^3$, alwey Lt$^2$Ii$^2$Br hit] *om.* T$^4$PT$^3$

29 good thoght] god RLt$^2$Br, gode SVFfH$^3$Ii$^2$ if] þogh RSVFfT$^4$Lt$^2$Ii$^2$Br, al þow P ware] neuer so *add.* T$^3$ and] also *add.* SV al] maner of *add.* T$^3$

30 so . . . loue$^1$] *om.* Ii$^2$ no] maner of *add.* T$^3$ quenche] slakne RSVDdFfH$^3$T$^4$ Lt$^2$BrT$^3$, lette P loue$^1$] but euere hit is stable in god *add.* SV is] also called *add.* T$^3$ inseperabile] þat tyme *add.* T$^3$ when] qwil H$^3$

31 and$^1$] ⟨also T$^3$⟩ alle thi *add.* RT$^3$, þi *add.* SVDdFfH$^3$T$^4$PBr holely] only FfH$^3$Lt$^2$Ii$^2$, saddely and lastandly T$^3$ in] swet *add.* T$^3$

32 Criste] and in noon oþer þinge *add.* T$^3$ tyme] not *add.* V 32–3 bot . . . hym] *om.* Lt euer] ay RDdH$^3$T$^3$, alwey Lt$^2$Ii$^2$Br þou$^2$] most *add.* SV, *om.* H$^3$Lt$^2$Ii$^2$Br, besily with stedfaste beleefe T$^3$

33 þynkest] þenken SV, þinke BrT$^3$ on] in P hym] before all oþer creatures þat euer was or ȝit sall be for whi he is þi maker and of his grete mersy he sall be þi saueour *add.* T$^3$ forþi] þerfore RFfP, *om.* T$^4$Ii$^2$, forwhi Lt$^2$, whi Br, for þat ilke skille T$^3$ hit is] *trs.* Br hit] þat loofe T$^3$ cald] verryly *add.* T$^3$ inseperabile] is *add.* Lt$^2$

34 þe] *om.* RH$^3$Lt$^2$ þoght] loue SVFfT$^3$ of] suet *add.* T$^3$ Crist] nor ȝit fro þe longhand þought of suet ihesu was godenes lastȝ aye T$^3$ Thi] that RPLt$^2$Br, þe Ii$^2$ loue] also *add.* T$^3$ is] callede *add.* T$^3$ syngulcr] and sothely þat is þat tyme *add.* T$^3$ þi] þe R

loue] also *add.* T$^{3}$ is] callede *add.* T$^{3}$ synguler] and sothely þat is þat tyme *add.* T$^{3}$ þi] þe R

35 delite] delites FfH$^{3}$, loue T$^{4}$PT$^{3}$ is] ben Ff, *om.* H$^{3}$ oþer] *om.* T$^{3}$ thynge] þou *add.* SVH$^{3}$, þanne *add.* Ff, hit may *add.* P, þat es vpon erthe *add.* T$^{3}$ fyndeth] fynd LtRT$^{4}$P, fyndes Dd, fyndest SVH$^{3}$Lt$^{2}$Ii$^{2}$Br, fyndest þou Ff, felys T$^{3}$ and] or RPLt$^{2}$Ii$^{2}$Br, ne SVT$^{3}$, noþer T$^{4}$

36 comfort] nyght nor daye *add.* T$^{3}$ degre] of loue *add.* Br stalwarth] myȝti T$^{4}$, strong PLt$^{2}$Ii$^{2}$Br and] as T$^{4}$, also *add.* T$^{3}$ hard] stronge T$^{4}$ helle] pyne *add.* T$^{3}$ for] riht *add.* SV, whi right *add.* T$^{3}$

37 al] *om.* Ii$^{2}$ thynge] thynges T$^{4}$P, here *add.* T$^{3}$ world] riht *add.* SVT$^{4}$P, vnsekir duellynge place rygth T$^{3}$ so] sothely withouten any maner of doute *add.* T$^{3}$ 37–8 in . . . soule] *om.* SV a] *om.* Ii$^{2}$Br

38 al . . . and$^{1}$] of lustes and likynges and wikked desires þe warped stirrynge ȝa and þat in all maner T$^{3}$ and$^{1}$] in P erthly] *om.* T$^{4}$ coueitynge] couaytise RSVDd FfH$^{3}$T$^{4}$Lt$^{2}$Ii$^{2}$BrT$^{3}$ and$^{2}$] also *add.* T$^{3}$ 38–41 as . . . loue] *om.* SV

39 spareth . . . men] sparres in to it all þat þedir come and noon spares þat dede þer in ben T$^{3}$ to] þe *add.* Ff bot] scharpely and vggely with [. .] tormentȝ and peynes *add.* T$^{3}$ tormenteth] doith turmentes to T$^{4}$ þerto] þedur withouten any cessynge T$^{3}$ also] so RH$^{3}$T$^{4}$PLt$^{2}$Ii$^{2}$Br

40 man] what so euer he be þat es to saye on þis maner for oppen vndrestandynge *add.* T$^{3}$ wreched] wrecchidnesse and Lt$^{2}$, wlhidnes and Ii$^{2}$, and þe nakede *add.* T$^{3}$

41 lif] werd Ff, vnsekir lyfynge T$^{3}$ also] he *add.* DdFfP, full sore and ofte he þat T$^{3}$ to suffre] *om.* Lt pyne] pynes RDdH$^{3}$Lt$^{2}$Ii$^{2}$Br, penauncȝ T$^{4}$P, many peynes anguyche and tribulaciones T$^{3}$ loue] þat hym has wrought to his awne fourme and lykenes *add.* T$^{3}$

42 Therfor] man *add.* T$^{3}$ þe$^{1}$] þou T$^{4}$PLt$^{2}$Br list] to *add.* FfBr, wylt T$^{4}$ loue$^{2}$] þou *add.* P þe$^{2}$] *om.* RSVFfH$^{3}$T$^{4}$PLt$^{2}$Ii$^{2}$BrT$^{3}$ fairest] swettest SV

43 rychest] feirest *add.* SV wisest] that euer may ben yn heuyn or yn erthe *add.* T$^{4}$ lesteth] euere *add.* SV, aye *add.* T$^{3}$

44 witeth] vanisching SV, wit is Ff, wen a deþe T$^{4}$, wendiþ PLt$^{2}$Ii$^{2}$BrT$^{3}$ sone] *om.* SV, clene Br away] and *add.* SVFfT$^{4}$PT$^{3}$, for *add.* Lt$^{2}$Ii$^{2}$Br 44–5 noght . . . deserueth] *om.* Dd noght] *om.* T$^{4}$, no þyng PBr þat] is *add.* T$^{4}$ falleth] fallynge T$^{4}$, longeþ PIi$^{2}$ dwellynge] euer foydyng T$^{4}$, abidynge Ii$^{2}$

45 bot . . . deserueth] and hit deseruyth peyne but it be refreyned T$^{4}$ þat . . . deserueth] and wo SV deserueth] deserued R, þerfore *add.* SV, But *add.* T$^{4}$ good] god LtFfT$^{3}$

46 hym$^{1}$] ⟨þou p⟩ ihesu cryst T$^{4}$P and$^{1}$] þat SV shalt haue] hast RSVFfH$^{3}$T$^{4}$P Lt$^{2}$Ii$^{2}$Br good] godnes of SV, god Ff hym$^{2}$] ihesu crist T$^{4}$ þe] þou SVIi$^{2}$Br

47 want] non good nyn *add.* Ff, lacke T$^{4}$, faile P no] gode *add.* Ii$^{2}$ If] þe *add.* Ff hym] swetliche *add.* SV

48 may perisshe] schal faile Ii$^{2}$ þe] *om.* Br of] in Br þis] the T$^{4}$T$^{3}$ feynt] fayre T$^{3}$

49 and fals] *om.* Br and$^{1}$] *om.* Ii$^{2}$ and$^{2}$] but SV, in T$^{4}$, *om.* P fallynge] failyng RSVDdFfH$^{3}$T$^{4}$PLt$^{2}$Ii$^{2}$T$^{3}$, fayle Br nede] for *add.* Lt$^{2}$Ii$^{2}$Br þai . . . in] þe beyen vn Ff and$^{3}$] but SVBr

50 bitterer] ⟨as Br⟩ bitter SVH$^{3}$PBr þan] eny *add.* SVT$^{3}$, þe *add.* DdFfH$^{3}$T$^{4}$, as Br galle] worse þen eny atter and *add.* SV can nat] coueyte P withouten] with P felewship] forþi *add.* H$^{3}$

51 lift] vp *add.* SVLt$^{2}$Ii$^{2}$Br, hef vp P þoght] herte SVBr, vp *add.* Ff þat] and Ii$^{2}$ may] schalt Ii$^{2}$ fele] fynd Dd, *om.* T$^{4}$ and] alle *add.* Ff, with ⟨his Br⟩ *add.* T$^{4}$Br

52 halowes] holy men T$^{4}$P, in heuen *add.* Lt$^{2}$BrT$^{3}$, seyntis in heuene Ii$^{2}$ þe$^{1}$] *om.* P which] the *add.* T$^{4}$ wil] *om.* T$^{3}$ þe$^{2}$] well *add.* T$^{3}$ God] gode and preye for þe SV let] lede SVT$^{4}$PT$^{3}$ þi] *om.* Ff

53 dothe] þerfore *add.* SV Restreyne] Refreyne T$^4$Lt$^2$Ii$^2$Br a while] ay wele H$^3$, *om.* P al] thy *add.* T$^4$ lust] lustis FfBr and] yn T$^4$ lykynge] likyngis FfBr

54 aftreward] *om.* Br hit shal] to T$^4$PT$^3$ clensed] of synne *add.* T$^4$

55 þe$^1$] ȝe T$^4$, þou Lt$^2$Br shal] wil R, ne wol SV, *om.* DdFfH$^3$ lust] to *add.* RLt$^2$Ii$^2$BrT$^3$ do] *om.* T$^4$P þat$^2$] þat *add.* SVDdFfPT$^3$, *om.* Lt$^2$ is] to ⟨þe V⟩ *add.* VH$^3$Lt$^2$, xal be to þe Br, may be T$^3$ paynge] plesyng T$^4$PIi$^2$BrT$^3$ to] of DdH$^3$Lt$^2$Br, almyghty *add.* T$^4$ God] and *add.* SVLt$^2$Ii$^2$Br þe$^2$] þou Ii$^2$Br

56 list] to *add.* FfT$^4$Lt$^2$Ii$^2$Br hit at] all T$^4$ þe] þi Lt, *om.* H$^3$, þo T$^3$ Goddis loue] þe loue of god Ii$^2$T$^3$ when] þou art and *add.* Ff

57 feleth] fyndeþ Lt$^2$Ii$^2$ in] ihesu *add.* SVFfT$^4$Ii$^2$T$^3$ þe] thou T$^4$PLt$^2$Br nat] luitel SV, speke ne *add.* T$^4$ to] *om.* RFfH$^3$ ne iangle] *om.* T$^4$ ne] or to SV, to *add.* Lt$^2$Ii$^2$ of] to SV, ihesu *add.* FfT$^4$ Crist] þi lord and *add.* S, þi frend and *add.* V

58 dure] dreghe RSVDdFfH$^3$, suffir T$^4$P, endure T$^3$ sit] or to be *add.* T$^4$ on] selfe T$^4$PLt$^2$Ii$^2$Br vse] enforse T$^3$ stalwarthly] myȝtli T$^4$T$^3$, strongly P his] þis Lt, cristis T$^4$

59 shal$^1$] woll T$^4$ stabilly] stable þe and SV þat] to Ii$^2$ þe$^2$] thi T$^4$ solace] ioye SV þis] þe ST$^4$ shal$^2$] miȝte SV

60 mowe] *om.* SVDdT$^4$Br for] fro H$^3$ þe$^2$] ne *add.* SV, þou Lt$^2$Ii$^2$Br wil] schalt Lt$^2$Ii$^2$Br þerof] And *add.* Lt$^2$Ii$^2$Br

61 on] self RSVDdFfH$^3$T$^4$PLt$^2$Ii$^2$BrT$^3$ be euer] And þerfore SV euer] ay RDdH$^3$, all gate T$^4$, alwey PLt$^2$Ii$^2$BrT$^3$ til] to that T$^4$ cum] on þe *add.* SV oþer] beo euere SV praier] or in redynge or in writynge *add.* T$^3$

62 oþer] or in good deuocioun or Ff gode] *om.* Lt$^2$Ii$^2$ meditaciouns] meditacioun RSVDdFfH$^3$T$^4$PLt$^2$Ii$^2$BrT$^3$ ordeyn] ordand Dd praiynge] prayingis T$^4$ and$^2$] *om.* SVLt$^2$Ii$^2$BrT$^3$ wakynge] werkynge Ff, walkynge T$^4$

63 þat . . . be] *om.* P be] don *add.* SVLt$^2$Ii$^2$BrT$^3$ in] with SV, be Br discrecioun] and *add.* H$^3$, but *add.* Lt$^2$Ii$^2$Br

64 litel] but in a good mene *add.* SV Bot] and SV þynke] *om.* SV euer] ay RDdH$^3$, þenkynge *add.* SV, alwey Lt$^2$Ii$^2$BrT$^3$ þat . . . þynge] on þeose þinges þat SV of . . . þynge] *om.* Ii$^2$ of al] *om.* P of] ouer Ff þynge] thinges RFf, þat *add.* PLt$^2$Br most] þat *add.* Ff coueiteth] quemeth RFfLt$^2$BrT$^3$, pleseþ SVT$^4$PIi$^2$, conueniens H$^3$ God] þe whuche is stable *add.* SV, þe *add.* Dd, ys *add.* PLt$^2$Br loue] lufs H$^3$, *om.* Br of] a *add.* SV, *om.* Br

65 forþi] þarefore RSVT$^4$P, þerfore y rede þe ⟨þat þoue Ii$^2$⟩ Lt$^2$Ii$^2$Br seke] þinke T$^3$ any] vnskilful *add.* Lt$^2$Ii$^2$Br

66–7 for . . . penaunce] *om.* SV 66–72 bot . . . ioy] *om.* T$^4$P

67 euer] ay RDdFfH$^3$, alwei Ii$^2$BrT$^3$ þe] *om.* Br wheþer] wher Lt$^2$, þat *add.* Br litel] mykel RSVDdH$^3$Lt$^2$Ii$^2$Br mych] lytel ⟨but SV⟩ RSVDdH$^3$, lytel And þerfore Lt$^2$Ii$^2$Br Be] euer *add.* SV aboutward] aboute ⟨inwardli Lt$^2$Ii$^2$⟩ SVLt$^2$Ii$^2$, about in worldely Br

68 in] al *add.* RSVFfH$^3$, wiþ alle Lt$^2$Ii$^2$Br þi myght] þat þou maiȝt SV, þin herte Br þat . . . gyfen] to ȝeue þe Lt$^2$Ii$^2$Br loue] *om.* H$^3$ Crist] so *add.* Lt$^2$Ii$^2$Br

69 for . . . soule] *om.* Lt$^2$Ii$^2$Br noght] what so SV, na thyng DdLt$^2$Ii$^2$Br þat] *om.* SV, eny *add.* Lt$^2$Ii$^2$Br men] man Lt$^2$Ii$^2$Br myght] may RDdH$^3$T$^3$, *om.* SV, can Lt$^2$Ii$^2$Br say] do Dd do] to þe *add.* SVLt$^2$Ii$^2$Br, say Dd 69–70 mak . . . sory] be it good or euyl be þou neiþer (neuer Br) glad ne sori þerof þat is to sey be þou noȝt glad whanne men preisen þee ne sory whanne men lacken þe Lt$^2$Ii$^2$Br mak þe] þou beo not SV mak] made RFfH$^3$

70 þy] þe Br within] þe *add.* H$^3$, *om.* T$^3$ in] þe *add.* RDdH$^3$BrT$^3$, with Ff of] ihesu *add.* Ff loue] and *add.* SVDdLt$^2$Ii$^2$BrT$^3$

71 in$^1$] þe *add.* Ff delite . . . ese] eorþliche vanites SV erthly] worldely T$^3$ ese] ne *add.* RSVDdFfT$^3$, gude H$^3$ 71–2 in$^2$ . . . þe$^1$] *om.* H$^3$ in$^2$] and Lt$^2$Ii$^2$Br

praysynge] louyng RSVDdFfLt$^2$BrT$^3$ 71–2 if . . . ioy] But Lt$^2$Ii$^2$Br if] when Dd begyn] began RFf

72 ne . . . ioy] þenk not þeron SV ne] *om.* Dd ioy] but *add.* SV in$^2$] to SVIi$^2$ he] *om.* T$^4$ to] *om.* SVT$^4$P þe$^2$] thing *add.* R, skilfully *add.* T$^3$

73 praiest] to *add.* SV for] *om.* RSVDdFfH$^3$Lt$^2$Br, of T$^4$PIi$^2$T$^3$ skylfully] for *add.* Lt$^2$Ii$^2$Br, in ryghtwisnes and resoun T$^3$ 73–4 to . . . to] that a cristen soule T$^4$P Cristen . . . soule] skylful men Ii$^2$ mannys] mennes RFf

74 seche] þe loue *add.* SV and$^1$] to *add.* SV aske] of god *add.* H$^3$ of] vr lord *add.* SV Ihesu] *om.* Br hit] we SV, he Lt$^2$Ii$^2$Br, þai T$^3$

75 hym$^1$] hertiliche swetliche deuoutliche and *add.* SV outcastynge] caste awei þe SV, all *add.* T$^4$

76 worldes . . . bisynesse] alle þe þouȝtis and besynes of þe (þis Br) worlde Lt$^2$Ii$^2$Br il] iuel RSVT$^4$PT$^3$, wickede Ff bisynesse] bisynesses V And] For SV þou$^1$] *om.* Lt$^2$

77 and] in T$^4$ no] *om.* Ff loue] lust RSVFfH$^3$T$^4$PLt$^2$Ii$^2$BrT$^3$ þi] *om.* Ff, þe Ii$^2$Br anguys] angrynge RFfH$^3$Lt$^2$Ii$^2$Br, anger SV, angers DdT$^4$PT$^3$

78 world] worldli T$^4$ ne hatreden] *om.* Br ne$^2$] of H$^3$ men] mon SV þe$^1$] *om.* RH$^3$, nat *add.* Ii$^2$ nat] thoght H$^3$, *om.* Ii$^2$ in] to bodili *add.* Lt$^2$, to worldly *add.* Ii$^2$, to *add.* Br

79 of] and Lt$^2$Ii$^2$ bodily] *om.* Lt$^2$, worldly Ii$^2$ þynges] þing ⟨þenne SV⟩ SVDd FfH$^3$T$^4$PT$^3$, and *add.* Ii$^2$

80 þat$^1$] *om.* SV hit] *om.* Ii$^2$ is] *om.* SV delitabiler] more dilytable SVLt$^2$Ii$^2$, more delectable Br in . . . houre] more merie Br al] þe *add.* RSVDdFfH$^3$Lt$^2$Ii$^2$ BrT$^3$ welth] of þis world *add.* SV þat . . . se] in þis worlde or Br here] in þis worlde *add.* Lt$^2$Ii$^2$ se] þat *add.* Ff, in all þis brood warld or elles þat *add.* T$^3$ may] be *add.* RFfH$^3$T$^4$PLt$^2$Ii$^2$BrT$^3$, þauȝ we mihte lyue *add.* SV

82 And] þenne SV and] or T$^4$PBrT$^3$ for$^1$] from FfIi$^2$ temptacíouns] temptacion V for$^2$] fro FfIi$^2$, *om.* Br for$^3$] fro Ii$^2$

83 ouer] *om.* SVT$^4$ myche] *om.* SV of] to Ii$^2$ if] þow PLt$^2$Ii$^2$Br þe] that *add.* T$^4$Br, þo *add.* Ii$^2$ þynge] þingis Lt$^2$Ii$^2$

84 nat trewly] vntreuli Lt$^2$Ii$^2$Br, not of hym T$^3$ nat] Nou SV He] god P, crist Ii$^2$ þat$^1$] *om.* SVH$^3$T$^4$P

85 þay . . . hym$^2$] *om.* SV þay] tho T$^4$, ho P, he Lt$^2$Ii$^2$Br hym$^1$] þay *add.* T$^4$P shal] shold R

86 sithes] tyme Ii$^2$ þan] *om.* SV

87 right] wel SV, ryghtfulliche T$^4$, weel *add.* Lt$^2$Ii$^2$Br euer] *om.* RSVH$^3$T$^4$PLt$^2$Ii$^2$ Br, ay Dd, o Ff, in all tyme T$^3$ erthly] erly P ioy] ioyes Ff, þinge Br

88 þogh] *om.* SV, if DdH$^3$T$^3$ þou wake] *trs.* SV Crist . . . fynd] þou maiȝt not fynde him SV fynd] *om.* H$^3$ he] crist Ff is nat] wol not beo SV

89 har] þat SV lyveth in] loue T$^4$

90 willet] went SVLt$^2$Ii$^2$, *om.* T$^4$P, whylede awaye T$^3$ hir] scho *add.* DdT$^4$PLt$^2$Ii$^2$ Br, whedir þat his will was sche *add.* T$^3$ soght] him ⟨sore SV⟩ *add.* SVDdFfT$^4$PLt$^2$Ii$^2$BrT$^3$ gretynge] wepyng RSVPLt$^2$Ii$^2$Br, bothen *add.* Ff, full T$^4$ his] hir SVT$^4$PIi$^2$ kynreden] frendis Ii$^2$

91 hirs] hisen SVT$^4$PIi$^2$ sechynge] schetyng and her sorowyng R, serwynges SV, and hir (*om.* Ii$^2$) sorwynge *add.* FfH$^3$Lt$^2$Ii$^2$Br til] forte P

92 in] *om.* H$^3$ 92–3 sittynge . . . hyrynge] techinge SV sittynge] *om.* T$^3$

93 answarynge] and *add.* Lt$^2$Ii$^2$Br þe] to *add.* SVFfT$^4$PLt$^2$Ii$^2$Br do] *om.* T$^3$ wil] wolde Br

94 sek] him *add.* SVDdFfH$^3$T$^4$PT$^3$ inwardly] in wordly T$^4$ in] *om.* T$^4$ trouth] þat is feiþ *add.* P, feiþ Ii$^2$, trewe Br and$^1$] in SVP, *om.* H$^3$Lt$^2$Ii$^2$Br, yn *add.* T$^4$ and$^2$] in SV, in *add.* T$^4$P of . . . chirche] *om.* Ii$^2$

95 al$^1$] þi *add.* SV, of T$^4$ syn] synnes SVFf and] *om.* SVDdP hatynge] hate T$^4$Br hit] hem SV þi] his Ff þat] oonly synne T$^4$ hym]hem SV, out *add.* Ii$^2$

96 þe] *om.* T$^4$PY þou] ne *add.* SV herdes] herdemen T$^3$, shepherds P hym$^2$] *om.* RY

97 crib] cracche T$^4$, cradel P, maniowr Br, full straytte stalle T$^3$ by] *om.* LtRDd FfH$^3$Lt$^2$Ii$^2$BrT$^3$Y, in ensaumple SV, bytokenynge T$^4$P þat] *om.* T$^4$, schal *add.* Lt$^2$Ii$^2$ Br, and T$^3$ þou knowe] *om.* T$^4$P þou] þerfore T$^3$ knowe] him *add.* SV if] that *add.* T$^4$

98 þou] wolte *add.* T$^4$P verraily] warly H$^3$, for þan *add.* Ii$^2$ þe] þou SV behoueth] most SV, to *add.* FfT$^4$Lt$^2$Ii$^2$Br to] *om.* RSVDdFfH$^3$T$^4$PLt$^2$Ii$^2$Br nat] in þe wei *add.* SV

99 sterre] sterres T$^4$ þre] *om.* T$^4$PT$^3$ in] *om.* Br Bedleem] and *add.* T$^4$P

100 swedled in] in swethil R, in swaþelyng SVFfLt$^2$Ii$^2$BrY, yn symple T$^4$P, in suylke araye and T$^3$ cloutes] clathes H$^3$T$^4$P, *om.* T$^3$ sympilly] symple FfH$^3$BrT$^3$Y, *om.* T$^4$P barne] childe ⟨and T$^4$Lt$^2$Ii$^2$Br⟩ RSVT$^4$PLt$^2$Ii$^2$Br Therby] þou maiȝt *add.* SV, maist þou *add.* Lt$^2$Br, herby þou miȝt Ii$^2$ vndrestond] þat *add.* RFfH$^3$PLt$^2$Ii$^2$ BrY, þe *add.* SV, the that *add.* T$^4$

101 in pride] *om.* Br and] in *add.* SV vanyte] vanites Ff 101–9 How . . . forbedeth] Also SV

102 bot] a *add.* H$^3$T$^4$PLt$^2$Ii$^2$BrT$^3$ seruaunt] and subiecte *add.* T$^3$ riche] riches T$^4$P

103 spouse . . . þi] *om.* Ii$^2$ yed] but *add.* Ii$^2$, deied Br a] on R

104 al] þat *add.* T$^4$, þe cloþis *add.* Ii$^2$ had] weryd P on] vppon hym Ff, And *add.* Lt$^2$Ii$^2$Br Forþi] þarefore RFfT$^4$PLt$^2$Ii$^2$Br rede] þe *add.* T$^4$Lt$^2$Ii$^2$Br þat$^2$] *om.* Y þou] *om.* H$^3$P

105 of] with H$^3$, þyn *add.* P outrage] outragiousnesse Lt$^2$Ii$^2$Br wil] wolde T$^4$

106 hast] *om.* H$^3$ mestier] nede T$^4$PLt$^2$Ii$^2$Br of] to T$^4$ more] as *add.* Br seid] bad FfH$^3$

107 þai] one T$^3$ two . . . haue] *om.* RDdT$^4$PLt$^2$Ii$^2$BrT$^3$Y as] so Lt$^2$Ii$^2$

108 with] and *add.* Ii$^2$

109 outrageous] owtrage DdT$^4$Y, outtragiousnesse and ⟨veyn Lt$^2$Ii$^2$⟩ FfLt$^2$Ii$^2$, gret outrage and T$^3$ bisynesse] and *add.* P, drede T$^3$ 109–11 þat . . . on] *om.* T$^3$ forbedeth] profrith þe to haue Br

110 loue] son *add.* T$^4$ is] a *add.* Br tresoure] and *add.* Lt$^2$Ii$^2$Br ful$^2$] a Br and] *om.* Ff, a *add.* Br

111 to . . . on] ⟨for FfBr⟩ a (*om.* T$^4$Lt$^2$) mon to trusten on (þervppon FfBr, theron T$^4$) SVFfT$^4$PLt$^2$Ii$^2$Br to] *om.* H$^3$ a] *om.* RDdH$^3$Y man] men RH$^3$ on] and *add.* P Forþi] þarefore RP, forwhi Lt$^2$Ii$^2$Br he] ne *add.* V

112 and] ne SVH$^3$PLt$^2$Ii$^2$Br to] *om.* H$^3$ þe] þat SVP, *om.* Ii$^2$ which] *om.* SV

113 wil] not *add.* Lt$^2$ hit] *om.* Ff ar] *om.* R, rather FfT$^4$Lt$^2$Ii$^2$Br, titter H$^3$, raþerly P þay] *om.* PLt$^2$Ii$^2$Br wold] wil RDdH$^3$Lt$^2$Y or . . . wold] than any tyme T$^4$, þan P wold] schulde Ff, wolen Lt$^2$

114 And] For SV, in *add.* Br, þer wille T$^3$ wise] a *add.* Br doth] wol do no (*om.* V) SV precious] þinge or *add.* T$^4$

115 in . . . clene] *om.* SV clene] vessell *add.* T$^4$ as] also RFfH$^3$Lt$^2$BrY, riht so doþ SV, so T$^4$P, so þerfor Ii$^2$ Crist] he *add.* SV foul] soule Br herte] which is harde Br 115–16 in$^2$ . . . and] *om.* SVLt$^2$Ii$^2$Br in$^2$] fyled with many diuers T$^3$

116 bounden] in synne or *add.* SV, wiþ synne and *add.* Lt$^2$Ii$^2$Br in$^1$] with Lt$^2$Br, *om.* Ii$^2$ vile] ful Ff, foule T$^4$Lt$^2$Ii$^2$Br lust] lustis Ii$^2$Br of] þe *add.* FfT$^4$PIi$^2$Br fleishe] flesschlyche T$^4$ 116–17 in$^2$ . . . in] he setteþ his loue in a fair herte and in a clene and ful of SV clene] fayre DdFfH$^3$T$^4$PLt$^2$Ii$^2$BrT$^3$Y

117 faire] clene DdFfH$^3$T$^4$PLt$^2$Ii$^2$BrT$^3$Y in vertuȝ] and vertuouse Ff in] and ful of Br Natforþi] neuerþeles T$^4$Lt$^2$Ii$^2$Br, neuerþelater P made] so *add.* RDdP Lt$^2$Ii$^2$BrT$^3$Y, so fayre and *add.* T$^4$ so] *om.* RSVDdFfH$^3$T$^4$PLt$^2$Ii$^2$BrT$^3$Y a] *om.* RSVFfH$^3$T$^4$PLt$^2$Ii$^2$T$^3$Y

118 der] derwarde P thynge] ful *add.* Ff, and precious *add.* Lt$^2$Ii$^2$Br sauely] *om.* SVIi$^2$ done] put Ii$^2$T$^3$ sith] tyme Ii$^2$ purgeth] clanseþ SV

119 many] a SV, a *add.* T$^4$PLt$^2$Ii$^2$BrT$^3$ synful] foule T$^4$ mannys] *om.* T$^4$PLt$^2$Ii$^2$Br his] *om.* SV to] taken and *add.* Ff

120 þe] that T$^4$ his$^2$] owne derlynge yn (and P) his *add.* T$^4$P wonnyngested] dwellyng place (stede Br) PBr

121 holynesse] almesse Ff euer] ay RDdH$^3$Y, *om.* SVT$^3$, alwey Lt$^2$Ii$^2$Br clenner] more clene þat SV, þat *add.* Br 121–2 of heuyn] *om.* SV

122 heuyn] ihesu *add.* Ff þerin] and *add.* P forþi] þarefore RP, for H$^3$Lt$^2$Ii$^2$BrT$^3$ at] þat Ff, *om.* Br when] þat Br

123 God] good P, gode Ii$^2$ fele] flele V, fle Br swet licour] swetnes SV bene] *om.* T$^4$ wel] *om.* H$^3$T$^4$ 123–4 þe . . . God] goddes seruice RSVDdFfH$^3$T$^4$PLt$^2$Ii$^2$BrY, cristes seruice T$^3$

124 and$^1$] til *add.* T$^4$, forto *add.* P, þat *add.* Ii$^2$ be] clene *add.* SV prayers] preyere SV and$^2$] *om.* H$^3$

125 and] in T$^4$ in$^1$] of T$^3$

126 in] his *add.* T$^4$PBr, goddis *add.* Lt$^2$Ii$^2$ loue] to god *add.* Ff if] þat *add.* SV do] sett T$^4$ myght and] *om.* H$^3$ myght] trauayle T$^4$PY trauail] all his myght T$^4$PY, euery *add.* Br

127 blessed] blisful Ff, suet T$^3$ is] fastned *add.* Lt$^2$Ii$^2$Br

128 to$^1$] *om.* SVDd euer] ay RDdH$^3$, *om.* T$^4$PY, alwey Lt$^2$Ii$^2$Br, sodenly T$^3$

129 sum] *om.* Br lykynge] plesyng SV in$^1$] *om.* P prayinge] wakynge *add.* SV, paying T$^4$ in$^2$] *om.* SVP

130 worchynge] sum *add.* SV, is *add.* T$^4$ þynge] thynges DdFfIi$^2$ Ihesu Crist] cristes passyon Dd 130–1 and . . . thoght] *om.* SV 130–1 and . . . Criste] *om.* Br

131 þat . . . thoght] *om.* T$^4$P neuer] not RDdFfH$^3$Lt$^2$Ii$^2$BrT$^3$Y his] þis Br, þi T$^3$

132 glad] bodily affye T$^3$ þe] *corr. to* þenke P 132–3 and . . . hym] *om.* FfT$^4$ nat in] in no Br in$^2$] non *add.* SV other] veyne *add.* Ii$^2$

133 þynge] þynges of vanyte P and] þenne *add.* SV wil] *om.* Dd kastynge] cast Ii$^2$Br thoghtes] thoght H$^3$

134 Bot] *om.* T$^4$P if] *om.* H$^3$Br and tak] takyng P, of *add.* Ff, an *add.* T$^4$P oþer] in delyt *add.* SV þan] of *add.* Ff and$^2$] or SV, If þou H$^3$ thynge] þinges SVFfBr

135 dost] hast don RVDdFfH$^3$T$^4$Lt$^2$Ii$^2$BrT$^3$Y, hast forsaken SP

136 syn] vayne louynge T$^3$

137 Wherfor] þerfore SVIi$^2$, for *add.* Ff, where Br 137–8 þat$^1$ . . . worchynge] *om.* SV trewly] I wole þat þou *add.* Lt$^2$Ii$^2$Br, weel abouen all oþer þinge T$^3$ vndrestond] vndirstode Br

138 þynges] þat is *add.* Ii$^2$ in$^3$] *om.* Br and] in RDdH$^3$T$^4$T$^3$Y, in *add.* FfPLt$^2$Ii$^2$

139 Chaunge] Couche Ii$^2$ cast hit] thynke T$^3$ hit] al *add.* SVT$^3$ holy] only FfT$^4$PT$^3$Y on] to T$^4$, in P

140 þe] and *add.* SV Chaunge] Couche Ii$^2$ þi] þouȝt and þi *add.* SV mouth] thouȝt T$^4$ vnnayte] variytee Lt, vnprofitable R, vanites SV, vanite Ff, veyn T$^4$PT$^3$Y, ydel Lt$^2$Ii$^2$Br and$^1$] fro *add.* SV 140–1 and$^2$ . . . hym] *om.* SV

141–4 Chaunge . . . perfitnes] and kepe þe and þerfore loue him treweliche stalworþliche studefastliche and sweteliche and SV 141 Chaunge] Couche Ii$^2$ hand] honden RDdH$^3$T$^4$PLt$^2$Ii$^2$Br fro] þe *add.* Dd workes] werk RH$^3$, werkyng Ff

142 vanytees] vanyte T$^4$PLt$^2$Br lift] loue T$^4$, let P ham] hym T$^4$, vp *add.* Lt$^2$Ii$^2$ for] to gete *add.* T$^4$P

143 so] *om.* R, þan DdH$^3$T$^4$PIi$^2$ þou louest] salte þou loofe T$^3$ louest] him *add.* RFfH$^3$T$^4$PLt$^2$Ii$^2$BrT$^3$ þou gost] sal þou go T$^3$ þou$^2$] *om.* Dd gost] þan *add.* T$^4$P þe$^2$] perfyȝt *add.* T$^4$

144 so] *om.* SV hym] so *add.* SV receyue] no *add.* T$^4$

145 ioy . . . worldes] *om.* SV sorowe] worschipe Lt$^2$Ii$^2$Br and . . . nat] so þat noon T$^3$ and] ne SVIi$^2$ nat] ne SV, no Dd, neyþer Ff anguys] angres SVFfIi$^2$, angyre H$^3$, anguissches Lt$^2$ or] ne DdFfIi$^2$Br, and Lt$^2$ noy] nuyȝees or mischeef or seknes SV, noys FfLt$^2$Ii$^2$Br, sorowe T$^4$ bifal] by fals T$^4$ bodily] *om.* SV

146 on . . . frendes] deth of þi frendes draugh þi mynde from hym T$^3$ on$^1$] to SV on$^2$] to SV, of H$^3$Br, in T$^4$, *om.* Lt$^2$Ii$^2$ bot] bothe T$^4$ al] *om.* T$^4$ to] *om.* SVT$^4$

147 euer] ay RDdH$^3$, alwey Lt$^2$Ii$^2$Br, þan mekely T$^3$ of] for Ff sondes] sonde T$^4$P may] *om.* R

148 in] to Br 148–9 For . . . loue] *om.* SVH$^3$ if] *om.* Br hert] owther *add.* Dd led] ouer hyed T$^4$ oþer] *om.* DdT$^4$ worldes] lufe or *add.* Ii$^2$ drede] dede Ff or] with *add.* T$^4$P

149 ferre] feire Lt þe . . . loue] cristis loue and his swetnesse T$^4$PT$^3$ of] ihesu *add.* Ff

150 And] *om.* T$^4$P wel] *om.* T$^4$P, varly T$^3$ be] *om.* T$^3$ as] þis *add.* SV

151 þe] *om.* RP þat is] *om.* P peynted] poynted T$^4$ richely] *om.* H$^3$

152 within] it is *add.* Ii$^2$, ben *add.* Br, is nouȝt elles founden bot *add.* T$^3$ reten . . . bones] stinkynde bones rotynge SV reten] *om.* T$^4$, beþ P, rotyn and (*om.* BrT$^3$) Lt$^2$Ii$^2$BrT$^3$ stynkynge] stynke and Lt bones] and *add.* SVLt$^2$Ii$^2$Br

153 þe$^1$] *om.* Br name] man Ff þat$^1$] *om.* SVT$^4$ þe$^2$] *om.* SV

154 falleth] longiþ Ii$^2$ to] þe *add.* FfT$^4$ religione] of *add.* SV, for *add.* Lt$^2$Ii$^2$Br habit] þen to þe name for hit *add.* SV, clothynge wydde and sydde what of coloure so it be wylke is called þin abyte makes þe nether frere ne monke ne chanon ne heremite bot it T$^3$ þat$^1$] *om.* SV world] and *add.* H$^3$T$^4$PLt$^2$Ii$^2$Br 154–5 þat$^2$ . . . gyffen] and ȝiuen þe SV

155 seruyce] loke þou þenne *add.* SV, and *add.* H$^3$T$^4$PIi$^2$Br, so *add.* T$^3$ delite] delited Lt$^2$ þe] *om.* H$^3$T$^4$PIi$^2$Br in] none *add.* Ii$^2$ erthly] wordly P

156 thynge] þinges bot SV þan] *om.* SVT$^3$, þou H$^3$ þat] *om.* Ii$^2$ hit$^1$] so *add.* P hert] withinne *add.* SV in$^2$] to SV mennys] mannes Lt$^2$Ii$^2$ sight] withouten *add.* SV, eghen H$^3$

157 may . . . þe] makeþ SV make] be in H$^3$ religious] religiouns H$^3$ 157–8 vertuȝ . . . in] clennes and vertus in soule of Lt$^2$, clennes of soule and vertu of Ii$^2$ of] in SVBr

158 in] and SV, and in Br charitee] þen *add.* SV, and *add.* Lt$^2$Ii$^2$Br ordre] asketh and *add.* Ff

159 within] for *add.* PLt$^2$Ii$^2$Br þi] þe Ff

160 fro] of SVFfH$^3$ and$^1$] lett it ben *add.* Br lapped] happed RSVDdFfH$^3$Lt$^2$Ii$^2$ BrT$^3$, wrappid T$^4$P in] with SV loue] of god *add.* P and$^2$] in *add.* SVIi$^2$ mekenesse] and *add.* Lt$^2$Ii$^2$ 160–6 Drede . . . thynge$^2$] *om.* SV Drede] so *add.* Ii$^2$, And Br

161 so] *om.* Ii$^2$ nat] and *add.* Lt$^2$Ii$^2$Br

162 hel] helde RDd*FfT$^3$, hald H$^3$, holde T$^4$PLt$^2$Ii$^2$Br out . . . þe] the out of FfT$^4$P, fro þe T$^3$ al] maner of *add.* Lt$^2$Ii$^2$Br synnes] and *add.* Lt$^2$Ii$^2$Br away] all *add.* T$^4$ slownes] and *add.* Lt$^2$Br, slouþe and Ii$^2$, ydulnes T$^3$ Vse] be T$^3$ þe] also T$^3$ manly] namly H$^3$T$^4$PBr goodnesse] and *add.* Lt$^2$Ii$^2$Br

163 debonair] þou boner Ff, debour Br, boner Dd$^2$ meke] buxum Ff men] and *add.* Lt$^2$Ii$^2$Br in] *om.* RDd

164 ir] wretthe FfP or] ne to T$^4$, ne in P, in to *add.* Br, and T$^3$ enuy] and *add.*

Br   Dight] make Lt$^2$Ii$^2$Br   soule] þer *add.* Br   faire] and *add.* DdLt$^2$Ii$^2$Br   make] þer *add.* T$^4$Lt$^2$, meke Br   þerin] in Br   toure] trone RFfH$^3$T$^4$PLt$^2$Ii$^2$BrT$^3$ Dd$^2$

165 mak] gar DdFfH$^3$, put T$^4$, ȝif Lt$^2$Ii$^2$BrDd$^2$, compelle T$^3$   be couaitous] *om.* T$^4$P   to] *om.* T$^4$

166 loued] louyst Br   thynge$^2$] þingeȝ and Lt$^2$Br, þingis þan Ii$^2$

167 þoght] þouȝtes SVT$^3$   167–84 and . . . hym] *om.* SV   and] with a (*om.* T$^4$) *add.* T$^4$P   desire] ȝernyng DdFfDd$^2$, ȝernyngs H$^3$, ȝernynge yn to god T$^4$, desires T$^3$   no] not Br

168 in$^1$] withynne Ff   þe] þi saule ne ȝit in þi consciens T$^3$   when] þat RDdFf H$^3$T$^4$PLt$^2$Ii$^2$BrT$^3$Dd$^2$   art] be RDdFfH$^3$T$^4$PLt$^2$Ii$^2$BrT$^3$Dd$^2$   faire] as blosme *add.* Ff

169 eghen] egh H$^3$, siȝht Lt$^2$BrT$^3$, siȝt þe Ii$^2$   Fairhede] Fayrenesse T$^4$PLt$^2$Ii$^2$Br   þe] þi R*DdFfLt$^2$Ii$^2$BrDd$^2$, *om.* H$^3$T$^4$PT$^3$   þat] *om.* T$^4$P   that is] *trs.* RDdFfH$^3$Lt$^2$ Ii$^2$BrT$^3$Dd$^2$, as that T$^4$P   to] þou RDdFfH$^3$T$^4$PLt$^2$Ii$^2$BrDd$^2$, þou þan þorough þat T$^3$   and] *om.* PIi$^2$T$^3$

170 and$^1$] *om.* RDdFfH$^3$T$^4$PLt$^2$T$^3$Dd$^2$   suffrynge] pacient P, and *add.* Lt$^2$Ii$^2$Br   neuer] and be not T$^4$   gurche] irk RDdFfH$^3$Dd$^2$, slow T$^4$, wery PLt$^2$Ii$^2$Br, full ne yrke T$^3$   his] godis FfDd$^2$   wille] but *add.* Lt$^2$Ii$^2$Br   euer] ay RDdH$^3$Dd$^2$

171 hatynge] hate T$^4$   al$^1$] *om.* Ff   wikednesse] and *add.* Lt$^2$Ii$^2$, wrechidnesse BrT$^3$   euer] ay RDdH$^3$T$^3$Dd$^2$   171–2 to$^1$ . . . fairhede] þat inough of his noble fayrehed sal come vnto þe T$^3$   cum] in *add.* Dd   to$^2$] þe *add.* RDdFfH$^3$PLt$^2$Ii$^2$Br Dd$^2$, the of *add.* T$^4$

172 fairhede] godhede P   cum] in *add.* Dd

173 oght] shold P, is hoth Br   to] *om.* P   be] þe *add.* DdFfPT$^3$Dd$^2$, oure *add.* Br   of] at Ii$^2$   al] *om.* Ii$^2$Dd$^2$

174 lyve] dwelle Ii$^2$   174–5 þat$^1$ . . . lange] to comyn Ff, *om.* H$^3$Dd$^2$   þat$^1$] þe T$^4$   sight] off godis face *add.* T$^4$   in . . . hert] *om.* T$^4$   in] with PBr   þat$^2$] *om.* T$^4$   vs] we DdT$^4$Lt$^2$Ii$^2$Br, we may P

175 euer] ay RDdLt$^2$, *om.* T$^4$PIi$^2$, fulle T$^3$   þerto] to and H$^3$, thereafter T$^4$PT$^3$, til Dd$^2$   Also] þou xalt *add.* Br   in] *om.* T$^4$P   hert] þat *add.* H$^3$, to *add.* T$^4$P   his] the T$^4$, þe bitter T$^3$   passioun] of our lorde ihesu criste *add.* T$^3$

176 his] bitter *add.* Lt$^2$Ii$^2$Br   woundes] and *add.* P   and swetnesse] *om.* H$^3$   þou$^1$] fynde and *add.* Lt$^2$Ii$^2$, haue and T$^3$   fele] haue H$^3$, fynde T$^3$

177 þi] þis H$^3$   þoght] mynde BrT$^3$   in] and þi BrT$^3$   mynd] þoght Br, entente T$^3$

178 right] trewly PT$^3$   loue] lyfe Dd$^2$   brennyngly] the *add.* T$^4$   alle] and Lt

179 and$^1$ . . . il] of ill and dredys H$^3$   of il] *om.* T$^4$PT$^3$   il] euel R, wicke Ff, helle Lt$^2$Ii$^2$BrDd$^2$   defoul] þam *add.* H$^3$P   vndre] with H$^3$   þi] *om.* T$^4$

180 fete] fote DdT$^4$PT$^3$   he$^2$] and T$^4$

181 helpeth] kepeth Lt, helpe T$^4$   ham] *om.* Br   al har] his Br   rereth] reiseth RDdFfT$^4$Lt$^2$Ii$^2$BrT$^3$Dd$^2$, rayse H$^3$   al$^2$] *om.* RFfH$^3$Lt$^2$BrDd$^2$

182 þynge] thynges T$^4$PLt$^2$Ii$^2$   may] *om.* PT$^3$   sauour and] *om.* T$^3$   and solace] *om.* R   in] of RT$^3$   þe] *om.* T$^3$   of] in T$^3$

183 heuyn] Also *add.* Br   Purchace the] Purge Lt   wel] will T$^4$Br   gretynge] wepyng RT$^4$PIi$^2$Br   and] *om.* T$^4$   sese] þou *add.* Lt$^2$Ii$^2$   til] þat *add.* RFfT$^4$P   haue] founden *add.* T$^3$

184 hym] it T$^4$PLt$^2$Ii$^2$Br   þe$^1$] þin FfT$^3$Dd$^2$   hert] hertis Lt$^2$   where] þe *add.* SVBr, þere þat Ff, will T$^3$, þore Dd$^2$   spryngeth] and *add.* T$^3$   þer] *om.* P, þe Ii$^2$

185 be kyndled] kendelyn FfT$^4$, ytend P, kyndelle and abyde T$^3$   and . . . loue] *om.* SV   seþen] þen P, siȝen Br   þat shal] alle FfDd$^2$   hert] and *add.* FfDd$^2$   wil] and SV

186 bren] brynge RSVFfH$^3$T$^4$PLt$^2$Ii$^2$BrT$^3$Dd$^2$, bryn Dd   al$^1$] at Br   þe] *om.*

FfH$^3$Dd$^2$ al$^2$] synne and *add.* Ff, *om.* Ii$^2$, þe *add.* Dd$^2$ filth] syn H$^3$ as clene] and þat T$^3$

187 þe$^1$] *om.* SVT$^4$PT$^3$ þat] *om.* T$^3$ proued] clensid Br in þe] with T$^4$, in a P fourneys] forsoþ *add.* SV, fyre T$^4$Lt$^2$Ii$^2$Br, hote fiere meltande T$^3$, sikerly P$^1$ wot] weel ⟨þer is Ii$^2$⟩ *add.* Lt$^2$Ii$^2$, knowe P$^1$ 187–8 no . . . shal] inwardly þat no þinge mai Br

188 shal] woll T$^4$ take . . . hert] make þe Lt$^2$Ii$^2$Br Goddis loue] þe loue of god SV Goddis] wil and *add.* Ii$^2$ 188–9 and . . . heuyn] *om.* SV þe] *om.* Ii$^2$ ioy] ioyes T$^4$P

189 of heuyn] *om.* LtRH$^3$Lt$^2$Ii$^2$Br to] *om.* S þe] *om.* FfT$^4$PIi$^2$Dd$^2$ þis] þe SVIi$^2$P$^1$ as] þan is þis for to be of T$^3$, a *add.* Dd$^2$

190 of] on Ii$^2$P$^1$ mescheuous . . . greuous] *om.* SVIi$^2$ mescheuous and] *om.* Br mescheuous] mysese RFfH$^3$PLt$^2$T$^3$Dd$^2$, mysesis T$^4$P$^1$ greuous] of þe FfT$^4$PDd$^2$, þe H$^3$, of þe hedous and wondurful T$^3$, on þe P$^1$ woundes] woun[dy]ng of god H$^3$ and . . . deth] *om.* P$^1$ and] *om.* Br þe] hidous *add.* SV, peyneful *add.* Ii$^2$, bitter *add.* T$^3$ deth] passioun T$^3$ of$^2$] oure lord *add.* PP$^1$

191 Crist] for *add.* SVPP$^1$ rer] reise RSVDdFfH$^3$T$^4$Lt$^2$Ii$^2$BrT$^3$Dd$^2$, rere vp PP$^1$ abouen] al *add.* SVT$^4$PIi$^2$, fram al P$^1$ erthly] þinges and *add.* SVFf lykynge] lykynges of þe world SV, likynges Ff, thyngs H$^3$, þyng PP$^1$

192 hert] saule T$^3$ brennynge] ⟨to P$^1$⟩ brenne T$^4$PP$^1$ Cristis loue] þe loue of god P$^1$ and] to *add.* SV, hit wul *add.* P$^1$ purchace] purgeth Lt, purges Dd, þe þe welle of wepyng and *add.* SV, peraventure T$^3$ 192–3 in . . . heuyn] þe sauour and þe swetnesse in to þi sowle P$^1$ in$^2$] to *add.* RSVFfH$^3$T$^4$PLt$^2$Ii$^2$BrDd$^2$, vnto T$^3$ delitabilte] grct dilitable delyt SV, a delitable swetnesse T$^4$, delitable Lt$^2$Ii$^2$Br

193 and] of H$^3$, *om.* Lt$^2$Ii$^2$Br heuyn] heuenli comfort Lt$^2$Ii$^2$Br

194 perauentur] percas T$^4$, haply Ii$^2$ wil] *om.* P$^1$ say] þus *add.* Lt$^2$Ii$^2$P$^1$ despise . . . nat] *om.* H$^3$ þe] þis SV world] ne *add.* Ii$^2$ 194–5 I$^2$ . . . to] ne P$^1$

195 fynd] it *add.* RDdFfH$^3$Lt$^2$Ii$^2$T$^3$Dd$^2$ pyne] punysche RSVFfH$^3$T$^4$PLt$^2$Ii$^2$BrT$^3$Dd$^2$P$^1$ body] fleche T$^3$P$^1$ and] þat SV, also *add.* Br me behoueth] I ⟨ne SV⟩ moste SVLt$^2$Ii$^2$BrP$^1$, to *add.* FfT$^4$P fleishly] flesch and my SV

196 take] myn *add.* SVT$^4$PP$^1$ when . . . cometh] *om.* SV when] what tyme so T$^3$ 196–7 If . . . þoghtes] *om.* P$^1$

197 þoghtes] poyntes T$^4$ I . . . þou] *om.* Ii$^2$ I . . . þe$^1$] loke Lt$^2$Br I] Nowe y P$^1$ þe$^1$] *om.* R, at þe begynnynge *add.* T$^3$ þat þou] *om.* SV, wolte *add.* T$^4$PP$^1$ þe$^2$] wel *add.* SV 197–8 fro . . . world] *om.* T$^3$ þis] *om.* T$^4$, þe P$^1$

198 whare] alle *add.* P$^1$ þe$^2$] þis SVT$^4$P worldes louers] louers ⟨þat haue bene Ii$^2$⟩ of þis worlde Lt$^2$Ii$^2$Br worldes] wordly PP$^1$ now] becomen *add.* SVPP$^1$, bycome T$^4$ 198–9 and . . . God] *om.* SV and whar] war H$^3$ ben$^2$] *om.* H$^3$, now *add.* P

199 Certes] Sekirly T$^4$PP$^1$ and wommen] *om.* P$^1$ ben] nou *add.* SV

200 and laghet] as we do nou (*om.* T$^4$) SVT$^4$, as we do *add.* PP$^1$, as nede was Lt$^2$Ii$^2$Br and$^2$] but SV þe] þis V, thoo T$^4$P$^1$ loued] louen SV þis] the T$^4$ world] and *add.* T$^4$PP$^1$ toke . . . body] *om.* SV toke] to kep H$^3$, to Ii$^2$

201 lyued] loued Lt, liuen SV, *om.* T$^3$ as . . . in] aftir þe luste and Br 201–2 of . . . and$^2$] and in lust of heore flesch atte laste SV 201–2 lad . . . and$^1$] in P$^1$

202 lust] lustis FfH$^3$Lt$^2$Ii$^2$Br and$^1$] yn *add.* T$^4$Lt$^2$, *om.* P delites] and lykyng ⟨of the flessche T$^4$⟩ at her deyng *add.* T$^4$P, At her deyng *add.* P$^1$ in$^2$] at P a] þat T$^3$ fel] fallen SV, doun *add.* FfT$^4$P in] *om.* RSVFfT$^4$PP$^1$ helle] ther to dwelle without ende *add.* T$^4$PP$^1$ 202–8 Now . . . helle] *trs. to l. 211* SV

203 greet] *om.* RSVDdFfH$^3$T$^4$PLt$^2$Ii$^2$BrT$^3$Dd$^2$P$^1$ foul] *om.* H$^3$Ii$^2$ glotones] and also (*om.* P) fowle gouernyd hem selfe *add.* T$^4$P, gouernyd hemself P$^1$ þat] so *add.* T$^4$P yers] of þis wordle *add.* P$^1$

204 wasted] and distruiȝed *add.* SVP$^1$ endles] *om.* SV ioy] and blisse þat euer

schal laste *add.* SV þat] þe which SVIi$^{2}$ was] bowȝt and *add.* P$^{1}$ for] to SVP$^{1}$ haue] loued god and *add.* P$^{1}$

205 penaunce] in her lyues *add.* P$^{1}$ synnes] For *add.* SV sest] well *add.* T$^{4}$PP$^{1}$ al] *om.* P$^{1}$ þe] þo P richesse] and þe delyte *add.* H$^{3}$, ⟨and P⟩ likyngges *add.* T$^{4}$P, goodes P$^{1}$ 205–6 and delites] *om.* H$^{3}$P

206 delites] delite R, delite of it Ii$^{2}$, þe eesys and þe lykynges of eny creatures þat here lyueþ P$^{1}$ passeth] vanisseth RSVDdH$^{3}$T$^{4}$PLt$^{2}$BrT$^{3}$Dd$^{2}$P$^{1}$, gon and wastyn Ff, wastyn Ii$^{2}$ away] alwey Br cometh] bycomeþ T$^{4}$P doth] are SV al] *om.* SV har] þe worldes SV, þe DdLt$^{2}$Ii$^{2}$, þese FfP$^{1}$, swilke T$^{3}$

207 louers] þarof *add.* DdLt$^{2}$Ii$^{2}$ for . . . ground] *om.* P$^{1}$ for] þer may *add.* Ii$^{2}$ may] *om.* Ii$^{2}$ stabilly] *om.* SV on . . . fals] bot if it so be þat it be saddely sette and grownded on a sekir T$^{3}$ on] yn T$^{4}$ fals] glase Ii$^{2}$ ground] and *add.* S, For *add.* P

208 to$^{1}$] þe *add.* P$^{1}$ in erthe] *om.* P$^{1}$ in] þe *add.* H$^{3}$Ii$^{2}$Br þe] *om.* P deuelys] feondes SV, deuel FfH$^{3}$Lt$^{2}$Ii$^{2}$BrP$^{1}$ of] in RSVT$^{4}$PLt$^{2}$Ii$^{2}$Br helle] with hem (hym P$^{1}$) to dwell yn endles fyre *add.* T$^{4}$PP$^{1}$

209 Bot] And SV al] þo *add.* SVT$^{4}$PLt$^{2}$Ii$^{2}$BrT$^{3}$P$^{1}$ þat] loueþ god and *add.* SV forsaketh . . . lif] *om.* P$^{1}$ forsaketh] forsoke RFfH$^{3}$T$^{4}$PT$^{3}$Dd$^{2}$ þe$^{1}$] *om.* SV þe$^{2}$] *om.* S vanyte] pruide SV þis] þe SVIi$^{2}$ lif] world SVLt$^{2}$Ii$^{2}$Br and$^{2}$] studyed nyȝt and day to loue oure lord ihesu cryst with (in P$^{1}$) all her myghttis and sittid (sette PP$^{1}$) her likynge yn hym entierly (hollely PP$^{1}$) forsakynge vnskylfull ease of her flessche ⟨nowȝt recchyng of erthly þyng P$^{1}$⟩ and *add.* T$^{4}$PP$^{1}$ stond] stode RDdFfH$^{3}$T$^{4}$PT$^{3}$ Dd$^{2}$P$^{1}$ stalworthly] myȝtli T$^{4}$, strangly PP$^{1}$, stifly Ii$^{2}$

210 al] *om.* SVPP$^{1}$, the T$^{4}$ temptaciouns] and ȝif they eny tyme fille sone aryse aȝen (*om.* PP$^{1}$) and amendid hem *add.* T$^{4}$PP$^{1}$ endeth] ended LtRDdFfH$^{3}$T$^{4}$PIi$^{2}$Br T$^{3}$Dd$^{2}$P$^{1}$ þe] *om.* V þai] þoo Lt$^{2}$Br

211 ben . . . in] schal haue endles Ii$^{2}$ in] þe *add.* H$^{3}$ ioy] and blisse *add.* SV and] þei *add.* P$^{1}$ hath þe] *om.* H$^{3}$Ii$^{2}$ þe] her P$^{1}$ of] in P$^{1}$ heuyn] Now (202) . . . helle (208) *interposed* SV 211–24 þare . . . loued] dwellyng þere in endeles ioye and endles life so þat yuel and good lif and deþ ben showid to vs so þat we may putte forþ owr hond and take whuche þat we wul and þerfore defoule not þi flesch loue nat þe world hate synne lufe clennesse and pray hertili to god and to owre lady and to alle þe halewys of heuene and so shalt þou come to þat blisse þat neuer shal haue ende þat god graunte vs of his mercy amen P$^{1}$ 211–13 þare . . . nede] and SV 211–12 þare . . . end] *om.* Ii$^{2}$ won] dwelle T$^{4}$Br

212 restynge] *om.* Lt þe] *om.* PT$^{3}$ delites] delyt T$^{4}$ soght] toke Ii$^{2}$

213 reste ne] *om.* T$^{4}$ body] bodies Lt$^{2}$Ii$^{2}$Br of] and *add.* T$^{4}$P

214 O] *om.* T$^{3}$ þynge] ȝit *add.* Br, *om.* T$^{3}$ the] *om.* SVPDd$^{2}$ his] þis RSVFfH$^{3}$PIi$^{2}$T$^{3}$Dd$^{2}$, this glorious T$^{4}$, þat is þis Lt$^{2}$Br Iesus] ihesu RSVDdFfH$^{3}$T$^{4}$P Lt$^{2}$Ii$^{2}$BrT$^{3}$Dd$^{2}$ bot] bo Lt, *om.* T$^{3}$

215 hit$^{1}$] *om.* H$^{3}$T$^{3}$ hert] bothe *add.* T$^{4}$PBr and$^{2}$] as *add.* RFfH$^{3}$Dd$^{2}$ þi$^{3}$] *om.* Lt$^{2}$Ii$^{2}$T$^{3}$ dere] derrest T$^{3}$

216 lif] and *add.* SV Rot hit] put that euer T$^{4}$ hit] alwey *add.* P Ihesu] in al þin herte *add.* SV made . . . and] *om.* Br þe] *om.* SV

217 for . . . dette] *om.* T$^{3}$ his] *om.* LtT$^{4}$ dette] and *add.* P Forþi] þerfore RT$^{4}$PLt$^{2}$Ii$^{2}$Br 217–24 set . . . loued] loue ihesu with al þin herte with al þi soule with al þi þouȝt amen SV

218 on] yn T$^{4}$ his] this T$^{4}$PLt$^{2}$Ii$^{2}$Br þat . . . hele] and T$^{4}$, *om.* P is] þin *add.* Ff hele] saueoure and Ii$^{2}$ il] euel RFfT$^{4}$PLt$^{2}$Ii$^{2}$BrT$^{3}$ haue dwellynge] dwelle T$^{4}$Lt$^{2}$Ii$^{2}$, byde Br

219 in . . . hert] *om.* FfPDd$^{2}$ in] withyn T$^{4}$ þe] þat RH$^{3}$Lt$^{2}$Ii$^{2}$Br, thyn T$^{4}$ hert] parlance T$^{3}$ þer] þat Br holdyn . . . trewly] treuly kepte inne Br holdyn] had T$^{4}$ hit] he Br chaseth] alle *add.* Ff

220 deuylles] to *add.* T$^{4}$  hit] and DdFfIi$^{2}$, he Br  and] it RH$^{3}$T$^{4}$PLt$^{2}$Ii$^{2}$Dd$^{2}$, he Br  dredes] dedis Ff

221 þe] *om.* H$^{3}$, þi Br  Who] What Lt  so] þat Ii$^{2}$  loueth] lusteþ P  verrayly] he þat *add.* T$^{3}$

222 and$^{1}$] yn T$^{4}$  in$^{1}$] and T$^{4}$PIi$^{2}$, his *add.* T$^{3}$  comfort] comfortes Ff  in . . . lif] and in his loofe T$^{3}$  þis] his T$^{4}$Br

223 dey] ben dede out of þis werld Ff  þei] *om.* T$^{4}$P  in$^{1}$] *om.* H$^{3}$  ordres] ordre RFfH$^{3}$T$^{4}$PLt$^{2}$Ii$^{2}$BrT$^{3}$Dd$^{2}$

224 þat . . . loued] for þat þai hafe her hertily lofede hym now of his grete mersye vnto þat ilke ioye brynge vs he þat bouȝt vs with his precious blod on þe rode tree amen T$^{3}$  þat] whom P  haue] *om.* FfDd$^{2}$  loued] amen *add.* DdH$^{3}$, þat is iesus *add.* FfDd$^{2}$, to þat ioye þe holi trinite brynge vs amen *add.* T$^{4}$, to þat ioye he bryng vs amen *add.* P. *RLt$^{2}$Ii$^{2}$Br continue without a break with lines 610–25 of the 'Form'.*

## *Desire and Delight*

1 Desyre] Gernyng Th    in] of Th    thoght] thoghtes Th
2 pure] haly *add.* Th    And] when a man felis hym in þat degre *add.* Th
3 effectuous] affeccyons and Th    shorne] drawen Th
4 taryynge] tagillynge Th
5 þynge] thynges Th    when] *om.* Th
6 is$^{2}$] noghte *add.* Th
8 certeyn] clene Th
9 þe] *om.* Th    restregnynge] rest regnynge Lt
10 Anoþer] es *add.* Th    destruynge] restreynynge Th
11 of] or Th
12 he] *om.* Th    hold] haldis Th
13 thoght] thoghtes Th    comynge] comynynge Lt
14 Euery man] Ilk ane Th
17 affectuouse] affeccyouns and Th
18 þe] *om.* Th
21 meditacioun] medytacyons Th    orisone] orysouns Th
22 noght hath] *trs.* Th
23 myche] mekely Th    of heynesse] styrrynge Th    al] *om.* Th
24 and . . . skyl] *om.* Th
25 euer] ay Th
26 of] with Th    and] or Th
27 thoght] thoghteȝ etcetera explicit Th

## *Ghostly Gladness*

3 vmlappeth] unlappes Dd
5 lengthes] es lenthed Dd
6 to] *om.* Dd
7 maketh] gars Dd
9 let] it *add.* Dd    in$^{2}$] of Dd

## *Lyrics*

### (i)

1 hit] is *add.* La  is] made La

2 Whan] For Dd  chaunge] slake La

3 is] it DdLa  turned] tournes DdLa  to[1]] þe *add.* Dd  the] þe Dd, *om.* La  trauaille] it turneþ *add.* La

4 loue] þus *add.* Dd, do La  þe[1]] *om.* Dd  may] schalt þanne La

5 is] a *add.* La  desyre] And also *add.* La

6 I lykene] is lickned Lt  to] into La  quenchen] sloken DdLa  may] for *add.* La

7 vs clenseth] *trs.* La  our] vs Dd  bot] blis La

8 ioy] euere *add.* La

9 sete] settel Dd, socour La  set] lyft Dd, liftid La  ful] *om.* DdLa

10 þat[1]] *om.* DdLa  hit] *om.* DdLa  erth] it *add.* Dd, herte þat it La  man] men Dd, þe peple boþe La

11 þe] ȝou it La

12 þegh] þof Dd, þerof La  be] to La  dregh] For euere *add.* La  coupileth] compileth Lt  and] to La

13 love[2] . . . beswyke] To hem þat of it is fayn and frike La

14 myght] it *add.* DdLa  euer] ay Dd, euermore La  ylike] lijke La

15 couereth] comfortes Dd, heliþ La  lifteth] us up in *add.* La  rike] And *add.* La

16 wot] nowhere *add.* La  lust] loue La  hit] is *add.* La

17 hethen] hens La

18 hit] þe DdLa

19 Loke] þou *add.* La  þogh] if Dd  in] *om.* La  wandreth] wandrynge Lt, wandre La  ware] euery where La

20 hym weld] *trs.* La  with] and Dd  wyn] inne La  hym[2]] hertili *add.* La

21 lif] loue La  loue] þou *add.* La

22 be] to me *add.* La  desyrynge] ȝhernyng DdLa

23 Wo] And þat synne La  and] loue *add.* La  comyn] war *add.* Dd  my] owne *add.* La

24 If] *om.* La  praysynge] ⟨sweete La⟩ lovyng DdLa

25 is] to vs *add.* La  euer] ay Dd  lestynge] lastand Dd  þat] tyme þat *add.* La  hit] verrili *add.* La

26 me make] *trs.* Dd, make we euere La  brennynge] byrnand Dd  may] gar Dd  me] it ⟨uerrili La⟩ DdLa

27 take] it *add.* La  in] to *add.* DdLa  stable] þou *add.* La  euery] ylk a DdLa

28 nat] no þing La  holdynge] heldand Dd, hildande La  loue] uerrili *add.* La  þis] þe La

29 an] any DdLa

30 and my] in foule La

31 me] *om.* DdLa  of] at my La  departynge] partyng Dd  þat] it *add.* La  hote] attir La

32 welth] welþis La  is bot] ben La  shal] wolde La  spille] le *obscured in MS binding*

33 hath] heere La  likened to] ful likinge vnto La  haye] iȝee La

34 faire] freische *add.* La  now[2]] anoon aftir is La  witynge] wytes Dd, welkid La

35 Such] þis La þis] þe La I wene] alle men moun seen La shal] *om.* Dd, wole La be] bees Dd to] vnto La daye] All *add.* Dd

36 In] Ful greet La in] *om.* Dd, myche La for] *om.* Dd, To La fle] þat *add.* DdLa no . . . may] is ful hard in fay La

37 loue] leue yuel La

38 gif] ⟨to La⟩ hym *add.* DdLa þi] *om.* La hert] sawle Dd, *om.* La hit[1]] þee dere La hit[2] . . . wyn] þe dwell within Dd hit welde] weelde þee La wyn] inne La

39 As] crist *add.* Dd, Al La Crist] *om.* Dd, þi lord La þerof] he *add.* La blyn] mynne La

40 So] þus La þou shal] *trs.* La heuyn won] *trs.* La withjn] For siþe *add.* La

41 þis is] *trs.* DdLa trusty] trayst Dd

42 stond] styll *add.* Dd, euere *add.* La chaunge] it *add.* Dd, neuere *add.* La

43 The lif] þat wiȝt þat La myght] may La

44 kare] it *add.* DdLa and . . . glewe] Such a mirþe fyndiþ to fewe La lendeth] led Lt

45 Forþi] For now Dd þou] as *add.* La I] þee *add.* La Crist] is trewe loue *add.* La telle] and *add.* Dd

46 take] þou *add.* La sylle] felle La

47 þou hate] *trs.* La no . . . bot] I rede all Dd no] maner *add.* La bot] loke *add.* La myght] may DdLa felle] fele Lt, dwelle La

48 stalwarth] more strenger La as] þe *add.* Dd, þan La hard as] more harder þan La

49 a] *om.* La light] and a *add.* La birthyn] fyne *add.* La gladdeth] boþe *add.* La

50 withoutyn] wiþout ony La

51 a] *om.* La gostly] deliciouse as *add.* La wyne] wynne Dd maketh] men ⟨boþe La⟩ *add.* DdLa

52 Of] To þat La loue] sal he *add.* Dd, y schal me *add.* La no thynge] so faste La shal] *om.* DdLa hit] y La wil] it euermore La

53 man] heere La hath tane] men may han La

54 Goddis] owne *add.* La byndeth] boþe *add.* La

55 loue] þerfore *add.* La lyuynge] lykyng DdLa I] ne *add.* Dd wote] knowe La

56 me] oonly *add.* La be] but La

57 Bot] al *add.* La floure] flouris La in] of La

58 And] schal *add.* La lestynge be] *trs.* La than] But as La hit . . . bot] ane houre of Dd bot] an hour of La

59 soroweth sethen] sythen syghe Dd sethen] aftir þat La proudhede] lust þar pryde DdLa and] *om.* Dd, al *add.* La

60 til] in to La

61 erth . . . þay] þair bodys lyse in syn þair sawls mai Dd, her bodies in þe fen liggen þanne schulen her soulis La quake and] be in La

62 And] For Dd shal . . . men] aȝen as men schulen risen La to] and DdLa dede] mysdede La

63 seyn] fonden Dd, þan *add.* La as] and La now] heere *add.* La lede] ledde þan La

64 þay shal] *trs.* La sit] ligge La derkenesse] myrknes Dd

65 and] her *add.* La werkes] sal *add.* Dd

66 flaume] flawmes La fyre] bath *add.* Dd knyght . . . kynge] bitterli brennynge La sorow] care La and] *om.* Dd shame . . . lye] schamfully Dd, sorewe schamefastli La

67 to] þi lord *add.* La

68 in . . . dye] þarto þou traiste trewly Dd Amen] *om.* DdLa

## (ii)

1 son] þou art *add.* La  of] moost hiȝ *add.* La

2 Sen] verrili *add.* La  wil] loue La  in] *om.* Dd

3 world] land Dd

4 way] hand Dd, ward and La  set] þou *add.* La

5 Ihesu] þou *add.* La

6 spere] anoon *add.* La  þat] mykel *add.* DdLa  me] men DdLa

7 langeth] þou *add.* La  to] into La  light] siȝt La  festyn] þere *add.* La  þe] al *add.* Dd

8 fil] make La  hert] liȝt þat al *add.* La  make] *om.* La  wene] wane Dd, wexe La

9 God] ihesu *add.* Dd, and *add.* La  my$^2$] loueli *add.* La  forsake] þou *add.* La

10 hit] to *add.* Dd, to La  meke] meekinge La  haue] hate DdLa

11 is] al *add.* La  desyrynge] ȝhernynge Dd  loue] þou *add.* Dd  kyndel] þou *add.* La

12 in] with þi La

13 Wownd] þou *add.* La  hit] me La

14 On] Of La  make . . . skylle] fastne me þat y not spille La  make] gar Dd  my] me Dd

17 Root hit] ihesu putte La  in] to *add.* La

18 sekenes] lijknes La  and] eek *add.* La

20 wixynge euer] ay waxand Dd, *trs.* La  hit] y La

21 songe] loue La  is] euere *add.* La

22 lif] loue La  in] þee *add.* La

23 to] vnto La  þat] þere La  maye] aye Lt

24 in] and Dd

25 me] so *add.* La

26 My] His La  hit] he La  me] now *add.* La  sent] schent Dd  euery] ilk a Dd

28 me] awei *add.* La  shal neuer] neuere aȝen schulen La

29 brest] hert Dd  is] now *add.* La

30 why ne] whyn Lt

31 state] ȝernynge La  in$^2$] al *add.* La

32 in] *om.* DdLa  for] þe *add.* La  þou] hase *add.* DdLa  shadde] bleed La

33 Demed] he *add.* DdLa  was] on a crosse *add.* La

34 Ful sore] Wiþ scourgis La  hym] sore *add.* La  swynge] slynge Lt

35 bake] brist La  was] bloo *add.* La  and] Not La  his blessed] was his La

36 þe] þat La  naked] nayled Dd, doon La  on] þe *add.* DdLa

38 faire face] face fairest La

39 wand] þan reste La  hym] ⟨more La⟩ in *add.* DdLa

40 As . . . strand] Al he suffride þat was wisest La  on] of þe Dd  can] to lete La

41 eyen] And al *add.* La

42 was . . . vmset] þat alle men siȝe Ful myldeli he out gan lete La  sorowfully] saryful Dd  vmset] umbesette Dd

43 maistry mare] be maister þere La

44 When . . . sare] *om.* La

45 risen] rase DdLa  anoon] agayne DdLa  in fairhed] In to blis ful fair La

46 And . . . kare] *om.* La  deth] es *add.* Dd  noon] noght Dd

47 He] On hym Dd  þe$^2$] he it La  in] to *add.* La

48 þi$^2$] in La  and] so to *add.* La  Amen] *om.* DdLa

## *(iii)*

1 I] *om.* Dd and[1]] y La on] þat is *add.* La
2 bot] his *add.* La euer is] es ay Dd, is so La newe] true La
4 were] *om.* Dd, schulde La turned] turne La in to] til ioy ful Dd, ioie *add.* La langynge] sang Dd
5 he lyveth] *trs.* La
Lines 6 and 7 *trs.* La
6 I] to La
7 fro . . . al] wolde from him La wil] walde Dd þogh] *om.* La he ware] *trs.* La
8 That] He þat DdLa hym loued] *trs.* Dd loued] loueþ La so . . . a] fra euel he wil hym DdLa shilde] childe Lt
9 þan] *om.* Dd al . . . bete] may of al my bale be bote La
10 wil] may Dd swete] soote La
11 lacid] lauȝt La I shal] *trs.* Dd forlete] forgete Dd
12 blody] heed *add.* La
13 behoueth] boweth Lt, es bowne Dd, wole La faire] loue *add.* La
14 is[1]] ful *add.* La
16 vs] me ⟨haþ La⟩ DdLa
17 þegh] gyf DdLa sorow] woo al La be sette] bisett La
18 and] ȝhe La
19 pitte] To me *add.* La
20 syn wil] wolt þi synnes La
21 lif] loue Lt, tonge Dd of] þis *add.* La lest] *om.* DdLa
22 is] euere *add.* La
23 euer] *om.* DdLa loueth . . . is] of loue longinge kan not ceesse La
24 hym shold] *trs.* DdLa mak . . . lasse] þat he so his loue schulde lese La loue] lif Lt
25 is[1]] þe *add.* La
26 to[1]] þe *add.* Dd þe[2] . . . to] And derknes in to day La ebbynge] dawyng Dd
28 Ihesu] þou *add.* Lt as þou] þat La loue] þe *add.* DdLa Amen] *om.* DdLa

## *(iv)*

1 euery] ilk a DdTh
2 þis] þat is Lt hit] *om.* Dd wendeth] wytes DdTh
3 besy þe] fande DdTh wil . . . þe] with þe will Dd
4 þan] *om.* Dd and[2]] þi Dd
5 þou] *om.* Lt thoght] þou *add.* Dd
6 how] þat Th
7 hym] *om.* Th soght] full *add.* Th
8 þou] þe Dd þat] bot Dd
9–12 Thay . . . within] *om.* Dd
10 þar] þat Lt
13 Thou] *om.* Dd

14 þat] *om.* DdTh
15 synketh] ay *add.* Th ferre] downe *add.* Dd
16 Forþi] þarfore Dd þar] þat Lt
17–20 Lerne . . . laste] *om.* D 17 euer] more *add.* Th
18 þi] thy *add.* Th
20 and] be his for Th
21 couait] knyt þi Dd, thi *add.* Th chaungeth] chawnge DdTh
22 trace] grace Th seigh] seke Dd sit] seke Lt
24 his] þis Th loue] lyf LtTh
27 your] with Dd loue] lif Lt, þat *add.* Dd shal neuer] *trs.* Dd
28 to won heuyn] heuen to won Dd
29 on] of Th þat] *om.* Dd
30 his heed] *om.* Dd priketh] es prikked Dd, pungede Th þe] wit(h) DdTh
31 let] þat Th þe] þat was Dd
32 swetnesse] for *add.* Th þan] *om.* Dd, þat Th
33–6 Festyn . . . fare] *om.* Dd 33 þi[2]] þis Th
34 soul] saules Th
35 His] Thi Lt in] it Th
38 þe[1]] *om.* Dd stabilynge] stallyng Dd
39 euer] ay DdTh and] *om.* Dd
40 For] Ful Lt I haue] *trs.* Dd
41 to] at DdTh
42 vp to that] vnto þi Dd non] mon Th
43 hym] bath *add.* Dd
44 Wisse] Bryng Dd, Rayse Th me] vpe *add.* Th þi] þe Th right] lyght Dd for] *om.* DdTh
45 euer] ay DdTh lyuynge] louynge LtTh
46 wil . . . hym] with hym wil DdTh
48 þan] þat Lt he hath] *trs.* DdTh loue] ay *add.* Th
50 þou . . . bitake] til hym þou take Dd so] full Th
51 Thy] þe Dd may . . . man] na man may DdTh euery] ilk a DdTh
53 euer] ay DdTh
54 lok] let Dd hit nat] *trs.* Lt
55 hath . . . wirched] wirkes men sa Dd
56 til] with Dd
60 Whose] And with Dd loue] þat *add.* Dd in . . . ille] þi hert he wil fulfyll Dd in] and Th
62 þat] þai Dd, þan Th let ham] will þay Th
63 put hit] putted DdTh is] in Lt to] in Th
64 may] wil DdTh
65 whils] þat *add.* Dd
67 Thi] þe Dd turneth] in *add.* DdTh blisse] ioy Dd mow] sall Dd
68 I] þe *add.* Dd
69 þoght] hedes Dd, thoghtes Th we] be Lt
71 syn] synnes DdTh þe] þen Dd tythynge] tythans DdTh
72 non] man Th shal] may Dd
75 turne . . . kynd] ouer al thyng Dd kynd] and *add.* Th euer] ay Dd, *om.* Th loue] the *add.* Th
76 wel] will Th bale] bales Th may] wele Th
77 Of] Wyth DdTh
78 I . . . deth] me thare Th nat] may Lt, þe *add.* Th mankynde] mankyn DdTh side] sydes DdTh to] *om.* Dd
84 dar] thaie Th had] haue DdTh

85 fight] fande Dd
86 day] dayes DdTh that . . . shende] *om.* Th
87 þi] þe Dd
88 se hym] *trs.* DdTh
89–108 Afforce . . . Amen] *missing in Th*
90 Thou] And Dd
91 bos] bot Lt, burd Dd
95 For] Ful Dd sete] setell Dd to] for Dd
97 forþi] for þe Dd
98 þi] þe Dd
99 bot . . . hit] and þai þarof will Dd
100 that sorow] *om.* Dd hath] it *add.* Dd
102 þe$^{1}$] *om.* Dd
103 þe$^{1}$] þat Dd of þe] any Dd
104 lecheth] lennes Dd
107 Avise] And vse Dd þe$^{2}$] be Dd
108 And . . . loue] Swa þat þow hafe Dd in] I Lt end] endyng Dd Amen] *om.* Dd

## *(v)*

2 desyre] ȝherne Dd
8 the] *om.* Dd
9 beteth] dynges Dd
15 for] *om.* Dd
17 men] *om.* Dd
18 no thynge] noght Dd quemed] ed *obscured in MS binding*
23 setes] setels Dd
24 purchace] purgeth Lt, purges þe Dd Amen] *om.* Dd

## *(vi)*

*Introductory stanza* Who . . . ille] *om.* Ad$^{2}$TrH$^{4}$Ha$^{1}$Ha$^{2}$ so] ofte *add.* VS The] *om.* V
1–4 Ihesu . . . thynge] *om.* Ha$^{1}$Ha$^{2}$ 1 Ihesu swet] *trs.* VSAd$^{2}$Ro
3 to] *om.* VSAd$^{2}$
5–8 Ihesu . . . mysse] *om.* H$^{4}$Ha$^{2}$, l. 1 Ha$^{1}$ 5 Ihesu swet] *trs.* VSAd$^{2}$RoHa$^{1}$
6 hert$^{1\&2}$] hertus Ro lysse] blysse Lt
7 In . . . me] þou art suete myd y Ha$^{1}$ In] þi Ro, to þi *add.* Tr
8 And . . . to] wo is him þat he shal Ha$^{1}$ þi . . . to] þerof Ro to] *om.* VSAd$^{2}$
9–12 Ihesu . . . aright] *om.* Ha$^{2}$, l. 5 Ha$^{1}$ 9 Ihesu swet] *trs.* VSAd$^{2}$RoHa$^{1}$ hert] hertus Ro
10 nyght] þou *add.* Ha$^{1}$
11 me] lord *add.* Tr both . . . myght] grace of gostely lyght H$^{4}$ both . . . and] streinþe and eke Ha$^{1}$
12 For to] þat I may Tr, and the to H$^{4}$ þe aright] with all my myght H$^{4}$ þe] ihesu *add.* Tr

13–16 Ihesu . . . mote] *om.* Ha², l. 9 Ha¹ 13 Ihesu swet] *trs.* VSAd²RoHa¹ sowl] huerte Ha¹

15 swote] hote Lt

16 wet hit] lene Ha¹ hit] lord *add.* TrH⁴ grow] springe VSAd²RoHa¹

17–20 Ihesu . . . dreme] *om.* H⁴Ha², l. 13 Ha¹ 17 Ihesu swete] *trs.* VSAd²Ro her] hertus Ro

19 As . . . borne] ybore þou were Ha¹ was] weore VSAd²

20 in . . . loue] me of þi loue to Tr in me] me here Ha¹ loue] suete Ha¹

21–4 Ihesu . . . louer] *om.* H⁴Ha¹, l. 69 VSAd²Ro, l. 59 Tr, l. 5 Ha² 21 songe] þing Ha² be swetter] so swete be Tr

22 thoght . . . blestfuller] myrþe of þis world ne glee Tr thoght] noht Ha² hert] eorþe Ha²

23 Noght . . . lightfuller] lord as is þe loue of þe Tr feled] filled Lt lightfuller] lihtsomer VSAd², worthyer Ro, lykerusere Ha²

24 Than . . . louer] kynge of heuene þou graunte it me Tr a louer] alumere Ha²

25–8 Ihesu . . . tre] *om.* Ha¹, l. 73 VSAd²Ro, l. 61 Tr, l. 21 H⁴, l. 9 Ha² 25 loue] to *add.* H⁴ was vs] *trs.* H⁴ vs] *om.* Tr

26 hit . . . heuyn] froo heuene it Tr hit] we Ha²

27 loue . . . me] grete loue and pyte Tr þou . . . boght] ful deere bouȝtest þou VS

28 For . . . tre] on þe cros þou hongest for me Tr honge] hangest H⁴ on] or V, the *add.* H⁴

29–32 Ihesu . . . were] *om.* H⁴Ha¹Ha², l. 77 VSAd²Ro, l. 65 Tr

30 ful] *om.* Ro, a Tr

31 þei] a Ad², ȝe Ro setten] geten Tr

32 while] luytel VSAd²RoTr or] before Tr taken] i take S, take Ad²

33–6 Ihesu . . . ore] *om.* TrH⁴Ha¹Ha², l. 81 VSAdRo

34 of²] *om.* VSAd²Ro

35 þore] þo *add.* Ro

36 besoghtest] praydest Ro

37–40 Ihesu . . . swete] *om.* H⁴Ha¹Ha², l. 85 VSAd²Ro, l. 69 Tr 37 went] eodest VSAd², ȝedist Ro vpon] on VSAd²Ro

39 And] Riȝt Ad² or] er VSAd²Ro, þere Tr þou] *om.* Lt

40 þou . . . prayer] ffeyre wordes Tr prayer] boone VSAd²Ro

41–4 Ihesu . . . be] *om.* H⁴Ha¹Ha², l. 89 VSAd²Ro, l. 73 Tr 41 Ihesu] To him VS

42 to] *om.* VSAd²RoTr the] þat *add.* Tr

45–8 Ihesu . . . name] *om.* TrH⁴Ha¹Ha², l. 93 VSAd²Ro 45 tornedest] tornest Lt, agayne *add.* Ro than] *om.* Ro

46 euery] vch a VSAd² man] may men Ro

47 or] and er VSAd², and can Ro þou²] hom Ro blan] blame LtRo

48 ayeyn . . . way] þe wey aȝeyn SRo

49–52 Ihesu . . . mone] *om.* TrH⁴Ha¹Ha², l. 97 VSAd²Ro 49 after] þus eft VSAd², ȝit efte Ro

50 went] wont Lt, beefore bigonne VSAd²Ro for] *om.* VSAd²Ro

51 als] eke VSAd²Ro þe] þi Lt, þo Ro sone] eftsone Ro

52 madest] prayer *add.* Ro a] *om.* Ro

53–6 Ihesu . . . songe] *om.* TrH⁴Ha¹, l. 109 VSAd²Ro, l. 13 Ha² 53 suffredest] suffrest Lt, þoledest Ha²

55 peyn . . . was] rewful paynes were Ro peyn] peynes VSAd²Ha² rewful] rykene Ha² was] ⟨hit Ha²⟩ weore VSAd²Ha² ful] and VS, *om.* Ha²

56 may] me *add.* VSAd² hit] hem Ad²RoHa² tunge] ⟨in VSAd²⟩ spel VSAd²RoHa² nor] ne VAd²RoHa², and S

57–60 Ihesu . . . wailawo] *om.* Ha¹, l. 113 VSAd²Ro, l. 81 Tr, l. 24 H⁴, l. 17 Ha²

57 þou . . . loue] for loue þou suffredest (dree Ro, dreȝedest Ha$^2$) VSAd$^2$RoH$^4$Ha$^2$ soffredest] soffrest Lt for . . . so] boþe peyne and Tr so] *om.* H$^4$Ha$^2$

58 þat] *om.* Ha$^2$ blody stremys] stremes of blode Tr yow ran] ⟨dyd H$^4$⟩ ronne þe VSAd$^2$RoTrH$^4$Ha$^2$ ran] come Lt* fro] ffor luf *add.* Tr, þat *add.* Ha$^2$

59 white] swete Ro, *om.* TrHa$^2$ blo] for *add.* Ha$^2$

60 made] so *add.* RoH$^4$, wes Ha$^2$ wailawo] wel low Lt, so Ha$^2$

61–4 Mary . . . bene] *om.* TrH$^4$Ha$^1$Ha$^2$

62 Send] vs *add.* VSRo, ȝif me Ad$^2$

63 we] I Ad$^2$

64 to] *om.* VSAd$^2$ bene] Amen *add.* Ad$^2$

65–8 Ihesu . . . þe] *om.* H$^4$Ha$^1$, l. 21 Tr, l. 1 Ha$^2$

66 þer] Ne VSAd$^2$, Here Ro, *om.* Ha$^2$ may] nys Ro, *om.* Ha$^2$ swet] may *add.* Ha$^2$

67 Noght . . . or] al þat me may wiþ eȝen Ha$^2$ Noght] Ouȝt Ad$^2$

68 þay] Ne VS, *om.* Ad$^2$RoTrHa$^2$ no] *om.* VS swetnes] witnes Lt, wetenes Ro agayns] lord to Tr

69–72 Ihesu . . . wete] *om.* Ha$^2$, l. 21 VSAd$^2$Ro, l. 25 Tr, l. 13 H$^4$, l. 17 Ha$^1$ 69 Ihesu lord] Swete ihesu VSAd$^2$RoHa$^1$ lord] godd H$^4$

70 is] to *add.* H$^4$ hit shal] *trs.* Ro hit] þe Ha$^1$ lete] lorde *add.* Tr

71 Gyf . . . to] þerefore we shulden ofte þe Ha$^1$ grace] lorde *add.* H$^4$ for] and myȝt Tr grete] wepe VSTrH$^4$

72 For . . . wete] wiþ salte teres and eȝe wepe Ha$^1$ wete] lete S

73–6 Ihesu . . . bond] *om.* TrH$^4$Ha$^2$, l. 25 VSAd$^2$Ro, l. 21 Ha$^1$ 73 Ihesu swet] *trs.* VSAd$^2$RoHa$^1$ londe] þou *add.* Ha$^1$

74 Make] þou *add.* VSAd$^2$Ro to] for Ha$^1$

75 I . . . hert] min herte more Ha$^1$ with] in myn VSAd$^2$Ro

76 is þi] þai bi Lt

77–80 Ihesu . . . ore] *om.* H$^4$Ha$^2$, l. 29 VSAd$^2$RoTr, l. 33 Ha$^1$ 77 Ihesu dere] Swete ihesu VSAd$^2$RoHa$^1$ dere] *om.* Tr reweth] forþinkeþ Tr

78 Of my] ffor Tr, *om.* Ha$^1$ mysdedes] sunnus Ad$^2$, gultes þat Ha$^1$ done] wroȝt Ha$^1$

79 Foryeve . . . more] þare fore y bidde þin mylse and ore Ha$^1$ me Lord] hom me Ro

80 Bot . . . ore] merci lord ynul na more Ha$^1$ I . . . aske] aske þe of Ro mercy] myght Lt, milce VSAd$^2$, mylde Ro

81–4 Ihesu . . . engyne] *om.* H$^4$Ha$^2$, l. 33 VSAd$^2$RoTr, l. 25 Ha$^1$ 81 Ihesu good] Swete ihesu VSAd$^2$RoHa$^1$

82 lif] loue Lt, and *add.* Ro soule] huerte Ha$^1$ is al] *trs.* Tr al] *om.* Ro

83 lyth] liȝte VSAd$^2$TrHa$^1$, come Ro

84 saue] wite Ha$^1$ me] lord *add.* Tr wicked] þe (*om.* Ha$^1$) fundus Ad$^2$Ha$^1$, helle Tr engyne] pyn RoTr

85–8 Ihesu . . . mode] *om.* H$^4$Ha$^2$, l. 37 VSAd$^2$RoTrHa$^1$ 85 Ihesu swete] *trs.* VSAd$^2$RoHa$^1$ lord goode] vpon þe rode Tr

86 For . . . shedest] þou me bohtest wiþ Ha$^1$ shedest] bleddes Tr, al *add.* Ro hert] blessed VS, swete Ad$^2$Tr, *om.* Ro

87 hert] hit *add.* VSAd$^2$, þer *add.* Tr come] ran Ro, orn Ha$^1$ a] þe VSAd$^2$Ha$^1$

88 with . . . mode] þat by þe stod Ad$^2$Ha$^1$

89–92 Ihesu . . . sene] *om.* H$^4$Ha$^2$, l. 41 VSAd$^2$RoTrHa$^1$ 89 Ihesu swete] *trs.* VSAd$^2$RoHa$^1$

90 Hyre . . . mene] y preye þe þou here my bene Ha$^1$ Hyre . . . for] to þe lord Tr

91 For . . . myld] þourh erndyng of þe heuene Ha$^1$ For] þorw VSAd$^2$Ro Mary praier] preyere of marie VSAd$^2$

92 þi . . . me] my bone be nou Ha$^1$ loue] mercy Tr be . . . me] on me be VSAd$^2$

93–6 Ihesu . . . bloode] *om.* H$^4$Ha$^2$, l. 45 VSAd$^2$RoTr, l. 29 Ha$^1$ 93 Ihesu swete] *trs.* VSAd$^2$RoHa$^1$

94 Al] *om.* Ha$^1$ þi werkes] werkes of þe VSAd$^2$Ro ful] *om.* VSAd$^2$Ro, suete and Ha$^1$

95 vs] me VSAd$^2$RoTrHa$^1$ on] vppon VSAd$^2$RoTrHa$^1$

96 And] for me þou Ha$^1$ þeron . . . hert] *om.* Ha$^1$ hert] swete VSAd$^2$

97–100 Ihesu . . . reste] *om.* H$^4$Ha$^2$, l. 49 VSAd$^2$RoTr, l. 45 Ha$^1$ 97 Ihesu lord] Swete ihesu VSAd$^2$RoHa$^1$ lord] swete Tr child] sheld Lt, barn VSAd$^2$Ha$^1$, of alle þing Tr

98 þi . . . feste] In þi loue make me studefast Tr, wiþ þe ich hope habbe rest Ha$^1$ loue] þou *add.* VSAd$^2$Ro

99 Whan] Wheder TrHa$^1$ go] north *add.* VSAd$^2$Ro, be Ha$^1$ south] est *add.* VSAd$^2$Ro, este Tr

100 In . . . reste] þe help of þe be me neste Ha$^1$ In . . . alon] euer in þi loue Tr alon] a luf Ro fynd I] *trs.* Tr

101–4 Ihesu . . . the] *om.* Ha$^2$, l. 53 VSAd$^2$RoTr, l. 17 H$^4$, l. 49 Ha$^1$ 101 Ihesu swet] *trs.* VSAd$^2$RoHa$^1$ hym] he H$^4$

102 shal] *om.* Tr, may Ha$^1$ þi] *om.* RoHa$^1$ ioy] blisse VSAd$^2$RoHa$^1$, schal *add.* Tr

103 With . . . me] after mi soule let aungles be Ha$^1$ loue cordes] gode wille Ad$^2$

104 þat . . . the] for me ne gladieþ gome ne gle Ha$^1$ may] *om.* H$^4$ be] wone VSAd$^2$RoTr, dwell H$^4$

105–8 Mary . . . nyȝt] *om.* Ad$^2$TrHa$^1$Ha$^2$, l. 161 VS, l. 105 Ro, l. 49 H$^4$ 105 modyre] ladi VSH$^4$ lady] mooder VSH$^4$

107 hert] my *add.* H$^4$

108 be . . . help] prey for me (us H$^4$) VSH$^4$

109–12 Ihesu . . . þore] *om.* Ad$^2$Ha$^1$Ha$^2$, l. 117 VSRo, l. 85 Tr, l. 29 H$^4$ 109 þi . . . sore] whan þou crouned wore Tr corone] it *add.* Ro ful] þe VS

110 The] ⟨andH$^4$⟩ þi RoH$^4$ scornynge . . . wore] scharpe þornes pricked ful sore Tr scornynge] scourgyng VSRoH$^4$ betten] scourget VSRo

112 soffredest] soffrest Lt, þoledest VS

113–16 Ihesu . . . me] *om.* Ad$^2$TrHa$^1$Ha$^2$, l. 121 VSRo, l. 33 H$^4$

114 bot] al *add.* VSRo

115 For] with Ro þat] *om.* VSRoH$^4$ I] and VS did] gult VSRo agayns þe] so wo is me Ro

116 þou] hem VH$^4$, hit SRo

117–20 Ihesu . . . sore] *om.* Ad$^2$TrH$^4$Ha$^1$Ha$^2$, l. 125 VSRo 117 þou] i *add.* S

118 wexed] wexen VS, were Ro

119 Thy modyr] mary Ro euer] ay Ro

120 sekynge] sikynges VS, chere Ro hert] wiþ VS, sykynge Ro

121–4 Ihesu . . . begoo] *om.* Ad$^2$TrH$^4$Ha$^1$Ha$^2$, l. 129 VSRo

122 And] þat VSRo wroghtest] didist Ro

125–8 Ihesu . . . be] *om.* Ad$^2$TrHa$^1$Ha$^2$, l. 133 VSRo, l. 37 H$^4$ 125 sawe] sees Ro in] on VS.

*Lines 126 and 127 trs. Lt.*

127 Of] *om.* Ro

128 woldest . . . me] for me woldest VS

129–32 Ihesu . . . vicious] *om.* Ad$^2$TrHa$^1$Ha$^2$, l. 137 VSRo, l. 41 H$^4$ 129 so] *om.* H$^4$

130 curious] disirrous VS

133–6 Ihesu . . . goode] *om.* H$^4$Ha$^1$, l. 141 VSRo, l. 117 Ad$^2$, l. 89 Tr, l. 21 Ha$^2$ 133 vs] luf RoHa$^2$ hange] stehe Ha$^2$

134 yaue] seȝe Ha$^2$ blode] þi *add.* Tr

135 (l. 92 Tr) the made] is euer Tr, þou madest Ha$^2$   oure] my Tr

136 (l. 91 Tr) broght] bouȝt Tr

137–40 Ihesu ... me] *om.* H$^4$Ha$^1$, l. 145 VSRo, l. 121 Ad$^2$, l. 93 Tr, l. 25 Ha$^2$
137 my leman] my (*om.* Tr) lord Ad$^2$Tr   þou ... fre] I þanke it þe Tr

138 þat] For Ro   al] *om.* Ad$^2$Ha$^2$   þou ... of] þis luf hast schewed to Tr

139 for ... yeld] doo aȝeyne to Tr, þare fore ȝelde Ha$^2$

140 Noght ... me] þer nys noht bote hit loue be Ha$^2$   Noght ... kepest] þow kepest (askes Ro) not but þe (*om.* Ro) loue VSAd$^2$Ro   kepest of] axes Tr

141–4 Ihesu ... mournynge] *om.* Ha$^1$, l. 149 VSRo, l. 125 Ad$^2$, l. 97 Tr, l. 45 H$^4$, l. 29 Ha$^2$   141 god] good Ad$^2$   my lord] iesu Ha$^2$

142 þou me] ffor itt H$^4$   þou] ne *add.* Ad$^2$RoHa$^2$   me askest] *trs.* VSAd$^2$RoHa$^2$, askest of me Tr   askest] askethe H$^4$

143 hert] loue VSAd$^2$RoTrHa$^2$   in] and VSAd$^2$TrHa$^2$   loue] herte VSAd$^2$Tr, al Ro, eke Ha$^2$   longynge] wyrkynge Ro, servyng Ha$^2$

144 with] and VS   stil] swete RoHa$^2$

145–8 Ihesu ... nyght] *om.* H$^4$Ha$^1$, l. 153 VSRo, l. 129 Ad$^2$, l. 101 Tr, l. 33 Ha$^2$
145 Ihesu] my *add.* VSAd$^2$RoTr   dere] *om.* Ha$^2$   loue] lyf ⟨iesu Ha$^2$⟩ TrHa$^2$   light] hert Lt

146 wil] *om.* Ha$^2$   þe loue] *trs.* Ha$^2$

147 Do] make Ad$^2$Tr   the loue] *trs.* RoTrHa$^2$   the] *om.* Ad$^2$

148 for] after VSAd$^2$   both] *om.* VSAd$^2$RoHa$^2$

149–52 Ihesu ... se] *om.* TrH$^4$Ha$^1$, l. 157 VSRo, l. 133 Ad$^2$, l. 37 Ha$^2$   149 so loue] to luf so Ro   loue] seruen Ha$^2$

150 my ... euer] euer my þouȝt RoHa$^2$   euer] ay VS   on] vpon RoHa$^2$

151 eighen] swete eyȝe ⟨þou Ro⟩ RoHa$^2$, þou *add.* Ad$^2$   on] towart Ha$^2$

152 mildely ... þou] help me for ned I Lt   mildely] euermore Ad$^2$   nede] dede Ro, y preie al þat Ha$^2$   þou] *om.* VRo

153–6 Ihesu ... boght] *om.* Ha$^1$, l. 165 VS, l. 137 Ad$^2$, l. 161 Ro, l. 105 Tr, l. 53 H$^4$, l. 41 Ha$^2$   153 is] be Ad$^2$RoHa$^2$

154 þynge] ne *add.* VSAd$^2$RoTrHa$^2$   reche] kepe Tr   I] me Ro, ryght *add.* H$^4$

155 Bot ... þe] y ȝyrne to haue þi wille y Ha$^2$   þat ... þe] relesshe of synne þat I haue Tr   þat] *om.* H$^4$

156 And ... boght] Aȝeynes þi wille in word and þouȝt Tr   And] for Ha$^2$   þat] *om.* VSAd$^2$RoH$^4$Ha$^2$   hast me] *trs.* Ad$^2$H$^4$Ha$^2$   so] wel Ha$^2$

157–60 Ihesu ... fre] *om.* Ha$^1$, l. 169 VS, l. 141 Ad$^2$, l. 165 Ro, l. 109 Tr, l. 45 Ha$^2$
157 Ihesu ... be] *om.* H$^4$

158 (l. 57 H$^4$) Ful ... me] þurȝ loue and mercy bryng me to þe Tr   Ful] For Ro, wel Ha$^2$   longe] lord *add.* H$^4$   hast þou] *trs.* H$^4$

159 þe ... the] þat ich may þi ioy se Tr

160 þat ... fre] þere as þou regnes in deyte Tr   with] to Ro, *om.* Ha$^2$   fre] and I a traytor ageynst the *add.* H$^4$

161–4 Mary ... jugement] *om.* TrH$^4$Ha$^1$Ha$^2$, l. 105 VSAd$^2$, l. 169 Ro

163 þat] *om.* VSAd$^2$   went] nt *obscured in MS binding*

165–8 Ihesu ... kynge] *om.* TrH$^4$Ha$^1$Ha$^2$, l. 173 VSRo, l. 145 Ad$^2$

168 kynge] swetyng VSAd$^2$Ro

169–72 Ihesu ... þe$^2$] *om.* TrH$^4$Ha$^1$, l. 177 VSRo, l. 153 Ad$^2$   169–70 Ihesu ... tre] *om.* Ha$^2$   169 to] *om.* VSAd$^2$

170 þou] me *add.* VSAd$^2$, þat me Ro   shewedest] schewest VSAd$^2$   þi] þo Ro

171 (l. 49 Ha$^2$) corone] bac Ha$^2$   þorne] þornes VSAd$^2$Ro   and] þi RoHa$^2$

172 to hert] þorw VSAd$^2$RoHa$^2$

173–6 Ihesu ... showynge] *om.* TrHa$^1$, l. 181 VSRo, l. 157 Ad$^2$, l. 61 H$^4$, l. 51 Ha$^2$
173 I se] is (*om.* Ha$^2$) soþe RoHa$^2$

174 (l. 183 Ro) to] in S   loue clippynge] mankynde Ha$^2$   loue] lo H$^4$

175 (l. 182 Ro) hede] doun *add.* RoHa$^2$ swet] luf Ro

176 al] *om.* H$^4$ showynge] longynge Ha$^2$

177–80 Ihesu ... me] *om.* Ha$^1$, l. 185 VSRo, l. 161 Ad$^2$, l. 113 Tr, l. 65 H$^4$

177 euer] *om.* VSAd$^2$RoHa$^2$

178 þi] þe VSAd$^2$TrHa$^2$, þo Ro

179 þi ... se] Iche see þi body al blody Tr ymage] bodi VSAd$^2$RoH$^4$Ha$^2$ blody] bi bled VSAd$^2$Ro, to toren Ha$^2$

180 Lord . . . sith] hit makeþ heorte Ha$^2$ do . . . wound] þou suffurdest þat for Tr wound] smerte Ha$^2$

181–4 Ihesu . . . mode] *om.* Ha$^1$, l. 189 VSRo, l. 165 Ad$^2$, l. 117 Tr, l. 69 H$^4$, l. 59 Ha$^2$

181 þi modyr] þe quene Ha$^2$

182 Of] on H$^4$ lete] wepte VSRoHa$^2$, grette Ad$^2$, hade Tr

184 Hyre made] heo maden hire haue VS, made hyr hert RoHa$^2$, *trs.* H$^4$Tr a] of Ad$^2$, *om.* RoTrH$^4$Ha$^2$ ful] *om.* VSRoHa$^2$, of *add.* TrH$^4$

185–8 Ihesu . . . lete] *om.* Ha$^1$, l. 193 VSRo, l. 169 Ad$^2$, l. 121 Tr, l. 73 H$^4$, l. 63 Ha$^2$

185 Ihesu] þi *add.* Ad$^2$ loue . . . to] for luf þou dudes Tr þe dede] *trs.* Ro to] *om.* Ha$^2$ grete] wepen VSTr

186 dede þi] made RoHa$^2$, made þi Tr blode] lyue H$^4$ to] *om.* Ha$^2$ swete] lete Tr

187 were] wel *add.* Ro, ful *add.* H$^4$ sore] i *add.* STr, be *add.* Ro, a *add.* H$^4$

188 dede] þi *add.* VSAd$^2$TrH$^4$Ha$^2$, made Ro

189–92 Ihesu ... be] *om.* H$^4$Ha$^1$Ha$^2$, l. 201 VS, l. 173 Ad$^2$, l. 217 Ro, l. 125 Tr

189 þi] to Tr

191 on] þe *add.* Tr

192 loue] ne *add.* VSAd$^2$ may] mihte VS non] no man Tr

193–6 Ihesu ... dede] *om.* H$^4$Ha$^1$Ha$^2$, l. 205 VS, l. 177 Ad$^2$, l. 221 Ro, l. 129 Tr

193 first] word *add.* VSTr was] *om.* Tr as] *om.* Ro

194 þou] to *add.* Tr dere] swete Tr

195 he] *om.* Lt

196 Al] *om.* Tr þat] on þe cros *add.* Tr þe] *om.* Ro to] þo *add.* Ro

197–200 Ihesu . . . paradisse] *om.* H$^4$Ha$^1$Ha$^2$, l. 209 VS, l. 181 Ad$^2$, l. 225 Ro, l. 133 Tr

197 oþer] word *add.* Tr j-wisse] þis Tr

198 written] it *add.* Tr

199 haue] be in Ro

200 with . . . day] þat dey wiþ þe Tr

201–4 Ihesu ... Iohn] *om.* H$^4$Ha$^1$Ha$^2$, l. 213 VS, l. 185 Ad$^2$, l. 229 Ro, l. 137 Tr

201 þe þrid] þat oþer Ro, word *add.* Tr

202 shold . . . gone] þe schulde (*trs.* Tr) forgon VSAd$^2$Tr

203 A sone] Also Ro, þan Tr A] And Ad$^2$ betoke hire] hire betauhtest VSAd$^2$Ro one] to seynt ion Tr

204 take] lo RoTr Iohn] þi sonne Tr

205–8 Ihesu ... wore] *om.* H$^4$Ha$^1$Ha$^2$, l. 217 VS, l. 189 Ad$^2$, l. 237 Ro, l. 141 Tr

205 as] whan Tr more] ȝore Ro

206 firth] fyft Ro

207 A . . . þursteth] þou seydest I am aþurst ful Tr quod] seydest VS, now Ro þou] god Ro þursteth] þursted Ad$^2$

208 dampned] synful RoTr

209–12 Ihesu ... me] *om.* H$^4$Ha$^1$Ha$^2$, l. 221 VS, l. 193 Ad$^2$, l. 233 Ro, l. 145 Tr

209 fift] word *add.* VSTr, fyrthe Ro reweth] rewed LtAd$^2$

210 saidest] spake RoTr on] þe *add.* Tr

211 God$^1$] lord Tr

212 þat] it semes Ro hast] al *add.* VSAd$^2$, þus *add.* Tr

213–16 Ihesu ... was] *om.* H$^4$Ha$^1$Ha$^2$, l. 225 VS, l. 197 Ad$^2$, l. 241 Ro, l. 149 Tr

213 word] hit *add.* VSAd$^2$RoTr

215 þou] *om.* VSAd$^2$Ro betoke] betauhtest VSAd$^2$

216 his] þi Ro wil] it *add.* Tr

217–20 Ihesu . . . goste] *om.* RoH$^4$Ha$^1$Ha$^2$, l. 299 VS, l. 201 Ad$^2$, l. 153 Tr 217 in . . . peyne] þe seuent word greued me Tr in] al *add.* VSAd$^2$

218 Neuer . . . beste] whan þou seydest consummatum est Tr a] *om.* VAd$^2$

219 þou . . . est] þou bowest þi heued and ȝeld þe gost Tr

220 þi . . . goste] so meke was neuer man ne best Tr

221–4 Mary . . . go] *om.* RoTrHa$^1$Ha$^2$, l. 253 VS, l. 149 Ad$^2$, l. 77 H$^4$

222 Hel] Al Lt þou] *om.* VSAd$^2$H$^4$ shild] kepe H$^4$ me] us H$^4$

223 me] us H$^4$ so . . . do] ⟨to H$^4$⟩ do so VSAd$^2$H$^4$

224 I] we H$^4$ mot] *om.* VSAd$^2$H$^4$

225–8 Ihesu . . . me] *om.* TrH$^4$Ha$^1$Ha$^2$, l. 233 VS, l. 205 Ad$^2$, l. 197 Ro

226 gone] passen VSAd$^2$Ro in] be VS þe] *om.* Ro way] here *add.* Ro

227 Abide and] A while abydeþ VSAd$^2$Ro

228 peyn] ⟨in Ro⟩ serwe VSAd$^2$Ro like] to *add.* VSAd$^2$Ro

229–32 Ihesu . . . me] *om.* TrH$^4$Ha$^1$Ha$^2$, l. 237 VS, l. 209 Ad$^2$, l. 201 Ro

230 folke] fader Ro may hit] *trs.* VSAd$^2$Ro

231 What] þat Ro

232 þat . . . art] Why þis payne is so hard Ro

233–6 Ihesu . . . sore] *om.* TrH$^4$Ha$^1$Ha$^2$, l. 241 VS, l. 213 Ad$^2$, l. 209 Ro 233 þou] *om.* Lt

234 folk] ȝe *add.* VSRo, peple Ad$^2$ me] *om.* Ro yore] fore Ad$^2$, Why *add.* Ro

235 I] þe *add.* Ad$^2$ with] for Ro

236 And] ffor Ad$^2$ with] *om.* VSAd$^2$, for Ro yow] so VSAd$^2$, *om.* Ro

237–40 Ihesu . . . bette] *om.* TrH$^4$Ha$^1$Ha$^2$, l. 245 VS, l. 217 Ad$^2$, l. 205 Ro 237 yite] þet Ad$^2$

238 vynyard] he haue *add.* VSAd$^2$, kynreden Ro I] haf *add.* Ro þe] se Ad$^2$ sete] fette Ro

239 I] *om.* VS hete] bihet VSAd$^2$Ro

240 And] wiþ VSAd$^2$Ro I] al VSAd$^2$Ro

241–4 Ihesu . . . blisse] *om.* TrH$^4$Ha$^1$Ha$^2$, l. 249 VS, l. 221 Ad$^2$, l. 213 Ro

242 amisse] ⟨of Ro⟩ mis VSAd$^2$Ro

244 yeldest me] *trs.* VSAd$^2$ peyn] *om.* Lt, schome VS ayeyn] mi *add.* VSAd$^2$Ro

245–8 Ihesu . . . he] *om.* RoHa$^1$, l. 257 VS, l. 229 Ad$^2$, l. 157 Tr, l. 81 H$^4$, l. 67 Ha$^2$ 245 fyve] *om.* H$^4$ wellys] woundes Ha$^2$ fynd I] *trs.* VSAd$^2$Ha$^2$ in] on Tr

246 þat] þy Ha$^2$ to] *om.* VSAd$^2$Ha$^2$ sprynge] spryngyng Tr, sprenges Ha$^2$ drawen] to drawe VSAd$^2$, myght draw H$^4$, tacheþ Ha$^2$

247 rede] *om.* Ha$^2$ blode] and water *add.* Ha$^2$ þi] þe VSAd$^2$TrH$^4$Ha$^2$

248 My . . . he] us to whosshe from oure fon þre Ha$^2$ euer] of synnes VSAd$^2$, euen H$^4$ wosshen] washe H$^4$, reweþ on Tr he] heo VS, hee Ad$^2$, þe Tr, ye H$^4$

249–52 Ihesu . . . fordo] *om.* RoHa$^1$, l. 261 VS, l. 233 Ad$^2$, l. 161 Tr, l. 85 H$^4$, l. 71 Ha$^2$ 249 euer] *om.* VSAd$^2$TrH$^4$Ha$^2$ draw] me *add.* Lt to] And *add.* VSAd$^2$, vntoo And Tr

250 Make . . . hert] min heorte opene Ha$^2$

251 Yif . . . þe] þis hure of Ha$^2$ þi . . . drynke] to drynke of þi loue Tr

252 fleishely] flessches VSAd$^2$ be] al *add.* Ha$^2$ fordo] done me froo Tr

253–6 Ihesu . . . me] *om.* RoTrH$^4$Ha$^1$Ha$^2$, l. 265 VS, l. 237 Ad$^2$ 253 to] *om.* VSAd$^2$

254 Who] Wo Ad$^2$ yeld . . . se] al ȝelde þe VSAd$^2$

255 my] þi VSAd$^2$ to] hit VSAd$^2$

256 peynes] pyne VSAd$^2$ suffred] þoldust Ad$^2$

257–60 Ihesu . . . entierlyche] *om.* RoTrH$^4$Ha$^1$Ha$^2$, l. 269 VS, l. 241 Ad$^2$ 257 gif me] *trs.* Ad$^2$

258 þat] *om.* VS ground] þat VS

259 pershe] þurle VSAd$^{2}$

260 þat . . . þyn] þyn owne þat I be Ad$^{2}$ I] hit VS

261–4 Ihesu . . . fro] *om.* RoHa$^{1}$, l. 273 VS, l. 245 Ad$^{2}$, l. 165 Tr, l. 89 H$^{4}$, l. 75 Ha$^{2}$ 261 Ihesu] crist *add.* Ha$^{2}$ do] mak Ad$^{2}$TrH$^{4}$ me] to *add.* Ad$^{2}$Tr

262 and] or VSAd$^{2}$TrH$^{4}$ what] where Tr, so *add.* Ha$^{2}$ do] goo Tr

263 I . . . for] lyf ne deþ weole ne Ha$^{2}$ I] *om.* Lt ne] or H$^{4}$

264 Neuer . . . turne] turne my hert neuer Tr Neuer] Ne VSAd$^{2}$Ha$^{2}$ Neuer let] *trs.* H$^{4}$ let] do Ha$^{2}$

265–8 Mary . . . be] *om.* RoTrH$^{4}$Ha$^{1}$, l. 297 VS, l. 269 Ad$^{2}$, l. 79 Ha$^{2}$

266 Crist] *om.* VS, loue Ad$^{2}$ the] þat *add.* Ad$^{2}$

268 with . . . to] worþi þat (þay Ha$^{2}$) hit (I Ha$^{2}$) so VSAd$^{2}$Ha$^{2}$

269–72 Ihesu . . . þynge] *om.* RoH$^{4}$Ha$^{1}$Ha$^{2}$, l. 277 VS, l. 249 Ad$^{2}$, l. 169 Tr 269 my] *om.* VTr lord] mi ⟨dere Tr⟩ *add.* VSAd$^{2}$Tr

271 Make . . . derlynge] And ordeyne me euer at þi lykyng Tr

272 þat I þe] þe to Tr

273–6 Ihesu . . . blyn] *om.* RoHa$^{1}$Ha$^{2}$, l. 281 VS, l. 253 Ad$^{2}$, l. 173 Tr, l. 93 H$^{4}$

276 To] so S

277–80 Ihesu . . . gretynge] *om.* RoHa$^{1}$Ha$^{2}$, l. 285 VS, l. 257 Ad$^{2}$, l. 177 Tr, l. 97 H$^{4}$

278 þi . . . lykynge] ȝefe me here in my lyffyng Tr

279 My . . . longynge] pacience peyne and suffryng Tr

280 With . . . gretynge] þat to my soule were amendyng Tr to þe] *om.* VSAd$^{2}$Ro gretynge] wepyng VSAd$^{2}$

281–4 Ihesu . . . tame] *om.* RoTrH$^{4}$Ha$^{1}$, l. 289 VS, l. 261 Ad$^{2}$, l. 83 Ha$^{2}$ 281 yeue] do Ha$^{2}$ me] þat *add.* Ha$^{2}$

282 Paciens in] me likeþ to dreȝe Ha$^{2}$

283 hit . . . game] is (*om.* Ha$^{2}$) note and frame VSAd$^{2}$Ha$^{2}$

285–8 Mary . . . be] *om.* RoTrH$^{4}$Ha$^{1}$Ha$^{2}$, l. 197 VS, l. 255 Ad$^{2}$

286 sorowes] serwe VSAd$^{2}$

287 sorow here] *trs.* Ad$^{2}$

288 a] *om.* VSAd$^{2}$ to] *om.* VSAd$^{2}$

289–92 Ihesu . . . þe] *om.* RoTrH$^{4}$Ha$^{1}$, l. 293 VS, l. 265 Ad$^{2}$, l. 87 Ha$^{2}$ 289 þat] þis Lt se] þe VSAd$^{2}$, al *add.* Ha$^{2}$

290 fleisshly] þe (*om.* Ad$^{2}$) fflessches VSAd$^{2}$, fleyhs Ha$^{2}$

291 do . . . fle] to leten me Ha$^{2}$ me] to *add.* Ad$^{2}$

292 And . . . to] graunte for þe loue of Ha$^{2}$ yeue to] *trs.* Ad$^{2}$

293–6 Ihesu . . . besoght] *om.* RoH$^{4}$Ha$^{1}$, l. 301 VS, l. 273 Ad$^{2}$, l. 181 Tr, l. 91 Ha$^{2}$ 293 in] on Tr

294 Of] al Ha$^{2}$ þynge] blisse Ha$^{2}$ rech] kepe Tr

296 wel] in lykyng Tr besoght] of þouȝt VS, i douȝth Ad$^{2}$, brouȝt Tr, ywroht Ha$^{2}$

297–300 Ihesu . . . me] *om.* RoH$^{4}$Ha$^{1}$, l. 305 VS, l. 277 Ad$^{2}$, l. 185 Tr, l. 95 Ha$^{2}$ 297 forlet] forsake Tr

298 I lyke] me lyken VSAd$^{2}$Tr, mi likyng Ha$^{2}$

299 Blisse . . . me] glad may ich neuer Tr Blisse . . . may] mai ne god blisse Ha$^{2}$ ne may] may non VS, non *add.* Ad$^{2}$

300 Til] þat *add.* VSAd$^{2}$Tr, o þat Ha$^{2}$

301–4 Ihesu . . . noght] *om.* RoH$^{4}$Ha$^{1}$Ha$^{2}$, l. 309 VS, l. 281 Ad$^{2}$, l. 189 Tr 301 þou] þat VSAd$^{2}$Tr hast me] *trs.* VSAd$^{2}$ boght] abouht VSAd$^{2}$

302 to] *om.* Lt draweth] drawud Ad$^{2}$

303 I . . . of] Out of sunne put out Ad$^{2}$ I] *om.* VSTr holy] *om.* Tr hit] *om.* VS, fullych *add.* Tr out] *om.* Tr

304 þat] þurȝ synne *add.* Tr I] ne *add.* VSAd$^{2}$

305–8 Ihesu . . . me] *om.* RoH$^{4}$Ha$^{1}$, l. 313 VS, l. 285 Ad$^{2}$, l. 193 Tr, l. 103 Ha$^{2}$ 305 spoused] weddet VS

306 With . . . be] ofte ych habbe misdon aȝeynes þe Ha$^{2}$ hit] is Lt owet] ouhte VSAd$^{2}$Tr

307 þogh . . . þe] iesu þi merci is wel fre Ha$^{2}$

308 þi . . . me] iesu þi merci y crie to þe Ha$^{2}$ euer redy] *trs.* Ad$^{2}$

309–12 Ihesu . . . haue] *om.* RoH$^{4}$Ha$^{1}$, l. 317 VS, l. 289 Ad$^{2}$, l. 197 Tr, l. 107 Ha$^{2}$
309 þi mercy] wiþ herte Ha$^{2}$ by leue] euer Tr, þi loue Ha$^{2}$ by] wiþ Ad$^{2}$

310 Me] hit Ha$^{2}$ þe to] ⟨nede Ha$^{2}$⟩ þat I hit VSAd$^{2}$TrHa$^{2}$

311 dewe] wete Ad$^{2}$ me] þou *add.* Tr

312 worþi . . . haue] helpe me lord þat I be saue Tr, from alle harmes þou me saue Ha$^{2}$

313–16 Ihesu . . . langynge] *om.* RoTrH$^{4}$Ha$^{1}$, l. 321 VS, l. 293 Ad$^{2}$, l. 111 Ha$^{2}$
313 þou . . . yernynge] from me be al þat þyng Ha$^{2}$ yernynge] desiryng Ad$^{2}$

314 In . . . my] þat me may be to mis Ha$^{2}$ Lord be] *trs.* VSAd$^{2}$

315 My . . . mournynge] al þat is nede þou me bryng Ha$^{2}$

316 þe . . . langynge] þi loue is my ȝyrnyng Ha$^{2}$

317–20 Ihesu . . . blode] *om.* RoH$^{4}$Ha$^{1}$, l. 325 VS, l. 297 Ad$^{2}$, l. 201 Tr, l. 115 Ha$^{2}$
317 my . . . of] I aske wiþ Tr of myld] *trs.* VSAd$^{2}$

318 My . . . good] helpe þat my soule haue fode and Tr hath] gret *add.* Ha$^{2}$

319 Mak . . . clene] tak hire treufole Ha$^{2}$ þolemode] holy mode Lt

320 fulled] filled Lt, ful hit (hire Ha$^{2}$) VSAd$^{2}$TrHa$^{2}$ blode] flod VSAd$^{2}$Tr

321–4 Ihesu . . . þe] *om.* RoH$^{4}$Ha$^{1}$, l. 329 VS, l. 301 Ad$^{2}$, l. 205 Tr, l. 119 Ha$^{2}$
321 prayeth] precheth Lt, I prey Ad$^{2}$, bidde y Ha$^{2}$

322 Let . . . vncloþet] euermore wel us Ha$^{2}$ Let] suffur Tr vncloþet] to *add.* Tr be] but *add.* Tr

323–4 Cloth . . . þe] *om.* Ha$^{2}$ 323 Cloth hit] Clothed Lt þi] *om.* Tr so fre] and charyte Tr so] *om.* VS

324 liken þe] it lyȝt be Tr

325–8 Ihesu . . . þoght] *om.* RoH$^{4}$Ha$^{1}$Ha$^{2}$, l. 333 VS, l. 305 Ad$^{2}$, l. 209 Tr
325 Ihesu . . . I] ffor golde ne syluer axes þou Tr fairnes] beute ne VSAd$^{2}$ I] þe *add.* VSAd$^{2}$

326 nobily] noble i Ad$^{2}$

327 Broches . . . rynges] londes ne rentes (beutes S) VSAd$^{2}$ der j-boght] kepes þou noȝt Tr

328 hert] hertly VS, herte Ad$^{2}$, herty Tr

329–32 Ihesu . . . þe$^{2}$] *om.* RoH$^{4}$Ha$^{1}$Ha$^{2}$, l. 337 VS, l. 309 Ad$^{2}$, l. 213 Tr
329 whan . . . liketh] swete byseche I Tr so] *om.* S liketh] likud Ad$^{2}$

330 Loue sparkles] of þi loue þat Tr þou send] *trs.* VSAd$^{2}$ me] And *add.* Tr

332 in] me *add.* Lt

333–6 Ihesu . . . þynkynge] *om.* RoTrH$^{4}$Ha$^{1}$, l. 345 VS, l. 317 Ad$^{2}$, l. 121 Ha$^{2}$

334 is] his Ad$^{2}$ ful] wel Ha$^{2}$

335–6 May . . . þynkynge] *om.* Ha$^{2}$ 335 hit] i S fele] witen VSAd$^{2}$ techynge] e *obscured in MS binding*, knowyng VS

336 if] *om.* VSAd$^{2}$ þrogh] herte *add.* VSAd$^{2}$

337–40 Ihesu . . . fre] *om.* Ha$^{1}$Ha$^{2}$, l. 349 VS, l. 321 Ad$^{2}$, l. 245 Ro, l. 217 Tr, l. 101 H$^{4}$
337 me] grace *add.* TrH$^{4}$ þat I may] to Tr

338 þe] thy H$^{4}$ gret] muchele VS, *om.* Tr godnes] good ⟨þat Ro⟩ VSAd$^{2}$Ro þou hast] *om.* H$^{4}$ done] to *add.* RoTrH$^{4}$

339 And . . . agayn] Vnkynde agayne haf I ben to Ro the] haue be VSAd$^{2}$TrH$^{4}$

341–4 Ihesu . . . noght] *om.* Ha$^{1}$Ha$^{2}$, l. 353 VS, l. 325 Ad$^{2}$, l. 249 Ro, l. 221 Tr, l. 105 H$^{4}$

342 Won] dwelle Tr togeddre] ne *add.* S þay may] mouwe þi V, *trs.* SAd$^{2}$Ro noght] but *add.* Tr

343 broght] ffor *add.* Tr

344 bittyr] ne *add.* Ad$^{2}$

345–8 Ihesu . . . me] *om.* Ha$^{1}$Ha$^{2}$, l. 357 VS, l. 329 Ad$^{2}$, l. 253 Ro, l. 225 Tr
345 thanke] vak Ro

346 þogh] þat Ad² wreched] ⟨be S, a Ro⟩ wrecche VSAd²RoTr and] *om.* Ro
347 to] *om.* VSAd²Ro
348 þou graunt] *trs.* VSRoTr to] *om.* VSAd²RoTr
349–52 Ihesu . . . mercy] *om.* Ha¹, l. 361 VS, l. 333 Ad², l. 257 Ro, l. 229 Tr, l. 109 H⁴, l. 127 Ha² 349 be vnworþi] yuel bee Tr
350 The . . . almyghty] alle my truste lord is in þe Tr The . . . loue] to loue þe VSAd²RoHa² almyghty] ffor *add.* Tr
351 godenes] loue Ha² me] *om.* RoTrH⁴ make] maken Lt, maketh ⟨to ben Ha²⟩ VSAd²Ha²
352 My . . . do] To do (putte Tr) my soule RoTr, ant don me al Ha²
353–6 Ihesu . . . he] *om.* Ha¹, l. 365 VS, l. 337 Ad², l. 261 Ro, l. 233 Tr, l. 113 H⁴, l. 131 Ha² 353 þy mercy] swete þis Tr, þi mildenesse Ha² conforteth] froreþ Ha²
354 For] þat Tr non] no mon VSAd²RoTrH⁴Ha²
355 þat] ȝif TrHa² syn . . . leue] wold leue synne Ro, he synne leue Tr, he let sunne Ha² to . . . fle] turne (flee Tr) to þe RoTr, turne to me H⁴
356 þat] redy *add.* Ro, But H⁴ mercy . . . he] ne fynd socour at þe Ha² mercy . . . fyndeth] þou ne art euer redyer þan Tr ne] ful redi VS, redi ne Ad², and grace H⁴
357–60 Ihesu . . . lisse] *om.* TrH⁴Ha¹, l. 369 VS, l. 341 Ad², l. 269 Ro, l. 135 Ha² 357 Ihesu . . . is] For sunful folk swuete iesus Ha²
358 come . . . of] lihtest from VSAd²RoHa² blisse] hous Ha²
359 In . . . wisse] pore and loȝe þou were for ous Ha²
360 To . . . lisse] þin heorte loue þou sendest ous Ha² yif] brynge Ro al] to *add.* Ro lisse] blisse LtRo*
361–4 Ihesu . . . me] *om.* TrH⁴Ha¹Ha², l. 373 VS, l. 345 Ad², l. 265 Ro
362 I . . . in] Trysty hope I haue to Ro I] and Lt haue] i had *add.* Ad² truste] hope *add.* VS, good hope Ad²
363 Der] þerfore VSAd²Ro
364 þou mend] amende þou (to Ro) VSAd²Ro
365–8 Ihesu . . . leman] *om.* RoTrH⁴Ha¹, l. 377 VS, l. 349 Ad², l. 143 Ha² 365 þat] þou VSAd²Ha²
366 desyr I] *trs.* Ad², y ȝyrne Ha²
367 Me . . . nan] þarefore ne lette me noman Ha² suffre] þing *add.* VSAd² nan] vayn Lt, non VSAd²
368 Swet . . . leman] þah ich for loue be blac and won Ha²
369–72 Ihesu . . . fre] *om.* TrH⁴Ha¹, l. 381 VS, l. 353 Ad², l. 273 Ro, l. 139 Ha² 369 euer] forþi Ha²
370 þi] *om.* Ad² jnward loue] luf inwardely Ro jnward] suete Ha² þou graunt] *trs.* Ro
371 þogh] þat Ha² vnworthi] worþi Ha²
372 þou¹] *om.* RoHa² worthy] *om.* Lt? þou²] þat VSAd²RoHa²
373–6 Ihesu . . . food] *om.* TrH⁴Ha¹, l. 389 VS, l. 361 Ad², l. 277 Ro, l. 147 Ha² 373 Ihesu] al *add.* VSAd²Ha² swet . . . art] þou art al swete Ro þou] þat VSAd², iesu Ha² so] al VSAd²Ha², and Ro
374 Do] *om.* Ha²
375 me] *om.* Ro make] so *add.* VSAd²RoHa² swith] swete VSAd²Ro
376 wonder . . . food] y ne drede for no flod Ha² food] mood VSAd²Ro
377–80 Ihesu . . . ille] *om.* H⁴Ha¹Ha², l. 393 VS, l. 365 Ad², l. 281 Ro, l. 237 Tr 377 mak] do VSRo me] to *add.* RoTr
379 loue] lord *add.* Tr fulfille] þou fille Ro
380 suffre] neuere *add.* VSAd², me *add.* Ro nat] *om.* VSAd²Ro, noon Tr
381–4 Ihesu . . . amonge] *om.* H⁴Ha¹, l. 397 VS, l. 369 Ad², l. 285 Ro, l. 241 Tr, l. 151 Ha² 381 hote] swete VSAd²RoHa²
382 lif] soule hele Tr al] *om.* Tr þeron] i *add.* VSAd², on þe y Ha²

383 Lord] iesu Ha$^2$

384 swete] wete Ro [*corr. to* swete]

385–8 Ihesu . . . fro] *om.* H$^4$Ha$^1$, l. 401 VS, l. 373 Ad$^2$, l. 289 Ro, l. 245 Tr, l. 159 Ha$^2$
385 þou] be *add.* VSAd$^2$RoHa$^2$

386 hert] soule Ha$^2$

388 þou] my swete (lord Ad$^2$, god Ro) *add.* VSAd$^2$Ro, alle my helpe Tr, my lif Ha$^2$ art] is TrHa$^2$   gone . . . fro] me atgo Ha$^2$   gone] went VSAd$^2$

389–92 Mary . . . mercy] *om.* TrH$^4$Ha$^1$Ha$^2$, l. 341 VS, l. 313 Ad$^2$, l. 293 Ro

390 and] *om.* VSAd$^2$

391 þynk . . . jnwardly] wole enterly VSAd$^2$, now wil inwardely Ro   jnwardly] jwardly Lt

392 to . . . to] *om.* VSAd$^2$Ro   his] þi S

393–6 Ihesu . . . se] *om.* H$^4$Ha$^1$, l. 405 VS, l. 377 Ad$^2$, l. 297 Ro, l. 249 Tr, l. 163 Ha$^2$
393 þyn ore] lord Tr   me] for *add.* Ha$^2$

394 my soul] ich Ha$^2$

395 How . . . be] Iesu þi lore biddeþ me Ha$^2$   hit] I RoTr

396 þer . . . se] helpe me lord to wone with þe Tr, wiþ al myn herte louie þe Ha$^2$ þer] þat Ro   þe] *om.* Ad$^2$

397–400 Ihesu . . . me] *om.* H$^4$Ha$^1$Ha$^2$, l. 409 VS, l. 381 Ad$^2$, l. 301 Ro, l. 253 Tr
397 þi . . . þou] swete þi wille Tr   þou] *om.* VSAd$^2$Ro   teche] it *add.* Ad$^2$, þou *add.* Ro

399 With] þorw VSAd$^2$RoTr   myght] grace Tr   so] to *add.* Tr

400 And] þat V, *om.* S   þou] *om.* VAd$^2$Ro

401–4 Ihesu . . . brynge] *om.* H$^4$Ha$^1$, l. 413 VS, l. 385 Ad$^2$, l. 305 Ro, l. 257 Tr, l. 167 Ha$^2$
401 my lef] *om.* Ro   lef] lif Ad$^2$TrHa$^2$   my lord] iesu Ha$^2$   lord] ihesu *add.* Ro

402 To . . . soule] My soule to þe Ro   gret] *om.* Ha$^2$   longynge] lykyng Tr, ȝyrnyng Ha$^2$

403 þou . . . hit] þat hir Ro   hast . . . rynge] art suetest of alle þyng Ha$^2$   weddit] weddist Ro   þi] a Tr

404 to . . . hit] hir to þe Ro

405–8 Ihesu . . . þe] *om.* TrH$^4$Ha$^1$, l. 417 VS, l. 389 Ad$^2$, l. 309 Ro, l. 171 Ha$^2$

406 to$^1$] *om.* Ha$^2$

408 may . . . þe] in blys may þe se Ro, wiþ blisse þe mowe se Ha$^2$   dwel] wone VSAd$^2$

409–12 Ihesu . . . nyght] *om.* TrH$^4$Ha$^1$, l. 421 VS, l. 393 Ad$^2$, l. 313 Ro, l. 175 Ha$^2$
409 Ihesu] al *add.* VS, so *add.* RoHa$^2$   fayre] my lord Ad$^2$   my lemmon] ihesu so RoHa$^2$

410 I þe] þat i Ha$^2$   pray] beseche VSAd$^2$RoHa$^2$   hert of] al my VSRoHa$^2$   of] *om.* Ad$^2$

411 þi] þat Ad$^2$, þe Ha$^2$

412 þer] ioy *add.* Ro   is] ioye *add.* Ad$^2$, euer boþe *add.* Ro   withouten] and neuere VS, and Ad$^2$Ro

413–16 Ihesu . . . þynge] *om.* Ha$^1$, l. 425 VS, l. 397 Ad$^2$, l. 317 Ro, l. 261 Tr, l. 121 H$^4$, l. 179 Ha$^2$   413 þi] *om.* Tr, thow H$^4$   help] me *add.* Tr   endynge] and *add.* Tr

414 Take . . . deiynge] ant ine þat dredful out wendyng Ha$^2$   deiynge] endynge Lt, And *add.* Ro, partyng þou Tr

415 hit] vs Ro, *om.* Tr, mi soule Ha$^2$   socour] counfort Ro, god Ha$^2$   and] *om.* Ha$^2$   confortynge] sokeringe Ro, weryyng Ha$^2$

416 hit] ne *add.* VSAd$^2$, ho Ro, I ⟨ne Ha$^2$⟩ TrHa$^2$   wicked] eouel Ha$^2$

417–20 Ihesu . . . be] *om.* H$^4$Ha$^1$, l. 429 VS, l. 401 Ad$^2$, l. 321 Ro, l. 265 Tr, l. 183 Ha$^2$
417 for . . . mercy] þi grace þat is so Ha$^2$   for] form Ro   þi] grete *add.* Tr   mercy] ercie Ro   fre] *om.* Tr

418 In . . . help] Suche grace þen sende to Ro   hope] hape Lt   þou help] do þou VSAd$^2$Ha$^2$   help] sette Tr

419 scap] flee helle Tr     bid with] come to VSAd$^2$RoHa$^2$     bid] wone Tr

420 And . . . to] to þe blisse þat ay shal Ha$^2$     And] *om.* Tr     in . . . þe] with þe in blis Ro     in] ioy and *add.* Tr     with þe] *om.* Tr     to] *om.* VSAd$^2$

421–4 Ihesu . . . me] *om.* TrH$^4$Ha$^1$, l. 433 VS, l. 405 Ad$^2$, l. 325 Ro, l. 187 Ha$^2$
421 blessed] merci Ro, ful wel Ha$^2$     is] ben VSAd$^2$RoHa$^2$     he] heo VSAd$^2$

422 in þi] euer in Ro     ioy] blisse VSAd$^2$RoHa$^2$     þe shal] mowe þe (*om.* Ha$^2$) VSAd$^2$RoHa$^2$     se] be Ha$^2$

424 graunt] hit *add.* Ha$^2$

425–8 Ihesu . . . brynge] *om.* H$^4$Ha$^1$, l. 437 VS, l. 409 Ad$^2$, l. 329 Ro, l. 273 Tr, l. 191 Ha$^2$
425 Ihesu . . . no] þere ioy is euer wiþouten Tr     blisse] loue RoHa$^2$

426 þer . . . no] and neuer Tr     nor] ne no VSAd$^2$Ro, ne Tr     gretynge] wepynge VSAd$^2$RoTrHa$^2$

427 pitte] pees VSAd$^2$Tr, ioy RoHa$^2$     ioy] blis RoHa$^2$, myrþ Tr     with gret] and ful Ro, ant Ha$^2$     Amen] Amen *add.* Tr, per charite *add.* H$^4$

## *Meditation A*

20 teched] teche Ti
36 mekeli] mekel Ti
37 fader] *om.* Ti
39 an] and Ti
45 wote] vote Ti
66 wisse] wille Ti
72 him] *om.* Ti
75 tugged] tugge Ti
85 thei] *om.* Ti  fro] *om.* Ti
90 Herode] Horode Ti
103 ȝour sylues] ȝouris synnes Ti
111 satte] satten Ti
116 thefes] thefe Ti
129 that] than Ti
131 spere] spe Ti
159–60 Omnipotens . . . And] *om.* Ti
160 auees] Aue maria etcetera Ti
162 þe] *om.* Ti  whan] and Ti  wormys] and *add.* Ti
163 and . . . bestes] *om.* Ti  eighen] bodi Ti  nose] mouthe Ti
164 mouth] nose Ti  lippes] chekes thin eres and Ti  164–5 thy[2] . . . body] and thi membres of the Ti
166 þou wreche] *om.* Ti  shal þer] *trs.* Ti  the . . . comfort] *om.* Ti
168–9 Mercy . . . Ihesu] swete dere ihesu haue mercy on me Ti
169 Ihesu] etcetera *add.* Lt

## *Meditation B*

1 as . . . made] þat madist Add    þe] to *add.* Add
4 myȝt] myȝtis TiAdd    my[2]] *om.* Ti
5 occupaciouns] ocupacioun Add    bysynesse] and *add.* Add
7 þe[2]] to *add.* Add
8 wil] soule Add    luste] loue Add    soule] wil Add    loue] lust Add
9 with[3] . . . desyre] *om.* Add
10 lyf] with al my desirynge *add.* Add
11 verray] *om.* Add    shryft] confessioun to þee Add    and[2]] *om.* Ti
14 so . . . lemys] *om.* Add    al[2]] to be *add.* Add
15 bowe] bowinge Add    biddynge] biddingis Add
16 and[1]] *om.* Add    to þe] to the *add.* Ti    þe] *om.* Add
17 biddynge] biddingis Add
18 me[1]] *om.* Mu    and] *om.* Ti    me[2]] *om.* Ti    yiftis] ȝiltis Ti
20 þe[1]] to Add
21 be meke] meken me Add    yiftes] yifte Mu
22 apaid] wiþ þi ȝiftis *add.* Add    proud ne presumptuouse] *trs.* Add
23 know] knouleche Add
24 lyghted] aliȝtist Add
28 peynful] a *add.* UpTiAdd    þy] þat TiAdd
29 of] thi *add.* Ti
33 was] were UpTiAdd    dey] deeþ Up
36 laide] leftist Add
37 woldest] þou *add.* Add
38 profite] profre me Add    good] hool Add    and] in Add
39 and[2]] in Add    shrift] to þee *add.* Add
40 good[1]] *om.* UpAdd    of] in Ti
41 in] bi Add
42 temptacioun . . . tribulacioun] tribulacioun in ech temptacioun Add    my] man Add
44 þo] þe Add
45 Ihesu] *om.* Add
46 þe] þou *add.* Add
49 dere lord] *om.* Add    Crist] *om.* Add
50 and] of *add.* Add
51 holy passioun] passioun so holi Add    for vs] *om.* Add    on] opon Add
52 þer] þat UpTi    my wille] myn Add
54 one] ones UpTi    þy self] þee Add
55 haue] often *add.* Add    wille[1]] willis Add    for] fo Mu
56 of] in Add
57 euer] redi *add.* Add    put . . . wille] not at myn Add    out] not *add.* Up
58 with] to Add    þyne] þat is my ioie *add.* Add    grace] euere *add.* Add
59 and] so to *add.* Add    þerto] to þee Add
61 þat] þe Add    ferdnesse] drede Add
63 anguysshe] Here *add.* Add
64 al] my Ti, my *add.* Add
68 of] for Add    þy] þe Add    deseses] disese Add
69 þe] and *add.* Add    told] it *add.* Add    hym[2]] faire and *add.* Add    hit] þat Add

70 syn] synnes Add

71 kepe] scheelde Add    of$^{1}$] fro UpTiAdd    of$^{2}$] *om.* Add

72 euery] eche UpTiAdd    on] in Add

73 may] myȝte Add    lord] *om.* Add    73–4 for . . . þe] *om.* Add

75 desaises] diseis Add

76 þe$^{2}$] *om.* Mu    þe$^{3}$] somme *add.* UpTi

77 þe$^{4}$] *om.* Add

78 þou] *om.* Ti

79 þe] to *add.* Add

80 my] of þe Add

81 or] of *add.* Add    a . . . his] lordes Mu

82 sone] *om.* Mu    Yit] *om.* Add

84 cure] and come neer to me wiþ grace as þe samaritan dide and hilde in to my woundis oile of merci and wyn of counfort and brynge me in to þe stable of charite and euere holde me vndir þi cure *add.* Add

85 swet lord] *trs.* Add    fondynges] fondyng Ti, temptaciouns Add

86 þerfor] þanne Add

88 fordone] for loren Add

89 lyȝt] be Add

91 þe$^{1}$] for *add.* Add    is] *om.* Add    medeful] needful Add    spedeful] meedful Add

92 and . . . nedefulle] *om.* Ti    nedefulle] spedeful Add

93 þankynges] þankyng UpTi

94 shame] schames Add    a . . . as] *om.* Add

95 tribulacioun ne temptacioun] *trs.* Add

96 depart] parte Add    atwyn] asundir Add

97 il lore] euel teching Up, *om.* Add    ne] noon Add

100 beleued$^{1}$] leued Ti    leuynge] beleuynge Mu    beleued$^{2}$] leued Ti

101 to$^{1}$] *om.* Add    to$^{2}$] *om.* Add    and] in *add.* Add

102 and] in *add.* Add    of] al *add.* Add

103 þat] *om.* UpTi    103–4 trist . . . hope] *om.* Add

105 trist] rise Add    in] to *add.* Add

106 swete] *om.* Mu

107 and$^{1}$] *om.* Add    wilfully] skilfulli Add

108 to . . . and] *om.* Add    in$^{2}$] perfiȝt *add.* UpTi

109 hool be] *trs.* Add    hool] holy UpTi    or] and Add

110 as . . . dost] and lete me loue after þin heeste Add    or] and Add    let] þat *add.* UpTi, graunte me grace þat Add

111 let] graunte Add    lord] to *add.* Add

112 þe$^{2}$] *om.* Add    kunnyngely] kunnynge Ti

113 let] graunte Add    me] to *add.* Add

114 hatis] hatedist Up

115 yeld] to *add.* Add    þankynge] þankingis Add

117 goynge] goynges UpTiAdd

119 shame] shames ⟨and Up⟩ UpTiAdd    anguyshe] anguysches UpTiAdd

122 vpon] seint *add.* Add

123 neuer] neiþer Add

124 myȝt] myn Add    þe] þin Add

125 þy$^{1}$] *om.* MuAdd    and] thi *add.* Ti

126–7 so . . . come] *om.* Add

127 to . . . mercy] *om.* Add

129 accusours] accusaciouns Add

130 in$^{1}$] *om.* Add

131 stond] in *add.* Ti  þe] *om.* Mu

132 to] *om.* Mu  snybbynge] snybbyngis UpAdd, subbyngis Ti  al] *om.* Add

133 know] knouleche Add  man] for *add.* Add

137 Pater . . . etcetera] *om.* Mu

138 þankynge] þankingis Add

139 to] *om.* Add  face] in *add.* Add

140 deynte] deyntes Ti

141–2 þe inwardly] *om.* Add

143 and] *om.* Add

144 þe] *om.* Ti

145 graunt[1]] ȝeue Add

147 othyr] oþirs Add

148 swete] *om.* Mu  grace] *om.* UpTiAdd  blessed] blisful Add

150 þankynge] þankingis Add  þe[2]] *om.* Add

151 blasphemes] *om.* Add

152 al[1]] þe *add.* UpTiAdd  of[1]] al *add.* UpTi  þy] the Ti  holdes] housis Add

153 þe] helde the *add.* Ti

154 withjn] in *add.* Add

155 þank . . . I] *om.* Add

156 suffraunce] suffringe Add  stidfastly] stefastly Ti

157 and[1]] ne Add  or] ne Add  grace] *om.* Add

158 stidfastly] stifli Add  assaillynge] assailingis Add

161 þe[2]] *om.* Ti

162 and þederward] *om.* Mu  the] *om.* Add

163 gatys] goynges Up

164 and[1]] to *add.* Add

165 þy] *om.* Ti

166 mak] *om.* Ti

168 yeld] ȝele Ti  þankynge] þankingis Add

170 blyndynge] blindfelling Add  170–1 and . . . self] in latyng bi my silf moche UpTi, in wanhope in latinge to myche bi my silf Add

171 blyndynge] blindfelling Add

172 let] graunte Add  clerly] to *add.* Add

175 endlesly] endesly Ti

180 deseises] disese Add  tribulaciouns] tribulacioun Add

181 sekenesse] siiknessis Add

182 þe] god UpTiAdd  þy] his UpTiAdd  sondes] sonde Add

183 purgatory] to be poriede Add  hertely . . . hit] continuel herte lord þat Add lord] and *add.* UpTi

185 blesful . . . gracious] *om.* Add

186 þankynge] þankyngis UpTiAdd

188 naked] and *add.* UpTi, *om.* Add  fast] *om.* Ti

189 to scourgen] scourgers Add

190 chosen . . . weren] *om.* Mu, chosen men Add  stronge] *om.* Add  and[1]] *om.* UpTi

191 was[2]] weren UpTiAdd

193 wounde] woumde Mu  smytten] so *add.* Add

194 strok] þei *add.* UpTi  hit þe] *om.* UpTiAdd  deppyr] and deppere *add.* UpTi  yift] *om.* Add

195 a] *om.* Ti  shewynge] shedynge Mu

196 was] is Add  ful[2]] *om.* Ti

197 bettyr] briȝter Up, biȝtter Ti  shynen] not *add.* Add  nyght] nyȝtis Add

198 day . . . nyght] *trs.* Add

199 bot[1]] a *add.* Add
200 þe] *om.* Add   200–1 al . . . men] synne Add
202 my] oure Ti   202–3 nyght . . . medicyne] *om.* Add
204 cause] in erþe *add.* Add
206 grace] and *add.* Add
207 mynys] of *add.* Add   swet] lord *add.* Add
208 perle] perre Add
210 to] *om.* Add   þe] a UpTiAdd
211 swet] lord *add.* Add
212 to] *om.* Add   þis] þe UpTiAdd   scourgynge] skuournynge Ti
213 draweth] þe *add.* UpTi
214 hit] I Add
215 þe[2]] *om.* Add
216 to[2]] *om.* Add   216–17 þy . . . is] *om.* Add   þy] *om.* Ti
217 me] lord *add.* Add
218 me] lord *add.* Add   þe] þi Add   of . . . comaundementis] *om.* Add
219 þy] *om.* Add
221 Efte] Offte Up, ȝit Add   to] *om.* Add   for] as *add.* UpAdd
222 of[1]] dowue *add.* Add
223 cache] areche to Add
224 refuyt] refuse Ti   to vs] *om.* Add
226 abide] a byte Up, habite Ti
227 to] *om.* TiAdd   hit] þat Add
228 in] *om.* UpTiAdd   a] *om.* UpTiAdd   way] weies Add
229 yeld] ȝelding UpTiAdd
231 of] and Add
232 desyre] desiris Add   to] of Ti
233 contynuynge] contynuaunce Add
234 delitably] delicatly Mu, delitable Up, delectable Ti, delicat Add   to abyde] to habite Ti, abidinge Add
236 lyke] to *add.* Ti   al] *om.* Add
238 me] grace often *add.* Add   þy] þis Add
240 þe] þat Add
242 þis] þat Add   euche] euery UpTi
243 let] graunte Add   me] grace þat I may haue Add   study . . . my] *om.* Add and[2]] pryme Add   and[3]] *om.* Add
244 and[2] . . . be] *om.* Add
246 And] *om.* Add   yit] *om.* UpTi
249 and] in Mu, *om.* Ti
251 yeld] to *add.* Ti   þankynge] þankingis Add
252 for[1]] þoru Add   whan . . . purpur] *om.* Ti   purpur] for vs *add.* Up
253 corowned] þe *add.* MuTi, þin heed Add   peyn] preue Add   hede] suffraunce and pacience Add   and[2]] þanne *add.* Add
254 on . . . knelynge] fellen on knees and Add   scornynge] scorneden Add cleped] calliden Add
256 þay] *om.* Add   þo] þe Add
257 turnes] þat we haue wrouȝt *add.* Add   þe] þat Add   shame] schames Ti
259 þe[1]] *om.* Ti
263 let] graunte Add   me] grace to *add.* Add
264 let] graunte Add   me] grace *add.* Add   neuyre] to *add.* Add
267 al] þat *add.* Add
268 on[1]] *om.* Add   syde] *om.* Ti   despised] and hastid *add.* Add
269 stronge . . . foul] strongeful Mu

270 swete] *om.* Mu  and] worþi to be *add.* Add  þy] *om.* Add
271 swete] *om.* Ti
273 wilfully] wiseli Add
275 to] *om.* Add  þankynges] thankyng Ti  and graces] *om.* Add
277 drowen] þee *add.* Add  felly] þat greet ruþe was to se and þerto swete ihesu *add.* Add
278 putted] putten Add  þe[1]] *om.* Ti  and] *om.* Add  smot] smyten Add  þe[2]] so *add.* Add
279 what] þat Add  was] *om.* Ti
280 begynnynge] biddinge Add  Herodes] Eroud Add  comaundement] *om.* Add
281 so] *om.* Add
283 when] *om.* Ti
284 þy] þe Add  cloth] cloþinge UpTi  þe] þi skyn Add
285 so] in Add  of] *om.* Add  þay] þou Add
286 pitevous] dispiteuous Add
287 hit] *om.* Add  on] of Add
288 þe] þi Add
289 stremes] stremynge Add  and scorgynge] *om.* Add
290 on] *om.* Ti  þe[2]] *om.* Add
291 for] *om.* Add  prikked] sittiþ Add  Allas] allas *add.* UpTi
293 þy[2]] *om.* Add
294 al] *om.* Ti  coroned] crowneþ Add  þe[2]] al Add
295 þe[1]] *om.* Mu  lordes] þe emperour of helle *add.* Add  295–6 of . . . houndes] now hound Add
298 had] haþ Add  myght] mai Add  was] is Add
299 in] þe *add.* Add
300 for[2]] *om.* Add
301 as . . . synnys] *om.* Add  me . . . for] *om.* Up
302 in] *om.* UpTiAdd  wery ne] *om.* Add
303 þat] for that *add.* Ti
307 for . . . þe] of Ti  þe] þat Add
308 þe] þi Add
310 was] *om.* Add  harried] harien Add
311 and] þei Add  spurned] spurnen Add  haddist be] weere Add
312 A] A *add.* Ti  heere] is *add.* Add
313 is[1]] *om.* Ti  is[2]] al *add.* UpTi
314 is] al Add  defowled] desoilid Add  spittynge] spotil Add
315 so] *om.* Ti  besene] biseide Add
316 was] *om.* Add  hegh] huge Add  on] vpon Add  þat . . . bare] *om.* Add
317 crushed] to hepe *add.* Add
319 and[1]] *om.* Add  by] for Add
320 þe] *om.* Add  nyȝt] biforen *add.* Add
322 blode] blodi UpTi  þe] thi Ti  þy] þat Add
323 birthen] biryng Ti  styngeth] stiketh Ti
324 in] *om.* Ti  þe] thi Ti
325 gawren] gouliþ Add
326 suche] a *add.* UpTiAdd  Ihesu] *om.* Ti
327 to[1]] *om.* Add
328 and] *om.* Ti  compassioun] *om.* Ti
330 keste] castist Add  eyen] iȝe Add  vpon] toward Add
331 dere] *om.* Add  modyr] so dere *add.* Add  saw] siȝ Add  þe] *om.* Add  þat] þe Add

332–3 mynd . . . sorowes] *om.* Add
334 cast] castiþ Add  abrode] *om.* Mu, and spred hem on brode UpTi
335 in] *om.* Up  oft] of Ti  tymes] siþis Add  sorowe[1]] sorowis Add
336 and[1]] in Mu  aggregged] greued þee UpTi  manyfold] encreside UpTi
338 hir] sche Add  wel] þe *add.* UpTi  ether] of ȝou *add.* Add  for] *om.* Ti
339 euery] eiþir Add
340 your sorow] *trs.* Up  euery] eithere TiAdd
341 erth] for *add.* Add
342 stikked] stikiþ Add
343 folow] him *add.* Add  þat] þe *add.* Add
345 withdrawe] withdrawen Ti
346 to[1]] no *add.* Ti
347 as] *om.* Add  347–9 and . . . sone] *om.* Add  on] in Ti
349 sighynges] siȝghynge Ti, siȝhis Add  349–50 dele . . . breste] brest so ful of dole and sorewe Add  349–50 in . . . breste] birefte Mu, þe breste Up [*corr. in margin to* birefte], the breste Ti
350 bereft] bireckinge Add
351 bodily] wo or *add.* Add  lettynge] lettingis Add
353 was] *om.* Add  þo] þy MuTi, þe Up
354 by] wiþ Add
357 owne] desyre *add.* Mu  ne] *om.* Add  wrongful] wrongfully Ti, daungerous Add
358 þy] *om.* Ti
359 syghynge] siȝyngis Add  seighed] siȝhist Add
360 þis] þat Add
361 castelles] castel Up  tours] townes Add  ne[2]] noon *add.* Add  oþere] oþers Mu
362 ne mone] *om.* Mu
363 reuth] of *add.* Add  and] of *add.* Add
364 to[2]] and I Add
365 and] or ellis Add  drop] of his *add.* Add
366–7 mercy . . . al[3]] *om.* Add
368 deelful] of alle woful Add  my[1]] sike *add.* Add
369 Send . . . compassioun] *om.* Ti  me] *om.* Add
370 and] *om.* TiAdd
371 þe[2]] þat Add
372 and] þere *add.* UpTi
373 fete to] sette Ti
374 first] fast Add  þe] þat Add
375 þan] swete ihesu þei *add.* Add  swet Ihesu] *om.* Add  to . . . fete] til þi fete rauȝte ⟨to Add⟩ þe hoolis UpAdd, to thi fete there holis rauȝte Ti
376 þe[2]] þi Add
377 bruys] presse Up  þe[1]] þi Add
378 blody] bled Add  þe[2]] þi UpAdd
379 þy[1]] þe Add  to-drawen] and straitly streyned *add.* UpTi  brode] þat merueile is it halt *add.* Add
380 al] ful of *add.* UpTiAdd  in þy] *om.* Ti
381 in þe] þi Up, thei Ti  synwes] alle to reuen *add.* UpTi  þer[1]] is *add.* Mu  is[2]] *om.* Ti
382 for] to Add  382–3 a rake] þe harowe Add
383 is] al *add.* UpTiAdd  so] *om.* Ti
386 in mendynge] and mende Add
387 spek] steke Ti  lord] *om.* Ti  hey] þy Mu  deuocioun] and *add.* Add

388 nat] wote *add.* Ti, noot Add wot] *om.* Add in] þi *add.* Add
389 and[1]] I *add.* Add for] *om.* Add dym] wickid Add
390 and] han *add.* Add stopped] stoppeþ UpTi of] and Ti
391 man] creature Add
392 and[2]] or Add matier] Pater noster *add.* Add
394 syn] so *add.* Add
395 swetnesse of] *om.* Add lene] sende Add me] lord *add.* Add
397 and secheth] þee Add
398 þe] þy Mu fynd] þan late him *add.* UpTi
399 feble . . . outcast] *om.* Mu and] rebuke him silf and *add.* UpTi
400 lord] god *add.* Add
402 when] þanne Add heved] heuen Add hit] to *add.* Add
403 hole] holde Mu þan] *om.* Add
404 swete] *om.* Ti
405 þe[2]] þi Add of[2]] *om.* Add 405–6 al . . . peyns] and al parte Ti
406 peyns] peis Add jnow] þouȝh Ti
408 was[2]] so *add.* Add
409 carions many] diuers careines þat it loþide any man to neiȝe nyȝ Add were al] *trs.* Ti fyve] life Ti
410 peyne] peynes Add of] of *add.* Ti þy] *om.* Add
411 and[1]] *om.* Add þy . . . sawe] *om.* Mu ham] þan MuUp
413 of[1]] wiþ Add lord] *om.* Add
414 þe[1]] *om.* Ti
415 to] in Add
416 þe[1]] þi nose UpTiAdd swet] swe Ti
417 myche] *om.* Add causeth] is cause of Add and[1]] of *add.* Add
418 yaf] ȝeuen þee Add galle] eisil Add
419 accusynge] acusinggis UpAdd
420 of] a Ti
421 haue] þee *add.* UpTi, hange Add
422 may] wille UpTi, can Add
423 byndynge] and *add.* Add
424 of] *om.* Ti
425 and] in Add naylynge] of þi *add.* Add
426 þou] so *add.* Add and] so *add.* Add 426–7 þe goodes] good Add
427 had nat] ne haddist Add helle] hilen wiþ Add
428 al[1]] *om.* Add al[2]] *om.* Add
430 þe[2]] *om.* Ti
431 on] of Add
432 had] ne hast Add
435 fadyre] to *add.* Add
436 lord] *om.* Add
437 toke hede] tendist Add þy] the Ti
438–9 swete . . . þou] *om.* Add
439 to] *om.* Add Now] þanne Add
440 sethen] now Add now] þou UpTi
441 to] *om.* Add
442 was þe] were þou Add
449 and at] in Add doun] ful *add.* Add
450 on] in UpAdd, *om.* Ti
451 þe by] doun bi þi sidis Add
452 of sorow] *om.* Add
454 and] *om.* Add

455 þan] *om.* Add haue] *om.* Add
456 of] *om.* Ti
457 cas] haue *add.* Add
458 peynes] peyne Add
459 deth[1]] as *add.* UpTi, so *add.* Add
460 my] þi Add
463 swetly] *om.* Add
465 kelynge] likynge Ti of þyrst] þristis Add
466 poysone] poysome Mu þurst] wiþ *add.* Add
467 kele] kepe Ti, hele Add
468 þis] *om.* Ti, þi Add body] blodi Ti
469 þursted] thriste Ti to] þe *add.* Up, *om.* Ti
470 delyueraunce] dalyaunce MuUp
471 graunt] ȝeue Add 471–2 for . . . sake] *om.* Add
472 and[2]] to *add.* Add
473 of[3]] and of Ti, *om.* Add of[4]] *om.* Add
474 shadow] sadwe Ti
475 þurst] aftir *add.* Add and[2]] þi Add desyre] desiryng UpTi
476 yernynge] willynge Add
479 no . . . þou] þou no þinge Up þy] *om.* Ti vs] alle *add.* UpTiAdd
481 peyne] þat is *add.* Add tendyrly] tendir UpTiAdd was[2]] *om.* Add
482 heuyn] hangiþ *add.* Add al] *om.* Add
483 shold] *om.* Mu hit] *om.* Add
484 þe] þat Add
487 was] to *add.* Add wo] lo *add.* Add
488 þe] so *add.* Add
489 man] telle ne *add.* Add for] *om.* Ti
491 neþer] neuer arise Mu, neiþer Up, neythere Ti
492 al þy] þat Add
494 þe] þo UpTiAdd stynkynge] dede *add.* Add wlatfully] wlatsumli to se Add
497 and] am Add hem vpon] on hem Add
498 Ihesu] from *add.* Add þy] *om.* Ti
499 mad] markid Add þy] precious *add.* Add
500 softe] softid Add hit] I Mu, *om.* UpTiAdd
501 Ihesu] iesus Up my] hard *add.* Add hert] it *add.* Add is now] *trs.* Up and] to Add
502 and quyk] to quikene Add
503 rered] reised UpTiAdd
504 opened] openeþ UpTi helles] helle UpAdd þe[1]] *om.* Add
505 þat is] *om.* Add
506 any] *om.* Add
508 my] wickid *add.* Add þat . . . wikked] *om.* Add 508–9 is . . . is] *om.* Add
510 and þe] in Mu hert] soule Add lord] ihesu *add.* UpTi, ihesu Add þy] *om.* Mu
511 droped] dropping UpTiAdd vpon] on Add
512 in] to melte bi Add
514 of[1]] *om.* Ti þe] *om.* Add Ihesu] *om.* Ti
515 and[1]] to *add.* Add ryghtyn] þe holi soulis of oure holi fadris *add.* Add þat] lijk *add.* Add in[2]] *om.* Add
516 be] *om.* Ti
517 with[2]] *om.* Ti
519 vnworþynesse] vnworth me Ti besyde þe] bi þi side Add
520 also] so Add nat] as worþi *add.* Add 520–2 in . . . trespas] I aske itt as gilti Add

522 þerby] *om.* Add    522–3 to be] *om.* Ti

523 me nedeth] my nede Add    and] in Mu, my *add.* Add    wikkednesse] as hit *add.* Mu, wickenesses Ti

524 þan] þou Mu

525 for] *om.* Up    oo[2]] o good ihesu late þe UpTi    passioun] to *add.* Add

526 þy] *om.* Up

528 lykynge] likingis Add

529 bot] oonly *add.* Add

531 þan] that Ti    soule] spirit Add

532 hondes] euere *add.* Add

533 hit] I UpTi

538 and] *om.* Add    spirit] goost Add

539 cleue] to cleef Add    to-revyn] to bursten Add

540 witnesse] witnessis Add

541 were] þere *add.* Add

542 and fete] foot Add    in[2]] *om.* TiAdd    hangeth] hanged UpTi    vpon] on Add

543 þy[1]] *om.* Ti    þe] thi Ti

544 shewen] schewed Ti    al[1]] *om.* Ti    clotred] cloþed Add

547 vpon] on Add    with] þe *add.* Add

548 vpon[1]] on Add    þe] thi Ti    wyde] *om.* Add    on[1]] vpon Add    vpon[2]] on Add

549 al] *om.* Add    at] *om.* Ti    tyme] place Add

551 on þat] vpon þe Add    551–2 þcy . . . vpward] *om.* Add

552 loken] loked Ti

553 so] *om.* Add    har] hir Add    þe] *om.* Ti, her Add

554 sethen] þat *add.* Add

555 gret] *om.* Add    to[2]] *om.* Add

556 parte . . . sorow] *om.* Add    þat[2]] thi Ti

558 as[2]] and Ti, and as Add    hadden] it *add.* Add

559 stil] *om.* Add

# NOTES

## I *The Form of Living*

**2, 18, etc.** *wrechednes(se)*: the uninflected plural reflects the OE strong feminine.

**9** *is*: inserted above line in same hand.

**18** *worldisshe*: this rare adjectival form (*OED worldish*) is confined to Northern texts.

**25** *sych*: the only instance of this form in the MS; elsewhere *such(e)*.

**30** *wend*: 'think', showing an occasional instance of intrusive consonant.

**33** *nat*: subpuncted in the MS, suggesting that a reader had access to a text of the Dd group.

**40** *ham þynken*: *þynke* is often found uninflected in impersonal constructions in this MS, possibly due to confusion with the personal verb 'think', or because the Northern inflexion *-es* could be used in any person or number unless a personal pronoun preceded. Here the inflexion appears to be influenced by the preceding dative pronoun. This construction is not elsewhere recorded.

**56** *worke*: I have not thought it worth emending, but the evidence of the other MSS suggests 'thing' was the original reading.

**57** *fallen*: Northern form of 'fail', possibly misunderstood as 'fall'.

**63** *ne þynke*: MS *no þynge* was probably the result of mistaking 'think' for the unvoiced form of 'thing', and emending *ne* accordingly.

**64–5** 'Nota de iniuria abstinencia' in right hand margin.

**66** Ps. 58: 10 'fortitudinem meam ad te custodiam'.

**68** *waillynge*: the variants here provide an interesting example of manuscript transmission. Dd's *wanand* is original, to which U supplies a synonym *wastynge*. The Northern vowel is rounded by Ff to give *wonend* 'dwelling'. Ch's *monande* shows initial minim confusion, and a similar mistake must have given rise to Lt's synonym *waillynge*. D's *wauerynge* shows medial minim confusion: *wanand* > *wauand* > *wauynge*, with the *er* suspension mark introduced to make sense, and *tremblynge* (P[1]) and *quakyng* (P[2]) are synonymous substitutions. *Wending* (HT[2]) results from a further confusion of the original form, and *tornynge* (Ld) is a scribal variant of this new sense.

**69** *Ierom*: the text is attributed to St Jerome in the *Decretum* of Gratian (cap. Non mediocriter 24 dist. V de Consectatione): 'De rapina holocaustum offert qui temporalium bonorum sive ciborum nimia egestate vel manducandi vel somni penuria corpus suum immoderate affligit'; and also by Aquinas in Quaestiones Quodlibetales V art. xviii: 'Unde Hiero. dicit "De rapina holocaustum offert qui vel ciborum nimia egestate vel somni penuria immoderate corpus affligit."' Elsewhere Rolle draws on both these sources.

*ravyn offrynge*: 'a sacrifice of stolen objects'; cf. too Isaiah 61: 8 'odio . . . rapinam in holocausto'.

**71** *Bernard*: *P.L.* 184, 328 'Nam sunt et alia corporis exercitia, in quibus necesse est corpus laborare, sicut sunt vigiliae, jejunia et alia huiusmodi, quae spiritualia non impediunt, sed juvant, si cum ratione discretionis fiant. Quae si ex indiscretionis vitio sic agantur, ut vel deficiente spiritu, vel languente corpore spiritualia impediantur.'

**74** *thar* may show influence of ON *þár*; the usual MS spelling is *ther(e)*.

**79** 'Ihesu' is written in the margin here and at lines 88, 132, 140, 161, 212, 250, 422, 432, 489, 496, 652, 730, 756, 791, and 810.

**80** *an*: 'and' showing weak stress.

**88** *hit*: inserted above line in same hand.

**106** *vnstable and vnwise*: the original reading was clearly a form of *unquaint*, which Lt, in common with most other MSS, has deliberately altered. Dd has mistaken the *vn-* prefix for *&*.

**112–13** *hath* ... *confounden*: the Lt reading makes sense, but is supported only by B², and in view of the unhistorical form of the p.p. should perhaps be emended to *both* ... *confoundeth*. However the p.p. can be justified as a development from *confound* p.p., on the analogy of *founden* beside *found*.

**117** *whan*: the MSS are divided between *whan*, *þe which* and *whom*; possibly Northern *wham* is correct.

*deceyuet*: 3 sg. pr. ind. with *-et* for *-eþ*, particularly common in the MS before a following *þ-* or *th-*, where, if the spelling is phonetic, it may show dissimilation. Inflexional *-et* for *-eþ*, whatever its explanation, occurs in WM, Kentish and Norfolk texts (Gradon, p. 97, n. 6, with reference to Wallenberg).

**129** *loue*: 'e' inserted above line.

**131–2** 'Nota de gaudio beneuiuencium' in right hand margin.

**134** Josh.: 1: 7 'Confortare igitur et esto robustus valde'.

**139–40** Rev. 1: 9ff.

**147** *lereth*: MS *sheweth* reflects the presence of this word in the preceding MS line.

**162–7** cf. Cassian's *Collationes* (*P.L.* 49, 1025): 'Etenim saepe illud quod Apostolus dicit probatum est evenire "Ipse enim Satanas transfigurat se in angelum lucis" (2 *Cor.* 11: 14) ut obscuram et tetram caliginem sensum pro vero lumine scientiae fraudulenter effundat. Qui nisi humili et mansueto corde suscepti, maturissimi fratris vel probatissimi senioris reserventur examini, et eorum judicio diligenter excussi, aut abjiciantur aut recipiantur a nobis, sine dubio venerantes in cogitationibus nostris pro angelo lucis angelum tenebrarum, gravissimo feriemur interitu. Quam perniciam impossibile est evadere quempiam judicio proprio confidentem, nisi, humilitatis verae amator et executor effectus, illud quod Apostolus magnopere deprecatur, omni contritione cordis implerit.'

**169** *glaad*: the doubling of *a* to show length is a chiefly Northern characteristic.

**176** This temptation may have been suggested by an incident in Rolle's own life, and described by him in his *Comment on the Canticles*. A beautiful woman appeared to him in his cell, but vanished when he crossed himself and said 'O Ihesu, quam preciosus est sanguis tuis.'

**177** *anon she*: inserted above line in same hand but darker ink. The evidence of the majority of other MSS suggests that *anon* is misplaced, and should be after the third *and* of the line, not the first.

**182** cf. *Comp. theol. ver.* ii 66: 'diabolus in angelum lucis se transfigurat sub specie scilicet virtutum inducens vitium. Haec fit quando suadendo honestatem inducit superbiam, vel iustum iudicium inducit crudelitatem, vel suadendo largitatem inducit prodigalitatem et sic de aliis.'

**199** *wild*: the form may be influenced by ON.

**216–18** Eccles. 5: 2: 'Multas curas sequuntur somnia'; Ecclus. 34: 7: 'Multas enim errare fecerunt somnia, et exciderunt sperantes in illis.'

**220–6** cf. St Gregory's *Dialogues* (*PL* 77, 409): 'Sex modis tangunt animum imagines somniorum. Aliquando namque somnia ventris plenitudine vel inanitate, aliquando vero illusione, aliquando cogitatione simul et illusione, aliquando revelatione, aliquando autem cogitatione simul et revelatione generantur.'

**222** 'vi cause sompniorum' in right hand margin.

**223** *þe deuyl*: Lt is supported only by T³ and H².

**231** *vnstable*: a deliberate alteration of *unquaint*, cf. l. 106; MS *ben* for *heghen* is probably a misunderstanding.

**233** In her edition of the text of Dd, Miss Allen has supplied *I* in square brackets without comment. This is not in the MS of Dd, nor is there a space left for it; *knawe* has a capital and is thus an imperative, and *es* for *semeth* would then appear to be a deliberate alteration.

**239–40** 'Nota de amore dei et mundi' in left hand margin.

**250** *presentes*: retention of Northern inflexion, probably indicating a Northern exemplar.

**252–3** Miss Allen has taken *coueit*, *sek* and *haue* as imperatives. I prefer to punctuate as if they were subjunctives.

**255** The MS has a punctus after *blood.*

**258** *ham þynken*: see note to l. 40.

**262** *thaym*: retention of Northern pronoun.

**271** *modelynge*: the *OED* derives 'muddle' from 'mud', and compares Mod. Dutch *moddelen* 'to dabble in mud'. The earliest transitive use is cited for 1607, but the variant *grobbynge* indicates that this is indeed the meaning intended here.

**276** The omission of conjunction *þat* before *þou maist laste* in LtFCh and originally He considerably alters the sense, and I have punctuated accordingly. However Lt's reading seems fully justified; not only does it have the support of unrelated MSS, but the extract in B³ starts in the same way: *Foure þynges . . .*

*wix*: the *i* spelling may reflect the influence of old Northern pa.t. *wix*, probably caused by shortening of OE *ēo* (cf. *hild* < *hēold*, *fill* < *fēoll*).

**277** MS *self* is without support, and must represent a scribal slip.

**280** 'i' in right hand margin.

**281–3** *we . . . euer*: cf. *Emendatio Vitae*, ch. 1 'In puncto viuimus, imo minus puncto, quia si totum tempus nostrum eternitati comparatur, nihil est.' I am grateful to Nicholas Watson for drawing my attention to parallels between this text and Rolle's English epistles.

**283** 'ii' in right hand margin.

*Anoþer . . . endynge*: cf. *Emendatio Vitae*, ch. 1 'scientes quod mors nobis incerta est'.

**286** 'iii' in right hand margin.

**290** Lamentations 1: 15 'Vocavit adversum me tempus'.

**291** *oops*: this unique variant (alia *vse*, *werkes*, *þewes*) is used here in the OF sense 'works'. The *OED* cites *oeps* for 1428 etc., but only in the sense 'benefit', 'profit'.

**293** *punshed and demed*: transposed in most MSS, which is the more logical reading.

**297** *losten*: the strong form of the p.p. probably results from a blending of wk. *losian* (p.p. *lost*) and str. *lēosan* (p.p. *loren*).

'iiii' in right hand margin.

**298** *Goddis*: despite the support of B²Hh, MS *good* must be assumed to be scribal error.

**305–6** *loued . . . fileth*: the change in sequence of tense, if it is not simply anacoluthon, may indicate a change from action to duration.

**312–13** *I . . . hold*: 'I say (this) not because I wish that, if you have begun unreasonable abstinence, you should persist in it'.

**322** *wyxynge*: see note to l. 276.

**324–9** 'i', 'ii', 'iii', 'iiii', 'i' and 'peccata cordis' in left hand margin.

**329–98** Much of this section is a translation or adaptation of the *Compendium theologicae veritatis*, attributed originally to Albertus Magnus, but now thought to be the work of Hugo Argentinensis, and written *c.* 1265. I have cited the text of the 1573 edition, collated with the edition of 1564 and the text in MS Buchanan d. 13. Variant readings are marked /; variant additions are in brackets. Part of the fifth tabula of the *Speculum Christiani* draws on the same source, and its readings make an interesting comparison with those of the *Form.*

**329–48** cf. *Comp. th. ver.* iii, ca. 30: 'Peccata cordis sunt haec: cogitatio, delectatio, consensus, desiderium mali, voluntas peruersa, infidelitas, indeuotio, presumptio, desperatio, timor male humilians, amor male accendens, suspitio, ira, inuidia, odium, timere (deum) seruiliter, exultatio in aduersus proximi, contemptus pauperum vel peccatorum, personarum acceptio, perfidia, affectus parentum carnalis, inepta laetitia, seculi tristitia, impatientia, auaritia, superbia, perplexitas, (malicia), obstinatio mali, tedium boni, acedia, inconstantia, poena poenitentiae, dolor quia non fecit plus malum, hypocrisia, amor placendi, timor displicendi, verecundia de bono opere, amor priuatus, sensus singularis, ambitio dignitatum, vana gloria de bonis naturae vel gratiae vel fortunae, verecundia de pauperibus amicis, contemptus admonitionum, immisericordia.'

**333–4** *sorowe in har welfare*: although the LtURSVWT reading is not supported by the extant Latin, we do not know Rolle's immediate source, and this passage is not a direct translation. I would therefore still argue that it is original, and that its omission in the other MSS was caused by an early scribal error, the eye moving from one *fare* to the other. It is of note that the phrase is present in the *Spec. Chr.* MSS; two unrelated texts are unlikely to make the same independent addition.

**344** *faire*: comparative form.

**349** 'peccata oris' in left hand margin.

**349–63** cf. *Comp. th. ver.* iii, ca. 31: 'Peccata oris sunt haec: crebra iuratio, periurium, blasphemia, nomen Dei irreuerenter assumere, veritatem impugnare, de mendacio et vanis alios instruere, contra Deum murmurare, irreuerenter horas dicere, detraccio, adulatio, mendacium, vituperium, maledictio, infamatio, contentio, comminatio, impugnatio veritatis agnitae, impugnatio charitatis fraternae, seminatio discordiae, proditio, falsum testimonium, mala consilia, derisio, contradictio obedientiae, inuertere facta bona, in ecclesiis placitare, ad iram homines prouocare, reprehendere proximum in aliquo quod ipse facis, vaniloquium, (multiloquium), stultiloquium, proferre verba otiosa vel superflua vel curiosa, iactantia, verborum politio, peccatorum defensio, clamor, risus, cachinnus, turpiloquium, lenocinium, cantare cantilenas seculares, in cantu divino magis studere vocem frangere quam deuote psallere, murmurare, verba scurrilia proferre, in iniusta causa aduocare, malum commendare.'

**354** *wreyynge*: this should translate Latin *maledictio*, and appears to be an error for *waryynge* which has support from both sides of the stemma; possibly the Lt scribe did not recognize the word and substituted a homoeograph.

*cursynge*: here a translation of *contentio* is required, and of the variants Northern *flytyng* is the most suitable, with *chydynge* a Southern equivalent. Possibly Lt's *cursynge* was in his exemplar a marginal gloss on *waryynge*, and he mistook it for a gloss on *flytyng* and accordingly substituted here.

**357** Although the MSS are interestingly divided here, the Dd etc. reading *done ham* is preferable to MS *done ham woo.* It has the support of U, and taken with what follows it makes superior sense. The other scribes, not understanding that *ham* refers to *dedes*, have assumed a textual corruption and attempted to emend, commonly, as in Lt, by treating *ham* as an indirect object and supplying a direct object for *done.*

**359** *fool*: Latin *stultiloquium* supports this against the *foul* of UDdLCHeT³PFHaAr Hh.

**361** *and*: both MS *in*, though widely supported, and DdM *of* seem unsatisfactory here, the Latin is of no assistance, and the meaning obscure. The emendation is made on the grounds that it makes slightly better sense, and MS *in* and & are easily confused.

*mowe*: (Latin *cachinnus*). The Lt reading, supported by U, is taking *mowe* as an infinitive used as a verbal noun.

**364** 'peccata in facto' in right hand margin.

*glotony lechurie*: Ar has a major variant here, with two more at lines 397–8 and 404–7, which together suggest that its text of the *Form* had been adapted to form a rule for religious. The adaptation must have taken place in a predecessor, possibly at the same time as the treatise was condensed, because the present text appears corrupt; nevertheless it is of sufficient interest to cite separately: 'glutonie þat haues þire braunchis: ouer erly, ouer hastili, ouer deliciouseli, ouer ardantli, ouer mikil, ouer late, ouer ofte, and mare bifallis þis synne in drynk þen in mete. Licherie, þat haues þire kyndels: horedome, maiden losse, inceste, þat is bitwene sibbe fleshli or gasteli, foule wille to þe synne with consent, egge oþer þerto thorugh rageyng, foule spekyng or gig laghtre, lighte latis, giftis or flaterand speche, foule handeling, watte stede or tyme to come þerto, and on what maner eauer þis synne be done, wakand and wilfulli, it is heuid synne bot it be in wedlaik.'

**364–80** cf. *Comp. th. ver.* iii, ca. 32: 'Peccata operis sunt haec: gula, luxuria, ebrietas, symonia, sortilegium, violatio dierum solennium, sacrilegium, indigne communicare, votorum fractio, apostasia, dissolutio in diuino officio, scandalizare suo malo exemplo proximum et corrumpere, laedere hominum, vel in rebus, vel in persona, vel in fama, furtum, rapina, usura, deceptio, ludus, venditio iustitiae, exactio indebita, t(h)e(o)lonea iniusta, auscultare mala, iocularibus/ioculatoribus dare, necessaria sibi subtrahere, superflua sumere, vltra vires proprias quidam aggredi, consuetudo peccandi, recidiuatio, simulatio, tenere officium ad quod non sufficit vel quod sine peccata non agitur, chor(e)izare, nouitatem inuenire, maioribus rebellare, minores opprimere, delinquere/relinquere visu, auditu, odoratu, gustu et tactu, luctu, osculis, muneribus, itineribus, nutibus, mendaciis/mandatis, scripturis/scriptis, circumstantias aggravantas omittere, quae sunt tempus, locus, modus, numerus, persona, mora, scientia, aetas, tentationem praevenire, seipsum ad peccatum cogere.'

**365** *haly*: the Northern vowel uncharacteristically retained.

**376** *swelighynge*: (Latin *gustu* . . . *luctu*, *osculis*: variants *swellyng*, *schewyng*). If *handlynge* is accepted as an equivalent of *osculis*, *gustu* and *luctu* remain to be translated. 'Taste' is the obvious omission among the five senses, and it must be this that Lt's 'swallowing' represents.

**377** *reteyne*: not only do all the MSS of the *Form* read *receyue*, with the exception of Ch who has tried to make sense with *chargen nouȝt*, and Do, who omits, but also the word appears in the great majority of the 46 relevant MSS of the *Spec. Chr.*, but here the reading is *receyue not*, with seven related MSS emending, with the same intention as Ch, to *reherce not*. Holmstedt (p. 261), who had not identified the Latin source, considered *not* to be an early and inexplicable interpolation, and interpreted the original reading as 'voluntarily to receive > seize the subordinate circumstances of a sin whenever an opportunity offers itself'. But this does not explain how *omittere* came to be translated as *receyue*. Miss Allen (*English Writings*, p. 156) suggests that Rolle read *omittere* as *accipere*, but it is ridiculous to assume that Rolle was so ignorant of the Church's teaching on penance that he was able to render even faulty Latin into nonsensical English. Moreover it is assuming a similar extraordinary error on the part of the *Spec. Chr.* compiler. Unless *receyue* is correct, and had some obscure theological meaning corresponding to *omittere*, it would seem that, contrary to previous speculation, the *Form* and the *Spec. Chr.* passages must derive from a common *English* exemplar, which mistook *reteyne* in a translation it was copying for *receyue.*

**378** *þese*: MS *yere* is a mistaken reading of Northern *þere.*

**379** *ar*: see note to l. 365.

**381–98** cf. *Comp. th. ver.* iii, ca. 33: 'Peccata omissionis sunt haec: de Deo non cogitare, ipsum non timere vel amare, gratias de beneficiis non agere, opera quae quis facit ad ipsum non referre, de peccatis, sicut debet, non dolere, ad gratiam recipiendam/percipiendam se non praeparare, gratia accepta non vti nec eam seruare/conseruare, ad inspirationem diuinam se non conuertere, voluntatem suam voluntati diuinae non conformare, ad rationes dicendas non attendere, orationes debitas omittere, ea ad quam tenetur ex voto vel precepto vel officio negligere, communionem et confessionem semel in anno non expedire, parentes non honorare, seipsum non recognoscere et reprehendere, conscientiam negligere, ecclesias et praedictiones fugere, tentationibus non resistere, poenitentias iniunctas negligere/*om.* aut/*om.* negligenter facere, et quae statim facienda sunt diferre, bonis proximi non gaudere, et malis non condolere, iniurias non remittere, fidem proximo/*om.* non seruare et beneficiis eius non respondere, derelinquentes non corrigere, lites non sedare, ignorantes non instruere, afflictos non consolari, admonitionibus non acquiescere.'

**391–2** *foryeuen*: 'forgiving'; *-en* for the more usual verbal noun ending *-ynge* occurs elsewhere in the MS, and may show weakening of [ŋ] to [n].

**392** *heth*: possibly a false Southernization of *hes.*

**397–8** *&. . .foule*: Ar reads 'studis in foule thoughtis, be fayne of fals gladyng, be heuy and morneand or grucheand for mete or drink or oght ellis, in silence broken, of houres missaide withoute hert and deuocion or in vntyme, of some fals worde, of sweryng, of playing, or giglaghtre, of splillyng [*sic*] of cromes, brede or ale or oþer mete or drink, latyn brede moule, ale soure, flesh and fish be lost, clathes vnsewid, torne, unwaschen, broken cop or dish or dobeler, or oþer vessel or lomys as axes, wymbils, persours, or ani oþer swilk þat men with delis, or hurtyng of me self so þat I was vnabil til do þat to me fell, of alle þe thinges þat are in oure Reule þat I haue broken.'

**399** *þay*: 'those', from ON.

**399–477** cf. *Emendatio Vitae*, ch. 4: 'Secundo que sunt que mundificant hominem & sunt tria, scilicet contritio cogitationis, expulsio omnis affectionis que non pertinet ad laudem & honorem dei & amorem eius. Confessio oris, que debet esse tempestiua nuda & integra. Satisfactio operis, que habet tres partes, scilicet ieiunium quia peccat contra seipsum, orationem quia peccat contra deum, eleemosynam quia peccat contra proximum. Non tamen dico quod de bonis alienis faciat eleemosynam, sed restituat, quia non dimittitur peccatum nisi restituatur ablatum. Tertio que sunt que munditiam cordis seruant & sunt tria, scilicet vigil dei meditatio, vt nullum tempus sit in quo de deo non cogitet, exceptio somno qui est omnibus communis. Solicitudo custodie sensuum exteriorum, vt gustus & olfactus, auditus, visio, tactus, sub freno discipline sapienter arreantur, & honesta occupatio, vt legendo, aut aliquid de deo loquendo, aut scribendo aut aliquid vtile agendo. Similiter que obseruant munditiam oris, scilicet loquendi premeditatio, cauere multiloquia, mendacii detestatio. Item munditiam operis tria conseruant, scilicet alimentorum moderatio, praue societatis declinatio, & iugis mortis meditatio. Quarto que ad conformitatem diuine voluntatis nos illiciunt, & sunt tria, scilicet creaturarum exemplaritas, que attenditur per considerationem, dei familiaritas, que attenditur per orationem & meditationem, et regni celestis iucunditas, que admodum sentitur per contemplationem.

**399–403** 'i remedia cordis contricio', 'ii oris confessio' in left hand margin.

**404–7** *hasted . . . worth*: Ar reads 'wreiand and accusand him self, noght sai I was nedid þerto thorugh oþer or þe deuel. It sal also be bitter agayn þat þe thought þe synne swete, haleli made til an preste withoute departyng, nakidli made as þe syn was done, noght schewid in faire wordis, ofte made, sone made after þe syn is done, mekeli made, noght telle his gode dedes bot his il dedes, schamefuli made, dredeful, so þat þou drede þat þou has forgeten some of þe circumstances, hopeful of goddis merci, wise and to wise man made, sothe to sai, na mare ne lesse þen þou has done, wilfuli made, noght nedid þerto nor drawen o þe as þine vnthankis, awne, noght wreie oþer, stedfast to do þe penance and leue þe syn, bi thoughte lang bifore, in v maners, þe first, þat þou geder þi synnes of þi childehede and al þine elde, þe ii, þat þou geder þe stedes sunderli in ilk elde, þe iii, trie þi synnes after þi v wittes, þe iiii, bi alle þi lymes in whilk þou hast mast synnid with or oftisd, þe v, trie þi synnes bi daies and tymes.'

**406** 'iii et satisfaccio' in left hand margin.

**411–17** 'i', 'i', 'ii', 'iii', 'i', 'ii' in left hand margin.

**424** *þe*: MS punctuation shows that the scribe read *ye* as an exclamation instead of a pronoun.

**433** Ecclus. 7: 40: 'In omnibus operibus tuis memorare novissima tua et in aeternum non peccabis.'

**448** *quathis*: 'fainting fits', a variant not found in the *OED*, which records only *coth-*, *coath-* forms.

**450–1** *forþi whils*: the Lt reading, widely supported, is preferable to Dd's *for þe tyme*, but affects modern punctuation of the text.

**455** *whils*: I have taken this to mean 'sometimes' instead of the conjunction 'while' as Miss Allen. This again affects the punctuation.

**469** 'quare sequi in voluntatem dei' in left hand margin.

**475** *loued . . . trusteth*: see note to lines 305–6.

**485** *as*: Northern form, see note to l. 250.

**489** *Amore langueo*: Canticles 2: 5.

**500** Many MSS, including Lt, have a punctus after *heuyn*, not *mede.*

**510–12** 'De graciarum accione in hora prandi' in right hand margin.

This poem is found also in *The Lay Folks Mass Book*, ed. T. F. Simmons (EETS OS 71), a text thought to have been written in the mid twelfth century, probably in French, and of which English translations exist in many later MSS. Its editor, acting on the advice of Furnivall, prints the poem in a rhyme scheme of AAB, AAB, BAA, but the evidence of the *Form* MSS shows this to be unlikely. Miss Allen suggests on stylistic grounds that the poem was borrowed from the *Form*, and in the absence of any known MS of the *Mass Book* predating the *Form*, this cannot be disproved.

**525** 'Of iii degrees of loue' in right hand margin.

**525 ff.** Rolle's often repeated 'thre degrees of loue' appear to derive from a work of Richard of St Victor *De Quattuor Gradibus Violentiae Charitatis* (*PL* 196, 1213 ff.): 'Ecce iam habemus in ardenti dilectione quatuor violentiae gradus, de quibus superius proposuimus. Primo ergo violentiae gradus est, quando mens desiderio suo resistere non potest; secundus autem gradus est, quando illud oblivisci non potest; tertius vero gradus est, quando ei aliud sapere non potest; quartus autem, qui et ultimus, quando nec ipsum ei satisfacere potest. In primo itaque gradu amor est insuperabilis, in secundo inseperabilis, in tertio singularis, in quarto insatiabilis. Insuperabilis est qui alii affectui non cedit; inseperabilis qui a memoria nunquam secedit; singularis qui socium non recepit; insatiabilis cum ei satisfieri non possit.' Rolle omits the fourth degree of insatiable love.

**531** *auþer*: variants *oþer*. Lt's *auyer* must have been caused by misreading Northern *auþer*. The *y* is unmistakable in the MS; the preceding letter could be *n* or *u*.

**534** *spryngynge*: pr. p., dependent on *shal . . . be* in the previous line; cf. Dd's *spryngand*.

**538** 'ii' in left hand margin.

**549** 'iii' in left hand margin.

**558** *ondynge*: MS *and*. Dd's *anedande* is not recorded. It appears to derive from the Northern dialect word *ande* 'to breathe', and as a present participle should read *and(e)ande*. It is easy to see how the Lt scribe, faced with such a form in his exemplar, mistook it for a repetition of *and* and emended accordingly. This is further indication of Lt's closeness to the original.

**567** The omission of subject pronoun of a principal clause occurs sporadically.

**586** *takeled*: variants *takked* DdLT³MHa, *taglede* R²FfHT², *tangled* SVCDLd, elsewhere a synonym substituted. According to the *OED* (*tagle*), the word is found only in Rolle texts. Forms given include those of Lt, R² and S, but not the *takked* of DdLT³ MHa. It suggests *tagild* was the original word, *takild* perhaps a scribal variant, and *tangild* a nasalized phonetic form.

**592–3** 1 Cor. 15: 41 'Alia claritas solis, alia claritas lunae, et alia claritas stellarum.'

**597** *when*: MS *whombe* is inexplicable, even as a rendering of 'of whom', and it is an odd coincidence that a similar aberration occurs in *wom* for 'when' just before the second lyric of *Ego Dormio*. Possibly the original reading was *whonne* 'when', and the error the result of minim confusion.

*thy*: MS *his* must be an error, but it is remarkable that it occurs too in MSS from both sides of the stemma, and in W *þi* has actually been altered to *his*.

**598–9** 'Cantalena' in right hand margin.

**599** *may*: MS *me* may have been caused by an unthinking copying of Northern monophthongized *me* 'mei'.

**604** *His*: the LtD reading necessitates a different punctuation from that supplied by Miss Allen. Both Lt and D are metrically deficient, and the other MSS have compensated in a variety of ways.

**606** *place*: Miss Allen quotes a similar passage from the *Melum*: '. . . inclusus a ludo lasciuo'. Possibly the meaning here is 'appearing in public', which would correspond roughly to *inclusus* (*OED place* 1a).

**608** *walkynge*: Northern spelling of *wakynge*.

**610–12** 'Nota de nomine Ihesu' in left hand margin.

**613–14** cf. St Bernard's *Sermo in Cantica* (*PL* 183, 847): 'Jesus mel in ore, in aure melos, in corde jubilus', a passage quoted in the *Comp. th. ver.* iv, ca. 12. Of all the MSS only G follows St Bernard in its transposition of *ere* and *hert*.

**617, 635** *kyndels*: see note to l. 250.

**620** The MS has no punctuation between *man* and *haue*.

**621** *haille*: MS *hailleth* was probably caused by carelessly mistaking the Northern *hayls* for an inflected form.

**622** *lare*: see note to l. 365.

**624** Rom. 13: 10: 'Plenitudo ergo legis est dilectio.'

**625** 'Nota quinque interrogacionnes' in left hand margin.

**629** *louse*: 'to solve', cognate with ON *leysa*. It is an English formation from the adjective *lous* 'loose', which is from the ON adjective *lauss*, from which *leysa* is derived. It is first cited with this meaning by the *OED* for 1596; however the *Promptorium Parvulorum* glosses *solvo* as *losyn or vnbyndyn*, and the Northern derivation suggests that the word could be original to this text.

**633** 'Prima interrogacio quid est amor' in left hand margin.

**633–61** Much of this section is again taken from the *Comp. th. ver.* v, ca. 23, which is in turn quoting from Pomerius' *De Vita Contemplativa*, a work formerly ascribed to St Prosper of Aquitaine (*PL* 59, 463): 'Charitas est . . . recta voluntas ab omnibus terrenis ac praesentibus ac futuris prorsus aduersa, iuncta Deo inseperabiliter et unita, igne quodam spiritus sancti, a quo est et ad quem refertur, incensa, inquinamenti omnis extranes, corrumpi nescia, nulli vitio mutabilitatis obnoxia, super omnia quae carnaliter dicuntūr/diliguntur excelsa, affectionum omnium potentissima, diuinae contemplationis auida, in omnibus semper inuicta, summa bonarum actionum, salus morum, finis coelestium praeceptorum, mors criminum, vita virtutum, virtus pugnantium, palma victorum, sanctarum mentium armatura/anima, causa meritorum bonorum, praemium perfectorum, sine qua nullus Deo placuit, cum qua aliquis Deo displicere/peccare non potuit, fructuosa in poenitentibus, lacta in proficientibus, gloriosa in perseuerantibus, victoriosa in martyribus, operosa in omnibus omnino fidelibus, ex qua quicquid est boni operis vivit. Charitas quantum ad actum diffinitur quatuor modis. . . . Charitas est dilectio, qua diligitur Deus propter se, et proximus propter Deum et in Deum. . . . Quid est charitas? Vita copulans amantem cum amato. . . . Charitas est virtus qua videre Deum et perfrui desideramus. . . . Charitas est virtus, quae animi nostri rectissima affectio est.'

**637** *swete*: I have taken MS *subiect* as an error, possibly a misreading of *suiete* 'sweet' as *sujete* 'subject', but it is interesting that, although Dd has the support of UTG against RSVW, Lt is supported by Ad and Tr², and partly by P's *suget swetnesse*. The error may have therefore occurred the other way round.

**641** The MS punctuation, with a capital for *than*, suggests that the omission had already occurred in Lt's exemplar.

**646** *þynge*: MS *loue* caused by the proximity of the same word.

*al . . . loue*: 'completely deadly is inordinate love'. Although the MSS are divided on both sides of the stemma here, Lt's reading makes sense, and is also the more difficult. Dd's emendation is the obvious one to make if scribes thought the phrase corrupt, and it would thus be wrong to attach too much importance to the support of URGSVWT for it here. The whole sentence seems to have caused widespread confusion.

**652–4** cf. 1 Cor. 13: 2–3: 'Et si habuero prophetiam, et noverim mysteria omnia et omnem scientiam . . . et si distribuero in cibos pauperum omnes facultates meas, et si tradidero corpus meum ita ut ardeat, charitatem autem non habuero, nihil mihi prodest.'

**654** *ordeyned*: MS *or deeth* caused by mistaking the form *ordende* (perhaps abbreviated to *ordēde*) for Northern *or dede* 'or death'.

**655** MS omission caused by eye skip.

**661** *gnedy*: this form is unique to Lt. The *OED* gives the OE forms *gneað*, *gnieðe* (*gneðe*) which seem to represent OTeut. **ga-nauþo*, **ga-nauþjo*, **ga-naudjo*; the last of these occurs in OHG *ginoti*, *gnote* (MHG *genæte*) 'eager for', which corresponds to the Lt sense. Elsewhere in ME the meaning seems restricted to 'sparing' 'miserly' 'scanty'; although the phrase *gnedy glotoun* occurs in a *Piers Plowman* MS as a variant to *gredy*, this is normally regarded as an error. However the form *gnedely* 'greedily' is found in the Lt text of *The Parson's Tale*, so the spelling here is probably a genuine one.

**664** *corone*: MS *sorow* is clearly a careless error (Latin *palma*). So too is Dd's *mirynes* for *armes* (Latin *armatura*).

**665–6** cf. Pomerius, *PL* 59, 496: 'quem si ex toto corde diligamus, nihil erit in nobis unde peccati desideriis serviamus.'

**669** *parsonel*: a corruption of *parcener* 'sharer' (*OED parcenal*). The form is used elsewhere by Rolle. The Lt spelling may show ignorance of this meaning, but *personal* is not recorded as a noun until 1678.

**671–3** cf. St Bernard, *PL* 183, 865: 'instar profecto ignis, qui aurem, quem inflammat, dum suum ei totum calorem imprimit, induitque colorem, non ignitum, sed ignem fecisse cernitur', and *PL* 182, 991: 'quomodo ferrum ignitum et candens, igni simillimum fit, pristina propriaque forma exutum, et quomodo solis luce perfusus aer in eamdem transformatur luminis claritatem.'

**678** 'ii interrogacio vbi est amor' in left hand margin.

**684** cf. Matt. 7: 15: 'Attendite a falsis prophetis . . . intrinsecus autem sunt lupi rapaces.'

**705** 'iii interrogacio est quo modo diligam deum veraciter' in left hand margin.

**709** cf. Isa. 66: 2: 'Ad quem autem respiciam, nisi ad pauperculum et contritum spiritu.' Unlike Miss Allen I have punctuated accordingly; the MS has only a demi punctus after *goste.*

**715–16** cf. Canticles 8: 6: 'Quia fortis est ut mors dilectio, dura sicut infernus aemulatio.'

**719** *peynt*: 'pain', with intrusive consonant, cf. lines 30, 756 and 877.

**723–4** The omission suggests earlier transposition of *peyn* and *angre* at l. 723.

**756** *ploumbe*: see note to l. 719.

**762** *offres*: see note to l. 250.

**765–70** cf. St Bonaventura, *De sex gradibus dilectionis Dei* (*Opera*, Quaracchi, viii, 10): 'Quintus gradus est securitas . . . tantam concepit anima spem de adiutorio divino ut nullo modo existimet se posse separari a Deo. . . . Sextus gradus est vera et plena tranquillitas, in qua est tanta pax et requies ut anima quodam modo sit in silentio et in somno et quasi in arca Noe collocata, ubi nullo modo perturbatur.'

**771** In her printed text Miss Allen has transposed the order of *loue* and *lif*, but the Dd MS reads as Lt *lufe . . . lyf.*

**772** cf. Ps. 75: 3: 'Et factus est in pace locus eius.'

**773** 'iiii interrogacio' in left hand margin.

**780–2** Eccles. 9: 1–2: 'Sunt iusti atque sapientes et opera eorum in manu Dei; et tamen nescit homo utrum amare an odio dignus sit, sed omnia in futurum servantur incerta.'

**791–810** 'i', 'ii', 'iii', 'iiii', 'v', 'vi', 'vii' in right hand margin.

**803–5** Dd ascribes the quotation to St Augustine, who has a similar passage in his 70th Sermon (*PL* 38, 444): 'Omnia enim saeva et immania, prorsus facilia et prope nulla efficit amor', somewhat misquoted in the *Comp. th. ver.* as 'Omnia grauia et immania leuia facit amor.' However Cassiodorus, whose work was much influenced by Augustine, has such strong support from MSS unrelated to Lt that it is probable that the ascription to him is original, and that a similar quotation exists in his work. Most scribes apparently found the sentence confusing, and emended accordingly; the Lt rendering is closer to the Latin than most.

**819** 'quinta interrogacio' in right hand margin.

**827** *gret doctour*: reference untraced.

**830** *þat*: inserted above line in same hand.

**836** 'De vita actiua et contemplatiua' in left hand margin.

**849** 'De vita actiua' in left hand margin.

**861** 'Contemplatiua vita' in right hand margin.

**876** *forsaake*: see note to l. 169.

**877** *þerof*: see note to l. 719. I have emended for the sake of clarity.

**878** Hos. 2: 14: 'Propter hoc ecce egȯ lactabo eum, et ducam eam in solitudinem, et loquar ad cor eius, et dabo ei vinitores eius ex eodem loco.'

**881** *suffred*: a partial analogy for MS p.p. *suffren* might be provided by OE Class II strong verbs with *ū* > ME *ŭ* in the infinitive; thus *suck*, which has in ME both a surviving strong p.p. and a new weak one. If the two could co-exist, it might have been felt that an adopted word with *u* in the infinitive was capable of forming its p.p. with *-(e)n* as well as with *-(e)d.* However *OED* records no irregular forms for the pa.t. or p.p. of *suffer*, and the unhistorical form therefore seems more likely to be the result of scribal error.

## II *Ego Dormio*

**1** Canticles 5: 2.

*et* inserted above line.

'Ihesu' in margin (also at lines 16, 33, 51, 68, 99, 105, 121, 132, 139, 256).

**16–20** The nine orders of angels were first enumerated by the fourth-century Pseudo-Dionysius. The names derive from St Paul's description (Col. 1: 16, Eph. 1: 21).

**29** *Seraphyn . . . brennynge*: Hebrew *sārāph* was thought to derive from the verb *sārāph* 'to burn', and seraphim were identified with lightning.

**50** *þe wil loth with*: there seems to be confusion here between the use of *loth* as an impersonal verb and *loth* noun. The latter is suggested by the presence of *with*, but this construction requires *be* after *wil* as Tr. RSVG supply *þinke* instead.

**56** Dd's *for þe lufe of god* is pleonastic. It occurs also in the Latin text of *Ego Dormio*.

*forsaak*: see note to l. 169 of the *Form.*

**60–1** I have punctuated to make sense of the MS reading, but the text should possibly read: '. . . loue þat þou may hire and se. And God . . .' as Dd. But against this, Dd is isolated. P and AdAr have omissions here; RSVWG, while supporting Lt's *þat*, have taken it for a relative and omitted *God*, thus altering the sense. Lt is supported by R[1] and Br, and also by the Latin 'propter multitudinem obstaculorum per que totum humanum genus sepe ab amoris dei retardatur; verumtamen, audiendo et videndo scire potes, plus amatores suos deus confortat . . .'. The MS has a punctus after *hath* at l. 60 and then nothing until a second punctus after *nat* at l. 62.

**66–9** 'Of þe þre degrees of loue i' in left hand margin.

**66** *hire þese*: 'hear these' as R[1]DdBrTr is to be preferred to MS *here ben*, and I have emended accordingly. Lt and the other Southern MSS RSVWG, possibly not recognizing the Northern demonstrative *þere*, have taken the verb 'hear' for the adverb 'here', and independently substituted *ben* for *þere*, an obvious way of rectifying the sense. The verb 'hear' is regularly spelt *hire* in Lt, and indeed this spelling is a recognized feature of Anglo-Irish. The Latin gives 'tres gradus amoris pulchre tibi describam'.

**67** *ryse*: MS *ryve* could be an aphetic form of 'arrive', but being unsupported is more probably a simple error.

**82–4** 'nota de dulcedine peccandi' in left hand margin.

**95** *entres*: the Northern inflexion has been retained.

**113** *an*: 'and' showing weak stress.

**116** *life*: this form of the pr. pl. may represent Northern unvoicing of [v] when brought into final position by loss of final *-e*.

**125** *þe*: *þ* and *y* are regularly distinguished as graphs, so MS *ye* must here be regarded as an error.

**135** *hopis*: as l. 95.

**137–8** *hold hit*: Dd is alone among the English MSS in reading 'halde þe', which Miss Allen (*English Writings*) has taken to be an imperative with reflexive pronoun, instead of infinite and direct object. The Latin agrees with Dd inasmuch as it reads *te* for *þe*, but its verbal form *abducet* is future 3 sg.

**164** *hath*: probably an unthinking Southernization of *has* 'hast'.

**165–6** *if þou liue*: MS *þi lif* might result from confusing the Northern verb form in *-f* (see note to l. 116), and emending *þou* accordingly, but this does not explain how the error came to be shared by R[1], itself a Northern text, and the fault is thus better ascribed to carelessness in a common ancestor. Br's *þine* may show an independent attempt to emend the same reading.

**167** *standis*: as l. 95.

**175–211** As Carleton Brown (*RL XIV*, pp. 241–2) and Miss Allen (*English Writings*, pp. 148–9) have pointed out, lines 175–83 derive ultimately from a fragment of Latin meditation, the *Respice in Faciem Christi*, ascribed in the Middle Ages to Augustine (*PL* 158, 861) and later to Anselm, which Rolle used also, only slightly altered, in his *Incendium Amoris*: 'Respicite in eum, et uidebitis caput Diuinum spinis coronatum, faciem consputam . . . dorsus flagellatum, nudum pectus cruentatum, uenerabiles manus perforatas, latus dulcissimum lancea sauciatum, pedes confossos.' Lines 182–4 derive from the *Candet Nudatum Pectus*, which follows in the same text, and of which many vernacular translations exist (*IMEV* 4088). Lines 190–206 again reflect the *Incendium*: 'Ipse uero Christus quasi nostro amore languet, dum tanto ardore ut nos adquireret ad crucem festinauit; sed uerum dicitur quia amor preit in tripudio, et coream ducit. Quod Christum ita demissum posuit, nihil nisi amor fuit. Ueni saluator meus animam meam consolari. Stabilem me fac in dileccione, ut amare nunquam desistam. . . . Reminiscere misericordie tue, dulcissime Ihesu, ut lucens sit uita mea uirtute repleta. . . . Ex quo enim sancto amore mens mea incensa est, positus sum in langore uidenti maiestatem tuam . . . despicio dignitatem terre, nec curo de ullo honore. . . . Quando amare inceperam, amor tuus cor meum suscepit, et nihil me concupiscere permisit, preter amorem; deinde tu deus de dulci lumine animam meam inardescere fecisti, ex quo per te et in te mori potero, et tristiciam non sentire.'

A version of this lyric with additions and some textual dislocation is found in BL MS Add. 37049 (*IMEV* 3416), followed by an even more dislocated version (*IMEV* 4076) incorporating passages from the *Form* lyric and the second *Ego Dormio* lyric. This manuscript also contains disjointed sentences from Rolle's prose.

Lt's Southernizations have sometimes destroyed or weakened the rhyme, as at lines 181, 188, 190, 196, and 205.

**179** Although Lt's omission of *faire* is supported by the Latin of the *Incendium*, the adjective is present in all other MSS including R[1] and Ca, and it seems more probable that Lt inadvertently omitted an alliterating word than that it has been independently added. See too E. J. Dobson and F. Ll. Harrison, *Medieval English Songs* (London, 1979), p. 146, lines 25–6 for alliterating pairs of adjective and noun where the Latin original has no corresponding adjective.

**186** *kan*: in Northern dialect used to form a periphrastic pa.t. without ingressive significance.

**187** *stronde*: there is a fifteenth-century recording of MS *strone*, described by the *OED* as 'Anglo-Irish, sense obscure': 'The suynerd of the towne shulde not suffre the swyne to cum into the strone of the said cite on the one party of the watir ne of the other.' This is interesting for its Anglo-Irish affiliation, but not particularly relevant to the sense here, and the word in the present text could as well represent a phonetic spelling of 'strand' showing loss of final *-d* after *n*, or, more simply, a scribal slip. The last is indicated by the spelling *strand* in the similar phrase at l. 40 of text VI(ii).

**205** *forþe*: *hit* is written in the left hand margin in the same hand with a caret mark for insertion before *fle*. However this would result in a less metrical line, and is only necessary to the sense if Dd's word order is preferred. I have therefore chosen to ignore the insertion, and to emend MS *forþi* to *forþe*, as all other MSS except Dd. This is also supported by the Latin 'Nichil preter te cupiens, totum mundum pro te fugiens'.

**216** *entres*: as l. 95.

**224** *onely*: probably confused with the adverb 'only' and omitted by the scribe as unnecessary. The Latin gives 'solomodo'.

**225** *ryngen*: 'ringing'. The spelling *-en* for *-ing* occurs several times in the MS; see too note to l. 391 of the *Form.*

**231** *gref*: see note to l. 116.

**249** *deile*: the spelling is Northern, the *i* denoting length.

**259** *þar*: retention of the Northern possessive.

**267** sq. Miss Allen (*English Writings*, pp. 149–50) points out verbal similarities to the *Melum*, *Incendium*, *Iesu Dulcis Memoria* and *Wohunge of Ure Lauerd.*

**273** *more*: Lt by Southernizing has lost the rhyme. Elsewhere the scribe often retains *mare* in rhyme.

**280** An obscure line, found only in Lt, Dd and Br. Miss Allen adopts the suggestion that the image is of the knight's stall with his arms above it, giving the translation 'My heart paints the banner (with some badge of Jesus) by which we know our place.' The alliterative phrase *stid in stalle* is used elsewhere by Rolle (cf. text VI(iv) l. 94 *Thou stid hym in þi stalle*) and glossed by Miss Allen as 'take him home with you', but this is not very satisfactory. Br's reading *standith* suggests that the phrase is a variant on *to stand in stall*, meaning 'to be of help' (*OED stall* n[1]. 26). *Palle* could refer to the cloth covering the chalice at the altar, and so be a reference to the Eucharist, or, less specifically, be an unrecorded ME derivation of Latin *palus* 'prop, support'. The line would then mean 'My heart imagines/depicts the Eucharistic sacrifice/support which is the cause of our salvation.'

**291** *lykynge*: R[1] and Dd both read *lyfynge*, which is perhaps an error for *lufynge*, for which Lt provides a synonym. Alternatively, as Lt is supported by RSVWGBrAd, *lyfynge* could just be a coincidental misreading of *lykynge*, influenced by preceding *lif.*

**300** *yif my desyrynge*: the R[1]DdBr reading *yif me my ȝernynge* is probably original, but by its customary substitution of *desyrynge* for *ȝernynge* Lt has produced an ametrical line, and rectified this by omitting *me.*

**303** *fayere*: an unusual spelling, but apparently deliberate; the first *e* is an insertion.

## III *The Commandment*

**24–8** 'Of þre degrees of loue. Insuperabile i' in right hand margin.

**24–36** cf. *Emendatio Vitae*, ch. 11: 'Sunt quidem tres gradus amoris Cristi. Primus gradus vocatur insuperabilis, secundus inseparabilis, tertius singularis. Tunc quippe amor est insuperabilis, quando nulla affectione alia potest superari, & quando libenter propter Cristum omnia impedimenta abiicit, omnes tentationes & omnia carnalia desideria extinguit, quando propter Cristum omnia angusta patienter patitur & nulla delectatione vel blandimento superatur. . . . Amor inseparabilis est, quando iam vehementi dilectione succensa mens, atque Cristo inseparabili cogitatione adherens nullo quidem momento ipsum a memoria recedere permittit, sed quasi in corde ligaretur, ipsum cogitat & ad ipsum suspirat. . . . Cum autem illum cogitando nulla occasione illum obliuiscendo Cristo inseparabiliter inheret, inseparabilis & sempiternus nuncupatur. . . . Sed adhuc restat tertius gradus que dicitur singularis. Aliud est eum solum esse & aliud summum esse: sicut aliud est semper presidens esse, & aliud confortem non admittere. . . . Ad singularem ergo gradum amor ascendit, quando omnem consolationem, preter vnam que est in Iesu, excludit: quando nihil preter Iesum sibi sufficere poterit.' Rolle seems to have drawn on this passage both here and in lines 525–51 of the *Form*.

**30** 'Inseperabile ii' in right hand margin.

**34** 'iii Synguler' in right hand margin.

**35** *fyndeth*: the other MSS vary between the 2 and 3 sg. pr. ind., and I have chosen to emend to the latter as making the better sense. However it is possible that the Lt scribe intended his form *fynd* as a subjunctive, and that it should therefore stand.

**42** 'Ihesu' in margin; also at lines 64, 72, 106, 137, 167, 175, 187, 194 and 214.

**45** *good*: there is only one other instance in the MS of the spelling *god* for 'good', and there too the meaning is ambiguous in the context. It is therefore probable that the scribe was here intending 'God', and I have emended accordingly.

**49** *fallynge*: late fourteenth-century Northern spelling of *a* for *ai*: cf. *Ego Dormio* l. 279.

**84–5** Prov. 8: 17: 'Ego diligentes me diligo, et qui mane vigilant ad me, invenient me.'

**86** *fyndes*: retention of the Northern inflexion.

**107** Luke 3: 11: 'Qui habet duas tunicas, det non habenti.'

**117** *so*: in same hand in right hand margin.

**140** *vnnayte*: this, the difficilior lectio of DdH³, is preferable to MS *variytee* or other variants.

*wordys*: 'worldly'.

**149** *ful*: in her printed text of Dd, Miss Allen appears to have misread this as *still*. The MS reading is *full*.

**152** *stynkynge*: there are no other instances of the scribe mistaking a Northern present participle; probably the word was split between two lines in his exemplar.

**183** *Purchace*: it is probable that Lt's exemplar read *purges* (cf. Dd's reading at l. 192), and that the scribe misunderstood the text and emended accordingly.

**192** *purchace*: MS *purgeth* shows the same mistake as l. 183 above.

**201** *lyued*: MS *loued* is a common result of minim confusion.

**201–2** cf. Job 21: 13: 'Ducant in bonis dies suos et in puncto ad inferna descendunt.'

**221** *Who*: MS *what* suggests a Northern *wha* in exemplar.

## IV *Desire and Delight*

**7** *blyndet*: 'blended', showing raising before covered *n* (Jordan, §34.2).

# VI *Lyrics*

(i) **17–20** The Lt scribe is not averse to retaining Northern *a* from OE *ā* in rhyme; see too lines 57–60, (ii) 43–8, (iv) 33–6, 81–4, but cf. (v) 9.

**19** *wandreth*: this Dd reading, from ON *vandrǣði*, was obviously unfamiliar to the non-Northern scribes of both Lt and La.

**25–8** The Northern present participle is required for medial rhyme; see too (iv) 45–8, (v) 13.

**31** *departynge*: Latin *separacione.*

**44** *turneth*: DdLa *it turnes*, *Incendium conuertitur.*

**47** *felle*: there is no spelling recorded of MS *fele* 'fell' vb., and it must therefore be regarded as an error.

**48** *dede*: 'death', retention of Northern form for rhyme.

**50** *haue*: I previously printed this as *hane* when less familiar with the script. Similarly I did not expand final looped *r* and final crossed *ll.*

**54–6** Northern reflex of OE *ā* required for rhyme.

**60** *casten*: for the strong p.p. see d'Ardenne, p. 161 with reference to Wallenberg, s.v. *Keste.*

(ii) **4** *way*: Dd's variant *hand* has the merit of internal rhyme, but only because in the preceding line it reads *land* for Lt's *world*, possibly a scribal emendation as La here supports Lt. Medial rhyme is not a regular feature of this lyric.

**8** *wene*: if this is not an error for *wane* as Dd, such a form not being recorded, it means 'go', and shows sporadic loss of final *-d* after *n* in this MS.

**30** *why ne*: MS *whyn* repeats a similar error or contraction in an *Ego Dormio* lyric, l. 285.

**35** *in betynge*: for Rolle's fondness for verbal nouns in all constructions, see Miss Allen's note, *English Writings*, p. 141.

**37–40** For similar lines, see *Ego Dormio* 184–7 and note.

**43** *maistry*: suffixal *-y* from OF *-ir*, *-ier* is usually regarded as a Southern or Kentish feature.

(iii) **13** *behoueth*: MS *boweth* is probably a misreading of **boues*, Northern 3 sg. pr. ind. of **bōve(n)*, with *u* standing for the /v/ consonant, this being a contracted form of OE *bi-hōfian* (cf. OE *bufan* from *bi-ufan*, and ME *blive* from OE *bi-līfan*). Although the indicative form is not recorded, a pr. subj. form *bove* is cited (*OED bus* vb.).

**28** The emendation, suggested by DdLa, is metrically preferable.

(iv) **14** The DdTh reading is metrically preferable.

**17** *wose*: the only example in the MS of this spelling.

**27** *your*: correct use of the plural possessive.

**56** *too*: 'take', originally *taa*, but altered to fit the Southernized rhyme.

**62** *thar*: retention of Northern possessive.

**64** *dwyne*: glossed above 'idest ebbe' in the same hand.

**79** *mankynde*: the variant *mankyn* is needed for rhyme. The Lt reading might evidence an intrusive consonant (see note to *Form* lines 30 and 719), but these are not common in the MS, and the spelling is more probably occasioned by a failure to realize that the two words are etymologically distinct.

**91** *bos*: MS *bot* suggests a misunderstanding of the Northern contracted form *bos* written with a high *s*.

**99** *þat*[1]: written above line in same hand.

(v) **9** *sore*: Northern *sare* is required for medial rhyme.

(vi) **6** *lysse*: MS substitution of *blysse* occurs again at l. 360, and it would appear that the scribe was unfamiliar with this word in the sense of 'joy', although it is used or retained in the sense of 'remission' at l. 243.

The metre would be improved if final *-e* were added to the following: *hert* (lines 6, 9, 22, 40, 75, 98, 107, 190, 258, 264, 284, 328, 374); *sowl/soul* (lines 13, 296, 394); *grow* (l. 16); *peyn* (lines 43, 55); *tel* (l. 56); *swet* (lines 66, 190, 267, 280, 384); *herd* (l. 124); *mak* (l. 268); *der* (l. 363); *pray* (l. 363); *swith* (l. 375). At lines 81 and 85 the scansion requires not *lord*, but the earlier form *laferd* as in Ha[1].

**15** *swote*: this spelling is not found in Lt, and MS *hote* may be a deliberate change to retain the rhyme while avoiding an alien form.

**33–52** Matt. 26: 38–9; Mark 14: 34.

**45** *tornedest*: the omission of *-ed-* in the inflected weak pa.t. occurs several times in the MS, giving MS reading *tornest*. In this text it occurs also in *suffrest/soffrest* at lines 53, 57 and 112. I have emended for the sake of clarity.

**47** *blan*: MS *blame*, although supported by Ro, is probably the coincidental result of minim confusion, or failure to understand an unfamiliar word. The verb 'blame' is not recorded in intransitive use.

**48** *way*: in right hand margin in same hand, with caret mark for insertion.

**49–52** The sense required is that of Matt. 26: 44 'iterum abiit et oravit tertio, eundem sermonem dicens', and I have emended accordingly, but *for* should perhaps read *befor*.

**58** *yow* should perhaps be emended to *þe*, but the plural pronoun sometimes alternates with the singular in addressing the Divinity.

*ran*: MS *come*, placed as it is in the margin of the text, might suggest scribal improvisation to supply a lacuna in his exemplar.

**60** *wailawo*: for the emendation I have adopted the spelling found at l. 387. MS *wel low*, presumably meant to mean 'very humbled', could reflect a misunderstanding of the exclamation *we loo*, as in *Sir Gawain and the Green Knight*, l. 2208.

**80** *mercy*: MS *myght* is probably a misunderstanding of *mylth* 'mercy', a word not recorded after the early fourteenth century.

**83** *lyth*: 'alight'; a similar instance of this spelling is seen at l. 180 in *sith* 'sight'.

**133** *hange*: Northern pa.t. from ON causal verb *hengja*, which in ME became *hing*, and was then conjugated like a strong verb of Class III.

**152** This line suggests a corruption somewhere in transmission which forced the scribes variously to extemporize. The adoption of the S reading is only tentative.

**174–5** cf. *Ancrene Wisse* (Corpus MS) fol. 205, 19–20.

**185** *dede* (also lines 186, 188, *deden* 196): pa.t. forms of 'do' in *e* are generally SE in ME, but they can be Northern with *e* for earlier *i*: either *ĕ* by lowering of *ĭ*, or *ē* by open syllable lengthening of *ĭ*.

**193–220** The conventional order of the Seven Words, established from the early Middle Ages (see A. Wilmart, *Revue Bénédictine*, xlvii (1935), 236–8) was Ignosce, Hodie,

Mulier, Sitio, Deus meus, Consummatum and Commendo. Here the last two are transposed.

**193** Luke 23: 34.

**198** Luke 23: 43.

**204** John 19: 26.

**207** John 19: 28.

**211** Matt. 27: 46; Mark 15: 34.

**214** Luke 23: 46.

**219** John 19: 30.

**217–20** Either the original rhyme scheme for this stanza was ABBA, or the poet was being less than exact. There was an OE variant *gǣst* of *gāst*, but it is not recorded as surviving into ME.

**225** Lam. 1: 12.

**229** Mic. 6: 3.

**234** John 18: 23.

**238** Isa. 5: 4.

**241** John 10: 32.

**248** *he*: 'they'.

**255** *my self to be*: understand 'the one who will repay'. The construction is awkward, but the variants more unsatisfactory.

**259** *pershe*: this spelling, beside *perce*, appears to be a scribal idiosyncrasy; similar instances are seen in *mysshe* 'miss' beside *mysse*, *wisshynge* beside *wissynge*, and *greishe* 'grease'.

**296** *besoght*: 'reconciled', a variant spelling, with prefix, of ME *saught* from late OE *sæht.*

**303** Possibly *I* should be omitted.

**306** *hit owet*: the MS reading clearly needs emending, and I have substituted *hit* for *is*, but retained *owet* as a possible instance of *-t* for *-þ* before following *þ-*; cf. note to l. 117 of the *Form.*

**320** *fulled*: 'baptized'. MS *filled* indicates that the Lt scribe had misunderstood the sense here, but in the context the Lt variant *blode*, supported by $Ha^2$, is preferable to $VSAd^2Tr$ *flod.*

**351** *make*: MS *maken* has *n* falsely added. The subj. sg. is required, expressing a prayer.

**356** The evidence of the other MSS suggests that Lt may have omitted *redy*. Of the variants the reading of $Ad^2$ is metrically superior.

**357** 1 Tim. 1: 15.

**367** *nan*: MS *vayn* is probably a misreading of *nayn*, Northern spelling for *none.* The other texts appear to have misunderstood *let* as 'allow' instead of 'hinder', and *suffre* as 'suffer' instead of 'allow', and altered their readings accordingly.

**414** *deiynge*: the MS repetition of *endynge* was possibly caused by the form *dyynge* in the scribe's exemplar.

## VII *Meditation* A

Evidence of a Northern prototype for this text is seen in the following:

**17** *thaire* 'their' (normal MS form *here*); **59** *commes* 2 sg. pr. ind. (normal MS form *-est*); **127** *thristes* 3 sg. pr. ind. (normal MS form *-eth*); **76** *denyande* pr. p. (normal MS form *-yng(e)*); **34** *er* 'are' (normal MS form *ben(e)*); **35** *ilkone*, **65, 94** *ilka*, **101** *thilke*; **49** *titter* 'rather'; **47, 111** *ay* 'always'; **117** *eke* 'increase'; **14** *louyng* 'praising'; **6, 63** *til* 'to'; **29** *wisshe* pa.t.3 sg. 'washed'.

**7–11** *Domine . . . tuum*: this prayer forms part of the York litany. *Adiuua . . . tuum* is taken from Ps. 78: 9, v. 9 being included in the litany between *retribuas nobis* and *Adiuua.*

**11** *Te . . . ago* is reminiscent of the post-Missal thanksgiving, but the remainder of the prayer is not part of the liturgy, and I have been unable to trace it.

**15–16** *schorene away*: cf. *Desire and Delight* 3.

**25–7** *Aue . . . omnium*: I have been unable to identify this prayer, which again seems to have no liturgical connections.

**34–5** John 13: 35.

**36** *mekeli*: MS *mekel* could be a further sign of Northern origin, but in view of the frequent carelessness of this scribe, I have preferred to regard it as an error.

**66** *wisse*: the emendation is made on the supposition that high *ss* was mistaken for *ll*, but further textual corruption may lie behind the MS reading.

**82–3** Ps. 50.

**83–4** *Absolue . . . tuarum* appears to be a plural adaptation of a prayer in the Mass for the Commendation of Souls, where it is also coupled with the *Miserere* as one of the Penitential Psalms.

**102–3** Luke 23: 28 'nolite flere super me sed super vos ipsas flete'. The emendation is made in accordance with the Biblical text.

**112** *seiȝe*: etymology obscure. The obvious sense is 'protrude', 'stand (out)', but no suitable word accommodates the MS form. If this is not corrupt, it is possibly a form of *OED sye* v.[1] 2 *fig.* 'to come from a source', here used literally, or in the general sense of 'move'.

**117** *rowed*: 'rotated' (*OED roll* v.[2] II, 11). The spelling is Northern, though not recorded as such until the sixteenth century (but cf. Jordan §292 B).

**159–60** *Omnipotens . . . tuis*: the opening words of the prayer which begins the Mass of the Holy Trinity. It continues 'in confessione uere fidei eterne trinitas gloriam agnoscere et in potencia maiestatis adorare unitatem quesumus ut eiusdem fidei firmitate ab omnibus semper muniamur aduersis.'

**162–4** The Lt MS now has a large blot on the left hand side of fol. 58[v], which makes it difficult to deciper, so for the words in square brackets I have relied on Miss Allen's earlier transcription.

## VIII *Meditation* B

The rare use of the surname 'Rolle' need not be regarded as proof of authorial authenticity; indeed the combination of the name and date of death in Ti and Add may itself be indication that the ascription is apocryphal, for its first recorded mention is in the *Office*. Apart from the three *Meditation* MSS, which probably derive from a common source, the name appears only six times in conjunction with Rolle's undisputed writings, compared to the several hundred attributions to Richard hermit or Richard Hampole. None of these six manuscripts can be dated within fifty years of Rolle's death, and in three of them the ascription is appended in a different hand. The remaining three (R, $Tr^2$ and $Lt^2$) are not authoritative textually, and it is further remarkable that where two MSS can be shown to derive from a common source, as the *Commandment* text of $Lt^2$ and Br, or the *Ego Dormio* text of R and S, the surname occurs in one but not in the other.

**13** *graeȝ*: an unrecorded spelling, but phonetically possible.

**38** *profite*: 'advance' is possibly the meaning here (*OED profit* v. I, 1), but the more common meaning 'be of use' also makes sense.

**46–8** The prayers to be said after each meditation are only briefly indicated in Mu, although fuller versions are found sporadically in the other MSS. The Lord's Prayer and the Hail Mary are followed by excerpts from the York Hours of the Cross: the Antiphon for Matins precedes the Versus 'Adoramus te Christe et benedicimus tibi' and the Responsus 'Quia per sanctam crucem tuam redemisti mundum.' Then comes the Prayer 'Domine Iesu Christe, fili dei vivi, pone passionem crucem et mortem tuam inter iudicium tuum et animas nostras, nunc et in hora mortis nostre, et largiris digneris vivis misericordiam et gratiam, defunctis veniam et requiem, ecclesie regnoque pacem et concordiam, infirmis sanitatem, et nobis peccatoribus vitam et gloriam sempiternam. Qui vivis et regnas deus per omnia secula seculorum. Amen.'

**52–3** Luke 22: 42.

**97** 'fides' in left hand margin in same hand.

**100** *leuynge*: MS *beleuynge* results from the confusion of *leue* 'leave' and *leue* 'believe'.

**102** 'Spes' in right hand margin in same hand.

*bynd* in left hand margin in same hand.

**107** *wilfully*: Lindkvist suggests the Add reading *skilfulli* is preferable in the context, but the agreement of Mu with UpTi argues against emendation; cf. too l. 269.

'Caritas' in left hand margin in same hand.

**111** *let*: *t* inserted above line in same hand.

**114** *hatis*: retention of Northern inflexion.

**143** *and*: 'also'.

**152** *tyme of* in left hand margin in same hand.

**170–1** *and . . . self*: this may be a deliberate simplification of a clumsy phrase shared substantially by UpTiAdd.

**190** MS *stronge stronge* (first crossed through).

**194** *hit þe*: although UpTiAdd agree in omitting these words, UpTi have further variants which may be additions on their part, and I have not considered it necessary to emend.

**202** *meditacioun*: *medicacioun* might seem preferable in the context, but *t* is clearly distinguishable in all MSS.

**214** *hit*: Lindkvist prefers Add's reading *I*, but cf. note to l. 107.

**221** For similar comparisons, see note to *Wisdom*, l. 1106 (*The Macro Plays*, ed. M. Eccles, EETS os 262).

**234** *delitably*: the emendation is suggested by Up's reading.

**294** *persheth*: see note to VI (vi) 259.

**295** *blessed*: read as noun 'company of heaven'. Although the MS renders it as an adj., the emendation is supported unanimously.

**317** *shrynkes*: cf. note to l. 114.

**318** *fright*: 'burdened'. The spelling may be inverted, but more probably reflects raising of *e*. *MED* (*fraughten*, v.) records two further instances, in pr. 3 sg. (an Irish MS), and pa.t.pl.

**321** *biffetynge*: spelling unrecorded and may show minim loss.

**334** *abrode*: the emendation here follows Add, on the assumption that the UpTi reading could be an independent addition.

**342** 'Ihesu' in right hand margin in same hand.

**349–50** If the emendation is accepted, the loss of *in (þy)* would appear to have occurred in the prototype of MuUpTiAdd. Ll reads '. . . þe sorewe þat styked in þi breest refte þe þe reckyng of bodyly drede . . .'. MS *birefte* was possibly influenced by the appearance of *bereft* in the following line; the scribe of Up has made a tentative alteration by inserting *i* after the *b* of *breste*, and Ti, regarding *breste* as a verb, supplies pron. *þe* as object. Add rearranges the phrase to make sense.

**357** *Set me on*: all four MSS agree in this reading, but the sense is more readily conveyed by Ll's 'gete me of'. Mu's unique addition of *desyre* after *owne* may reflect scribal misunderstanding.

**375** *to*: 'until'.

**386** *vnmythty*: unique instance of this spelling by the scribe.

**388** *nat wot*: this peculiar construction, also in UpTi, suggests misunderstanding of original contracted negative verb *not*, as Add.

**389** *dym*: the only instance of this adj. meaning 'wicked' cited by *MED*.

**393** *turnes*: cf. note to l. 114.

**397** 'Nota bene' in right hand margin, in different but contemporary hand.

**410** 'Visus' in right hand margin in same hand.

**411** *ham*: MuUp *þan* must derive from independent misreading of Northern *þam*.

**413** 'Olfactus' in right hand margin in same hand.

**416** 'Gustus' in left hand margin in same hand.

**418** 'Auditus' in left hand margin in same hand.

**420** Matt. 27: 29, Mark 15: 18.

**422** Luke 23: 35.

**423** 'Tactus' in left hand margin in same hand.

**431–2** Matt. 8: 20.

**433–5** Lamentations 1: 12.

**478–9** Matt. 27: 46, Mark 15: 34; *þat . . . me* has no Biblical authority.

**481** *tendyrly*: the only example of this adjectival form cited by *OED* is Scottish, dated 1567.

**487–8** *losse* . . . *sore*: a confusing statement, because man's soul was saved, not lost, by the Crucifixion. Possibly *þat* should be interpreted as 'who', and it is a specific reference to those who assisted in the torture.

**498** *kepe*: this may represent the Northern verb *kep* 'catch falling liquid', rather than the obvious but less satisfactory sense 'ward off'.

**531** Luke 23: 46.

**534** 'in' inserted above line in same hand between *neuyre* and *wel.*

John 19: 30.

# APPENDIX

## VARIANT LYRICS IN *EGO DORMIO*

(*a*) *From MS* P

Haf mynde vpon þi kyng, how he þe water wepte
þat is þi dere swetyng, and how his blod he swette.
Ful sore beten was he, so þat his blood hym wette,
And al hit was for þe, þe fendes power to lette.
Defouled was his face with dispitous spyttynge,
And þis kyng corowned was with þornes sore prikkynge.
Allas, my dere swetyng and al my loue so fre,
Demyd he was to hyng; þerfore ful wo is me.
Nailed were his hondes and nayled were his feet,
And þirled was his hed so semly and so sweet.
Naked was his white brest and red his blody syde,
Al wan was his fair hew, his wowndes deep and wyde.
Drawen als hit is to dole þat is owr gostly good,
And defouled as a fole, of heuen þe hiest food.
A wonder hit is to se, who so vnderstood,
How god of mageste was deyng on þe rood.
But sothe þen is hit seid þat loue ledyþ þe ryng:
þat þat hym lowe haþ leyd but loue hit was no þyng.
Ihesu, al myn herte, vnto þy loue me bryng;
Al my desir þou erte, y longe after þi comyng.
þou make me clene of of (*sic*) synne, and lat vs neuer twynne;
Teend þi fir me ynne þat y þi loue may wynne
And se þi blessid face, þi blisse þat neuer shal blynne.
Ihesu, graunte me þat grace and bryng me to þat ynne;
In loue þou wynde my þouȝt, and lifte myn herte to þe;
þis sowle þat þou hast bouȝt þi louer make hit be.
But þe y coueite nouȝt, þis wordle fro (*sic*) þe y fle;
þou art þat y haue souȝt; þi face when may y se?
How longe shal y be here? When may y come to þe
þi mel[odi]e to here and þi fair face to se?
þou bryng me to þat place, Ihesu, my der swetyng,
Wher y may se þi face and alwey be dwellyng. Amen.

(*b*) *From MS* Tr

Ihesu, grete loue moued þe
To suffur þe peyne on þi feyre bode
Of þat wicked lede and bolde.
For grete sorowȝe it is a lord to se
Of his deceyple betrayed to be,
As Iudas, lord, þe solde
To þe Iewes, Ihesu, þat þe duden bete,
þat her scourges duden mete,
As fast as þei knouþen dynge.
Her peynes þan weren drede,
For of hym þei token non hede,
But defouled hym wiþ spittyng.
Hard þei duden him þring to a pyler of stone;
Wiþ þornes þei crouned hym kynge;
Hard was þat prykkyng
þat he suffurd þan of hem.
Alas, my dere swetyng, wiþ her hard yron dynge
Grete peyne was þe þanne on.
Swete Ihesu, þei demed þe honged for to be
Wiþ falshede and wiþ wrong,
And to a cros of tree ful fast þei nayled þe
Wiþ yrnen neyles strong.
Ihesu, boþe hande and fete of þe i were nayled to a tree,
And þerled was þi feyre syde.
þow hongest al one on rode,
By ronnen with spetel and blod,
þat semely was and whyte.
þi feyre body was defouled þere,
And grymly stongen wiþ a spere;
For deel now may I wepe.
Ihesu, þi flesche þei duden to tere
þat pyte it is þer of to here,
Wiþ woundes and depe.
In fyue places, lord, wiþouten moo,
þe stremes of blode rannen þe froo,
As water from a welle.
Alas, lord, why dude þei soo
þi feyre body so muchel woo

More þan I may telle?
Ihesu, ful of pyte þou suffurst hem milde
To spitte in þi faire face.
Gret peyne it was to see
þe nayled to an tree,
Wiþouten gult or trespasse.
Now may I hauc mournyng,
And of care may I syng,
Of peyne ȝif I take hede.
To see þe Iewes so dyng,
Hit is a rewþful þing,
Hym þat is angel brede.
For sorowȝ now may I wepe
For my loue þat is so swete,
Of loue ȝif I be trewe.
For he suffurd woundes depe,
Now may I teres lete,
For more loue neuer man knewe.
Ihesu, boþe hende and free,
Lorde, ful of pyte,
þurȝ þi holy grace
Graunte me þat I may se þe,
Lord in maieste,
In þi ioyful place. Amen.

## Cantus secundus

Ihesu, receyue my hert, for my desire þou art,
And to þi loue me bring,
þat I may gostly se þe bryȝtnesse of þe,
For I coueyte þi comyng.
þou make me clene of synne,
And lete me neuer fro þe twynne,
For þe chaunges my hew.
þi grace be me wiþinne, þat I þi loue may wynne
And se þi face, Ihesu,
To blisse þat neuer schal blynne, Ihesu, my soule þou wynne
þat heuen and erþe hast wrouȝt,
And my þouȝt to þe bynde
To haue þe moste in mynde,

þat mannes soule dere hast bouȝt.
þi louer make me to be,
I coueyte nouȝt but þe;
þis world for þe I flee,
þou art þat I haue souȝt.
þi face whan schal I see
Wiþouten ende to be
In ioy þat þou hast wrouȝt?
Make my soule bryȝt and clere,
þi loue chaunges my chere,
How long schal I be here?
When may I come þe nere
þi melodye to here
þat is ay lastynge?
þan myȝt I in reste be
Wiþouten ende with þe,
And of ioy euer to synge.

# GLOSSARY

The Glossary attempts to record every word which occurs, and every form, whether inflexional or orthographical. Brackets enclose letters which are optionally alternative spellings. Preference for a particular variant is proportionate to the number of occurrences listed. However all occurrences of every word or form are not recorded, and in the case of more common words only a few instances are given, usually one for each text.

Verbs are recorded under the infinitive, when it occurs, followed by the present indicative in order of person, subjunctive, imperative, past tense indicative and subjunctive, past participle and present participle; forms identical to the headword are not shown when they follow immediately after it. Cross-references are as full as possible. The gloss, or glosses if the senses are too close to distinguish with certainty or if particular application is obvious, extends to all variants unless otherwise stated.

In the arrangement of the entries, initial and medial [j] is placed alphabetically as modern *y*, and no distinction is made between *y* and *ȝ* in this function. Medial and final *ȝ*, where it represents the voiceless front and back fricative, is treated as *gh*. The vowel spelt *i*, *j* or *y* is treated as *i*. Initial and medial *i* or *y*, where it stands for modern *j*, is treated as such. No distinction is made between *th* and *þ*. The vowel written as *u* or *v* is treated as modern *u*, and the consonant written *u* or *v* as modern *v*. An asterisk following a word indicates that it is an editorial emendation. Scribal errors, being noted in the textual apparatus, are not normally recorded.

**a** *interj.* ah I. 88, VI (vi). 207, VIII. 287
**a** *prep., adj. see* **on**
**a(n)** *indef. art.* a, any, some I. 21, I. 56, II. 41, III. 6, III. 80, IV. 2, VII. 48, VIII. 23 *etc., and see* **on(e)** *adj.*
**abide, abyde** *v.* stay, remain VIII. 226, VIII. 234; *pr.pl.* **abiden** VIII. 559; *imp.pl.* **abide** VI (vi). 227, **abyde** VIII. 434
**abydynge** *n.* continuance VIII. 239
**ab(i)le** *adj.* suitable, fitted I. 138, III. 119; ~ **to** I. 314 capable of
**aboundance** *n.* superfluity I. 872
**about** *adj.* busy, concerned I. 97; **aboutward** II. 169, III. 67
**about** *adv.* around II. 136, VII. 117
**about(e)** *prep.* around, surrounding VII. 67, VII. 106, VIII. 309; concerning I. 739, I. 864
**aboue(n)** *prep.* above I. 660, II. 214, III. 181, IV. 16, VII. 116
**abrode*** *adv.* widely apart VIII. 334
**abstynence, abstinence** *n.* abstinence I. 49, II. 157
**accompt** *v.* consider, reckon I. 296
**accordeth** *pr.3 sg.* agrees, unites VIII. 58; *pl.* **accordeth** I. 873, **accorden** VI (vi). 344
**accusaciouns** *n.pl.* accusations, blame VIII. 132
**accused** *p.p.* accused VII. 87
**accusynge** *n.* censure VIII. 419
**accusours** *n.pl.* accusers, prosecutors VIII. 129
**actif** *adj.* active I. 836
**adoun** *adv.* down VII. 62, VIII. 450
**adresse** *subj.pl.* direct I. 211
**aduersite** *n.* trouble, hardship I. 814
**affeccioun** *n.* emotion, love I. 332, I. 648; *pl.* **affeccioun**s VIII. 117, manifestation of affection I. 595
**affectuouse** *adj.* ardent, desirous IV. 17
**afflicciou**n *n.* pain, suffering I. 196
**afforce** *v.refl.* exert I. 670; *subj.sg.* II. 12; *pl.* I. 294; *imp.sg.* VI (vi). 89
**afor** *adv.* before VIII. 478
**afor(e)** *prep.* in the sight of I. 88; in front of VIII. 128
**aftre, after, aftyr** *prep.* after VII. 55, VIII. 299; according to I. 622; in pursuit of II. 120, III. 45
**aftre, after, aftreward** *adv.* afterwards I. 124, I. 150, III. 54, II. 244, II. 251, VI (vi). 49; **efter** VII. 146
**agayn(e), agayns** *prep.* against I. 450, III. 7, III. 78, III. 181, VI (vi). 115, VI (vi). 155, I. 391, II. 264, III. 210; in comparison with VI (vi). 68
**agaynward** *adv.* in return VIII. 241
**age** *n.* age VIII. 285

**aggregged** *pa.t.pl.* increased VIII. 336
**agreved** *p.p.* troubled VIII. 419
**ay(e)** *adv.* always I. 605, II. 236, VI (i). 1, VI (i). 60, VI (ii). 24, VI (iii). 25, VII (iv). 3, VII. 47, *and see* **ayeyne(e)** *adv.*
**aire, ayre** *n.* air I. 671, VI (i). 61; **eyre** VIII. 430
**aise** *see* **ese**
**al** *adv.* entirely, totally I. 320, I. 645, IV. 23, VI (iii). 7, VI (vi). 82, VIII. 14
**al(le)** *adj.* all, every, everything, everyone I. 15, I. 17, I. 75, I. 603, II. 13, II. 25, II. 56, III. 9, III. 104, IV. 3, VI (iii). 6, VI (iv). 49, VI (v). 9, VI (vi). 4, VII. 4, VII. 22, VII. 2, VIII. 295 *etc.*; *as n.* II. 279
**al(l)as** *interj.* alas II. 181, VIII. 291
**aleynth** *see* **draw**
**alyȝt** *v.* alight, descend VIII. 513
**almyghty** *adj.* almighty VI (vi). 333, **almiȝti** VII. 173
**almysdede** *n.* almsgiving I. 408, **almusdede** I. 685 alms, charity
**alon(ly)** *adv.* only VI (vi). 100, III. 11
**als** *see* **as, also**
**also** *adv.* also, in addition I. 497, III. 13, VII. 17, VIII. 227; similarly I. 734, II. 23, III. 39, **als** VI (vi). 51
**alson** *adv.* immediately IV. 19
**am** *pr.1 sg.* am I. 630, II. 287, VII. 62, VIII. 23
**amen** *interj.* amen, so be it I. 897, II. 313 *etc.*
**amend** *v.* correct, improve VIII. 39; *pr.pl.* I. 47; *subj.sg.* I. 137; *imp.sg.* **mend** II. 201; *pr.p.* **amendynge** I. 394
**amendement** *n.* correction VIII. 469; **amendynge** VIII. 10
**amyd** *prep.* amidst VIII. 482
**amisse** *adv.* wrongly VI (vi). 242
**amonestynge** *n.* exhortation I. 318
**among(e)** *prep.* amongst I. 22, II. 39, VII. 19, VIII. 331, **amonges** III. 92
**amonge** *adv.* at the same time VI (vi). 384
**an** *see* **and, on, a**
**and** *conj.* and I. 5, II. 3, III. 5, IV. 1, VI (i). 10, *etc.*, **ande** I. 65, **an** I. 80, II. 113, VI (iv). 15; if III. 14, III. 103; also VIII. 143; even III. 96
**a(u)ngel** *n.* angel VII. 3, VIII. 62, ~ **of light(e)** angel dwelling in heaven I. 163, I. 182; *pl.* **a(u)ngels** I. 12, II. 16, III. 51, VI (i). 46, VI (ii). 12, VIII. 43, VIII. 140; *gen.* II. 54, VI (ii). 33, VI (ii). 44
**angre, anger** *n.* anger, resentment I. 338, I. 617; affliction II. 53, **angyr(e)** I. 811, VIII. 158; *pl.* **angres** afflictions I. 805, III. 82
**anguysshe** *n.* suffering I. 135, VIII. 63, **anguys** I. 352, II. 113, III. 28, **anguysh(e)** VIII. 65, VIII. 119, **anguisse** VII. 40, **angwishe** VIII. 61, **angwise** VII. 99; *pl.* **anguysshes** I. 124
**any** *pron.* anyone I. 35, I. 783, III. 146, IV. 19; anything I. 427
**any** *adj.* any I. 37, II. 5, III. 17, IV. 17, VI (vi). 228, VII. 110, VIII. 72 *etc.*, **eny** II. 105, VIII. 400, **ony** VIII. 533
**ano(o)n** *adv.* at once I. 175, I. 177, VI (ii). 45, VI (vi). 48
**another, anoþer** *pron.* someone else II. 218, I. 834, II. 34
**anothre, another, anoþer** *adj.* another I. 394, III. 150, IV. 10, IV. 20
**answare** *v.* answer I. 287, VI (i). 62; *pr.1 sg.* **answar(e)** I. 705, I. 633; *3 sg.* **answareth** I. 721; *pa.t.sg.* **answered** VII. 48; *pr.p.* **answarynge** III. 93
**apaid** *p.p.* satisfied VIII. 22
**apertly** *adv.* plainly, openly I. 805
**apostasie** *n.* apostasy I. 366
**apostle** *n.* apostle I. 246; *pl.* **apostles** I. 443
**appeireth** *pr.pl.* damage III. 16
**appereth** *pr.3 sg.* appears I. 163; *pa.t.sg.* **appered** I. 168
**appetit(e)** *n.* appetite I. 448, VIII. 364
**appil(le)** *n.* apple I. 740, I. 754
**ar** *conj.* before I. 58, I. 379, III. 104, **or** VI (vi). 32, VI (vi). 39, VIII. 191, **er** VIII. 193
**ar** *adv.* rather III. 113
**archangels** *n.pl.* archangels II. 17
**arghnes** *n.* timidity VIII. 344
**aright, aryȝt** *adv.* correctly VI (vi). 12, VIII. 397
**arly** *adv.* early I. 587, **erly** III. 85
**arme** *n.*[1] arm VII. 111; *pl.* **armes** VI (vi). 174, VIII. 334, **armys** VIII. 493
**armes** *n.*[2]*pl.* armour I. 664
**armed** *adj.* armed VIII. 310
**array** *n.* dress VIII. 260
**art** *pr.2 sg.* art, are I. 87, II. 129, III. 61, VI (iv). 14, VI (vi). 10, VIII. 88 *etc.*
**as** *adv.* & *conj.* as, like I. 51, II. 7, III. 36, IV. 21, VI (i). 2, VI (vi). 44, VII. 41, VIII. 23 *etc.*, **als** I. 198, VI (iv). 79; inasmuch as I. 481, II. 139, VI (vi). 19, VIII. 1; similarly I. 498; because VI (i). 39; **als** VI (vi). 31

while; **als(o) . . . as** II. 48, VII. 153, VIII. 258, **as . . . as** I. 308, III. 13 *etc.*, as . . . as
**as** *v. see* **haue**
**ascendeth** *pr.3 sg.* rises I. 872
**ask(e)** *v.* ask I. 626, III. 74, VII. 22; *pr.1 sg.* VI (vi). 325, VIII. 360, VI (vi). 80, VII. 156; *2sg.* **askest** VI (vi). 142; *3sg.* **asketh** II. 9, requires VIII. 523; *pl.* **ask** II. 148, **asketh** I. 165; *imp.sg.* **aske** VII. 152; *pa.t.sg.* **asked** VII. 39, VIII. 438
**askynge** *n.* question I. 633
**assailynge** *n.* assault VIII. 159
**assent** *n.* agreement I. 329
**assent** *v.* agree, submit VIII. 145
**assiduel** *adj.* constant I. 432
**at** *prep.* at II. 178, II. 225, III. 122, VII. 14, VII. 119, VIII. 355, VIII. 432, **atte** I. 267; according to I. 79, I. 211, VI (ii). 13, VIII. 16; against IV. 13; in I. 235
**aþurst** *adj.* thirsty VIII. 464
**atyre** *n.* clothing VIII. 261
**attyre** *n.* poison II. 83
**atwyn** *adv.* asunder VIII. 96
**auþer** *see* **oþer(e)** *pron.*
**auees** *n.pl.* Hail Marys VII. 160
**avise** *imp.sg.refl.* instruct VI (iv). 107
**away(e)** *adv.* away I. 704, II. 249, III. 44, IV. 3, V. 9, VI (iv). 2, VI (iii). 7, VII. 16
**ayeyne, ayeyns, ayayn, aȝeyns** *prep.* against III. 4, VIII. 72, VIII. 166, VII. 155; **ayeyn** VI (vi). 244 in return for
**ayeyn(e), ayayn, aȝein, aȝeyne** *adv.* again VI (vi). 48, VIII. 37, VI (vi). 300, VII. 90, VII. 101, **aye** I. 178

**bacbiters** *n.pl.* slanderers III. 16
**bacbitynge** *n.* slander, calumny I. 353, II. 75; *pl.* **bacbytynges** I. 712
**bad** *see* **bidden**
**bak** *n.*[1] bat (mammal) III. 19
**bak(e)** *n.*[2] back VI (ii). 35, VII. 71, VIII. 275, VIII. 316
**bale** *n.* suffering II. 299, VI (ii). 26, VI (iii). 9, VI (iv). 76, VIII. 365
**band(es)** *see* **bond**
**bank** *n.* riverbank VIII. 214
**baptisede** *p.p.* baptized VII. 20
**bare** *adj.* naked VI (v). 12, VIII. 316
**barne** *n.* child III. 100
**bath** *imp.sg.* bathe VIII. 527
**bath** *n.* bath VIII. 500
**be-** *see* **bi-**
**be(n)** *v.* be I. 17, I. 84, II. 15, III. 33, IV. 26, VI (i). 4, VII. 18, VIII. 21, VII. 162 *etc.*, **bene** VI (vi). 64; *pr.3 sg.* (*with fut. implications*) **beth** I. 607; *pl.* **ben(e)** I. 1, I. 73, I. 93, I. 360, II. 16, III. 9, III. 151, IV. 3, VI (i). 60, VI (iv). 10, VI (vi). 94, VIII. 54, VIII. 224 *etc.*, **be** I. 63, VI (vi). 247, **beth** I. 396, VI (v). 7, **er** VII. 34; *subj.sg.* **be** I. 318, II. 244, III. 8, IV. 14 *etc.*, *pl.* **be** I. 72, II. 59, VIII. 14 *etc.*; *imp.sg.* **be** I. 134, III. 61, III. 163, VI (vi). 108, VII. 52 *etc.*; *p.p.* **bo** I. 319, **ben** I. 75, VI (vi). 160, VII. 112, **bene** I. 288, III. 123, VIII. 455, *&see* **am, art, is, was**
**becum** *v.* become II. 7, **bicum** II. 95, **become** VIII. 386, **bicome** VIII. 502; *p.p.* **becomyn** VIII. 499, **become** VIII. 544
**bed** *n.* bed II. 8, II. 245; resting place VI (i). 11
**bede** *see* **bidden**
**befalle** *v.* happen, occur I. 352, **bifal** III. 145; *pr.3 sg.* **befalleth** I. 77, **bifalleth** I. 807; *pl.* **befalleth** I. 222; *subj. sg.* **befalle** I. 180
**befor(e), bifor(e), byfore** *prep.* in front of I. 287, I. 346, I. 394, II. 38, VII. 98, VIII. 120, VIII. 131; above I. 33, III. 17
**before** *adv.* before I. 223, VIII. 50, **befoor** I. 416, **bifore** II. 238, VII. 29, VIII. 172, **byfore** VIII. 321, **biforne** VIII. 69
**begger staf** *n.* a prop or support for beggars, a symbol of poverty I. 653
**begile** *v.* deceive I. 166; *pr.3 sg.* **begileth** I. 26; *subj.sg.* **begil** I. 119; *p.p.* **begiled** I. 48
**begyn** *v.* begin, undertake I. 370, **bigyn** VI (v). 21; *pr.pl.* **begynneth** I. 54, **begynnen** I. 311, **begyn** III. 49; *subj.pl.* **begyn(ne)** I. 146, III. 71; *imp.sg.* **begynne** VII. 150; *pa.t.sg.* **began** VIII. 360; *pl.* **bigan** VI (ii). 43, **kan** VI (ii). 34; *p.p.* **begun(n)e** I. 189, I. 313
**begynnynge** *n.* beginning, start, origin I. 267, II. 225, III. 56, VIII. 280, **begennynge** II. 3, **bigynnyng** VII. 136
**begoo** *p.p.* beset VI (vi). 124, **bygone** VIII. 446
**behynd** *prep.* behind III. 104, VIII. 290, **behinde** VII. 65
**behynd(e)** *adv.* behind VI (iv). 73, VII. 69
**behoueth** *pr.3 sg.* is necessary I. 401; needs, must II. 73, VI (iii). 13, VII. 45, **bos*** VI (iv). 91, **bihoueth** VII. 45; *impers.* **behoueth** I. 560, II. 152, III. 12, V. 6, VI (vi). 255, **bihoueth** I. 200; *pa.t.sg.* **behoued** I. 175

**belde** *pr.1 sg.* shelter II. 307
**beleue** *v.* believe VIII. 101; *pr.1 sg.* VIII. 34; *p.p.* **beleued** VIII. 100; *pr.p.* **belevynge** VIII. 99
**beleue** *n.* belief, faith VIII. 98, **byleve** VIII. 96, **bileue** VIII. 97
**beme** *n.*[1] trumpet VI (v). 14
**beme** *n.*[2] ray VI (vi). 18
**benfaites** *n.pl.* benefits I. 383
**benysone** *n.* blessing I. 858
**ber** *v.* carry I. 785, VIII. 262; *pr.3 sg.* **bereth** produces VIII. 205; *pa.t.sg.* **bare** VII. 97, VIII. 276; *pl.* **bare** VIII. 405; *p.p.* **borne** born VI (iv). 29, VI (vi). 19; *pr.p.* **berynge** producing VIII. 206
**bereft** *pa.t.sg.* deprived VIII. 350; *pr.p.* **berevynge** I. 116
**berynge** *n.* carrying VIII. 424
**beseche** *v.* beseech, implore VIII. 364; *pr.1 sg.* **besech(e)** VI (vi). 266, VI (vi). 369, VIII. 7; *pa.t.2 sg.* **besoghtest** VI (vi). 36; *p.p.* **besoght** reconciled VI (vi). 296
**besene** *p.p.* treated VIII. 315
**beset** *p.p.* surrounded I. 845
**besy** *imp.sg.refl.* occupy, concern VI (iv). 3
**besyly** *adv.* assiduously VIII. 113
**besoght(est)** *see* **beseche**
**beste** *n.* animal VI (vi). 218; *pl.* **bestes** III. 97, VII. 163
**best(e)** *adj.* & *adv. see* **better**
**beswyke** *v.* betray, deceive VI (i). 13
**betake** *pr.1 sg.* commit, entrust VIII. 531; *imp.sg.* **bitake** III. 146, VI (iv). 50; *pa.t.2 sg.* **betoke** VI (vi). 203, **bitok** VIII. 443; *3 sg.* **bitauȝte** VII. 37; *p.p.* **bitoke** VIII. 448
**bete** *v.*[1] cure II. 299, VI (ii). 26, VI (iii). 9, VI (iv). 76
**bete** *v.*[2] beat, scourge VII. 81; *pr.3 sg.* **beteth** VI (v). 9; *p.p.* **bet(e)** II. 176, VI (vi). 187, **bette(n)** VI (vi). 110, VIII. 282
**beth** *see* **be(n)**
**beþynke** *v.* consider, reflect VIII. 489; *subj.sg.refl.* **bethynke** I. 416, III. 197; *imp.sg.refl.* **bethynk(e)** I. 433, II. 94, VII. 161, **bethinke** VII. 150
**betyde** *v.* happen, befall VI (iv). 7
**betynge** *n.* beating, scourging VIII. 320; **in** ~ VI (ii). 35 lacerated
**betraied** *pa.t.sg.* betrayed VIII. 69
**bette(n)** *see* **bete, better** *adv.*
**better, bettre** *adj.comp.* better I. 32, I. 207, III. 21, VII. 137, **bettyr(e)** II. 254, VI (i). 55, VIII. 133; *sup.* **best(e)** I. 31, I. 358, II. 288, III. 67, VI (vi). 97, VIII. 224; *as n.* VI (i). 4
**better, bettre** *adv.comp.* better I. 33, II. 94, **bettyr(e)** VIII. 112, VIII. 439, **bette** VI (vi). 240; *sup.* **best** VI (v). 20, VIII. 525
**betwix, bitwix** *prep.* between I. 642, VIII. 482, III. 97
**bi-, by-** *see* **be-**
**by, bi** *prep.* (of place) beside VI (vi). 226, VIII. 455; across VIII. 288; (of time) during VIII. 197; (of means or cause) by VII. 75, VIII. 319, VIII. 354; according to I. 853
**by** *v.* buy I. 740, VI (vi). 131, **bye** pay for VI (i). 65; *pa.t.2 sg.* **boghtest** VI (vi). 405, VIII. 89, **boght** VI (vi). 27; *3 sg.* **boght(e)** III. 217, VI (ii). 5, VI (ii). 47, VI (iv). 6; *p.p.* **boght** II. 8, VI (iii). 12, VI (vi). 301, **j-boght** VI (vi). 156, VI (vi). 327, **bouȝt** VII. 45
**bid** *v.* stay, remain VI (vi). 419
**bidden** *pr.pl.* ask, order I. 42; *imp.sg.* **bid** I. 171; *pa.t.2 sg.* **bad** VI (vi). 35, **bede** VI (vi). 194 prayed; *3 sg.* **bad** VII. 57; *pl.* **bad** VII. 95
**biddynge** *n.* command I. 497, VI (iv). 59, VIII. 17; *pl.* **biddynges** I. 376, VI (iv). 25
**bye** *adv.* at hand, imminent VI (v). 14
**biffetynge** *see* **buffetynge**
**bigge** *pr.1 sg.* dwell II. 307
**bigge** *adj.* strong VI (i). 51
**biholde** *pr.1 sg.* look at, contemplate VI (iii). 13; *imp.sg.* **bihold(e)** VI (iv). 30, VII. 122; *pl.* **behold** VIII. 434; *pa.t.2 sg.* **beheld** VIII. 122; *3 sg.* **bihilde** VII. 75
**biholdynge** *n.* contemplation I. 866
**bynd** *v.* bind, fetter I. 109; *pr.3 sg.* **byndeth** II. 302, VI (ii). 22, restrains, holds in check VI (i). 54; *imp.sg.* **bynd** VI (iv). 74, VIII. 95; *pa.t.sg.* **bonde** VII. 106; *pl.* **bonde(n)** VII. 64, VIII. 94; *p.p.* **bounden** I. 1, III. 116, VI (ii). 34, **bound** VIII. 188, **ybounden** VII. 67
**byndyng(e)** *n.* fettering VII. 64, VIII. 423
**byneth** *prep.* below I. 437, **benethen** VII. 117
**byrdes** *n.pl.* birds VIII. 431
**birthe** *n.* birth VII. 14
**birthyn, birthen** *n.* burden VI (i). 49, VIII. 323
**bisy, bisi** *adj.* occupied, assiduous II. 152, IV. 14

**bisynes(se), bisinesse, bysynesse, besynesse** *n.* activity I. 269, III. 76, IV. 3, VI (iv). 55, II. 240, VIII. 5, II. 36, II. 138 *etc.*; assiduity I. 149, I. 413, I. 421; *pl.* **bisynesse** I. 217 troubles

**bitauȝte** *see* **betake**

**bitter, bittyr** *adj.* harsh, cruel VI (vi). 232, VIII. 189; sour VI (vi). 344, VIII. 417; *comp.* **bitterer** II. 83, III. 50 sourer

**bitternesse** *n.* suffering VI (iv). 53

**blaber** *v.* babble II. 135

**blak** *adj.* black VI (vi). 59

**blame** *n.* **to** ~ I. 64 at fault

**blan** *see* **blyn**

**blasphemes** *n.pl.* blasphemies VIII. 151

**blede** *v.* bleed VI (iv). 79; *pa.t. 2 sg.* **bled(de)** VIII. 188, VIII. 267; *pl.* **blede** VII. 122; *p.p.* **bled** VIII. 283

**blemesshynge** *pr.p.* damaging, impairing I. 115

**blesful, blisful** *adj.* blissful, blessed VI (vi). 376, VIII. 185, VIII. 172, VII. 122; *comp.* **blestfuller** VI (vi). 22

**blesse** *v.* bless VIII. 528; *imp.sg.* II. 110; *p.p.* **blessed** VI (vi). 421, VIII. 269, **blissed** VII. 170

**blessed** *adj.* blessed I. 513, III. 127, VI (ii). 35, VIII. 142, *as n.* VIII. 295, **blissede** VII. 2; *comp.* **blesseder** I. 536

**blyn** *v.* cease II. 200, VI (i). 39, VI (ii). 14, VI (vi). 11, VI (vi). 276; *pa.t.2 sg.* **blan** * were silent VI (vi). 47

**blynd(e)** *adj.* blind VI (v). 7, VII. 23, VIII. 391

**blyndet** *p.p.*[1] blended, mingled IV. 7

**blyndet** *p.p.*[2] blinded VI (ii). 41

**blyndfelled** *p.p.* blindfolded VIII. 410

**blyndfellynge** *n.* blindfolding VIII. 168

**blyndynge** *n.* blinding VIII. 170

**blis(se)** *n.* joy, bliss II. 117, II. 200, VI (i). 11, VI (ii). 14, VI (iv). 67, VI (vi). 5, VII. 126, VIII. 140 *etc.*, **blys(se)** VI (vi). 64, VIII. 27, I. 273

**blisful** *see* **blesful**

**blo** *adj.* livid VI (vi). 59

**blod(e)** *n.* blood II. 175, VI (i). 54, VI (ii). 5, VI (vi). 86, VII. 6, VIII. 63 *etc.*, **blood(e)** I. 255, II. 176, VI (ii). 35, VI (vi). 96; ~ **rewes** VIII. 322 streams of blood

**blody** *adj.* bloody II. 184, VI (ii). 37, VI (iii). 12, VI (iv). 30, VI (vi). 58, VII. 122, VIII. 365

**blody** *adv.* bloodily VI (ii). 41, VI (iii). 18

**blondre** *pr.1 sg.* blunder, stumble VIII. 391

**blont** *adj.* blunt VIII. 376

**bloweth** *pr.3 sg.* blows VI (v). 14

**body** *n.* body I. 71, II. 80, III. 158, VI (vi). 59, VII. 165, VII. 21, VIII. 66 *etc.*; form I. 176, **bodi** VII. 122; *pl.* **bodies** III. 207, celestial bodies VIII. 362

**bodily** *adj.* physical II. 14, III. 79, IV. 17, VIII. 18, **bodili** I. 258, **bodilye** VIII. 140

**bodily** *adv.* physically I. 575, III. 145

**boke** *n.* book I. 489, VIII. 238; the Psalter II. 136; *pl.* **bokes** I. 623, IV. 22

**bold(e)** *adj.* brave VI (i). 51, VI (iii). 15, VIII. 343

**bolned** *adj.* swollen VII. 74, VIII. 314

**bond** *n.* fetter, tie VI (vi). 76, **band** I. 605; obligation VIII. 111; *pl.* **bondes** I. 108, **bondis** VIII. 218

**bondman** *n.* vassal VIII. 82

**bone** *n.*[1] flesh VI (i). 54; *pl.* **bones, bonys** III. 152, VIII. 494 bones

**bone** *n.*[2] prayer, petition VI (vi). 49

**borne** *see* **ber**

**bos** *see* **behoueth**

**boste** *n.* arrogance, ostentation VI (v). 16

**bot** *conj.* but I. 12, II. 4, III. 10, V. 5, VI (i). 57, VIII. 22 *etc.*, **but** VII. 51; unless II. 74, ~ **if** I. 33, I. 320, I. 462, III. 126; except I. 388, I. 478, VIII. 57

**bot** *prep.* except I. 143, I. 636, III. 55, VI (iii). 2, VII. 63, VII. 166

**bot** *adv.* only I. 96, II. 52, III. 102, VI (i). 32, VI (vi). 80, VII. 90, VIII. 192

**bot(e)** *n.* spiritual healing VI (i). 7, VI (vi). 13, VIII. 368

**bote** *v.* remedy VIII. 410

**both** *adv.* both I. 14, I. 151, VI (iii). 1, **boþ** I. 621

**both(e)** *adj.* both II. 115, VI (i). 56, VI (ii). 10, VI (vi). 11, VII. 120

**bounden** *see* **bynd**

**bowe** *subj.pl.* submit, incline VIII. 15; *p.p.* **bowed** VI (vi). 175

**brayne pan** *n.* skull VIII. 291

**brand-** *see* **bren-**

**bred(e)** *n.* food II. 189, VI (ii). 44

**bred(e), bredde** *p.p.* engendered II. 284, VI (iv). 47, VI (ii). 29

**brek** *v.* break VIII. 111; *pr.3 sg.* **breketh** harms I. 446; *subj.sg.* **brek** VIII. 217; *p.p.* **broken** harmed I. 447

**brekynge** *n.* violation I. 365

**bren(ne)** *v.* burn, consume with fire I. 555, III. 185, VI (i). 61, VI (iv). 27, **brand** I. 108, I. 307; *pr.3 sg.* **brenneth** I. 886; *pl.* **brandyn** I. 240; *p.p.* **brent** II. 249, VI (ii). 27; *pr.p.* **brennynge** I. 499, II. 28, III. 126, VI (iv). 48, VI (vi). 332, VIII. 339, **brendynge** I. 314

**brennynge** *n.* fire, burning I. 605, II. 29, III. 11, **brandynge** I. 144, **brendynge** I. 635

**brennynge** *adj.* burning I. 553, I. 633, III. 167, VI (i). 26; *comp.* **brennynger** I. 465 more ardent

**brennyngly** *adv.* ardently II. 37, III. 178

**bresed** *see* **bruys**

**brest(e)** *v.* burst, break I. 601, II. 289, VI (iii). 13, VI (iv). 91; *pa.t.sg.* **brast** VII. 65, VIII. 504, **brest** VII. 86; *pl.* **brest** VII. 121, **brosten** VIII. 403

**brest(e)** *n.* breast, chest II. 184, VI (ii). 37, VI (iv). 47, VIII. 543; heart VI (ii). 29

**bright, bryght** *adj.* bright, radiant, attractive II. 21, II. 189, II. 303, VI (vi). 89, VI (vi). 105, **bryȝt** II. 21; *as n.* VI (iii). 4 happiness; *comp.* **brighter** II. 21, VI (vi). 18

**bryght** *adv.* brightly VI (v). 22

**brighthede** *n.* clarity I. 592

**brynge** *v.* bring I. 25, I. 56, II. 8, III. 163, IV. 6, VI (i). 7, ~ **vpe** I. 374 initiate; *pr.3 sg.* **bryngeth** II. 81; *pl.* **bryngeth** I. 2; *subj.pl.* **brynge** I. 50; *imp.sg.* **brynge** II. 196, VI (i). 21, VI (ii). 32, VI (vi). 404, VIII. 216; *pa.t.sg.* **broght** I. 176, VI (vi). 26, **brouȝte** VII. 142; *pl.* **brouȝt** VII. 78; *p.p.* **broght** I. 891, VI (i). 40, VI (ii). 46, VI (vi). 343

**broches** *n.pl.* brooches VI (vi). 327

**brode** *adv.* widely VIII. 379

**broght, brouȝt(e)** *see* **brynge**

**broken** *see* **breke**

**brosten** *see* **brest(e)** *v.*

**broþer** *n.* brother I. 474, **brothere** VII. 172; *pl.* **breþere** I. 299

**bruys** *v.* bruise VIII. 377; *p.p.* **bresed** VII. 101

**buffeted** *pa.t.pl.* beat VIII. 255

**buffetynge** *n.* beating VIII. 178, **biffetynge** VIII. 321

**buffetys** *n.pl.* blows VIII. 314

**bury** *v.* bury I. 856

**but** *see* **bot**

**buxumnesse** *n.* obedience II. 99

**cache** *v.* catch VIII. 223; *imp.sg.* VIII. 212

**caitife** *see* **kaitif**

**calle** *v.* summon VI (iv). 95, **kalle** II. 278; *p.p.* **cald** named I. 526, II. 224, III. 26, **called** I. 490, **callet** I. 290 invoked

**came** *see* **come**

**can** *v.*[1] *aux. with inf. as equiv. of pa.t.* did II. 178, VI (ii). 40, **kan** II. 186; *pl.* **can** II. 178, **kan** VI (ii). 34

**can** *v.*[2] (i) know, be skilled in I. 653; *pr.1 sg.* II. 283; *3 sg.* VI (vi). 167; *pl.* III. 111; *subj.pl.* I. 653. (ii) be able to *pr.1 sg.* II. 58, VI (i). 11, VI (ii). 25, VI (vi). 366, VIII. 61; *2 sg.* II. 147, III. 50; *3 sg.* I. 698, I. 797, VI (iii). 22, *pl.* I. 27, I. 92, II. 52, VI (iv). 11, **kan** I. 722, II. 84; *pa.t.sg.* **kouth** VIII. 422; *pl.* **couth** VIII. 255

**candel** *n.* candle II. 22

**care, kare** *n.* trouble, distress I. 598, II. 272, VI (i). 18, VI (ii). 46, VI (iv). 4 *etc.*

**carions** *n.pl.* corpses, carcases VIII. 409

**cas** *n.* chance, fortune VIII. 457

**cast(e)** *v.* cast, throw, project VIII. 496, VI (iv). 19 overthrow; *subj.sg.* **cast** III. 78; *imp.sg.* II. 139, VI (iv). 5, **kast** III. 162; *pa.t.2 sg.* **keste** VIII. 330; *3 sg.* **cast** VIII. 334; *pl.* **kest** VII. 95; *p.p.* **cast** VIII. 372, VII. 162, **casten** VI (i). 60, **kasten** VI (ii). 46; *pr.p.* **castynge** III. 94, **kastynge** II. 132

**castelle** *n.* castle I. 755; *pl.* **castelles** VIII. 361

**cause** *n.* reason VIII. 207

**causeth** *pr.3 sg.* causes VIII. 417

**celle** *n.* cell, small compartment VIII. 228; *pl.* **cellis, cellys** VIII. 228, VIII. 230

**certeyn** *adj.* sure, confident IV. 8

**certeynly** *adv.* surely I. 778

**certes** *adv.* certainly, truly I. 697, III. 86

**cessen** *pr.pl.* cease I. 242; *subj.sg.* **cesse** I. 703; *imp.sg.* **sese** III. 183

**charite** *n.* love I. 61, I. 618, II. 167, III. 11, VII. 33, VIII. 97, **charitee** III. 158

**chaseth** *pr.3 sg.* chases away I. 618, III. 219

**chaste** *adj.* chaste, pure I. 762, II. 98, III. 169

**chaunge** *v.* change VI (i). 2; *pr.3 sg.* **chaungeth** II. 207, VI (iv). 21; *imp.sg.* **chaunge** III. 139; *p.p.* **chaunget** I. 798

**chaungynge** *n.* exchange I. 9, VIII. 453

**chekes** *n.pl.* cheeks VIII. 288

**chere** *n.* appearance, demeanour II. 207, VI (iv). 21, VI (vi). 30, VIII. 147

**cherubin** *n.pl.* cherubim II. 19
**chese** *v.* choose VII. 49; *pr.3sg.* **cheseth** II. 219; *pl.* **chesen** I. 12; *imp.sg.* **chese** VII. 136; *pa.t.sg.* **chese** VI (iv). 90, VIII. 34; *p.p.* **chosen** * VIII. 190
**chydynge** *pr.p.* complaining I. 815
**child(e)** *n.* child I. 741, VI (vi). 97*; young man VI (iii). 5; *pl.* **children** I. 754
**childhode** *n.* infancy I. 91
**chyn** *n.* chin VIII. 542
**chirch(e)** *n.* church II. 70, III. 94, VII. 14, VIII. 101
**circumcised** *p.p.* circumcized IV. 2
**circumstances** *n.pl.* circumstances, adjuncts I. 377
**cite** *n.* city VIII. 484
**clarifieth** *pr.3 sg.* makes clear I. 617
**cled** *see* **cloth(e)** *v.*
**clene** *adj.* clean, pure I. 159, II. 98, III. 115, VI (ii). 16, VI (iv). 78, VI (vi). 319, VIII. 230; healthy VIII. 315; *comp.* **clenner** III. 121
**clennesse** *n.* purity I. 160, I. 326, III. 157
**clenseth** *pr.3 sg.* purifies III. 221; *pl.* I. 399; *p.p.* **clensed** III. 54
**cleped** *pa.t.pl.* called, named VIII. 254
**clere** *v.* cleanse VIII. 201
**clere** *adj.* pure, unclouded, translucent II. 207, VI (iv). 23
**clerly** *adv.* plainly VIII. 172
**cleue** *v.*[1] *subj.sg.* cling, adhere VIII. 90; *pa.t.sg.* **cleued** VIII. 281
**cleue** *v.*[2] *pa.t.sg.* split asunder VIII. 539; *pl.* **cleued** VIII. 281
**clymynge** *pr.p.* ascending I. 310
**clippynge** *n.* embrace VI (vi). 174
**close** *n.* enclosure VIII. 219
**closed** *p.p.* enclosed VIII. 154; shut, excluded I. 414, **closet** I. 551
**cloth(e)** *v.* clothe I. 670, I. 854; *pr.3 sg.* **cloth** I. 671; *imp.sg.* **cloth** VI (vi). 323; *p.p.* **cled** III. 158; **cloþed** VIII. 252
**cloth(e)** *n.* garment VIII. 284; cloth VIII. 427, VII. 95; *pl.* **clothes** II. 162, **cloþes** I. 91, III. 102, VI (vi). 326
**cloþynge** *n.* apparel VIII. 260
**clotred** *p.p.* clotted VIII. 544
**cloud** *n.* cloud VIII. 199; *pl.* **cloudes** VIII. 200
**cloutes** *n.pl.* rags III. 100
**cold(e)** *n.* cold I. 751, VII. 24
**cold(e)** *adj.* cold, unimpassioned VI (iii). 14, I. 190
**cole** *n.* coal I. 670, **cool** I. 671, **colle** VI (i). 13
**coloure** *n.* complexion VIII. 451
**coma(u)ndement** *n.* commandment I. 389, III. 1, VIII. 280; *pl.* **comandementȝ** I. 662, II. 92, **commaundementȝ** I. 496, **comma(u)ndementis** VII. 20, VII. 35, **comaundementis** VIII. 218
**comber** *v.* overwhelm, destroy I. 882
**come** *v.* come II. 135, VI (vi). 104, VIII. 127, **cum** I. 127, II. 73, III. 171, VI (i). 30, VI (ii). 16, VI (iv). 58, **comme** VII. 6; *pr.2 sg.* **comest** I. 767, II. 226, **commes** VII. 59; *3 sg.* **cometh** I. 148, III. 196, VI (v). 15, VII. 184, **commeth** VII. 158; *pl.* **cometh** I. 438, III. 39, **comen** I. 9, I. 312, **comyn** I. 46, VIII. 325; *subj.sg.* **cum** I. 612, II. 61, VI (ii). 23, VI (vi). 300, **come** VIII. 214, **comme** VII. 152; *imp.sg.* **come** VIII. 524, **comme** VII. 153; *pl.* **cum** VI (vi). 227; *pa.t.sg.* **come** III. 92, VI (vi). 87, VII. 38, VIII. 62, **came** I. 178, **comme** VII. 42; *2 sg.* **come** VI (vi). 358; *pl.* **come** VII. 69; *p.p.* **comen** I. 164, I. 559, II. 274, **comyn** VI (i). 23; *pr.p.* **comynge** I. 582
**comers** *n.pl.* arrivals I. 585, I. 823
**comfort-** *see* **confort**
**comynge** *n.* arrival II. 197, III. 166, IV. 13*, VIII. 515
**comynly** *adv.* in common, without exception I. 183
**company** *n.* company, companionship VIII. 458
**compassioun** *n.* pity II. 45, VIII. 328
**compleccioun** *n.* physical constitution IV. 10
**complyne** *n.* Compline VIII. 244
**comprehend** *v.* grasp, fully understand II. 111
**conceyue** *v.* understand, apprehend VIII. 240; *pr.3 sg.* **conceyueth** I. 765
**confessioun** *n.* confession VII. 153
**confort** *v.* comfort, succour, encourage I. 164, III. 141, **comfort(e)** I. 598, VII. 166, VIII. 62, VIII. 443; *pr.3 sg.* **conforteth** I. 141, II. 61, VI (vi). 353; *subj.sg.* **comforte** VII. 171; *pa.t.sg.* **comforted** VII. 52; *p.p.* **comforted** I. 134; *pr.p.* **confortynge** I. 396
**confort, comfort** *n.* comfort, support I. 125, I. 103, II. 217, III. 51, III. 36, VII. 52, VIII. 165, VIII. 103 *etc.*
**confortable** *adj.* sustaining, cheering I. 206, I. 552

**confortynge** *n.* comfort, support II. 294, VI (vi). 415
**confortour** *n.* comforter II. 276
**confounden** *p.p.* defeated I. 113
**confourme** *v.* conform, shape in a similar fashion I. 386; *pr.3 sg.* **confourmeth** I. 274; *subj.pl.* **confourme** I. 469; *p.p.* **confourmed** I. 462
**conynge** *adj.* clever I. 166; *comp.* **connyngre, connynger** I. 32, I. 372
**connynge** *n.* knowledge, skill, intelligence I. 377, I. 488, VI (iv). 40, VIII. 50, **conynge** I. 651, **kunnynge** VIII. 3
**consail(le)** *n.* advice I. 107, I. 347, I. 498
**conscience** *n.* conscience VIII. 173
**constreyne** *v.* force, compel I. 379; *imp.sg.* **constrayn** VI (vi). 400
**contemplacioun** *n.* meditation I. 253, VIII. 253
**contemplatif** *adj.* contemplative I. 487, I. 619, II. 224
**conteneth** *pr.3 sg.* contains, holds II. 17; *p.p.* **contened** II. 16
**continuaunce** *n.* perseverance VIII. 40
**continue** *v.* continue VIII. 106
**continuely** *adv.* continually I. 616, VIII. 183, **continualy** VIII. 459
**contynuynge** *n.* perseverance VIII. 233
**contrarie** *adj.* opposed I. 528, III. 9, IV. 7
**contrarious** *adj.* contrary VIII. 55
**contre** *n.* country, homeland I. 748
**contricioun** *n.* repentance VIII. 11
**cool** *see* **cole**
**cordes, cordis** *n.pl.* ropes VI (vi). 103, VIII. 373, VIII. 425
**corone** *n.* crown I. 664*, VI (vi). 109, **croun(e)** VIII. 294, VIII. 547
**corone-** *see* **crowneth**
**coronynge** *n.* coronation VIII. 267
**corrupcioun** *n.* depravity I. 659
**cost** *n.* sufficient money I. 856
**coupileth*** *pr.3 sg.* unites VI (i). 12; *p.p.* **cowpled** II. 15; *pr.p.* **coupelynge** I. 636
**coueit(e)** *v.* desire, covet I. 249, I. 379, II. 25, **couait** I. 623, II. 57, III. 188, VI (ii). 2; *pr.1 sg.* **couait** II. 197; *2 sg.* **coueiteste** I. 595, **couaitist** II. 139, **couaitest** III. 84; *3 sg.* **coueiteth** I. 718, II. 41, IV. 14, **couaiteth** II. 10, III. 169; *pl.* **coueiteth** I. 23, I. 143, **couaiteth** II. 30, **couait** I. 796; *subj.sg.* **coueit** I. 252, **couait** III. 76; *pl.* **couait** II. 260; *imp.sg.* **couait** VI (iv). 21; *pa.t.pl.* **couaited** I. 893
**coueitynge** *n.* desire, longing I. 317, II. 274, III. 38, VI (i). 23, **couaitynge** II. 158, VI (iv). 89
**coueitise** *n.* greed, avarice I. 792, **coueitys** I. 557, **couetise** I. 825, **couaitise** I. 268, II. 76, IV. 17; desire I. 636
**coueitouse** *adj.* desirous III. 45; **couaitous** III. 165
**couer(e)** *v.* hide I. 90, VII. 107; **keuer** II. 272 shield, protect; *pr.3 sg.* **couereth** VI (i). 15 restores to health
**couerchief** *n.* headscarf VII. 106
**couetise** *see* **coueitise**
**cowpled** *see* **coupileth**
**craftes** *n.pl.* skills I. 106
**craue** *pr.1 sg.* demand VI (vi). 309
**creature** *n.* created thing I. 732, II. 79, VIII. 146; *pl.* **creatur(e)s** VIII. 270, VIII. 297, VII. 102 women
**cry** *n.* shout VIII. 420
**crib** *n.* manger III. 97
**cried** *pa.t.2 sg.* called out VIII. 463; *pl.* VIII. 421; *pr.p.* **cryinge** I. 575
**criynge** *n.* shouting, clamour I. 361, II. 225; appeal for VIII. 39
**cristen** *adj.* Christian III. 73, VIII. 292
**cros(se)** *n.* cross VIII. 276, VII. 98
**crowneth** *pr.3 sg.* crowns II. 180; *pa.t.sg.* **crowned** VI (ii). 36, **coroned** VIII. 294; *pl.* **corouned** VII. 93; *p.p.* **coroned** I. 111, VIII. 486, **corowned** VIII. 296
**crucifix** *n.* crucifix VIII. 553
**cruel** *adj.* harsh, pitiless I. 112
**crushed** *p.p.* crushed VIII. 317
**cum** *see* **come**
**cure** *n.* care VIII. 84
**curious** *adj.* solicitous VI (vi). 130
**cursynge** *n.* swearing I. 354
**custume** *n.* habitual practice I. 613
**custume** *v.* become accustomed I. 371

**day(e)** *n.* day I. 131, II. 12, III. 74, IV. 14, VI (i). 3, VI (ii). 22, VI (iii). 1 *etc.*; death day I. 604; *pl.* **daies, dayes** I. 365, III. 202
**dayntees** *see* **deynte**
**dale** *n.* valley of hell II. 89
**dalyaunce** *n.* conversation VIII. 245
**dampnacioun** *n.* damnation VIII. 171
**dampne** *v.* damn, condemn III. 136; *pr.2 sg.* **dampnest** I. 693; *p.p.* **dampned** VI (ii). 44, VI (vi). 208
**dar** *v.*[1] *pr.1 sg.* dare I. 321; *2 sg.* **darest** VI (vi). 106

**dar** *v.*[2] *impers.pr.sg.* needs I. 120, I. 424. I. 622, VI (iv). 84; *pers.pl.* I. 456
**daungerous** *adj.* reluctant to give VIII. 441
**debonair** *adj.* mild III. 163
**debonerly** *adv.* meekly II. 102
**debonerte** *n.* mildness I. 275
**deceyte** *n.* deceit I. 368
**deceyue** *v.* deceive I. 25; *pr.2 sg.* **deceyuest** I. 694; *3 sg.* **deceyueth** I. 34, I. 711, **desceyueth** I. 164, **deceyuet** I. 117; *pl.* **deceyueth** I. 232; *p.p.* **deceyued** I. 45, **desceyuet** I. 214
**deddly** *see* **dedely**
**dede** *n.*[1] deed, action I. 77, II. 5, III. 14, VI (vi). 315, **deed(e)** I. 394, I. 364; *pl.* **dedes** I. 60, VI (vi). 236, VIII. 16, **deedes** I. 36, **dede** VI (i). 62
**dede** *n.*[2] *see* **deth**
**dede** *adj.* dead I. 285, II. 78, III. 39, VI (iv). 14, VIII. 335 *etc.*, *as n.* VIII. 393, **ded** VI (v). 17, VII. 112
**dede(n)** *see* **do**
**dedely** *adj.* mortal, perishable I. 1, **deddly** II. 93, **dedly** I. 647, III. 9, VI (iv). 25, VIII. 350, **deedly** II. 70
**deed-** *see* **dede-**
**deelful** *adj.* unhappy VIII. 477; *as n.* miserable people VIII. 368, **deleful** VIII. 454
**deelfully** *adv.* miserably VIII. 463
**deeth** *see* **deth**
**defend** *v.* avert, repel VI (v). 9
**defense** *n.* defence I. 361
**defoul** *v.* suppress III. 179; maltreat I. 374; *p.p.* **defouled, defowled** VIII. 297, VIII. 314 defiled
**degre(e)** *n.* rank, order I. 94, I. 239, III. 25, VIII. 209; *pl.* **degrees** I. 525, II. 39, III. 25
**dey(e)** *v.* die I. 284, II. 251, II. 307, III. 113, VI (v). 16, VIII. 33, **dye** VII. 47; *pr.2 sg.* **deyest** II. 248; *pl.* **dey** I. 890, III. 223; *subj.sg.* **deye** VIII. 183; *pl.* **dey** II. 108, **dye** VI (i). 68; *pa.t.sg.* **deyed** I. 504; *pr.p.* **deynge** II. 193
**deiynge*** *n.* death VI (vi). 414
**deiynge** *adj.* dying I. 651
**deile** *see* **dele**
**deynte** *n.* pleasure VIII. 141; *pl.* **dayntees** I. 458 luxuries
**delayynge** *n.* procrastination I. 404
**dele** *n.*[1] grief II. 190, VIII. 336, **deile** II. 249
**dele** *n.*[2] part II. 304, VI (i). 27, VI (iv). 1
**delitabil(i)te** *n.* pleasure I. 810, III. 192
**delitable** *adj.* delectable I. 556, III. 110; *comp.* **delitabeller** I. 840, **delitabiler** III. 80
**delitably*** *adv.* pleasurably VIII. 234
**delit(e)** *n.* pleasure I. 117, II. 153, II. 233, III. 35, III. 75, IV. 1, **delyte** I. 10, I. 144; *pl.* **delites** I. 155, I. 329, II. 51
**delite** *subj.sg.refl.* take pleasure III. 134; *imp.sg.* **delit** III. 144; *pr.p.* **delitynge** IV. 8
**delyueraunce*** *n.* salvation VIII. 470
**delyuereth** *pr.3 sg.* saves I. 667
**deme** *v.* judge I. 93, VIII. 274; *pr.3 sg.* **demeth** VI (v). 16; *pa.t.pl.* **demed** VII. 97; *p.p.* **demed** I. 293, II. 188, VI (ii). 33, VI (v). 17, VIII. 135
**denyande** *pr.p.* disowning, repudiating VII. 76
**dennes** *n.pl.* lairs, earths VIII. 431
**depart** *v.* separate, divide II. 77; *pr.3 sg.* **departeth** I. 145, I. 540; *subj.sg.* **depart** VIII. 96; *p.p.* **departed** I. 767, II. 78, III. 34
**departynge** *n.* division I. 405; separation I. 658, VI (i). 31
**depe** *adj.* deep II. 185, VI (ii). 38, VI (iv). 6
**depeynt** *imp.sg.* paint VIII. 272
**deppyr** *adv.comp.* more deeply VIII. 194
**der(e)** *adj.* dear, precious II. 143, III. 110, III. 118, V. 5, VI (iv). 42, *etc.*; *as n.* II. 292
**dere** *adv.* dearly III. 217, VI (iii). 12, VI (vi). 27
**dere** *v.* harm VI (v). 18
**derkenesse** *n.* darkness VI (i). 64
**derlynge** *n.* precious thing VI (i). 54, VI (vi). 271
**derne** *adj.* secret VI (vi). 334
**derworth(i)** *adj.* precious VIII. 361, VII. 47, **derward** VII. 166
**desaise** *n.* suffering, misfortune VIII. 203; *pl.* **desaises** VIII. 75, **deseises** VIII. 180, **deseses** VIII. 68
**desceyuet(h)** *see* **deceyue**
**deserue** *v.* deserve I. 847; *pr.3 sg.* **deserueth** III. 45; *p.p.* **deserued** VIII. 257
**desire, desyr(e)** *n.* desire, longing II. 66, I. 634, II. 133, III. 167, IV. 1, VI (i). 5, *etc.*, *pl.* **desires, desyres** I. 6, II. 106, III. 38
**desire, desyre** *v.* wish, want, ask I.5, II. 123, III. 188, VI (v). 2, VIII. 261; *pr.1 sg.* **desyr** VI (vi). 366; *2 sg.* **desirest** I. 486; *3 sg.* **desireth** I. 796, **desyreth** VIII. 397;

**desire, desyre** (*cont.*) *pl.* **desire** I. 636; *subj.sg.* **desyre** III. 178, VIII. 533; *pl.* **desyre** III. 174; *imp.sg.* **desyre** III. 46; *pr.p.* **desyrynge** I. 557

**desyrynge** *n.* object of desire II. 300, VI (i). 22, VI (ii). 11

**despise** *v.* despise, scorn II. 105, III. 189, **dispise** I. 175, II. 163; *pr.2 sg.* **despisest** I. 247; *3 sg.* **despiseth** I. 473; *pl.* **dyspisen** I. 41, **despiseth** I. 239, III. 17; *pa.t.pl.* **despised** VIII. 77; *p.p.* **despised** VIII. 268; *pr.p.* **dispisynge** I. 444

**despit(e), dispite** *n.* contempt I. 334, VIII. 157, I. 347

**destrue** *v.* destroy I. 192, **destroy** I. 108, I. 200, II. 106, **destroi** I. 882; *pr.3 sg.* **destrueth** III. 220, **destroieth** II. 81; *pl.* **destruen** I. 48

**destruynge** *n.* destruction, obliteration IV. 10

**deth** *n.* death I. 2, II. 82, III. 36, VI (ii). 43, VI (iv). 78 *etc.*, **dethe** V. 4, VII. 130, **deeth** I. 67, I. 433, **dede** VI (i). 48, VI (vi). 196

**dette** *n.* due III. 217

**deuyl** *n.* devil I. 21, II. 151, VI (v). 18, **deuil** I. 308, **deuylle** II. 166; *gen.* **deuels** I. 684; *pl.* **deuelys** I. 668, II. 40, III. 208, **deuylles** III. 220

**deuocioun** *n.* reverence I. 260, II. 131; love III. 8, VIII. 387; assiduity VIII. 10

**deuout** *adj.* pious I. 762, VIII. 248

**deuoutly** *adv.* devoutly I. 707

**dewe** *n.* dew VI (vi). 311

**diche** *n.* ditch II. 86

**dye** *see* **deye**

**dight** *imp.sg.* array, dress III. 164

**dignite** *n.* high position I. 343; worth, honour, nobility VIII. 481

**dym** *adj.* wicked VIII. 389

**dyn** *n.* noise II. 225

**dinge** *v.* thrash, flog II. 178; *pa.t.pl.* **donge** VII. 69

**disciple** *n.* disciple VII. 21, VIII. 122; *pl.* **disciples(se)** VI (vi). 29, VII. 29, III. 106; *gen.* **disciples** VII. 30

**discord** *n.* strife I. 355

**discrec(c)ioun** *n.* moderation I. 52, I. 158, III. 63; judgement II. 223, VIII. 107

**discrete** *adj.* prudent II. 157

**disfamynge** *n.* calumny I. 354

**disgysynge** *n.* fantastic clothing VIII. 261

**dispaire** *n.* despair I. 156, I. 210

**dispend** *v.* waste II. 257; spend I. 291; *pr.2 sg.* **dispendest** I. 736; *p.p.* **despended** VII. 155 occupied time

**dispis-, dispite** *see* **despise, despit(e)**

**dispitous** *adj.* pitiless VIII. 168

**displese** *v.* displease I. 342

**dispose** *v.* prepare, make fit I. 384; control I. 485; *p.p.* **disposed** constituted I. 199, I. 835

**dissolucioun** *n.* unseemly behaviour I. 366

**dyuers** *adj.* various I. 151, I. 222, II. 136

**dyuersite** *n.* difference, variety I. 500

**do, don(e)** *v.* (i) do, perform I. 42, I. 57, I. 106, II. 146, III. 65, VI (vi). 50, VI (vi). 377, VII. 63, VIII. 307; (ii) act (*intr.*) I. 42, I. 63, I. 697, VIII. 79; (iii) put, place I. 518, III. 114, III. 118, VI (vi). 352, VII. 97; (iv) cause I. 256, VI (vi). 3, VI (vi). 147, VI (vi). 185; *pass.* to be done I. 337, I. 390; ~ **away** dispose of, disperse I. 818, III. 10, VIII. 200; *pr.1 sg.* **do** I. 696; *2 sg.* **dost** I. 426, II. 10, III. 135, VIII. 110; *3 sg.* **doth** I. 256, I. 670, II. 80, III. 114, VII. 41, **dothe** I. 359; *pl.* **done** I. 31, II. 187, III. 151, **doon** I. 36, I. 311, **don** I. 75, **do** I. 65, **doth** I. 409, I. 755, II. 251, III. 206, VI (ii). 40, **dothe** III. 53; *subj.sg.* **do** I. 694, II. 12, III. 67, III. 126, VI (vi). 380; *pl.* **do** I. 294; *imp.sg.* **do** I. 197, III. 143, VI (iv). 13, VI (iv). 59, VI (vi). 3, VI (vi). 147; *pa.t.sg.* **did** I. 34, I. 173, II. 48, VI (vi). 115, **dede** VI (vi). 185, **dide** VII. 96; *2 sg.* **didde** VIII. 301, **did** I. 544, VI (vi). 138, **dede** VIII. 302; *pl.* **didden** VIII. 469, **did** I. 465, VIII. 169, **deden** VI (vi). 196; *p.p.* **don(e)** I. 51, I. 172, III. 118, VI (vi). 78, VII. 52, VIII. 414 *etc.*, **doun** VII. 18, **do** VI (vi). 242; *pr.p.* **doynge** I. 852, II. 5

**doctour** *n.* teacher I. 827; *pl.* **doctours** VII. 19

**dogge** *n.* dog VIII. 311

**dome** *n.* judgement I. 79, VI (v). 14, VII. 145, VIII. 135; *pl.* **domes** II. 110, III. 161, **domys** I. 816

**domes day, domys day(e)** *n.* Judgement day I. 858, III. 81, VI (i). 35

**dominaciones** *n.pl.* dominations II. 18 (*see note*)

**domysman** *n.* lawful judge VIII. 131

**donge** *see* **dinge**

**doumb** *adj.* dumb I. 115

**doun(e)** *adv.* down I. 312, II. 40, IV. 6, VI (ii). 40, VI (vi). 220, VII. 41, VII. 95, VIII. 288, **downe** I. 813, **done** VII. 107
**dout** *n.* doubt I. 336, II. 38
**doue** *n.* dove VIII. 222; *pl.* **doves** II. 40
**downward** *adv.* down I. 270
**dranke** *see* **drynk(e)**
**draw** *v.* pull, drag II. 213, VIII. 124; attract, entice I. 469; ~ **aleynth** I. 389 protract, prolong; *pr.3 sg.* **draweth** I. 326, VI (vi). 302, VIII. 215; *pl.* **draweth** II. 60, II. 88, **drawen** VI (vi). 246; *subj.sg.* **draw** III. 78; *imp.sg.* **draw(e)** VI (vi). 103, VIII. 213; *pa.t.pl.* **drowen** VIII. 76, **drow** VIII. 373, **drowe** VII. 114, **drewe** VIII. 284, **drouȝe** VII. 77, **drourȝe** VII. 118; *p.p.* **drawen** VIII. 153
**drawynge** *n.* pulling VIII. 425
**dred(e)** *n.* fear I. 341, I. 619, II. 252, VI (v). 13, VIII. 346, **dreed** I. 332; *pl.* **dredes** III. 179
**dred(e)** *v.* fear I. 483, II. 115, VI (i). 61, *refl.* VI (i). 31, **dreed** I. 120; *pr.1 sg.* **dred** V. 3; *3 sg.* **dredeth** I. 809; *subj.sg.* **drede** VI (iv). 78, VI (vi). 416; *imp.sg.* **dred(e)** III. 145, III. 160, **dreed** I. 135; *p.p.* **dreded** I. 344; *pr.p.* **dredynge** I. 382
**dregh** *adj.* difficult, wearisome VI (i). 12
**dreme** *n.* dream I. 228, VI (vi). 20; *pl.* **dremes** I. 217
**dremynge** *pr.p.* dreaming II. 6
**drery** *n.* sweetheart II. 292; *pl.* **dreries** II. 87 valuables
**drery** *adj.* sad VI (vi). 30, VIII. 350
**dried** *adj.* dried VIII. 284
**drynes** *n.* aridity VIII. 417
**drynk(e)** *n.* drink I. 46, I. 49, **drinke** VII. 128
**drynk(e)** *v.* drink VI (vi). 251, VI (vi). 374; *subj.sg.* **drynke** I. 451; *imp.sg.* **drynk** I. 195; *pa.t.pl.* **dranke** III. 199
**dryueth** *pr.pl.* rush headlong II. 88; *imp.sg.* **dryve** VIII. 82 force, compel; *p.p.* **dry-vyn** II. 190 forced
**dronken** *adj.* drunk I. 765
**dronkenes** *n.* intoxication I. 364
**drop(e)** *n.* droplet, small particle VIII. 355, VIII. 365
**dropped** *pa.t.sg.* fell VII. 41, VIII. 334; *p.p.* **droped** dropped VIII. 511
**drow-, drou-** *see* **draw**
**dufhouse** *n.* dovecot VIII. 221
**dulefulli** *adv.* grievingly VII. 138
**dure** *v.* endure III. 58
**durke** *adj.* dark I. 676
**dwel(le)** *v.* live VI (iv). 69, VI (vi). 408; remain, persist IV. 25, VI (iii). 22, VI (vi). 35; *pr.1 sg.* **dwel** II. 287, VI (ii). 21; *3 sg.* **dwelleth** I. 144; *pl.* **dwellen** I. 8, I. 827, **dwelleth** IV. 16; *imp.sg.* **dwel** VI (iv). 39
**dwellynge** *n.* continuance, persistence I. 378; residence III. 218
**dwellynge** *adj.* lasting III. 44
**dwyne** *v.* fade, wither VI (iv). 64; *subj.sg.* VI (ii). 20

**ease** *see* **ese**
**ebbynge** *n.* decline VI (iii). 26
**eche** *v.* increase VIII. 418, **eke** VII. 117; *pr.p.* **echynge** I. 310
**echynge** *n.* increasing VIII. 408
**effectuous** *adj.* urgent, earnest IV. 3
**efte** *adv.* moreover VIII. 221; again VII. 36, **eft** I. 371
**efter** *see* **aftre** *adv.*
**eggeth** *pr.3 sg.* incites, encourages I. 185; *pl.* **eggen** VIII. 174
**egre** *adj.* sharp, bitter VIII. 187
**e(i)gh, eygh** *n.* eye, sight I. 86, I. 477, II. 85, III. 19, VI (vi). 88; attention II. 215; *pl.* **e(i)ghen** I. 395, III. 169, VI (vi). 151, VII. 163, VIII. 449, **eyghen** VIII. 543, **eiȝen** VII. 73, **eyeghen** VIII. 174, **eyghne** VIII. 334
**eyre** *see* **aire**
**eysel** *n.* vinegar VIII. 465, **eiselle** VII. 128
**eke** *see* **eche**
**eld** *n.* age I. 378
**els, elles** *adv.* else, otherwise I. 268, I. 547, II. 11, IV. 15, VIII. 346
**enclosed** *p.p.* in a state of recluse I. 461
**encresceth** *pr.3 sg.* increases VIII. 385
**end(e)** *n.* finish, conclusion I. 8, I. 56, II. 41, VI (iv). 108; purpose, objective I. 662, III. 173, VIII. 20; time of death VI (v). 12
**endeth** *pr.pl.* end II. 222, III. 210*; *p.p.* **ended** VII. 129, **endet** VIII. 537
**endynge** *n.* conclusion, end I. 51, II. 313, III. 50, VI (iii). 28, VI (iv). 60, VI (vi). 425; death I. 298, III. 173, VI (vi). 413
**endles** *adj.* endless, eternal III. 43, IV. 14, VI (ii). 46, VI (iii). 22, VIII. 488, **endlees** I. 10
**endlesly** *adv.* eternally VIII. 175
**enemy(e)** *n.* enemy I. 21, I. 112, VI (v). 15, **enmy** VIII. 43; *pl.* **enemy(e)s** I. 467, II. 150, III. 181, VI (iii). 24, VII. 123, VIII. 85

**enemy** *adj.* hostile III. 10
**enforce** *imp.sg.refl.* exert I. 263
**enfourme** *v.* teach I. 409
**engyne** *n.* cunning, trickery VI (vi). 84
**englisshe** *adj.* English I. 493, **engglische** VII. 136
**eny** *see* **any**
**enyoynte** *p.p.* ordered I. 389
**enlumyneth** *pr.3 sg.* illuminates I. 274; *p.p.* **enlumyned** II. 227
**enoynt** *imp.sg.* anoint VIII. 271
**ensample** *n.* example I. 367, VIII. 241
**entent** *n.* purpose, object I. 102, I. 689, VI (i). 22; heed, attention I. 387, II. 65, III. 172, **entencioun** VIII. 3
**ententif** *adj.* assiduous I. 471
**entier** *adj.* whole I. 405
**entierly** *adv.* wholly I. 83, II. 243, **entierlyche** VI (vi). 260
**entisseth** *pr.3 sg.* provokes, incites I. 191
**entremetteth** *pr.pl.refl.* concern, occupy I. 801
**entres** *pr.2 sg.* enters II. 95; *3 sg.* **entreth** IV. 20
**enuy** *n.* envy I. 38, II. 75, III. 164, VIII. 111 *etc.*
**er** *see* **ar**
**e(e)re** *n.* ear I. 477, I. 613, VI (v). 17
**erly** *see* **arly**
**erre** *v.* go astray I. 146
**errynge** *n.* straying III. 3
**errour** *n.* false belief I. 29, I. 332, VIII. 98
**erth(e)** *n.* earth, world III. 208, VI (i). 10, VI (iii). 21, VII. 160, VII. 162, VIII. 24
**erthly** *adj.* worldly, material I. 887, II. 43, III. 38, IV. 13, VI (i). 29, VI (iv). 9, **ertly** II. 51
**eschape** *v.* escape, avoid I. 221, VII. 50
**e(e)se** *n.* comfort I. 529, II. 114, III. 28, I. 185, **ease** III. 196, **aise** I. 258
**esely** *adv.* calmly VIII. 305
**estate** *n.* material condition I. 239
**ete** *v.* eat VII. 163; *pr.2 sg.* **etest** I. 515; *subj.sg.* **ete** I. 451; *pl.* **et** I. 187; *imp.sg.* **et** I. 194; *pa.t.pl.* **ete** III. 199
**ether** *pron.* either of two VIII. 338
**etynge** *n.* eating I. 457
**euch(e)** *adj.* each, every VIII. 42, VIII. 43, VIII. 104
**euaungeliste** *n.* evangelist VII. 2
**euene** *n.* evening VII. 152
**euer** *adv.* always I. 270, II. 4, III. 21, IV. 25, VI (i). 25, VI (ii). 20 *etc.*, **euyr(e)** VIII. 213, VIII. 244
**euery** *adj.* every, each I. 1, II. 212, III. 21, IV. 14, VI (i). 27, VIII. 35 *etc.*
**euery** *pron.* each I. 640, II. 23
**euermore** *adv.* always I. 212, II. 229, III. 173, V. 9, VIII. 177, **euermoor(e)** I. 484, I. 703, **euermare** I. 599, VI (i). 20, VI (ii). 48
**euyl** *see* **yuel**
**euynsonge** *n.* evensong VIII. 244
**excellent** *adj.* supreme VIII. 482
**excludynge** *n.* exclusion VIII. 172
**excuse** *v.* excuse VIII. 136
**excusynge** *n.* prevarication I. 405
**exercise** *n.* occupation I. 800
**exile** *n.* exile I. 747
**exite** *v.* provoke I. 358
**experimentȝ** *n.pl.* tests I. 791

**face** *n.* face I. 891, II. 38, VI (ii). 38, VI (iv). 23, VII. 72, VIII. 139
**fadyd** *p.p.* made dim VIII. 143
**fadyr(e)** *n.* father, God II. 96, VI (vi). 39, VIII. 52, VIII. 435, **fader** VI (vi). 36, VII. 36; *gen.* **faderes** VIII. 53, **fadris** VII. 51, **fadyr** VIII. 482, **fader** VI (vi). 239
**faille** *v.* fail, faint I. 50; *pr.3 sg.* **failleth** I. 572; *pl.* **faillen** I. 64, I. 567, **failleth** I. 567; *subj.sg.* **faille** III. 82; *and see* **falle**
**fayn** *adj.* glad I. 602
**fayne** *adv.* gladly VIII. 44
**fair(e)** *adj.* pleasing, handsome, beautiful II. 99, III. 168, VI (i). 5, VI (ii). 33, VI (iii). 1, VI (vi). 289, **fayre** VI (ii). 24, VI (vi). 409, VII. 43, VIII. 383, **fayere** II. 303; *as n.* VI (iii). 13; *comp.* **faire** I. 344; *sup.* **fairest** I. 176, III. 42
**faire** *adv.* well, pleasingly III. 164
**fairhed(e)** *n.* beauty I. 14, II. 256, III. 169, VI (ii). 45, VI (iv). 40, **fairheed** I. 300, I. 868
**fayrnesse, fairnes(se)** *n.* beauty II. 11, VI (vi). 325, II. 276
**faithfully** *adv.* truly, with faith VIII. 130
**fal(le)** *v.* fall, befall, concern, be relevant I. 210, I. 258, II. 213, VIII. 402; fail II. 279; *3 sg.* **falleth** III. 44, III. 154, VI (iv). 15, VIII. 551, VII. 53; *pl.* **falleth** I. 225, I. 814, I. 849, II. 91, **falle** I. 725, **fallen** I. 7, I. 57 fail; *subj.sg.* **fal** II. 153, III. 82, **falle** VIII. 105; *pa.t.sg.* **fel** VI (vi). 220, VIII. 330, VIII. 450, **felle** VII. 99; *pl.* **fel** I. 217, III. 202, **felle** II. 40, III. 62, **fellen** VIII. 451; *pr.p.* **fallynge** III. 49 failing

**fallynge** *n.* lapsing I. 371
**fals(e)** *adj.* treacherous III. 49, III. 207, VIII. 129
**falsly** *adv.* wrongly VII. 154
**fame** *n.* reputation I. 368
**fand** *see* **fynde**
**fandynge(s)** *see* **fondynge**
**fantasie** *n.* speculation I. 830; *pl.* **fantasies** I. 620 hallucinations
**fare** *v.* go I. 602, II. 274, VI (i). 17, VI (iv). 36; prosper, fare VI (v). 10; die VI (i). 57, VI (ii). 45
**fast** *v.*[1] fast I. 696
**fast** *v.*[2] *imp.sg.* secure, make firm I. 135; *p.p.* **fasted** I. 539; *and see* **festyn**
**fast(e)** *adv.* quickly II. 283; vigorously II. 178, VI (iv). 53, VIII. 449; securely I. 611, II. 263, VI (iv). 74, VIII. 91, VIII. 188, VIII. 281, **feste** VI (iv). 18; nearly VI (v). 14
**fast(e)** *adj.* secure IV. 2, IV. 7, **feste** II. 288, VI (i). 1, VI (iii). 14
**fastynge** *n.* fasting I. 71, I. 157, III. 63, VIII. 319
**fauour** *n.* preference I. 683
**feble, febel, febyl** *adj.* weak I. 62, I. 629, VIII. 319; inferior I. 194, VIII. 399*
**fede** *v.* feed I. 854; *imp.sg.* II. 270, VI (iv). 39; *p.p.* **fedde** II. 287, VI (ii). 31, VI (iv). 48, **fed** I. 16, III. 70 nourished
**feel-** *see* **fele**
**feet(e)** *see* **fote**
**feynynge** *n.* pretence I. 371
**feynt** *adj.* weak III. 48
**feith** *n.* belief I. 228
**fel-** *see* **falle, felle**
**feld** *n.* field VI (iv). 103
**fele** *v.* feel I. 27, II. 305, III. 51, VI (i). 25, VI (iv). 3, VI (vi). 295 *etc.*, **feel(e)** II. 228, I. 554; *pr.2 sg.* **felest** I. 505, II. 159; *3 sg.* **feleth** I. 499, III. 57; *pl.* **felen** I. 242, **feleth** II. 31; *subj.sg.* **fele** VI (vi). 336, VIII. 397; *p.p.* **felet** I. 795, **feled** VI (vi). 23*
**felew** *n.* companion VIII. 517; *pl.* **felewes** I. 299
**felewship(e)** *n.* company I. 434, II. 25, III. 50, **feleweshipe** I. 668, **felauschepe** VII. 43
**felynge** *n.* sensation I. 843
**fel(le)** *v.* destroy VI (iv). 85, VI (v). 15, VI (i). 47*, VI (iv). 72
**felly** *adv.* cruelly VIII. 277
**felonyes** *n.pl.* villainies VIII. 119
**fend(e)** *n.* devil I. 4, VI (iv). 85, VIII. 81, VIII. 474; *gen.* **fendes** I. 669, VIII. 505; *pl.* **fendis** VI (vi).intro. st.
**fer(re)** *adv.* far I. 659, I. 39, I. 587, III. 149*, VI (iv). 15, VI (iv). 72, VIII. 349 deeply
**ferd** *adj.* afraid I. 205
**ferde** *n.* fear VII. 62
**ferdnesse** *n.* terror VIII. 61
**fere** *n.* company VI (vi). 31
**ferly** *adj.* marvellous I. 549
**ferth** *adj.* fourth I. 223, I. 773, **fourth** I. 297, **firth** VI (vi). 206
**ferþer** *adj.comp.* further, greater VIII. 264
**feruent** *adj.* ardent VI (vi). 130
**feruour** *n.* ardent longing I. 252, VIII. 398
**feste** *n.* feast VII. 28
**feste** *adj.* & *adv.* *see* **faste**
**festyn** *v.* fasten, secure VI (ii). 7, **fest(e)** I. 883, VI (ii). 14, VI (iv). 89; *imp.sg.* **festyn** III. 175, VI (iv). 33, **fest(e)** I. 611, VI (iv). 18, VII. 97, VI (vi). 98; *pa.t.pl.* **fest** VII. 67, **festned** VII. 109; *p.p.* **fest(e)** I. 602, VI (iii). 14, **fested** I. 758, **festned** III. 31
**fet** *imp.sg.* fetch VIII. 81; *p.p.* **fette** VI (iv). 72, VIII. 349
**few(e)** *adj.* few I. 128, III. 203; *comp.* **fewer** I. 590, II. 59
**few(e)** *pron.* few I. 589
**fyfte, fift** *adj.* fifth I. 224, VI (vi). 209
**fyght** *n.* fight VI (iv). 10
**fight** *imp.sg.* fight VI (iv). 85; *pr.p.* **fyghtynge** I. 816
**fightynge** *n.* strife I. 663, II. 151
**fileth** *pr.3 sg.* defiles I. 324; *pl.* I. 306
**fylynge** *n.* defilement I. 659
**fille** *v.* fulfil VI (vi). intro. st.; *elsewhere* fill; *imp.sg.* **fil** VI (ii). 8, **fille** VI (ii). 15; *p.p.* **fild** I. 508, II. 118, II. 143; *pr.p.* **fillynge** II. 229
**fille** *n.* capacity VI (v). 4
**filth** *n.* corruption I. 13, I. 887, III. 186, VI (i). 37; dirt VI (iv). 62
**filthed(e)** *n.* corruption I. 158, I. 399
**fynd(e)** *v.* find I. 42, II. 57, III. 79, VI (i). 43, VI (iv). 76, VIII. 398; provide with I. 851; *pr.1 sg.* **fynd** I. 164, II. 2, VI (vi). 100, VIII. 387; *2 sg.* **fyndest** III. 101, **fyndes** III. 86; *3 sg.* **fyndeth** VI (vi). 356, III. 35*; *subj.sg.* **fynd** III. 167; *pa.t.sg.* **fand** III. 91, **fond** III. 92, VI (iv). 83, VIII. 549, **fonde** VII. 38; *2 sg.* **fond** VI (vi). 46; *pl.* **fand** III. 97, **fond** III. 99; *p.p.* **founden** III. 89

**fynger** *n.* finger I. 555; *gen.* VII. 65
**fyre, fire** *n.* fire I. 102, I. 108, I. 885, II. 199, III. 184, VI (i). 6, VI (ii). 11
**first(e)** *adj.* first I. 3, I. 633, III. 122, VI (vi). 193
**first** *adv.* first VI (iv). 82, VII. 67, VIII. 374
**firth** *see* **ferth**
**fyshe** *n.pl.* fish VIII. 213
**fyue** *adj.* five II. 164, VI (vi). 245, VIII. 409
**flat(te)** *adj.* stretched out VIII. 372, VIII. 491
**flattrynge** *n.* flattery I. 354
**flaume** *n.* flame VI (i). 14
**fle(e)** *v.* fly from, flee I. 434, II. 12, VI (i). 36, VI (iv). 33, VI (vi). 291, **fleen** VI (vi). 62; *pr.1 sg.* **fle** II. 205; *subj.sg.* **fle** VIII. 80; *imp.sg.* **fle** VI (iv). 53
**fleish(e)** *n.* flesh II. 107, III. 28, VIII. 42, **fleissh(e)** I. 13, I. 117, II. 186, VI (ii). 41, VI (iv). 30, VI (v). 22, I. 415 body, **fleyshe** VIII. 473, **flesche** VII. 6
**fleisshely** *adj.* bodily, carnal I. 6, II. 13, I. 630 mortal, **fleishly** I. 257, II. 101, III. 38, **fleisshly(e)** II. 44, VI (vi). 290, I. 660, **flessh(e)ly** IV. 10, VI (vi). 341, VI (i). 57, **fleishely** I. 270, VI (vi). 252, VIII. 528
**fleisshely, fleishely** *adv.* physically II. 55, VI (iv). 61
**flemed** *p.p.* banished VI (v). 19
**flitte** *v.* depart VIII. 498
**flode** *n.* flood VI (vi). 87; *pl.* **flodes** VIII. 542
**floure** *n.* flower VI (i). 57; most excellent example II. 276, VI (iv). 102; *pl.* **flours** VIII. 246
**fode, food(e)** *n.* food VI (vi). 93, II. 191, VI (vi). 376, VI (ii). 33
**fole, fool(e)** *n.* fool II. 191, I. 742, VII. 91; *pl.* **foles** I. 164, **fools** I. 311, **folis** III. 111, **folys** III. 203
**foly** *n.* stupidity I. 656
**folk(e)** *n.* people VI (vi). 234, VIII. 267
**folow(e)** *v.* follow, obey I. 5, I. 107, I. 134, II. 97, III. 103, VIII. 327; *pr.pl.* **foloweth** I. 217, **folwen** VIII. 325, **folowen** I. 247 serve; *subj.pl.* **folow** I. 472; *imp.sg.* **folow** I. 245; *pa.t.sg.* **folowed** VIII. 287; *pl.* **folowed** VII. 102
**fol(o)wers** *n.pl.* adherents II. 59, I. 590
**folwynge** *adj.* ensuing I. 224
**fond** *see* **fynde**
**fonde** *v.* test, prove VI (vi). 75
**fondynge** *n.* temptation VIII. 473, **fandynge** VI (iv). 37; *pl.* **fandynges** I. 529, II. 167, **fondynges** VIII. 85
**foo** *n.* enemy VIII. 110; *pl.* **foes** VIII. 133, **foos** VIII. 160
**food(e)** *see* **fode**
**fool(e)** *n. see* **fole**
**fool** *adj.* stupid I. 359
**for** *conj.* for, because I. 6, I. 744, II. 9, III. 10, IV. 19, VI (i). 9, VII. 53 *etc.*; in order that VIII. 483
**for** *prep.* because of II. 41, III. 69, VIII. 24; in spite of III. 91; on account of I. 644, II. 231, III. 56, III. 102, VI (iii). 1, VI (v). 13, VIII. 12; on behalf of I. 58, II. 41, II. 310, VII. 7, VIII. 33; in place of I. 10; to prevent VII. 69
**forbedeth** *pr.3 sg.* forbids III. 109
**forber** *imp.sg.* abstain, refrain from III. 56
**forbette** *p.p.* severely beaten VI (ii). 41, VI (iii). 18
**forcried** *p.p.* shouted at VIII. 268
**fordo(ne)** *p.p.* destroyed VI (vi). 252, VIII. 88
**forgyf** *see* **foryeue**
**forlete** *v.* abandon VI (iii). 11; *subj.sg.* **forlet** VI (vi). 297
**forlorne** *p.p.* lost, doomed VI (iv). 31
**forsake** *v.* abandon, renounce I. 133, III. 135, **forsaake** I. 876; *pr.2 sg.* **forsakes** I. 246; *3 sg.* **forsaketh** I. 274, III. 40; *pl.* **forsaketh** III. 209, **forsaken** I. 247; *subj.sg.* **forsake** I. 748, **forsaak** II. 56; *pl.* **forsake** II. 64; *imp.sg.* **forsak(e)** VI (iv). 26, VI (ii). 9, VI (iv). 49; *pa.t.sg.* **forsoke** VIII. 122; *p.p.* **forsaken** I. 122, III. 154, VI (vi). 212, VII. 126, VIII. 480, **forsak** VIII. 478
**forsoth** *adv.* truly, indeed VI (iii). 6, VI (vi). 165
**forswerynge** *n.* perjury I. 349
**forth(e)** *adv.* forward I. 176, VII. 309, VII. 76
**forþi** *conj.* because II. 6
**forþi** *adv.* therefore I. 31, II. 114, III. 33, IV. 22, VI (i). 45, VI (iv). 16 *etc.*, **forthy** II. 164, **forþy** I. 796
**foryet** *v.* forget I. 256, II. 107, III. 32, **foryit** I. 544; *subj.sg.* **foryet** II. 140, III. 214, VIII. 527; *p.p.* **foryeten** II. 169
**foryetynge** *n.* distraction, lack of concentration III. 5
**foryeve** *v.* forgive I. 409; *subj.sg.* VI (vi). 195; *imp.sg.* VI (vi). 79, VIII. 257, **forgyf**

VI (vi). 407; *pa.t.sg.* **forȝaf** VII. 125; *pr.p.* **foryeuen** I. 391
**forȝyuenesse** *n.* forgiveness VII. 156
**fote** *n.* step, VIII. 323; base VIII. 493; *pl.* **fete** feet III. 180, VI (vi). 37, VII. 164, VIII. 312, **feet(e)** II. 182, VI (iii). 12, VII. 30
**foul(e)** *adj.* unclean, disgusting, spiritually blemished I. 32, I. 155, I. 328, III. 115, VIII. 143, VIII. 480; *sup.* **foulest** VIII. 414
**fouled** *p.p.* defouled II. 179; maltreated II. 191
**founden** *see* **fynde**
**foure** *adj.* four I. 324
**fourme** *n.* shape I. 168; manner I. 265, I. 894
**fourneys** *n.* furnace III. 187
**fourth** *see* **ferth**
**foxes** *n.pl.* foxes VIII. 431
**fre** *adj.* noble, not in bondage I. 346; not bound VI (v). 8; generous VI (vi). 25, VI (vi). 137; guiltless III. 55
**freelte** *n.* weakness I. 146, I. 844
**frend(e)** *n.* friend I. 475, VI (iv). 88, VII. 59, VIII. 110; *pl.* **frendes** I. 332, II. 56, III. 53, VIII. 412
**fresshe** *adj.* vigorous VIII. 17; **freshe** VIII. 285 youthful
**fright** *p.p.* burdened VIII. 318
**frith** *n.* wood VI (iv). 103
**fro** *prep.* from I. 97, II. 24, III. 34, V. 5, VI (i). 19 *etc.*, **froo** VI (iv). 53, **from(e)** VII. 6, VII. 151; *forming conj.* from the time I. 770*, II. 47, II. 244, VI (i). 25
**froyt, fruyt** *n.* harvest, produce I. 650, VIII. 205
**frowardenesse** *n.* perversity I. 52
**ful** *adj.* full (of) II. 143, III. 23, VI (vi). 34, VIII. 85; complete, total VIII. 45; sated I. 221
**ful** *adv.* very, exceedingly I. 292, II. 38, III. 110, VI (i). 9, VI (ii). 31 *etc.*
**fulfil(le)** *v.* fulfil, carry out, perform II. 34, III. 127, IV. 15, VIII. 234; *pr.3 sg.* **fulfilleth** I. 618; *imp.sg.* **fulfille** VI (vi). 379 totally fill; *p.p.* **fulfilled** I. 498, VIII. 53
**fulled*** *p.p.* baptized VI (vi). 320
**fully** *adv.* totally VI (vi). 423, VIII. 533, **fullyche** VI (vi). 257
**fulnes** *n.* fulfilment I. 624
**gaddre** *v.* gather I. 883; *p.p.* **gedered** III. 31
**gaynsigge** *v.* contradict I. 351
**galle** *n.* gall, bitter liquid II. 83, III. 50, VI (vi). 343, VII. 127, VIII. 416
**galows** *n.pl.* gallows VIII. 279
**game** *n.* pleasure VI (vi). 283; *pl.* **games** II. 51
**gangerels** *n.pl.* vagabonds I. 585
**gate** *n.* way VI (v). 2; *pl.* **gatys** VIII. 163 goings, journeys
**gawren** *pr.pl.* gape VIII. 325
**gedered** *see* **gaddre**
**gefen, gefynge, geuen** *see* **yeue**
**gelus** *adj.* devoted VI (vi). 129
**gent** *adj.* gracious VI (vi). 161
**gentil** *adj.* noble I. 346
**gerarchi** *n.* rank, hierarchy II. 17; *pl.* **gerarchies** II. 16
**get** *v.* obtain, acquire I. 547, II. 217, VIII. 400; *imp.sg.* VIII. 354; *p.p.* **getten** I. 770
**gif-** *see* **yeue**
**giftes** *see* **yifte**
**giles** *n.pl.* tricks I. 54
**gilt(e)** *n.* guilt, sin VI (vi). 114, VIII. 436
**gilt** *p.p.* offended, sinned VI (vi). 231
**gilty** *adj.* guilty VIII. 492
**gyses** *n.pl.* fashions, styles I. 374
**gla(a)d** *adj.* joyful, happy I. 37, I. 169; *comp.* **gladdir** I. 96
**glad** *v.* rejoice III. 132 (*refl.*); *pr.3 sg.* **gladdeth** VI (i). 49
**gladynge** *adj.* cheering I. 553
**gladly** *adv.* joyfully I. 473, III. 165
**gladnes(se)** *n.* rejoicing V. 1, V. 9, VIII. 103
**gleme** *n.* bright light VI (vi). 17
**gle(w)e** *n.* mirth, melody V. 10, VI (i). 44, VI (iii). 4
**glide** *v.* flow II. 186, VI (ii). 40
**glorious(e)** *adj.* full of glory, illustrious I. 39, VII. 1, VIII. 172, VIII. 496
**glotones** *n.pl.* gluttons III. 203
**glotony** *n.* gluttony II. 76
**gnedy (to)** *adj.* eager (for) I. 661
**go** *v.* go, walk II. 44, III. 98, VI (v). 2, VI (vi). 224, VII. 80, VIII. 165, **gone** VI (vi). 202; *pr.1 sg.* **go** VI (vi). 99, VII. 170; *2 sg.* **gost** III. 143, VIII. 323; *3 sg.* **goth** II. 165, VI (i). 11, VIII. 299, **gooth** I. 789; *pl.* **go** I. 62, **gone** VI (vi). 226; *subj.sg.* **go(o)** VI (vi). 385, VI (iv). 54; *pa.t.sg.* **yed** III. 103, **ȝede** VII. 76; *2 sg.* **yede** VIII. 116; *p.p.* **gone** II.

**go** (*cont.*) 166, VI (vi). 388, VII. 54, VIII. 559; *pr.p.* **goynge** I. 832, II. 5

**god** *n.* God I. 5, II. 15, VIII. 102 *etc.*; *gen.* **goddis** I. 67, II. 56, III. 56, V. 26, VI (ii). 1, **godis** I. 781

**gode** *see* **good**

**god(e)nes(se)** *see* **goodnesse**

**godhede, godheed** *n.* divinity VIII. 398, I. 479

**goers** *n.pl.* travellers I. 585, I. 823

**goynge** *n.* departure I. 597, VIII. 117

**gold** *n.* gold II. 87, III. 187

**good** *adj.* good I. 36, II. 25, III. 15, IV. 25, VI (vi). 81, VIII. 38, **goode** VII. 52, **gode** III. 62

**good(e)** *n.* goodness III. 21, III. 45*, III. 129; benefit I. 191; provision I. 440; wellbeing I. 10, VI (vi). 136; joy II. 190; good people I. 576, VI (iv). 70; *pl.* **goodes** properties I. 72, I. 114; belongings II. 122, VIII. 427

**goodnes(se)** *n.* goodness I. 140, II. 32, II. 147, III. 22, VIII. 11, **goodenes** VII. 158, **godenes(se)** I. 847, VI (vi). 351, **godnes** VI (vi). 338

**go(o)ste** *n.* spirit, life VI (vi). 220, I. 449; **þe holy** ~ I. 126, III. 184 *etc.* the Holy Ghost

**go(o)stly** *adj.* spiritual I. 3, I. 72, II. 100, II. 226, III. 69, IV. 1, VI (i). 51, VIII. 18, **gostely** VI (iv). 64

**gostly** *adv.* spiritually I. 574, IV. 2

**gouernance** *n.* guidance VIII. 87

**gouerneth** *pr.3 sg.* guides I. 710

**grace** *n.* divine grace I. 103, II. 106, III. 20, VI (ii). 15, *etc.*, **graeȝ** VIII. 13; *pl.* **graces** I. 494, gifts, advantages; thanksgiving VIII. 93, **gracis** VIII. 115

**gracious** *adj.* kind, generous VIII. 185, VIII. 442

**graciously** *adv.* by means of divine grace VII. 144

**graunt** *v.* grant, allow VIII. 327; *subj.sg.* VI (vi). 348; *imp.sg.* VI (vi). 392, VIII. 19; *pa.t.2 sg.* **graunted** VIII. 439

**grave** *n.* grave VII. 142; *pl.* **gravis, grauys** VIII. 503, VIII. 539

**gref** *see* **greue**

**grene** *adj.* green VI (i). 34, VIII. 204

**gret(e)** *adj.* great, large I. 259, I. 508, II. 154, III. 176, VI (i). 5, VII. 54, VIII. 71 *etc.*, **greet** I. 741, III. 203; *sup.* **grettest** VIII. 70

**grete** *v.* weep VI (iv). 74, VI (vi). 71, VI (vi). 185; *pa.t.sg.* **gret(t)e** II. 175, VI (iii). 19; *p.p.* **grette** VI (iv). 71; *pr.p.* **gretynge** III. 90, VI (vi). 280

**gretynge** *n.* weeping I. 157, II. 119, III. 183, VI (vi). 426

**gretly** *adv.* much I. 64, III. 29, VIII. 336

**greue** *v.* distress, afflict VIII. 73, VIII. 495, **gref** II. 231; *pr.3 sg.refl.* **greueth** I. 717, VIII. 73, VIII. 323; *pa.t.sg.* **greuet** VIII. 286, **greved** VIII. 337

**greuous** *adj.* severe III. 190; distressing VIII. 415; *comp.* **greuouser** I. 153

**greuously** *adv.* harshly I. 292

**gryntynge** *n.* grunting VIII. 293

**grisful** *adj.* terrifying I. 204

**grisly** *adj.* terrifying VIII. 486

**grith** *n.* sanctuary VI (iv). 101

**groned** *pa.t.2 sg.* groaned VIII. 317; *pr.p.* **gronynge** I. 78; *as n.* VIII. 293

**ground(e)** *n.* foundation III. 207, VI (vi). 258; earth VIII. 372, VII. 62

**grow** *v.* grow VI (vi). 16; *pr.3 sg.* **groweth** VIII. 205; *pr.p.* **growynge** VIII. 206

**gruch, gurch(e)** *v.* grumble, complain I. 351, III. 170, VIII. 157, VIII. 181; *pr.pl.* **gurch** I. 814; *pr.p.* **gurchynge** VIII. 303; *as n.* IV. 26

**haat** *see* **hate**

**habergeone** *n.* sleeveless coat of mail worn for penance I. 196

**habit(e)** *n.* nun's clothing III. 154, I. 90

**haye** *n.* grass VI (i). 33

**hail** *interj.* salutations VIII. 420

**haille*** *imp.sg.* greet I. 621

**half** *adv.* half II. 166

**half** *n.* side VIII. 551

**halle** *n.* hall, dwelling place II. 278, VI (iv). 96

**halowes** *n.pl.* saints I. 350, II. 124, III. 52, VII. 4; *gen.* II. 191*

**halt** *adj.* crippled VII. 23

**ham** *see* **thay**

**ham self** *pron. refl.* themselves I. 36, I. 802, VI (iv). 100, *and see* **one**

**han** *see* **haue**

**hand** *n.* hand I. 679, VIII. 374; keeping VI (i). 27; **hond(e)** I. 781, VII. 109; **at** ~ VI (v). 15 nearby; *pl.* **hand** II. 182, III. 141, VI (i). 65, **handes** VIII. 380, **hond** VI (iii). 12, **hondes** VII. 70, VII. 164, VIII. 333, **handis** VIII. 531, **hondis** VII. 65

**handlynge** *n.* handling I. 376
**hang-** *see* **henge**
**happe** *n.* chance I. 345
**har(e)** *see* **thay**
**hard** *adj.* difficult I. 629; II. 43, **herd** I. 802, I. 844; harsh, unyielding I. 716, III. 36, VI (i). 48, VII. 120, VIII. 369, painful VII. 130; *comp.* **harder** VIII. 505 less yielding
**hard, herd** *adv.* harshly VIII. 316, VI (vi). 124; much VIII. 318
**hardy** *adj.* bold VI (vi). 351
**hardily** *adv.* boldly I. 563
**hardynes** *n.* strength I. 805
**harlotes** *n.pl.* jesters I. 369
**harme** *n.* harm, injury I. 392
**harried** *pa.t.pl.* drove forth VIII. 310; *p.p.* **harred** VIII. 153
**harrynge** *n.* harassment VIII. 423
**hart-** *see* **herte**
**hasted** *p.p.* done quickly I. 404
**hate** *v.* hate VI (v). 1, VIII. 113, **haat** I. 55; *pr.2 sg.* **hatis** VIII. 114; *3 sg.* **hateth** I. 731, III. 29; *pl.* **hatyn** I. 241; *subj.sg.* **hate** VI (i). 37; *imp.sg.* **hate** I. 425, II. 100, VI (iv). 5, VI (v). 24; *pr.p.* **hatynge** II. 171
**hate, hatreden** *n.* hatred VIII. 111, I. 782, III. 78
**hauk** *n.* hawk VIII. 223
**haue** *v.* have, possess, receive I. 31, I. 726, II. 6, III. 46, IV. 4, VI (i). 64, VI (iv). 91, VI (vi). 199, VIII. 141 *etc.*; *pr.1 sg.* I. 829, II. 2, VI (ii). 10, VI (vi). 78, VI (iv). 40, VII. 154, VIII. 364; *2 sg.* **hast** I. 105, II. 92, III. 154, VI (iv). 37, VI (v). 3, VI (vi). 156, VII. 149, VIII. 18, *with pron.* **hastou** VII. 126, **haste** I. 452, II. 204, **as** I. 485, **hath** II. 164; *3 sg.* **hath** I. 15, II. 54, III. 19, IV. 1, VI (i). 21, VI (iii). 11, VII. 157, VIII. 397, **haþ** I. 444; *pl.* **haue** I. 6, II. 252, III. 18, VI (i). 50, VII. 43, VIII. 55, **hath** I. 141, I. 576, II. 31, III. 211, VI (i). 2, VI (iv). 58, VI (vi). 68, VIII. 359, **han** I. 287, I. 880, II. 27, II. 42, VI (iv). 71, **heth** I. 392; *subj.sg.* **haue** I. 385, II. 55, III. 106, III. 123, VI (ii). 47, VI (vi). 164, VIII. 219; *imp.sg.* **haue** I. 620, VI (iv). 18, VIII. 135; *pa.t.sg.* **had** III. 104, VI (i). 24, VI (iv). 84, VII. 128, VIII. 298, VIII. 352, **hadde** VIII. 344; *2 sg.* **haddest** VIII. 68, **haddist** VIII. 311, **had(de)** VIII. 356, VIII. 94; *pl.* **had** I. 860, **hadden** VIII. 558; *subj.sg.* **had** I. 783, VI (iii). 3, VII. 112; *pl.* **had** I. 51; *p.p.* **hadden** I. 52; *pr.p.* **hauynge** I. 390, II. 133, VIII. 328
**he** *pron.3 sg.masc.* he I. 14, II. 4, III. 21, IV. 4 *etc.*; *acc., dat.* **hym, him** I. 110, II. 9, III. 32, V. 5, VI (i). 18, VII. 91, VIII. 69 *etc.*; *refl.* **hym** I. 162, I. 379, II. 69, **him** VII. 96; *poss.adj.* **his, hys** I. 98, II. 5, III. 120, III. 135, IV. 4, VII. 2 *etc.*; *and see* **thay**
**hede** *n.*[1] attention VIII. 437
**hede** *n.*[2] head VI (vi). 175, VII. 164, VIII. 253, **heed** VI (iv). 30, **heued** VII. 70
**heel** *see* **hele** *n.*
**heer(e)** *n.* hair VIII. 312, VII. 75
**heete** *see* **hete** *n.*
**hegh** *adj.* high, lofty, noble I. 459, II. 38, IV. 5, VI (i). 9, VI (vi). 358, VIII. 316, **heigh** IV. 15, VIII. 24, **heygh** VIII. 26; *comp.* **hegher** I. 94, II. 59; *sup.* **heghest** I. 272, II. 18
**hegh** *adv.* highly VI (iv). 24; **on heigh** VIII. 478 aloft; *comp.* **hegher** I. 111, I. 785
**hegheth** *pr.3 sg.* ascends VI (iv). 66; *pl.* **heghen*** exalt I. 231; *imp.sg.* **hegh** raise VI (iv). 85
**heght** *n.* height I. 535
**heighynge** *n.* exaltation IV. 11
**heynesse** *n.* exaltation II. 232, IV. 23
**hel** *imp.sg.* pour III. 162
**hele, heel** *n.* health, wellbeing II. 114, VI (iv). 66, I. 529, I. 662; salvation II. 220, III. 218, IV. 14, V. 2, VI (iv). 14, VII. 46; restoring power I. 650
**helid** *pa.t.sg.* healed VII. 22
**helle** *v.* conceal, cover II. 68, VIII. 427
**helle** *n.* hell I. 2, II. 46, III. 36, VI (i). 48, VI (iii). 23, VII. 142, VIII. 429, **hel** I. 667; ~ **fyre** VI (v). 19 damnation; ~ **houndes** VIII. 295 fiendish people; *gen.* **helles** VIII. 504
**helpe** *v.* help, profit, benefit I. 649, III. 52; *pr.3 sg.* **helpeth** III. 15; *pl.* **helpeth** I. 72; *imp.sg.* **help** VI (vi). 418
**help(e)** *n.* help, assistance, remedy I. 112, I. 631, II. 277, VI (vi). 108, VII. 165, VIII. 30, VIII. 64
**helth(e)** *n.* health, spiritual wellbeing V. 2, VIII. 66, VII. 150
**hem** *see* **thay**
**hen** *see* **hethen**
**henge** *v.* hang II. 181, VI (ii). 33, **honge** VIII. 519; *pr.2 sg.* **hongest** VIII. 384; *3 sg.* **hangeth** VIII. 542, **hongeth** I. 625 depends; *pa.t.2 sg.* **henge** VI (vi). 113, VIII. 484, **honge** VI (vi). 28, **hange** VI (vi). 133, **hanged** VIII. 426; *3 sg.* **honge**

**henge** (*cont.*)
VII. 130, **hanget** VIII. 283, **honged** VIII. 404, **henged** VIII. 451; *pr.p.* **hongyng** VII. 122
**hent** *p.p.* apprehended VI (i). 24
**herbes** *n.pl.* herbs VIII. 247
**herbrow** *v.* give lodging to I. 854
**herd** *see* **hard, hyre**
**herdes** *n.pl.* shepherds III. 96
**her(e)** *adv.* here I. 124, II. 37, III. 24, V. 6 *etc.*, *and see* **thay, heere**
**heremyt** *n.* recluse VIII. title
**heresy** *n.* heresy, false belief VIII. 98
**heritage** *n.* inheritance I. 669, III. 211
**herknynge (of)** *n.* listening (to) I. 369
**hert** *v. see* **hurt**
**hert(e)** *n.* heart I. 3, I. 133, II. 3, II. 11, III. 20, V. 1 *etc.*; courage VIII. 184, **hart(e)** III. 65, VI (iv). 13; *gen.* **hert(e)** VI (vi). 6, VI (vi). 17 *etc.*; *pl.* **hertes** II. 31, **hartys** VIII. 553, **herte** I. 142
**hertely, hertily** *adv.* earnestly, sincerely VIII. 183, VI (vi). 389
**hestes** *n.pl.* commands VIII. 234
**hete** *pr.1 sg.* promise II. 141, VI (iv). 75; *pa.t.sg.* VI (vi). 239
**he(e)te** *n.* heat I. 751, I. 764
**heth** *see* **haue**
**hethen** *adv.* hence II. 291, VI (i). 17, VI (iv). 36, **hen** VI (vi). 224
**heved** *pa.t.pl.* heaved VIII. 402
**heued** *n. see* **hede**
**heuy** *adj.* heavy VIII. 316
**heuyn** *n.* heaven, sky I. 14, II. 9, III. 51, V. 2, VI (i). 9 *etc.*, **heuene** VII. 4; *gen.* **heuyn** VI (vi). 277
**heuynesse** *n.* oppressiveness, gloom IV. 26, V. 8
**heuynrike** *n.* kingdom of heaven VI (i). 15
**heuynward** *adv.* towards heaven I. 62
**hewe** *n.* dye I. 671; colour, complexion II. 185, VI (iii). 1
**hiddreward** *adv.* hither VIII. 162
**hide** *v.* hide, conceal, protect I. 97, VIII. 199; *pass.* II. 187; *pr.3 sg.* **hideth** I. 183; *subj.sg.* **hyde** VI (iv). 8; *pa.t.pl.* **hid** VII. 73
**hide** *n.* skin VII. 105
**hym self** *pron.refl.* himself I. 143, I. 644, III. 22, VI (iv). 7, VI (v). 20, VIII. 388, **hym selfe** I. 359, I. 789; *and see* **he**
**hire, hyre** *v.* hear, listen I. 150, I. 477, I. 614, II. 209, II. 61, VI (iv). 44; *pr.2 sg.* **hirest** II. 247; *imp.sg.* **hyre** II. 2, VI (vi). 90, VIII. 46; *pa.t.2 sg.* **herd** VIII. 455; *p.p.* **herd** I. 105, I. 485, VI (i). 24, VIII. 455; *pr.p.* **hyrynge** III. 93
**hire, hyre** *n.* reward, payment II. 82, VI (ii). 12; *and see* **she**
**hyrynge** *n.* hearing, listening I. 375; sense of hearing VIII. 418
**hirs** *see* **she**
**his** *see* **he, hit**
**hit** *pron.3 sg.neut.nom.acc.dat.* it I. 51, I. 88, II. 2, II. 132, II. 137, III. 7, III. 117, VIII. 194 *etc.*, **hyt** I. 484, III. 27, VI (iv). 82, **hitte** VIII. 301, **it** VII. 114, VII. 22, VII. 50 *etc.*; *refl.* **hit** I. 275; *poss.adj.* **his** VIII. 505
**hit self** *pron.refl.* itself IV. 8
**hitte** *v.* hit VII. 71
**hold(e)** *v.* (i) hold, keep I. 82, I. 201, I. 372, II. 137, III. 111, VI (i). 52; ~ **þyn ere** II. 1 listen; *pr.3 sg.* **holdeth** I. 325, II. 69, III. 95, VI (iv). 70; *pl.* **holdeth** I. 496; *subj.sg.* **hold** I. 313, III. 83, IV. 12; *pl.* **hold** II. 263; *imp.sg.* **hold** I. 623, II. 165, V. 8, VI (iv). 25, VI (vi). 270, VIII. 532; *pa.t.pl.* **helden** VIII. 153; *p.p.* **holden** I. 373, obliged I. 388, VIII. 412, **holdyn** III. 219; *pr.p.* **holdynge** II. 14, II. 240, VI (i). 28 continuing; (ii) consider, regard VIII. 21, VIII. 134, *pr.1 sg.* **hold** I. 95, VI (iv). 92, VIII. 519; *3 sg.* **holdeth** III. 21; *pl.* **hold** VI (iii). 27, **holden** I. 39, I. 244; *subj.sg.* **hold** I. 745, VIII. 399; *pl.* **hold** I. 265; *p.p.* **holden** I. 44, I. 343
**holdes** *n.pl.* strongholds VIII. 152
**holdynge** *n.* preservation II. 155
**hole** *adj.*[1] healthy, sound II. 109, VII. 23, **hool** VIII. 203
**hole** *adj.*[2] whole, entire VII. 93, VII. 110, **hool** VIII. 109; *and see* **hoole** *n.*
**hol(e)ly** *adv.* wholly I. 22, I. 880, II. 11, II. 124, III. 139, VI (vi). 303, III. 31, **hooly** I. 539, VIII. 89; *sup.* **holyest** II. 35
**holy** *adj.* holy, pious I. 107, I. 682, II. 25, III. 94, IV. 22, VI (iii). 16, VII. 3, VIII. 50, **haly** I. 365; *comp.* **holier** I. 372
**holynesse** *n.* piety, purity of life I. 90, II. 68, III. 121
**holys** *see* **hool**
**holsom(e)** *adj.* salutary VIII. 247, VIII. 249
**home** *adv.* homewards VIII. 81
**homelier** *comp.adj.* more familiar I. 474
**hond-** *see* **hand-**
**hondwerk** *n.* creation, handiwork VIII. 87
**honest** *adj.* honest, decent I. 415

**hong-** *see* **henge**
**hony** *n.* honey I. 562, I. 613, II. 294, VI (vi). 343, VIII. 228; ~ **combe** VIII. 227 honeycomb
**honour** *v.* respect I. 335; *p.p.* **honoured** I. 44
**honour** *n.* honour VII. 1; worship I. 100, I. 683; respect I. 343
**hooge** *adj.* immense VII. 24
**hool(e), hole** *n.* hole VIII. 223, VIII. 226, VIII. 374, VII. 115; *pl.* **holys** VIII. 373
**hoot** *see* **hote**
**hope, hoope** *n.* hope, trust I. 810, II. 304, III. 94, V. 2, VI (vi). 347, VIII. 96, I. 61, I. 777, IV. 25
**hope** *v.* trust, expect VIII. 107; *pr.1 sg.* **hop(e)** II. 68, I. 107, II. 32, **hoop** I. 179; *2 sg.* **hopis** II. 135; *pl.* **hopeth** I. 778; *pa.t.pl.* **hopped** I. 217
**horrible** *adj.* horrible I. 482, **orrible** I. 668
**hoste** *n.* army VI (v). 15; **oste** VII. 60 company
**hote** *adj.* burning VI (i). 31; **hoot** I. 556 hot; *comp.* **hottyre** VI (i). 13
**houre** *n.* hour III. 80, VII. 39; *pl.* **hours** VIII. 243 canonical hours
**hous(e)** *n.* house VIII. 223, VII. 66
**housynge** *n.* lodging I. 855
**how(e)** *adv.* how I. 42, I. 284, II. 58, III. 101, VI (iii). 19, VI (vi). 241, VII. 5, VIII. 285
**hundred** *adj.* hundred II. 134
**hungre** *n.* hunger I. 458, **hungyr** VIII. 472, **hungur** VII. 24
**hungri** *n.* hungry people I. 854
**hurt** *v.* harm I. 367; *p.p.* **hert** VI (vi). 236
**hurtynge** *n.* damaging I. 114, VII. 69

**I** *pron.1 sg.nom.* I I. 107, II. 2, III. 24, V. 3, VI (i). 4, VI (vi). 1 *etc.*; *acc.dat.* **me** me I. 546, I. 598, II. 169, V. 3, VI (i). 10 *etc.*; *refl.* **me** myself II. 7, VII. 170, VIII. 528; *poss. adj.* **my(n)** I. 601, II. 3, V. 3, VI (i). 22 *etc.*, **myne** VI (vi). 81, **mi** VI (vi). 230; *pron.* **myn(e)** mine VI (v). 23, VI (ii). 18, VIII. 357
**ydel, idel** *adj.* empty, casual I. 35, II. 43, III. 72, I. 360; **ydul** I. 289 idle
**if** *conj.* if I. 62, II. 9, III. 55, VI (iii). 20, VI (vi). 41 *etc.*, **yf** I. 157, VIII. 223, **yif** VIII. 80, **ȝif** VII. 34; although V. 4
**ignorance** *n.* ignorance I. 146
**il(le)** *n.* wickedness, sin I. 330, II. 101, III. 179, VI (iv). 60, VI (v). 2, VI (vi). 380
**il(le)** *adj.* evil I. 329, II. 102, III. 19, IV. 10, VIII. 97, I. 44, VI (i). 31; *as n.* I. 576
**il** *adv.* badly VI (v). 10
**ile** *n.* island I. 139
**ilfare** *n.* misfortune I. 333
**ilike, ylike** *adj.* & *adv. see* **lyke**
**ilka** *adj.* each VII. 65
**ilkone** *pron.* each one VII. 35
**illusioun** *n.* delusion I. 222
**ymage** *n.* appearance I. 227; likeness VI (vi). 179; *pl.* **ymages** I. 205 apparitions
**ymagyn** *v.* imagine II. 46
**impossibil, impossible** *adj.* impossible I. 578, I. 804
**in** *prep.* (of place) in I. 108, II. 2, VI (vi). 3, VII. 162 *etc.*, on VII. 31; (of time) in I. 128, III. 80, VIII. 159 *etc.*; (of condition) I. 13, II. 85, III. 8, VI (i). 3; according to III. 63; concerning III. 125; occupied in VIII. 15; as, representing VI (iv). 94, VI (iv). 104; *with ellipsis of vb. of motion* II. 278
**incarnacioun** *n.* incarnation VIII. 29
**inderly** *adj.* inner VIII. 332
**ynke** *n.* ink VIII. 237
**inogh, ynogh** *adv.* enough I. 195, VIII. 200, II. 164, VIII. 407, **ynowe** VIII. 223, **inow** VIII. 406
**inseperabil(e)** *adj.* inseparable I. 537, I. 538, III. 26
**insyght** *n.* insight VIII. 396
**inspiracioun** *n.* divine influence I. 386
**inspireth** *pr.3 sg.* divinely influences I. 876
**insuperabile** *adj.* insuperable I. 526, III. 26
**inward** *adj.* deep VI (vi). 370; internal I. 840
**inwardly** *adv.* inwardly II. 148, VIII. 142; deeply III. 68, III. 188, VI (vi). 391, **inwardliche** VI (vi). 259
**ypocrisi** *n.* hypocrisy I. 341
**ypocrites** *n.pl.* hypocrites III. 151
**ir(e)** *n.* anger I. 155, II. 74, III. 164, VI (ii). 10
**iren** *n.* iron I. 670
**irkynge** *n.* weariness, dislike I. 277
**is, ys** *pr.3 sg.* is, exists I. 15, I. 632, II. 4, III. 80, IV. 2, V. 2 *etc.*; *neg.* **nys** I. 16
**yuel, yville** *n.* evil I. 183, I. 96
**yuel** *adj.* wicked, sinful I. 167, **euyl** VIII. 132, **evil** VIII. 150
**iwisse** *adv.* indeed VI (vi). 197, VI (vi). 359

**iay** *n.* jay VIII. 388
**iangle** *v.* chatter III. 57, V. 8

**ianglers** *n.pl.* chatterers, jesters I. 585, III. 15
**ioy(e)** *n.* joy, pleasure I. 10, I. 78, II. 50, III. 43, V. 1, VI (i). 8 *etc.*; *pl.* **ioies** I. 241
**ioyeth** *pr.3 sg.* rejoices I. 641; *pl.* **ioyeth** I. 873
**ioyful** *adj.* joyful I. 169, II. 232, **ioiful** II. 38
**ioynge** *n.* cause of joy I. 513, VI (ii). 30
**ioyneth** *pr.3 sg.* joins I. 638; *p.p.* **ioyned** I. 658
**ioyntes** *n.pl.* joints VIII. 378
**iues, iewes, iewis** *n.pl.* Jews VI (ii). 39, VIII. 76, VII. 60
**iuge** *n.* judge I. 287
**iugement** *n.* judgement VI (vi). 164, VIII. 277
**jugge** *v.* judge VIII. 273

**kaytif** *n.* worthless creature VII. 161, **caitife** VII. 147
**kaitif** *adj.* wretched, worthless I. 816
**kake** *n.* cake VII. 74
**kalle** *see* **call**
**kan** *see* **begyn, can**[1], **can**[2]
**kare** *see* **care** *n.*
**karolles** *n.pl.* ring dances I. 374
**kastynge** *n.* calculation, consideration VI (v). 1
**kele** *v.* cool II. 305, VI (i). 26, VI (iv). 52, VIII. 466; *pr.3 sg.* **keleth** I. 703
**kelynge** *n.* cooling, alleviation VIII. 465
**kene** *adj.* bitter VIII. 343
**kene** *adv.* sharply VIII. 348
**kep(e)** *v.*[1] keep, maintain VII. 33, guard, protect I. 66, I. 413, III. 112, VI (iv). 50, VII. 33, VIII. 174, VIII. 444; *pr.2 sg.* **kepest** VI (vi). 140 desire; *3 sg.* **kepeth** I. 710, II. 69; *pl.* **kepeth** I. 412, I. 497; *subj.sg.* **kepe** I. 897, VII. 174; *pl.* **kepe** VII. 35; *imp.sg.* **kep(e)** VIII. 217, VI (iv). 25, VI (vi). 275, VIII. 71; *pa.t.sg.* **keped** VI (iv). 82; *p.p.* **kept(e)** I. 411, II. 93, VIII. 471; *pr.p.* **kepynge** I. 392
**kepe** *v.*[2] catch falling liquid VIII. 498
**kepers** *n.pl.* innkeepers I. 585
**kepynge** *n.* custody, defence VI (vi). 270; maintenance IV. 11
**kest(e)** *see* **caste**
**keuer** *see* **couer**
**kyn** *n.* family I. 345, II. 97; manner of I. 579
**kynd(e)** *n.* nature I. 114, I. 344, VI (i). 41, VI (i). 44, VI (iv). 75, VIII. 72, VIII. 344; health, constitution I. 186
**kyndel, kyndil** *v.* kindle, rouse, enflame II. 24, II. 122; *pr.3 sg.* **kyndels** I. 617, **kyndyls** I. 635; *subj.sg.* **kyndel** VI (iv). 97; *imp.sg.* **kyndel** II. 199, VI (ii). 11, VIII. 526; *p.p.* **kyndled** I. 658, III. 185, **kyndlet** II. 227
**kyndly** *adv.* in accordance with nature VIII. 340
**kynge** *n.* king II. 175, VI (i). 66, VI (ii). 9, VI (iii). 27, VI (iv). 17, VIII. 295 *etc.*; *gen.* **kynges** II. 8, VI (i). 8, VI (v). 4; *pl.* **kynges** III. 99, VII. 16, VIII. 295
**kynreden** *n.pl.* family II. 107, III. 90
**kyrtel, kyrtil** *n.* man's tunic III. 103, VIII. 280; *pl.* **kyrtels** III. 107, **kirtils*** II. 162 gowns
**kysse** *imp.sg.* kiss VII. 160; *pa.t.sg.* **kissed** VII. 30
**kyssynge** *n.* kissing VI (vi). 175
**knees** *n.pl.* knees I. 177, VIII. 254
**knelynge** *pr.p.* kneeling I. 832, VIII. 254
**knyght** *n.* knight VI (i) 66; *pl.* **kneghtes** VIII. 310 soldiers
**knottes** *n.pl.* knots VIII. 193
**knowe** *v.* know I. 628, VII. 34; acknowledge II. 258, VIII. 23; *pr.1 sg.* **know** I. 233, VIII. 516; *2 sg.* **knowest** I. 453, VI (v). 12, VIII. 525; *3 sg.* **knoweth** I. 657; *pl.* **knowen** I. 77; *subj.sg.* **knowe** I. 181, III. 97; *pa.t.sg.* **knew(e)** I. 34, I. 831, VI (iv). 82, VIII. 337; *pl.* **knewe** I. 26; *subj.sg.* **knewe** VI (i). 43, VI (iii). 3; *p.p.* **know** I. 51
**knowynge** *n.* knowledge, understanding I. 785, VI (iv). 57
**konnynge** *see* **connynge**
**kunnyngely** *adv.* intelligently VIII. 112

**lacid** *p.p.* fastened, secured VI (iii). 11
**lad** *see* **lede** *v.*
**lady** *n.* mistress I. 130; the Virgin VI (vi). 105, VII. 7, VIII. 342
**laghet** *pa.t.pl.* laughed III. 200
**laghtre** *n.* laughter I. 361
**lay** *v.* lay, place VIII. 491; *pr.3 sg.* **leith** I. 54; *pa.t.sg.* **laide** VIII. 36 relinquished; *pl.* **leid(e)** VIII. 372, VII. 107, **laide** VII. 141, *p.p.* **laid(e)** VI (ii). 42, **leyd** II. 195; ~ **lowe/logh** II. 195, VI (ii). 42 abased; *and see* **lye** *v.*[1]
**laike, layke** *v.* play, divert VI (iv). 102 (*refl.*), VI (v). 4
**layry** *adj.* earthly IV. 16

**laken** *pr.pl.* disparage, blame I. 38
**lakynge** *n.* blaming I. 464
**lame** *adj.* unable to move VIII. 16; lame VII. 23
**land** *see* **londe**
**lang(e), langer, langeth, langynge** *see* **long, longeth, longynge**
**languyssh(e)** *pr.1 sg.* long, pine I. 493, I. 601, **langwisshe** I. 565
**languysshynge** *n.* pining I. 566
**lap** *v.* ~ **in þe best** represent in the best way I. 357; *p.p.* **lapped** enfolded III. 160
**lare** *see* **lore**
**large** *adj.* excessive VIII. 99; generous VIII. 194, VIII. 358
**lasse** *adj.comp.* lesser, smaller I. 87, VI (iii). 24, VI (iv). 56; inferior I. 375; *sup.* **lest(e)** I. 281, VI (iii). 21, VII. 146, **leest** I. 244 most insignificant
**lasse** *adv.comp.* less I. 195; *sup.* **lest** II. 30
**last** *adj.* last I. 433, VIII. 535; **at þe last(e)** III. 91, VI (iv). 20 finally
**last** *adv. see* **late**
**laste** *v. see* **lest**
**lastynge** *see* **lestynge**
**late** *adv.* late I. 585, III. 90; *comp.* **lattre** I. 228 more slowly; *sup.* **last** VIII. 537 finally
**latyn** *adj.* Latin VII. 135
**laue** *imp.sg.* pour VI (vi). 311
**law(e)** *n.* commandment I. 624; *pl.* **lawes** VIII. 471
**lecheth** *pr.3 sg.* heals VI (iv). 104
**lecherie, lechurie** *n.* lechery, lewdness I. 92, II. 76, I. 364, I. 306
**led(e)** *v.* lead, guide, conduct I. 373, VI (ii). 7, VII. 79; *pr.3 sg.* **ledeth** I. 118, II. 194, VI (v). 4; *pl.* **lede** VI (i). 63, **leden** I. 40, **ledeth** I. 495; *subj.sg.* **led(e)** VI (ii). 47, V. 8; *imp.sg.* **lede** II. 269, VI (iv). 77; *pa.t.sg.* **led** III. 99; *pl.* **lad** III. 201, **led** VII. 68, VIII. 309, **lede** VII. 73, **ledde** VII. 66; *p.p.* **led(de)** I. 842, III. 148, VIII. 326, II. 285, VI (ii). 30; *pr.p.* **ledynge** I. 127
**lede** *n.* lead (metal) VI (iv). 15
**leest** *see* **lasse**
**lef** *adj.* beloved VI (vi). 401, **leue** VIII. 144; **lefe** VIII. 358 precious; *comp.* **leuer** I. 531, II. 306 preferable
**lefte** *see* **leue**
**lei-** *see* **lay**
**lem(m)an** *n.* beloved one II. 235, VI (vi). 137, VI (vi). 396, **lemmon** VI (vi). 409
**len** *v.* grant VI (iv). 28; *imp.sg.* **lene** VIII. 395; *p.p.* **lent** I. 291, VI (i). 21
**lend** *v.* live, dwell II. 202, VI (v). 11, VI (vi). 106; *pr.3 sg.* **lendeth** V. 2, VI (i). 44*; *p.p.* **lent** arrived II. 296, VI (ii). 25
**lendys** *n.pl.* loins VIII. 427
**lenger(e)** *see* **longe**
**lengthes** *pr.3 sg.* becomes more distant V. 5
**lennynge** *n.* support VIII. 382
**lepre** *n.* leper VII. 72
**ler(e)** *v.* teach I. 488, VI (iv). 83; *pr.1 sg.* **lere** I. 518; *3 sg.* **lereth*** I. 147; *pa.t.2 sg.* **lered** II. 282 (*and see* **lerne**)
**lere** *adj.* empty I. 221
**lerne** *v.* learn VIII. 241, **lere** VI (iv). 24; *imp.sg.* **lerne** VI (iv). 17, **lere** V. 6, VI (i). 17; *pr.p.* **lernynge** teaching I. 127
**lernynge** *n.* instruction I. 107
**lese** *v.*[1] deliver, release V. 6
**leseth** *v.*[2] *pr.3 sg.* loses I. 15; *pl.* **lese** VI (iv). 12, **lesyn** I. 14, **lesen** I. 52; *subj.pl.* **lese** II. 115; *pa.t.sg.* **lost(e)** VIII. 505, VIII. 538; *p.p.* **lost** I. 683, **losten** I. 297
**lesynge** *n.* falsehood I. 354, I. 423
**lesse** *v.* lessen VI (iv). 31
**lest** *conj.* lest VIII. 105
**lest(e)** *v.* endure, persevere I. 188, II. 254, VI (iv). 3, VI (iv). 17, **last(e)** I. 276, VII. 110; *pr.3 sg.* **lesteth** I. 282, I. 663, II. 72, III. 29, VI (i). 1, VI (ii). 24, VI (iii). 25; *pl.* **lesteth** I. 298; *pa.t.sg.* **lested** I. 831
**lest(e)** *adv.* & *adj. see* **lasse**
**lestynge** *adj.* continuing I. 9, I. 553, III. 8, VI (i). 25; **in lastynge** I. 609 eternal; *comp.* **lestynger** I. 840
**lestynge** *n.* continuance VIII. 11
**lestyngly** *adv.* continually I. 85, II. 145, III. 77
**lestyngnesse** *n.* durability I. 642
**let(e)** *v.* (i) let, allow, permit III. 113; *pr.pl.* **let** VI (iv). 62; *subj.sg.* **let** I. 330, II. 135, VI (vi). 264; *imp.sg.* **let** II. 198, II. 305, III. 163, V. 9, VI (vi). 8, VIII. 87; *pa.t.2 sg.* **lete** VIII. 79; (ii) abandon, forsake II. 298, VI (ii). 25, VI (vi). 70, VI (vi). 188, **lette** VI (iii). 20; *subj.sg.* **let** II. 146 (*intr.*); *pa.t.sg.* **lete** VI (vi). 182 emitted; *2 sg.* **lete** VI (vi). 39 left, went away; (iii) hinder, obstruct I. 769, III. 52, VI (vi). 367, **lette** VIII. 346; *pr.3 sg.* **letteth** II. 13, III. 11; *pl.* **letteth** I. 72, I. 845; *subj.sg.* **let** VIII. 536; *p.p.* **letted** I. 259, I. 315, I. 823; *pr.p.* **lettynge** I. 59

**lettynge** *n.* hindrance VIII. 351
**lettres** *n.pl.* Scripture I. 649
**leue** *v.*[1] leave, abandon I. 338, II. 12, VI (vi). 355, VIII. 55; *pr.pl.* **leuen** I. 381; *subj.sg.* **leue** I. 443, II. 55; *pa.t.sg.* **lefte** VII. 31; *pl.* **lefte** VII. 80; *pr.p.* **leuynge** * VIII. 100
**leue** *v.*[2] believe I. 630
**leue** *n.* permission I. 121, I. 179, VI (vi). 309; leave VIII. 443
**leue-takynge** *n.* farewell VIII. 449
**leue(r)** *see* **lef**
**ly(e), ligge** *v.*[1] lie prostrate VI (i). 66, VI (iv). 62, I. 68, VIII. 497; **low** ~ VI (v). 13 hide; *subj.pl.* **ligge** I. 187; *pa.t.2 sg.* **lay** VIII. 493; *pl.* **lay** VIII. 494; *pr.p.* **liggynge** III. 97
**licour** *n.* liquid III. 114
**lieth** *v.*[2] *pr.3 sg.* tells a lie I. 702; *subj.sg.* **ly** I. 423
**lyf(e), lif(e)** *n.* life I. 16, I. 132, II. 104, III. 9, V. 2, V. 8, VI (i). 1, VI (ii). 43, VI (iv). 10, VII. 154, VIII. 10 *etc.*; way of life I. 20, II. 35, I. 245, VI (iv). 45; human being VI (i). 43, VI (iii). 21; *gen.* **lyves** I. 8, II. 72; *pl.* **lifes** I. 836 ways of living
**life** *v.* see **lyue**
**lifte** *adj.* left VII. 109
**lifte** *v.* raise I. 5; *pr.3 sg.* **lifteth** IV. 16, VI (i). 15; *imp.sg.* **lift** II. 203, III. 51, **lifte** VII. 28; *pa.t.pl.* **lifte** VII. 120; *pr.p.* **liftynge** II. 132, VI (iv). 13, **lyftynge** II. 229
**ligg-** *see* **lye**
**liggynge** *n.* lying supine II. 245
**light** *v.*[1] lighten, illumine; *subj.sg.* **lyght** I. 103; *pr.pl.* **lygheten** VIII. 199
**light** *v.*[2] relieve VI (iii). 2
**light** *adj.* easy I. 803; not heavy VI (i). 49; *comp.* **lightre, lighter** easier I. 303, II. 47
**light(e)** *n.* brightness, radiance, illumination I. 635, II. 123, VI (ii). 7, VI (iv). 12, VI (iv). 77, VI (vi). 9, VI (vi). 107, **lyȝt** VIII. 395
**lighteth** *v.*[3] *pr.3 sg.* alights, descends I. 886; *subj.sg.* **lyȝt** VIII. 89; *imp.sg.* **lyth** VI (vi). 83, **lyȝt** VIII. 524; *pa.t.2 sg.* **lyghted** VIII. 24, **lyȝted** VIII. 514; *pp.* **light** II. 302 arrived, lodged, **lyghted** VIII. 523 visited
**lightfuller** *comp.adv.* more lightly VI (vi). 23
**lightly** *adv.* readily, easily I. 462, II. 104
**lightnynge** *n.* descent IV. 12
**lightsomnes** *n.* joy V. 3
**lyynge** *n.* falsehood I. 425
**lyk(e), like** *adj.* like, similar to III. 151, VI (i). 16, VI (vi). 228, VII. 72, VIII. 7, VIII. 210, VIII. 221, **ylike** VI (i). 14, **ilike** I. 457; *comp.* **lyker** VIII. 315
**like** *adv.* similarly I. 346
**like** *v.* (i) please, *pr.3 sg.* **liketh** VI (vi). 329; *pl.* **liken** VI (vi). 324; *subj.sg.* **lyk** VIII. 529; *pl.* **like** III. 47; *pr.p.* **lykynge** III. 129; (ii) like, take pleasure in **lyke** VI (vi). 298
**likene** *pr.pl.* compare I. 282; *p.p.* **lik(e)ned** I. 591, VI (iv). 61, VI (iii). 33
**lykynge** *adj.* pleasing VIII. 27
**lykynge, likynge** *n.* pleasure I. 7, I. 340, II. 13, III. 28, VI (ii). 3, VI (iv). 58, VI (vi). 166, VIII. 9, VIII. 226, VI (i). 30 *etc.*; *pl.* **lykynges** II. 262
**liknes(se), lyknesse** *n.* form, shape, guise I. 184, I. 191, VIII. 143
**lym** *n.* limb VI (iv). 104; *pl.* **lymmys** VIII. 13, **lem(m)ys** VIII. 14
**lippes** *n.pl.* lips VII. 164, VIII. 543
**lisse** *n.* remission VI (vi). 243; **lysse** peace, delight VI (vi). 6*, VI (vi). 360
**list** *v.*[1] *imp.sg.* listen V. 6
**list** *v.*[2] *see* **lust**
**litel(le)** *adj.* little, small I. 11, I. 199, I. 417, II. 41, III. 14, VI (iii). 46, VI (iv). 40, VIII. 73; *as n.* VIII. 359
**litel** *adv.* little II. 49, VIII. 199
**lyth** *n.* limb VI (iv). 104, VIII. 485
**lyth** *see* **lighteth**
**lyue** *v.* live I. 478, II. 79, II. 223, III. 50, V. 6, VI (i). 17; *pr.2 sg.* **lyvest** II. 37, **leuest** II. 152; *3 sg.* **lyveth** VI (iii). 5; *pl.* **lyuen** I. 836, **lyue** I. 281, II. 250, III. 174, **lyveth** III. 89; *subj.pl.* **life** II. 116, **lyve** II. 108, VI (i). 68; *pa.t.pl.* **lyued*** III. 201; *p.p.* **lyved.** I. 288, II. 92; *pr.p.* **lyvynge** I. 481, I. 890, VI (iv). 41
**lyuynge** *adj.* living I. 715, I. 874, III. 37
**lyuynge** *n.* way of life I. 894, II. 156, VI (i). 55, VIII. 40
**logh** *see* **lay**
**loghest** *see* **low(e)**
**loke** *v.* look, watch, take care II. 215, VIII. 141; contemplate VIII. 142; *pr.1 sg.* **lok** VI (vi). 178; *2 sg.* **lokest** I. 419; *pl.* **loken** VIII. 552; *subj.sg.* **loke** I. 885; *imp.sg.* **lok(e)** VI (iv). 54, I. 520, II. 99, III. 150, V. 8, VI (i). 19, VI (iv). 42, VI (vi). 151, **look** I. 483; *pa.t.sg.* **loked** VIII. 546
**lokynge** *n.* looking, regarding IV. 21, VIII. 121; countenance VIII. 313

**lombe** *n.* lamb VII. 88
**lond(e)** *n.* land VI (iv). 12, VI (vi). 73, VIII. 215, **land** III. 89
**longe** *adj.* long I. 59; (of time) I. 149, VI (vi). 55, VII. 139, VIII. 170
**longe** *adv.* for a long time I. 747, II. 208, VI (vi). 158, VI (vi). 382, VIII. 282, **lange** III. 175; *comp.* **lenger** VIII. 112, **langer** I. 831
**longeth** *v.*[1] *pr.3 sg.* longs, yearns I. 609; *impers.* II. 236, **langeth** I. 565, II. 278, VI (ii). 7; *pr.p.* **langynge** VI (iii). 23
**longeth** *v.*[2] *pr.3 sg.* belongs VIII. 88
**longynge** *n.* desire I. 596, VIII. 10, **langynge** II. 213, II. 267, VI (ii). 22, VI (iii). 4, VI (iv). 28
**look** *see* **loke**
**lord(e)** *n.* lord, master II. 7, III. 107, VI (ii). 1, VI (vi). 69, VII. 1, VII. 166, VIII. 1; *gen.* **lordes** VIII. 363; *pl.* **lordes** VIII. 295
**lordship** *n.* dominion, authority VIII. 25
**lore** *n.* teaching, instruction VI (vi). 235, VIII. 97, **lare** I. 603, I. 622, IV. 13, V. 6, VI (ii). 47, VI (iv). 83
**losse** *n.* loss VIII. 487
**lost(e)** *see* **lese**
**loth** *adj.* unwilling, averse VIII. 166; displeased I. 205
**loth** *v.* feel disgust with I. 258; *impers.* + *with* II. 50
**loud** *adv.* openly VI (vi). 378
**louse** *v.* solve I. 629
**loue** *n.* love, affection I. 5, II. 2, III. 18, V. 3, VI (i). 1, VI (ii). 6, VI (iii). 2, VII. 5, VIII. 8 *etc.*; beloved one I. 129; pleasure VIII. 495
**loue** *v.* love, value I. 149, I. 471, II. 13, III. 42, VI (i). 4, VI (iii). 28, VI (iv). 17, VI (vi). 4, VIII. 7 *etc.*; *pr.1sg.* I. 628, II. 6; *2sg.* **louest** I. 333, II. 142, III. 143, VIII. 113; *3sg.* **loueth** I. 15, I. 491, II. 224, III. 84, VI (iii). 5; *pl.* **louen** VI (iv). 61, **loueth** I. 23, I. 240, II. 28, II. 236, III. 17, VI (iv). 9, **loue** I. 492, VI (iv). 11, VI (iv). 57; *subj.sg.* **loue** I. 698, II. 10, III. 132, VI (i). 29, VI (iv). 65, VI (vi). 272; *pl.* **loue** VII. 35, *imp.sg.* **loue** III. 42, VI (i). 45, VI (ii). 48, VI (iv). 41, VI (v). 24; *pa.t.sg.* **loued** I. 831, II. 90, III. 166, VI (iii). 8; *pl.* **loued** I. 305, III. 200, VII. 143, **louet** I. 482; *p.p.* **loued** I. 84, I. 829, II. 27, III. 224, VIII. 270, **louede** VII. 47; *pr.p.* **louynge** I. 229, I. 382, II. 246, VI (iv). 47
**loued** *n.* loved one I. 637
**louely** *adj.* beautiful VIII. 544; *comp.* **louelier** I. 841; *sup.* **louelieste** I. 603
**loue-langynge, loue-longynge** *n.* desire for love VI (vi). 2, VI (vi). 143; **his** ~ I. 604 longing for his love
**louer** *n.* lover I. 621, II. 139, VI (vi). 24; *pl.* **louers** I. 254, II. 61, III. 48, VI (i). 50
**louereden** *n.* love I. 804
**louesom(e)** *adj.* worthy of love III. 168, VI (ii). 42
**louynge** *adj.* loving I. 493
**louynge** *n.* lover I. 637, II. 211, VI (i). 5; praising I. 425, VI (ii). 12; love VII. 155; **louyng** VII. 14 rejoicing; **loouynge** VII. 149 praising
**low(e)** *adj.* low, humble VIII. 25; *comp.* **lower** I. 95; *sup.* **lowest(e)** I. 244, II. 17, **loghest** I. 312
**lowe, lowly** *adv.* humbly VIII. 262, VII. 36
**lust(e)** *n.* pleasure I. 45, I. 189, II. 81, VI (i). 16; desire III. 53, IV. 10, VIII. 8, VIII. 145; *pl.* **lustes** pleasures I. 7, III. 89, VI (vi). 252, desires II. 261, **lustis** desires IV. 16, VIII. 472
**lust(e)** *v.impers.* please II. 49, **list** II. 246, III. 56; *pr.3sg.* **lust** I. 491, II. 1, **list** I. 552, III. 42, VI (iii). 9, VI (v). 23; *pers.* **lust** VIII. 147 desire; *pa.t.sg.* **lust** III. 201

**mageste** *n.* majesty I. 301, II. 193, VI (ii). 1, VI (iv). 65
**may** *see* **mow**
**maye** *n.* May VI (i). 57
**mayd(en)** *n.* maiden, virgin VIII. 447, II. 156, VI (vi). 265; *gen.* **maiden** VI (ii). 5
**maydenhede** *n.* virginity II. 155, VIII. 344
**maist** *see* **mow**
**maistyr** *n.* master VIII. 254; *pl.* **maistres** III. 93 learned men
**maistry** *n.* control II. 308
**maistry** *v.* master, overcome VI (ii). 43
**mak(e)** *v.* make, cause I. 26, I. 205, I. 807, II. 100, II. 213, VI (iii). 24, VI (iv). 51, VII. 111, VIII. 365 *etc.*; *pr.3sg.* **maketh** I. 30, I. 70, I. 500, I. 803, II. 248, III. 119, V. 7, VI (i). 10, VI (iii). 15, VI (v). 10; *pl.* **make** I. 76, IV. 9, **maketh** I. 159, II. 77, IV. 18, **maken** I. 328, VIII. 552; *subj.sg.* **mak(e)** III. 69, VI (iv). 98, VI (vi). 351*; *pl.* **make** I. 60; *imp.sg.* **mak(e)** II. 198, III. 164, VIII. 166, V. 10, VI (i). 26, VI (ii). 8, VI (iv). 23, VI (v). 12, VI (vi). 20, VIII. 80; *pa.t.sg.* **made** III. 216, VI (vi). 135, VII. 14, VIII.

**mak(e)** (*cont.*) 340; *2sg.* **madest** VI (vi). 52, VIII. 7, **mad** VI (vi). 40, VIII. 13; *pl.* **made** VI (vi). 60, VII. 17, VIII. 402; *p.p.* **mad(e)** II. 8, III. 55, VIII. 499, I. 444, III. 117, VIII. 191, **make** VI (iv). 95, **maked** I. 215, I. 315, I. 772, **j-made** VIII. title composed
**makles** *adj.* without equal VIII. 341
**malice** *n.* malice, spite I. 109, VIII. 508
**malisone** *n.* curse I. 859
**man** *n.* man, person I. 1, I. 739, II. 69, III. 111, IV. 2, VI (vi). 46, VIII. 133; mankind VI (i). 10, VI (iii). 20, VII. 16, VIII. 435; *gen.* **mannys** I. 86, I. 333, III. 6, VIII. 346, **mannes** I. 119, II. 53, IV. 24, VII. 45; *pl.* **men** I. 12, II. 40, III. 39, VI (i). 2 *etc.*; *gen.* **mennys** II. 120, **mennes** I. 92
**manacynge** *n.* threatening I. 355
**maner(e)** *n.* manner, way I. 24, I. 378, II. 220, III. 5; kind of VIII. 71, VIII. 351; *pl.* **maner(e)s** I. 113, I. 151, I. 220; customs I. 662, **manere** I. 400 sorts
**manhede** *n.* manhood VIII. 479
**many** *adj.* many I. 217, II. 60, III. 102, VI (vi). 123, VII. 24, VIII. 18
**many** *pron.* many I. 8, I. 214, II. 131, VI (v). 10
**manyfold** *adv.* in many ways VIII. 336
**mankynd(e)** *n.* mankind I. 21, VI (iv). 79, VII. 7, VIII. 24
**manly** *adv.* vigorously I. 294, II. 264, III. 162
**mare** *see* **more**
**matier** *n.* subject VIII. 392
**matyns** *n.* matins, midnight office of breviary VIII. 243
**me** *see* **I**
**mede** *n.* profit, reward I. 194, II. 114, VI (i). 64, VI (iv). 97, **meed** I. 211; **in ~ with** I. 246 equal in merit
**medeful** *adj.* profitable I. 841, VIII. 91
**medew** *n.* meadow VIII. 246
**medicyne** *n.* remedy VIII. 83
**meditacioun** *n.* meditation, contemplation IV. 21, VIII. 202; *pl.* **meditaciouns** I. 509, III. 62
**meed** *see* **mede**
**meen** *n.* mean, average I. 200
**meyne** *n.* household I. 850
**mek(e)** *adj.* meek, humble I. 708, I. 40, III. 163, VI (ii). 10, VI (vi). 218, VIII. 21; *sup.* **mekest** VI (iii). 6
**meke** *v.refl.* humble oneself VIII. 134
**mekely, mekeli** *adv.* humbly IV. 20, VII. 20, VII. 18
**mekenes(se)** *n.* meekness, humility I. 423, I. 248, I. 709, II. 99, III. 160, VI (iv). 29, **meknes** VIII. 66
**melle** *v.* speak V. 7
**melody(e), melodi** *n.* sweet music I. 144, I. 614, II. 54, II. 209, II. 233, VI (i). 67, VI (iv). 44
**membris** *n.pl.* private parts VII. 107
**memorie** *n.* mind I. 620, VI (ii). 17
**men-** *see* **man**
**mend** *v.* amend VI (iv). 107; *subj.sg.* VI (vi). 364; *imp.sg.* II. 201; *pr.p.* **mendynge** VIII. 386
**mene** *v.*[1] *pr.1 sg.* intend, signify VIII. 388
**mene** *v.*[2] *pr.1 sg. refl.* mourn, lament VI (vi). 90
**menged** *p.p.* mingled VII. 128
**mercy** *n.* mercy I. 853, II. 170, VI (vi). 308, VII. 21, VII. 167, VIII. 30
**mercyfulle** *adj.* merciful VIII. 121
**mercyfulli, mercyfully, mercifulli** *adv.* mercifully VII. 21, VII. 22, VII. 124
**merit(e)** *n.* reward I. 52, I. 779; worth, value I. 318; *pl.* **merites** I. 843
**mescheuous** *adj.* terrible III. 190
**meschief** *n.* misfortune VIII. 26, VII. 23
**messager** *n.* envoy II. 7
**meste** *see* **more**
**mestier** *n.* need III. 106
**mesure** *n.* length I. 280; moderation, discretion I. 46, I. 442, VIII. 99
**metaille** *n.* metal VIII. 208; *pl.* **metailles** VIII. 207
**met(e)** *n.* food I. 45, I. 436; *pl.* **mettis** I. 443
**mete** *v.* meet VI (ii). 28; *subj.pl.* III. 105; *pa.t.sg.* **met** VII. 59; *pl.* **met** II. 177; *p.p.* **mett** VI (iv). 70
**meve** *v.* move VIII. 16
**my(n)** *see* **I**
**mych(e)** *adj.* great, large I. 45, II. 141, VIII. 123, VIII. 436, **mich(e)** I. 504, II. 3, **moche** I. 359, VIII. 456, **mychel** VI (v). 22, **mykel** I. 572
**mych(e)** *adv.* much, greatly I. 74, I. 88, I. 504, II. 27, III. 13, V. 4, VI (vi). 167 *etc.*, **mich** I. 80
**myddel** *n.* waist VII. 68; **in myddes** I. 50 in the middle of
**myddis** *adj.* middle II. 27; **mydel** II. 18
**myght** *n.* strength I. 6; power I. 478, III. 126, VI (vi). 11, VI (vi). 106; capability I. 370, I. 804, III. 68, VI (iv). 41, **myȝt** VIII. 2

**myght, myȝt** *v. see* **mow**
**myghtful** *adj.* powerful, efficacious VI (vi). 277
**myghty** *adj.* strong VIII. 386
**mykel** *see* **myche** *adj.*
**myld(e)** *adj.* gentle, meek III. 170, VI (iii). 6, VI (vi). 52
**mildely*** *adv.* gently VI (vi). 152
**mynd(e)** *n.* memory II. 173, III. 131, VII 171, VIII. 226, VIII. 557; thought VIII. 9
**mynd** *subj.sg.* think II. 121
**mynys** *n.gen.pl.* mines' VIII. 207
**mynstralcie** *n.* music I. 583
**myrroure** *n.* mirror VIII. 139
**myrth, mirth** *n.* joy, pleasure I. 615, II. 49, II. 54, VI (i). 44, VI (iii). 5, VI (iv). 51
**mysaise** *n.* discomfort, distress I. 751
**mysdede** *n.* sin VI (vi). 195; *pl.* **mysdedes** VI (vi). 78, VIII. 126
**mysel** *n.* leper VIII. 315
**my self** *pron.refl.* myself VI (vi). 240, VI (vi). 255, VIII. 171
**myslike** *v.impers.* displease V. 7
**myspay** *v.* displease I. 533
**myspaynge** *adj.* displeasing I. 136
**mysse** *v.* fail to attain VI (vi). 8
**myssiggynge** *n.* slander, abuse I. 354
**moche** *see* **myche** *adj.*
**mode** *n.* heart, feeling VI (vi). 88
**modelynge** *pr.p.* wallowing I. 271
**modyr(e), moder** *n.* mother II. 96, VI (vi). 61, VIII. 331, III. 89, VI (vi). 202, VII. 2; *gen.* **moderes** VIII. 517
**mone** *n.*[1] moon I. 591, II. 22, VIII. 362*
**mone** *n.*[2] moan VI (vi). 52, VI (vi). 201
**mor(e), moor(e)** *adj.comp.* greater I. 13, I. 152, II. 32, III. 18, III. 121, I. 78, I. 110, I. 379 *etc.*; *as n.* II. 10; *as pron.* **moo** VI (vi). 123; *sup.* **most(e)** I. 193, I. 738, II. 31, III. 49, VIII. 141, **moost** I. 64, **meste** VI (vi). 217
**mor(e)** *adv.comp.* more I. 85, I. 182, I. 362, II. 28, III. 65, VI (iv). 35, VI (vi). 118, **moor(e)** I. 80, I. 182, VI (vi). 118, I. 401 again, **mare** I. 601, VI (i). 43, VI (iv). 35, VI (i). 58 longer; ~ **yit** VIII. 236 moreover; *sup.* **most(e)** I. 819, II. 28, III. 64, III. 166, VI (iii). 9, VIII. 91
**morne** *n.* morning VII. 151
**morsel** *n.* bite, mouthful I. 511, II. 80
**most(e)** *see* **more, mot**
**mot(e)** *pr.1,3 sg.* may VI (vi). 16, VI (vi). 44, VI (vi). 224; *pa.t.pl.* **most** must I. 293, I. 480, I. 859
**mount** *n.* hill VI (vi). 38, VII. 103, VIII. 51
**mourne** *v.* lament, pine VI (vi). 148; *pr.1 sg.* II. 290
**mournynge** *n.* lamentation I. 603, VI (iii). 4, VI (vi). 144, VIII. 313
**mouth** *n.* mouth, speech I. 575, II. 241, III. 140, VII. 164
**mowe** *v.*[1] be able, have power to III. 60; *pr.1,3 sg.* **may** can, may I. 25, I. 665, II. 79, II. 199, III. 18, III. 194, IV. 4, V. 3, VI (i). 6, VI (iii). 21, VII. 25, VIII. 65 *etc.*, **mow** VI (iv). 67, VIII. 223; *2 sg.* **may** I. 42, I. 263, II. 15, III. 24, VI (i). 4, VI (iv). 26, VI (iv). 65, VI (v). 4, VII. 63, **maist** I. 261, **mayist** VII. 153, **mow** I. 523, I. 561; *pl.* **may** I. 4, II. 89, III. 13, VI (i). 25, VI (iv). 99, VIII. 126, **mow(e)** I. 4, I. 472, II. 250, VIII. 126, **mowen** I. 56; *pa.t.sg.* could, might **myght** I. 16, I. 176, II. 6, II. 274, V. 5, VI (i). 14, VIII. 298, **myȝt** I. 525, VIII. 124; *pl.* **myght** I. 101, I. 69, **myȝt** VII. 39
**mowe** *v.*[2] make a grimace I. 361
**mowes** *n.pl.* grimaces VIII. 151
**multitude** *n.* abundance I. 578

**nayle** *n.* nail VII. 108; *pl.* **naylles** VI (vi). 171, VIII. 276, **nailles** VIII. 380, **nayllys** VIII. 384, **nales** VII. 86
**nayled** *pa.t.pl.* nailed VII. 108, VIII. 374; *p.p.* **naillet** II. 182, **nailled** II. 189, VIII. 548, **nayled** VI (iii). 18
**naylynge** *n.* nailling VIII. 425
**naked** *adj.* naked II. 184, III. 159, VI (ii). 36, VII. 105, VIII. 188; unembellished I. 404; *as n.* I. 854
**naked** *pa.t.pl.* stripped VII. 91
**name** *n.* reputation I. 90; name I. 611, II. 140, III. 142, VI (vi). 281
**name** *v.* name II. 247, **neune** I. 350; *p.p.* **named** II. 239, **nempned** I. 615
**name** *pa.t.2 sg.* took VI (vi). 48
**namely, nameli** *adv.* especially I. 418, I. 492, III. 14, I. 262, **namly** VIII. 121
**nan** *see* **none** *pron.*
**nat** *adv.* not I. 5, II. 7, III. 10, V. 3, VI (i). 19, VI (v). 3, VI (vi). 114, VIII. 52 *etc.*, **noght** I. 444, II. 156, VI (iii). 8, VI (iv). 99, VI (vi). 294, **noȝt** I. 419, **nouȝt** VII. 39, **not** VII. 63; otherwise VI (v). 10
**nat** *n.* nothing I. 75, I. 143, I. 547, I. 636, II. 205, VIII. 427, **noght** I. 463, I. 654, II. 11, III. 44, IV. 22, VI (ii). 8, VI (vi). 23, VIII. 1, **noȝt** VIII. 346, **nouȝt** VII. 93

**natforþi** *adv.* nevertheless I. 151, III. 117

**natwithstondynge, natwithstandynge** *prep.* in spite of VIII. 436, VIII. 438

**ne** *adv.* nor I. 4, II. 161, III. 28, VI (i). 2, VI (vi). 22, VII. 25, VIII. 22 *etc.*; not I. 137, I. 630, II. 67, VI (vi). 56, VII. 112 *etc.*

**necessaries** *n.pl.* necessities I. 369, I. 851

**nede, need** *n.* need II. 244, III. 49, VI (iv). 37, VI (vi). 318, I. 64, I. 147, I. 186 necessity; *pl.* **nedes** I. 821

**nedeful(le)** *adj.* necessary VI (vi). 126, VIII. 92

**nedeth** *pr.3 sg.intr.* is necessary II. 163, VIII. 523

**need** *adj.* necessary I. 360; *& see* **nede**

**negh** *adv.* nearly I. 804; near VI (i). 11, VI (iv). 87, **nere** II. 208, VI (iv). 22, VIII. 343, **ney** VIII. 450

**negh** *v.* approach VI (iv). 43; *pr.3 sg.* **negheth** VI (iv). 87

**neghbore** *n.* neighbour, fellow being I. 393, II. 74, III. 23; *gen.* **neghbors** I. 390

**negligently** *adv.* carelessly I. 388

**ney** *see* **negh** *adv.*

**nek(e)** *n.* neck VII. 68, VII. 79

**nempned** *see* **name** *v.*

**nere** *see* **negh** *adv.*

**nesshe** *adj.* soft VIII. 502

**nestes** *n.pl.* nests VIII. 431

**neþer, nether** *adv.*[1] nor, neither I. 4, I. 456, III. 27, VIII. 361, **noþer** I. 63, III. 144

**neþer*** *adv.*[2] lower VIII. 491

**net(te)** *n.* net VIII. 212, VIII. 215

**neuer** *adv.* never I. 56, II. 4, III. 48, VI (ii). 20, VI (iii). 7, VI (vi). 8, VIII. 22 *etc.*, **neuyr(e)** VIII. 157, VIII. 264

**neuerþelatre, neuerþelattre, neuerþelatter** *adv.* nevertheless I. 170, I. 243, I. 483, II. 151

**neune** *see* **name**

**new(e)** *adj.* new, fresh VI (iii). 2, VI (iv). 83, VIII. 549; *as n.* VI (i) 42.

**next** *adj.sup.* nearest I. 501, II. 19

**nyght** *n.* night I. 471, II. 12, III. 74, IV. 14, VI (i). 3, VI (ii). 22, VI (iii). 1, VI (vi). 10, VIII. 197; darkness I. 608; **nyȝt** VI (vi). 108, VIII. 198; *gen.* **nyghtes** VI (iii). 15

**nyghtgalle** *n.* nightingale I. 572

**nys** *see* **is**

**no** *adv.* not I. 334

**no(n), none, noon** *adj.* no I. 6, I. 466, II. 9, III. 7, IV. 5, VI (i). 6, III. 25, VIII. 73 *etc.*

**nobely** *n.* noble estate VIII. 26

**nobily** *adv.* finely VI (vi). 326

**noght, noȝt** *see* **nat**

**noy** *n.* trouble, distress I. 135, I. 352, II. 52, III. 145; displeasure I. 338; *pl.* **noyes** I. 806, disturbances I. 825

**non(e), noon** *pron.* none, nobody I. 197, I. 428, I. 657, VI (i). 13, VI (iv). 72, VI (v). 9, VI (vi). 354, VII. 166, VIII. 362, **nan** VI (vi). 367; **noon** VI (ii). 46 nothing

**nor** *adv.* nor VI (vi). 56

**nose** *n.* nose VII. 163

**notable** *adj.* useful II. 172

**noþer** *pron.* neither I. 439; *& see* **neþer** *adv.*[1]

**nothynge** *adv.* in no way VI (v). 18

**noumbre** *n.* frequency I. 378

**now(e)** *adv.* now I. 105, I. 756, II. 42, III. 198, V. 5, VI (i). 34 *etc.*

**nurisshe** *v.* nourish III. 140

**o(o)** *see* **one** *adj.*

**obleged** *p.p.* bound I. 659

**obstakle** *n.* hindrance IV. 13

**obstinacioun** *n.* obduracy I. 338

**occupacioun** *n.* occupation, activity I. 288, III. 14; *pl.* **occupaciouns** I. 269, VIII. 5

**ocupien** *pr.pl.refl.* busy, concern oneself I. 238; *p.p.* **occupied** I. 237, I. 821, VIII. 15

**of** *adv.* off VII. 104, VIII. 284 *etc.*

**of** *prep.* (*in gen. & partitive functions*) of; (*of motion*) from VIII. 65; (*of person or place*) from I. 31, I. 229, IV. 4, VII. 140; (*of origin*) belonging to, from I. 2, I. 114, IV. 1, VII. 56, VIII. 4; (*of cause*) for, because of I. 513, I. 847, III. 147, V. 1, VI (iv). 27, VIII. 514; (*of agent*) by I. 44, I. 223, I. 863, II. 227, VIII. 76, VIII. 295, VII. 21, from II. 221; (*of concern*) about, for I. 36, I. 166, VI (vi). 78, VIII. 102, VII. 5, VII. 66; (*with vbs. of request*) for II. 148, VIII. 29 *etc.*

**office** *n.* appointment, position I. 373

**offre** *v.* offer, sacrifice II. 35; *pr.2 sg.* **offres** I. 762; *subj.sg.* **offre** I. 251; *p.p.* **offred** VII. 18, **offerd** VII. 43

**offryng(e)** *n.* sacrifice, offering VII. 17, I. 70

**oft(e), often** *adv.* often I. 57, II. 173*, VIII. 193, VIII. 460 *etc.*; ~ **tymes** I. 27, VIII. 335, ~ **sith(e)** I. 94, II. 5, III. 118, ~ **syth** I. 77, ~ **sithes** I. 349, III. 86

**oft** *adj.* frequent VIII. 41

**oght** *adv.* in any respect I. 146, VI (vi). 302, **ouȝte** VII. 173

**oght** *n.* anything I. 281, I. 462, VI (vi). 126 *etc.*, **ouȝte** VII. 157
**oght** *v. see* **owe**
**olde** *adj.* (*as n.*) old VI (i). 49
**omyssioun** *n.* omission I. 381
**on** *prep.* (*of place*) on, in III. 207, VI (vi). 28, VII. 119, VIII. 72, VIII. 372; (*of time*) on, in VII. 17; (*of regard*) on II. 133, VIII. 135; (*of concern*) of, about III. 4, VIII. 431, VII. 38; (*with vbs. of belief etc.*) in I. 475, *etc.*
**on(e)** *adj.* one I. 638, II. 67, III. 150, IV. 9, VI (i). 56, VII. 116, VIII. 54, **oon** I. 131, I. 406, I. 432, II. 148, III. 107, VIII. 70, VIII. 193, **o** I. 581, III. 214, **oo** I. 531, VIII. 525, **a** I. 114, I. 465, I. 828, VII. 39; *with* **by** *& poss.adj.* alone I. 129, II. 125, III. 58; *with* **by** *& acc.pron.* I. 162, I. 877; **by one** II. 44
**on(e), oon** *pron.* one I. 42, I. 428, VI (iii). 1, VIII. 499
**ondynge*** *pr.p.* panting I. 558
**onely** *adj.* solitary II. 224
**ony** *see* **any**
**only** *adv.* only I. 18, II. 56, III. 11, VI (ii). 2, VIII. 104 *etc.*, **oonly** I. 239
**oops** *n.pl.* works I. 291
**opyn** *v.* open VIII. 501; *pr.3 sg.* **openeth** I. 619; *pl.* **opyn** VIII. 379; *pa.t.sg.* **opened** VIII. 504; *p.p.* **open** VI (vi). 176
**opynly** *adv.* without concealment VIII. 123
**oppyn** *adj.* overt I. 99, I. 19
**or** *conj.* or I. 21, II. 5, IV. 10, VI (iii). 3, VI (vi). 99, VIII. 65 *etc.*; *& see* **ar**
**ordeyn(e)** *v.* direct, rule, conform I. 326, I. 850; prepare I. 12, II. 52; *pr.3 sg.* **ordeyneth** VI (iv). 24; *subj.pl.* **ordeyn** II. 63; *imp.sg.* **ordeyn** III. 62, **ordayn** II. 309; *p.p.* **ordeyned** I. 645 fittingly placed; destined I. 654*, II. 38, I. 519, III. 204, VIII. 32, **ordeynet** I. 875; directed II. 124; allotted VII. 149 **ordened**
**ordeynour** *n.* ruler I. 210
**ordynaunce** *n.* decree VIII. 35; *pl.* **ordinaunces** VIII. 102
**ordre** *n.* rank I. 504; religious order III. 158; *pl.* **ordres** II. 16, III. 223
**ore** *n.* mercy VI (vi). 36, VI (vi). 80
**orisone, orisoun** *n.* prayer IV. 21, VIII. 50, VII. 83
**orrible** *see* **horrible**
**orwhiles** *see* **oþer while**
**oste** *see* **hoste**
**oþer(e), other(e), oþre** *adj.* other, second I. 6, I. 381, II. 5, II. 237, III. 16, IV. 3, VI (vi). 142, VI (vi). 197, VII. 68, VII. 163, VIII. 340 *etc.*, **othyr** VIII. 147; (*with* **þe**) **toþer, tother** I. 403, I. 526, II. 95, II. 238, III. 26, VII. 113
**oþer(e), other(e)** *pron.* the other, someone else, some I. 592, I. 640, II. 24, III. 134, VIII. 338, **othyr(e)** VIII. 339, VIII. 179; *pl.* **others** I. 333, **oþre** I. 347, **oþer** I. 42, **othre** I. 31, I. 343; **auþer*** I. 531 either of two
**oþer, other** *conj.* either, or I. 34, I. 175, II. 171, III. 61, III. 148
**oþer/other/othre while** *adv.* sometimes I. 154, I. 205, I. 208, **orwhiles** I. 204
**ouȝte** *see* **oght**
**our(e)** *see* **we**
**oure self** *pron.refl.* ourselves I. 192
**out** *adv.* away I. 403, III. 95, VIII. 57, VIII. 534; outside I. 747
**outcast** *p.p.* rejected, thrown out VIII. 399*, VIII. 415; *pr.p.* **outcastynge** III. 75
**outrage** *n.* intemperance, excess I. 46, I. 213, I. 437, III. 105
**outrageous** *adj.* immoderate III. 109
**outrageouslye** *adv.* excessively I. 70
**outtake** *pr.1 sg.* omit, except I. 441
**outtaken** *prep.* except I. 541
**outward** *adj.* external I. 838
**ouene** *adj.* oven VII. 74
**ouer** *prep.* above, beyond I. 305, VI (vi). 4, VI (vi). 272, VIII. 527
**ouer** *adv.* too I. 45, I. 181, III. 63
**ouercomers** *n.pl.* victors I. 664
**ouercum** *v.* defeat I. 528, II. 150, III. 27, III. 179; *pr.3 sg.* **ouercometh** VI (i). 68; *pl.* **ouercomen** I. 153; *subj.pl.* **ouercum** I. 711; *p.p.* **ouercome(n)** I. 112, I. 453, II. 166
**ouerhope** *n.* overconfidence, presumption VIII. 71
**ouer-ron** *adj.* overflowing VIII. 322
**ouertrist** *n.* overconfidence VIII. 171
**owe** *v.* (i) owe VI (vi). 253; (ii) be obliged to VI (vi). 159 *& elsewhere*; *pr.1 sg.* **ow(e)** VI (vi). 169, VI (vi). 159, VI (vi). 253; *3 sg.* **oweth** I. 101, I. 337, **owet** VI (vi). 306; *impers.* I. 385; *pl.* **owen** I. 357; *pa.t.sg.* **oght** II. 154, III. 173
**owne, owen** *adj.* own I. 390, III. 17, VI (vi). 306, VIII. 116; **myn** ~ VIII. 354 that which is mine

**paciens, pacience** *n.* patience VI (vi). 282, I. 249, VIII. 184
**paciently** *adv.* patiently VIII. 132
**pacis** *n.pl.* paces VIII. 116, **pases** steps I. 62
**pay(e)** *v.* please, satisfy I. 665, II. 57, VI (iv). 1; *pr.3 sg.* **payeth** II. 144, VI (i). 29; *p.p.* **paied** I. 519, III. 148, **payed** IV. 26; *pr.p.* **paynge** III. 55
**paynge** *n.* pleasure II. 295
**pale** *adj.* pale II. 281, VI (i). 10, VIII. 452
**palle** *n.* altar cloth II. 280
**paradis(s)e** *n.* heaven VIII. 446, VI (vi). 200
**parchemyn** *adj.* parchment VIII. 382
**parsonel** *n.* sharer, partaker I. 669
**parte** *n.* portion, share VIII. 456, **partie** part I. 105, I. 676
**partener** *n.* sharer VI (vi). 288
**parteth** *pr.3 sg.* departs VI (iv). 63; *subj.sg.* **part** share III. 104, VI (vi). 286; *imp.sg.* **part** share VIII. 358
**passe** *v.* (i) *intr.* go, stray II. 134, I. 252, III. 113; *pr.3 sg.* **passeth** II. 84; *pl.* **passe** II. 26, VIII. 433, **passeth** III. 206; *subj.sg.* **passe** III. 131, VI (vi). 43; *pa.t.sg.* **passed** VIII. 332; *p.p.* past, ended **passed** I. 154; *pr.p.* **passynge** I. 883; (ii) exceed, surpass I. 197; *pr.3 sg.* **passeth** I. 843; *pl.* **passen** I. 46; *pr.p.* **passynge** I. 40
**passynge** *adj.* transitory I. 10, I. 757, III. 44
**passyngely** *adv.* briefly I. 758
**passioun** *n.* suffering, the Crucifixion II. 45, III. 175, VII. 1, VIII. 29, **passione** II. 174, **passion** VII. 170
**paued** *p.p.* paved VII. 78
**pece** *n.* piece VIII. 286
**pees** *n.* peace I. 632, I. 772
**peyn(e), pyne** *n.* pain, punishment, distress I. 130, I. 341, I. 723, III. 46, III. 113, III. 41, III. 177, VI (i). 32, VI (ii). 17, VI (iv). 4, VI (v). 21, VI (vi). 43, VII. 99, VIII. 27, VIII. 124 *etc.*, **payn(e)** VII. 40, VIII. 187, **peynt** I. 719; *pl.* **peyn(e)s** VI (vi). 54, VI (vi) 222, VII. 54, VIII. 251, VIII. 406
**peyn(e), pyne** *v.* punish, afflict, torture I. 74, VIII. 253, III. 195, VI (ii). 39; *pa.t.sg.* **pyned** VIII. 488; *p.p.* **p(e)yned** VI (vi). 121, VIII. 423
**peynful** *adj.* painful VIII. 28
**peynteth** *pr.3 sg.* depicts, visualizes II. 280; *p.p.* **peynted** painted III. 151
**peyntynge** *n.* cosmetic adornment II. 86
**penaunce, penauns** *n.* penance I. 11, II. 41, II. 231, III. 66, VIII. 12, I. 291
**peple, pepil** *n.* people VIII. 310, VIII. 325
**perauentur, peraduenture** *adv.* perhaps III. 194, I. 833, II. 42
**pere** *n.* equal I. 550
**perfeccioun** *n.* consummation I. 649; perfect state I. 895, III. 9
**perfit(e)** *adj.* perfect I. 278, I. 466, II. 95, III. 37; righteous II. 105
**perfitly** *adv.* completely I. 83, I. 235, II. 15, II. 261; perfectly III. 12
**perfitnes** *n.* righteousness III. 144
**peril(le)** *n.* danger I. 69, I. 839
**perillous** *adv.* dangerously I. 182
**perisshe** *v.* perish, die I. 410, III. 48; *pr.3 sg.* **perisshethe** II. 84; *p.p.* **perist** VII. 51
**perle** *n.* pearl VIII. 208
**perles** *adj.* unequalled VIII. 240
**perpetuel** *adj.* eternal VIII. 171
**perplexite** *n.* moral indecision I. 336
**persecucioun** *n.* persecution II. 113
**persheth** *pr.3 sg.* pierces VIII. 294; *subj.sg.* **pershe** VI (vi). 259; *pa.t.pl.* **persed** VIII. 540
**persone** *n.* person, identity I. 378
**pesynge** *pr.p.* appeasing I. 395
**piller(e)** *n.* whipping post II. 178, VIII. 188, **piler** VII. 91
**pyn-** *see* **peyne**
**pitevous** *adj.* piteous VIII. 286
**pitte** *n.* pit VII. 162
**pitte** *n.* pity, mercy VI (vi). 427, VII. 156, VII. 169; cause for regret II. 188, VI (iii). 19, **pite** VII. 168
**place** *n.* dwelling place VI (iv). 24; location VI (vi). 215, VIII. 32, **plas** VIII. 408; public appearance I. 606; *pl.* **places** VIII. 155
**play(e), playnge** *n.* amusement, diversion VI (i). 59, VI (iv). 100, I. 606; delight VI (iv). 4
**plenerly** *adv.* fully I. 730
**plente** *n.* abundance VIII. 417
**plenteuous** *adj.* abundant VIII. 195
**plenteuously** *adv.* lavishly VIII. 267
**plese** *v.* please, satisfy I. 80; *pr.3 sg.* **pleseth** VIII. 260
**ploumbe** *n.* plum I. 756
**poynt(e)** *n.* small part, detail I. 486, VIII. 35, VIII. 507; instant I. 281, III. 202; **in** ~ on the verge of I. 410
**poysone*** *n.* poison VIII. 466

**poysoned** *p.p.* poisoned II. 80
**polisshynge** *n.* over-refinement I. 361
**pompe** *n.* ostentation III. 209
**pore** *see* **pouer**
**porely** *adv.* wretchedly VI (iv). 63
**possible** *adj.* possible I. 804
**possyng** *pr.p.* trampling VII. 111
**potestates** *n.pl.* embodiments of spiritual power II. 18
**pouer** *adj.* poor, wretched, humble I. 334, I. 651, II. 108, III. 100, VI (iv). 29, VIII. 298, *as n.* VIII. 359, **pore** II. 165, VIII. 426
**pouert(e)** *n.* poverty I. 248, I. 396, I. 458, I. 685, II. 97, III. 98, VIII. 25
**power(e)** *n.* ability I. 113, I. 370, I. 853
**pray** *v.* pray, beseech I. 409, II. 44, VIII. 52, **prey** I. 128; *pr.1 sg.* **pray(e)** II. 139, III. 197, VI (iv). 68, VI (vi). 42, VIII. 169, VII. 172; *2 sg.* **praiest** I. 516, III. 73; *3 sg.* **prayeth*** VI (vi). 321; *imp.sg.* **pray(e)** I. 896, VI (vi). 162, VII. 172; *pa.t.2 sg.* **prayed** VII. 44, VIII. 54; *3 sg.* **praide** VII. 40, **praiede** VII. 123, **prayde** VII. 36, **prayed** VII. 37; *pr.p.* **praiynge** I. 867
**prayer(e), praier** *n.* prayer I. 102, III. 61, VI (vi). 40, VI (vi). 91, VIII. 50, **prier** I. 157; *pl.* **prayers, praiers** III. 124, II. 127, **priers** I. 60, I. 251
**prayinge, praiynge, praynge** *n.* act of prayer III. 129, III. 62, II. 133, I. 509, VI (iv). 107
**praise, preise** *v.* praise I. 461, I. 362; *pr.3 sg.* **prayseth** I. 580; *pl.* **praise** I. 460, **preisen** I. 37, I. 813; *imp.sg.* **preise** I. 511; *p.p.* **praised** I. 512, **preiset** I. 89; *pr.p.* **praisynge** I. 300
**praysynge, praisynge, preisynge** *n.* praise, praising I. 97, I. 98, I. 457, III. 71, I. 573, VI (i). 24, I. 89
**prech** *pr.1 sg.* preach, advise II. 11; *pa.t.sg.* **preched(e)** VII. 19, VII. 21
**precious(e)** *adj.* precious, estimable I. 739, III. 114, VI (vi). 131, VIII. 152, VIII. 272, VII. 31
**prey** *see* **pray**
**preis-** *see* **praise, praysynge**
**pres(e)** *n.* throng VIII. 310, VIII. 331
**presens, presence** *n.* presence I. 173, VIII. 175
**present** *adj.* present I. 842; readily accessible VI (vi). 162
**presentes** *pr.2 sg.* offer I. 250
**prest** *n.* priest I. 406
**presumpcioun** *n.* arrogance I. 156
**presumptuouse** *adj.* arrogant, unduly confident VIII. 22
**price** *n.* value, cost I. 817, VI (vi). 131
**prickynge** *n.* pricking II. 180
**pride, pryde** *n.* pride I. 33, II. 74, III. 101, VI (ii). 10, VI (iv). 5, VIII. 146, VIII. 261 *etc.*
**prier(s)** *see* **prayere**
**prike** *n.* cause of remorse VIII. 355
**priketh** *pr.3 sg.* pricks VI (iv). 30; *pa.t.sg.* **prikked** VIII. 291
**principaly, principali** *adv.* particularly II. 172, III. 130
**principatis** *n.pl.* high ranking spiritual beings II. 18
**prisone** *n.* prison I. 397, I. 856, VII. 77; *pl.* **prisons** VIII. 153
**prisoned** *p.p.* imprisoned VII. 77
**priue, pryue** *adj.* secret, intimate I. 99, I. 427, II. 110, VIII. 484
**priuelege** *n.* favour I. 775
**priuely** *adv.* stealthily I. 27, I. 182
**pryuetees** *n.pl.* divine mysteries I. 140
**processioun** *n.* procession VIII. 326
**profecied** *p.p.* prophesied VII. 129
**profered** *pa.t.sg.* offered, sacrificed VIII. 31
**profitable** *adj.* beneficial, useful I. 415, III. 130, II. 34
**profite** *n.* profit, benefit I. 111, I. 390
**profite** *v.* avail, be of benefit to VIII. 38; *subj.sg.* I. 896, VII. 173
**prophecie** *n.* prophecy I. 650
**prophet** *n.* prophet I. 66
**prosperite** *n.* good fortune VIII. 215
**proud** *adj.* arrogant, proud II. 39, VIII. 22; ostentatious VI (vi). 326; *as n.* VI (v). 16; **prout** I. 724
**proudhede** *n.* arrogance VI (i). 59
**proueth** *pr.3 sg.* proves, shows I. 694; *p.p.* **proued** III. 138; tested III. 187, **prouet** I. 453
**psalme** *n.* psalm VII. 82; *pl.* **psalmes** I. 561, II. 129
**psauter** *n.* psalter II. 130
**pul** *subj.sg.* pull VIII. 215; *pa.t.pl.* **pulled** VIII. 76, VIII. 277
**punysshe** *subj.sg.* punish I. 749, VI (v). 5; *p.p.* **punshed** I. 293
**purchace*** *v.* obtain III. 192*; *imp.sg.* III. 184*, VI (v). 24*
**pure** *adj.* true, unsullied IV. 2

**purgatorie, purgatory** *n.* purgatory II. 261, VIII. 183
**purge** *v.* cleanse, purify III. 186; *pr.3 sg.* **purgeth** I. 126, I. 616, III. 118; *p.p.* **purget** III. 124
**purpos** *n.* intention VIII. 533
**purpur** *n.* purple clothing VIII. 252
**pursued** *p.p.* pursued VIII. 222
**purtee** *n.* cleanness I. 637
**put** *v.* place; *with* **out/away** dispel; *pr.1 sg.* VI (vi). 303; *3 sg.* **putteth** I. 29, I. 619, III. 220; *pl.* **putteth** I. 158; *subj.sg.* **put** I. 555, VIII. 57; *pa.t.pl.* **putted** shoved VIII. 278; *p.p.* **put** I. 403, II. 125, VI (iv). 63

**quaynt** *adj.* cunning I. 162
**quayntise** *n.* trick, stratagem VI (iv). 19
**quake** *v.* shiver, tremble VI (i). 61, VI (v). 13; be unsteadfast VI (iv). 52
**quathis** *n.pl.* fainting fits I. 448
**quede** *n.* wretchedness, evil VI (i). 47
**quelle** *v.* kill VI (iii). 24
**queme** *v.* please I. 136; *p.p.* **quemed** VI (v). 18
**quenche** *v.* extinguish III. 30, VIII. 467, **quenchen** VI (i). 6; *p.p.* **quenched** I. 792
**quene** *n.* queen VI (vi). 61
**quert** *n.* health II. 294, VI (i). 15, VI (ii). 18, VI (iv). 15
**questions** *n.pl.* questions I. 629
**quyet** *n.* silence I. 768
**quyk** *adj.* alive VIII. 502
**quykkest** *pr.2 sg.* animate, bring to life VIII. 393; *imp.sg.* **quyken** VIII. 394
**quyt** *p.p.* free of debt I. 857
**quod** *pa.t.2 sg.* said VI (vi). 207

**rabble** *v.* gabble I. 387
**rabil** *n.* disorderly mob II. 89
**raght** *see* **reche**
**rake** *n.* rack VIII. 383
**ran** *see* **ren**
**rased** *p.p.* cut, slashed VIII. 282
**rauyn** *n.* robbery I. 368; **of** ~ stolen I. 70
**rauyssheth** *pr.3 sg.* transports, carries away VI (i). 16; *p.p.* **rauist** I. 887, **rauyst** II. 146
**rauysshynge** *adj.* plundering I. 684
**rebelle (to)** *v.* rebel (against) I. 374
**rebukynge** *n.* reproach VIII. 157
**receyue** *v.* receive, accept I. 159, III. 120; ~ **god** I. 365 take communion; *pr.3 sg.* **receyueth** I. 473; *subj.sg.* **receyue** III. 7; *imp.sg.* **receyue** II. 196, VIII. 535; *p.p.* **receyued** II. 30
**rech-** *see* **rek**
**reche** *v.* reach IV. 6; *pr.3 sg.* **recheth** VIII. 379 stretches; *pa.t.pl.* **raght** VIII. 375
**recluse** *n.* recluse I. 166
**rede** *v.* (i) advise *pr.1 sg.* I. 451, III. 104, III. 214, VI (i). 45; (ii) read *pr.1 sg.* VI (vi). 193; *3 sg.* **redeth** II. 218; *pl.* **rede** I. 119
**rede** *adj.* red II. 184, VI (vi). 247, VIII. 236, **reed** VI (ii). 37
**redy** *adj.* prepared, willing I. 286, I. 448, VIII. 15; available VI (vi). 308
**redynge** *n.* reading VIII. 240
**reed** *see* **rede** *adj.*
**ref(t)** *see* **reue**
**refuyt** *n.* refuge VII. 165, VIII. 224
**regard** *see* **reward**
**reghtest** *see* **ryght** *adj.*
**rek** *v.* care I. 387; *pr.1 sg.* **rech(e)** VI (vi). 294, VI (vi). 154; *imp.sg.* **rech** VI (iv). 8
**rekenyng** *n.* account VII. 146
**rekkynge** *n.* regard, care VIII. 350
**religioun** *n.* religious order III. 153
**religious** *adj.* (*as n.*) a genuine member of a religious order III. 157
**remedy** *n.* redress I. 156
**remeve** *v.* remove, take away III. 60; *pr.3 sg.* **remoueth** I. 617
**ren** *v.* run, flow II. 136, VIII. 288; *pr.pl.* VIII. 384; *imp.sg.* VII. 168; *pa.t.sg.* **ran** II. 283, extended VI (i). 9; *pl.* **ran** VI (vi). 58*, VIII. 449; *pr.p.* **rennynge** I. 828
**rent** *p.p.* lacerated VIII. 282
**repente** *v.* repent VIII. 126
**repressynge** *n.* suppression IV. 10
**reproue** *v.* censure, reproach I. 358; *pr.pl.* **reproue(n)** I. 720, I. 38; *subj.sg.* **reproue** III. 105
**repro(e)ues** *n.pl.* rebukes I. 712, VII. 24
**rer** *v.* raise, lift III. 191; *pr.3 sg.* **rereth** III. 181; *pa.t.sg.* **rered** VIII. 503
**reserued** *p.p.* kept I. 782
**resonable** *adj.* sensible, moderate II. 157
**resseit** *n.* remedy VIII. 250
**rest(e)** *n.* rest I. 124, I. 584, II. 41, III. 147, IV. 4, VI (i). 3, VI (iii). 15, VI (vi). 100, VII. 170, VIII. 6 *etc.*
**rest(e)** *v.* rest VII. 57, VIII. 16; *pr.3 sg.* **resteth** I. 709; *pr.p.* **restynge** I. 558, III. 212*
**restfuller** *adj.comp.* more restful I. 840
**restore** *imp.sg.* bring back VIII. 142

**restregnynge** *n.* restraint IV. 9
**restreyne** *v.* restrain, hold back II. 261; *imp.sg.* III. 53
**reteyne*** *v.* keep back, fail to disclose I. 377
**reten** *see* **roteth**
**reul** *v.* rule, govern I. 485, I. 610; *subj.sg.* **reule** VIII. 117
**reuth** *n* pity VIII. 287
**reuthful** *adj.* piteous VIII. 312
**reue** *v.* take away II. 137; *pr.3 sg.* **reueth** I. 254, VI (iii). 15; *imp.sg.* **ref** VI (ii). 3; *pa.t.pl.* **rof** VII. 104; *p.p.* **reft** I. 448, II. 214
**reuelacioun** *n.* revelation I. 224; *pl.* **reuelaciouns** I. 139 visions; I. 148 disclosures
**reuerence** *n.* respect I. 351
**reward** *n.* heed VIII. 285; **in regard of** I. 846 in comparison to
**rewe** *v.* have pity II. 309; regret VI (iv). 84; *pr.3 sg. impers.* **reweth** VI (vi). 77 grieves, *pers.* VI (vi). 209*; *imp.sg.* **rew** VI (vi). 393
**rewes** *see* **blode**
**rewful** *adj.* pitiful VI (vi). 55
**rich(e)** *adj.* rich I. 335, II. 109, III. 102, VI (i). 65, **ryche** I. 354; *comp.* **richer** I. 344; *sup.* **rychest** III. 43
**richely** *adv.* richly III. 151
**riches(se)** *n.pl.* wealth I. 23, I. 335, I. 651, II. 51, III. 99, III. 205, VI (iv). 8, **richesses** II. 86
**right** *adj.* true, proper, fitting I. 147, VI (vi). 146; **ryȝt** righthand VII. 111, VIII. 437; *sup.* **reghtest** truest I. 647
**right** *adv.* correctly I. 199, I. 741, II. 145, III. 87, III. 178; directly I. 272; very I. 169; exactly I. 721
**right, ryght, ryȝt** *n.* justice I. 727, VIII. 354, VIII. 357, VI (i). 306; correct course VI (iv). 44
**ryghtyn** *v.* put to rights VIII. 515; *p.p.* **ryȝted** VIII. 524
**rightwise** *adj.* virtuous I. 457, I. 657, **rightuous(e)** I. 287, I. 780
**rightwisly** *adv.* virtuously II. 117
**rightwisnesse** *n.* virtue, righteousness I. 456; justice I. 368, I. 481
**rynge** *n.* ring VI (vi). 403; dance II. 194; *pl.* **rynges** VI (vi). 327 rings
**ryngen** *n.* resonant noise II. 225
**ryngeth** *pr.3 sg.* resounds VI (v). 17
**rise, ryse** *v.* rise, arise I. 11, I. 256, II. 67*, VI (i). 62, VII. 58, VIII. 507; *imp.sg.* VII. 153; *pl.* VI (v). 17; *pa.t.sg.* **rose** VII. 143; *pl.* **rissen** VIII. 539; *p.p.* **risen** VI (ii). 45
**robes** *n.pl.* fine clothes III. 86
**rod(e), rood(e)** *n.* the Cross VI (vi). 133, VII. 123, VIII. 378, I. 514, II. 193, VI (ii). 36, VI (vi). 95, VII. 138; ~ **tre** VI (vi). 28, VI (vi). 178
**rof** *see* **reue**
**roosynge** *n.* boasting I. 360
**root(e)** *see* **rote, rot**
**rope** *n.* rope VII. 67
**rot** *imp.sg.* root, establish III. 216, **root** VI (ii). 17
**rote** *n.* root VI (vi). 14; innermost part VII. 139; *pl.* **rootes** VII. 75
**roteth** *pr.pl.* rot II. 86, **reten** III. 152
**roughe** *adj.* rugged VII. 95
**roust** *n.* rust, moral corrosion II. 249, III. 186
**rowed** *pa.t.pl.* rotated VII. 117
**rowt** *n.* mob VIII. 345

**sacrementes, sacrementȝ** *n.pl.* sacraments VIII. 101, I. 650
**sacrilege** *n.* sacrilege I. 365
**safe** *see* **saue**
**say, sey, sei** *v.* say I. 424, II. 129, III. 69, I. 10, I. 353; *pr.1 sg.* **sei** I. 179, **say** I. 579, II. 218, VI (i). 4, VI (iii). 6, VI (iv). 68, VII. 147; *2 sg.* **saist** I. 520, **seist** I. 522; *3 sg.* **seith** I. 66, III. 154, **saith** III. 84; *pl.* **seith** I. 74, I. 713, II. 102, VI (v). 7, **saith** I. 714, **sey** I. 41, **seyn** II. 78, **seien** VIII. 457; *subj.sg.* **say** I. 425, II. 131; *pl.* **sigge** I. 96; *imp.sg.* **say** VI (iv). 14, VII. 81, VII. 168, **sey** I. 172; *pa.t.1,3 sg.* **said** I. 177, **seid** I. 168, III. 106, **seyd** I. 173, **saide** VII. 34, **sayde** VII. 44; *2sg.* **saidest** VI (vi). 33, VI (vi). 198, VIII. 52, **seidest** VI (vi). 30, VI (vi). 206, **said** I. 561, VIII. 478, **seid** VI (vi). 204; *pl.* **seid** VIII. 152, **said** VIII. 256, **saide** VII. 61; *p.p.* **said** II. 194, **seid** VIII. 431, I. 894 narrated, **seide** I. 388, **saide** VII. 136; *pr.p.* **seiynge** I. 541
**sake** *n.* sake, account VIII. 181
**saluacioun** *n.* salvation VIII. 102
**same** *adj.* same I. 290
**sare** *see* **sore**
**satisfaccioun** *n.* atonement I. 407
**sauf** *see* **saue**

**saue** *v.* save VI (ii). 44, VI (iv). 79, VIII. 422; *pr.2 sg.* (*with fut. implication*) VI (iv). 34; *imp.sg.* VI (vi). 84; *pa.t.sg.* **saued** VI (iv). 31; *p.p.* **saued** II. 73, **sauf** I. 779, **safe** III. 18, **sauede** VII. 50

**sauely** *adv.* safely III. 118

**sauyour** *n.* saviour II. 276

**sauorynge** *adj.* smelling VIII. 247

**sauour(e)** *n.* sweetness, delight I. 253, II. 160, III. 148, V. 2; scent VI (iv). 103, VIII. 249, VIII. 390

**scap** *v.* escape VI (vi). 419

**schal-, schold-** *see* **shal**

**schedyng** *n.* shedding, spilling VII. 46

**schewed** *see* **shewe**

**scornynge** *n.* mocking, derision I. 356; *pl.* **scornynges** VIII. 151; **scornys** VIII. 419

**scourgen** *v.* whip VIII. 189; *pa.t.pl.* **scourged** VII. 92; *p.p.* **scourged** VIII. 189, **scourget** VIII. 549

**scourges** *n.pl.* whips VIII. 191, II. 177

**sco(u)rgynge** *n.* flagellation VIII. 212, VIII. 289

**se(e)** *v.* see I. 173, II. 61, II. 192, III. 203, III. 223, V. 5, VI (ii). 24, VI (iv). 36, VI (vi). 67, VII. 63, VIII. 148 *etc.*, **seen** VI (vi). 63; *pr.1 sg.* **se** I. 462, II. 287, VI (vi). 173, VIII. 288; *2 sg.* **se(e)st** II. 21, II. 286, III. 205, VI (iv). 2; *3 sg.* **seth** I. 21, III. 180; *pl.* **se(e)** I. 461, I. 460, II. 85, **seth** I. 132, I. 891, **seen** I. 132; *subj.sg.* **se(e)** I. 454, I. 446; *imp.sg.* **see** I. 652; *pl.* **se** VI (vi). 227; *pa.t.sg.* **saw(e)** I. 174, VIII. 406, VI (vi). 88, VII. 98; *2 sg.* **saw(e)** VI (vi). 125, VIII. 331, VIII. 411; *subj.sg.* **saw** I. 739; *pl.* **saw** I. 133; *p.p.* **sene** I. 85, VI (i). 33, VI (vi). 92, **seyn** VI (i). 63, **seen** VIII. 456, *pr.p.* **seynge** I. 300

**seche** *v.* seek, search, look for I. 24, III. 74, VIII. 58; *pr.1 sg.* **seke** V. 5; *2 sg.* **sechest** III. 87; *3 sg.* **secheth** I. 823, VIII. 397; *pl.* **sechen** I. 100, **secheth** I. 143, I. 726, **secheeth** I. 682, **seke** I. 826; *subj.sg.* **sek(e)** I. 252, III. 86; *imp.sg.* **sek** III. 94, **seke** III. 65 endeavour; *pa.t.sg.* **soght** III. 90; *pl.* **soght** I. 892, III. 212, **souȝte** VII. 61; *p.p.* **soght** II. 206, VI (i). 39, VI (iv). 7; *pr.p.* **sechynge** VI (iv). 23

**sechynge** *n.* looking III. 91

**seculere** *adj.* secular I. 362

**secunde** *adj.* second I. 570

**seghynge** *see* **sigh, sighynge**

**sey-, sei-, seyn, seigh** *see* **say, se, sigh**

**seiȝe** *v.* ? move VII. 112 (*see note*)

**seynt, seint(e)** *adj.* sainted VIII. 127, VII. 2, VII. 5

**seyntes** *n.pl.* saints VIII. 140

**sek-** *v. see* **seche, sighynge**

**sek(e)** *adj.* sick, ill II. 109, VIII. 83, VIII. 318; *as n.pl.* I. 855

**sekenes(se)** *n.* ill health II. 116, VI (ii). 18, VIII. 158

**seldome** *adv.* seldom VIII. 441

**self** *adj.* same II. 39, VI (vi). 49; own VIII. 332 (*& see* **my self, hym self** *etc.*)

**semblant** *n.* outward appearance VIII. 147

**seme** *v.* seem, appear I. 372; *pr.2 sg.* **semest** I. 264; *3 sg.* **semeth** I. 233, II. 52, III. 156; *pl.* **semen** I. 206, I. 261, **semeth** I. 682; *subj.sg.* **seme** III. 150; *pl.* **seme** II. 62; *pa.t.sg.* **semed** VI (v). 20; *pr.p.* **semynge** I. 235

**semly** *adj.* fair, handsome II. 183; **semely** VIII. 345 befitting

**sen** *see* **seþen** *conj.*

**send** *v.* send VI (iv). 105; *pr.3 sg.* **sendeth** I. 441; *imp.sg.* **send** II. 201, VI (ii). 2, VI (vi). 62, VIII. 369; *pa.t.sg.* **sent(e)** I. 82, VII. 144, *intr.* VII. 90 sent a message; *pl.* **sente** VII. 89; *p.p.* **sent** II. 296, VI (ii). 26

**sensualite** *n.* sensual nature IV. 18

**sepulcre** *n.* tomb III. 151, VIII. 514

**seraphyn** *n.pl.* seraphim II. 20

**seruaunt** *n.* servant I. 466, III. 102; *pl.* **seruauntȝ** I. 309

**serue** *v.* serve I. 188, VI (iv). 32, VIII. 1; labour VI (iv). 1; *subj.pl.* I. 666 render service; *pa.t.pl.* **serued** I. 308; *p.p.* **serued** I. 85

**seruice, seruyce, seruys** *n.* service, fealty I. 67, II. 63, III. 124, III. 155, VIII. 15, VIII. 107; servitude I. 668; divine office I. 353, I. 366

**sese** *see* **cesse**

**set(te)** *v.* set, place, put, direct I. 33, I. 200, III. 59, VI (iv). 69; *pr.1 sg.* **set** III. 24; *3 sg.* **setteth** I. 688, III. 122, I. 879 causes; *pl.* **set** II. 149, **setteth** I. 568, II. 237, **sette** VI (iv). 69; *subj.sg.* **set** I. 320, IV. 13, VI (i). 30; *pl.* **set** II. 64; *imp.sg.* **set** I. 463, II. 137, III. 172, VI (ii). 4, VI (iv). 104, VI (vi). 14, VIII. 84; *pa.t.sg.* **set** I. 177, **sete** VI (vi). 238 laid before, made available; *pl.* **set** VII. 119; *p.p.* **set(te)** I. 57, II. 2, II. 65, IV.

24, VI (i). 9, VI (iii). 17, VI (v). 8, VIII. 348 (*& see* **sit**)
**sete, seet** *n.* throne, seat II. 38, VI (i). 9, VI (iv). 95, I. 753; *pl.* **setys** VI (v). 23
**seþen, sethen** *conj.* since VIII. 489, II. 297, VI (ii). 27, VIII. 360, **sithen** VII. 147, **sen** VI (iv). 82
**seþen, sethen** *adv.* afterwards I. 83, I. 877, II. 176, III. 185, VI (i). 59, VI (iii). 17, VII. 20, **setheþen** I. 68, **seþyn** I. 74, **sithe(n)** VII. 118, VII. 15, **sythen** VII. 22
**seþenforward** *adv.* henceforth I. 887
**sevyn, seven** *adj.* seven II. 21, II. 132
**shadde** *see* **shedest**
**shadow** *n.* shadow VIII. 474
**shal** *v.* (i) shall, will (*future*); (ii) must, be obliged to (*two senses often hard to distinguish*) *pr.1,3 sg.* I. 66, I. 179, II. 127, III. 46, V. 7, VI (i). 7, VI (vi). 139, VII. 49, VII. 161, VIII. 134, VIII. 400 *etc.*, **schalle** VII. 34; *2 sg.* **shalt** I. 127, I. 107, II. 57, III. 46, VI (iv). 87, VII. 162, **shal** I. 422, II. 103, III. 54, VI (i). 17, VI (iv). 36, VI (v). 1, VI (vi). 88, **schalt** VII. 146; *pl.* **shal** I. 17, I. 670, II. 26, VII. 163, **schal** VII. 54; *pa.t.* (i) should, would (*conditional & indirect future*); (ii) ought to, were to *pa.t.1,3 sg.* **shold** I. 40, I. 136, III. 107, VI (ii). 31, VI (vi). 199, VIII. 99, VIII. 242, VI (iii). 23 *as v. of motion*, **schulde** VII. 41; *2 sg.* **sholdest** VIII. 513; *pl.* **shold** I. 51, I. 382, II. 257, III. 107, VI (iii). 24, VIII. 376 *etc.*, **sholden** I. 316, I. 63*, I. 80*, **schulde** VII. 32
**shame** *v.* shame, dishonour VIII. 253; *pa.t.pl.* **shamed** VIII. 259
**sham(e)** *n.* shame I. 178, I. 342, II. 230, III. 102, VI (i). 66, VI (vi). 282, VIII. 94, VIII. 177; modesty VIII. 351; *pl.* **shamys, shames** VIII. 151, VIII. 251
**shameful, shamful(le)** *adj.* opprobrious VIII. 321, VIII. 256, VIII. 276
**shamfully** *adv.* ignominiously VIII. 278
**shamynge** *n.* modesty VIII. 344
**sharp(e)** *adj.* sharp VI (vi). 172, VIII. 540; harsh I. 192
**she** *pron.3 sg.fem.* she I. 177, II. 92, VI (vi). 182, VIII. 223, **sho** I. 94, I. 169, II. 91, VIII. 546; *acc.dat.* **hir(e), hyr(e)** I. 169, I. 178, II. 90, VIII. 331, VIII. 338, VI (vi). 184; *poss.adj.* **hyr, hir(e)** I. 177, II. 91, VII. 106, VIII. 223; *pron.* **hirs** II. 91
**shedest** *pa.t.2 sg.* shed, let fall VI (vi). 86, **sheddest** VI (vi). 96, **shadde** VI (ii). 32
**shendshipe** *n.* disgrace VIII. 177
**shene** *adj.* radiant VI (vi). 89
**shew(e)** *v.* show, reveal, manifest I. 98, I. 631, I. 701, VIII. 262; *pr.3 sg.* **sheweth** I. 147, II. 4, III. 22; *pl.* **sheweth** I. 691, **shewen** VIII. 544; *subj.sg.* **shew(e)** VIII. 43, I. 171; *pa.t.1,3 sg.* **shewed** I. 140, **schewed** VII. 31; *2 sg.* **shewedest** VI (vi). 170, VIII. 33, **shewedist** VIII. 28, **sheweddest(e)** VIII. 123, VIII. 78; *p.p.* **shewed** I. 429 revealed
**shewynge*** *n.* revelation, disclosure VIII. 195, **showynge** VI (vi). 176
**shild** *subj.sg.* forbid VI (iii). 23; *imp.sg.* protect VI (vi). 222, VIII. 169
**shilde*** *n.* shield VI (iii). 8
**shildynge** *n.* protection VIII. 87
**shyne** *v.* shine VI (v). 22; *pr.pl.* **shynen** VIII. 197; *pr.p.* **shynynge** I. 676
**shynynge** *n.* radiance I. 300, II. 268, II. 312, VI (ii). 24
**shipe** *n.* ship, ark I. 769
**sho** *see* **she**
**shold** *see* **shal**
**shope** *pa.t.sg.* formed, created VIII. 297
**shorne** *p.p.* cut IV. 3, **schorene** VII. 15
**short** *adj.* brief I. 68, II. 41
**shortly** *adv.* briefly I. 894
**shot** *pa.t.sg.* cast, propelled VI (v). 20; *p.p.* VIII. 390
**shoven** *pa.t.pl.* pushed VIII. 76
**showynge** *see* **shewynge**
**shrift, shryft** *n.* confession I. 403, VIII. 11, VIII. 39; ~ **fadyre** I. 170 confessor
**shrynkes** *pr.2 sg.* shrivel, recoil VIII. 317; *pl.* **shrynken** VIII. 543
**sib** *adj.* intimate II. 56
**side, syde** *n.* side II. 183, VI (ii). 37, VI (iv). 79, VI (vi). 176, VII. 94, VIII. 268
**sigge** *see* **say**
**syggynge ayeyne** *n.* contradiction III. 4
**sygh** *v.* sigh VIII. 360, **seigh** VIII. 555; *pr.1 sg.* **sigh** VI (iii). 1; *imp.sg.* **seigh** VI (iv). 22; *pa.t.2 sg.* **seighed** VIII. 359; *3 sg.* **seighed** VIII. 407; *pr.p.* **se(i)ghynge** I. 558, VI (iii). 17, VIII. 333
**sighynge, syghynge** *n.* sighing VI (ii). 21, VIII. 359, **seghynge** II. 267, VIII. 293, **sekynge** VI (vi). 120; *pl.* **s(e)ighynges** VIII. 349, VIII. 450

**syght, sight** *n.* eyesight II. 303, III. 156, VI (iii). 3, VIII. 410; vision, spectacle I. 607, I. 888, II. 312, III. 171, VI (iv). 42, **syȝt** VIII. 172, **sith** VI (vi). 180; *pl.* **syghtes** apparitions I. 206, VIII. 174
**signe** *n.* sign, token I. 686, III. 20; *pl.* **signes** I. 376 nods
**siker, syker, sikyre** *adj.* sure, secure I. 428, II. 248, VI (vi). 418, VIII. 223, III. 76, I. 337; *comp.* **sykerer** I. 840
**sikernesse** *n.* security I. 634, IV. 25
**silence** *n.* silence I. 769, II. 241, III. 14
**sylle** *subj.sg.* sell VI (i). 46
**syllynge** *n.* selling I. 368
**symony** *n.* simony I. 364
**sympilly** *adv.* plainly III. 100
**syn(ne)** *n.* sin I. 1, I. 646, II. 198, III. 10, VI (i). 7, VI (ii). 16, VI (iv). 9, VI (v). 6, VIII. 16, I. 158, VIII. 174 *etc.*, **synn** VI (vi). intro.st.; *pl.* **synnes, synnys** I. 25, II. 75, III. 9, VI (v). 1, VI (vi). 60, VIII. 71, VI (vi). 364, VIII. 12, **synns** II. 70
**syn** *v.* sin I. 434, II. 82, VIII. 147; *pr.2 sg.* **synnest** I. 212; *3 sg.* **synneth** I. 665, *pl.* **synneth** I. 47, I. 327; **synnen** I. 394; *pa.t.2 sg.* **synned** I. 449; *p.p.* **synned** VI (vi). 307
**synful** *adj.* sinful I. 1, II. 81, III. 119, VI (vi). 157, VIII. 23, *as n.* VI (vi). 357, **synfulle** VIII. 125; *comp.* **synfuller** I. 43; *sup.* **synfullest** I. 789
**synge** *v.* sing I. 362, II. 90, VI (i). 8, VI (i). 67, VI (vi). 1; *pr.1 sg.* I. 284, VI (ii). 29; *pr.p.* **syngynge** I. 574
**syngynge** *n.* singing I. 575, II. 225
**singulere, synguler** *adj.* unique, special I. 527, III. 26; unorthodox I. 342; egotistical I. 30
**synketh** *pr.3 sg.* sinks VI (iv). 15
**synwes, synuȝ, synewes** *n.pl.* sinews VIII. 381, VII. 110, VII. 112
**sit** *v.* sit I. 753, I. 829, II. 246, III. 58, V. 9, VI (v). 23; *pr.1 sg.* I. 284, VI (ii). 29; *3 sg.* **sitteth** I. 273, VIII. 322; *pl.* **sytteth** VI (iv). 12; *subj.pl.* **sit** I. 188; *pa.t.sg.* **sat** VI (vi). 109, **sate** VIII. 318, **satte** VII. 19; *pl.* **setten** VI (vi). 31, **saten** VIII. 450; *pr.p.* **sittynge** II. 4, III. 92
**syth** *n.* time I. 77; *pl.* **sithes** I. 349, III. 86 (*& see* **ofte**)
**sith** *see* **syght**
**sithe(n) sythen** *see* **sethen, seþen** *adv. & conj.*
**syttynge** *n.* sitting I. 832
**six** *adj.* six II. 164, VI (vi). 216 sixth
**sky** *n.* sky II. 215
**skyl(le)** *n.* reason I. 51, I. 635, IV. 19, VI (ii). 14, VI (iv). 57, VI (v). 1
**skylful** *adj.* proper III. 73
**skylfully** *adv.* properly III. 73; justly VIII. 136
**skylwise** *adj.* reasonable I. 437
**skylwisly** *adv.* reasonably I. 749
**skyn(ne)** *n.* skin VIII. 283, VII. 94
**skynles** *adj.* without skin VIII. 322
**sklaundre** *pr.pl.* blaspheme against I. 815
**sklaundrynge** *n.* blasphemy I. 350
**skorned** *pa.t.pl.* mocked, derided VIII. 77; *pr.p.* **scornynge** VI (vi). 110, VIII. 254
**slak** *v.* reduce, abate; cease II. 86; *pr.2 sg.* **slakest** VI (vi). 221; *p.p.* **slaked** VIII. 457
**sle(e)** *v.* kill I. 198, I. 199, VIII. 190; *pr.3 sg.* **sleth** I. 715, III. 37, **sleeth** II. 80, III. 37; *pl.* **sleeth** II. 76; *p.p.* **slayn(e)** I. 652, II. 79, VI (ii). 45, VI (iv). 10
**slegh** *adj.* skilful VI (i). 10
**slepe, sleep(e)** *n.* sleep I. 543, III. 61, I. 49, I. 195
**slepe** *v.* sleep VII. 57; *pr.1 sg.* II. 3, II. 235, **sleep** I. 564; *pl.* **slep(en)** I. 203, I. 227; *subj.pl.* **sleep** I. 187; *pr.p.* **slepynge** I. 152, I. 180, VI (vi). 46, VII. 38
**slepynge** *n.* sleep I. 541
**slowe** *adj.* slow, dilatory I. 190, III. 125
**slownes(se)** *n.* sloth I. 277, I. 618, II. 75, III. 162
**smel** *n.* smell VIII. 415
**smellynge** *n.* act of smelling I. 375, VIII. 413
**smert** *v.* sting, smart VI (iv). 16
**smert** *adj.* smarting VIII. 192
**smyte** *v.* strike, beat VIII. 179; *pa.t.sg.* **smote** VIII. 453; *pl.* **smot** VIII. 194, **smytten** VIII. 193, **smote** VII. 70
**smytynge** *n.* beating VI (iv). 16
**snakys** *n.pl.* snakes VII. 162
**snybbynge** *n.* reprimands VIII. 132
**so** *conj.* in order (that) II. 66, III. 7, VI (i). 20, VIII. 14 *etc.*
**so(o)** *adv.* in such a way, to such an extent I. 8, II. 110, III. 55, III. 93, IV. 5, VI (iv). 101, VI (vi). 15, VII. 25, VII. 68, VIII. 25 *etc.*; as II. 21 *etc.*
**sob** *pr.1 sg.* weep VI (iii). 1; *pa.t.sg.* **sobbed** VIII. 550

**socour(e), sokour** *n.* help, comfort VI (vi). 415, VIII. 86, VIII. 367, II. 277, VI (vi). 104
**soffr-** *see* **suffre**
**soft** *adv.* comfortably I. 187
**soft** *v.* soften VIII. 511
**softe** *adj.* soft VIII. 500
**softhed** *n.* softness, comfort I. 185
**sokour** *see* **socoure**
**solace** *n.* comfort, consolation I. 104, II. 48, III. 41, VI (iv). 21, VIII. 103
**solitarie, solitary** *adj.* solitary I. 123, I. 259, I. 495
**solitude** *n.* solitude I. 138
**some, sum** *adj.* some II. 172, VIII. 226, I. 20, I. 702, III. 129, VI (iv). 57, VIII. 396 *etc.*
**some, sum** *pron.* some VIII. 76, I. 29, I. 753, II. 26, VI (v). 7, VII. 68
**somwhate** *adv.* to some extent VIII. 238
**son(e)** *n.*[1] sun I. 592, I. 671, II. 21, III. 19, VI (v). 22, VIII. 297
**son(e)** *n.*[2] son I. 669, II. 9, VI (ii). 1, VI (vi). 63, VII. 45, VIII. 347, **sun** III. 165; *gen.* **sones** VIII. 452; *pl.* **sonnes** I. 684
**son(e)** *adv.* soon, immediately, quickly I. 137, I. 541, II. 87, III. 44, VI (iv). 95, VI (vi). 51, VIII. 81 *etc.*, **soone** VII. 54; *comp.* **soner** I. 730; *sup.* **sonest** VIII. 400
**sond** *n.* dispensation VIII. 158; *pl.* **sondes** III. 147, IV. 26, VIII. 182
**songe** *n.* song, refrain I. 490, I. 615, II. 2, VI (i). 24, VI (ii). 21, VI (iv). 20, VI (vi). 2; *pl.* **songes** I. 362; ~ **of songes** I. 490 Canticles
**sore** *adj.* painful II. 180, VIII. 178; sorrowful, afflicted VI (vi). 34, **sare** VI (ii). 44, VI (iv). 34
**sore** *adv.* sorely II. 176, VI (ii). 34, VI (v). 9, VI (vi). 77, VII. 76, VIII. 189, **sare** VI (i). 59, VI (iv). 84
**sory** *adj.* sorrowful I. 642; distressed I. 807; resentful I. 37, III. 70; wretched, worthless VIII. 505; *comp.* **sorier** I. 96
**sorynes(se)** *n.* vexation I. 277, I. 814; grief V. 9
**sorow(e)** *n.* grief III. 145, VI (iii). 17, VI (iv). 86, VI (vi). 34, VII. 98, VIII. 27, VIII. 335; vexation I. 110, II. 87, VI (i). 66; repentance I. 400, I. 747, VI (v). 6; ~ **of þe world** I. 336 regret for worldly things; *pl.* **sorowes** VI (vi). 286, VIII. 333
**sorow** *v.* grieve I. 384, VI (vi). 287, VIII. 556; *pr.pl.* **soroweth** VI (i). 59 come to grief; *pr.p.* **sorowynge** I. 391
**sorowful** *adj.* mournful VI (vi). 120
**sorowfully** *adv.* grievously VI (ii). 42
**sorowynge** *n.* grief, anguish II. 89, VIII. 293
**soth** *n.* truth I. 181, I. 424
**soth** *adj.* true I. 229
**soth** *adv.* truly II. 194
**sothfaste** *adj.* true II. 167
**sothfastnes(se)** *n.* truth I. 351, I. 427
**sothly** *adv.* truly III. 206
**souke** *v.* suck I. 878
**soul(e), sowl(e)** *n.* soul, inner being, mind I. 145, I. 554, II. 77, III. 19, IV. 4, V. 1, VI (i). 24, VI (ii). 6, VI (vi). 82, VII. 45, VIII. 4 *etc.*; person VIII. 292; *gen.* **sowl(e)** VI (vi). 13, VI (vi). 135, **soule** VI (vi). 93; *pl.* **soules** II. 161, VI (ii). 44
**south** *adv.* southwards VI (vi). 99
**souereyn(e)** *adj.* supreme I. 584, VIII. 83
**sowynge** *n.* dissemination I. 355
**sowir** *adj.* bitter VI (iv). 101; *comp.* **sowrer** II. 83
**space** *n.* respite VII. 169
**sparcle** *n.* spark VIII. 369; *pl.* **sparkles** VI (vi). 330
**spare** *v.* spare VI (v). 11; refrain VIII. 165; *pr.2 sg.* **sparest** VIII. 479; *3 sg.* **spareth** I. 716, III. 39; *p.p.* **spared** VI (vi). 158
**spech(e)** *n.* speech, conversation I. 82, III. 43, III. 14, VIII. 4
**special** *adj.* particular I. 430, III. 215
**speciali, specialy** *adv.* particularly II. 33, III. 143
**specials** *n.pl.* favourites II. 236
**specialte** *n.* special favour VIII. 400
**spede** *v.* prosper, succeed II. 270, VI (iv). 38
**spedeful** *adj.* profitable VIII. 91
**speer** *see* **spere**
**spek(e)** *v.* speak I. 77, I. 615, III. 57, III. 56, VI (iii). 9; *pr.1 sg.* VIII. 387, I. 576, VIII. 391; *2 sg.* **spekest** I. 427; *3 sg.* **speketh** I. 877, III. 21; *pl.* **spek** I. 720, **speketh** I. 680; *subj.sg.* **spek(e)** I. 419, I. 692, **speeke** I. 417; *pl.* **speke** I. 464; *imp.sg.* **spek** III. 141; *pa.t.2 sg.* **spake** VI (vi). 191; *subj.pl.* **spake** I. 830; *p.p.* **spoken** I. 38; *pr.p.* **spekynge** II. 101
**spekynge** *n.* speaking III. 130
**spende** *v.* pass time VII. 149; *pr.pl.*

**spende** (*cont.*)
**spend** I. 738 waste; *p.p.* **spended** VII. 149
**spere** *n.* spear VI (ii). 6, VI (v). 20, VIII. 540, III. 131*, **speer** VI (vi). 172
**spetynge, spittynge** *n.* spittle II. 179, VIII. 314
**spille** *v.* spill, shed; kill VI (i). 32; *pa.t.sg.* **spilet** I. 514, **spild** VI (ii). 35
**spirit** *n.* life, soul VIII. 538, VII. 129; *pl.* **spirites** I. 165 apparitions
**spitten** *pa.t.pl.* spat VIII. 139, VII. 72, **spit** VIII. 255, **spitted** VIII. 420
**spouse, spowse** *n.* bride, bridegroom I. 129, II. 144, III. 103
**spoused** *p.p.* wedded VI (vi). 305
**spred** *p.p.* outstretched VI (vi). 174
**sprynge** *v.* rise, flow, gush VI (vi). 3; *pr.pl.* **spryngeth** III. 184; *pr.p.* **spryngynge** I. 534
**sprynge** *n.* fount VI (vi). 246; forward flow VI (iii). 26
**spurned** *pa.t.pl.* kicked VIII. 311
**stabil** *imp.sg.* establish, make firm III. 161, VI (i). 27, VI (iv). 16; *p.p.* **stablet** I. 418, I. 539, **stabled** I. 829
**stabilynge** *n.* steadfastness VI (iv). 38; means of making steadfast I. 650
**stabilte** *n.* steadfastness VI (ii). 4
**stable, stabil(e)** *adj.* firm, steadfast, trustworthy I. 529, I. 413, II. 70, III. 22, IV. 8, VI (iii). 8
**stablenesse** *n.* stability VI (i). 42
**stably, stabilly** *adv.* steadfastly, firmly I. 616, II. 37, III. 207
**staf** *n.* staff, stick I. 653
**stalle** *n.* security II. 280, VI (iv). 94
**stalworth** *adj.* steadfast, strong I. 65, I. 528, I. 715, **stalwarth** I. 134, III. 36, VI (i). 48, VIII. 190
**stalworthly** *adv.* steadfastly, strongly I. 84, I. 706, II. 241, III. 209, **stalwarthly** I. 715, III. 58
**stamake** *n.* stomach, digestion I. 447
**stand-** *see* **stond**
**state** *n.* condition I. 138, II. 286, III. 17, VI (ii). 31, VI (v). 3, VIII. 264
**sted-** *see* **stid-**
**stel*** *v.* creep II. 125
**steppis** *n.pl.* footsteps VIII. 115, **stappis** VIII. 161
**sterre** *n.* star III. 99; *pl.* **sterres, sterris** I. 593, II. 215, II. 23, VIII. 197
**stid(de)** *n.* place I. 83, I. 726, VI (iv). 16, **stede** VI (i). 46; *pl.* **stiddes** II. 186, **steddes** II. 136
**stid** *v.* place, establish VI (iv). 38; *pr.3 sg.* **stiddeth** II. 280 takes the place of; *imp.sg.refl.* **stid** VI (iv). 94, **sted** VI (iv). 45; *p.p.* **stedde** II. 286
**stidfast** *adj.* steadfast, true III. 189
**stidfastly** *adv.* faithfully, resolutely I. 125, VI (iii). 22, VIII. 156, **stidfast** VIII. 113
**stykketh** *pr.3 sg.* remains fixed VIII. 553; *subj.sg.* **stik** VI (vi). 258; *pa.t.sg.* **stikked** VIII. 342
**stil** *adj.* silent I. 603, VI (vi). 144; **stille** motionless I. 827, VIII. 128
**stil(le)** *adv.* still, continually I. 8, VIII. 559; **stylle** secretly VI (vi). 378
**styngeth** *pr.3 sg.* pierces VIII. 323; *pa.t.sg.* **stong(e)** VII. 131, VI (vi). 172; *p.p.* **stonggede** VII. 139
**stynk, stynch** *n.* stench VIII. 409, VIII. 413
**stynke** *v.* be abhorrent II. 87
**stynkynge** *adj.* illsmelling III. 152, VIII. 494; disgusting I. 32; filthy III. 114
**stirreth** *pr.3 sg.* rouses, incites III. 128, VIII. 510; *p.p.* **stirred** I. 17, I. 722, VIII. 529
**stirrynge, styrrynge** *n.* incitement, prompting I. 643, II. 103, III. 6, IV. 11; *pl.* **stirrynges** I. 414
**stody** *see* **study**
**stond** *v.* stand VI (i). 42, VIII. 156, **stand** III. 207, resist II. 152, stay VI (iv). 46; ~ **ayeyns** I. 4, I. 391 resist; *pr.1 sg.* **stand** I. 603, **stond** VIII. 131; *2 sg.* **standis** II. 167, **stondest** VIII. 384; *3 sg.* **standith** II. 72; *pl.* **stonden** I. 153, **stond** III. 209; *subj.pl.* **stand** II. 264; *pa.t.sg.* **stode** VII. 88, **stoode** VI (ii). 34, VI (vi). 181; *pr.p.* **standynge** I. 391, I. 832, II. 4
**stondynge** *n.* standing VIII. 128
**stone** *n.* stone VII. 78, VIII. 369; *pl.* **stones, stonys** VI. 70, VIII. 539; gems I. 739, VIII. 207
**stopped** *p.p.* closed up, stoppered VIII. 390
**strait, streite** *adj.* narrow, restricted VIII. 100, VIII. 105
**straytly** *adv.* strictly II. 93
**strand** *n.* shore VI (ii). 40, **stronde*** II. 187

**straunge** *adj.* niggardly, sparing VIII. 441
**streyned** *pa.t.pl.* stretched VIII. 374; *p.p.* VI (vi). 117, VIII. 378
**streynth(e)** *n.* strength, fortitude I. 506, VIII. 2, VIII. 156
**streynthful** *adj.* steadfast I. 99
**stremed (on)** *p.p.* running (with) VIII. 287
**stremes, stremys** *n.pl.* streams, rivers II. 187, VI (ii). 40, VI (vi). 247, VIII. 289, VI (vi). 58
**striffes** *n.pl.* quarrels I. 395
**strypynge** *n.* stripping VIII. 286
**stryue** *v.* fight, struggle I. 351, VI (ii). 43; *pa.t.sg.* **strof** VIII. 179
**strok(e)** *n.* blow VIII. 178, VIII. 194
**stroke** *pa.t.pl.* struck VII. 115
**stronde** *see* **strand**
**stronge** *adj.* powerful VI (vi). 54, VI (vi). 381, VIII. 190
**study** *v.* endeavour mentally II. 97, VIII. 243; *pr.1 sg.* **stody** VIII. 388
**study, stody** *n.* mental labour VIII. 242, VIII. 234
**studious** *adj.* assiduous VIII. 239
**studiously** *adv.* assiduously VIII. 558
**substanciali** *adv.* intrinsically I. 673
**such(e)** *adj.* such I. 43, I. 148, II. 59, III. 196, VI (i). 35, VI (iv). 91, VI (vi). 166, VIII. 23, VIII. 260 *etc.*
**suffiseth (to)** *pr.3 sg.* is adequate (for) I. 174; *intr.* I. 806; *pl.* **suffice** I. 373
**suffrayne** *n.* sovereign, superior I. 374
**suffraunce** *n.* patience, forbearance VIII. 156
**suffre** *v.* (i) suffer, endure I. 123, III. 41*, VII. 41, VIII. 132, **soffre** VIII. 292; *pr.1 sg.* **suffre** VIII. 302; *3 sg.* **suffreth** I. 193, I. 718; *pl.* **suffren** I. 36, **suffreth** I. 681, VI (v). 21; *subj.sg.* **suffre** I. 751; *pl.* **suffre** I. 652; *imp.sg.* **suffre** II. 102; *pa.t.1,3 sg.* **suffred** III. 177, VII. 24, VIII. 480; *2 sg.* **suffred** VI (vi). 256, VIII. 62, **soffred** VIII. 371, **suffred(d)est(e)** VI (vi). 53, VIII. 75, VIII. 178, **soffredest*** VI (vi). 57; *p.p.* **suffred** II. 42, VI (iii). 20, VI (iv). 84, I. 881* (MS **suffren**); (ii) tolerate, allow I. 203, III. 128; *pr.3 sg.* **suffreth** I. 110, I. 151; *imp.sg.* **suffre** VI (vi). 367; *pa.t.sg.* **suffered** VI (iv). 79; *pr.p.* **suffrynge** II. 134, VIII. 328
**suffrynge** *adj.* long-suffering III. 170
**suffrynge** *n.* endurance II. 99
**sum*** *n.* total I. 661
**sum** *adj. see* **some**
**sun** *see* **sone** *n.*[2]
**suple** *v.* soften VIII. 370
**supposeth** *pr.pl.* think, believe I. 692
**suspeccioun** *n.* expectation I. 330
**sustenaunce** *n.* support, sustenance I. 437
**sustene** *v.* keep up, sustain I. 67; *p.p.* **sustened** III. 108
**sustre** *n.* sister I. 474
**sutil(e)** *adj.* cunning, sly I. 106, I. 162
**swapped** *pa.t.pl.* banged VII. 121
**swedled** *p.p.* wrapped III. 100
**swelighynge** *n.* swallowing, tasting I. 376
**swerd** *n.* sword VIII. 452
**swere** *v.* swear I. 349; *p.p.* **sworne** VI (iv). 32
**swet(e)** *adj.* sweet, pleasing, dear I. 8, II. 80, III. 123, VI (ii). 12, VI (iii). 5, VI (vi). 1, VII. 44, VII. 169, VIII. 31, VIII. 37 *etc.*, **swote*** VI (vi). 15; *comp.* **swetter** I. 562, II. 47, VI (iv). 64, VI (vi). 21; *sup.* **swet(t)est** VI (vi). 53, I. 600
**swete** *n.*[1] loved one VI (iii). 10, VI (iv). 73; **swetynge** I. 607, II. 181, VI (iv). 20, VI (iv). 91, VI (vi). 269
**swete** *n.*[2] sweat VII. 41
**swete** *v.* sweat VI (vi). 186; *pa.t.2 sg.* **swettest** VIII. 63; *3 sg.* **swete** II. 175
**swetly** *adv.* sweetly I. 707, VIII. 463
**swetnes(se)** *n.* pleasure, sweetness I. 103, II. 31, III. 8, III. 120, V. 1, VI (ii). 8, VI (iii). 21, VI (iv). 32, VIII. 229, VIII. 239 *etc.*; **swettnesse** I. 242, III. 149
**swyne** *n.pl.* pigs VI (iv). 61; *gen.* **swynes** I. 16
**swynge** *v.* beat, flog II. 178, VI (ii). 34*
**swith** *adv.* quickly VI (vi). 375
**swowne** *n.* swoon, faint VIII. 335

**tak(e)** *v.* take, capture I. 54, III. 188, VII. 6, VIII. 492; *pr.3 sg.* **taketh** I. 29, II. 80; *pl.* **taketh** I. 849, II. 221; *subj.sg.* **take** I. 319, I. 685, **tak** III. 134, VI (ii). 12, **too** VI (iv). 56; *imp.sg.* **tak(e)** VI (i). 22, VI (ii). 19, VI (iv). 105, VIII. 79, II. 130, VI (i). 46, VI (iv). 22, VI (vi). 204, VIII. 89; *pa.t.2 sg.* **tak** VIII. 37, **toke** VIII. 437; *3 sg.* **toke** VII. 56; *pl.* **toke** III. 200, VII. 64, VIII. 285; *subj.pl.* **toke** I. 80; *p.p.* **take** I. 27, I. 123, VIII. 280, **taken** I. 385, II. 26, III. 223, VI (vi). 32, **takyn** VIII. 76, **tane** VI (i). 53, VI (v). 3

**takeled** *p.p.* entangled I. 586
**tale** *n.* regard, heed I. 464
**tame** *adj.* docile VI (vi). 284
**tane** *see* **take**
**taryynge** *n.* vexation, hindrance IV. 4
**tast(e)** *n.* feeling, appreciation VIII. 389; sense of taste VIII. 418
**tasted** *p.p.* tasted VII. 128
**teche** *v.* teach, instruct VIII. 54; *pr.1 sg.* I. 264; *imp.sg.* VI (i). 397, **tech** VI (vi). 383; *pa.t.2 sg.* **teched** VI (vi). 189, **taghtest** VIII. 52; *3 sg.* **tauȝt** VII. 32, **teched*** VII. 20; *pr.p.* **techynge** I. 395
**techynge** *n.* instruction VI (vi). 335
**tel(le)** *v.* tell, narrate I. 302, VI (iii). 21, VI (iv). 40, VI (iv). 71, VI (vi). 56, VII. 25; *pr.1 sg.* VI (i). 11, VI (ii). 45; *3 sg.* **telleth** I. 208; *imp.sg.* **tel** I. 626, VI (vi). 229; *pl.* **tel** VI (vi). 234; *pa.t.1,3 sg.* **told** I. 18, I. 170; *2 sg.* **told** VIII. 69; *pl.* **tolde** VI (iii). 16; *p.p.* **told(e)** I. 871, VI (i). 50
**temperaunce** *n.* moderation I. 436
**temple** *n.* temple III. 92, VII. 19, VIII. 539
**temptacioun** *n.* temptation I. 4, I. 152, IV. 11, VIII. 42; *pl.* **temptaciouns** I. 881, II. 264, III. 83, VIII. 159 *etc.*
**tempt(e)** *v.* tempt I. 110, I. 179; *pr.3 sg.* **tempteth** I. 161; *p.p.* **tempted** I. 155, III. 29
**ten** *adj.* ten II. 69
**tendyrly** *adj.* frail, easily broken VIII. 481
**tendre, tender, tendyr** *adj.* tender, sensitive I. 255, VIII. 286, VIII. 284
**tendrely, tenderly** *adv.* tenderly, caringly II. 142, III. 112, VI (iii). 19, VII. 47
**tene** *n.* vexation VI (i). 36
**tent** *n.* attention VI (vi). 292
**teres, teris, terys** *n.pl.* tears III. 167, VI (vi). 72, VIII. 407, I. 880, VI (vi). 144, III. 184
**terre** *v.* tear VIII. 376
**tethe** *n.pl.* teeth VIII. 544
**thay, thai, þay, þai** *pron.3 pl.nom.* they I. 7, I. 507, II. 26, II. 61, III. 13, III. 224, VI (i). 61, VI (iv). 61, VI (v). 7, VII. 39, VII. 77, VIII. 77 *etc.*, **they, thei, þey, þei** I. 3, I. 7, I. 31, II. 108, III. 113, VI (i). 60, VII. 61, VIII. 309 *etc.*, **he** VI (vi). 248; *acc.dat.* **ham** them I. 8, II. 83, III. 12, III. 181, VI (vi). 46, VIII. 19 *etc.*, **hem** VI (vi). 45, VII. 22, VIII. 79, **thaym** I. 262; *refl.* **ham** themselves I. 11, I. 82, I. 244, VI (iv). 62; *poss.adj.* **har(e)** their I. 5, II. 82, III. 17, III. 181, VI (i). 59, VIII. 154, I. 3, I. 850, VI (i). 62 *etc.*, **her(e)** I. 142, VII. 70, **thar** VI(iv). 62, **þar** II. 259, **thaire** VII. 17
**þay** *adj.dem. see* **that**
**than, þan** *adv.* then I. 55, II. 216, II. 58, IV. 2, VI (vi). 45, VII. 14, VII. 165, VIII. 54 *etc.*; therefore III. 86, III. 156, VI (iv). 32, VIII. 89
**than, þan** *conj.* than I. 13, II. 22, II. 58, III. 19, VI (i). 13, VI (vi). 18, VII. 50, VIII. 133
**thanke** *n.* gratitude I. 80, **þankynge** VIII. 115; *pl.* **þankynges** VIII. 93
**þank(e)** *v.* thank II. 258, VIII. 185; *pr.1 sg.* **thank(e)** VI (i). 345, VIII. 31, **þank** VIII. 32; *imp.sg.* **þank** II. 109, **thanke** I. 896, III. 147; *p.p.* **þanked** I. 512, VIII. 270; *pr.p.* **thankynge** I. 383
**thar(e), þar(e)** *see* **thay, there**
**that, þat** *adj.dem.* that I. 5, I. 58, I. 573, II. 20, III. 127, VI (i). 44, VI (iii). 13, VII. 57, VII. 166, VIII. 20 *etc.*; *pl.* **tho, þo** those I. 694, VII. 44, **þay** I. 399
**that, þat** *pron.dem.* that I. 95, II. 60, II. 68, I. 313, I. 567, I. 731, V. 3, VII. 34, VII. 119; *pl.* **tho, þo** I. 495, VIII. 539
**that, þat** *pron.rel.* that, which, who(m) I. 1, II. 2, III. 5, IV. 1, VI (i). 1, VI (iii). 5, VI (vi). 15, VII. 14, VIII. 7 *etc.*
**that, þat** *conj.* that I. 3, II. 6, II. 34, III. 7, IV. 4, VI (i). 22, VI (iv). 86, VI (vi). 16, VII. 31; because I. 228, II. 259; **in** ~ inasmuch as VII. 49
**the, þe** *def.art.* the I. 2, II. 2, III. 18, IV. 5, VI (i). 3, VI (vi). 48, VII. 1, VII. 19, VIII. 4 *etc.*, **te** VII. 170
**the, þe** *pron. see* **thou**
**þederward*** *adv.* thither VIII. 162
**thef(e), þef(f)** *n.* thief VI (vi). 199, VIII. 94, VII. 111, VIII. 437; *pl.* **theues** VIII. 482, **þefes** VIII. 520, **thefes** VII. 116
**thefte** *n.* theft I. 368
**þegh** *see* **thogh**
**they, þey, thei, þei** *see* **thay**
**þens** *adv.* thence VIII. 498
**ther(e), þer(e)** *adv.* there III. 92, VI (iv). 70, VIII. 33, VIII. 458; where I. 273, II. 39, III. 219, VI (i). 1, VI (i). 41, VI (vi). 396, VIII. 321, VIII. 414; *impers.* VI (iii). 2, VII. 140, VIII. 85 *etc.*, **thar(e), þare** I. 74, II. 227, III. 211, VI (iii). 21, VI (v). 4; **thore, þore** VI (vi). 35, VI (vi). 112, VI

(vi). 119; *prefixed to adv. or prep.* ~ **as** VIII. 381 where; ~ **about** III. 108; ~ **by/bi** III. 100, VIII. 522; ~ **for(e)** I. 630, III. 42, VII. 167, VIII. 84, VII. 49; ~ **fro(o)** I. 588, VI (iv). 53; ~ **in** I. 47, II. 47, III. 172, VI (i). 26, VI (iv). 107, VI (vi). 83; ~ **of** II. 6, III. 11, VI (i). 39, VI (iv). 11, VII. 154, VIII. 353; ~ **on** II. 257, VI (vi). 96, VII. 108, VIII. 373; ~ **to** I. 5, II. 217, III. 39, III. 175, IV. 6, VI (vi). 371, VIII. 59, I. 584 in comparison with; ~ **vndre** VIII. 317; ~ **with** I. 581, III. 8, VIII. 504

**these, þese** *see* **this** *adj.dem.*

**thewes** *n.pl.* manners, customs I. 275

**thy(ne), thi, þi, þyn** *see* **thou**

**thyng(e), þyng(e), thing(e), þing(e)** *n.* thing I. 30, I. 58, II. 14, II. 105, III. 7, III. 214, IV. 1, VI (i). 6, VI (iii). 2, VI (iv). 19, VI (vi). 4, VII. 109 *etc.*; *pl.* **thynges, þynges** I. 432, II. 43, I. 157, I. 399, III. 138, IV. 9, **thinges** VII. 54, **thynge** I. 644

**thynk(e), þynk(e)** *v.*[1] think, consider I. 127, I. 518, I. 477, II. 44, III. 133, VI (iii). 19, VI (vi). 67, VIII. 72; imagine II. 52, **thinke** VII. 25; *pr.1 sg.* **þynke** VI (iii). 10, VI (vi). 177; *2 sg.* **þynkest** * III. 33; *3 sg.* **þynketh** I. 189 intends; *pl.* **thynke** I. 93, II. 82, **þynke** I. 492, **thynketh** I. 296, **thynken** I. 31, I. 243, **þynken** I. 7, I. 61; *subj.sg.* **thynk** I. 616, **þynk(e)** VI (vi). 391, VIII. 398, II. 140, III. 214; *pl.* **thynke** III. 4, **þynke** I. 297; *imp.sg.* **thynk(e)** II. 169, III. 171, II. 254, **þynke** I. 246, III. 64, VI (iii). 27, **thinke** VII. 14; *pr.p.* **thynkynge** I. 543, II. 172, **þynkynge** I. 382, II. 5

**thynke, þynke** *v.*[2] *impers.* seem II. 47, I. 562, I. 614; *pr.3 sg.* I. 530, VI (i). 10, VI (iii). 10, I. 445, I. 530, VI (i). 12, VI (v). 17, **thynk** II. 42, **þynketh** II. 288, VIII. 288, **þynken** I. 40, I. 258; *subj.sg.* **thinke** VII. 137, **þynke** III. 175

**thynkynge, þynkynge** *n.* meditation II. 121, III. 190, VI (vi). 336; act of thinking III. 138; thought, mind VI (iv). 18, VI (iv). 105

**thynnest** *adj.sup.* weakest I. 195

**thirle** *imp.sg.* pierce VI (ii). 6; *p.p.* **þurlet** II. 183

**þyrst** *see* **þurste**

**þirstlew** *adj.* thirsty VIII. 464

**this, þis** *adj.dem.* this I. 13, II. 26, II. 33, III. 5, IV. 15, VI (i). 35, VI (ii). 3, VI (vi). 43, VII. 47, VIII. 85 *etc.*; *pl.* **these, þese** these I. 18, I. 329, II. 26, VIII. 202

**this, þis** *pron.dem.* this I. 32, II. 24, VI (iii). 20

**thy self, þy self** *pron.refl.2 sg.* thyself I. 454, I. 693, VIII. 54

**tho, þo** *see* **that** *adj. & pron.*

**thogh, þogh** *conj.* although I. 319, II. 62, III. 88, VI (i). 19, VI (iii). 7, VI (vi). 157, VIII. 358, **þegh** VI (i). 12, VI (iii). 17

**thoght, þoght** *n.* thought, mind, consideration, intellect I. 115, I. 612, II. 34, III. 2, III. 51, IV. 1, VI (i). 5, VI (ii). 7, VI (iii). 11, VI(iv). 52, VI(vi). 22 *etc.*, **þoȝt** I. 235, VIII. 4, **thouȝt** VII. 146; *pl.* **thoghtes, þoghtes, thoghtis, thoghtys** I. 61, III. 15, IV. 3, I. 517, II. 126, III. 31, I. 329, II. 125, IV. 17

**þolemode*** *adj.* submissive VI(vi). 319

**þolle** *v.* endure VI(i). 14

**thore, þore** *see* **there**

**þorne** *n.* thorn II. 180, VI(ii). 36, VI(iv). 30, VI(vi). 171, VIII. 291; *pl.* **thornes** VII. 94, **þornes** VIII. 253

**thou, þou** *pron.2 sg.nom.* thou, you I. 87, I. 105, II. 9, III. 45, V. 8, VI(i). 4, VI(iv). 13, VI(iv). 78, VI(vi). 7, VII. 59, VIII. 75 *etc.*; *acc.dat.* **the, þe** thee, you I. 109, I. 450, II. 1, II. 231, III. 42, III. 78, V. 7, VI(i). 4, VI(iii). 20, VI(vi). 2, VII. 7, VIII. 349 *etc.*; *refl.* **þe** I. 123, I. 319, II. 12, III. 132, VI(v). 3, VI(iv). 102, **the** VII. 5, VII. 67; *poss.adj.* **thy(n), þy(n)** thy, your I. 129, I. 250, II. 10, III. 69, VI (vi). 63, VI(vi). 118, VII. 164, VIII. 535 *etc.*, **thi, þi** I. 88, II. 10, II. 231, III. 30, V. 8, VI(i). 25, VI(vi). 8, VI(vi). 29, VII. 150, VII. 164 *etc.* **thin** VII. 28; *pron.* **thyne, þyn(e)** thine VI(ii). 19, VI(v). 24, VI(vi). 260, VIII. 58

**thourȝ** *see* **throgh**

**þousand** *n.* thousand I. 22

**thre, þre** *adj.* three I. 2, I. 113, II. 16, III. 24, IV. 9, VI(vi). 171, VII. 160

**thridde, þrid** *adj.* third I. 9, II. 216, III. 26, IV. 11, VI(vi). 51, VII. 143

**thrist-** *see* **þurst** *v.* & *n.*

**throgh, þrogh** *prep.* through, by means of I. 35, I. 117, II. 155, II. 312, III. 119, VI(v). 1, VI(vi). 335, VIII. 65 *etc.*, **þrugh** VIII. 453, **thourȝ** VII. 108

**thronus** *n.pl.* positions of domination II. 19

**throuȝt** *prep.* completely through VII. 113

**þrow** *n.* pang VIII. 454

**þurlet** *see* **thirle**

**þurst** *v.* thirst, desire VIII. 475, *pr.3 sg. impers.* **þursteth** VI(vi). 207, **thristes** VII. 127; *pa.t.2 sg.* **þursted** VIII. 469

**þurst(e)** *n.* thirst I. 751, VIII. 417, **þyrst** VIII. 416, **thriste** VII. 24

**þursty** *n.* thirsty people I. 854

**thus, þus** *adv.* thus, in this way I. 193, III. 143, VIII. 324

**tyde** *n.* time, occasion VI (ii). 39, VIII. 242

**til, tyl** *conj.* until I. 181, I. 278, II. 67, III. 61, V. 6, VI (ii). 23, VI (vi). 300, VIII. 282 *etc.*, **tille** VII. 65

**til(le)** *prep.* to I. 51, II. 285, VI (i). 30, VI (i). 60, VI (ii). 16, VI (ii). 30, VI (iv). 56, VI (iv). 58, VI (v). 3, VII. 6, VIII. 339

**tyme** *n.* time, occasion I. 68, III. 32, VI (vi). 51, VII. 167, VIII. 34, VII. 151; *pl.* **tymes** VII. 171, VIII. 335

**tyne** *v.* lose VI (i). 52, VI (iv). 62

**tythynge** *n.* tidings, news VI (iv). 71

**titter** *adv.* sooner, rather VII. 49

**to** *prep.* (*of direction*) to II. 67, VII. 168, VIII. 24, up to II. 24; (*of place*) upon VIII. 94; (*of emotion*) towards I. 22, III. 15, VIII. 16, VIII. 174; (*of purpose*) for I. 598, VII. 117; (*of benefit*) for I. 66, I. 444, II. 7, II. 113, III. 73, VI (iv). 95; (*of regard*) concerning VIII. 346; according to, in compliance with I. 431, IV. 19, VI (iv). 41

**to** *adv.* too VIII. 440

**to** *conj.* until VII. 118, VIII. 375

**tobreke** *v.* break asunder VI (iii). 10

**todis** *n.pl.* toads VII. 162

**todrawen** *p.p.* pulled taut VIII. 379

**tofore** *prep.* in front of VII. 89

**togh** *adj.* tough VIII. 208

**togiddre, togyddre** *adv.* together I. 636, VIII. 283, **togeddre** III. 31, VI (vi). 342, **togedyre** VI (iv). 69

**token** *n.* sign I. 798, **tokenyng(e)** VII. 31, VI (vi). 173

**tong(e)** *n.* tongue, speech I. 476, I. 798, II. 135, VII. 164, **tunge** VI (vi). 56, **tounge** VII. 25

**too** *see* **take**

**toren** *pa.t.pl.* pulled asunder VIII. 77

**torenten** *pa.t.pl.* tore to pieces VIII. 290; *p.p.* **torente** VIII. 485

**torevyn** *pa.t.pl.* split apart VIII. 539

**torment** *see* **tourment**

**tornedest** *see* **turne**

**toshaked** *pa.t.pl.* shook to pieces VIII. 404

**tother, toþer** *see* **oþere** *adj.*

**touche** *v.* touch VIII. 232; *pr.3 sg.* **toucheth** I. 227 affects; *p.p.* **touched** affected II. 48, VIII. 229

**touchynge** *n.* touching I. 375

**toumble** *imp.sg.* fall VI (v). 3

**toun** *n.* town VIII. 415

**toure** *n.* dwelling place, stronghold II. 277, III. 164; *pl.* **tours** VIII. 361

**to(u)rment** *n.* torment, anguish I. 304, I. 654

**tourne** *see* **turne**

**toward** *prep.* towards VIII. 116

**trace** *n.* way of life VI (iv). 22

**trail** *subj.sg.* trail, drag III. 103

**traitour** *n.* traitor VII. 59

**transfigureth** *pr.3 sg.* transforms I. 182

**trape** *n.* trap I. 27; *pl.* **trappes** I. 108

**trauail(le)** *n.* labour, toil, affliction I. 149, I. 188, I. 509, II. 42, III. 126, VI (i). 3, **trauaile** VII. 42

**trauaille** *v.* labour III. 108; *subj.sg.* III. 178

**tre** *n.* the Cross II. 189, VI (iii). 18, VI (vi). 113, VIII. 94, **tree** VII. 120

**trembled** *pa.t.sg.* shook VIII. 504; *pr.p.* **tremblynge** VI (iv). 13

**tresone** *n.* treachery I. 355, VIII. 93

**tresour(e)** *n.* treasure II. 88, III. 110

**trespas** *n.* sin, guilt VIII. 126

**trespased** *pa.t.sg.* sinned VIII. 292; *p.p.* **trespassed** VII. 152

**trew(e)** *adj.* faithful, loyal III. 5, VI (i). 41, VI (iv). 81, VI (vi). 143

**trew(e)ly** *adv.* honestly, faithfully II. 71, III. 46, III. 77, III. 219

**tribulacioun** *n.* affliction VIII. 42; *pl.* **tribulaciouns** I. 123, VIII. 180

**trinite** *n.* trinity VII. 159

**trist(e), tristy** *see* **trust, trusty**

**trone** *n.* throne I. 827

**trouth** *n.* faith I. 61, I. 392, I. 648, II. 70, III. 94

**trow (to)** *v.* believe (in) I. 165; *pr.1 sg.* I. 124; *pl.* **troweth** I. 777; *subj.sg.* **trow** I. 181

**trussed** *p.p.* laden VIII. 316
**trust** *v.* trust III. 111, **trist** II. 117, VIII. 102; *pr.pl.* **trusteth** I. 475; *subj.sg.* **trist** VIII. 105; *imp.sg.* **trist** III. 72
**truste** *n.* trust VI (vi). 362, **trist(e)** VIII. 103, VIII. 104
**trusty** *adj.* faithful, loyal VI (i). 41, **tristy** VI (iv). 81
**tugged** *pa.t.pl.* tugged VIII. 77, VII. 75*
**tunge** *see* **tonge**
**turment** *v.* harass, distress VII. 81; *pr.3 sg.* **turmenteth** I. 70, **tormenteth** III. 39; *pr.p.* **tourmentynge** I. 118
**turmentours** *n.pl.* torturers VIII. 309
**turne** *v.* turn, convert, direct I. 11, I. 109, I. 356, I. 386, II. 68, VI (vi). 264, VIII. 41, **tourne** II. 291; *pr.2 sg.* **turnes** VIII. 393; *3 sg.* **turneth** I. 560, VI (i). 44, VI (iii). 26, VI (iv). 67; *pl.* **turne** VI (iv). 9, **turneth** II. 232; *subj.sg.* **turne** VIII. 90; *imp.sg.* **turne** I. 235, VI (iv). 75, VIII. 124; *pa.t.2 sg.* **tornedest*** VI (vi). 45 (*MS* **tornest**); *3 sg.* **turned** VII. 101; *p.p.* **turned** III. 122, IV. 19, VI (i). 3, VI (iii). 4, VIII. 44; *pr.p.* **turnynge** VIII. 121
**turnes** *n.pl.* tricks VIII. 257
**turnynge** *n.* turning, redirecting I. 268, I. 657, IV. 18
**twelftday** *n.* Twelfth night VII. 16
**twin, twyn** *v.* separate II. 198, II. 311, VI (iv). 27, VI (v). 8; *pr.pl.* **twynnen** VIII. 378; *subj.sg.* **twyn** VI (i). 19
**two** *adj.* two I. 184, II. 164, III. 107, IV. 18, VIII. 482

**umbithinke, umbethinke** *imp.sg.* consider, reflect VII. 5, VII. 85
**vmlappeth** *pr.3 sg.* completely envelopes V. 3
**vmset** *p.p.* set upon VI (ii). 42
**vnbuxomnes** *n.* intractability I. 356
**vncerteyne** *adj.* unknown I. 283, I. 782
**vncerteyntee** *n.* ignorance I. 283
**vnclennesse** *n.* impurity IV. 20
**vncloþet** *p.p.* naked VI (vi). 322
**vnconynge** *adj.* ignorant I. 395
**vncouenable** *adj.* unseemly I. 335
**vnder(e), vndre** *prep.* under I. 91, III. 179, VII. 162, **vndyr** VIII. 84
**vndeuocioun** *n.* lack of active worship or piety I. 330
**vndeuoutly** *adv.* irreverently I. 353
**vndo** *v.* open, unlatch VI (vi). 250; *imp.sg.* VI (vi). 83; *p.p.* **vndone** VIII. 383 rent apart
**vndregh** *adj.* joyful VI (iv). 86
**vndrestond(e)** *v.* understand II. 65, VI (vi). 74, VIII. 238; *imp.sg.* III. 100; *pa.t.sg.* **vndrestood** II. 192
**vndrestondynge** *n.* comprehension III. 2, VIII. 3
**vnkynd** *adj.* ungrateful VI (vi). 339
**vnlyke** *adj.* dissimilar VIII. 340
**vnmythty** *adj.* weak VIII. 386
**vnnayte*** *adj.* useless, unprofitable III. 140
**vnneth(e), vnnethes** *adv.* scarcely, with difficulty I. 280, VIII. 283, I. 589
**vnordeynt, vnordynat** *adj.* inordinate I. 645, I. 646, IV. 22
**vnouercomen** *p.p.* undefeated I. 661
**vnryght** *n.* sin VI (iv). 11
**vnshrift** *n.* failure to confess VIII. 170
**vnskylful** *adj.* unreasonable, intemperate I. 315, III. 66, VIII. 110
**vnskylfully** *adv.* unjustifiably VIII. 136
**vnstable** *adj.* unsteadfast I. 106
**vnstablenesse** *n.* inconstancy I. 340
**vnþanke** *n.* disfavour I. 74
**vntholmodnesse** *n.* impatience I. 376
**vntil** *prep.* unto VII. 18
**vnto** *prep.* up to, to the point of I. 2; to VII. 97
**vnwise** *adj.* foolish I. 106
**vnwisely** *adv.* foolishly I. 427
**vnworthy, vnworthi, vnworþi, vnworþy** *adj.* unworthy, undeserving VI (vi). 371, VIII. 399, VI (vi). 349, VI (vi). 390, VIII. 497
**vnworþynesse** *n.* unworthiness VIII. 519
**vp** *adv.* up I. 5, II. 213, III. 223, IV. 12, VI (i). 62, VI (iv). 13, VII. 28, VII. 75, VIII. 402
**vpon** *prep.* on, upon VI (iii). 18, VI (vi). 37, VII. 74, VIII. 91
**vpward** *adv.* upwards I. 272, VIII. 496
**vs** *see* **we**
**vse** *n.* practice I. 6, III. 11
**vse** *v.* practise, make use of I. 385, VIII. 19; *pr.pl.* **vsen** I. 19, **vseth** I. 442; *imp.sg.refl.* **vse** III. 58, III. 162; *p.p.* **vsed** III. 123, IV. 21, **vset** II. 47, IV. 24
**vsure** *n.* usury I. 368
**uttyr** *adj.* entire VIII. 282

**vayn(e)** *see* **veyn**
**vaynglorie** *n.* unwarranted pride I. 35, I. 344
**vanyte, vanite** *n.* worthlessness, a worthless thing I. 23, II. 64, III. 209; vanity III. 101; *pl.* **vanitees, vanytees, vanyteeȝ** I. 230, II. 134, III. 142, VI (iv). 49, I. 257, I. 292, II. 236
**vansheth** *pr.3 sg.* vanishes I. 704, II. 85; *pa.t.sg.* **vansshed** I. 178
**veyn, vayn(e)** *adj.* worthless, ineffectual III. 19, I. 359, III. 20, **in** ~ I. 207 uselessly
**venyal** *adj.* venial, pardonable III. 10
**venym** *n.* poison II. 80, II. 138
**venymous** *adj.* deadly II. 75, VII. 163
**verray, verrey** *adj.* true I. 131, II. 145, III. 5, VI (iv). 98, VIII. 11
**verray** *adv.* truly I. 729
**verrayly, verrayli, verraili, verraily(e)** *adv.* truly I. 627, III. 75, I. 847, II. 154, I. 700, I. 705, II. 14, III. 98, I. 885
**vertu(e)** *n.* virtue I. 37, I. 647, VIII. 66, VIII. 502; strength, power I. 649, I. 663, VIII. 198; *pl.* **vertues, vertuȝ** I. 48, VIII. 219, I. 275, I. 663, II. 100, III. 117
**vessel** *n.* container III. 115
**vices** *n.pl.* vices I. 73, II. 76, III. 160
**vicious** *adj.* sinful VI (vi). 132
**vile** *adj.* foul, disgusting I. 13, I. 155, III. 116, IV. 16; *sup.* **vilest** I. 244
**vynyard** *n.* vineyard VI (vi). 238
**violence** *n.* intensity I. 818
**virtus** *n.pl.* embodiment of power inherent in divine being II. 17
**visage** *n.* face VIII. 314
**visite** *v.* visit I. 855, VIII. 515; *imp.sg.* VIII. 368
**vowe** *n.* promise I. 389; *pl.* **vowes** I. 250, **voues** I. 366

**way(e), wey** *n.* path, road, way of life I. 58, I. 147, III. 98, VI (i). 12, VI (ii). 21, VI (ii). 4, VI (vi). 48; manner VIII. 228; *pl.* **wayes** VIII. 163, **waies** I. 376 journeys
**wailawo** *interj.* alas VI (vi). 387, VI (vi). 60*
**waillynge** *pr.p.* lamenting I. 68
**wake** *v.* awaken, watch, keep vigil I. 696, II. 44, VI (vi). 47, VII. 39; *pr.2 sg.* **wakest** I. 541; *3 sg.* **waketh** I. 564, II. 3, II. 235; *pl.* **waketh** III. 85; *subj.sg.* **wake** III. 88; *pr.p.* **wakynge** I. 213, I. 544, III. 86
**wakynge** *adj.* vigilant I. 413
**wakynge** *n.* vigil I. 72, I. 157, III. 62, VIII. 320, **walkynge** I. 608
**wan** *adj.* pale II. 185, VI (i). 10, VI (ii). 38, VIII. 313
**wand** *v.* refrain VI (ii). 39
**wandreth*** *n.* misery, trouble VI (i). 19
**wanhop(e)** *n.* despair VIII. 71, VIII. 105
**wanynge** *pr.p.* decreasing I. 322
**want** *v.* be lacking III. 47
**ware** *see* **was**
**warly** *adv.* cautiously VII. 79
**warm(e)** *adv.* warmly I. 188, III. 160
**warne** *pr.1 sg.* warn I. 466; *pa.t.2 sg.* **warned** VIII. 69
**warre** *adj.* cautious I. 180
**warto** *see* **where**
**was** *pa.t.1,3 sg.* was I. 119, II. 185, III. 90, VI (ii). 33, VI (iii). 18, VI (vi). 55, VII. 15, VIII. 35 *etc.*; *2 sg.* **were** VI (vi). 33, **wore** VI (vi). 110, VI (vi). 117, **was** I. 271, I. 465, VI (vi). 19, VIII. 33, VIII. 342; *pl.* **wer(e)** III. 199, VII. 67, **ware** III. 203, VI (ii). 41, **weren** I. 314, VIII. 189, VIII. 376, **wore** VI (vi). 208, **was** I. 470, II. 182, VIII. 191; *subj.sg.* **were** I. 85, VI (iii). 4, VIII. 278, **ware** I. 328, I. 718, II. 170, III. 29, V. 4, VI (i). 19, VI (iii). 7, VI (iv). 81
**waste** *v.* waste I. 68; *subj.pl.* **wast** I. 292; *pa.t.pl.* **wasted** III. 204
**watyr(e)** *n.* water II. 175, VIII. 334, VIII. 366
**wax** *see* **wix**
**we** *pron.1 pl.nom.* we I. 54, II. 62, III. 1, VI (i). 25, VI (vi). 63, VII. 31, VIII. 126 *etc.*; *acc.dat.* **vs** us I. 54, II. 261, VI (i). 7, VI (iii). 16, VI (vi). 25, VII. 32, VIII. 33 *etc.*; *refl.* **vs** ourselves I. 55, I. 74, II. 63, II. 261; *poss.adj.* **our(e)** our I. 74, II. 64, III. 2, III. 174, IV. 18, VI (i). 7, VI (iii). 25, VI (vi). 60, VII. 1, VIII. 126 *etc.*
**wed** *v.* marry II. 9; *p.p.* **weddit** VI (vi). 403
**wedde** *n.* pledge; **to** ~ VI (iv). 46 as a pledge
**wedded** *adj.* pledged VI (iv). 90
**wey** *see* **waye**
**wel(le)** *adv.* well I. 119, I. 212, II. 92, VI (ii). 31, VI (iv). 50; in favour I. 610; much I. 266, III. 128, VI (vi). 169, VIII. 338;. fully VIII. 33; easily, readily II. 54, III. 22, VI (iii). 28, VI (iv). 76; **wele** VII. 45 truly, indeed

**wel** *n.*[1] spring, fount I. 632, III. 183, VI (vi). 3; *pl.* **wellys** VI (vi). 245
**wel(e)** *n.*[2] wellbeing, prosperity I. 104, II. 90, II. 305, III. 27, V. 4, VI (i). 28, VI (iv). 2, VI (vi). 101, VIII. 26, **welle** VIII. 361
**weld** *v.* (i) rule II. 308; *imp.sg.* VI (ii). 13; (ii) possess VI (i). 20; *subj.sg.* VI (i). 38
**welfare** *n.* good fortune I. 334
**welth** *n.* prosperity I. 608, II. 114, III. 80, VI (i). 32, VI (v). 5
**wende** *v.* go VI (iv). 87, **wene** VI (ii). 8; *pr.3 sg.* **wendeth** I. 607, VI (iv). 2, VI (iv). 66; *pa.t.2 sg.* **went** VI (vi). 37, **whente** VII. 142; *p.p.* **went** II. 297, VI (i). 23, VI (ii). 28, VI (vi). 163
**wene** *v.* think, believe I. 207, I. 439, **wend** I. 30; *pr.1 sg.* **wene** II. 249, VI (i). 35; *pl.* **wene** II. 61, **weneth** I. 47, I. 57; *subj.sg.* **wene** I. 236; *pa.t.pl.* **wend** I. 58, VI (v). 10 expected; *subj.sg.* **wend** I. 33
**wepeth** *imp.pl.* weep VII. 102; *pa.t.3 sg.* **wept(e)** VIII. 407, VII. 76; *pr.p.* **wepynge** VII. 102, VIII. 333
**wepynge** *n.* weeping, grief II. 213, VI (i). 32
**were** *n.* danger, plight VI (v). 19
**were(n)** *see* **was**
**wery** *adj.* tired II. 4, VIII. 191
**werk-** *see* **worke**
**werre** *imp.sg.* wear I. 196
**weshe** *v.* wash, lave VIII. 366; *pr.pl.* **wosshen** VI (vi). 248; *imp.sg.* **wesshe** III. 166, **weshe** VIII. 271; *pa.t.sg.* **wisshe** VII. 29
**weste** *adv*. westwards VI (vi). 99
**wet** *imp.sg.* water VI (vi). 16; *pa.t.sg.* **wette** II. 176 drenched
**wete** *adj.* wet VI (vi). 72
**wex-** *see* **wix**
**whan, when** *adv.* & *conj.* when I. 21, I. 35, II. 25, II. 49, III. 56, III. 127, IV. 3, VI (i). 2, VI (vi). 99, VII. 15, VII. 161, VIII. 34, VIII. 52 *etc.*
**what** *adj.* what, whatever, which I. 24, I. 239, I. 289, I. 819
**what(e)** *pron.* what; *interrog.* VI (vi). 139, I. 288; *rel.* VIII. 388, I. 93, ~ **so** whatever I. 57, I. 807; *indef.* ~ **by** VIII. 319, ~ **with** VIII. 320, ~ **for** VII. 99
**what** *adv.* to what an extent I. 88, VII. 17, VIII. 279
**when** *see* **whan**
**wher(e), whar(e)** *adv.* & *conj.* where I. 133, I. 284, I. 678, II. 136, III. 184, III. 198, VI (vi). 262, VII. 71, VIII. 32 *etc.*; *prefixed to prep. or adv.* ~**for** therefore I. 169, I. 219, III. 137; ~**so** II. 141 wherever; **warto** VII. 59 why
**wheþer, whethere** *pron.* whichever VI (ii). 43, VII. 136
**wheþer, whethre** *conj.* whether I. 96, I. 334, II. 108, III. 67
**whi, why** *adv.* why I. 288, III. 86, VI (vi). 121, VIII. 455
**which(e)** *pron.rel.* who, which, that I. 26, II. 216, III. 9, III. 52, IV. 23, VII. 149, VIII. 140, **whoch(e)** I. 301, II. 35, VIII. 20
**whil(e), whils** *conj.* while I. 271, I. 295, I. 451, I. 515, II. 14, III. 87, III. 174, VI (ii). 21, VI (iv). 41, **whiles** VII. 110
**whil(e)** *n.* space of time III. 53, VI (vi). 32
**whils** *adv.* sometimes I. 455
**whit(e)** *adj.* white II. 184, VI (ii). 37, VI (vi). 59; *as n.* VIII. 543
**who** *pron.interrog.* who II. 235, VI (i). 14, VII. 165; *rel.* **whom** I. 308, I. 429, II. 79, VII. 61; *gen.* **whose** I. 772, II. 170, III. 43, VI (iv). 60, **wose** VI (iv). 17
**whoch(e)** *see* **whiche**
**whodre** *adv.* whither I. 284
**who-so(m)** *pron.* whoever I. 582, I. 721, II. 192, II. 222, VI (iii). 3, VI (iv). 81, VIII. 396
**wichecraft** *n.* witchcraft, sortilege I. 365
**wicked, wik(k)ed, wickid** *adj.* sinful I. 155, I. 209, I. 414, I. 695, II. 106, III. 16, VI (i). 65, VI (vi). 84; *as n.* II. 88, VI (v). 19; perverse, contrary I. 330
**wickedly** *adv.* sinfully VII. 155
**wickednesse, wik(k)ednesse** *n.* sin VI (iv). 54, III. 171, VIII. 523
**wide, wyde** *adj.* broad II. 185, VI (ii). 38, VI (iv). 6, VIII. 486
**wyde** *adv.* widely VI (vi). 250
**wil(le)** *n.* intention, desire, volition I. 5, I. 6, I. 327, II. 10, II. 219, III. 3, III. 6, IV. 11, VI (i). 29, VI (ii). 2, VI (vi). 216, VII. 51, VIII. 8, VIII. 38 *etc.*; *pl.* **willes** III. 31, **wilnes** II. 275
**wil(le)** *v.* (i) wish, desire, intend, be willing I. 255; *pr.1,3 sg.* I. 219, I. 381, II. 121, II. 137, II. 219, III. 105, III. 158, VI (iv). 59, VI (vi). 79, VII. 49, VII. 80, **wol** I. 84, I. 180; *2 sg.* **wil(le)** I. 424, I. 579, II. 94,

**wil(le)** (*cont.*) VI (iv). 49, VI (vi). 44, VI (vi). 240, **wilt** I. 246, VI (vi). 106, **wolt** I. 401; *pl.* **wil** I. 474, III. 12, VI (iv). 99; (ii) *as aux. forming future, often implying wish etc. pr.1,3 sg.* **wil** I. 518, I. 702, II. 7, II. 47, II. 122, II. 148, II. 272, III. 52, III. 184, V. 6, VI (i). 31, VI (i). 52, VI (iv). 28, VI (v). 11, VI (vi). 1 *etc.*, **wille** VII. 77, VIII. 491, **wol** I. 11, I. 203; *2 sg.* **wilt** I. 106, **wolt** I. 107, **wil** II. 161, II. 243, III. 93, III. 132; *pl.* **wil** I. 42, I. 431, III. 52, VI (iv). 62, **wol** I. 31, I. 165, I. 279; *pa.t.1,3 sg.* would, wished **wold** I. 236, II. 7, VI (i). 39, VI (vi). 254, VIII. 545, **wolde** VII. 6, **wild** I. 199, **willed** I. 393; *2 sg.* **woldest** VI (vi). 128, VIII. 34, VIII. 386, **wold** III. 165, VIII. 36; *pl.* **wold** I. 133, III. 113, III. 204, VI (ii). 39, VIII. 79, **wolde** VII. 22

**wylde** *adj.* violent VI (iii). 7

**wiles** *n.pl.* tricks, stratagems I. 24

**wilful** *adj.* voluntary I. 248; **wylful** III. 6 deliberate

**wilfully** *adv.* deliberately I. 586; willingly VIII. 107, VIII. 165

**willet** *v.*² *p.p.* lost, gone astray III. 90

**willy** *adj.* willing, desirous VIII. 33, VIII. 190

**wilnes** *see* **wille** *n.*

**wyn(ne)** *n.* joy VI (i). 20, VI (v). 22, VI (vi). 273

**wyn** *v.* attain I. 525, II. 199, III. 24, IV. 15, VI (i). 8, VI (ii). 15, VI (iv). 10, VI (v). 5

**wynd** *n.* wind I. 725

**wyne** *n.* wine VI (i). 51

**wirch-** *see* **worche**

**wirre** *adv.comp.* worse I. 451

**wyrship** *see* **worship**

**wisdom(e)** *n.* wisdom I. 738, II. 223, VIII. 392, VII. 145

**wise** *adj.* wise I. 44, I. 735, III. 114; *sup.* **wisest** I. 738, III. 43, VI (i). 2

**wise** *n.* manner, way VII. 49, VIII. 73; *pl.* VIII. 258

**wisely** *adv.* wisely I. 706, II. 63

**wisse** *imp.sg.* guide, show VI (iv). 44, VI (vi). 7, VII. 66*

**wisshe** *see* **weshe**

**wysshe** *n.* wish, desire VIII. 9

**wist** *see* **witte** *v.*

**wit(te)** *n.* understanding I. 631, VI (iv). 80, VII. 145; opinion I. 30, I. 342; *pl.* **wittes** senses I. 414, IV. 19, VIII. 5, **wittis** VIII. 263

**wit(te)** *v.* know, understand, have knowledge of I. 229, I. 411, I. 579, II. 55, VI (v). 22, VIII. 483; *pr.1,3 sg.* **wot(e)** I. 44, I. 65, I. 579, II. 58, III. 187, V. 4, VI (i). 16, VI (i). 55, VI (ii). 31, VI (v). 11, VIII. 388, VIII. 396, VII. 45*; *2 sg.* **wost** I. 193, I. 406, **wot** II. 165; *pl.* **wot(e)** I. 93, I. 283, I. 779; *subj.sg.* **witte** I. 219; *imp.sg.* **wit(te)** I. 119, I. 212, I. 327, III. 135; *pa.t.2 sg.* **wist** VIII. 32; *3 sg.* **wist** VII. 40; *subj.pl.* **wist** I. 779

**witeth** *pr.3 sg.* vanishes III. 44, *pr.p.* **witynge** VI (i). 34 fading

**with** *prep.* (*of association, emotion, etc.*) with I. 12, II. 15, IV. 7, VI (i). 4, VI (vi). 30, VII. 16, VII. 39, VIII. 127 *etc.*; (*of instrument*) with, by I. 356, I. 447, VIII. 2; (*of benefit*) for I. 450

**withal** *adv.* in addition VII. 105

**withdrawe** *p.p.* removed VIII. 345

**withhold** *v.* hold back I. 369, VIII. 358

**within** *adv.* within, inside I. 3, I. 79, II. 63, VI (i). 40, VI (ii). 13, VI (iv). 77, VI (v). 7, **withjnnen** I. 824; internally III. 68

**within, wythin** *prep.* within VI (i). 64, VI (iv). 12, VI (v). 23, VIII. 87, **withjnne** VI (vi). 274

**without(en)** *prep.* without I. 213, I. 405, II. 37, III. 20, IV. 4, VI (iii). 28, VI (iv). 60, VI (v). 2, VI (vi). 10, VIII. 231, **withoutyn** VI (i). 50, **witouten** III. 3, **withowten** VII. 55

**withouten** *adv.* outwardly, externally I. 78, I. 462, II. 62, III. 150

**withstond** *v.* resist I. 6, VIII. 472

**witnes(se)** *n.* testimony, evidence I. 355, VIII. 540

**witterly** *adv.* undoubtedly II. 46

**wittyngely** *adv.* knowingly I. 586

**wix** *v.* grow I. 276, **wax** I. 523; *pr.1 sg.* **wax** II. 281; *3 sg.* **wixeth** III. 121, **wexeth** VIII. 338; *subj.sg.* **wix** I. 317; *pa.t.sg.* **waxed** VIII. 452, **wox** VIII. 451; *pl.* **wexed** VI (vi). 118; *pr.p.* **wyxynge, wixynge** I. 322, III. 25, VI (ii). 20

**wlatfully** *adv.* loathsomely VIII. 494

**wlatsome** *adj.* loathsome VIII. 408

**wo(o)** *n.* grief, misfortune I. 104, I. 812, II. 84, III. 27, V. 4, VI (i). 2, VI (ii). 8, VI (iv). 55, VI (vi). 57, VIII. 26, VIII. 341

**wo(o)** *adj.* woeful VIII. 406, II. 89

**wodenesse** *n.* madness I. 96

**wogh** *n.* wall I. 69

**woke** *adj.* weak I. 3, I. 62
**wol(e)** *n.* wool I. 671, I. 673
**wol, wolt, wold-** *see* **wille** *v.*
**wolfes** *n.pl.* wolves I. 684
**womb(e)** *n.* womb VI (vi). 359; stomach I. 221
**womman** *n.* woman I. 1, I. 167, VI (vi). 204, VIII. 332; *gen.* **wommanes** VIII. 344; *pl.* **wommen** I. 106, II. 40, III. 199
**won** *v.* dwell II. 306, III. 211, VI (i). 40, VI (ii). 23, VI (iv). 28, VI (vi). 342; *pr.pl.* **wonneth** I. 892
**wonder, wondre** *n.* strange sight, marvel II. 192, III. 83, V. 4, VI (iii). 17, VI (v). 6, VII. 100, VII. 112, **wondyr** VIII. 464; *pl.* **wondres** VIII. 509
**wonder, wondyr** *adv.* marvellously VI (vi). 376, VIII. 310
**wondre (on)** *v.* marvel (at) I. 26; *pr.pl.* **wondreth** VIII. 325
**wondre** *adj.* wonderful I. 476, **wondre-ful, wonderful** IV. 5, I. 634
**wondrefully** *adv.* marvellously I. 141
**wondrynge** *n.* admiration I. 78
**wone** *n.* dwelling place VI (i). 55
**wonet** *p.p.* accustomed I. 799
**wonnynge(sted)** *n.* dwelling place I. 12, VI (ii). 32, III. 120
**woobigone** *adj.* oppressed with grief VIII. 279
**wood** *adj.* passionate VI (vi). 375
**worch(e)** *v.* work, do I. 63, I. 128; **wirch** V. 4 cause; *pr.3 sg.* **worcheth** I. 354; *imp.sg.* **wirche** III. 142; *pa.t.2 sg.* **wroghtest** VI (vi). 122; *3 sg.* **wroght** VIII. 509; *p.p.* **wroght** VI (ii). 6, VI (iv). 98, VI (vi). 155, **wirched** VI (iv). 55; *pr.p.* **wirchynge** I. 702, II. 171
**worchynge** *n.* action I. 703; performing III. 130
**word(e)** *n.* word, speech, utterance I. 356, II. 102, VI (vi). 206, III. 13, VII. 48, VIII. 43, VIII. 109, *pl.* **wordes** I. 360, III. 16, VI (vi). 190, VIII. 132
**wordys** *see* **world**
**wore** *see* **was**
**worke, werk(e)** *n.* work, deed, action I. 50, II. 153, III. 6, VIII. 43; *pl.* **workes, werkes** III. 141, VIII. 206, II. 110, VI (i). 65, VI (iii). 16, VI (vi). 94, VIII. 5
**world** *n.* world, earth I. 14, II. 26, II. 150, III. 28, VI (i). 35, VI (ii). 3, VI (iv). 73, VI (vi). 166, VIII. 42 *etc.*, **worlde** VIII. 473; *gen.* **worldes** III. 198; *forming adj.* worldly I. 824, II. 239, III. 76, VIII. 361, **worldis** I. 335, II. 125, II. 263, III. 144, IV. 1, VI (i). 28, VI (iv). 2, VI (vi). 291, **worldisshe** I. 18, **wordys** III. 140; *pl.* **worldes** I. 130
**worldly** *adj.* temporal VIII. 19
**worme** *n.* worm VIII. 309; *pl.* **wormes, wormys** III. 208, VII. 162
**wors** *adj.comp.* worse I. 261, I. 347, II. 83, VIII. 338; *sup.* **worst** I. 358, VI (iv). 92
**worship** *v.* honour, worship VIII. 258, **wyrship** VIII. 146; *subj.sg.* **wyrship** VIII. 20
**worship(e)** *n.* honour VIII. 164, VIII. 263, **worschipe** VII. 17, VII. 158
**worth** *n.* value III. 66
**worth(y), worþi, worþy** *adj.* deserving I. 98, I. 407, VI (vi). 312, VIII. 513, VIII. 521; *comp.* **worþier** I. 789
**wose** *see* **who**
**wosshen** *see* **weshe**
**wost, wot(e)** *see* **witte** *v.*
**wound** *v.* wound VI (vi). 180; *pr.3 sg.* **woundeth** I. 618; *imp.sg.* **wound** II. 203, VI (iv). 77, **wownd** VI (ii). 13
**woundes** *n.pl.* wounds II. 185, III. 190, VI (ii). 38, VI (iv). 6, VI (vi). 54, VII. 171, VIII. 192, **woundis** VII. 121
**wowe** *pr.1 sg.* woo II. 6
**wox** *see* **wix**
**wrath** *see* **wreth** *v.*
**wrech(e)** *n.* despicable being I. 43, II. 81, VI (vi). 390, VII. 166, VIII. 23; *pl.* **wreches** III. 200, VIII. 367
**wreched** *adj.* wretched, miserable II. 77, III. 40, VI (vi). 132, VII. 161, **wrecched** VII. 147; *sup.* **wrochedest** I. 244 most worthless
**wrechednes(se)** *n.* sinfulness I. 55, I. 89, I. 467; poverty II. 85; *pl.* I. 2, I. 18 causes of sin
**wreyynge** *n.* accusing, denouncing I. 354
**wreth** *n.* anger I. 91, II. 103, VI (iv). 5, VIII. 111
**wreth** *v.* anger I. 531, I. 809, II. 71, **wrath** III. 114; *subj.sg.* **wreth** III. 161, **wrath** VI (vi). 304; *pl.* **wreth** II. 259
**wrynge** *v.* wring VI (i). 65; *pr.pl.* VIII. 551, *pa.t.sg.* **wronge** VIII. 333
**writ(e)** *v.* write I. 624, II. 58; *pr.1 sg.* II. 32, II. 265; *p.p.* **written** I. 166, II. 2, VI (i). 2, VI (vi). 198, VIII. 236

**writynge** *n.* written material II. 3, VIII. 239; **holy** ~ I. 862 Scripture
**wrochedest** *see* **wreched**
**wroght** *see* **worche**
**wronge** *v. see* **wrynge**
**wronge** *n.* sin VI (vi). 122; injustice VI (vi). 53; harm I. 409, *pl.* **wronges** VIII. 181 injustices
**wrongefully** *adv.* unjustly VIII. 269
**wrongful** *adj.* unjust VIII. 357
**wroth** *adj.* angry I. 713

**yate** *n.* gate, means of entry I. 884, VI (v). 2; *pl.* **yatis** VIII. 504
**ye** *pron.2 pl.nom.* you II. 115*, VI (vi). 225, VIII. 433, **ȝe** VII. 34; *acc.dat.* **yow** VI (vi). 58, VI (vi). 236, **ȝow** VII. 35; *poss. adj.* **your(e)** your VI (iv). 27, VIII. 340, VIII. 341, **ȝour(e)** VII. 44, VII. 103
**yed(e), ȝede** *see* **go**
**yeld** *v.* yield, give, return VI (vi). 139, VI (vi). 254; *pr.1 sg.* VIII. 93; *2 sg.* **yeldest**VI (vi). 244; *pa.t.2 sg.* **yelded** VI (vi). 220; *3 sg.* **ȝeldid** VII. 129; *pr.p.* **yeldynge** I. 393
**yeld** *n.* yield VIII. 229
**ȝere** *n.gen.* year's VII. 15; *pl.* **yers** years I. 128, III. 203
**yernynge** *n.* object of desire VI (vi). 313; longing VIII. 476
**yet** *see* **yite**
**yeue** *v.* give, grant I. 228, I. 387, VI (vi). 292, **ȝeue** VII. 146, **yif** I. 854, II. 148, VI (vi). 360, **ȝiue** VII. 148, **gif** I. 449, II. 34, III. 72, VI (iv). 38, **gyf** I. 408, II. 98; *pr.3 sg.* **yeueth** I. 121, II. 256, III. 47, **gif(f)eth** II. 220, I. 430, **gyfeth** III. 112; *pl.* **yeueth** I. 848, **yeuen** I. 142, I. 10 exchange, **gyf** I. 755; *subj.sg.* **gif** I. 685, II. 11, VI (i). 38; *pl.* **gif** I. 652, I. 801; *imp.sg.* **yyve** VI (i). 18, **yeve** VI (vi). 281, VIII. 1, **yif** VI (vi). 223, VIII. 184, **gif** I. 464, II. 65, III. 217, VI (ii). 48, VI (iii). 28, VI (iv). 46, VI (vi). 337, **gyf** II. 129, VI (iv). 74, VI (vi). 11; *pa.t.2 sg.* **yave** VI (vi). 134, VIII. 467, **yaf** VIII. 20; *3 sg.* **yaue** I. 171, **ȝaue** VII. 21; *pl.* **yaf** VIII. 418, **yaven** VIII. 465, **yoven** VIII. 466, **ȝaue** VII. 127; *subj.sg.* **yaue** I. 740; *pl.* **yeven** I. 83; *p.p.* **yeuen** I. 233, VIII. 18, **gyf(f)en** I. 797, I. 847, III. 68, II. 259, III. 155, **gefen** III. 208, **geven** I. 775; *pr.p.* **gefynge** II. 101
**yif, ȝif** *conj. see* **if**
**yift(e)** *n.* gift VIII. 194, VIII. 298; *pl.* **yiftes** I. 513, II. 221, VIII. 21, **yiftis** VIII. 18, **giftes** I. 376
**yit(e)** *adv.* nevertheless VIII. 122; moreover VI (vi). 237, VIII. 82; **yet** yet I. 535, I. 595
**yonge** *adj.* young I. 451, VIII. 285; *as n.* VI (i). 49
**yore** *adv.*[1] formerly, of old VI (vi). 78
**yore** *adv.*[2] without delay VI (vi). 234
**your(e), ȝour(e)** *see* **ye**
**ȝour sylues*** *pron.* yourselves VII. 103

# INDEX OF NAMES